COMMON CORE ACHIEVE

Mastering Essential Test Readiness Skills

SCIENCE

Mc Graw Hill Education

Bothell, WA • Chicago, IL • Columbus, OH • New York, NY

MHEonline.com

Send all inquiries to:
McGraw-Hill Education
8787 Orion Place
Columbus, OH 43240

ISBN: 978-0-02-140015-7
MHID: 0-02-140015-6

Printed in the United States of America.

4 5 6 7 8 9 QLM 17 16 15 14

Table of Contents

To the Student

Congratulations! If you are using this book, it means that you are taking a key step toward achieving an important new goal for yourself. You are preparing to take your high school equivalency test, an important step in the pathway toward career, educational, and lifelong well-being and success.

Common Core Achieve: Mastering Essential Test Readiness Skills is designed to help you learn or strengthen the skills you will need when you take your high school equivalency test. The program includes four core student modules – *Reading & Writing, Mathematics, Science,* and *Social Studies.* Each of these modules provides subject-level pretests and posttests, in-depth instruction and practice of the core skills and practices required for high school equivalency tests, and a number of additional features to help you master all the skills you need for success on test day and beyond.

How to Use This Book

Before beginning the lessons in each module, take the **Pretest**. This will give you a preview of the types of questions you will be answering on the high school equivalency test. More importantly, it will help you identify which skill areas you need to concentrate on most. Use the evaluation chart at the end of the Pretest to pinpoint the types of questions you have answered incorrectly and to determine which skills you need to work on. The evaluation chart will also help you identify where to go within the module for instruction and practice. You may decide to concentrate on specific areas of study or to work through the entire module. It is highly recommended that you work through the whole module to build a strong foundation in the core areas in which you will be tested.

Common Core Achieve: Mastering Essential Test Readiness Skills includes a number of features designed to familiarize you with high school equivalency tests and to prepare you for test taking. At the start of each chapter, the **Chapter Opener** provides an overview of the chapter content and a goal-setting activity. The lessons that follow include these features to help guide and enhance your learning:

- **Lesson Objectives** state what you will be able to accomplish after completing the lesson.

- **Key Terms and Vocabulary** critical for understanding lesson content is listed at the start of every lesson. All boldfaced words in the text can be found in the Glossary.

- The **Key Concept** summarizes the content that is the focus of the lesson.

- **Core Skills** are emphasized with direct instruction and practice in the context of the lesson. Each of the Core Skills aligns to the Common Core State Standards.

- **Core Practices** build important reasoning and application skills. Core Practices align to key skills specified in the Common Core State Standards and other assessment targets.

- Special features within each lesson include **21st Century Skills**, **Technology Connections**, **Workplace Skills**, and **Test-Taking Skills** to help you activate high-level thinking skills by using real-word application of these skills.

- The **Calculator Skills** feature will help you practice using a calculator with mathematical concepts or numerical data.

- **Think about Science** questions check your understanding of the content throughout the lesson.

- The end-of-lesson **Vocabulary Review** checks your understanding of important lesson vocabulary, and the **Skill Review** checks your understanding of the content and skills presented in the lesson.

- **Skill Practice** exercises appear at the end of every lesson to help you apply your learning of content and skill fundamentals.

In addition to the above lesson-level features, this module also includes these features to help you check your understanding as you prepare for the test.

- The end-of-chapter **Review** tests your understanding of the chapter content.

- **Check Your Understanding** charts allow you to check your knowledge of the skills you have practiced, and reference where you can go to review skills that you should revisit.

- The **Answer Key** provides the answers for the questions in the book.

- **Application of Science Practices** helps you demonstrate scientific reasoning and synthesize information.

- After you have worked through the book, take the **Posttest** to see how well you have learned the skills presented in this book.

Good luck with your studies, and remember: you are here because you have chosen to achieve important and exciting new goals for yourself. Every time you begin working within the material, keep in mind that the skills you develop in *Common Core Achieve: Mastering Essential Test Readiness Skills* are not just important for passing the high school equivalency test, they are keys to lifelong success.

Directions: Use the diagram to answer questions 1 and 2.

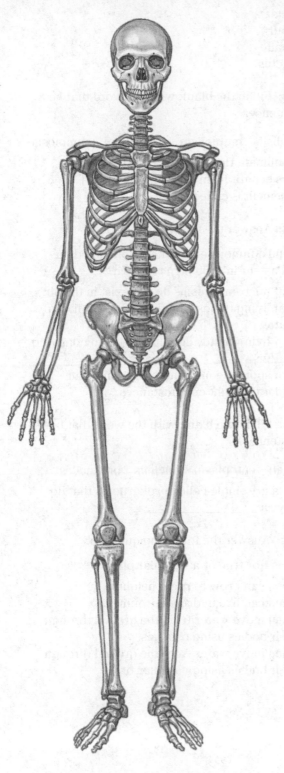

1. Bones at joints are covered in flexible cartilage, which is a tough, elastic connective tissue. If cartilage is damaged at a joint, what might happen?

   A. two bones might rub together
   B. the lungs might not be protected
   C. the brain might become exposed
   D. your body might not make blood cells

2. Different types of joints allow for different types of movement. What kind of joint is located at the shoulder?

   A. pivot joint
   B. hinge joint
   C. gliding joint
   D. ball-and-socket joint

Directions: Fill in the blank with the word that best fits the sentence

   follicles   gametes   glands   hormones

3. Two chemical messengers, called _____ that are important for human reproduction are testosterone and estrogen.

Directions: Answer the following questions.

4. On a very hot day, how does the human body maintain homeostasis?

   A. by sweating
   B. by shivering
   C. by heating up
   D. by gasping for air

5. Explain how a vaccine can prevent disease.

6. Which of the following is **not** a biotic part of an environment?

   A. grass
   B. rabbit
   C. sunlight
   D. bacteria

7. There are four levels of organization within an environment. Which is the correct arrangement of the levels from smallest unit to largest.

   A. organism → population → community → ecosystem

   B. community → population → ecosystem → organism

   C. population → ecosystem → organism → community

   D. ecosystem → organism → community → population

Directions: Use the diagram below to answer questions 8–9.

8. Food webs show complex feeding relationships in ecosystems. The arrows in the diagram lead from one organism to an organism that eats it. Which relationship is represented in the food web diagram?

   A. cactus → tortoise → coyote → pronghorn

   B. grass → horned lizard → weasel → rattlesnake

   C. seeds → kangaroo rats → rattlesnake → raven

   D. jackrabbit → coyote → roadrunner → pronghorn

9. Which of the following is a producer shown in the food web?

   A. ants

   B. toad

   C. quail

   D. cactus

Directions: Fill in the blank with the word that best fits the sentence.

commensalism mutualism parasitism symbiosis

10. Bees pollinate flowers, and both bees and flowers benefit from this arrangement. This arrangement is called _____ .

Directions: Answer the following question.

11. What did a famous experiment conducted by Louis Pasteur in 1859 help to prove?

   A. that microorganisms do not exist in the air

   B. that living things can arise from nonliving matter

   C. that living things do not arise from nonliving matter

   D. that spontaneous generation can occur under the right circumstances

Directions: Fill in the blank with the word that best fits the sentence.

cell wall cytoplasm nucleus organelles

12. Bacteria are single-celled prokaryotes that do not have a _____ .

Directions: Answer the following question.

13. Which is **not** true of a vascular plant?

   A. They can grow to great heights.

   B. They can live in dry environments.

   C. They move water from the ground through their bodies using osmosis.

   D. They move water from the ground through their bodies using vascular tissue.

Directions: Use the diagram below to answer questions 14–15.

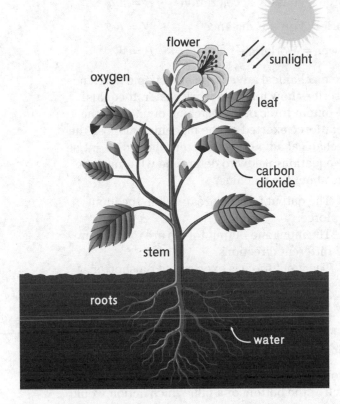

flower

sunlight

oxygen

leaf

carbon dioxide

stem

roots

water

14. According to the diagram, where do plants get the light energy needed to undergo photosynthesis?

   A. from water
   B. from the soil
   C. from sunlight
   D. from other plants

15. According to the diagram, where does most photosynthesis in a plant take place?

   A. in the roots
   B. in the seeds
   C. in the leaves
   D. in the flowers

Directions: Answer the following questions.

16. Tallness in an organism is a dominant trait. Suppose a mother has two tall genes, and a father has one tall gene and one short gene. How likely is it that an offspring will be short?

   A. 0%
   B. 25%
   C. 50%
   D. 75%

17. Which of the following is **not** a trait that is influenced by genes?

   A. eye color
   B. blood type
   C. hair texture
   D. musical skill

18. Besides his theory of evolution, Charles Darwin also proposed the Theory of Universal Common Ancestry. What does this theory state?

   A. that all life has slowly changed over time
   B. that all humans are related to each other
   C. that all life descended from a single organism
   D. that all species that look alike are related to each other

19. Explain why mutations that affect body cells do not get passed on to offspring.

20. How might a long neck help a species of tortoise survive better?

   A. A long neck will help it digest food better than shorter-necked tortoises.
   B. A long neck will help it escape predators better than shorter-necked tortoises.
   C. If its food source is high off of the ground, a long neck will help it get more food than shorter-necked tortoises.
   D. If its food source is close to the ground, a long neck will help it to walk less than shorter-necked tortoises.

Directions: Use the graph to answer questions 21 and 22.

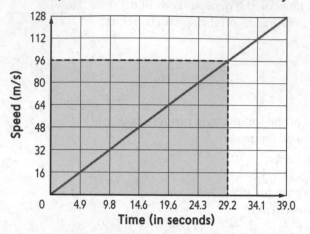

Speed v. Time for Freefall in Earth's Gravity

21. Draw two conclusions about the object's motion based on the slanted line in the graph.

22. What will the speed of an object be after 4 seconds of free fall?
- A. 4.9 m/s
- B. 9.8 m/s
- C. 14.6 m/s
- D. 39.0 m/s

Directions: Answer the following questions.

23. A horse pulling on a sled causes it to accelerate at 5.0 m/s². Suppose passengers get out of the sled, causing the mass to be halved. If the horse continues to pull with the same force, what will happen to the acceleration?
- A. It will stay at 5.0 m/s².
- B. It will increase to 7.5 m/s²
- C. It will decrease to 2.5 m/s².
- D. It will increase to 10.0 m/s².

24. A small forklift exerts a force of 16 Newtons to move a crate 10 meters in 8 seconds. The power of the forklift is _____ joules.

Force = mass × acceleration	$F = ma$
Work = Force × distance	$W = Fd$
Power = Work/time	$P = W/t$

25. The mechanical advantage of a simple machine describes how it makes work easier. It equals the output force of the machine divided by the input force exerted on the machine. Suppose the mechanical advantage is determined to be $\frac{1}{3}$. Use the equations below to determine what must be true about the machine?
- A. The output force is greater than the input force.
- B. The input and output forces are exerted in different directions.
- C. The input force is exerted over a shorter distance than the output force.
- D. The work done on the machine is less than the work the machine does.

Directions: Answer the following question.

26. A roller coaster car is at rest on a flat section of track at the bottom of a hill. Which action would increase the gravitational potential energy of the car?
- A. attaching the car to other cars
- B. adding passengers to the car
- C. pushing the car to the top of a hill
- D. pushing the car backward along a flat track

Directions: Use the diagram to answer questions 27 and 28.

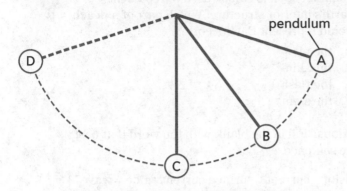

pendulum

27. The pendulum is released at point A and swings to point D before returning. At which point is the kinetic energy of the pendulum greatest?

A. point A
B. point B
C. point C
D. point D

28. At which point is KE = PE?

A. point A
B. point B
C. point C
D. point D

Directions: Answer the following questions.

29. Name a renewable energy resource and a nonrenewable energy resource. Tell how they are alike and how they are different.

30. A piano string produces a sound with a frequency of 264 Hz. If the wavelength of the sound wave in air is 1.40 m, what is the speed of the sound in air?

$$\text{speed} = \text{frequency} \times \text{wavelength}$$
$$v = f \times \lambda$$

A. 124 m/s
B. 189 m/s
C. 370 m/s
D. 404 m/s

31. Atomic radius decreases from left to right across the periodic table. Explain why this is true based on the structure of atoms.

32. Which of these chemical equations is balanced?

A. $2AgNO_3 + H_2S \rightarrow Ag_2S + 2HNO_3$
B. $Li_2O_2 + 2CO_2 \rightarrow Li_2CO_3 + O_2$
C. $Fe_2O_3 + H_2 \rightarrow 2Fe + H_2O$
D. $C_4H_8 + O_2 \rightarrow 2CO_2 + 2H_2O$

Directions: Use the diagram to answer question 33.

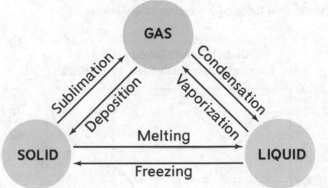

33. Sublimation is most like which of the following processes in terms of energy change?

A. freezing
B. condensation
C. melting
D. deposition

Directions: Fill in the blank with the word that best fits the sentence.

thermal energy   state   temperature   arrangement
of particles

34. During each of the labeled processes, the _____ of the substance stays the same.

Directions: Answer the following question.

35. A student adds $AgNO_3$ to 100 g of water at 10°C and records the amount that dissolves. The student repeats the same process at 20°C, 40°C, 60°C, and 80°C. What is the dependent variable in the investigation?

   A. the solute used
   B. the solvent used
   C. the temperature of water
   D. the solubility of $AgNO_3$

Directions: Use the graph to answer questions 36 and 37.

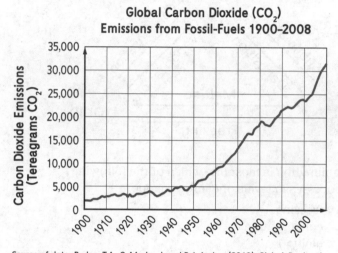

Global Carbon Dioxide (CO_2) Emissions from Fossil-Fuels 1900–2008

Source of data: Boden, T.A., G. Marland, and R.J. Andres (2010). Global, Regional, and National Fossil-Fuel CO2 Emissions. Carbon Dioxide Information Analysis Center, Oak Ridge National Laboratory, U.S. Department of Energy, Oak Ridge, Tenn., U.S.A. doi 10.3334/CDIAC/00001_V2010.

36. What can you infer about the relationship between fossil fuels and carbon dioxide from this graph?

37. What will happen to the line on the graph if people do not reduce their use of fossil fuels?

   A. It will fluctuate.
   B. It will flatten out.
   C. It will continue to rise.
   D. It will begin to go down.

Directions: Answer the following questions.

38. Common objects can be used to represent Earth's interior structure. Which part of a peach would represent Earth's core?

   A. the pit
   B. the skin
   C. the flesh
   D. the stem

Directions: Fill in the blank with the word that best fits the sentence.

   density   current   surface current   tide   wave

39. A cold _____ in the top part of the ocean brings water from the poles toward the equator.

Directions: Answer the following question.

40. A friend tells you that severe weather is headed for your area. Weather forecasters have spotted a rapidly moving, swirling column of air a few kilometers away. What safety precautions should you take?

   A. Move to higher ground to avoid a storm surge from a hurricane.
   B. Gather warm blankets to avoid exposure to cold during a blizzard.
   C. Seek shelter in a basement to avoid the strong winds of a tornado.
   D. Lay flat in an open area to avoid lightning strikes from a thunderstorm.

Directions: Use the information to answer questions 41 and 42.

> Our solar system formed from a cloud of dust and gas called a solar nebula. Scientists have a hypothesis about how the solar nebula began to collapse and eventually form the Sun, Earth, and other objects in the solar system. They believe that a disturbance, possibly from a nearby supernova, sent shock waves through the nebula. These shock waves caused much of the gas and dust in the nebula to be pushed toward the center of the nebula. As the nebula compressed, the gravitational forces overcame the internal pressure of the nebula's hot gases and it collapsed. This resulted in a spinning pancake shape of hot gas with a bulge in the middle. The dense, hot center portion became the Sun. The heavy, rocky material pulled in strongly by gravity stayed near the central bulge. This heavy material became the inner planets. The lighter elements, mainly hydrogen, stayed near the outer edge and became the outer planets.

41. Cite evidence in the text that supports the conclusion that gravity played a role in forming the solar system.

42. What inference can you make based on this passage?
  A. Our solar system is unique in that it formed from a nebula.
  B. Scientists know everything about how our solar system formed.
  C. Without a disturbance, the solar nebula would not have compressed.
  D. The planets in Earth's solar system are all made of the same materials.

Directions: Fill in the blank with the word that best fits the sentence.

cluster elliptical irregular spiral

43. Galaxies are classified according to their shapes. The Milky Way galaxy is a(n) _____ galaxy.

Directions: Answer the following questions.

44. A student is using common objects to model structures in the universe. He uses a marble for Earth, a basketball for the Sun, and a baseball for the solar system. How would you evaluate the student's model?
  A. The model should be changed because the baseball should represent Earth.
  B. The model is fine because each object shows the correct model size of each structure.
  C. The model should be changed because the basketball should represent the solar system.
  D. The model is fine because it includes three round objects to represent three round structures.

45. An exposed cliff contains four layers of sedimentary rock. A scientist labels the layers 1 through 4, with 1 representing the bottom layer and 4 representing the top layer. Each layer of rock contains fossils. In which layer would the scientist most likely find the oldest fossils?
  A. layer 1
  B. layer 2
  C. layer 3
  D. layer 4

1. **A** Without cartilage between them, two bones in a joint might rub together at a joint. The lungs and the brain are protected by bone and red blood cell production is not a function of cartilage.

2. **D** The movement of the shoulder is similar to that of the hip. The shoulder joint is a ball-and-socket joint.

3. **hormones**
   Hormones are chemicals produced by glands that regulate body functions. Glands produce hormones. Female eggs grow inside follicles. Gametes are sex cells, called sperm in men and eggs in women.

4. **A** The body maintains homeostasis, or balance, by sweating to cool down its internal temperature.

5. A vaccine is a dead or weakened portion of a pathogen. When a vaccine enters the body, the body produces an immune response to the vaccine, which it remembers. Later, if you are exposed to the real disease, your body knows how to fight it.

6. **C** Biotic refers to living organisms in an environment, such as grass, rabbits, and bacteria. Abiotic refers to nonliving parts of an environment, such as sunlight.

7. **A** An organism is the smallest unit. Many organisms form a population. Populations form a community. Communities are part of an ecosystem.

8. **C** Seeds are eaten by kangaroo rats, which are eaten by rattlesnakes, which are eaten by ravens.

9. **D** Many producers, like the cactus, are plants that use energy from the Sun to make their food.

10. Bees pollinate flowers and both bees and flowers benefit from this arrangement. This arrangement is called [mutualism].

11. **C** Pasteur's experiment helped to prove that living things arise only from other living things. He showed the organisms cannot spontaneously appear, but rather that all organisms come from parent organisms.

12. **nucleus**
    A prokaryotic cell has a cell membrane, cell wall, and cytoplasm but does not have a nucleus or membrane-bound organelles.

13. **C.** Vascular plants have tube-like tissues that transport water and other substances throughout the plant. They do not use osmosis to transport water throughout the plant.

14. **C** Plants capture light energy from the sun and change it into chemical energy in a process called photosynthesis.

15. **C** Most photosynthesis takes place in the leaves, but it can also take place in green stems.

16. **A** Each offspring will have at least one gene for tall height, so they will all be tall.

17. **D** Musical skill is influenced by practice more than by genes.

18. **C** The Theory of Universal Common Ancestry states that all life descended from a single primitive ancestor. You can tell from the name of this theory that it has to do with the fact that all organisms come from a common ancestor.

19. If a mutation occurs in the combined cells in a fertilized egg, all of the cells of the offspring will have the mutated DNA. But if a mutation occurs in a body cell, that cell is not part of reproduction to form new offspring.

20. C If a long neck helps the tortoise get more food, it will be healthy and reproduce more. This will help the species survive.

21. The slanted line indicates that the object is accelerating. The slope of the line is the acceleration. The fact that it is a straight line indicates that the acceleration is constant.

22. D The point on the line directly above 4 seconds on the x-axis aligns with the point 39.0 on the y-axis.

23. D Acceleration is directly related to force and indirectly related to mass. If the mass is reduced by one-half, the acceleration will be doubled.

24. A small forklift exerts a force of 16 N to move a crate 10 m in 8 seconds. The power of the forklift is [20] joules.

25. C Mechanical advantage (MA) is equal to the output force divided by the input force. If MA is less than 1, the output force must be less than the input force. If the output force is not greater, then the distance must be so the machine allows the user to exert the input force over a shorter distance.

26. C Gravitational potential energy (GPE) depends on the mass of an object, its height, and the acceleration due to gravity. Increasing the height will increase the GPE.

27. C The kinetic energy of the pendulum is greatest when its height is lowest and speed is greatest. This occurs at point C.

28. B As the pendulum falls from its initial height, its potential energy is converted into kinetic energy. At the bottom of its path, the pendulum is at its lowest height and is moving at its greatest speed. Therefore, kinetic energy is greatest at the bottom of the swing.

29. Wind is a renewable energy resource whereas coal is a nonrenewable energy resource. Both can be converted into other forms of energy, such as electricity, that can be used to do work. However, wind will be replaced through natural processes as it is used whereas coal is not replaced at a rate close to the rate at which it is used, so it will eventually run out.

30. C Speed equals frequency times wavelength. Both the frequency and the wavelength are provided so substitute them into the given equation: $v = f \times \lambda$, so $v = 264$ Hz(1.40 m) $= 370$ m/s. Note that 1 Hz is 1 cycle per second, so Hz multiplied by m gives m/s.

31. While moving from left to right across a period of the periodic table, each successive element has one more proton and electron. This increases the attraction between the positively charged nucleus and the negatively charged outer electrons. As a result, the electrons are pulled in closer to the nucleus and the atomic radius decreases.

32. A An equation is balanced if the total number of each type of atom is the same on both sides of the equation. In this equation, there are 2 Ag atoms, 2 N atoms, 6 O atoms, 2 H atoms, and 1 S atom on each side of the equation.

33. C During sublimation, matter gains energy and its particles become less structured. The only other process listed in which matter gains energy is melting.

34. **temperature**
During each of the labeled processes, the [temperature] of the substance stays the same. The amount of thermal energy changes as the substance absorbs or releases thermal energy. However, the energy affects the arrangement of the particles of matter and therefore does not affect the temperature.

35. The dependent variable is the factor being measured or observed. In this case, the student is changing temperature and measuring the amount of $AgNO_3$ that dissolves. The amount that dissolves is determined by its solubility.

36 Fossil fuels emit carbon dioxide when they are burned to generate energy.

37. C According to the graph, emissions of carbon dioxide by fossil fuels have steadily risen over the past 100 years. If rates of usage of fossil fuels are not reduced, emissions would continue to rise.

38. A Earth's core is the innermost layer of Earth. It would correspond to the pit of a peach, which is the innermost part of the fruit.

39. **surface current**
Both surface currents and density currents move ocean water from place to place. However, surface currents are driven by wind and affect only the top part of the ocean. Density currents move along the bottom of the ocean.

40. C A tornado is a swirling column of air that can move very quickly. It is characterized by strong winds that can harm living things and damage property. The winds can lift rooftops off houses and cause debris to fly through the air. To avoid injury from the winds and flying debris, it is best to seek shelter in a basement or under a strong piece of furniture, away from windows.

41. As the nebula compressed, the gravitational forces overcame the internal pressure of the nebula's hot gases and collapsed . . . The heavy, rocky material pulled in strongly by gravity stayed near the central bulge.

42. C A disturbance was necessary to push gas and dust toward the center of the nebula. This began the process that led to the formation of our solar system.

43. **spiral**
The Milky Way galaxy has long arms that extend outward and bend around a large central bulge. Therefore, it is a spiral galaxy. A cluster is not a type of galaxy shape. An elliptical galaxy has a smooth, regular shape without spiral arms. An irregular galaxy does not have a uniform shape.

44. C The solar system is larger than the Sun, so the object that represents the solar system should be larger than the object that represents the Sun.

45. A Sedimentary rocks are often deposited in layers. The bottom layer forms first; subsequent layers are deposited on top of the bottom layer. If the layers are not disturbed, then fossils found in the bottom layer would be older than fossils found in the upper layers.

Check Your Understanding

On the following chart, circle any items you missed. This helps you determine which areas you need to study the most. If you missed any of the questions go back and review the reference pages.

Item #	Reference	Item #	Reference	Item #	Reference	item #	Reference
1	p. 15	13	p. 110	25	p. 201	37	p. 293
2	p. 16	14	p. 119	26	p. 214	38	p. 305
3	p. 32	15	p. 119	27	p. 212	39	p. 298
4	p. 36	16	p. 150	28	p. 213	40	p. 325
5	p. 50	17	p. 153	29	p. 220	41	p. 339
6	p. 62	18	p. 157	30	p. 237	42	p. 339
7	p. 63	19	p. 163	31	p. 251	43	p. 341
8	p. 71	20	p. 170	32	p. 267	44	p. 344
9	p. 71	21	p. 185	33	p. 259	45	p. 348
10	p. 81	22	p. 186	34	p. 258		
11	p. 99	23	p. 185	35	p. 274		
12	p. 106	24	p. 186	36	p. 293		

Chapter 1

Human Body and Health

The systems within the body work together to keep the body functioning. Eating healthful foods, staying active, and drinking plenty of water help to maintain the body systems. Good hygiene and regular hand washing can prevent diseases and help keep the body healthy. A healthy body is better able to regulate itself and to return to a normal state during times of stress or illness.

Purestock/Getty Images

Lesson 1.1

Skeletal, Muscular, and Nervous Systems

The skeletal, muscular, and nervous systems work together to help the body move. Learn about the structure and function of each of these body systems.

Lesson 1.2:

Digestive, Excretory, Respiratory, and Circulatory Systems

The respiratory, circulatory, digestive, and excretory systems deliver oxygen and nutrients and remove wastes. Learn how oxygen and nutrients are taken in and processed.

Lesson 1.3:

Endocrine and Reproductive Systems

The endocrine system controls hormones that carry messages throughout the body. Learn how hormones regulate growth and development.

Lesson 1.4:

Homeostasis

Homeostasis is responsible for keeping balance between all body systems and the environment. Learn how different body systems maintain body temperature, oxygen levels, and other values that are essential for our survival.

Lesson 1.5:

Nutrition

Nutrients provide hydration, energy, and structural elements that help our cells to function properly. Learn about six different nutrients the body needs for optimal health.

Lesson 1.6:

Disease Prevention

Harmful substances such as bacteria, viruses, and parasites can cause diseases in the body and disrupt the function of a body system. Learn how the body fights against disease and learn strategies for preventing disease.

Goal Setting

Set some goals for learning about human body systems by creating a three-column chart. In the first column list each body system covered in this chapter. Write a question you have about each body system in the second column. As you read, look for an answer to your question or conduct additional research and record your answer in the third column.

LESSON OBJECTIVES

- Identify the components and functions of the skeletal, muscular, and nervous systems
- Describe how each system works with other body systems to perform different functions

CORE SKILLS & PRACTICES

- Integrate Content Presented in Different Ways
- Determine Central Ideas

Key Terms

cartilage
strong but flexible material found in some parts of the body

joint
point of connection between bones

neuron
cell that transmits or receives signals within the nervous system

tendon
strong, fibrous connective tissue that joins muscle to bone

Vocabulary

integrate
bring parts together to make a whole

muscle
tissue that can contract

Key Concept

The skeletal, muscular, and nervous systems work together to allow your body to react to the sights, sounds, tastes, odors, and physical contact that you encounter daily.

The Skeletal System

Marathon runners travel more than 26 miles from start to finish. Running that far challenges the body both physically and mentally. Those who finish can take pride in achieving such a difficult goal. Running a marathon requires muscle strength and endurance. It also requires a sturdy skeletal system to support those muscles.

The skeletal system is a framework of bones that provides structure to your body and protects your internal organs. The skeleton also serves as a reservoir for the storage of minerals, produces blood cells, and allows movement of the body. A typical human skeleton is made up of 206 bones. The skull contains bones that surround and protect the brain, while bones of the spine support the skull and allow movement in the back. The ribs protect important internal organs. Bones in the hand allow for many tasks, and bones in the feet support the body when walking or running.

Each bone is composed of living, growing tissue. If a bone breaks, one type of bone cell breaks down the damaged tissue while another type of bone cell begins to rebuild the bone. Calcium and vitamin D are nutrients that help build strong bones. You may think of bones as hard, solid objects. Although the outside of a bone is hard, the inside is filled with soft tissue called marrow. Bone marrow produces new blood cells.

Two types of bone marrow, red and yellow, run through the center of many long bones, such as those in the legs and arms. Red bone marrow produces red blood cells, which transport oxygen throughout the body. It also produces certain types of white blood cells, which help to fight disease. Yellow bone marrow is made up mostly of fat cells that are a source of stored energy.

U.S. Air Force photo by Tech. Sgt. Tracy L. DeMarco

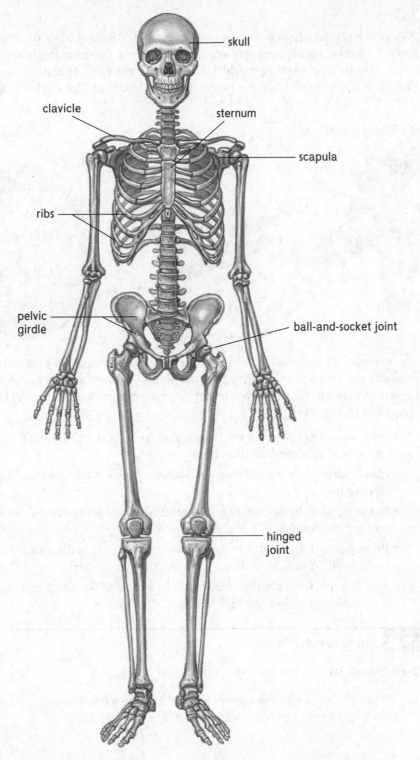

skull

clavicle

sternum

scapula

ribs

pelvic
girdle

ball-and-socket joint

hinged
joint

TECHNOLOGY SKILLS

Use Internet Resources

The most common kinds of bone injuries are broken bones, which heal in time with proper treatment and care. Using reliable Internet resources, research other kinds of bone injuries and common types of bone disease. What are the risk factors for developing bone disease? What causes bone injuries and disease? What can you do to help keep your bones healthy and strong as you get older? Write a paragraph to summarize your findings.

Bones come in different shapes and sizes, and are based on their functions. For example, short, slender bones in your fingers allow your fingers to move and grasp things. Bones are classified as:

- long bones, found in the legs and arms
- short bones, found in fingers and toes
- flat bones, found in the skull and pelvis
- irregular bones, found in the backbone and ears

Joints

Joints are places where two or more bones meet. Tough strands of connective tissue called ligaments connect bones at most joints. Bones at joints are covered in flexible **cartilage**, which is a tough, elastic connective tissue. Cartilage covers bones to prevent them from rubbing against each other.

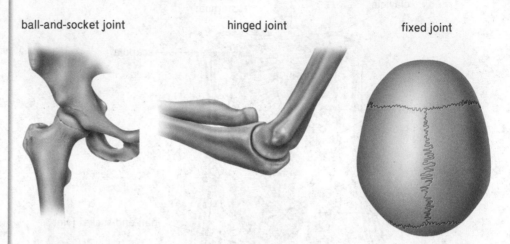

ball-and-socket joint   hinged joint   fixed joint

The amount of bone movement at a joint varies. For example, joints in the skull are not movable, while joints in the shoulder allow a wide range of motion. Joints are classified by the type of movement they allow and the shapes of their parts.

- Ball-and-socket joints, found in the shoulders and hips, allow for movement in almost all directions.
- Hinge joints, found in elbows and knees, allow for movement in one direction.
- Gliding joints, found in wrists and ankles, allow limited movement in many directions.
- Pivot joints, found between vertebrae in the spine, mainly allow rotating movement from side to side.
- Fixed joints, found in the skull, hold the bones of the skull together and do not allow for any movement.

Think about Science

Directions: Answer the following questions.

1. As people grow older, which component of the skeletal system can wear down and cause bones to rub together at the knee joint?

   A. marrow
   B. ligament
   C. cartilage
   D. calcium

2. Which of these protects the lungs from injury during a fall?

   A. ribs
   B. skull
   C. cartilage
   D. marrow

The Muscular System

The skeletal and muscular systems are interrelated. The muscular system uses muscles to move the bones of the skeletal system. **Muscles** are tissues that contract. Contraction occurs when muscle fibers shorten and pull together. Many muscles attach to bones, allowing you to walk, run, throw, dance, or do any other type of activity. Other muscles allow your heart to beat or move food through your body.

Voluntary Muscles

Skeletal muscles, or the muscles that are used to control bone movement, are all voluntary muscles you can consciously control. These muscles are connected to bones by **tendons**, which are bands of strong, fibrous connective tissue. Because a muscle can only contract, every joint is controlled by opposing muscles. This allows back-and-forth movement to occur. As shown in the image, you contract your biceps muscle to bend your arm. When your biceps muscle contracts, your triceps muscle relaxes and becomes stretched. You contract your triceps muscle to straighten your arm. When your triceps muscle contracts, your biceps muscle relaxes and becomes stretched.

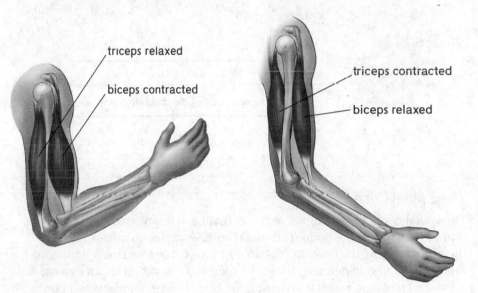

triceps relaxed

biceps contracted

triceps contracted

biceps relaxed

Involuntary Muscles

Muscles in the lungs, intestines, bladder, blood vessels, and heart are all involuntary muscles. You have limited control over involuntary muscles. In other words, these muscles function without you consciously controlling them. Some involuntary muscles move materials into, through, or out of the body, such as the smooth muscles in the blood vessels, lungs, or intestines. The involuntary muscle in the heart is called cardiac muscle. Cardiac muscle causes the heart to beat, which pumps blood throughout the body.

🔗 Think about Science

Directions: Fill in the blank.

1. The _____ muscle is used to bend your elbow.
2. The joint in your thumb is an example of a _____ joint.

Integrate Content Presented in Different Ways

In this section, information about the skeletal and muscular systems was presented using both text and diagrams. When you **integrate**, or bring together, content that is presented in different ways, you are likely to improve your understanding of a concept. For example, look at the information about voluntary muscles on this page. The text gives you details about what voluntary muscles are and how they can cause movement. The diagram uses pictures and text to further explain these concepts. What are some other ways that the concept of skeletal muscle movement could be presented?

Determine Central Ideas

Most informational text you read is organized into paragraphs containing central ideas that summarize the material. Paragraphs also contain supporting statements that provide details about the central ideas. To understand the material in informational text, you must be able to recognize central ideas. You must also be able to evaluate supporting statements to determine if the central ideas are valid.

Read each of the paragraphs on this page again. Can you determine one or two central ideas in each paragraph? What are the key words or statements in these paragraphs that support the central ideas? Use a graphic organizer such as the one below to organize each central idea and its supporting statements. This can help you understand the most important ideas in any text.

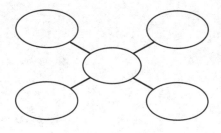

The Nervous System

When you want to move, what causes your muscles to contract? Muscles move in response to electrical and chemical signals that travel through the nervous system. The nervous system includes the brain, spinal cord, and a network of specialized nerve cells called **neurons.** When you decide to move your arm or leg, your brain sends a nerve impulse down the spinal cord. The impulse reaches the muscles involved, causing muscle contraction and movement.

Neurons

A neuron consists of three main parts: dendrites that receive messages from other neurons, a cell body that contains the nucleus, and an axon that allows an electrical signal to travel to other neurons and muscles. Axons are surrounded by a myelin sheath that insulates the axon and improves the speed at which impulses are conducted. At the gap between neurons, called a synapse, the electrical message is changed to a chemical message that is picked up by the next nerve cell.

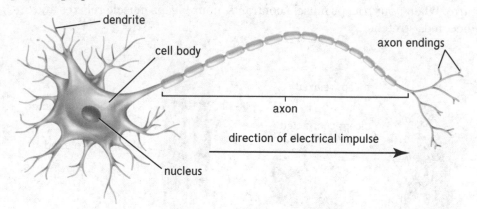

The Spinal Cord

The spinal cord consists of nerve fibers that send impulses to and from the brain to the rest of the body. The spinal cord sends many messages from the brain to allow the body to function. At times, however, the spinal cord functions as a body defense system by immediately acting on an emergency nerve-cell message without involving the brain. For example, when you touch a hot stove, a sensory neuron sends a message to your spinal cord that the stove is hot. The spinal cord immediately sends a message to the motor neurons in your arm and hand that causes you to pull your hand away from the stove. This reflex response is used to prevent injury when it would take too long for the message to travel to the brain, down the spinal cord, and then out to the affected area.

The Brain

The brain is a complex organ that contains 90 percent of the neurons in the body. The brain controls all actions except reflex responses. Different portions of the brain control different body functions.

There are three main structures at the base of the brain. The cerebellum controls coordination, posture, and balance. The medulla oblongata governs involuntary body functions like breathing and digestion. The pons helps control the rate of breathing and relays signals between the cerebellum and the cerebrum.

The cerebrum is the large structure at the top of the brain. It controls motor coordination and interpretation of sensory information from inside and outside the body. The cerebrum is divided into two halves called hemispheres. Each hemisphere contains four lobes that perform specific functions:

- The frontal lobe regulates voluntary movements and is involved with decision making and problem solving.
- The temporal lobe regulates memory, emotions, hearing, and language.
- The parietal lobe processes sensory signals from the body.
- The occipital lobe is involved with sight and visual memory.

The Human Brain

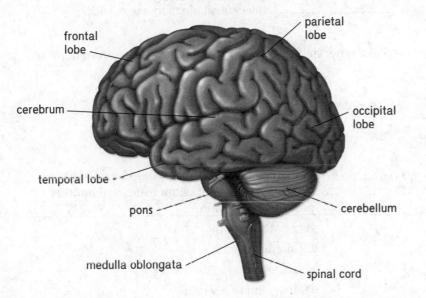

Health Literacy

A car or motorcycle accident can damage parts of the nervous system. When the nervous system is damaged, certain parts of the body can become paralyzed, or immobile. Think about how the brain and spinal cord receive sensory messages and then relay responses throughout the body. Prepare a presentation that explains how damage to the brain or spinal cord can cause paralysis. Suggest safety measures that could be taken to prevent nervous system damage due to accidents.

Think about Science

Directions: Fill in the blank with the correct answer.

1. When I pet a cat, the area of the brain that senses softness is the

   _____ .

2. The _____ keeps me from falling down when I trip on the sidewalk.

3. Signals to the _____ cause me to pull my hand away when I touch a sharp object.

4. The area of the brain that is helping me to answer these questions is the _____ .

Vocabulary Review

Directions: Write the missing term in the blank.

cartilage   muscle   neuron

joint   tendon   integrate

1. One function of _____ is to prevent contact between bones.

2. Two bones are held together at a _____ .

3. A _____ is tissue that can shorten and lengthen.

4. A _____ connects tissues in two different body systems.

5. A concept can become clearer when you _____ the central ideas in a text with experience from your own life.

6. A _____ is a specialized cell in the nervous system that conducts signals throughout the body.

Skill Review

Directions: Answer the following questions.

1. Which of these is a major function of the bone marrow?

   A. intercellular communication

   B. movement of materials

   C. avoidance of pain

   D. production of blood cells

2. Which of these best describes the pathway a nerve impulse takes through the body when you touch a hot stove with your hand?

   A. "hot" message—arm—spinal cord—arm

   B. "hot" message—brain—arm—spinal cord

   C. "hot" message—arm—brain—arm

   D. "hot" message—brain—spinal cord—arm

3. Which structure in the nervous system is most like a joint in the skeletal system?

   A. axon

   B. synapse

   C. nucleus

   D. cell body

4. Which of these activities would be most likely to activate the cerebellum instead of another portion of the brain?

   A. reading a book

   B. singing a song

   C. dancing to music

   D. listening to a lecture

5. During a softball game, a batter attempts to hit the ball that has been pitched toward her. Explain how the muscles, bones, and tendons of the batter's arms interact as the bat makes contact with the ball and the batter drives the ball into left field.

6. A reflex response occurs in the nervous system under certain circumstances. Explain how the reflex response improves survival in humans.

Skill Practice

Directions: Use the diagram to answer questions 1 and 2.

The Human Brain

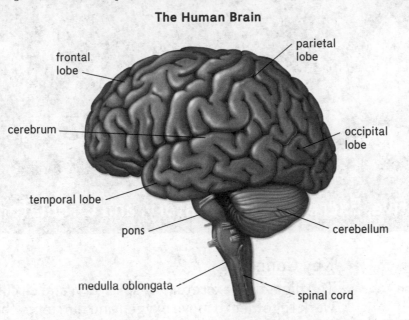

1. A man sustains an injury to his brain during a motorcycle accident that causes him to become temporarily blinded and unable to stand or walk without falling. Which area or areas of the brain shown in the diagram were most likely damaged?

   A. medulla oblongata
   B. medulla oblongata and frontal lobe
   C. cerebellum and temporal lobe
   D. cerebellum and occipital lobe

2. A concussion causes swelling in the frontal lobe. Which two symptoms might be a predicted result of this injury?

   A. short-term memory loss and loss of coordination
   B. increased rate of breathing and uncontrolled crying
   C. poor decision making and inability to move arms or legs
   D. temporary hearing loss and numbness in legs and arms

Directions: Answer the following questions.

3. When you swallow, which type of muscle moves food from your throat all the way down into your stomach?

   A. skeletal muscle
   B. cardiac muscle
   C. smooth muscle
   D. voluntary muscle

4. Which of these has a function that is most similar to the function of a tendon?

   A. ligament
   B. joint
   C. cartilage
   D. marrow

5. Why does the cardiac muscle need to be involuntary muscle instead of voluntary muscle?

6. The axon of a neuron is covered with a myelin sheath. How does a myelin sheath improve communication within the nervous system?

7. Compare the movements performed by the knees to the movements performed by the ankles. Considering their functions, why would these two structures have different types of joints?

LESSON OBJECTIVES

- Identify the components and functions of the digestive, excretory, respiratory, and circulatory systems

- Describe how each system works with other body systems to perform different functions

CORE SKILLS & PRACTICES

- Evaluate Validity of Conclusions
- Interpret Text or Graphics

Key Terms

alveoli
tiny air sacs within the lungs where gas exchange occurs

capillaries
microscopic blood vessels that connect arteries and veins

esophagus
a muscular tube that moves food from the throat to the stomach

Vocabulary

arteries
blood vessels that carry oxygen-rich blood away from the heart

summarize
to provide a short statement that includes the main ideas of a larger topic

veins
blood vessels that carry oxygen-poor blood toward the heart

Key Concept

The digestive, excretory, respiratory, and circulatory systems work together to move oxygen and nutrients through and out of your body.

The Digestive System

No matter what you eat, everything that goes into your mouth is processed by your body's digestive system. Three main processes occur within the digestive system: digestion, absorption, and elimination.

- Digestion is the breakdown of food into nutrients, which are molecules that your body's cells can use.
- Absorption is the movement of nutrients from the digestive system into the bloodstream, where they can be carried to all parts of the body.
- Elimination is the removal of undigested material from the body.

These processes occur in a series of organs called the digestive tract. The organs of the digestive system help the process by moving food around or by producing chemicals used in digestion.

The Esophagus and Stomach

Digestion starts as soon as you put food in your mouth. Chewing breaks food into smaller pieces and enzymes in your saliva help to chemically break down food. Smooth muscle in the digestive tract moves food through the digestive system. In this way, the digestive system interacts with the muscular system. Food moves from your mouth to your stomach through a muscular tube called the **esophagus**. Your stomach is the body's main organ of digestion. Food is broken down by the stomach's digestive juices.

The Small and Large Intestines

Partially digested food moves from the stomach to the small intestine, where absorption occurs. Digested nutrients and water pass through the walls of the small intestine and into the bloodstream. Waste materials continue through the small intestine and move into the large intestine. In the large intestine, waste materials are prepared for elimination, which is the passage of undigested material out of the body through an opening called the anus.

Tanya Constantine/age fotostock

Human Digestive System

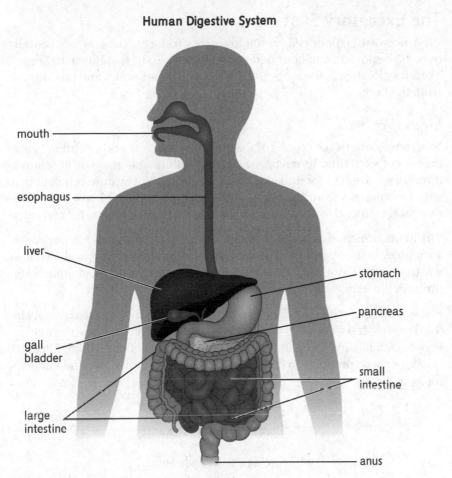

- mouth
- esophagus
- liver
- gall bladder
- large intestine
- stomach
- pancreas
- small intestine
- anus

The Liver, Gallbladder, and Pancreas

Even though food does not move through them, the liver, gallbladder, and pancreas are important parts of the digestive system. These three organs aid digestion in the small intestine. The liver is the largest internal organ of the body and has many functions. Its job in digestion is to make bile, which breaks down fat. Excess bile made by the liver is stored in a small organ called the gallbladder. The gallbladder releases bile into the small intestine as needed. The pancreas is a leaf-shaped organ that produces digestive enzymes. Enzymes from the pancreas are proteins that speed up biological reactions. The enzymes the pancreas makes help break down proteins, carbohydrates, and fats in the small intestine.

Think about Science

Directions: Fill in the blank.

1. Absorption, the process by which nutrients move from the digestive system into the bloodstream, occurs in the _____.

2. Digestion begins in your _____.

3. The pancreas, gall bladder, and _____ have important roles in digestion, but food does not pass through these organs.

4. Your esophagus connects your mouth with your _____, the body's main organ of digestion.

Digestive, Excretory, Respiratory, and Circulatory Systems

CORE PRACTICE

Evaluate Validity of Conclusions

The table below lists digestion times for six adults between the ages of 28 and 30.

Subject	Total digestion time (hours)
1	60
2	49
3	47
4	55
5	56
6	55

Evaluate the two conclusions listed below. Explain whether the conclusion is supported by the evidence provided in the table. Provide a thorough explanation for your answer.

1. Digestion may take different amounts of time, depending on a variety of factors.

2. People between the ages of 28 and 30 digest food in less than 60 hours.

Some jobs in the field of healthcare involve working in the home of a patient instead of in a clinical setting. This field of work is often called "in-home care." The work may involve helping senior citizens or adults with disabilities to maintain independence. The responsibilities of a caregiver may range from providing companionship to providing medical care.

Research the types of businesses that employ in-home health care workers. What challenges and opportunities do they face? What makes this type of business successful? **Summarize,** or provide a brief explanation of, your findings citing evidence from multiple sources to support your findings.

The Excretory System

Processes within your cells result in waste products. These waste products must be removed from your body to keep your body systems in balance. The excretory system is the system that removes liquid, solid, and gas wastes from the body.

Liquid Waste

Your skin is one of the organs of the excretory system, and sweating is one process of excretion. Your skin sweats in conditions such as warm weather and during exercise. The sweat helps your body with temperature regulation. As sweat evaporates from your skin, this helps your body cool down. When your skin sweats, this also allows your body to get rid of excess water and salts.

The lungs, which are part of the respiratory system, are also important structures in the excretory system. Carbon dioxide is a gas produced as a waste product from cell processes. Most of it is removed from your body through the lungs when you exhale.

Urine is produced by the kidneys, which are organs that are separate from the digestive tract. Kidneys are the main organs of the excretory system. People usually have two kidneys. The kidneys use millions of tiny filters to separate waste products in the blood from the water, glucose, and minerals the body needs.

Human Excretory System

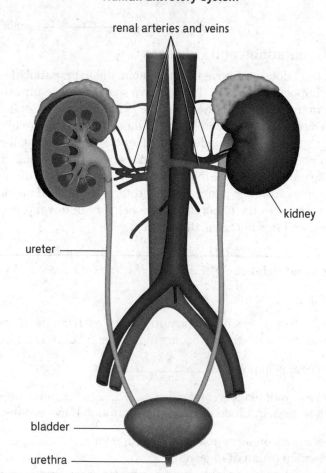

renal arteries and veins

kidney

ureter

bladder

urethra

Digestive, Excretory, Respiratory, and Circulatory Systems

Liquid waste produced by the kidneys is carried in urine, which passes through a tube called the ureter and is stored in the bladder. When the bladder is full, it contracts and pushes urine out of the body through the urethra. In most instances, the emptying of the bladder is under the control of voluntary muscles.

Blood enters each kidney through a large artery. Inside the kidney, the artery divides into many networks of capillaries that surround the filtering units of the kidney, which are called nephrons. Each kidney has about one million nephrons. Each nephron looks like a long coiled tube with a cup at one end. The cups of the nephrons are found in the outer rim of the kidney. Fluid from the blood is pushed through the walls of the capillaries and into the nephron. Some of the material that is moved into the nephron is waste material, and some is material the body needs. The material the body needs is returned to the blood through a process called reabsorption. The material that is waste, along with water, leaves the body as urine.

The Human Kidney

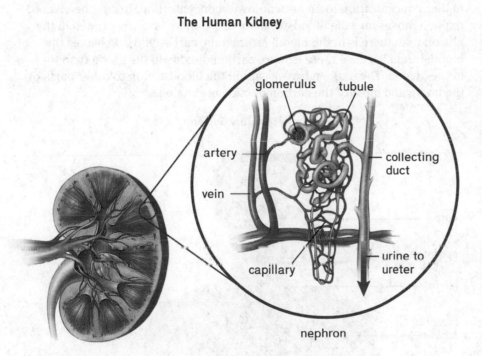

nephron

Solid Waste

Solid waste from the digestive system is prepared in the large intestine for elimination. Water is removed from the waste material, which eventually leaves the body through the anus as feces.

Think about Science

Directions: Fill in the blank.

1. The excretory system excretes wastes through processes such as exhalation, urination, and _____.

2. The _____ contains millions of tiny filters called nephrons that remove wastes from blood.

3. Urine exits the body through the _____.

Interpret Text or Graphics

Graphics such as diagrams, illustrations, charts, and tables can provide additional information or support text. They can help a reader better understand the text.

The text on this page describes the process in which blood enters the kidney and is filtered into either liquid waste or materials the body needs. The illustration shows the parts of the kidney that aid in this process. How does the graphic help you understand how blood is filtered in the kidneys? Looking at the graphic, what role do you think the collecting duct plays?

The Respiratory System

Did you know that your digestive system is closely connected to your respiratory system? Oxygen, which enters your body through the respiratory system, is required for the process your cells use to release energy from food molecules. Specifically, oxygen is the gas that cells use for cellular respiration. Through cellular respiration, organic molecules from the food you eat are broken down, and energy and carbon-dioxide gas are released. The released energy is used by body cells for all the cells' activities.

Gas Exchange Within the Lungs

When you breathe, you pull air into a pair of organs inside the chest called lungs. The inside of a lung is divided into many small air sacs, called **alveoli,** which are surrounded by tiny blood vessels called pulmonary capillaries. Oxygen in the lungs enters the body by diffusing across the alveoli and into the blood vessels. Diffusion is the movement of molecules from an area of higher concentration to an area of lower concentration. Inside the alveoli, oxygen moves into the bloodstream because there is more oxygen in the alveoli than there is in the blood. Meanwhile, carbon dioxide leaves the bloodstream because there is more carbon dioxide in the blood than there is in the alveoli. The oxygen travels within the bloodstream to other parts of the body, and most of the carbon dioxide is exhaled.

Human Respiratory System

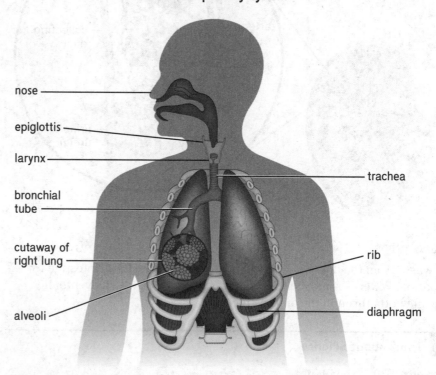

nose
epiglottis
larynx
bronchial tube
cutaway of right lung
alveoli
trachea
rib
diaphragm

Think about Science

Directions: Answer the following questions.

1. What is the main role of the respiratory system?
2. Name and describe the main organ(s) of the respiratory system.

Digestive, Excretory, Respiratory, and Circulatory Systems

The Circulatory System

The circulatory system transports blood through the human body. Blood delivers water and nutrients from the digestive system, and oxygen from the respiratory system, to all cells in the body. Blood also carries wastes from body cells to the organs that remove wastes.

The Heart

The center of the circulatory system is the heart, which pumps blood. The heart is a fist-sized muscle divided into two upper chambers called atria and two lower chambers called ventricles.

The Human Heart

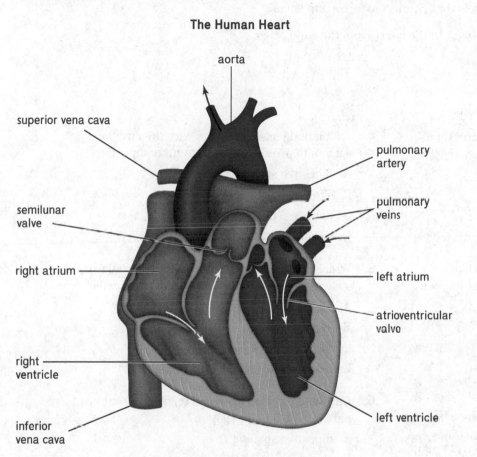

aorta

superior vena cava

pulmonary artery

pulmonary veins

semilunar valve

right atrium

left atrium

atrioventricular valve

right ventricle

left ventricle

inferior vena cava

Oxygen-poor blood from the body enters the right side of the heart. The right atrium and right ventricle pump oxygen-poor blood to the lungs. While in the lungs, the blood takes up oxygen gas and releases waste carbon-dioxide gas it has carried away from body cells. Oxygen-rich blood returns to the left side of the heart from the lungs. The left atrium and left ventricle pump oxygen-rich blood to the rest of the body. When it reaches body cells, the oxygen-rich blood gives up its oxygen and nutrients and picks up carbon-dioxide gas. The blood returns back to the right atrium, and the cycle continues.

Blood Vessels

There are three kinds of blood vessels inside the body: arteries, capillaries, and veins. In general, **arteries** carry oxygen-rich blood away from the heart. As blood moves away from the heart, the arteries get smaller and narrower. **Capillaries** are microscopic vessels that connect arteries and veins. Capillaries are only one cell thick. **Veins** carry blood back to the heart from the capillaries.

TEST-TAKING SKILL

Eliminate Unnecessary Information

Some test questions contain information you may not need to answer the question. This information may distract you from the actual focus of the question. To identify the information that is most important, you may wish to draw a line through the information that does not help you answer the question. You may also wish to underline or circle the information that is most important or relevant. Be sure you can still read any information you cross out.

Read the question below:

> The digestive system is one of the main body systems. Smooth muscles in the stomach and in other organs help move food through the digestive system. In which body structure do nutrients from the digestive system pass into the circulatory system?

Which part or parts of the question above provides unnecessary information? Explain your answer.

Vocabulary Review

Directions: Write the missing term in the blank.

arteries   esophagus   veins
capillaries   alveoli

1. Oxygen-rich blood is carried by the _____ to all parts of the body.

2. The _____ transports food to the stomach.

3. The exchange of gas occurs in the _____.

4. The _____ are vessels that connect arteries and veins.

5. _____ carry blood back to the heart from the capillaries.

Skill Review

Directions: Answer the following questions.

1. Which body systems interact most directly to produce urine?

   A. muscular and digestive

   B. digestive and excretory

   C. circulatory and excretory

   D. digestive and circulatory

2. Which part of the respiratory system is responsible for the actual exchange of oxygen and carbon dioxide?

   A. trachea

   B. alveoli

   C. esophagus

   D. arteries

3. A patient was diagnosed with gallstones, hard particles within the gall bladder. Gallstones can block the duct through which bile passes. Which part of digestion is most likely to be directly affected if this duct were blocked?

   A. The breakdown of food within the stomach

   B. The breakdown of fats in the small intestine

   C. The movement of food through the esophagus

   D. The rates of reactions within all organs of digestion

4. Which body system works with the circulatory system to provide oxygen to all body cells?

   A. digestive system

   B. skeletal system

   C. nervous system

   D. respiratory system

5. Which body system works with the circulatory system to provide nutrients to all body cells?

   A. digestive system

   B. skeletal system

   C. nervous system

   D. respiratory system

6. Carbon dioxide is excreted by organs that are part of which body system?

   A. digestive system

   B. skeletal system

   C. nervous system

   D. respiratory system

Digestive, Excretory, Respiratory, and Circulatory Systems

Directions: Use the diagram to answer questions 7 and 8.

7. This diagram shows a representation of the circulatory system. Red represents arteries, and blue represents veins. Based on what you know, explain which part of the diagram represents the capillaries.

8. Based on what you have learned about the circulatory system, explain why capillaries are only one cell thick.

The Human Circulatory System

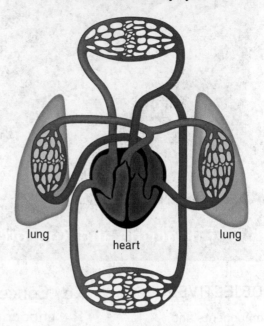

lung   lung

heart

Skill Practice

Directions: Answer the following questions.

1. Summarize the interactions between the excretory system and the respiratory system.

2. What is one main similarity between the digestive system and the respiratory system?

   A. Both use the mouth, esophagus, lungs, and alveoli to move materials in the body.

   B. Both receive waste materials and toxins that were filtered out by the kidneys.

   C. Both rely on the circulatory system to transport materials throughout the body.

   D. Both depend on chemicals released by the pancreas and the liver to function properly.

3. Write a hypothesis about an interaction between two of the following: digestive system, respiratory system, and circulatory system. Briefly describe how you could test your hypothesis.

4. A crew of Emergency Medical Technicians (EMTs) are called to an accident scene. They find an unconscious victim. Based on what you know, which body system—digestive, respiratory, or circulatory—do you think the EMTs will need to support first? Explain your answer.

5. Diabetes is a disease that occurs when the body cannot regulate levels of blood sugar. People with diabetes must use devices to monitor blood-sugar levels. Imagine you are in a medical setting and talking to a young patient who was recently diagnosed with diabetes. Describe to the patient, in detail, how sugar enters a person's bloodstream.

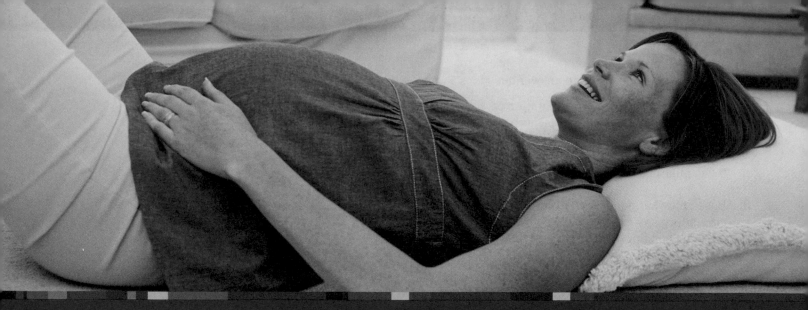

LESSON 1.3 Endocrine and Reproductive Systems

▌LESSON OBJECTIVES

- Identify components and functions of the endocrine and reproductive systems
- Describe how each system works with other body systems

▌CORE SKILLS & PRACTICES

- Reconcile Multiple Findings
- Compare and Contrast Information

Key Terms

gamete
sex cell

glands
organs that produce and release a substance

hormones
chemical messengers released by glands into the blood that regulate body functions

placenta
uterine membrane that creates a connection between the mother and embryo or fetus

Vocabulary

fetus
stage of development of an organism eight weeks after fertilization until birth

reconcile
explain how two ideas are true at the same time

Key Concept

The endocrine and reproductive systems are examples of body systems. Hormones in the endocrine system influence functions throughout the body, including the functions of the reproductive systems.

The Endocrine System

The endocrine system is similar to the nervous system, in that both systems send messages around the body. The endocrine system releases chemicals called **hormones** into the bloodstream. When these hormones reach target cells within the body, receptors on the target cells react, triggering a particular body response. For example, when you are feeling nervous, the hormone epinephrine is released into the bloodstream. When epinephrine reaches receptors on target cells, your heart rate increases, and your skeletal muscles become tense as part of the fight-or-flight response.

The speed at which hormones travel in the bloodstream is slow compared with the speed of nerve impulses. Thus, the endocrine system tends to regulate body processes that happen slowly over a long period of time. These processes include cell growth and development, metabolism, sexual function, and reproduction.

Glands are organs that produce and release substances. In the case of the endocrine system, these substances are hormones. Glands are found in the head and body, but not in the arms or legs. Different types of glands produce different types of hormones, and each hormone produces a unique effect.

Pituitary Gland

The pituitary gland is located in the brain and is connected to and controlled by the hypothalamus. The hypothalamus is an area of the brain that connects the nervous system to the endocrine system.

The pituitary gland secretes nine different hormones that either control other glands or directly regulate body processes. These hormones include adrenocorticotropic hormone (ACTH), which responds to stress and triggers the adrenal glands to release epinephrine; follicle-stimulating hormone

Endocrine and Reproductive Systems

The Primary Glands

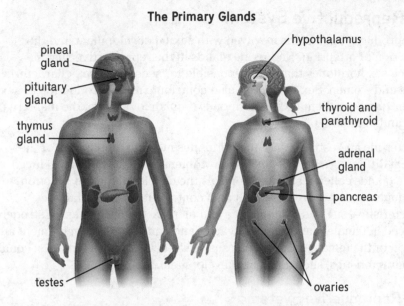

- pineal gland
- pituitary gland
- thymus gland
- testes
- hypothalamus
- thyroid and parathyroid
- adrenal gland
- pancreas
- ovaries

(FSH), which triggers the production of sperm and the maturation of egg cells; and prolactin, which triggers the production of milk in females.

Other Glands

Other glands are located in the head or upper body, as shown in the diagram. The pineal gland secretes melatonin, which is involved in regulating body rhythms. The thyroid gland releases thyroxine, which regulates the process through which cells break down chemicals and produce energy. The parathyroid glands release hormones that help regulate the amount of calcium in the bloodstream. The thymus gland produces hormones that help the body fight disease.

Still other glands are located near the center of the body. The adrenal glands produce the hormone epinephrine, which causes the fight-or-flight response in your skeletal and heart muscles. The pancreas, which is also an organ of the digestive system, releases hormones called insulin and glucagon, which stimulate the liver to either take up or release sugar into the blood. Reproductive glands produce testosterone and estrogen hormones that control reproduction and the development of secondary sex characteristics.

Think about Science

Directions: Answer the following questions.

1. Which statement is true about hormones?
   A. All hormones produce similar effects in the body.
   B. Hormones act on the site at which they are produced.
   C. Hormones travel throughout the bloodstream.
   D. Most organs in the body can produce hormones.

2. Hormones produced by the endocrine system can have a variety of effects within the body. Which of these is an example of a hormone effect on the muscular system?
   A. Decrease in blood calcium levels
   B. Increase in how fast the heart beats
   C. Increase in blood-sugar levels
   D. Development of reproductive organs

CORE PRACTICE

Reconcile Multiple Findings

Sometimes you may be asked to **reconcile** information, or explain how two findings or ideas are true at the same time. On this page, the text states that the pancreas is part of the endocrine system. However, the text also states that the pancreas is an organ of the digestive system. Write an explanation that reconciles these two statements.

The Reproductive System

The reproductive system is involved with sexual development and the production of offspring. Endocrine glands in the reproductive system produce sex hormones that are responsible for secondary sex characteristics in men and women. Sex hormones also contribute to the production of sex cells, or **gametes.** Female sex hormones regulate ovulation, the menstrual cycle, and pregnancy.

Testosterone and estrogen are the hormones mostly responsible for the physical differences between men and women. Testosterone is produced in male glands called testes and controls the development and function of the male reproductive system. It also controls male secondary sex characteristics, such as a deep voice and increased muscle mass. Estrogen is produced in female glands called ovaries and controls the development and function of the female reproductive system. It also controls female secondary sex characteristics, such as breast development.

Male Reproductive System

The male reproductive system includes the testes, epididymis, scrotum, penis, urethra, and a variety of glands. The testes produce male gametes, called sperm and the hormone testosterone. Millions of sperm are produced each day and stored in the epididymis. The testes and epididymis are suspended in the scrotum, which is a sac that hangs outside the body. The position of the scrotum keeps sperm at a cooler temperature, so the sperm are able to mature. During sexual activity, the sperm travel toward the urethra, which is a tube that spans from the urinary bladder through the penis. A series of glands add fluids to the sperm to form semen. Semen leaves the body through the penis during ejaculation.

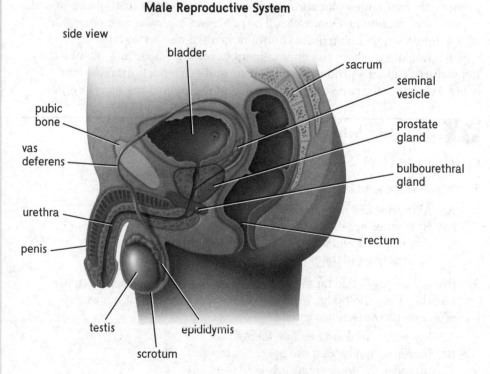

Male Reproductive System

side view

bladder
sacrum
seminal vesicle
pubic bone
prostate gland
vas deferens
bulbourethral gland
urethra
rectum
penis
testis
epididymis
scrotum

Endocrine and Reproductive Systems

Female Reproductive System

The female reproductive system includes the ovaries, fallopian tubes, uterus, and vagina. Female gametes, called eggs, are produced in the ovaries. The female reproduction system has several functions, including producing female sex hormones and storing and releasing the eggs.

Female Reproductive System

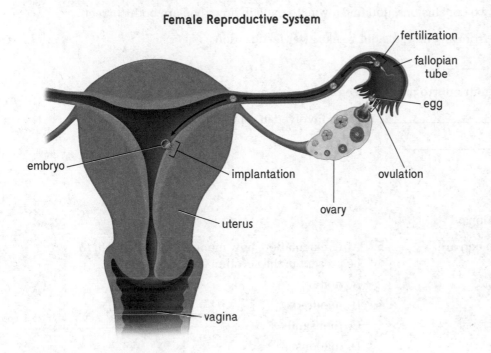

fertilization

fallopian tube

egg

ovulation

ovary

implantation

embryo

uterus

vagina

The Menstrual Cycle

Every month, sexually mature women release an egg from one of their ovaries and shed their uterine lining. This process is referred to as the menstrual cycle. The cycle starts when an egg begins to mature inside a follicle in the ovary. The follicle produces estrogen, which causes the tissue that lines the uterus to thicken. In about 14 days, the egg is released from the follicle in a process called ovulation. The empty follicle continues to release estrogen and also begins to release another hormone, progesterone. These two hormones cause the uterine lining to grow even thicker. If the egg is not fertilized as it travels down the fallopian tube, it dies and disintegrates. The lining of the uterus breaks down and is shed through the vagina as menstrual blood. The cycle typically takes about 28 days and then begins again. If a mature egg and sperm unite, pregnancy results, and the menstrual cycle stops.

Fertilization

When an egg is fertilized by a sperm cell, it begins to divide. This ball of cells moves down the fallopian tube to the uterus and attaches itself to the uterine lining. Upon implantation, the ball of dividing cells is called an embryo. Some of the cells differentiate to form the **placenta,** which is an organ that allows nutrients and other materials to pass between the mother and the developing offspring. The embryo becomes a **fetus** eight weeks after fertilization. The fetus undergoes rapid development until about nine months into the pregnancy. At this point, the mother's body produces hormones that cause labor. During labor, muscles in the uterus contract and relax, causing the baby to move down the birth canal until it is born.

CORE SKILL

Compare and Contrast Information

Some glands that are part of the endocrine system are also part of the reproductive system. Construct a Venn diagram that will allow you to compare and contrast these two systems. Place the glands that are part of both systems in the overlapping area of the Venn diagram. Place other structures that are part of only the endocrine or reproductive system in the areas of the diagram that do not overlap.

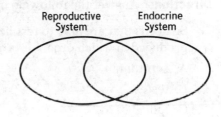

Reproductive System

Endocrine System

Vocabulary Review

Directions: Write the missing term in the blank.

fetus   gametes   glands

hormones   placenta   reconcile

1. When you _____ two conclusions, you find a way to explain how they are both correct.

2. A _____ develops from an embryo eight weeks after fertilization.

3. Sperm cells are male _____.

4. The _____ allows nutrients to pass between the mother and fetus.

5. Testosterone and estrogen are _____ that are involved in reproduction.

6. Hormones are released by _____.

Skill Review

Directions: Answer the following questions.

1. Sex cells that are able to fertilize an egg are produced in which organ or organs?

   A. scrotum

   B. testes

   C. kidneys

   D. ovaries

2. The growth of beards in men is most likely caused by which hormone?

   A. epinephrine

   B. estrogen

   C. progesterone

   D. testosterone

3. Which gland regulates levels of calcium in the body?

   A. parathyroid gland

   B. pancreas

   C. adrenal gland

   D. thyroid gland

4. The female reproductive system has four major parts. Which of these parts is most similar to the testes in the male reproductive system?

   A. uterus

   B. fallopian tubes

   C. ovaries

   D. vagina

5. After ejaculation, how many sperm are likely to be present in the scrotum 24 hours later?

   A. none

   B. hundreds

   C. thousands

   D. millions

6. Endometriosis is a condition that occurs when uterine tissue grows in the ovaries, fallopian tubes, or the lining of the pelvic cavity. Based on this information, what can you infer about endometriosis?

   A. It stops the menstrual cycle

   B. It can result in infertility

   C. It increases the chances of fertilization

   D. It can result in multiple births

7. Receptors on target cells trigger a body response in the presence of particular hormones. Explain why only certain cells are targeted by a particular hormone.

8. Describe how the reproductive systems of males and females are similar.

9. How do the endocrine and reproductive systems work together during childbirth?

Skill Practice

Directions: Identify the function of each gland. Fill in the blank with the correct term.

pineal	pituitary	thyroid
thymus	adrenal	reproductive

1. The _____ glands produce the hormone epinephrine, which causes the fight-or-flight response.

2. Hormones that help the body fight disease are produced by the _____ gland.

3. Melatonin, which helps to regulate body rhythms, is released by the _____ gland.

4. The _____ secretes hormones, which control other glands or help to regulate body process.

5. Thyroxine, which regulates the process through which cells break down chemicals and produce energy, is released by the _____ gland.

6. The _____ glands control the development of secondary sex characteristics.

Directions: Answer the following questions.

7. Changes in estrogen, progesterone, and other hormone levels are tied to events in the menstrual cycle. If disease caused progesterone levels to remain at their peak throughout an affected woman's menstrual cycle, how would the increased progesterone levels affect the woman's uterine lining?

   A. The uterine lining would thicken without being shed.

   B. The uterine lining would be unaffected.

   C. The uterine lining would cease to thicken.

   D. The uterine lining would thicken and be shed suddenly.

8. Cells in the ovaries would have receptors for which of these hormones?

   A. follicle-stimulating hormone

   B. thyroxin

   C. growth hormone

   D. glucagon

9. A woman begins having menstrual cycles on her 12th birthday. These cycles continue uninterrupted until she becomes pregnant on her 33rd birthday. How many menstrual cycles has she experienced by the time she becomes pregnant?

   A. about 252 cycles

   B. about 274 cycles

   C. about 365 cycles

   D. about 548 cycles

10. What reactions occur in the body during the fight-or-flight response?

11. Explain how yoga and meditation might influence levels of epinephrine to help a person calm down after a frightening experience.

12. During an ectopic pregnancy, the embryo implants outside the uterus. Why would it be difficult (and dangerous) for an embryo to develop in one of a woman's fallopian tubes? Use what you have learned to explain your answer.

LESSON 1.4 Homeostasis

■ LESSON OBJECTIVES

- Explain why homeostasis is vital for living organism survival
- Understand how organisms adjust to changes

■ CORE SKILLS & PRACTICES

- Evaluate Evidence
- Express Scientific Information or Findings Visually

Key Terms

homeostasis
the regulation of an organism's internal environment to maintain conditions necessary for life

negative-feedback mechanism
a system that responds to a change by shifting values in the opposite direction

positive-feedback mechanism
a system that responds to changes by increasing the change

Vocabulary

infer
to form an opinion or reach a conclusion based on evidence

response
the reaction to a stimulus

stimulus
a condition that causes an organism to react in a certain way

Key Concept

Human body systems work to maintain a balanced state of internal physiological conditions even when there are changes in the external or internal environment.

Homeostasis

What happens to our bodies on a cold, winter day? If we are not wearing enough layers of warm clothing, chances are we will start to shiver. By shivering, our body works to maintain a constant temperature when the external temperature is low.

Changes in the outside temperature are detected by our nervous system, which includes receptors in our skin. These receptors send a signal to the hypothalamus portion of our brain. The hypothalamus sends a signal to the muscular system so that muscles rapidly contract and relax, causing us to shiver in an attempt to produce body heat. In addition, smooth muscles in the circulatory system contract to constrict blood vessels, retaining body heat so the skin stays warm. The nervous system also sends signals so that we instinctively curl up as much as possible to bring all our body parts closer together. This behavior serves to expose less surface area so that less heat escapes our body.

If anything happens to or within a living organism that affects its normal state, processes to restore the normal state begin. The regulation of an organism's internal environment to maintain and balance the conditions needed for life is called **homeostasis.** Through homeostasis, body systems in organisms maintain characteristic conditions. Parts of the nervous system and endocrine systems are dedicated to maintaining homeostasis, and their action is coordinated by the hypothalamus. Conditions that are regulated to maintain homeostasis include the following:

- body temperature
- heart rate
- breathing rate
- blood glucose levels
- blood pH

Responses to Stimuli

A **stimulus** (plural, stimuli) is anything that causes a reaction or a change in a living organism. An increase in temperature in an environment is a stimulus to the human body, but the act of sweating to cool the body down is a **response,** or reaction to the stimulus. When sensory receptors in the nervous system detect stimuli, they send a message to the hypothalamus. The hypothalamus interprets the information and sends out a signal indicating how the body should respond to the stimuli.

A particular response to a stimulus is often recognized by a certain behavior or action. For example, a hunger response is triggered when our stomach is empty. The common behavior in response to hunger is to eat a snack or a meal. Behavior patterns of an organism are usually connected to its constant struggle to survive or reproduce. Other responses include an increased heart rate in response to fear, and an increase in white blood cell production in response to an infection.

External Stimuli

External stimuli come from outside an organism and influence the organism's behavior. Temperature, sound, light, and other organisms act as external stimuli and cause different responses in organisms. Oxygen is an external stimuli required to sustain life. Low levels of oxygen in our immediate surroundings trigger a behavioral response in humans. If we cannot take in enough oxygen from our environment, we will gasp for air, breathing faster and more deeply, trying to bring more oxygen to our blood cells. This behavior is due to the response in our body in which cells sense the lack of oxygen.

Internal Stimuli

Internal stimuli such as hunger or thirst come from inside an organism's body and also influence behavior patterns. When humans lose water on the surface of the skin in the form of sweat, the brain triggers specific hormones that let us know our body needs more water, and we feel thirsty. Other examples of internal stimuli include fatigue, a full stomach or a full bladder, and internal pain.

Think about Science

Directions: Answer the following questions.

1. Which body system is essential for maintaining all conditions of homeostasis throughout the human body?

   A. muscular
   B. circulatory
   C. nervous
   D. skeletal

2. Which of the following is an example of a response to a stimulus?

   A. shivering
   B. thirst
   C. hunger
   D. temperature

Evaluate Evidence

A text can give you information that can be used to support an idea that is not stated directly in the text itself. Read the section *Responses to Stimuli.* Explain how homeostasis of humans is affected by their environment. Include multiple pieces of evidence from the text to support your answer.

Express Scientific Information or Findings Visually

Diagrams, such as the one on this page, help explain the function of a complicated system. Following a diagram in a step-by-step fashion can help you understand complicated biological systems.

Read the passage. Then make a diagram that illustrates how homeostasis is restored when blood pressure is low. Include the stimulus and response.

Receptors in the circulatory system detect changes in blood pressure against the walls of vessels that carry blood to and from the heart. When a change in blood pressure occurs, a signal is sent to the hypothalamus. When blood pressure is low, the hypothalamus sends signals back to the circulatory system to increase the heart rate and constrict smooth muscles in the blood vessels.

Feedback Mechanisms

In general, the human body remains in homeostasis when it is functioning properly and all basic needs are met. Every body system contributes to maintaining homeostasis in some way, and this maintenance is similar to a very complex balancing act. Variables such as body temperature, heart rate, blood pressure, blood glucose, blood pH, and hydration levels all have a normal range. If these values deviate significantly from their norm, body systems work together to restore the normal value. Feedback mechanisms are systems set up to respond to changes in these variables. The diagram below provides a visual explanation as to how homeostasis is maintained.

Maintaining Homeostasis

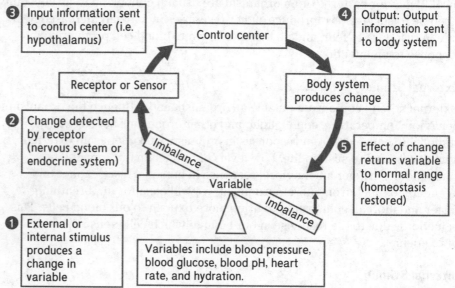

Negative-Feedback Mechanism

When a condition in the body, such as temperature, deviates from its normal value, or set point, due to an internal or external stimulus, the body activates certain systems or chemicals. These systems or chemicals help reverse the change and return the value to its set point. This process is called a **negative-feedback mechanism.** For example, when the internal body temperature in humans gets too high due to high external temperatures, a signal is sent from the brain to dilate blood vessels. Dilated blood vessels are closer to the skin's surface, so excess heat can escape. Another signal from the brain activates sweat glands to produce sweat, which also cools the body. Both of these systems work to return the body's temperature to its set point.

Negative Feedback Mechanism

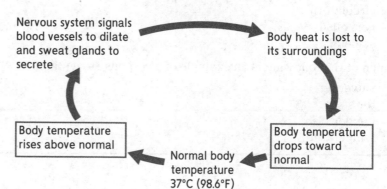

If the negative-feedback mechanism is not activated, homeostasis cannot be restored and the body temperature will continue to rise. This can lead to hyperthermia, which can cause dehydration, dizziness, and nausea. It is often called heat exhaustion. More severe hyperthermia leads to heat stroke, brain damage, organ-system shutdown, or possibly death.

Blood glucose levels are also controlled by a negative-feedback mechanism. After a meal, especially one high in carbohydrates, blood glucose levels rise. Receptors in the body sense the change and the pancreas, which acts as a control center for this feedback mechanism, releases a chemical called insulin into the blood. Insulin acts to lower the level of glucose in the blood and return it to its normal range, or set point.

Positive-Feedback Mechanism

In some cases, the body may activate a **positive-feedback mechanism.** A positive-feedback mechanism is a system set in motion to accelerate a change in an effort to maintain homeostasis. A fever is the result of a positive-feedback mechanism that acts to kill an infecting virus or bacteria. During an infection, a positive-feedback mechanism in the body accelerates an increase in internal body temperature in an effort to kill the infecting agent. Once the infecting agent is killed, the temperature returns to its set point.

The process of blood clotting when you are bleeding from an injury is also controlled by a positive-feedback mechanism. When a blood vessel is damaged, platelets in the blood cling to the injured site and release chemicals that attract even more platelets to the injured site. The platelets continue to accumulate until they form a clot, which stops the bleeding at the site.

Think about Science

Directions: Determine whether each of the following examples illustrate negative-feedback or positive-feedback mechanism.

1. The action of blood vessels constricting to conserve heat in the body.
   _____

2. The production of oxygen-carrying red blood cells in response to a low concentration of oxygen in the blood. _____

3. The release of hormones during childbirth to increase the rate of contractions and speed up the birthing process. _____

Interpret Information

Set up an experiment to measure the heart rate (pulse) of a group of ten people. Have each person rate their exercise level on a scale of 0 to 5 (0 = no regular exercise, 5 = intense exercise). Measure the resting heart rate of each subject and record this value. Next, measure the heart rate of the same individuals immediately after performing one minute of a physical activity such as jumping jacks or running. Then measure each person's heart rate at one-minute intervals to determine when it returns to the initial resting rate. Record all data for each person in a separate column.

To **infer** means to reach a conclusion based on facts. What can you infer from your results? What role does exercise play in helping a person maintain homeostasis? Use what you have learned in this lesson to explain your reasoning.

Vocabulary Review

Directions: Write the missing term in the blank.

| homeostasis | infer | negative-feedback mechanism |
| response | stimulus | positive-feedback mechanism |

1. When the body's temperature gets too high, the it's _____ activates to dilate blood vessels so heat can escape

2. An example of _____ is blood clotting when bleeding from an injury.

3. Maintaining a balance to sustain life is call _____.

4. While examining data from an experiment, you may _____ conclusions based on the evidence.

5. Oxygen is an external _____ required to sustain life.

6. When you sweat to cool down, your body is using a _____.

Skill Review

Directions: Answer the following questions.

1. In order to maintain homeostasis in hot climates, dogs pant, and humans _____.

2. Which of the following best illustrates the sequence of events that will lead to a response when the body experiences an increase in blood pressure?

   A. sensors detect increased pressure → signal sent to brain → blood vessels dilate → pressure decreases

   B. sensors detect increased pressure → signal to brain → signal to circulatory system → blood vessels dilate → pressure decreases

   C. brain detects increased pressure → signal from brain to sensors → signal from sensors to circulatory system → pressure decreases

   D. brain detects increased pressure → signal from brain to sensors → blood vessels dilate → pressure decreases

3. Which of the following is an example of an internal stimuli that can decrease the heart rate?

   A. decreased blood pressure

   B. increased blood pressure

   C. decreased environmental temperature

   D. increased environmental temperature

4. In which way are smaller animals better suited to maintain homeostasis than humans?

   A. Smaller animals do not have complex body systems.

   B. Smaller animals consume less food and water.

   C. Smaller animals have less surface area than larger animals.

   D. Smaller animals require less energy for cellular function.

5. Explain how hunger is an internal response that can help a person maintain homeostasis.

6. Inside the body, the chemical insulin is released to lower blood glucose levels after a person eats a meal. Of which type of mechanism is this an example? Explain.

7. A fever is one way the body attempts to return to its normal homeostatic conditions through a positive-feedback mechanism. Explain a situation in which this positive-feedback mechanism might be harmful rather than helpful to the body.

Skill Practice

Directions: Use the graph to answer questions 1 and 2.

The heart rate of an individual is measured at five-minute intervals over the span of one hour. The data is recorded in the graph.

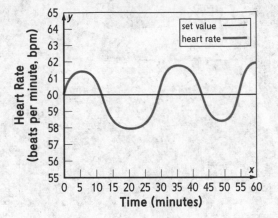

Fluctuations in Heart Rate

1. What is the heart rate (bpm) of the individual when homeostasis is maintained?

   A. 50 bpm

   B. 60 bpm

   C. 70 bpm

   D. 80 bpm

2. Explain why the heart rate is not constant over time.

Directions: Use the information to answer questions 3–5.

A Journey Through the Eye

The human eye works together with the brain to help us see. The eyes let in the light and send signals to the brain, and these signals create the pictures, or images, we see.

When light goes into the eye, it first passes through the cornea, which is a clear layer on the outside of the eyeball. The cornea protects the eye at its surface and moves light deep into the eye. Next, light travels through the pupil, an opening that appears to be a black spot in the center of the eye. The pupil controls how much light enters the eye. Around the pupil is the colorful iris. The muscles of the iris relax and become looser to open the pupil so that when you try to see in a dark or dim room, the pupil lets more light in. In a very bright room, the iris becomes tighter to make the pupil smaller so that less light passes into the eye.

From the pupil, light travels through a clear circular disk called a lens. The lens focuses light and can change its shape to focus on objects located at different distances from the eye. Focused light from the lens hits the retina, which is on the back of the eyeball. The retina is made up of nerve cells called rods and cones. Rods help us see in black and white in low lighting or the dark. Cones help us see colors when we are in brighter light. When a person enters a dark room after being in bright light, his or her eyes have to adapt to the change. The pupil grows wider to let in as much light as possible. But changes in the pupil are not enough to help us see when light conditions *quickly* change to dark. Along with pupil changes, a pigment found in the rods of the retina make it possible for us to see in the dark. Bright light bleaches this pigment and stops it from working. Therefore, when external conditions quickly turn dark, it takes time to activate the release of more pigment so the eyes can perceive objects.

3. Explain how the eyes' ability to see in the dark is due to a negative-feedback mechanism.

4. What do you think might happen if the mechanisms that return the eyes to homeostasis in the presence of bright light are disrupted? Explain.

5. Which body systems are involved in maintaining homeostasis in the eye?

LESSON 1.5 Nutrition

■ **LESSON OBJECTIVES**

- Identify the six key nutrients: carbohydrates, proteins, fats, vitamins, minerals, and water
- Identify key nutrient sources
- Explain the role calories play in a healthful eating plan

■ **CORE SKILLS & PRACTICES**

- Reconcile Multiple Findings, Conclusions, or Theories
- Represent Real-World Arithmetic Problems

Key Terms

calories
a measure of the energy stored in food

nutrients
raw materials needed to sustain healthy life functions

nutrition
the process by which an organism takes in and uses food

Vocabulary

minerals
inorganic elements the body needs for metabolic functions

vitamins
complex organic molecules that help the body build new tissues and important molecules

Key Concept

Your body depends on six key nutrients. Because nutrients come from food, eating a balanced diet contributes to your health.

Nutrients

All living things get energy through **nutrition,** which is the process by which an organism takes in and uses food. Foods supply **nutrients,** or raw materials needed to sustain healthy life functions. Nutrients provide energy, heal wounds, help to transport oxygen to cells, and regulate body functions. In other words, the body needs nutrients to maintain basic functions and to provide energy for daily activities.

Nutrients are constantly being consumed and depleted by bodily functions. Different foods provide different nutrients for the body, so eating a variety of healthful foods is important to get the nutrients needed. Key nutrients include carbohydrates, proteins, fats, vitamins, minerals, and water.

Carbohydrates

Carbohydrates are molecule chains made up of carbon, hydrogen, and oxygen that provide people with fuel and energy when consumed. There are three different kinds of carbohydrates: simple, starches, and fiber.

Simple carbohydrates are sugars, such as sucrose (table sugar), fructose, and lactose. Sugars occur naturally in fruits, vegetables, and milk. They can also be added to processed food, such as cookies, cakes, and breads. Refined simple carbohydrates such as white rice and white bread should be eaten in moderation.

Starches are complex carbohydrates that can be found in breads, pastas, potatoes, rice, and other grains. These are long chains of sugars that must be digested before the body can use them as fuel. Starches are a more sustained energy source than simple sugars and act as fuel for metabolic functions.

Nutrition

Fiber is a complex carbohydrate that comes from the cell walls of plants, and is found in peas, beans, fruits, vegetables, and whole-grain breads and cereals. Fiber is essential for the smooth running of the digestive system.

Protein

Proteins provide the basic structural and functional components of all cells. Each protein is made up of combinations of 20 different amino acids. Amino acids are the building blocks of proteins, nine of which are considered essential. This means they cannot be built by the body. The nine essential amino acids need to be consumed in order to maintain healthy body structures, including skin, muscles, and hair.

Both plant and animal food sources contain proteins. Proteins that come from fish, milk, meat, and eggs contain all 20 amino acids and are known as complete proteins. Nuts, beans, and some grains are rich in protein, but lack some of the 20 amino acids. Quinoa is an example of a grain that is a complete protein containing all 20 amino acids. People on a vegetarian diet must plan their meals carefully so they obtain all the amino acids they need.

Fats

Fats and other lipids are an important part of cell membranes, nerve insulation, and hormones. The three types of fat molecules—saturated fats, unsaturated fats, and trans fats—are classified based on their chemical structure. Fats support some of the body's functions and provide energy, but trans fats should be avoided.

- *Saturated fats* usually come from animals. Saturated fats are also known as solid fats because they are solid at room temperature. Butter and lard are examples of saturated fats.

- *Unsaturated fats* usually come from plants. Extracted unsaturated fats, such as corn oil and olive oil, are typically liquid at room temperature. Nuts, avocado, and fish are just a few other foods rich in unsaturated fats. Unsaturated fats are, in general, considered more healthful than saturated fats. Eating unsaturated fats in moderate amounts may lower your risk of heart disease.

- *Trans fats* are manufactured by adding hydrogen to vegetable oils. They are often used in processed foods and may have adverse effects on health, including an increased risk of stroke and heart disease.

Water

All of the body's cells contain water. Water is essential for most body functions. Cells cannot reproduce or grow without water. Water also lubricates the joints of the body and reduces protein breakdown of muscle tissue. Without water, neurotransmitters do not work efficiently, slowing down brain function, reaction time, and the ability to reason.

Every day the human body loses between two to three liters of water through respiration, perspiration, and urination. A person needs to consume at least two liters of water daily to maintain homeostasis in the body. While the human body can go weeks without food, it can survive only a few days without water. Dehydration can cause severe medical issues, including muscle weakness, slow reaction times, and even death.

■ **21ST CENTURY SKILL**

Critical Thinking and Problem Solving

In an effort to reduce consumption of soda and junk food, lawmakers in many cities and states have considered a special tax on soft drinks. Research has shown that a price increase in soda is associated with a decrease in consumption. Write a persuasive paragraph arguing either in support of or against taxes on soft drinks. Use the information you learned about sugars and additional research to support your argument.

CORE PRACTICE

Reconcile Multiple Findings, Conclusions, or Theories

Scientific research in the early 1900s led to the first discoveries about vitamins. In 1929, a Nobel Prize was awarded to two scientists to recognize their work on vitamins. Research on vitamins, minerals, and nutrition continues today and ideas about nutrition continue to change as new evidence emerges. For example, there have been multiple different findings and conclusions about whether or not women should take calcium supplements. Using reliable resources on the Internet or in print, research this topic. After reading about multiple findings and conclusions, write a statement to reconcile these findings and summarize what is known.

Vitamins

Complex organic molecules that help the body build new tissues, regulate body functions, and fight disease are called **vitamins.** There are 13 different vitamins. Their sources, functions, and results of deficiencies are shown in the table below. Even though only a few hundredths of a gram of each vitamin is needed every day, deficiencies can cause severe health problems.

Vitamin	Source	Function	Result of Deficiency
A	orange and dark green vegetables, eggs, dairy	used to form visual pigments	progressive blindness
B1	grains, meat, legumes, nuts	carbohydrate metabolism	beriberi (neurological symptoms)
B2	milk, eggs, leafy vegetables, grains	coenzyme for many metabolic reactions	dermatitis, sensitivity to light
B3	grains, meat, legumes, nuts	important part of nicotinamide coenzymes	pellagra; dermatitis and neurological symptoms
B6	meat, fruit, grains, legumes, vegetables	amino-acid metabolism	skin lesions, irritability, anemia, convulsions
B12	meat, eggs, dairy	used to maintain nerve cells; fatty acid and amino-acid metabolism	anemia, neuropathy
folate	vegetables, legumes	important part of DNA synthesis, red-blood-cell formation	anemia, digestive disorders, neural-tube defects in developing embryo
C	citrus fruit, green vegetables, potatoes	used in synthesis of collagen	scurvy (bleeding gums, loss of teeth, listlessness)
D	fatty fish, eggs, fortified milk	assists calcium absorption	rickets (unmineralized bones)
E	green vegetables, nuts, grains, oils, eggs	prevents damage to cell membranes	hemolytic anemia
K	leafy green vegetables	intestinal flora; formation of clotting factors	bleeding disorders

Minerals

Inorganic elements the body needs for most of its metabolic functions are called **minerals.** Minerals contribute to making bones strong, enabling nerves to send impulses and allowing muscles to contract.. Some of the many minerals the body needs, their sources, functions, and results of deficiencies, are shown in the table on the next page.

Mineral	Source	Function	Result of Deficiency
calcium	milk, eggs, green vegetables, fish	mineralization of bone	rickets, osteoporosis
sodium	most foods	fluid balance; muscle contraction; nerve conduction	weakness, cramps, diarrhea, dehydration
potassium	most foods	major cellular action	muscular and neurological disorders
iodine	seafood, iodized salt	required for synthesis of thyroid hormones	goiter (enlarged thyroid gland)
iron	red meat, liver, eggs, legumes, dried fruit	part of hemoglobin	anemia, indigestion
magnesium	green vegetables, grains, nuts, legumes	part of carbohydrate metabolism	muscular and neurological disorders, arrhythmic heartbeat

Eating a Healthy, Balanced Diet

When you eat meals that provide a variety of the nutrients your body needs, you are eating a balanced diet. Most foods contain more than one nutrient. For example, vegetables contain fiber, carbohydrates, vitamins, and minerals. Quinoa is a grain that contains carbohydrates, minerals, and protein. In order to have a healthy diet, it is important to include a variety of nutrient-rich foods that are low in fat and added sugars.

Calories and Maintaining a Healthy Weight

Calories measure the energy stored in food. People get all the calories they need from the foods they eat. Foods that are high in calories include foods high in fats, starches, simple carbohydrates, and many processed foods. Foods that are low in calories include lean meats, fruits, and vegetables. All metabolic functions, including respiration and maintaining body temperature, burn calories to maintain homeostasis in the body. However, most of these processes do not require a large amount of calories.

The number of calories a person needs depends on gender, age, and activity level. To maintain a healthy weight is to balance the calories consumed with the calories expended through physical activity. If a person eats more calories than his or her metabolism burns, the body will store the extra calories as fat.

Think about Science

Directions: Answer the following question.

1. Which nutrient is responsible for building muscle tissues?
   A. carbohydrates   C. water
   B. protein   D. fats

CORE SKILL

Represent Real-World Arithmetic Problems

Math skills are used to solve real-world arithmetic problems every day. Read the scenario below and then answer the question.

According to her current age, weight, and level of activity, Sarah has calculated that she needs a minimum of 1,620 calories per day to maintain her current weight and metabolic functions. She decides to start a new wellness program for which she eats on average 1,800 calories per day and also increases her activity level, burning 430 more calories per day. Is Sarah likely to lose, gain, or maintain her weight based on these changes? Explain.

Vocabulary Review

Directions: Write the missing term in the blank.

calories	**minerals**	**vitamins**
nutrients	**nutrition**	

1. The raw materials the body gets from food are called _____.

2. _____ are inorganic elements the body needs for most of its metabolic functions.

3. The energy stored in food can be measured in _____.

4. _____ are complex organic molecules that help the body build new tissues and important molecules.

5. _____ is the process of consuming and using nutrients to sustain life.

Skill Review

Directions: Answer the following questions.

1. Which foods provide the most proteins?
   A. meats
   B. vegetables
   C. grains
   D. nuts

2. Many foods contain more than one nutrient. Which of these nutrients can be found in broccoli?
   A. carbohydrates, protein, vitamins
   B. protein, fats, vitamins
   C. fats, carbohydrates, minerals
   D. carbohydrates, vitamins, fiber

3. According to the vitamin and mineral tables on pages 44 and 45, which vitamin(s) or mineral(s) are important for bone health?
   A. vitamin A and folate
   B. vitamin D and calcium
   C. iron and magnesium
   D. vitamins A, B, and K

4. Why is it important to drink more water during exercise?

5. The body may store energy from excess calories as _____.

Directions: Use the passage below to answer questions 6–7.

Cholesterol is a wax-like substance found in all body tissues. In small amounts, cholesterol is important to good health. The human body uses it in digestion. However, excess cholesterol can cause clogging of blood arteries, a condition that can interfere with proper blood flow and may lead to death. To lower cholesterol levels, doctors recommend limiting foods high in saturated fats such as red meat, fried foods, butter, and some processed foods. In general, a healthier diet can be achieved by eating a diet rich in lean proteins, fruits, vegetables, and complex carbohydrates.

6. Which of the following can you infer to be true from the information given in the passage?
   A. Even a small amount of cholesterol in the body is unhealthy.
   B. Excess cholesterol in the body can lead to heart disease.
   C. Plants that have a high oil content, such as olives, contain cholesterol.
   D. Family medical history is related to cholesterol level.

7. Avocadoes contain a nutrient that may help lower blood cholesterol. What are avocadoes likely rich in?
   A. proteins
   B. saturated fats
   C. unsaturated fats
   D. carbohydrates

Skill Practice

Directions: Answer the following questions.

1. John is a vegetarian and does not eat meat or fish. He wants to start a weight-lifting regimen. Which of the following meals offers the most protein needed to help him build muscle?

   A. Pasta and a spinach salad

   B. Pork chop with beans

   C. Rice and steamed broccoli

   D. Peanut butter and jelly

2. A patient is put on strict diet of lean proteins, unsaturated fats, and vegetables after experiencing a heart attack. He is also asked to eliminate processed or refined foods. Which of the following meals would be acceptable according to the new diet?

   A. Steak stir-fry with white rice, peas, and green beans

   B. Baked chicken with tomatoes and corn tortilla chips

   C. Baked chicken with broccoli and brown rice

   D. Roast-beef sandwich on a white bread roll with salad

3. Look at the table of vitamins on page 44. Which vitamin is important for eye function?

   A. A

   B. B_{12}

   C. folate

   D. K

4. A young adult's energy needs increased as she begins training for a half marathon. If her typical healthy calorie consumption is about 1,900 calories, and her energy needs increased by 30 percent, how many calories does she now need to consume daily?

Directions: Use the passage below to answer questions 5–7.

> **John Smith's Meal Plan**
>
> **Breakfast:** Three scrambled eggs with peppers, spinach, ham, and mushrooms. Coffee with cream and sugar. Two slices of white toast with butter.
>
> **Lunch:** Cheeseburger with ketchup and mayo. Spinach salad with almonds and an olive-oil vinaigrette dressing. Can of soda.
>
> **Dinner:** Baked rosemary chicken breast, side of steamed broccoli, and a baked potato with butter and sour cream.
>
> **Snack:** Yogurt

5. John is training in martial arts. Do you think this meal plan supports his training? Explain.

6. Do you think John's food choices represent a healthy, balanced diet? Explain.

7. What suggestions would you make to John's diet to create a more healthful meal plan? List the changes per meal.

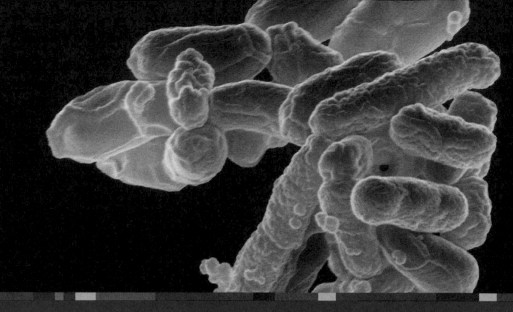

LESSON 1.6 Disease Prevention

■ LESSON OBJECTIVES

- Explain the causes of disease and how diseases are spread
- Describe how the immune system fights disease
- Explain the effects diseases can have on populations

■ CORE SKILLS & PRACTICES

- Explain a Nontextual Scientific Presentation
- Distinguish Between Cause and Effect

Key Terms

disease
any condition that disrupts the normal functioning of the body

immunity
a condition of being able to resist a particular disease

vaccine
dead or incomplete portions of pathogens or antigens

Vocabulary

analyze
to understand the relationship of parts through examination

epidemic
a disease or illness affecting a large number of people

pathogen
something that causes disease

Key Concept

Disease can be caused by something introduced into the body, like a virus, or by improper care of the body. Many diseases can be prevented by taking advantage of advances in medical science and by practicing healthy behaviors.

Disease

Automobiles require the right fuel and proper maintenance to work properly. Similarly, our bodies need proper care and nutrition to function. If the wrong substances enter the body, they can cause problems with the way the body works. A **disease** is any condition that disrupts the normal functioning of the body. Disease-causing agents, including certain types of bacteria, viruses, and parasites, are called **pathogens.** Each type of pathogen invades the body in a different way and causes specific diseases. Once pathogens get inside the body, they produce an infection. Diseases that are caused by pathogens, such as influenza and the common cold, are called infectious diseases.

Infectious Diseases

Pathogens are generally unable to move to a new host on their own. They must be carried in some form from one host to another. A person can be infected with a virus by breathing in the virus-filled saliva that spreads through the air when someone sneezes. Contaminated food can transmit pathogens such as *E. coli*. Insects, rodents, and other animals can transmit pathogens, as well. Some pathogens, such as human immunodeficiency virus (HIV) and hepatitis, can be transmitted through the blood.

Noninfectious Diseases

Not all diseases are caused by pathogens. Some diseases are caused by improper nutrition, a lack of exercise, smoking, or alcoholism. Other diseases are passed genetically from parent to child. Such diseases are noninfectious, which means they cannot be passed through the air or by contact with another person. Cardiovascular disease, cancer, diabetes, cirrhosis, and arthritis are a few examples of noninfectious diseases.

The Immune System

The immune system is the body's defense against pathogens. The defenses may be either nonspecific or specific. The nonspecific defenses of the body help keep pathogens out of the body and the specific defenses fight pathogens after they enter the body.

Nonspecific Defenses

Nonspecific defenses include the skin, mucous membranes, and inflammation. The skin is a dry, acidic environment unsuitable for most microorganisms. Body cavities exposed to the outside world, such as the nose and throat, are lined with mucus, a sticky liquid that traps germs and other foreign particles before they can invade cells.

Once a pathogen enters the body, for example, through a cut, cells near the injury release chemicals that cause inflammation. These chemicals cause blood vessels to expand and allow platelets to flow through gaps to seal out microorganisms.

Specific Defenses

If a pathogen gets past the skin or mucus membranes and enters the body, it causes an infection. At that point, the body's immune system begins to work against the pathogen. The immune system has several unique features that combat pathogens.

First, the immune system responds to specific pathogens. Antigens are proteins located on the cell walls of pathogens that trigger an immune response by the immune system. White blood cells called B cells and T cells that target the specific invader are produced. B cells produce proteins, called antibodies, which attach to the antigens on the pathogen. Killer T cells seek out infected cells and pathogens marked by antibodies and destroy them.

Second, the immune system has the ability to respond to millions of different threats. The B cells that respond to each antigen are present in the bone marrow of a newborn baby. The immune cells are inactive until each one is awakened by the presence of a specific antigen in the body.

Third, the immune system is capable of distinguishing between body cells and cells from other organisms. Immune cells respond to pathogens, cancerous cells, transplanted tissues, and insect venoms. Finally, the immune system is able to remember pathogens and develop **immunity**, a condition of being able to resist a particular disease.

Think about Science

Directions: Answer the following questions.

1. Which of the following is a nonspecific defense against pathogens?

   A. killer T cells
   B. skin
   C. antibodies
   D. antigens

2. Which of the following triggers the body's defenses against specific pathogens?

   A. killer T cells
   B. skin
   C. antibodies
   D. antigens

3. Compare and contrast infectious and noninfectious diseases.

4. What are some causes of noninfectious diseases?

Distinguish Between Cause and Effect

You have learned how the skin protects the body against pathogens. Explain what features of the skin cause pathogens to die and what effect this has on the body.

Look at the 2012 Foodborne Illness in the US chart on page 51. The chart shows that 14.30 out of 100,000 people were diagnosed with campylobacter in 2012. The last column states that for every case of this disease that is reported, 30 cases are not diagnosed. Determine how many total cases out of 100,000 people— reported and unreported— are estimated to have had campylobacter in 2012.

You can use a calculator to solve this problem. First determine the number of cases per 100,000 diagnosed in 2012. Next, determine the number not diagnosed. Multiply the number diagnosed by the number not diagnosed. This will give you the estimated number of undiagnosed cases. Add that number to the number of cases that were diagnosed, and you will have the total number of reported and unreported cases of campylobacter out of 100,000 people.

Preventing Disease

In the midnineteenth century, Louis Pasteur and other scientists discovered that pathogens, commonly called germs, cause many diseases. This discovery was later called germ theory. Doctors learned that washing their hands and using clean surgical instruments could inhibit the spread of disease.

Washing our hands is only one way to prevent disease. A healthy, balanced diet, including fruits, vegetables, grains, dairy, and proteins, gives your body the vitamins, minerals, and other materials it needs to function. Eating healthful foods strengthens your immune system and keeps all the systems in your body running smoothly. Foods high in fat, sugar, or salt should be used only sparingly. Obesity is a widespread problem in the United States and contributes to many diseases, such as diabetes and cardiovascular disease.

There are other things we can do to prevent disease or catch it in early stages. Regular, aerobic exercise is important to keeping our bodies healthy. Running, walking, swimming, and playing basketball are just a few examples of aerobic exercise.

Alcohol, tobacco, and illegal drugs can cause many serious diseases. Misuse of prescription and over-the-counter drugs is also harmful to our bodies. Regular doctor visits and routine screenings can help identify problems early. Early treatment can often prevent or slow the serious effects of a disease.

Vaccines

The development of **vaccines,** which contain weakened, dead, or incomplete portions of pathogens or antigens, was a great step forward in medicine. Vaccines work because the dead or incomplete agents produce the same response in humans that the actual disease does. After receiving a vaccination, the immune system produces a response to the pathogen and creates memory cells against it. Vaccines against polio, smallpox, and measles have saved millions of lives around the world.

Sexually Transmitted Diseases

Sexually transmitted diseases (STDs) such as chlamydia and syphilis are transmitted from person to person during sexual activity. Abstinence, or refraining from sex, is the best way to prevent a sexually transmitted disease. Limiting the number of sexual partners and using condoms can also help prevent STDs.

Public Health

The United States government organization that oversees public health issues is called the Centers for Disease Control and Prevention (CDC). The CDC works to fight disease and promote health. One of the main goals of the CDC is to prevent an **epidemic,** a disease or illness affecting a disproportionately large number of individuals. During the fourteenth century, an epidemic of the "Black Death," a bacterial infection believed to be the bubonic plague, killed about 25 million people worldwide.

The CDC is also tasked with educating the public in ways to prevent disease. You can protect yourself and others from disease in several ways. Covering your mouth when you cough, washing your hands, and keeping surfaces clean are some ways to prevent the spread of disease.

Proper handling of food also helps eliminate foodborne illness. The CDC tracks cases of foodborne illness in the United States. The table shown compares the changes in reported cases of various foodborne illnesses from 2006–2008 and 2012. The CDC can use the information in the table to know which diseases it should focus its efforts on.

2012 Foodborne Illness in the United States

Disease Agents	Percentage change in 2012 compared with 2006–2008	2012 rate per 100,000 Population	2020 target rate per 100,000 Population	CDC estimates that . . .
Campylobacter	14% increase	14.30	8.5	For every case reported, there are 30 cases not diagnosed
Escherichia coli O157	No change	1.12	0.6	For every case reported, there are 26 cases not diagnosed
Listeria	No change	0.25	0.2	For every case reported, there are 2 cases not diagnosed
Salmonella	No change	16.42	11.4	For every case reported, there are 29 cases not diagnosed
Vibrio	43% increase	0.41	0.2	For every case reported, there are 142 cases not diagnosed
Yersinia	No change	0.33	0.3	For every case reported, there are 123 cases not diagnosed

Source: U.S. Department of Health and Human Services Centers for Disease Control and Prevention "Food Safety Progress Report for 2012"

Think about Science

Directions: Answer the following questions.

1. Why do some diseases still spread even though vaccines to prevent them exist?
2. How can salmonella, a bacteria commonly found in poultry, spread to other foods?
3. Why are vaccines made of dead or weakened pathogens?
4. Why is it important to cook food thoroughly?

Understand and Explain a Nontextual Scientific Presentation

Analyze means to learn the nature and relationship of the parts of something by a close and careful examination. Analyze the different types of information given in the table on this page. On which disease agents should the CDC concentrate their efforts? Explain your reasoning.

Vocabulary Review

Directions: Write the missing term in the blank.

analyze   disease   epidemic
immunity   pathogen   vaccine

1. A(n) _____ contains dead or weakened pathogens.

2. When something affects a disproportionately large number of individuals in a population, it is called a(n) _____.

3. A(n) _____ disrupts normal body functions.

4. _____ is a condition of being able to resist a particular disease.

5. A(n) _____ is something that causes disease.

6. You _____ when you learn the nature and relationship of the parts of something by a close and careful examination.

Skill Review

Directions: Answer the following questions.

1. Which of the following describes infectious diseases but does not apply to noninfectious diseases?

   A. Infectious diseases disrupt the normal functions of the body.

   B. Infectious diseases are caused by poor nutrition.

   C. Infectious diseases can cause epidemics.

   D. Infectious diseases are caused by the transmission of pathogens.

2. Why do you think many vaccines are injected?

   A. Vaccines are injected to prevent inflammation.

   B. Vaccines taken orally cause the immune system to fail.

   C. Vaccines are injected in order to slow down the immune system.

   D. Vaccines will not work unless they get past the skin.

3. Why might the immune system attack cancer cells?

   A. The immune system attacks pathogens.

   B. Cancer cells are different from other body cells.

   C. Viruses are attacked by the immune system.

   D. The genetic makeup of cancer cells is similar to bacteria.

Directions: Use the Foodborne Illness in the US table on page 51 to answer questions 4–5.

4. A greater percentage of *Escherichia coli* O157 cases were diagnosed than *vibrio* cases. What is the most likely reason?

   A. *E. coli* may be caused by a virus instead of a bacterium.

   B. *Vibrio* may cause symptoms that are worse than *E. coli*.

   C. *E. coli* may cause symptoms that are worse than *vibrio*.

   D. *Vibrio* may be caused by a virus instead of a bacterium.

5. What policies could be implemented in an office environment to prevent the spread of infectious diseases? Justify your answer.

Skill Practice

Directions: Answer the following questions.

1. Which of the following is the most likely way hepatitis could be transmitted?
   A. coughing
   B. genetically
   C. through dirty water
   D. from mother to baby

2. Antibiotics are given to people with bacterial infections. How are antibiotics similar to vaccines?
   A. They both fight infectious disease.
   B. They both kill pathogens.
   C. They both prevent disease.
   D. They are both given to people with infections.

3. Which of the following produce antibodies?
   A. killer T cells
   B. B cells
   C. antigens
   D. pathogens

4. What diseases can be transmitted during a blood transfusion if the blood is not properly tested?
   A. hepatitis, common cold, influenza, AIDS
   B. hepatitis, influenza, multiple sclerosis, AIDS
   C. cardiovascular disease, common cold, syphilis, AIDS
   D. hepatitis, cardiovascular disease, common cold, influenza

5. Which of the following actions would be the most effective in preventing an epidemic?
   A. Encouraging people to stay home when they are ill
   B. Teaching people about nutrition
   C. Administering a vaccine to as many people as possible
   D. Encouraging people to wash their hands often

6. If malaria has been eradicated in the United States, why might there still be some cases of malaria in the US? Explain what led you to this conclusion.

7. Analyze your lifestyle and explain some ways you can change your habits to better prevent infectious and noninfectious diseases. Explain your answer.

Directions: Use the passage to answer questions 8 and 9.

Influenza is a serious disease that can lead to hospitalization and sometimes even death. Every flu season is different, and influenza infections can affect people differently. Even healthy people can get very sick from the flu and spread it to others. Over a period of 31 seasons between 1976 and 2007, estimates of flu-associated deaths in the United States range from a low of about 3,000 to a high of about 49,000 people. During a regular flu season, about 90 percent of deaths occur in people 65 years and older.

8. Make an inference about flu-associated deaths based on the data presented in the passage. Explain your answer.

9. Based on the passage and what you have read in this lesson, suggest at least three things individuals can do to prevent themselves from getting the flu and from spreading it to others.

Directions: Answer the following questions.

1. Which of the following best describes the function of the skeletal system in the human body?
   A. control center
   B. energy source
   C. protective shell
   D. supportive structure

2. The spongy tissue inside the bone is called _____.

3. How does the function of red blood cells differ from the function of white blood cells?

4. Which type of joint allows the ankle to have limited movement in most directions?
   A. pivot joint
   B. hinge joint
   C. gliding joint
   D. ball-and-socket

5. Explain how the muscles in the front and back of the thigh work together to bend and straighten the knee.

6. Which part of the nerve cell is responsible for relaying an electrical impulse to neighboring nerve cells?
   A. axon
   B. dendrite
   C. nucleus
   D. synapse

7. The region of the brain that controls motor coordination and interprets sensory information is the _____.

8. In which type of blood vessel does oxygen-rich blood travel from the heart to the left foot?
   A. aorta
   B. artery
   C. capillary
   D. vein

9. Which of the following explains why oxygen moves from alveoli into the blood stream?
   A. Pressure in the alveoli forces oxygen into the bloodstream.
   B. There is a higher concentration of oxygen in the blood than in the alveoli.
   C. There is a higher concentration of oxygen in the alveoli than in the blood.
   D. Blood is pumped out of the alveoli into the blood by contractions of smooth muscle.

10. Explain why the kidneys can be thought of as a "sorting station" for blood?

11. To relay chemical messages to different areas of the body, _____ are released directly into the bloodstream.

12. Which gland in the endocrine system becomes more active in people with high levels of calcium in their bloodstream?
    A. adrenal gland
    B. thyroid gland
    C. pituitary gland
    D. parathyroid gland

13. From where does a developing fetus obtain oxygen and nutrients necessary for growth and development?

    A. embryo

    B. hormones

    C. placenta

    D. uterus

14. Which of the following best describes the sequence of events in the menstrual cycle?

    A. uterine lining thickens → egg matures → egg released into uterus → lining breaks down

    B. egg released into uterus → uterine lining thickens → egg matures → lining breaks down

    C. egg matures → uterine lining thickens → egg released into uterus → lining breaks down

    D. egg released into uterus → egg matures → uterine lining thickens → lining breaks down

15. List three facts that support the statement, "Water is the single most important nutrient in the body."

16. Consuming which type fat molecules is beneficial to your health?

    A. lipids

    B. trans fats

    C. saturated fats

    D. unsaturated fats

17. Which of the following is the most effective way to prevent the spread of pathogens?

    A. wearing a face mask

    B. wearing latex gloves

    C. avoiding crowded spaces

    D. washing hands frequently

18. Antigens are a specific type of protein on a pathogen that can trigger the immune system's response to that pathogen. White blood cells, called killer T cells, seek out infected cells and pathogens that are marked by antibodies specific to the pathogen's antigen proteins and destroy them. Explain why killer T cells in the immune system may not destroy newly infected cells immediately.

19. A healthy immune system is capable of distinguishing between body cells and pathogens. An autoimmune disorder affects the functioning of the immune system. The prefix *auto-* means *self*. Explain what occurs in a person with an autoimmune disorder?

20. Weakened, killed, or incomplete viruses can be used to produce a _____ that can prevent the infection of that particular virus.

Directions: Questions 21–22 are based on the following passage.

In general, the human body remains in homeostasis when it is functioning properly and all basic needs are met. Every body system contributes to maintaining homeostasis in some way, and this maintenance is similar to a very complex balancing act. Variables such as body temperature, heart rate, blood pressure, blood glucose, blood pH, and hydration levels all have a normal range. If these values deviate significantly from their norm, body systems work together to restore the normal value.

21. Choose one variable mentioned in the reading passage and explain how it can be controlled by a feedback mechanism to maintain homeostasis.

22. Explain why the maintenance of homeostasis in the human body is referred to as a "complex balancing act?"

Directions: Use the image to answer questions 23–25

Human Digestive System

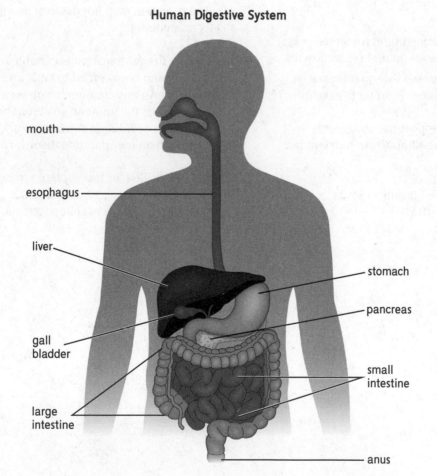

23. Excess bile provided by the liver is stored in which organ?

A. stomach

B. pancreas

C. gallbladder

D. small intestine

24. Enzymes that help break down nutrients are produced by which organ?

A. pancreas

B. stomach

C. small intestine

D. large intestine

25. Describe how nutrients in the food you eat get to the cells in the body.

Check Your Understanding

On the following chart, circle the items you missed. The last column shows pages you can review to study the content covered in the question.

Lesson	Item Number(s)	Review Page(s)
1.1: Skeletal, Muscular, and Nervous Systems	1, 2, 3, 4, 5, 6, 7	14–19
1.2: Digestive, Excretory, Respiratory, and Circulatory Systems	8, 9, 10, 23, 24, 25	22–27
1.3: Endocrine and Reproductive Systems	11, 12, 13, 14	30–33
1.4: Homeostasis	21, 22	36–39
1.5: Nutrition	15, 16	42–45
1.6: Disease Prevention	17, 18, 19, 20	48–51

Fighting the Flu

Core Practices

- Reconcile multiple findings, conclusions, or theories

Question

How effective is the influenza vaccine at preventing seasonal flu?

Background Concepts

Over the past few years there has been a greater need for the influenza vaccine as outbreaks of different strains of the flu have affected many countries around the world. Influenza, also called, the flu, is a virus that attacks the respiratory system.

A vaccine can reduce the risk of infection by imitating an infection without actually causing illness. The immune system will react the same way to a vaccine as it does to a real infection, so that the body can build up immunity to the particular virus or bacteria. Then the body is able to fight that disease in the future.

In the case of the flu, different strains of the virus infect populations from year to year. Scientists and doctors at the Centers for Disease Control (CDC) determine which flu strains to include in the vaccine each year. This decision is based on which strains of the flu are already circulating, how they are spreading, and how well current vaccines will protect against newly identified strains. A vaccine usually protects against various flu viruses. According to the CDC, at least two factors play a role in the effectiveness of the flu vaccine: the age and health status of the individual being vaccinated and the similarities between the infecting virus in a population and the vaccine administered.

Each flu season, researchers try to determine the effectiveness of a particular vaccine to decide whether the flu vaccine is a necessary public health intervention. Study results often vary based on the design of the study, the population being studied, and the season studied.

Hypothesis

A hypothesis is an explanation based on what evidence is available. It is a starting point for a scientific investigation that will either be confirmed, need to be revised, or be shown to be incorrect based on more evidence gathered. Review the background information provided about the flu and flu vaccines. Develop a hypothesis about the effectiveness of the flu vaccine for preventing the flu in a given population.

✅ Test-Taking Tip

When you are answering a test question that asks you to reconcile multiple findings or conclusions, it is important to read all of the information in the question or the accompanying passage. Ask yourself what the differences are between the two findings, or conclusions. If the question is multiple choice, try to come up with your own answer before you look at the answer choices. If the question is short answer, list the differences and then come up with an explanation that will make sense of the differences you have listed.

Investigation

After developing a hypothesis, the next step is to gather information and data to determine whether your hypothesis is supported or not. Research information about the flu vaccine and its effectiveness using various sources including the Internet, the library, and media sources. Information about the flu and the vaccine can be found on many government websites such as the Centers for Disease Control (CDC) website. On this site you will find information of how researchers determine which flu virus to make a vaccine against. You will also find information about how the vaccine affects different age groups and types of people. Try to find information on this website and in other sources that both supports and argues against the effectiveness of the flu vaccine. Weekly reports for each flu season can be found at the CDC website. Use this information to gather data relevant to your hypothesis.

Collect and Analyze Data

Collect data from the CDC website and other sources. Create a two column chart and label one column, "Supports hypothesis" and the other column, "Does not support hypothesis." As you collect data about the flu and the flu vaccine, place each piece of information into one of the two columns of your chart.

Interpretation

Record and summarize the data collected and interpret the evidence to determine if your hypothesis is supported. When you find data that is conflicting or presents different findings, reconcile these differences by finding more reliable sources that can help you determine which data is most accurate.

When evaluating and interpreting the information or data you collected, ask yourself these questions:

- How many cases of the flu have been reported in a given area or population in the U.S. last flu season?

- Determine what strains of influenza virus were included in the vaccine for the last flu season. Were these the same or different strains than those that caused infection or outbreak in the U.S in the same flu season?

- What percentage of the population that received the flu vaccine contracted the flu virus anyway?

Results

Discuss your results using evidence to support your conclusions. Discuss any observations about the information you gathered from reliable sources, possible sources of error, unexpected results, and any remaining questions. If your hypothesis was not supported, discuss your recommendations for formulating a new hypothesis or changes you would make to the investigation.

Consider these questions as you discuss your results:

- How many cases of the flu were reported in people who did not receive a vaccine compared to people that did receive the vaccine during the last flu season?

- What are some potential negative effects of the flu vaccine?

- Does the data suggest that it is beneficial to receive the flu vaccine even if it is not 100 percent effective?

Chapter 2

Ecosystems

In every environment you will find many organisms that depend on each other and their surroundings. Diversity in populations is a key element to maintaining a healthy environment. However, when you study an ecosystem, you will notice that some populations are much larger than others even though food, water, and energy sources seem plentiful. You might also notice that changes or disruptions in an ecosystem can change the sizes and types of populations either very quickly or over time.

Lesson 2.1
Living Things and Their Environment

Every living thing on Earth interacts with both living and nonliving elements that surround it. Learn how organisms adapt to the climate in their environment in order to increase their chances of survival.

Lesson 2.2
Movement of Energy and Matter

Energy passes through an ecosystem in a complex network of organisms called a food web. Learn how energy and matter flow through an ecosystem, and how living and nonliving elements are affected by changes to the ecosystem.

Lesson 2.3
Interactions Among Populations

Many factors influence the size of a population, including the interaction between organisms and the amount of resources in the ecosystem. Learn about the different ways in which organisms can interact with each other and how these interactions can affect the size of a population.

Lesson 2.4
Disruptions to Ecosystems

Disruptions in an ecosystem can be caused by human activity and by environmental disturbances including flood, fire, and the introduction of a new species. Sometimes these disruptions are catastrophic and upset the balance of an ecosystem. In this lesson, learn about both natural and unnatural causes of ecological disruption.

Goal Setting

It may be difficult to determine what type of ecosystem you live in, especially if you live in a city or a suburb. But, before the land was developed for human use, it was most likely a balanced ecosystem. Find out about the region you live in, and compare the species that once lived there to those that live there today, Use the information in this chapter to help you identify and describe any changes that might have occurred to the ecosystem.

LESSON 2.1 Living Things and Their Environment

■ LESSON OBJECTIVES

- List the biotic and abiotic components in an environment
- Explain the levels of organization in an environment
- Explain how climate decides the global distribution of biomes and organisms

■ CORE SKILLS & PRACTICES

- Analyze Relationships Between Sources
- Make a Prediction Based On Data or Evidence

Key Terms

abiotic
relating to nonliving things

biome
a major ecological system in a large region characterized by its organisms and climate

biotic
relating to living things

ecosystem
a community of organisms and its nonliving surroundings

niche
the role an organism plays in an ecosystem

Vocabulary

organize
to arrange or order things so they can be easily found

Key Concept

Organisms interact with the living and nonliving parts of their environments. Climate and other environmental factors influence how populations and communities develop around the world.

The Living Environment

Look around. Everything you see and feel is a part of your environment. An environment includes living things such as plants, animals, people, and even the tiniest of microbes. The living portions of the environment are called the **biotic** parts. The nonliving portions, such as rocks, sunlight, and air, are called the **abiotic** parts.

Interactions among organisms and their environments can be very complex because an organism gets everything it needs to survive from the biotic and abiotic parts of its environment. For example, a tree gets the energy it needs from sunlight, carbon dioxide from the air, and water and minerals from the soil. All organisms rely on the abiotic factors of their environment in addition to relying on other organisms for survival.

Organisms that live in the same environment affect other living organisms within that community. For example, prairie dogs are rodents that can be found in the grasslands of western North America. They rely on the grasses in their environment as a food source and energy supply. The black-footed ferret is a predator of prairie dogs, relying on them as a food source. Suppose a drought results in a drastic reduction of the abiotic factor of water in their environment. The drought kills the grass and the prairie dog population starts dying out. Since the ferrets depend on the prairie dog as a food source, the ferret population is also affected. All these organisms are interconnected. Something that affects one part of an environment can affect all the organisms that live there. Each abiotic and biotic factor of an environment must be in place for energy to flow from one organism to another.

Levels of Organization Within the Environment

To **organize** means to arrange or group items so they can be easily found and understood. There are four basic levels of organization within an environment: organisms, population, community, and ecosystem.

- **Organisms** All living things in the environment are organisms, such as plants, animals, fungi, and microorganisms.

- **Population** A population of organisms is a group of individuals from the same species living in a specific area at the same time. Green-winged macaws, anacondas, and capuchin monkeys are three populations of organisms in the Amazon rain forest.

- **Community** A biological community is made up of all the interacting populations of organisms in an environment. Interacting populations may compete for food, or one species may hunt the other as a food source. Species in a community may also be helpful to the survival of another species. For example, in the rain forest, the capuchin monkey feeds on the nectar of flowering trees. As it drinks the nectar, the pollen from the flower attaches to the fur on its face. As the monkey drinks the nectar of another flower, it passes the pollen from its face to the flower and helps pollinate the flowers of that tree.

- **Ecosystem** An **ecosystem** is made up of both the community of organisms in an area and their abiotic surroundings. The Amazon rain forest—including all the plants, animals, and abiotic factors such as sunlight, water, soil and rocks—is an example of an ecosystem. Other ecosystems include grasslands, wetlands, deserts, and oceans.

A group of capuchin monkeys represents a population. Several populations together form a community. All organisms and the abiotic factors in their environment make up an ecosystem.

Living Things and Their Environment

CORE SKILL

Analyze Relationships Between Sources

When researching a specific topic, it is often necessary to use multiple sources. Choose a type of ecology that interests you: population, community, or ecosystem. Next, choose a specific topic within that field. Research the topic you have chosen using multiple sources you find on the Internet or in the library. Analyze the relationship between the sources you find. Compare the facts presented in each text and also compare any data tables or charts that give you useful information on the topic. Ask the following questions about each source: Is the information coming from a reliable source? Are the facts consistent with other sources I have found?

Ecologists

Ecology is the branch of biology that examines the interactions among organisms and the interactions between organisms and their environment. Scientists who study ecology are called ecologists.

An ecologist studying a population may look at the ways in which organisms compete for resources such as food and water. Ecologists also examine how the organisms in a population cooperate to avoid predators or raise young.

Ecologists that study communities in an ecosystem investigate the factors that contribute to the diversity of populations in an area. Ecologists studying a community may look at the relationships between predators and prey, the ways in which different species compete for the same kinds of food, or how the presence of one species may benefit or harm another species.

Ecologists studying the ecosystem as a whole seek to answer questions such as how sunlight and nutrients affect the plants that all other organisms in the ecosystem depend on, or how changes in the composition of the atmosphere affect an ecosystem. Ecologists are also interested in studying changes in ecosystems brought about by climate change.

Ecologists call the unique strategy a species has for survival its niche. More specifically, a **niche** is an organism's role in the larger ecosystem. If you think of a species' habitat as its home address, its niche is its occupation. Species hunt, eat, hide, or reproduce in different ways to avoid occupying the same niche as other organisms or to avoid competing with them.

woodpecker   tufted titmouse   nuthatch

To avoid competition, woodpeckers, tufted titmice, and nuthatches each have a beak adapted for eating different types of insects that live in different parts of the trees their shared habitat.

Think about Science

Directions: Answer the following questions.

1. Soil is a(n) _____ factor in the environment, and a flowering plant is a(n) _____ factor.

2. Name three animal populations in your area.

3. Which of the following is the most likely habitat for a mosquito?
   A. grassy field
   B. oak tree
   C. puddle
   D. desert

Biomes

Around the world, similar communities develop in places of similar climate. Some regions have short, cool summers and long, cold winters, while other regions are warm all year long with little change of temperature. A **biome** is a large region that contains similar ecosystems or communities and contains similar organisms that have adapted to the conditions of that region.

Influence of Climate

Species adapt to live in a particular climate. Climate is the typical pattern of weather that is observed over a long period of time in an area. A place with water-conserving plants and very little rain is a desert. Climate is determined by such factors as temperature, precipitation, latitude, elevation, nearness to water, and land features.

The patterns of temperature and precipitation throughout the year are the most important features of climate. Species adapt to survive in specific climates. Their physical features and their behaviors are influenced by the ecosystem's temperature range as well as by the availability of food and water in the region.

Latitude, or distance from the equator, has an influence on the temperature and precipitation of a region. Regions close to the equator or the poles have more extreme conditions than those between the two. While warm temperatures and large amounts of precipitation are characteristic near the equator, cold temperatures and low amounts of precipitation are characteristic of climates at the poles. Regions at higher altitudes, or distance above sea level, also have a colder and drier climate than those at lower altitudes.

Large bodies of water, including the ocean and large lakes, also have an effect on climate. The climate near water is warmer and wetter than inland climates. Mountain ranges near the coast also affect climate. The climate between the ocean and the mountain will be warmer and wetter, while the climate beyond the mountain will be hotter and drier. These factors influence the communities that develop in a particular region.

Land Biomes

There are two main types of biomes: land biomes and water biomes. The seven major land biomes are shown on the map.

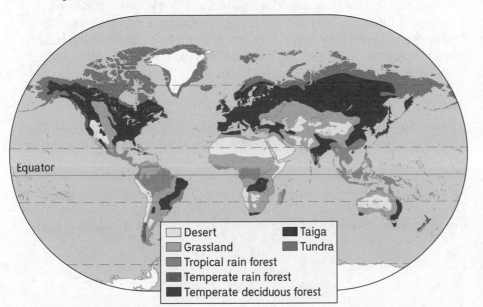

Equator

Desert
Grassland
Tropical rain forest
Temperate rain forest
Temperate deciduous forest
Taiga
Tundra

Make a Prediction Based on Data or Evidence

When scientists try to anticipate something that will happen based on something that is happening now, they are making a prediction. To make a prediction, scientists must interpret the data they have. *Interpret* means "to explain the meaning of something." Read the description of the two climates below and predict what might happen if a plant growing in Climate A was transported and planted in Climate B.

Climate A: Average annual temperature of 82°F (28°C). Chance of frost from October to May is 2 percent. Average rainfall of 82 inches (208 cm) per year. Latitude is 25° North of the equator. Distance from coast is 2 miles (3.2 km), and altitude is 9 feet (2.74 m) above sea level.

Climate B: Average annual temperature of 61°F (16 °C). Chance of frost from October to May is 76 percent. Average rainfall of 46 inches (117 cm) per year. Latitude is 40° North of the equator. Distance from the coast is 6 miles (9.6 km), and elevation is 82 feet (25 m) above sea level.

Informational Literacy

Investigation is the key to gathering information and developing hypotheses in science. Investigation involves asking questions, developing hypotheses, and designing innovative experiments or plans to test the hypothesis. Good science must be able to be repeated with similar results by other researchers.

Universities and government organizations often post information about research conducted by their scientists on their websites. Use the Internet to search for information on group behavior within a population. For example, you could choose to study why certain species live and travel in herds, why some species live in small family units, and why still others live a more solitary life. Search for information about investigations that are being conducted by researchers and write a short report on your findings. What is the scientific question being investigated? What are some valid hypotheses? What methods are being used to test these hypotheses?

Tundra

The tundra is a cold, dry, treeless plain. Permanently frozen soil called permafrost lies beneath the surface and prevents trees from taking root. In the short summer season, the tundra is filled with flowering plants, lichens, insects, birds, and grazing mammals. During the long, cold winters, most plants and animals become inactive or travel to warmer lands.

Taiga

As you travel south from the tundra, tall trees appear. This is the taiga, an evergreen forest that covers more area on Earth than any other biome. Winter is still long and cold, but during the short summer, temperatures are milder. The precipitation in the taiga is mostly snow. Animals that stay active in the winter adapt by growing thick coats and living in burrows to keep warm.

Temperate Rain Forest

South of the taiga, several different biomes form. Temperate rain forests form between oceans and coastal mountains. A temperate rain forest is a cool, wet, evergreen forest receiving up to 400 cm of rain per year. The nearby ocean keeps the average temperature mild. The temperate rain forest has a higher density of living and dead matter of any biome.

Deciduous Forest

Deciduous forests contain hardwood trees that drop their leaves in cold temperatures. Deciduous forests receive up to 150 cm of precipitation per year. The year is divided into four distinct seasons. Summer temperatures may reach 30°C, while winter temperatures can dip below freezing. The soil of a deciduous forest is rich from the leaves that fall and decay.

Grassland

Grasslands form where there is not enough precipitation to support trees. Grasses dominate, and trees are found only along the banks of streams and rivers. Grasslands receive up to 75 cm of precipitation per year. Grasslands have cold winters and hot, dry summers. Many animals live on grasslands, from large grazing mammals to insects.

Tropical Rain Forest

Tropical rain forests form near the equator, where it is warm and rainy year-round. They receive up to 600 cm of precipitation per year. The climate conditions are ideal for many plants, insects, and birds. In the rain forests there is competition for sunlight and nutrients from the soil. Lush growth blocks the Sun from many plants and animals.

Desert

A desert forms where there is not enough rainfall to support grasslands. They are the driest places on Earth, with fewer than 25 cm of precipitation per year. In many cases, deserts form because moisture from ocean breezes is blocked by coastal mountains. Temperatures vary greatly because the dry air does not block the Sun's rays or trap heat. The temperatures may rise above 40°C during the day and fall below freezing at night. Organisms that live in the desert have adapted to temperature extremes and lack of water.

Water Biomes

About 75 percent of Earth's surface is covered by water. The water may be deep or shallow, fresh or salty, moving or still. Each of these factors affects the kinds of organisms that live in the water and the biome that develops.

Freshwater Biome

Freshwater, which contains very little salt, can be found in wetlands, ponds, lakes, streams, and rivers. Wetlands are land areas where the soil is so saturated with water that aquatic plants are able to grow. These plants allow nutrient-rich soil to form. Oxygen allows many different animal species to thrive. Marshes, bogs, and swamps are examples of wetlands.

Ponds and lakes form where water pools in a low-lying area. Rivers and streams are biomes that contain moving water. Slow-moving rivers have muddy bottoms with plants growing in them. Swift streams have rocky bottoms, which doesn't allow for much plant growth.

Marine Biome

The oceans and seas of the world make up the marine, or saltwater, biome. The marine biome covers most of Earth's surface. Like freshwater lakes, oceans can be divided into shallow and deep layers. Sunlight penetrates about 200 m into the water, creating a warm shallow layer where plants can grow. The plants produce oxygen, allowing many sea creatures to live in this shallow underwater layer. The deep water of the ocean is cold, dark, and largely lifeless except for areas around undersea volcanoes. Coral reefs are regions of marine biomes that can support a diverse array of sea life.

⤜ Think about Science

Directions: Answer the following questions

1. Which two factors are the most influential on a region's climate?

2. Which two biomes are dominated by evergreen trees?
   A. deciduous forest and taiga
   B. taiga and temperate rain forest
   C. taiga and tundra
   D. temperate rain forest and tundra

Vocabulary Review

Directions: Write the missing term in the blank.

1. Grasslands, wetlands, deserts, and oceans are examples of _____.

2. To _____ means to arrange things so they can easily found and understood.

3. The _____ parts of the environment are the living portions.

4. Rocks, sunlight, and air are called the _____ parts of the environment.

5. A _____ is a large region with similar ecosystems and organisms that have adapted to the regional conditions.

6. The role that an organism plays in the ecosystem is called a _____.

Skill Review

Directions: Answer the following questions.

1. All the interacting biotic factors in an environment form a
   A. biome.
   B. community.
   C. ecosystem.
   D. population.

2. An ecologist focused on the effect of climate change on an ecosystem might study
   A. competition among species.
   B. global warming.
   C. herd characteristics.
   D. parasites and hosts.

Directions: Use the illustration to answer questions 3 and 4.

3. Identify five different habitats in the illustrated environment.

4. Name at least three abiotic factors in the illustration.

Skill Practice

Directions: Answer the following questions.

1. Which of the following organizes the environment from the most basic relationships to the most complex?

   A. community → ecosystem → population

   B. ecosystem → community → population

   C. population → community → ecosystem

   D. ecosystem → population → organism

2. Which two regions likely have similar climates?

   A. Arctic region and equatorial region

   B. Arctic region and mountaintop region

   C. Arctic region and regions below sea level

   D. Equatorial region and regions at sea level

3. How do plants play a role in the flow of energy in a freshwater biome?

4. A region of Earth in which trees lose their leaves in October and bud and flower in April is likely located

   A. at or close to the north pole.

   B. between the north pole and the equator.

   C. at or close to the equator.

   D. at or close to the south pole.

5. The brittle bush plant has leaves covered with tiny hairs that insulate the plant against extreme heat and cold; the hairs also trap moisture from the air for the plant. Which biome is the plant best adapted for?

   A. desert

   B. grassland

   C. rain forest

   D. taiga

Directions: Use the map to answer questions 6 and 7.

6. In which regions would you expect to find a cold, dry climate and almost no vegetation?

   A. A and B

   B. B and C

   C. C and D

   D. A and D

7. In which region would you find a herd of animals competing for nutrients in grasses?

   A. Region A

   B. Region B

   C. Region C

   D. All four regions

LESSON OBJECTIVES

- Describe how energy and matter flow through an ecosystem
- Explain how energy is lost at each step in a food web
- Analyze how cycles of matter affect ecosystems

CORE SKILLS & PRACTICES

- Identify and Refine Hypotheses for Scientific Investigations
- Analyze Relationships Among Terms

Key Terms

autotrophs
organisms that capture matter and energy from a nonliving source (a producer)

biogeochemical cycles
the recycling of chemical elements throughout an ecosystem

biomass
the total mass of living tissue in a trophic level

eutrophication
when excess nutrients in a body of water cause oxygen depletion

heterotrophs
organisms that eat other organisms (a consumer)

trophic level
each step in a food chain or ecological pyramid

Key Concept

Organisms move energy and matter through ecosystems. Energy is converted to heat as it passes through a community of organisms, but matter is recycled and used over and over again.

Energy Flow in an Ecosystem

Energy in an ecosystem is conserved. In other words, energy is neither created nor destroyed but changed from one form into another. As energy moves through organisms, some energy is absorbed by organisms, and some energy is released by those organisms as heat.

Organisms Move Energy and Matter

Living things that can capture matter and energy from abiotic sources are called producers. Producers, such as plants and green algae, use photosynthesis to turn the Sun's energy, water, and carbon dioxide in the air into complex organic compounds. Other producers, such as the bacteria living near deep-sea vents, can capture energy from other materials. Producers are also called **autotrophs,** or "self-feeders," because they make organic compounds from inorganic compounds and do not need to eat food.

Most organisms have to eat other organisms to obtain the energy they need to survive. Organisms that eat other organisms are called consumers, or **heterotrophs.** Herbivores are consumers that eat only autotrophs. Carnivores are consumers that eat only other heterotrophs. Consumers that eat both autotrophs and heterotrophs are called omnivores.

When an organism dies, small organisms such as fungi, bacteria, and protozoans break down the complex organic molecules in its body for food. These heterotrophs are called decomposers. Decomposers are important parts of every ecosystem. They release the elements stored in dead tissues into the environment, where they can be reused.

Food Chains and Food Webs

Ecologists make models to study how energy and matter flow through an ecosystem. The simplest model of the flow of matter and energy in an ecosystem is called a food chain. A food chain can be constructed by writing the names of the organisms in an ecosystem according to the role each plays and drawing arrows between them. The arrows show that one organism is eaten by the next. For example, a food chain from a desert ecosystem could be shown as the following:

seeds → kangaroo rats → rattlesnakes

Each step in a food chain is called a **trophic level**. In the food chain shown, seeds make up the first trophic level, and the next trophic level contains the kangaroo rats that eat the seeds. Organisms that eat plants are called first-order heterotrophs, or primary consumers. In this example, the final trophic level contains the rattlesnakes that eat the kangaroo rats. Organisms that eat first-order heterotrophs are called second-order heterotrophs, or secondary consumers.

A food chain can illustrate and help explain one feeding pathway, but it does not show the complex feeding relationships in a real ecosystem. Biological communities have many species at each trophic level. Organisms may also eat more than one kind of food. These relationships can be drawn as a series of food chains, or they can be connected to form a food web. A food web is a model that shows all the possible feeding relationships at each trophic level.

Food webs show complex feeding relationships in ecosystems.

Movement of Energy and Matter

CORE SKILL

Analyze Relationships Among Terms

Write a paragraph that explains the relationship among these terms: *food chain, trophic level, autotrophs, heterotrophs, food web.*

Percents

If only 10 percent of the energy from a trophic level passes to the next higher trophic level, how much energy from the first trophic level makes it to the third trophic level? How much energy from the first trophic level makes it to the fourth trophic level? Use a calculator to find the answer.

1. Key in 100 to show you are beginning with 100 percent.
2. Multiply by 0.1 to find 10 percent of 100.
3. Continue in this manner until you have the answer.

Energy Pyramids

Food chains and food webs show ecologists "who eats whom" in a community. Another type of model, an energy pyramid, helps ecologists see the relationships among trophic levels. Each layer of an energy pyramid represents a different trophic level. Autotrophs make up the base of the pyramid, and higher trophic levels are stacked above them.

One type of energy pyramid shows how energy moves through an ecosystem. Energy is lost as it moves through heterotrophs. Each trophic level contains less energy than the level below it. This happens because a heterotroph uses most of the energy it gets from food as fuel for life processes. Only about 10 percent of the energy a heterotroph takes in is stored in new body tissues. Most of the energy is lost as heat.

Another way to show the stored energy in each trophic level is with a pyramid of biomass. **Biomass** is the total mass of living tissue in a trophic level.

A pyramid of numbers can show how many organisms are in each trophic level. Typically population sizes get smaller in higher trophic levels. There are more autotrophs than herbivores, and there are more herbivores than carnivores.

Think about Science

Directions: Fill in the blank.

1. A(n) _____ shows how much energy is found at each level in an ecosystem.

2. The levels of an energy pyramid are called _____ levels.

Cycles of Matter

Have you ever recycled a plastic bottle and wondered what happens after you dropped it off? After you send the bottle to the recycling center, it is melted down and reused in a new product. The plastic may become part of an automobile, a cell phone, or a fleece jacket, but it is still the same plastic that made up the original bottle.

This process is similar to the movement of matter through an ecosystem. Water molecules and elements such as nitrogen and carbon constantly move among the ocean, the atmosphere, and terrestrial ecosystems. Energy is converted to heat as it passes through a community, but matter is recycled and reused over and over again. The recycling systems of an ecosystem are called **biogeochemical cycles.**

Oxygen Cycle

Oxygen is an element that is important to many life processes. Carbon and oxygen make up molecules essential for life, including carbon dioxide and simple sugar.

In the oxygen cycle, green plants and algae convert carbon dioxide and water into carbohydrates and release oxygen gas into the air during a process called photosynthesis. The carbohydrates are used as a source of energy for all organisms in the food web. Carbon dioxide is recycled as organisms take in the oxygen from photosynthesis and release it as carbon dioxide through cellular respiration.

Oxygen also participates in parts of the carbon, nitrogen, and phophorus cycles by combining with these elements and cycling with them through the biosphere. When oxygen cycles with these other nutrients, it is indirectly transferred through an ecosystem.

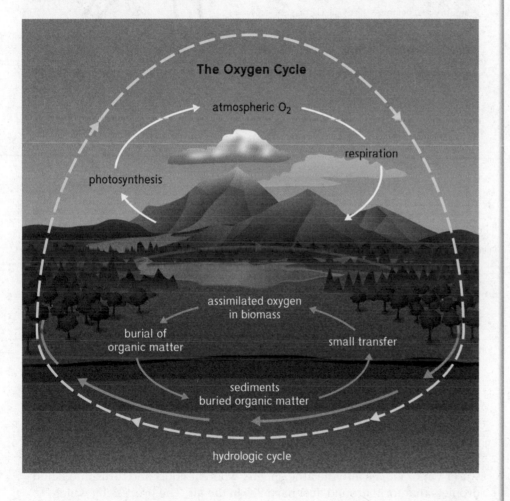

The Oxygen Cycle

atmospheric O_2

respiration

photosynthesis

assimilated oxygen in biomass

burial of organic matter

small transfer

sediments buried organic matter

hydrologic cycle

Write a hypothesis about what will happen to plants after a specific change to the water cycle in an environment, such as a flood or drought. Then write a brief outline of an experiment you could conduct to help you refine your hypothesis.

The Carbon Cycle

Carbon is the main building block of molecules in living things. It constantly moves among the ocean, the atmosphere, and Earth's ecosystems. Every carbon atom in a living thing was, at some point in the past, part of a carbon-dioxide molecule in the air. Autotrophs use carbon dioxide from the air to make the complex organic molecules found in their tissues. Heterotrophs that eat autotrophs break down the autotroph's molecules. Some of the molecules are broken down for energy, and the carbon in these molecules then returns to the air as carbon dioxide. Heterotrophs use other molecules to form their tissues. When a heterotroph dies and decays, some of the carbon in its tissues returns to the air as carbon dioxide. The carbon dioxide given off by all living things is reused by autotrophs.

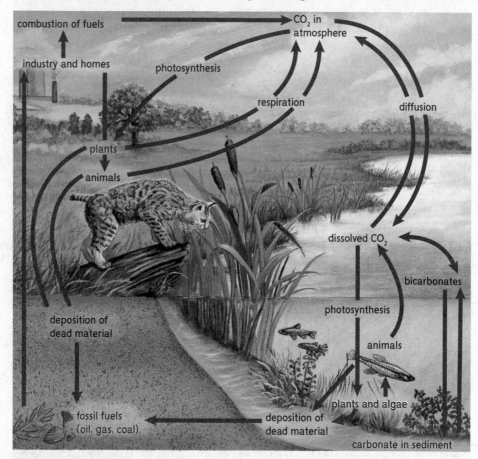

The Water Cycle

The water cycle starts with evaporation. Evaporation is the process by which heat from the Sun turns liquid water on Earth's surface into water vapor. The water vapor moves into the atmosphere, where it cools and turns into liquid droplets that form around dust particles in the air. The process by which water vapor cools and becomes a liquid is called condensation. The liquid droplets produce clouds, and as more water vapor condenses, more water droplets form. When the drops get heavy enough, they fall back to Earth as precipitation, which takes the form of rain, snow, sleet, or hail. Some water falls into lakes and oceans. Water that falls on land may flow to the ocean in streams and rivers or soak deep into the ground to form groundwater.

Water also moves through organisms. Plants pull water out of the ground through their roots and lose it by evaporation from their leaves during transpiration. Animals drink water and lose it when they urinate, sweat, and breathe.

The Nitrogen Cycle

Nitrogen makes up most of the air you breathe, but plants and animals cannot use it directly from the atmosphere. Most of the nitrogen in organisms comes from bacteria that convert atmospheric nitrogen into usable forms in a process called nitrogen fixation.

Plants absorb nitrogen compounds made by bacteria and use the nitrogen to build proteins and other molecules. When herbivores eat plants, they reuse the nitrogen in their own tissues. The nitrogen is reused every time one animal eats another. At each step, some nitrogen leaves an animal through that animal's urine. Animal wastes return nitrogen compounds to the soil, where plants and bacteria reuse them. Dead and decomposing organisms also leave nitrogen compounds in the soil, and soil bacteria convert these compounds into nitrogen gas, which returns to the air.

Fertilizers with nitrogen help plants grow and thrive. However, nitrogen also dissolves in water and can be washed away. If excess nitrogen enters aquatic (water) ecosystems, algae may grow uncontrollably. As the algae dies, decomposition consumes oxygen in the water. As the oxygen is depleted, marine animals and other organisms may suffocate and die. This kind of nutrient pollution is called **eutrophication.**

The Phosphorous Cycle

Most of Earth's phosphorous is found in sedimentary rock. When it rains, tiny bits of phosphates are dissolved from the rocks and spread through soil and water. Plants take up the phosphates from the soil. The phosphates then move from plants to animals when herbivores eat plants and carnivores eat herbivores. The phosphates absorbed by animal tissue eventually return to the soil through body wastes or from the decomposition of dead organisms.

Phosphorus is not highly soluble. It binds tightly to particles in soil and reaches water by traveling with eroded soil. Phosphates also enter waterways through fertilizer runoff, sewage seepage, natural mineral deposits, and wastes from other industrial processes. These phosphates settle on ocean floors and lake bottoms.

In lakes, excessive phosphorus is a pollutant. Phosphate stimulates the growth of algae, similar to nitrogen. As the excess algae dies, decomposition consumes the oxygen in the water, causing a lack of oxygen for other organisms. The result can be eutrophication.

Think about Science

Directions: Fill in the blank.

1. More than 99 percent of Earth's _____ is found in minerals in Earth's surface and interior.

2. _____ is the main building block of molecules in living things.

3. One step in the _____ is evaporation.

4. Most of the _____ in organisms comes from bacteria that convert atmospheric nitrogen into usable forms.

5. Most of Earth's _____ is found in sedimentary rock.

Summarize Information in Workplace Graphics

Ecologists and other scientists use energy pyramids. Look at the energy pyramids below and then answer the questions.

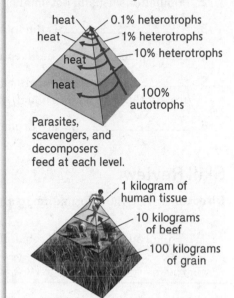

heat — 0.1% heterotrophs
heat — 1% heterotrophs
— 10% heterotrophs
heat
heat
100% autotrophs

Parasites, scavengers, and decomposers feed at each level.

1 kilogram of human tissue
10 kilograms of beef
100 kilograms of grain

1. How many kilograms of beef must a human eat to make 1 kilogram of tissue?

2. Based on the information in the first pyramid, how does the number of organisms change as you move to higher trophic levels?

Vocabulary Review

Directions: Write the missing term in the blank.

autotrophs   biogeochemical cycles   biomass
eutrophication   heterotrophs   trophic level

1. _____ are organisms that eat other organisms.

2. Populations usually get smaller at each higher _____.

3. _____ is the total mass of living tissue in a trophic level.

4. The recycling systems of an ecosystem are called _____.

5. _____ occurs when high levels of nutrients in a body of water support excessive algae growth that can lead to a lack of oxygen for other organisms.

6. _____ are organisms that capture matter and energy from a nonliving source.

Skill Review

Directions: Use the information to answer questions 1–3.

Phosphorous is an element that also takes part in a biogeochemical cycle. Phosphorous occurs in nature mainly in chemicals called phosphates. Most phosphates occur as salts in ocean sediments or in rocks.

Land plants absorb phosphates from soil, which helps them grow; ocean plants absorb phosphates from seawater. Plants are eaten by herbivores, and herbivores are eaten by carnivores. After death, both plants and animals decay, and the phosphates in each organism return to the soil or to the ocean.

Geological processes also play a role in this cycle. These processes bring ocean sediments to land, while weathering and runoff often carry phosphates back to the ocean. In the ocean, phosphates once again become part of bottom sediments; on land, phosphates may, over time, again become part of rocks.

1. Which element is found in phosphates?
   A. sulfate
   B. photons
   C. phosphorous
   D. carbon

2. In what commercial product would you most likely find phosphates?
   A. jet fuel
   B. garden fertilizer
   C. house paint
   D. wood glue

3. What processes move phosphorous from living organisms back to its storehouses in the ocean and in rock?
   A. death and decay
   B. birth and growth
   C. heat and pressure
   D. cooling and freezing

Directions: Answer the following questions.

4. What is the source of energy that drives the water cycle?

   A. Earth's internal energy

   B. water vapor

   C. rain

   D. The Sun

5. Imagine an ecosystem with large herbivores, such as cattle and deer, but no large carnivores. What might happen to cattle and deer if mountain lions were reintroduced to the ecosystem?

   A. All the cattle and deer would be killed by mountain lions.

   B. Some of the cattle and deer would be killed by mountain lions.

   C. Only deer would be killed by mountain lions.

   D. Only cattle would be killed by mountain lions.

6. Imagine an ecosystem in which deer are overgrazing. Which approach could prevent overgrazing?

   A. Introduce more grazing animals to compete with the deer.

   B. Introduce organisms, such as clover, from the lowest trophic level.

   C. Encourage deer to stop grazing on plants from the lowest trophic level.

   D. Introduce deer predators, such as wolves, from higher trophic levels.

7. Explain how energy is lost at each step in an energy pyramid. How does this energy loss help explain the shape of an energy pyramid?

Skill Practice

Directions: Answer the following questions.

1. Predict what would happen if an ecosystem had no decomposers.

2. Describe how plants, herbivores, carnivores, and decomposers move energy through ecosystems.

Directions: Use the information to answer questions 3–4.

The movement of carbon between some carbon storehouses may involve processes that take millions of years. Limestone, marble, and chalk are examples. Each of these is a common type of rock composed mainly of calcium carbonate. The carbon contained in these rocks comes from the bodies of marine organisms that were alive millions of years ago. These organisms took carbon from the atmosphere, took carbon that was dissolved in water, and took carbon from within soil components. When these organisms died, their remains eventually became part of sedimentary rocks, such as limestone, marble, and chalk, that formed during millions of years.

Today when deposits of limestone, marble, or chalk weather, the calcium carbonate chemically reacts with water. The byproducts of this reaction are carbon-dioxide gas and carbonic acid. Carbon returns both to the atmosphere and to oceans and lakes.

3. What carbon-based chemical is contained in limestone, marble, and chalk?

   A. carbon-dioxide gas

   B. carbonic acid

   C. calcium carbonate

   D. carbon monoxide

4. Based on the information in the passage, which other biogeochemical cycle reacts with calcium carbonate, resulting in the release of carbon dioxide?

   A. the water cycle

   B. the phosphorous cycle

   C. the nitrogen cycle

   D. the sulfur cycle

LESSON 2.3 Interactions Among Populations

©NPS photo by Doug Smith

LESSON OBJECTIVES

- Analyze the factors that affect a population's carrying capacity
- List three kinds of symbiosis
- Explain how predators and prey affect population size

CORE SKILLS & PRACTICES

- Evaluate Reasoning
- Describe a Data Set Statistically

Key Terms

commensalism
a symbiotic relationship in which one organism benefits and the other is not affected

mutualism
a symbiotic relationship in which both species benefit

parasitism
a symbiotic relationship in which one organism feeds off the living body of another

symbiosis
a close relationship between individuals of two or more species

Vocabulary

carrying capacity
the maximum number of organisms of one species that an environment can support

predation
when one organism kills and eats another organism

Key Concept

Many factors control the growth of a population in an area. The maximum size of a population a specific environment can sustain can be influenced by interactions among populations.

Factors That Affect Population Size

Populations of organisms must obtain food and other resources, or materials for living, within their ecosystem to survive. Factors that affect survival also affect population size.

Limiting Factors

Population density is a measure of the number of organisms per unit area. The size of any population in an ecosystem can be controlled by a number of limiting factors, or factors that set an upper limit on the growth rate of a population. Such factors include reproduction, natural resources, space and nesting sites, competition, and waste and disease.

Reproduction

The speed at which a population can grow is set by the species' reproductive cycle. Some species, such as whales, sharks, and humans, produce a single offspring after a long period of growth. These animals produce few young over their lifetimes. Other species, such as insects and small rodents, mature quickly and produce many young. This is because after only a short time, there will be many breeding members of the population.

A species' ability to reproduce also largely depends on the availability of resources. During periods when few resources are available, such as during a drought, many animals and plants produce fewer offspring. During periods of abundance, animals and plants produce more offspring.

Natural Resources

Natural resources, such as food and water, can be limiting factors. For example, the population size of an animal that eats only fruit will be limited by the amount of fruit available in the ecosystem. The population size of a predator will be limited by how many animals can be preyed on in the area.

Space and Nesting Sites

Living space and nesting sites can also be limiting factors. Some organisms live closer together than others. For example, millions of herb plants such as garlic mustard can exist in a square kilometer. Wolverines live very far apart with a population density of one individual per 100 square kilometers.

Certain animals must have places in which to construct their nests. For instance, many species of birds have plenty of space in which to live but are limited by the number of suitable nesting sites, such as holes in dead trees.

Competition

Competition will occur when when resources are limited. Competition is the interaction among living things for the resources they need to survive and to produce offspring. Competition can occur within a population or between individuals in different populations.

Wastes and Disease

As a population's density increases, its waste products can build up to unhealthy levels. Waste can poison an organism or spread diseases that can affect populations of animals that live close together in colonies, such as prairie dogs. It also can affect human population growth.

Carrying Capacity

The number of organisms of one species that an environment can support for a long time is called the environment's **carrying capacity.** In most cases, populations start small and grow until they are larger than the carrying capacity of their habitat. Limiting factors cause the population to drop below the carrying capacity for a period of time before growing once again. This graph shows how a population of sheep on the island of St. Kilda in Scotland has changed in size since 1985. The solid line shows how the population fluctuates dramatically each year.

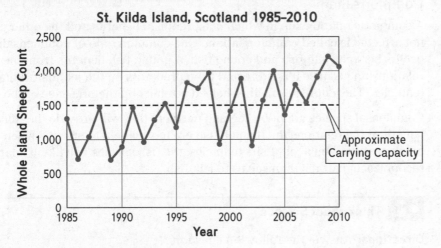

St. Kilda Island, Scotland 1985–2010

Natural Events and Carrying Capacity

Researchers studying the sheep population found that the timing of storms was an important factor influencing population fluctuations. The time it takes a population to return to its carrying capacity depends on the organisms' reproductive abilities. Aphids, tiny insects that are born pregnant, can repopulate an area in a matter of weeks. Sharks, however, produce only a few young each year, starting when they are several years old. It may take decades for a shark population to recover.

Evaluate Reasoning

When you evaluate reasoning, you determine whether arguments make sense based on evidence and your own experience. When experts testify in decisions over land-use permits, they often cite evidence from research others have done. When you cite a source, you quote it as evidence when supporting an argument.

Consider this scenario: A forest-products manufacturer approaches a state agency with a proposal to harvest trees from an old-growth forest. What types of evidence would an environmental organization cite to discourage the state from granting a permit?

To prepare for a test, it helps to gather all the information you can about the type of test and its length. It also helps to gather the information you are being tested on and put it into a form that will help you study. One useful form is an outline, with main topics and subsections that contain details underneath each topic. Make an outline of the material in this lesson so far, as a way to begin gathering and organizing information that will help you study.

Symbiosis

A close relationship between individuals of two or more species is called **symbiosis.** The partners in symbiosis typically have effects on each other's lives such as their ability to survive and reproduce. Symbioses are classified according to which species benefits from the relationship. There are three kinds of symbiosis: mutualism, commensalism, and parasitism.

Mutualism

A relationship in which both species benefit is called **mutualism.** There are many examples involving species from every kingdom of life. Most plants form a type of mutualistic relationship with fungi that is called a mycorrhiza. Fungi have hairlike structures that take up water and nutrients. The fungi live on sugars and other food they collect from plant roots. In turn, the fungi absorb water and minerals that are shared with the plant.

Mutualism results in many dramatic adaptations. Pollinators, such as birds and insects, and the flowers they pollinate are an example. Plants produce flowers with the shape, color, and smell preferred by their pollinators. Some flowers even look much like females of the insect pollinator's species.

Parasitism

Parasitism is a symbiotic relationship in which one organism, the parasite, feeds on the living body of the other organism. The parasite benefits, while the host, or the organism on which the parasite lives, is harmed. Some parasites, including fleas, mosquitoes, and ticks, live on the outside of the host. Other parasites, such as tapeworms, can live only inside the host's body.

Parasites have evolved to where they may hurt, but not kill, the host. If the host dies, the parasite can also die. Host species adapt by poisoning parasites or attacking them with their immune systems.

Commensalism

A symbiotic relationship in which one organism benefits and the other is not affected is called **commensalism.** One common type of commensalism occurs between jellyfish and young fish. A young fish benefits from the relationship because it is protected from predators by the jellyfish's stinging tentacles. The jellyfish is neither helped nor hurt by the presence of the fish.

Commensal species adapt by seeking partners that will provide the full benefit of the relationship. If small fish are more likely to survive when being protected by a jellyfish's tentacles, the fish species will likely adapt to recognize and attach themselves to jellyfish.

☍ Think about Science

Directions: Answer the following question.

1. In which of the following relationship types is one organism harmed when another benefits?

   A. commensalism
   B. cooperative
   C. mutualism
   D. parasitism

Predator-Prey Relationships

Predation is another type of mutualism in which one organism kills and eats another organism. Predation involves two organisms or species—a predator and its prey. The predator benefits by gaining food, while the prey that is eaten can no longer survive and reproduce. Unlike parasitism, which lasts a long time without killing the host, predation is a one-time relationship. Predator and prey species can affect each other's carrying capacity in a community.

Predation and Carrying Capacity

On Isle Royale in Lake Superior, moose colonized the island, and their population grew rapidly in the absence of predators. Food was one of the limiting factors that influenced the carrying capacity of the moose. When wolves colonized the island, predation became another factor that reduced the carrying capacity of the moose but increased the carrying capacity of the wolf.

How Changes Affect Food Webs

If the top predator in a food web is removed, all the other species in the web will be affected, for better or worse. For example, humans have killed off wolves throughout most of the United States to prevent wolves from eating livestock and to reduce competition between human hunters and wolves. One unexpected result was the significant increase in the number and range of coyotes. Coyotes were competing with wolves for small-animal prey. Also, wolves killed and ate many young coyotes. So, as the population of wolves decreased, the population of coyotes increased. Elk, rabbit, mouse, and deer populations also grew rapidly after the removal of wolves. These increases led to overgrazing and destruction of crops and plant communities.

Adaptation to Predation

Predators and prey both adapt to their relationships. Prey species adapt by becoming harder to find and less tasty to predators. They may also adopt a reproductive strategy of having many offspring at once. For example, all the maple trees in a population produce a heavy crop of seeds at the same time every few years. There are too many seeds for predators to eat them all. By the time the predator populations have grown larger, the young trees are too big to be eaten. Predators also adapt to increase their fitness. They can become better at catching and killing their prey. Behaviors such as speed, teamwork, and quiet movement help lions kill large animals. In addition, many predators can survive for a long time without catching any prey. Spiders can wait months between meals, and wolverines store meat under the snow.

Think about Science

Directions: Answer the following question.

1. Each of these pairs of animals lives in the same ecosystem. Which pair is most likely to be in a predator-prey relationship?

    A. eagle and hawk
    B. mouse and squirrel
    C. crab and sand flea
    D. dragonfly and fish

CORE PRACTICE

Describe a Data Set Statistically

You can perform a mathematical analysis on a data set using statistics. Statistics is a branch of mathematics concerned with the collection and analysis of numerical data. Statistics can be used on population data to produce a carrying-capacity graph. They can also be used to model how a population will grow in the future. When the growth of a population stabilizes, carrying capacity can be estimated by finding the mean, or average number of individuals, during that time of stability. Find the estimated carrying capacity of this stable crab population, using the data in the table.

Number of Individual Crabs

Year 10	245
Year 11	266
Year 12	264
Year 13	231
Year 14	260

Vocabulary Review

Directions: Write the missing term in the blank.

carrying capacity   commensalism   mutualism
parasitism   predation   symbiosis

1. _____ is when both organisms benefit in a relationship.

2. _____ refers to any close relationship between organisms of two or more species.

3. In _____, one organism benefits, while the other organism is not affected.

4. A population can stabilize around its _____ within an ecosystem.

5. A tick attached to a deer is an example of _____.

6. _____ is when one animal preys on another.

Skill Review

Directions: Answer the following questions.

1. Which of the following describes the relationship between a flower and its pollinator?

   A. mutualism

   B. commensalism

   C. parasitism

   D. competition

2. Space would likely be the most limiting factor for which of the following populations?

   A. A barnacle population on a boat

   B. A shark population in the open ocean

   C. A clam population on a sandy beach

   D. A seaweed population near a coastline

3. Each of these pairs of animals lives in the same ecosystem. Which pair is most likely to compete for food resources?

   A. butterfly and snake

   B. mouse and coyote

   C. crab and dolphin

   D. deer and rabbit

4. Prairie dogs eat grasses and live in burrows within a colony. They are hunted by a variety of predators, including hawks and black-footed ferrets. Describe how different factors could limit a prairie dog population.

5. Explain why the removal of a top predator such as a lion could cause an increase in populations of prey and other predators.

6. Explain why it would not be adaptive for a parasite to kill its host.

7. When food, water, and space are abundant and other factors are not an issue in an area, which of the following populations is likely to have the greatest number of individuals?

   A. mosquito population

   B. blue-jay population

   C. gray-squirrel population

   D. oak-tree population

8. A remora is a fish that attaches to a shark and eats scraps of food from the shark's meals. The remora does not help or harm the shark. What kind of relationship do the remora and shark have?

   A. commensalism

   B. competitive

   C. mutualism

   D. parasitism

9. After the removal of wolf populations in the United States, which of these populations decreased?

   A. coyote populations

   B. rabbit populations

   C. crop-plant populations

   D. deer populations

Skill Practice

Directions: Use the table to answer questions 1 and 2.

	Year 7	Year 8	Year 9	Year 10	Year 11	Year 12	Year 13
Number of Individual Gulls	175	212	199	187	170	184	200

1. A team of scientists monitors a nesting colony of gulls over a 13-year period. Their data are included in the table. During the last seven years, the population appears to stabilize. What is the approximate carrying capacity of this gull population?

   A. about 180 individuals

   B. about 190 individuals

   C. about 200 individuals

   D. about 210 individuals

2. What can you infer in year 11 that might have led to a drop in carrying capacity?

Directions: Use the graph to answer questions 3 and 4.

3. The graph shows the growth and stabilization of a population of paramecia that was cultured in a laboratory. What is the approximate carrying capacity for this population of paramecia?

   A. 25 paramecia

   B. 150 paramecia

   C. 275 paramecia

   D. 300 paramecia

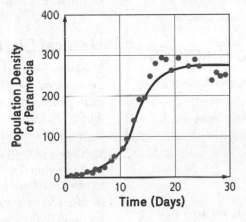

4. The graph shows that the paramecium population stabilized over time. If the population received a constant flow of nutrients, why did the population not continue to increase instead of stabilizing?

Directions: Answer the following questions.

5. A researcher transfers individual plants from the forest to pots in a greenhouse to use in a study. The first soil was replaced with sterile potting soil. All the plants die. Which of these relationships was interrupted when the researcher transferred the plants?

   A. commensalism

   B. parasitism

   C. mutualism

   D. predation

6. The predator-prey relationship limits moose and wolf populations on Isle Royale. What other factors might limit each of these populations?

LESSON 2.4 Disruptions to Ecosystems

■ LESSON OBJECTIVES

- Identify and analyze ways ecosystems are disrupted
- Describe the interdependence of organisms in an ecosystem

■ CORE SKILLS & PRACTICES

- Reason from Data or Evidence to a Conclusion
- Distinguish Among Reasoned Judgments

Key Terms

biodiversity
the variety of life in an area that is determined by the number of species in that area

extinction
the death of a species

habitat destruction
the changing of a natural area such that the habitat is no longer able to support the organisms

invasive species
an organism that is moved to a new, foreign environment in which that organism causes harm

Vocabulary

pollution
substances that have a harmful effect on an environment

valid
logical and justifiable

Key Concept

Ecosystems can be disrupted by both natural events and human activities. Disruptions can have a significant impact on organisms and the entire ecosystem.

Natural Disruptions to Ecosystems

You have learned that an ecosystem is a community of organisms that interact with each other and their environment. Ecosystems change over time. Sudden disruptions such as volcanoes, floods, or fires can affect which species will thrive in an environment. Other disruptions are caused by human activities. Some disruptions can be devastating for an individual species and may even cause an entire species to permanently disappear in a process called **extinction.** As species become extinct, the variety of species in the biosphere decreases, which decreases **biodiversity,** or the variety of life. Every organism plays an important role in the ecosystem to which it belongs. Whenever one species is removed, other species in the food chain are affected. These changes influence a community's biodiversity and can disrupt an entire ecosystem.

Wildfires

Fire is a common disruption to ecosystems that can be caused by nature or by human behavior. Natural wildfires can both help and harm an ecosystem. For example, wildfires kill many small animals and displace others that flee to safety. Animals looking to return after the fire will find their homes and much of their food supply destroyed. Also, bare soil that remains after a wildfire is particularly susceptible to soil erosion because the soil is no longer held in place by roots.

Wildfires can help an ecosystem by clearing out much of the dead and dying vegetation allowing surviving plants to benefit from increased light. Ash and charcoal left from burnt vegetation can help add nutrients to depleted soils. These nutrients provide a rich environment for surviving vegetation and sprouting seeds, allowing them to flourish. Eventually ecosystems rebound from fire disruption and are renewed with nutrient-rich soil and flourishing vegetation.

Flooding

Flooding can occur after a storm and may be disruptive to an ecosystem, depending on the extent of the flooding and how long the water stays. Flooding can result in saturated soils, or soils that are filled with water. Plant roots require oxygen, so saturated soils can kill plants by drowning the plant roots. Flooding may also cause water and nutrients to run off across land surfaces. Rushing water can cause soil to wash away, particularly bare soil. Burrows, dens, and nests can be destroyed, forcing surviving animals to relocate.

Some ecosystems, called flood plains, are made up of species that have adapted to occasional flooding. Flood plains are flat areas along rivers that flood when the river rises above its banks. The flooding deposits nutrient-rich sediment along stream banks. Adaptations of flood-plain species allow them to thrive in their ecosystem.

Volcanic Eruptions

On May 18, 1980, an earthquake under Mount St. Helens contributed to a tremendous volcanic eruption. The north face of the mountain slid away in a huge avalanche, releasing a blast of superheated, rock-filled gas that ripped up the trees in its path. Subsequently, slower flows of gas and rock destroyed trees and living organisms in the soil. Mature forests were turned into ash-covered wasteland. Since then, hardy plants have reappeared in the ash field. The plants attract herbivores that drop seeds from other plants in their dung. About three decades after the eruption, the forest began to regrow. The steady progression of species change and replacement in an ecosystem over time, as occurred after the eruption of Mount St. Helens, is called ecological succession.

Think about Science

Directions: Answer the following questions.

1. How can fires and floods be beneficial to ecosystems?
   A. They can change the pH of the water.
   B. They can provide nutrients for soils.
   C. They can kill predators.
   D. They can wash away soils.

2. After a volcanic eruption, which of these organisms would first reinhabit the disrupted ecosystem?
   A. carnivores
   B. grasses
   C. herbivores
   D. trees

Human Effects on Ecosystems

Humans impact the natural world more than any other species. Without limits on human activity, humans can damage the environment in many ways. As the human population grows, it requires more resources to keep its members healthy and comfortable. Each new family needs a place to live, food, water, clothing, medicine, and tools.

Media Literacy

The rapid decline of honeybees has been a mystery that concerns scientists. At first, scientists presumed that the decline in the honeybee population was due to poor nutrition. At least six more hypotheses to explain the decline in the honeybee population have been proposed, including disease, parasites, pesticide use, and electromagnetic radiation. One of the skills related to media literacy is the ability to analyze and evaluate the validity of media claims. A **valid** claim is one that is logical and justifiable based on evidence. With so many sources of information available, it is important to realize that not all information is reliable.

Describe some of the criteria you would use to determine which media resources are reliable and which resources are not. Explain your answer.

People often have to consider several options when making a decision or solving a problem. Consider this hypothetical situation: In the town of Springfield, homeowners planted trees in an effort to prevent soil erosion. These trees became an invasive species, and now the town must consider different ways to address the problem. One proposal is to clear-cut the plant and till the land to make sure the roots cannot continue to spread. The second possible solution is to introduce a beetle that eats the leaves of the tree, which kills it.

Use what you have learned about ecosystems to decide which, if either, of the proposed solutions is reasonable. You may suggest an alternate solution. Explain your answer.

Habitat Destruction

Habitat destruction occurs when a habitat is removed and replaced with some other type of habitat. No matter how careful the plan, land used to grow crops or build houses is no longer suitable for some of the organisms that once lived there. As a result, the organisms living at the site must move or be destroyed. Habitat destruction is the most important reason species are threatened with extinction today. Habitat destruction can have harmful effects on humans, too. Scientists believe that some of the destruction caused by Hurricane Katrina in 2005 resulted from the removal of wetlands that would normally take up much of the regional floodwaters. Natural coastal ecosystems, including thick vegetation, may be able to buffer the coastline from hurricanes and other storms.

Introduced Species

Wherever humans go, they take animals, plants, and microorganisms with them. Tulips—as well as most crop plants and many other highly-valued garden plants—are not native to the United States but rather are introduced species. Introduced species are an important part of the economy and of society. Some introduced species, however, can be disruptive to an ecosystem. An introduced species that has negative effects in its new ecosystem is called an **invasive species.**

Invasive species can have serious effects on an ecosystem and on the human population. For example, a vine called kudzu was introduced to the southern United States as a way to control soil erosion. However, the kudzu spread rapidly, choking the roots of some plants and blocking light for other plants, effectively killing them and changing the ecosystem.

Overhunting

Throughout history, humans have hunted or killed animals for several reasons. They obtained food and necessary materials from animals and eliminated competition for crops and prey. They protected livestock by trapping or hunting animals such as wolves. Many species were driven to extinction by hunting thousands of years ago. As the human population grew, more and more species of animals were threatened with extinction from overhunting. Laws were passed to limit hunting and to ban the killing of endangered species. Nevertheless, poaching, or illegal hunting, continues to threaten many populations.

Pollution and Environmental Change

As you can see in the graph on the next page, the human population has grown exponentially over the last few centuries. This population growth was a result of increasing resources and new technology to feed and provide for the growing population. Human activities cause **pollution**—the release of harmful substances into the environment—including air pollution, water pollution, and the production of hazardous waste. Air pollution in the form of carbon dioxide has contributed to global warming.

One effect of today's heavy use of fossil fuels—including coal, oil, and gas—is air pollution. Air pollution includes noxious compounds and particulate matter. Air pollution can result in respiratory trouble and other human sickness.

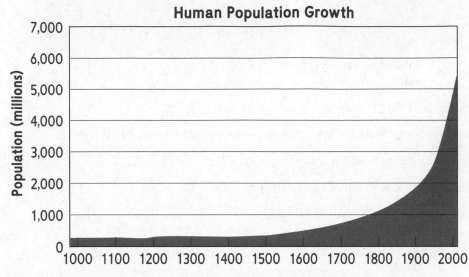

Human Population Growth

CORE PRACTICE

Reason from Data or Evidence to a Conclusion

Examine the data provided in the graph on this page. What do you notice about the human population in the last 400 years? Why do you think it has changed? According to geologic and biologic records, the number of extinctions has increased in the past 300 years. Do you think these facts are related? Explain.

Sources of water pollution include the runoff of fertilizer from lawns and agricultural fields, as well as runoff from oil and other urban pollutants. Water pollution is also caused by oil spills, in addition to smoke from power plants. Fertilizers introduce excess nutrients and result in major changes in water ecosystems, including changing the pH of the water, causing algae blooms, and reducing the oxygen in the water. Rainwater can wash all pollutants on Earth's surface into rivers, lakes, and the ocean. Oil spills kill animals and can affect several different food webs. Air pollution can lead to water pollution by causing acid rain that can damage—and even kill—living things. Water pollution can also occur when people do not properly dispose of toxic household or industrial materials.

Global Climate Change

Climate change can involve global warming, a slow rise in Earth's average temperature. While global temperatures have changed over time, most scientists agree that the release of carbon dioxide into the air from the burning of fossil fuels contributes to this rise in temperature. An increasing rise in temperatures could affect ecosystems around the globe. For example, rising temperatures can speed up the melting of glaciers and ice caps disrupting or destroying habitats along shorelines as waters rise. Climate change can affect precipitation patterns resulting in droughts or floods. Climate change can also alter ecosystems as populations unable to survive warmer temperatures migrate to cooler regions.

⚛ Think about Science

Directions: Fill in the blank.

1. The biggest threat to species extinction is _____ .

2. Air pollution is a consequence of the heavy use of _____ .

Vocabulary Review

Directions: Write the missing term in the blank.

biodiversity   extinction   habitat destruction
invasive species   pollution   valid

1. Development of a new housing complex is likely to cause _____ .

2. _____ are organisms introduced to a new area that cause harm to the ecosystem.

3. Bleach poured directly into a gutter that drains to a lake is an example of _____ .

4. _____ of a species may occur as a result of habitat destruction.

5. A(n) _____ explanation depends on logical reasoning.

6. _____ is the variety of life in an ecosystem.

Skill Review

Directions: Answer the following questions.

1. Which of the following would most likely be considered an invasive species?

   A. Goats shipped to Australia in the 1700s, causing vegetation loss

   B. An increased deer population in the United States due to fewer predators

   C. A tropical house plant introduced into gardens in the Pacific Northwest

   D. Coyotes raising their young in New York City's Central Park

2. Fertilizer is used to increase plant health and size. Why is fertilizer considered a human disruption to an ecosystem?

   A. It pollutes water, causing algae blooms.

   B. It kills insects that use the plants for food.

   C. It changes plant size, benefiting farmers who use them for crops.

   D. It changes the size of the animals that consume the plant.

3. When an ecosystem is disrupted, the balance between _____ and their _____ becomes unstable.

4. One of the risks of explosive human population growth is _____ as humans build towns and mine the land for resources.

5. Explain how weather systems, like a hurricane or a drought, may cause ecosystem disruption.

6. Why do you think habitat destruction has increased so significantly in the past 300 years? Defend your answer.

7. Explain how air pollution causes disruption to ecosystems.

Skill Practice

Directions: Answer the following questions.

1. Which condition will probably be the first to help an ecosystem rebound after a fire?

   A. extensive soil erosion

   B. areas of standing water

   C. ash and charcoal in the soil

   D. wildlife returning to their homes.

2. Why is farming considered a human disruption of an ecosystem?

   A. Clearing the land requires gas-powered machinery and tools.

   B. It removes an existing habitat and replaces it with a new habitat.

   C. It usually results in the extinction of sensitive plants and animals.

   D. The cleared land is more open to destructive weather like hurricanes.

3. Human effects on ecosystems can be lessened with proper planning or foresight. What are some ways humans can lessen their impact when building a new community? Provide a rationale for each suggestion you give.

4. Describe how the extinction of an animal can cause disruption in an ecosystem.

5. A fire burns through a large patch of forest. Describe how ecological succession will likely occur following this disruption.

Directions: Use the information to answer questions 6–7.

At the turn of the century, ranchers moved onto the grassy Kaibab Plateau in northern Arizona. They were attracted by the fine grazing areas and large numbers of deer for hunting. Fearing that the mountain lion, another inhabitant of the region, would prey on the cattle and deer, the ranchers waged a campaign to eliminate the mountain lion from the plateau. They were successful in their effort, and mountain lions disappeared within a few years. But their success produced terrible ecological results. Increased numbers of deer, along with herds of grazing cattle, stripped the land of all grasses. Soon heavy rains caused major erosion, and the land was reduced to a fraction of its usefulness. This problem has occurred repeatedly where humans have changed an ecosystem without considering the possible consequences.

6. Was the disruption to the ecosystem human induced, naturally induced, or both? Defend your answer.

7. Explain how the removal of mountain lions affected other species in the ecosystem.

Directions: Answer the following questions.

1. Which level in an environment encompasses the greatest amount of energy?

   A. habitat

   B. ecosystem

   C. population

   D. community

2. Black bears eat a diet of young plants, berries, aquatic plants, insects, small animals and rodents, deer, elk, and moose. How would you classify a black bear?

   A. producer

   B. primary consumer

   C. secondary consumer

   D. tertiary consumer

3. In which type of symbiosis would an organism be most likely end up with a disease spread through the blood?

   A. commensalism

   B. competition

   C. mutualism

   D. parasitism

4. Which of these is at the first trophic level or almost every food chain within a food web?

   A. water

   B. plants

   C. insects

   D. herbivores

5. If the population of primary consumers in an ecosystem is about 100, which of the following might be the population of secondary consumers in the same ecosystem?

   A. 50

   B. 200

   C. 500

   D. 1000

6. Which of the following factors determines how long it takes a population to return to its carrying capacity after an unusually severe winter?

   A. the reproductive ability of the surviving population

   B. the number of individuals in the original population

   C. the magnitude of the carrying capacity of the population

   D. the amount of space in the ecosystem occupied by the population

7. Which of the following is a benefit associated with destruction of an ecosystem by wildfires?

   A. Animal populations are decreased or eliminated from area.

   B. Soil erosion can clear the land for the growth of new plants.

   C. Development by humans is destroyed and the land is cleared.

   D. Dead matter is cleared and more sunlight gets to small plants.

8. What is a disadvantage of technology for an ecosystem?

   A. technology causes overhunting

   B. technology creates new plant species

   C. technology creates too much pollution

   D. technology causes too much biodiversity

9. Which type of ecology looks at the interaction between a coyote and a rabbit?

   A. community ecology

   B. competition ecology

   C. ecosystem ecology

   D. population ecology

10. In which biome would you expect to find animals growing a thick coat of fur and burrowing deep underground to keep warm in winter months?

    A. desert

    B. grassland

    C. taiga

    D. tundra

11. Mountain ranges close to coastal regions have an impact on climate. Which species is likely to be living in an ecosystem on the side of the mountain farthest from the coast?

A. cactus

B. hibiscus

C. oak

D. pine

12. Which of Earth's cycles can cause eutrophication by increasing the algae population in aquatic ecosystems?

A. carbon and nitrogen cycles

B. carbon and phosphorous cycles

C. nitrogen and phosphorous cycles

D. phosphorous and water cycles

13. Explain how animals can help the re-growth of plants after a major ecological disaster such as a volcanic eruption or a forest fire?

14. List four limiting factors for a population of freshwater fish.

15. Explain why many species are facing extinction because of human activity.

16. In which type of biome are wetlands found? Describe the environment of a typical wetland.

Directions: Read the passage and answer questions 17–19.

Wolves, once a top predator in the United States, have been mostly killed off by humans to prevent them from eating livestock. One unexpected result is the great increase in the number and range of coyotes. It turns out that coyotes were competing with wolves for small animal prey. Also, wolves killed and ate many young coyotes. So as the population of wolves decreased, the population of coyotes increased. Elk, rabbit, mouse, and deer populations also grew rapidly after the removal of wolves. These increases led to overgrazing and destruction of crops and plant communities. Without the wolf population, people have resorted to shooting, trapping, and poisoning many of wolves' former prey themselves.

17. According to this passage what was the limiting factor in the ecosystem?

A. the human population

B. the wolf population

C. the coyote population

D. the herbivore population

18. Which of the following is the cause of disruption in the relationship between all of the species mentioned in the passage?

A. human activity

B. wolves hunting

C. coyotes hunting

D. overgrazing herbivores

19. Which two species are likely to exist in a commensal relationship in this ecosystem?

A. elk and coyote

B. rabbit and deer

C. coyote and wolf

D. human and wolf

Directions: Use the diagram to answer questions 20–21.

20. According to the feeding relationship arrows drawn in the diagram, if the jackrabbit developed a disease that greatly reduced its population, how many other populations would be directly affected?

A. 0

B. 1

C. 2

D. 3

21. Which three species are in direct competition for a single food source? What is the food source they are competing for?

Directions: Read the passage and answer questions 22 and 23.

Invasive species can have serious effects on an ecosystem and on the human population. For example, a vine called kudzu was introduced to the southern United States as a way to control soil erosion. However, the kudzu spread rapidly, choking the roots of other plants and blocking light for other plants, effectively killing them and changing the ecosystem.

22. Describe the relationship between kudzu and plants native to the southern United States.

23. Explain why farmers or horticulturists may want to introduce a new plant species to an ecosystem and why this often ends up doing more harm than good.

Directions: Use the graph to answer questions 24–26.

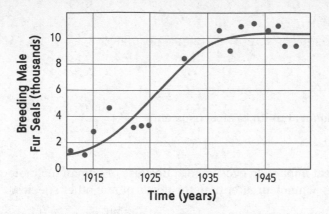

24. Approximately what year did the seal population on St. Paul Island off the coast of Alaska reach its carrying capacity?

25. Which of the following might have been a factor that caused the seals to reach their carrying capacity on the island?

A. limited daylight

B. increase in daylight

C. limited food supply

D. increase in food supply

26. What is the approximate carrying capacity for the seals in this population?

A. about 10

B. about 1,000

C. about 6,000

D. about 10,000

Check Your Understanding

On the following chart, circle the number of any item you answered incorrectly. Next to each group of item numbers, you will see the pages you can review to learn how to answer the items correctly.

Lesson	Item Number(s)	Review Page(s)
2.1: Living Things and Their Environment	1, 9, 10, 11, 16,	62–67
2.2: Movement of Energy and Matter	2, 4, 5, 12, 20, 21	70–75
2.3: Interactions Among Populations	3, 6, 14, 17, 18, 19, 24, 25, 26	78–81
2.4: Disruptions to Ecosystems	7, 8, 13, 15, 22, 23	84–87

What are the Consequences?

Core Practice

- Identify and refine hypotheses for scientific investigations

Question

How can we reduce the threat of human activity to an ecosystem?

Background Concepts

Human populations often have a great impact on ecosystems. Because of human technology and development, our need for resources is much greater than the needs of any other species.

To obtain some resources that all humans depend on, such as coal and oil, we must dig deep underground and destroy large areas of the environment. Humans also destroy forests to create more space for living and agriculture. They also cut down forests for lumber and paper products. Humans divert water from rivers or lakes to make room for new construction and land development. An increase in large scale commercial agriculture has caused an excess of chemical fertilizers to enter the soil in many ecosystems. We use chemical pesticides to decrease the number of insects that destroy crops or spread disease. These chemicals end up in many rivers and lakes and harm the organisms in those ecosystems.

The changes caused by human activity always have some consequence for the abiotic and biotic factors of an ecosystem. These activities may also have an effect on our own health and well-being.

Hypothesis

A hypothesis is a tentative explanation based on the available evidence. It is a starting point for a scientific investigation that will prove to be either supported or not supported by the evidence gathered. Develop a hypothesis that explains how a major ecological problem in your area, or in an area that interests you, affects various parts of the ecosystem.

✔ Test-Taking Tip

Some test questions will ask you to identify the most appropriate hypothesis for the scientific information or data presented. To determine the best hypothesis statement, review the variables and the data collected. Determine what question or questions the data might be answering. Then select the hypothesis that makes the most sense based on the information or data given.

Investigation

After developing a hypothesis, the next step is to gather information and data to determine whether your hypothesis is supported or not. Develop a list of sources that provide information about the ecosystem you choose. These sources can include government Internet sites and information gathered from local ecologists or environmental centers. Investigate how the ecosystem is directly or indirectly impacted by humans. Determine which human activities have caused negative changes in the ecosystem.

Collect and Analyze Data

Collect data that show ways in which human activity has impacted the ecosystem of your choice. List as many activities as you can that either directly or indirectly affect each component of the ecosystem such as plants, animals, soil, sunlight, air, and water.

Use a Concept Web graphic organizer like the one shown on page 447 to organize your research and record your findings. Place the human activity in the center of the graphic organizer. Create a web to show how changes in one biotic or abiotic factor affect other factors in the ecosystem. For example, a change in soil composition due to too many harmful chemicals will have an effect on plants, the primary consumers that eat those plants, and the secondary and tertiary consumers that eat the primary consumers.

Next, research some ways in which conservationists and ecologists are trying to promote changes to human activity to keep ecosystems from harm.

Interpretation

Summarize and interpret the information collected. Determine whether your hypothesis supports the cause of the problems facing the ecosystem you chose to study. Evaluate or refine a solution that has been tried or suggested to reduce the negative effects on the ecosystem you chose to study.

When evaluating and interpreting the information or data you collected, ask yourself these questions:

- Which human activity has most affected the ecosystem you chose to study? Was your hypothesis correct, or did you need to refine it?

- In what ways have ecologists and conservationists tried to educate the public so that humans make less of an impact on an ecosystem?

- Is there a solution that would be easy for the population to put into practice, and how would the ecosystem benefit?

Results

Discuss the results of your investigation using evidence to support your conclusions. Discuss any observations about the information you gathered, unexpected results, and any remaining questions. If your hypothesis related to the cause of disruption to an ecosystem was not supported, discuss how you were able to refine it based on the data collected.

Consider these questions as you discuss your results:

- Is the ecosystem you chose to study greatly impacted by human activity?

- What did you learn about the ways in which human activities have affected the ecosystem you chose to study?

- How would your proposal reduce the threat of human activity on the ecosystem?

Chapter 3

Structure and Function of Life

Every living organism on Earth is composed of one or more cells. Cells contain smaller parts called organelles that must work together in order for the cell to live and reproduce. Simple cells are found in organisms such as bacteria, and more complex cells are found in plants and animals. The cells of animals and plants contain similar cell parts; however, plants cells have additional parts that make them unique. Both plant and animal cells take in and convert energy from their environment to support cellular function.

Science Photo Library RF/Getty Images

Lesson 3.1
Cells: Basic Units of Life

Once the microscope was invented, scientists were able to see that each living organism was made up of very tiny units called cells. Learn how cells are grouped into several levels, including tissues, organs and body systems in multicellular organisms.

Lesson 3.2
Cell Structure and Function

Each cell is composed of smaller units called organelles that carry out a specific function in the cell. Learn about the two basic types of cells, and how they are similar and different in their structure and function.

Lesson 3.3
Plant Structure and Function

Plants have many different parts that function to ensure their survival and reproduction. Learn how plants can be grouped into different categories according to their structure and that each type of plant can better understood by examining the various parts that make up the whole plant.

Lesson 3.4
Energy and Cells

Both plant and animal cells need energy in order to function properly. Learn how plant and animal cells convert the energy molecules into sugar that is used in chemical reactions that produce energy-storing molecules called ATP. ATP is the energy source for all cellular functions.

Lesson 3.5:
Mitosis and Meiosis

In order for an organism to grow or maintain proper health, new cells must be continuously produced. Learn about the reproduction of cells through the processes of mitosis and meiosis.

Goal Setting

Choose one type of plant and one type of animal that interests you. Write down the name and a description of the physical characteristics that describe each organism. You can also include a drawing of each organism. Use the information in this chapter to describe how they are similar and different when you look at them on a cellular level.

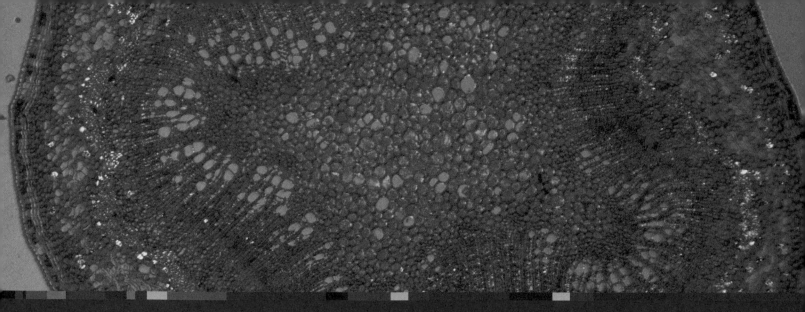

LESSON 3.1   Cells: Basic Units of Life

LESSON OBJECTIVES

- Explain the principles of the cell theory
- Describe the levels of cellular organization in animals

CORE SKILLS & PRACTICES

- Understand and Apply Scientific Models, Theories, and Processes
- Analyze Author's Purpose

Key Terms

cells
the smallest living unit that carries on the activities of an organism

cell theory
states that cells are the basic units of life, that all organisms are made of cells, and that cells produce new cells

spontaneous generation
a belief that living things come from nonliving matter

Vocabulary

subdivide
to organize into smaller units

Key Concept

Your tissues, organs, and body systems all have one thing in common—they are composed of cells. Cells are the basic units of structure and organization of all living organisms.

Cell Discovery and Cell Theory

The invention of the microscope in the seventeenth century was a great help in the study of living organisms. For the first time, biologists could see beyond the limits of the human eye. The discovery of **cells,** the smallest living unit that carries on the activities of an organism, would not have been possible without the work of many scientists and the development of the right scientific tools, such as the microscope.

In 1665, an English scientist named Robert Hooke made a simple microscope and looked at a slice of cork, the dead cells of oak bark. He was amazed at the tiny boxlike cavities the cork was made of. Because these cavities reminded him of the cells in which monks live at a monastery, he gave the name *cellulae* (the Latin word meaning "small rooms") to these tiny units of cork. It is from Hooke's work that we have the term *cell*.

Spontaneous Generation

By the mid 1800s, scientists had learned a great deal about cells. For example, they knew that cells were the basic units of plants and animals, and they knew about some structures inside cells. What they did not know was where cells came from. Many people believed that living things arose through **spontaneous generation,** which is the belief that living things come from nonliving matter. As early as the fifth century BC, philosophers had concluded that living things developed from nonliving elements in nature. Today this idea may seem unrealistic based on what you know. Yet these conclusions were based on people's observations. Some of the important research involving spontaneous generation is summarized below.

Francesco Redi

Even before the invention of the microscope, some critics had questioned the idea of spontaneous generation. In 1668, the Italian physician Francesco

Cells: Basic Units of Life

Redi proposed that maggots did not suddenly appear out of nowhere on rotting meat. Instead he believed that maggots came from eggs laid by flies that land on the meat. To test his hypothesis, Redi set out jars: Some of the jars were open to air, some were completely sealed, and some were covered with cheesecloth. Air can pass through cheesecloth, but flies cannot. Redi observed that maggots appeared only in the jars open to air that could be reached by flies.

John Needham

In 1745, an English clergyman named John Needham designed an experiment to test spontaneous generation. He boiled chicken broth to kill the microorganisms in it, and then he put the broth into a flask, sealed it, and waited. In time, microorganisms appeared in the broth. Needham concluded that spontaneous generation did indeed occur. Others thought that organisms in the air had grown in Needham's broth and that Needham was wrong.

Louis Pasteur

In 1859, a French chemist named Louis Pasteur designed an experiment to test spontaneous generation. He put broth in special S-shaped flasks and boiled it. This made it possible for air to reach the broth inside, but any microorganisms in the air would get stuck in the neck of the flask and be unable to reach the broth. Because no microorganisms grew in this broth, Pasteur knew that spontaneous generation did not occur. To confirm that microorganisms came from particles in the air, Pasteur then tilted the flasks so that air reached the broth without traveling through the bend in the tube. Microorganisms were then found in the broth. In this way, Pasteur showed that microorganisms exist in the air; they do not arise from nonliving matter.

While upright, the swan-necked flasks remained sterile. Dust and microbes were unable to reach the broth.

When Pasteur tilted a flask, microorganisms could now enter the broth and microorganisms grew.

The Cell Theory

Around the same time that Pasteur was conducting his experiments, a German physician named Rudolf Virchow was studying cells. Like Pasteur, Virchow did not support the idea of spontaneous generation. In 1855, Virchow presented a hypothesis that cells are produced only by other cells. This last piece of information about cells helped complete what is now one of the fundamental ideas of modern biology—the **cell theory.** The cell theory includes the following three principles:

1. All living organisms are made up of one or more cells.
2. Cells are the basic units of structure and function in all living organisms.
3. New cells are produced from existing cells.

CORE SKILL

Analyze Author's Purpose

An author writes with a specific purpose in mind. Authors who write informational texts write to inform and sometimes to persuade. Reread the paragraphs about spontaneous generation and ask yourself, "What is the author's purpose in writing these paragraphs?" Write a few sentences explaining what the author's purpose is. Cite evidence from the text to support your response.

CORE PRACTICE

Understand and Apply Scientific Models, Theories, and Processes

Conduct research to investigate other scientists who contributed to the cell theory, such as Antonie Van Leeuwenhoek, Matthias Schleiden, Theodor Schwann, and Lazzaro Spallanzani. Use what you learn to draw a timeline that shows the development of the cell theory.

Think about Science

Directions: Fill in the blank with *did* or *did not*.

1. Francesco Redi observed that maggots appeared only in the jars that were open to air and that could be reached by flies. This _____ support spontaneous generation.

2. John Needham concluded that spontaneous generation _____ occur because microorganisms grew in boiled broth in a sealed flask.

3. Louis Pasteur used flasks with S-shaped necks to prove that microorganisms exist in particles in the air, concluding that spontaneous generation _____ occur.

Specialized Cells and Cellular Organization

Your community could not function if many different people did not perform specific jobs to make life in the community possible. In thinking about your community, you can **subdivide,** or organize into smaller units, different groups of people. Groups of people with similar jobs often work together, for example, in a hospital or restaurant.

Just as people perform specialized jobs within a community, cells perform specialized tasks within an organism. Some cells are equipped to do a particular job. These cells are called specialized cells. For example, pancreatic cells produce insulin, and white blood cells fight infection. In most multicellular organisms, cells are organized into tissues, organs, and body systems as shown in the image on page 101.

Tissues

In most multicellular organisms, groups of similar cells are organized into tissues. There are four types of tissue, and each type has specific functions. Muscle tissues, for example, make the heart beat, the stomach digest food, and the body move. Nerve tissues form long fibers to carry impulses to the brain. Epithelial tissues form linings and coverings for body. Connective tissues form cartilage and ligaments.

Organs

A group of tissues can work together to form an organ, which performs a more complex function than individual cells and tissues perform. The heart, brain, and stomach are organs. The heart pumps blood throughout the body. It is made up of muscle tissue, blood tissue, epithelial tissue, and nerve tissue.

Body Systems

Organs that work together to perform a set of related tasks form a body system. Recall that the stomach is one of several organs of the digestive system. Other organs of the digestive system include the esophagus and the intestines. Together, all the body systems in a multicellular organism carry out the processes needed to keep the entire organism alive.

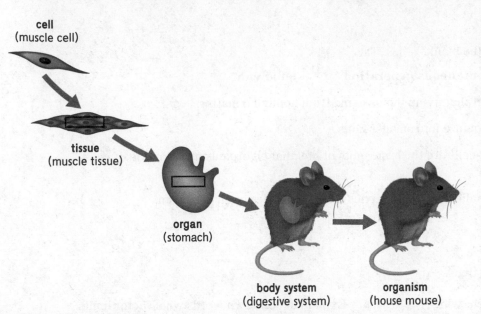

cell
(muscle cell)

tissue
(muscle tissue)

organ
(stomach)

body system
(digestive system)

organism
(house mouse)

Calculate how doubling the length of the sides changes the volume of each cube in the diagram. To calculate the volume of a cube, multiple the width by the length by the height of the cube, or cube the length of one side.

Then calculate how doubling the length of the sides changes the surface area of each cube. For a regular object, such as a cube, you can find the surface area by first finding the area of each face and then multiplying the area by the number of sides. Area is calculated by multiplying the length times the width.

Finally determine the surface-area-to-volume ratio. To do this, divide the surface area by the volume.

Limits on Cell Size

You may be wondering why many small cells group together in an organism instead of simply growing larger. Most cells are small for a reason. As a cell grows larger, both its volume and its surface area increase. Volume is the amount of space an object takes up. The surface area is a measure of the size of the outer surface of an object. For example, when you wrap a gift box, you cover the surface area of the box. The surface area of a cell determines the amount of material that can enter and leave the cell.

As a cell grows, the volume increases at a faster rate than the surface area. If the cell grows too large, it will require more materials than can pass through its surface area. Therefore there is a limit to how large a cell can grow. Instead of continuing to grow larger, cells form new cells that enable an organism to grow and develop tissues, organs, and body systems. The ratio of a cell's surface area to its volume is a factor that limits cell size. For example, when the sides of a cube double in length from 1 mm to 2 mm, the surface-area-to-volume ratio decreases from 6:1 to 3:1.

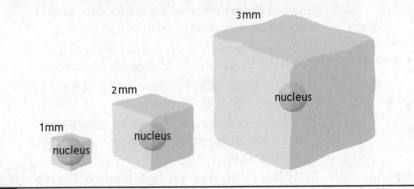

3 mm

nucleus

2 mm

nucleus

1 mm

nucleus

Think about Science

Directions: Answer the following question.

1. Which of these determines how much material can enter a cell?

   A. density
   B. mass
   C. surface area
   D. volume

Cells: Basic Units of Life

Vocabulary Review

Directions: Write the missing term in the blank.

cell   **cell theory**   **spontaneous generation**   **subdivide**

1. _____ is the belief that living things come from nonliving matter.

2. To _____ is to organize into smaller units.

3. _____ states that cells are the basic units of life, that all organisms are made of cells, and that cells produce new cells.

4. A _____ is the smallest unit that carries on the activities of an organism.

Skill Review

Directions: Answer the following questions.

1. What evidence did Redi's experiment with covered and open jars of meat—to see if maggots would grow on the meat—provide about spontaneous generation in organisms?

   A. It showed that maggots can appear out of nowhere, but it did not show that spontaneous generation occurs.

   B. It showed that maggots did not appear out of nowhere, but it did not show that microorganisms could not be produced by spontaneous generation.

   C. It showed that maggots do not appear out of nowhere; therefore it showed that spontaneous generation can never occur.

   D. It showed that maggots can sometimes appear out of nowhere; therefore it showed that spontaneous generation of microorganisms can sometimes occur.

2. John Needham experimented with boiled broth in a sealed jar. Why did he think he had proved that spontaneous generation occurred?

   A. In his experiment, microorganisms grew in air in a sealed flask.

   B. In his experiment, microorganisms grew in boiled broth in a sealed flask.

   C. In his experiment, microorganisms did not grow in boiled broth in a sealed flask.

   D. In his experiment, microorganisms grew in boiled broth once the flask was opened.

3. Describe the cellular levels of organization and give a specific example for each level.

4. Explain in your own words what factor limits the size of a cell.

5. In Pasteur's experiment, microorganisms in the air could reach the broth when the flask was tilted. Which statement explains how this could happen?

   A. The organisms had to travel up instead of down, which made it easier to reach the broth.

   B. The organisms in the air had a shorter distance to travel when the flask was tilted.

   C. The organisms were no longer trapped by the twisted neck of the flask.

   D. The organisms had enough air to survive when the flask was tilted.

6. How did the invention of the microscope help with the development of cell theory?

   A. Using a microscope, scientists realized that cork was made of little chambers called cells.

   B. Using a microscope, scientists could see maggots growing on meat.

   C. Without a microscope, Pasteur would not have been able to show that spontaneous generation did not occur.

   D. Without a microscope, Redi would not have been able to show that maggots do not arise from spontaneous generation.

Cells: Basic Units of Life

Skill Practice

Directions: Answer the following questions.

1. How did Pasteur's experiment improve upon John Needham's experiment?
   A. Pasteur's experiment used a more powerful microscope.
   B. Pasteur's experiment used a better method of sealing the flasks.
   C. Pasteur's experiment prevented microorganisms in the air from getting into the broth.
   D. Pasteur's experiment boiled the broth to kill microorganisms.

2. Which type of tissue is least likely to be found in the brain?
   A. blood tissue
   B. epithelial tissue
   C. muscle tissue
   D. nerve tissue

3. Cells divide before they become too large. Use what you know about cell volume and surface area to explain why this occurs.

4. The amount of space a cell takes up is known as its
   A. mass.
   B. surface area.
   C. volume.
   D. weight.

Directions: Use the information to answer questions 5 and 6.

In his famous experiment in the seventeenth century, Francesco Redi wanted to investigate the common belief that meat left to rot would change into maggots. Redi believed that living things, such as maggots, did not come from nonliving matter, such as meat; he believed that maggots came only through the reproduction of parent flies. To test this hypothesis, Redi placed pieces of meat to rot in three jars. The control jar was open to the air. The second jar was sealed with a cork. The third was sealed with cheesecloth. Maggots appeared only in the jar that was open to the air. In the jar that was covered with cheesecloth, maggots appeared on the cloth, but they were not able to get inside the jar to the meat.

Redi continued his experiments by capturing maggots. He observed that over time they turned into flies. He concluded that maggots in meat came from egg laying flies, not from spontaneous generation.

5. Why did Redi place cloth over the jar?
   A. To keep dirt off the meat in the jar
   B. To encourage flies to lay eggs on the cloth
   C. To keep fresh air from circulating in the control jar
   D. To prevent flies from laying eggs on the meat in the control jar

6. Which of the following factors should Redi have been most careful about when he began the experiment?
   A. Both pieces of meat should have been free of fly eggs.
   B. No flies should have been allowed to enter either jar.
   C. The temperature of each jar should have been kept constant.
   D. Both pieces of meat should have been exactly the same size.

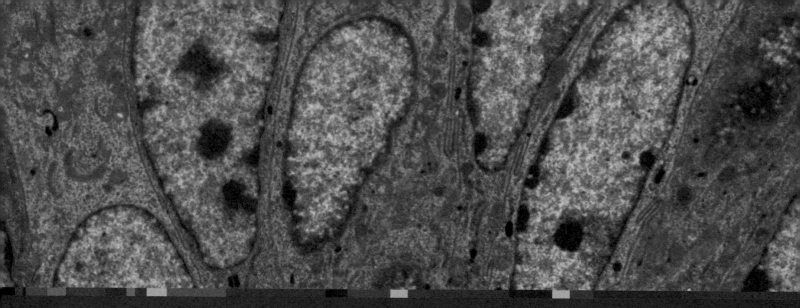

LESSON OBJECTIVES

- Identify the parts of animal and plant cells
- Differentiate between prokaryotic and eukaryotic cells
- Explain how materials move across cell membranes

CORE SKILLS & PRACTICES

- Determine the Meaning of Symbols, Terms and Phrases
- Make Inferences

Key Terms

eukaryotic cell
a cell with a nucleus and many organelles

nucleus
the organelle of a cell that contains the genetic material

organelles
cell structures that perform a particular function for the cell

osmosis
diffusion of water across a selectively permeable membrane

prokaryotic cell
a cell that does not have a nucleus or membrane-bound organelles

Vocabulary

differentiate
to see or state the differences between two or more things

Key Concept

Animal and plant cells have many of the same cell parts. The parts of a cell help the cell carry out the functions of life.

The Parts of a Cell

In many ways, living cells are like factories that produce goods. They take in raw materials, use them to build products such as proteins, package the products, and transport them to different parts of the cell or to other cells. They also eliminate waste and reproduce. The different jobs are performed by structures within the cell called **organelles.** The cells of animals and plants share most of the same kinds of organelles and other cell parts.

Animal and Plant Cells

Just as a factory needs a manager, a cell needs an organelle to direct the cell processes. The **nucleus** is the distinct central organelle that contains the cell's genetic material in the form of deoxyribonucleic acid (DNA). DNA is an organic molecule that stores the instructions for making proteins and other molecules needed by the cell. Two thin membranes make up the nuclear envelope that surrounds the nucleus.

The cell is generally divided into two parts—the nucleus and the cytoplasm that surrounds the nucleus. Cytoplasm is a jellylike substance made of water, amino acids, carbohydrates, fats, and nucleic acids. A variety of organelles are located in the cytoplasm.

Ribosomes

Ribosomes are organelles that use amino acids to assemble proteins according to instructions in DNA. A ribosome is made up of ribonucleic acid (RNA) and protein. Ribosomes are formed within a structure known as the nucleolus, which is in the nucleus of the cell. Unlike most other organelles, ribosomes are not surrounded by membranes.

Endoplasmic Reticulum

The cell contains a system of membranes and sacs known as the endoplasmic reticulum, or ER. The endoplasmic reticulum acts like a highway along which molecules can move from one part of the cell to another.

The part of the ER that is involved in the production of proteins has ribosomes along its surface. This type of ER, known as rough ER, is common in cells that make large amounts of proteins. Smooth ER, which does not have ribosomes, is involved in regulating processes in cells.

Golgi Apparatus

After products are made in a factory, they must be organized, boxed, and shipped. Similarly, proteins produced in rough ER are passed along to an organelle called the Golgi apparatus, which consists of a stack of membranes. Its job is to modify and package proteins and other molecules so they can either be stored in the cell or sent outside of the cell. In some glands, the Golgi apparatus packages and releases hormones.

Mitochondria

Some factories have their own generators that produce the electricity they need. Cells also have energy generators called mitochondria, which convert energy stored in organic molecules into compounds the cell can use. This happens through a process called cellular respiration. The greater the energy needs of a cell, the more mitochondria that cell will have.

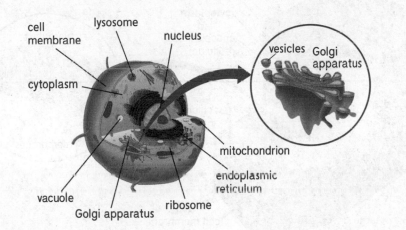

Lysosomes

Factories and cells also need cleanup crews. Lysosomes are small organelles filled with enzymes, proteins that speed up the rate of a chemical reaction. The enzymes enable the lysosomes to digest, or break down, organic molecules such as carbohydrates, lipids, and proteins.

Vacuoles

A factory needs a place to store materials and waste products. Similarly many cells have saclike organelles called vacuoles that store materials for the cell. In some cells, vacuoles store water, salts, carbohydrates, and proteins. Vacuoles may also digest food and store and dispose of waste.

Cell Membrane

The cell membrane is the soft, flexible barrier that surrounds the cell and holds it together. A cell must be able to take in nutrients and dispose of wastes. The cell membrane controls how these substances pass into and out of a cell.

Distinguishing Between Cells

Plant cells have many of the same parts animal cells have, including the nucleus, cytoplasm, ribosomes, endoplasmic reticulum, Golgi apparatus, mitochondria,

Cell Structure and Function

Lesson 3.2   105

lysosomes, vacuoles, and the cell membrane. It is, however, possible to **differentiate,** or recognize the differences, between plant and animal cells. For example, animal cells either do not contain vacuoles or have several small vacuoles, but plants usually have one large vacuole. The pressure of the liquid in this vacuole helps support the plant. Plant cells also contain parts that animal cells do not have, namely chloroplasts and a cell wall.

Chloroplasts

In addition to mitochondria, plant cells contain chloroplasts, which are organelles in which light energy is used to produce food for the cell through a process called photosynthesis. This food is then broken down to release chemical energy that is used to perform the functions of the cell.

Cell Wall

Another structure associated with plant cells is the cell wall, which is a rigid outer layer that supports the cell and protects it from harm. Plant cell walls are made of a carbohydrate called cellulose. Pores in the cell wall allow materials to pass into and out of the cell.

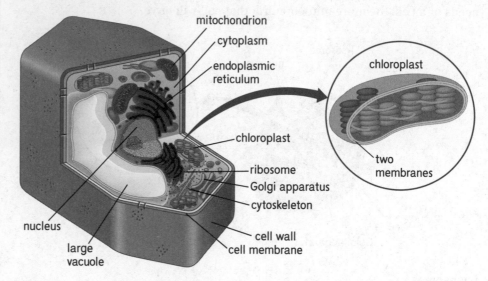

Two Main Types of Cells

There are two main types of cells. A **eukaryotic cell** has a membrane-bound nucleus and many organelles enclosed in their own membranes. Plant and animal cells, along with fungi, algae, and some single-celled organisms, have eukaryotic cells. A **prokaryotic cell** has a cell membrane, cell wall, and cytoplasm but does not have a nucleus or membrane-bound organelles. Prokaryotes include bacteria and archaeobacteria. All prokaryotes are single-celled organisms.

⌁ Think about Science

Directions: Answer the following questions.

1. Which organelle assembles proteins according to instructions found in DNA?

2. Differentiate between vacuoles in plant and animal cells.

3. Explain how the structure of a cell wall supports its function.

4. What is the difference between a eukaryotic cell and a prokaryotic cell?

Cell Structure and Function

Transport Across the Cell Membrane

Cell membranes are a selectively permeable membrane. This means that some substances can move through it, and others cannot. It is important for materials necessary for the cell's function to stay within the cell, for nutrients to move into the cell, and for waste products to move out.

Diffusion

Recall that diffusion is the movement of molecules from an area of high concentration to an area of low concentration. Diffusion is one way that molecules enter and leave a cell. Suppose, for example, that the concentration of a substance is different on either side of the cell membrane. If the substance can cross the cell membrane, its molecules will move toward the area where it is less concentrated.

Perhaps the most important substance that passes through the cell membrane is water. Water molecules pass through a selectively permeable membrane by a type of diffusion known as **osmosis**. During osmosis, water moves from a place of higher concentration of water to a place of lower concentration of water—either into or out of the cell.

If the concentration of water outside the cell is lower than the concentration inside the cytoplasm, water diffuses out of the cell, causing it to shrivel. If the concentration of water inside the cytoplasm is lower than the concentration outside the cell, water diffuses into the cell, causing it to swell.

Active Transport

Some substances need to move into or out of a cell, even though their concentration is higher in the direction they are moving. Therefore the cell must be able to move materials by another process. This is accomplished by active transport. During active transport, the cell moves molecules from an area of lower concentration to an area of higher concentration. Because this movement opposes the natural flow to areas of lower concentration, carrier proteins in the cell membrane pick up and transport materials. This work requires energy.

Think about Science

Directions: Answer the following questions.

1. Which form of cellular transport moves molecules from areas of lower concentration to areas of higher concentration?

   A. diffusion
   B. osmosis
   C. active transport
   D. selective permeability

2. With which process do molecules move from an area of high concentration to an area of low concentration?

   A. diffusion
   B. energy production
   C. active transport
   D. protein synthesis

Scientists often use square bracket symbols ([ ]) to mean "concentration." For example, [A] means "the concentration of A." When making notes about diffusion, you can use this symbol. For example, you could write "diffusion is the movement of molecules from an area of [↑] to an area of [↓]. How would you rewrite the sentence above in words without the use of symbols?

Vocabulary Review

Directions: Write the missing term in the blank.

differentiate   **eukaryotic cell**   **nucleus**

organelle   **osmosis**   **prokaryotic cell**

1. The movement of water across a selectively permeable membrane is called _____.

2. A(n) _____ is a cell that does not have a nucleus or membrane-bound organelles.

3. A cell structure that performs a particular function for the cell is called a(n) _____.

4. A(n) _____ is a cell that has a nucleus and many organelles enclosed in their own membranes.

5. You _____ when you see or state the differences between two or more things.

6. The _____ is the central organelle of the cell and contains the cell's genetic material.

Skill Review

Directions: Answer the following questions.

1. Iodine is more prevalent in sea plants than in the seawater that surrounds the plants, yet iodine still moves from the seawater into the cells of the sea plant. What process accounts for this phenomenon?

A. digestion

B. active transport

C. making proteins

D. diffusion

2. Which organisms are prokaryotic?

A. plants

B. animals

C. bacteria

D. insects

3. In plant cells, chloroplasts are active in the chemical processes required to make food. Animal cells have no chloroplasts. On this basis, what can we conclude?

A. Plant cells are more complex than animal cells.

B. Plant cells—not animal cells—generate chemical reactions.

C. Animal cells prey on plants cells to obtain food.

D. Animal cells do not make their own food.

4. Which of the following best describes why lysosomes are important to the health of a cell?

A. Lysosomes break down large molecules into smaller substances the cell can use.

B. Lysosomes speed up the chemical reactions that take place in the cell.

C. Lysosomes store enzymes that are used in chemical reactions in the cell.

D. Lysosomes use enzymes to provide energy for various cell functions.

5. Based on what you have learned about vacuoles, make an inference about why a plant wilts when it does not have enough water.

6. Integrate what you have learned about the nucleus, cytoplasm, ribosomes, endoplasmic reticulum, and the Golgi apparatus to explain how they work together.

Skill Practice

Directions: Answer the following questions.

1. Why might some cells have more mitochondria than other cells?

   A. Some cells have more waste than other cells.

   B. Some cells build more proteins than other cells.

   C. Some cells have more carbohydrates than other cells.

   D. Some cells need more energy than other cells.

2. Why might it be important for some organelles to be surrounded by membranes?

   A. Membranes can regulate what goes in and out of an organelle.

   B. Membranes contain proteins that aid in energy production.

   C. Membranes connect all the organelles in a cell.

   D. Membranes transport organelles across cell membranes.

3. Which of the following cell parts is most like a power plant?

   A. lysosome

   B. nucleus

   C. mitochondria

   D. ribosome

4. What might happen if a cell stopped producing ribosomes?

   A. The cell might start producing proteins in the endoplasmic reticulum.

   B. The cell may swell with extra deoxyribonucleic acids (DNA).

   C. The cell may not be able to repair itself because of lack of proteins.

   D. The cell may lose the amino acids it needs through osmosis.

5. Use a Venn diagram to compare and contrast the nucleus of a cell and the human brain.

6. Make a generalization about how the structure of something relates to its function. Use an example from this lesson to support your generalization.

7. Think about the how a cell is similar to a factory. Relate each organelle in a cell to a job in a factory using illustrations and descriptions for each analogy.

Directions: Use the information to answer questions 8 and 9.

One type of diffusion is facilitated diffusion. During this process, a few molecules pass through the cell membrane more easily than might be expected. The reason for this is that cell membranes have pathways in them known as protein channels. The channels allow specific types of molecules to pass into or out of the cell. Protein channels in red blood cells, for example, allow only glucose to pass through. Facilitated diffusion is still diffusion and occurs only if there is a difference in concentration.

8. Compare facilitated diffusion as described above with active transport.

9. Analyze the structure of the text in this lesson and explain how the structure can help you understand the parts of animal and plant cells.

LESSON 3.3 Plant Structure and Function

LESSON OBJECTIVES

- Describe different types of plants
- Explain the structures and functions of the parts of plants

CORE SKILLS & PRACTICES

- Design a Scientific Investigation
- Analyze Relationships Between Sources

Key Terms

phloem
tubelike structures that transport organic molecules from the leaves to the rest of the plant

pollination
the transfer of pollen from a stamen to a pistil

transpiration
the process by which water vapor exits the leaves of a plant through tiny openings in the leaves

vascular plants
true land plants that have evolved to survive independent of wet environments

xylem
tubelike structures that transport water and minerals from the roots to the rest of the plant.

Vocabulary

outline
a summary of the main points of a text

Key Concept

The parts of a plant work together to promote and sustain the life of the plant. The functions of the plant structures provide mechanisms for the plant's life processes.

Types of Plants

Plants provide people with many essential materials for shelter, food, and clothing. Plants also provide beauty in our lives, from vast gardens to flower boxes in our windows. The variety of uses we have for plants belies the great variety of plants that exist. Plants can be simple or complex, small or gigantic, flowering or nonflowering.

Nonvascular Plants

The most primitive types of plants lack vascular tissue, the tubelike structures through which water and other materials move inside a plant. Nonvascular plants are considered to be among the least complex living plants. They are usually small plants, which enables most materials to move through them easily. Nonvascular plants, such as liverworts and mosses, take in water through osmosis, the process that allows water to diffuse across a cell membrane. Because of this, their life cycles are dependent on damp places.

Liverworts and their relatives are small and grow on the surface of wet soil. Mosses are the small plants that form a green carpet on the floor of many forests. Mosses also grow on trees and rock surfaces. Liverworts and mosses, like all nonvascular plants, lack true roots, stems, and leaves.

Vascular Plants

Vascular plants, known as tracheophytes, are true land plants because they have evolved ways to survive independent of wet environments. They are able to move water from their surroundings through their bodies in vascular tissues. Vascular tissue allows plants to grow to a great height, like the giant redwoods of Northern California. Vascular plants include seedless plants like club mosses (which are not true mosses, despite their name), horsetails, and ferns, as well as seed plants—for example, violets, potatoes, and pine trees.

There are relatively few species of seedless vascular plants compared to vascular plants with seeds. The reproductive structures of seedless vascular plants are dustlike spores. Club mosses are small evergreen plants with needle-like or scale-like leaves. The leaves of horsetails encircle the shoots. Horsetails may or may not be evergreens and can grow to be rather tall. Fern leaves look a great deal like green feathers. These seedless vascular plants reproduce in a two-generation life cycle—one that produces spores, and one that does not.

Seed Plants

Seed plants are vascular plants that reproduce, as their name suggests, using seeds. They can be divided into two groups, gymnosperms and angiosperms, based on how their seeds are produced. Most of the plants people are familiar with, including trees, flowers, vegetables, and grains, are seed plants.

Gymnosperms

Gymnosperms are vascular plants that produce seeds that are not enclosed within a fruit. Gymnosperms, such as pines, firs, redwoods, and sequoias, do not produce flowers but form seeds in cones. The leaves of most gymnosperms are scale-like or needle-like. Many gymnosperms are called evergreens because some green leaves are always on their branches.

Angiosperms

Angiosperms are the most easily recognizable seed-producing plants. Angiosperms, or flowering plants, include familiar plants such as roses, corn, bamboo, orchids, daisies, and fruit trees. In angiosperms, seeds are enclosed in fruits. The fruit protects the seeds as they develop. Because most fruits are edible and the seeds not easily digested, animals often spread seeds far from the parent plants.

Although gymnosperms evolved long before flowering plants, today there are many more species of angiosperms than gymnosperms.

⤫ Think about Science

Directions: Answer the following questions.

1. What is the main difference between vascular and nonvascular plants?
    A. Vascular plants reproduce using flowers and seeds.
    B. Vascular plants can grow much taller than nonvascular plants.
    C. Vascular plants produce seeds encased in fruit.
    D. Vascular plants have tube-like tissue that transports water and other substances.

2. Which of the following applies to both gymnosperms and angiosperms?
    A. They both have needlelike leaves.
    B. They both grow flowers.
    C. They both produce seeds.
    D. They both produce fruit.

CORE PRACTICE

Design a Scientific Investigation

Scientists use a process called the scientific method to gain knowledge about the world. Refer to *The Scientific Method* on pages 454 and 455. Then begin your investigation by thinking of a question you have about plants. Design a simple investigation experiment to find the answer to your question. As you design your investigation, be sure to include a hypothesis, identify the independent and dependent variables, and record your procedure and observations. Explain the results of your investigation by writing a summary of your results or making a slide presentation.

The substances in some plants are used to develop medicines. Some entrepreneurs have created businesses hunting these valuable plants. Find an article from a reputable source about researchers who have developed medicines from plants. **Outline,** or summarize, the main points of the article you choose.

Parts of Plants

Plants have various parts that help them perform essential life functions. All vascular plants have roots, stems, and leaves, but only gymnosperms and angiosperms have seeds, and only angiosperms have flowers. Plants are made of cells, tissues, and organs that work together to perform specific functions that keep the plants alive. The four main organs of angiosperms are roots, stems, leaves, and flowers.

Roots

Roots come in various shapes and sizes. Roots give a plant the surface area it needs to absorb the water and minerals essential to its survival. The outermost cells of the roots absorb water and minerals. The more surface area, or outer part, the roots have, the more cells can absorb these essential substances. There are two main types of root systems: taproots and fibrous roots.

A taproot is a single thick structure that grows straight into the ground. Smaller branching roots grow out from its sides. A taproot securely anchors a plant in the soil and serves primarily as a storage organ for starch and sugar made by the plant. Taproots generally grow deep into the soil and can absorb water and nutrients there. Taproots are useful in areas where the water is deep in the soil.

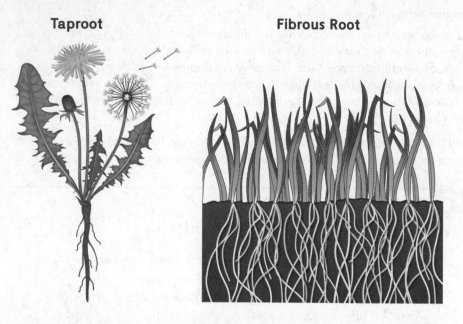

Taproot   **Fibrous Root**

Fibrous roots consist of a great many thin, branching roots that grow from a central point. They look like tufts of stringy hairs. Fibrous roots serve primarily to hold the plant in the ground and provide a large surface area for water and mineral absorption. The shallow branching nature of fibrous roots helps them absorb water quickly. Fibrous roots can help plants get water in sandy soil that does not hold water well.

Stems

Stems support the leaves, cones, fruits, flowers, and even seeds of plants. They hold a plant's leaves up toward the sunlight. Stems contain two types of vascular tissue. **Xylem** is vascular tissue made up of tube-shaped cells that transport water and dissolved minerals through the roots to the rest of the plant. Lignin, a hard substance in xylem, helps give structure to the plant. **Phloem** is tube-shaped vascular tissue that transports organic molecules from the leaves throughout the plant.

There are two classifications of stems: herbaceous stems and woody stems. Herbaceous stems are green, soft, and flexible. Cells in herbaceous stems contain chloroplasts that use light to make food for the plant. Woody stems are hard, strong, and rigid. Trees, shrubs, and roses have woody stems.

CORE SKILL

Analyze Relationships Between Sources

Information about the structure of a leaf is presented in the text and in the diagram. Carefully analyze the text and the diagram, noting similarities and differences, and explain the relationship between them. Explain the advantages and disadvantages of each presentation method.

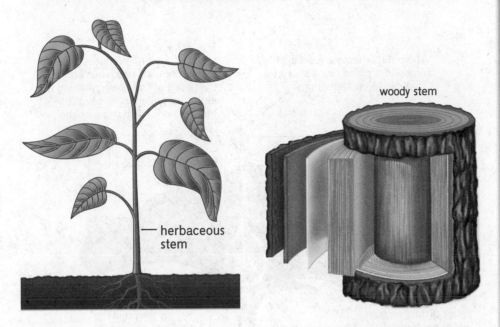

woody stem

herbaceous stem

Leaves

Leaves are plant organs whose main functions include capturing the energy of sunlight, making organic molecules, and exchanging gases with the environment. Most leaves are flat and have a relatively large surface area that receives sunlight.

Leaves have an outer layer of cells called the epidermis. The epidermis has various parts, two of which are the upper epidermis and the lower epidermis. The upper epidermis has a waxy, waterproof coating called the cuticle that prevents the plant from losing too much water. The lower epidermis has tiny pores, or openings, called stomata that allow molecules to move into and out of the plant. Between these layers is the tissue of the leaf where light energy is used to produce food for the plant in a process called photosynthesis.

The process by which most of the water passes out of leaves as water vapor through the stomata in the lower epidermis is called **transpiration.** Because water molecules attract other water molecules, water that exits the stomata by transpiration actually "pulls" water up from the roots.

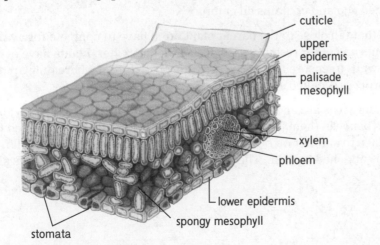

cuticle

upper epidermis

palisade mesophyll

xylem

phloem

lower epidermis

spongy mesophyll

stomata

Flowers

Flowers are the main reproductive organs of flowering plants. Most flowers have four main parts: petals, sepals, stamens, and a pistil. Each flower part plays an important role in a plant's ability to produce more of its kind.

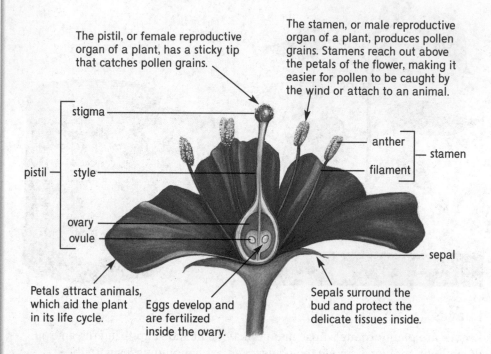

The pistil, or female reproductive organ of a plant, has a sticky tip that catches pollen grains.

The stamen, or male reproductive organ of a plant, produces pollen grains. Stamens reach out above the petals of the flower, making it easier for pollen to be caught by the wind or attach to an animal.

stigma

anther

stamen

pistil

style

filament

ovary

ovule

sepal

Petals attract animals, which aid the plant in its life cycle.

Eggs develop and are fertilized inside the ovary.

Sepals surround the bud and protect the delicate tissues inside.

Pollination is the transfer of pollen grains from stamen to pistil. With few exceptions, pollination must take place before seeds can form. Pollen grains can be carried by wind, water, gravity, insects, or other animals. Once a pollen grain lands on the female part of the plant, a pollen tube develops. The sperm cells move from the pollen down the tube and into the ovary. Fertilization can then take place between a sperm and an egg. The resulting fertilized egg develops into a seed, the offspring of a plant. The ovary surrounding the seed swells and becomes a fruit in many species of flowering plants.

Seeds

Seeds vary widely in appearance, but they all have the same basic structure: a protective seed coat, an embryo, and stored food. A seed develops from a fertilized egg and contains an embryo.

Seeds that fall close to the parent plant often have to compete for available nutrients and other resources, such as light and water. Plants have evolved many ways to ensure that seeds are transported from where they are formed. This process is called seed dispersal.

Coconuts seeds are encased in tough husks made of strong fibers with air spaces between them. The seeds can float in water and are dispersed from one place to another on ocean currents. Dandelion seeds have small fluffy threads attached to them. The threads help the wind carry the seeds aloft.

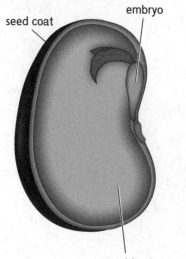

seed coat

embryo

stored food

The process by which the embryo in a seed begins to develop into a new plant is called germination. Germination begins when growing conditions are favorable. Water, oxygen, and favorable temperatures are common requirements of germination. Seeds often undergo a period of inactivity called dormancy until the conditions are right for germination.

Life Cycle of an Angiosperm

A life cycle is a continuous process and does not have a true beginning or end. One place to begin describing the process is at germination. The seed germinates, and a seedling begins to grow roots, stems, and leaves. An adult angiosperm grows flowers, which then go through the process of pollination. Once a flower has been pollinated, a seed begins to form with the fruit of the plant. Wind, water, or animals may carry the seed to a new location, and the life cycle continues.

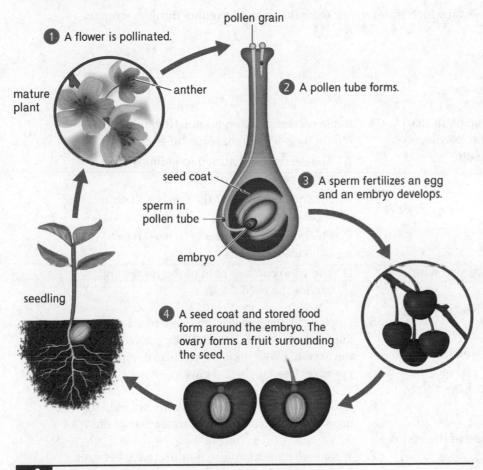

1 A flower is pollinated.

pollen grain

anther

mature plant

2 A pollen tube forms.

seed coat

sperm in pollen tube

embryo

3 A sperm fertilizes an egg and an embryo develops.

seedling

4 A seed coat and stored food form around the embryo. The ovary forms a fruit surrounding the seed.

Think about Science

Directions: Answer the following questions.

1. What are some of the functions of leaves?

2. How does the structure of fibrous roots help them perform their function?

3. What are the main parts of a flower?

4. What is germination?

Vocabulary Review

Directions: Write the missing term in the blank.

outline	phloem	pollination
transpiration	vascular plants	xylem

1. _____ is the transfer of pollen from a stamen to a pistil.

2. _____ are tubelike structures that transport food from the leaves to the rest of the plant.

3. _____ are tubelike structures that transport water from the roots to the rest of the plant.

4. You _____ a text when you make a summary of its main points.

5. _____ are true land plants that have evolved to survive independent of wet environments.

6. _____ is the process by which water vapor exits the leaves of plants through stomata.

Skill Review

Directions: Answer the following questions.

1. The saguaro cactus is a tall flowering plant that grows in the desert. In which of the following groups does the saguaro cactus belong?

   A. nonvascular plants

   B. gymnosperms

   C. liverworts

   D. vascular plants

2. Roots are the first part of a plant to grow. Why do you think this is so?

   A. Gravity causes the roots to develop first.

   B. Flowers need to be able to grow on roots.

   C. Roots hold the plant in place and absorb nutrients.

   D. Roots produce the food needed for the plant to grow.

3. What is the purpose of the sticky fluid at the end of the stigma?

   A. It contains the organelles needed for the plant to make food.

   B. It protects the pistil from insects.

   C. It helps pollen grains stick to the pistil.

   D. It captures insects to get nutrients for the plant.

4. Some seeds have tiny hooks. How might this characteristic help disperse the seeds?

   A. The seeds could attach to animals, which might carry them away.

   B. An animal could eat the seeds and scatter them.

   C. The hooks may protect the seed from animals.

   D. The wind catches hold of the hooks and carries the seed away.

5. Draw a diagram of the life cycle of an angiosperm. Using information from throughout the lesson, make your diagram as complete as possible. Use labels and captions.

6. How do you think vascular plants are able to grow so much taller than nonvascular plants?

7. What is the most significant difference between gymnosperms and angiosperms? Justify your answer.

Skill Practice

Directions: Answer the following questions.

1. Cherry seeds are surrounded by a sweet fruit. What method of seed dispersal is most likely to scatter cherry seeds?

   A. wind

   B. water

   C. animals

   D. gravity

2. A hive of bees in an area is killed by colony-collapse disorder. How might this affect plants in the area?

   A. The plants will be healthier.

   B. Seeds will not be scattered as far.

   C. Fewer flowers will be pollinated.

   D. More plants will survive.

3. Why might a plant with a woody stem survive better in a windy environment than a plant with an herbaceous stem?

   A. Woody stems can produce food for the plant.

   B. Woody stems are rigid and hold the plant up better.

   C. Woody stems break easily in the wind.

   D. Woody stems have more xylem and phloem.

4. Why do you think xylem and phloem are located in so many parts of a plant?

   A. All parts of a plant need to produce food for survival.

   B. All parts of a plant need the pollen xylem and phloem transport.

   C. All parts of a plant need the organelles in xylem and phloem cells.

   D. All parts of a plant need the water and food xylem and phloem transport.

5. Why is transpiration an important process?

   A. Water vapor could not enter the plant without transpiration.

   B. The plant could not cool itself.

   C. Water would not circulate through the plant without transpiration.

   D. Organic molecules would not circulate through the plant without transpiration.

6. Many plants grow differently in response to their environment. Phototropism is the growth of a plant toward light. Hydrotropism is the growth of a plant toward water. What do you think gravitropism is?

Directions: Use the diagram to answer questions 7 and 8.

7. How does the structure of the lower epidermis help it perform its function?

8. The _____ mesophyll receives more exposure to sunlight than the _____ mesophyll.

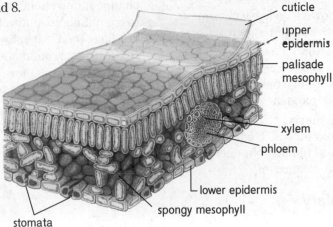

LESSON 3.4 Energy and Cells

▮ LESSON OBJECTIVES

- Discuss photosynthesis
- Explain cellular respiration

▮ CORE SKILLS & PRACTICES

- Express Scientific Information Symbolically
- Distinguish Between Facts and Speculation

Key Terms

cellular respiration
a process in which glucose and other organic molecules are broken down to release energy in the presence of oxygen

fermentation
a process that releases the energy stored in organic molecules in the absence of oxygen

photosynthesis
the process by which some organisms change light energy into chemical energy

Vocabulary

apply
to put to use, especially for some practical purpose

chlorophyll
pigment that allows plants to capture the energy of sunlight

enzymes
molecules that facilitate chemical reactions in organisms

Key Concept

Plant cells use energy from the Sun to make sugars. Plant and animal cells break down sugars and other food molecules to release energy cells can use.

Photosynthesis

Living things are made of cells, which use energy to perform all the functions needed for life. All organisms need energy to grow, to make repairs, and to move. Where does that energy come from? Almost all the energy used by living things comes from the Sun. Energy takes many forms, such as light and chemical energy. Chemical energy is stored in organic substances such as foods and fuels. Each form of energy can be changed into another form.

The process by which organisms capture light energy from the Sun and change it into chemical energy is called **photosynthesis.** Organisms that carry out photosynthesis are called producers because they make, or produce, food. All autotrophs, or organisms that capture matter and energy from their surroundings and use it to make their own food, are producers. Because plants capture matter and energy from their surroundings and use it to make their own food, they are autotrophs and producers.

Chloroplast

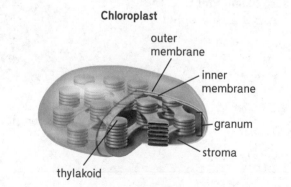

Most of the photosynthesis carried out in a plant takes place in the leaves but can also take place in green stems. The cells in leaves and green stems contain small structures, or organelles, called chloroplasts. Chloroplasts are the sites of photosynthesis. As shown in the diagram, chloroplasts have an inner and outer membrane that surround granum, or stacks of membranes called thylakoids. Thylakoids contain **chlorophyll**, the pigment that gives plants their green color and allows plants to capture the energy of sunlight. Chlorophyll is green because it reflects green light and absorbs other colors of light, particularly the red and blue light present in sunlight.

Materials of Photosynthesis

Plants need carbon dioxide and water to carry out photosynthesis. Carbon dioxide, a gas found in the air, enters the plant through stomata, small openings on the underside of leaves. Plants absorb water in their roots and then transport the water through xylem, up the stem to the leaves.

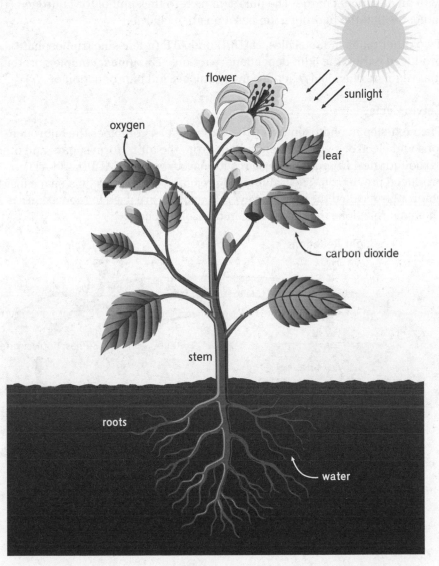

During photosynthesis, a plant uses the energy of sunlight to convert carbon dioxide and water into glucose and oxygen, which are the products of photosynthesis. The plant uses the glucose as energy to carry out life functions. Some of the oxygen produced from photosynthesis is used by the plant during cellular respiration, and the rest exits the plant through the stomata.

Scientists sometimes speculate, or make a guess, about something that is unknown. Speculation can be valuable in discovering new things. However, some speculation is based on information that is not always known as fact. There is some speculation that the earliest plants on Earth did not carry out photosynthesis. Conduct some research on how early plants may have captured and used energy. Using the information you find to identify what scientists consider a fact and what scientists identify to be speculation.

The entire process of photosynthesis can be summarized by the following equation. It shows that six molecules of carbon dioxide and six molecules of water are needed to form one sugar molecule and six molecules of oxygen.

$$\text{light energy} + 6CO_2 + 6H_2O \rightarrow C_6H_{12}O_6 + 6O_2$$

Light-Dependent Reactions

Many chemical reactions take place during photosynthesis. During the light-dependent reactions, chlorophyll molecules capture light energy from the Sun. A photon, or particle of light, hits an antenna-like structure that contains chlorophyll. This causes an electron to go to an excited state. The energy from the excited electron is used to split water molecules into hydrogen ions (H^+), oxygen molecules (O_2), and electrons. An ion is an atom or molecule with an electrical charge. The plus sign next to the symbol for hydrogen (H) indicates that the hydrogen ion has a positive charge.

Two other types of molecules, NADPH and ATP (adenosine triphosphate), are produced during the light-dependent reactions. **Enzymes,** complex proteins that regulate chemical reactions in organisms, aid in production of ATP.

Calvin Cycle

The next step in photosynthesis, the Calvin cycle, combines the hydrogen ions and electrons with carbon dioxide from the air to form sugars and other carbohydrates. Energy for these reactions is from the NADPH and ATP produced previously. The Calvin cycle reactions take place in a space inside chloroplasts called the stroma. Several enzymes are used in the various chemical reactions that take place in the Calvin cycle.

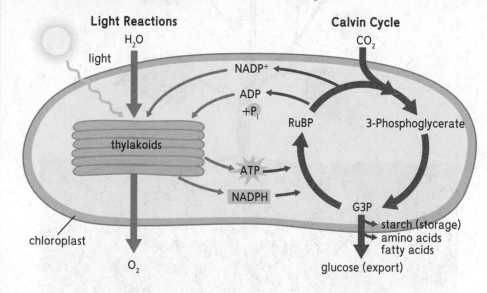

Think about Science

Directions: Answer the following question.

1. What are the substances that result from the splitting of water molecules during photosynthesis?
   A. carbon dioxide, sugar, oxygen molecules
   B. sugar, oxygen molecules, hydrogen ions
   C. electrons, hydrogen ions, carbon dioxide
   D. hydrogen ions, oxygen molecules, electrons

Cellular Respiration

Plants get the energy they need from the food they make during photosynthesis. Animals, on the other hand, cannot make their own food, so they eat plants and other animals to get the energy they need.

Plants, animals, and other organisms must release the energy stored in the organic molecules of food. One way they do this is through **cellular respiration,** a process in which glucose and other organic molecules are broken down to release energy in the presence of oxygen.

Most of the process of cellular respiration occurs in mitochondria, where the enzymes necessary for the chemical reactions are stored. As shown in the diagram, a mitochondrion has an outer membrane and an inner membrane.

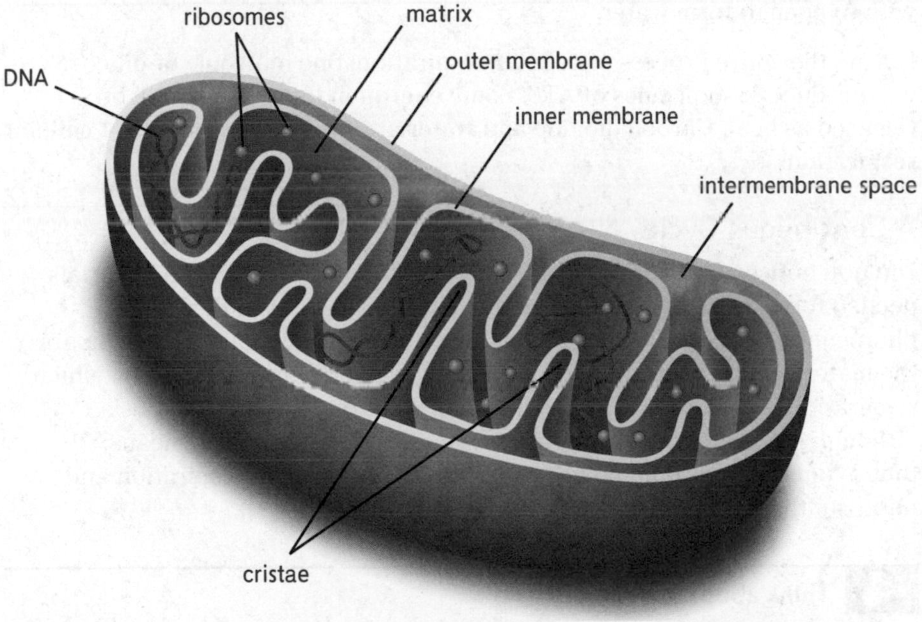
ribosomes
matrix
DNA
outer membrane
inner membrane
intermembrane space
cristae

The process of cellular respiration is summarized in the following equation. Despite the simple equation, cellular respiration does not take place in one simple step. Instead the process occurs in a series of steps. In each step, cells can trap bits of energy and change that energy into a form the cell can use.

$$C_6H_{12}O_6 + 6O_2 \ \backslash \ 6CO_6 + 6H_2O + Energy$$

Sugar (glucose) Oxygen Carbon Dioxide Water

CORE SKILL

Express Scientific Information Symbolically

This section of the lesson uses symbols to represent elements and molecules. In CO_2, the subscript 2 means there are two atoms of oxygen in each molecule of carbon dioxide. Using the example of a chemical equation shown for photosynthesis, write a chemical equation for what happens to two molecules of water during the light-dependent reactions. You do not need to include electrons, NADPH, and ATP in your chemical equation.

Communication and Collaboration

Collaboration is an important skill for scientists. When scientists collaborate, they must communicate with each other effectively. Scientists record their procedures and observations carefully so they can be shared with others. **Apply,** or put to practical use, your communication and collaboration skills by working with a partner to create a diagram, or other model, of what you know about cellular respiration.

Stages of Cellular Respiration

In the first part of cellular respiration, known as glycolysis, two molecules of ATP provide the energy to break apart a glucose molecule. This produces two molecules of a different sugar, pyruvate, and two molecules of ATP, a molecule for storing energy. Glycolysis can also break apart other organic molecules such as proteins, carbohydrates, and fats. Glycolysis occurs outside the mitochondria.

Kreb's Cycle

The next step of cellular respiration requires the presence of oxygen for the pyruvate molecules to enter the mitochondria. Inside the mitochondria, the pyruvate is changed into acetyl coenzyme A. The acetyl coenzyme A then enters the tricarboxylic acid cycle, also known as the Krebs cycle. During this stage, the acetyl coenzyme A is then changed in a long string of chemical reactions aided by enzymes. The Krebs cycle produces carbon dioxide and energy and occurs in the inner folded membrane of the mitochondrion.

Oxidative Phosphorylation

The last stage of cellular respiration is called oxidative phosphorylation and occurs in the folded inner membrane of the mitochondrion. Hydrogen atoms from the Krebs cycle have lots of energy. During this last stage, the hydrogen atoms are split into protons and high-energy electrons. The electrons are passed down an electron-transport chain. This transfer of electrons provides energy for the production of ATP. Eventually the protons and electrons join with oxygen to form water.

During the entire process of cellular respiration, one molecule of glucose will produce 38 molecules of ATP. Some energy in this process will be released as heat. Carbon dioxide and water are the waste products of cellular respiration.

A Continuous Cycle

Did you notice anything familiar about cellular respiration? The materials needed for cellular respiration are the materials produced during photosynthesis. And the materials produced during cellular respiration are the materials needed for photosynthesis. The chemical equation for cellular respiration is the reverse of the chemical equation for photosynthesis, although the processes are not the reverse of each other. This means that oxygen and carbon dioxide are both cycled through respiration and photosynthesis.

⚛ Think about Science

Directions: Fill in the blank.

1. The process of glycolysis breaks down _____ .

2. The main function of ATP is _____ .

3. The inner membrane of a mitochondrion is where _____ .

4. Cellular respiration and photosynthesis are related processes in that _____ .

Fermentation

Cellular respiration is said to be an aerobic process because it requires oxygen. When cells cannot get the oxygen they need, they use a process called **fermentation** to release energy stored in organic molecules. This process is said to be anaerobic because it does not require oxygen. Fermentation does not provide cells with as much energy as cellular respiration does. Two common types of fermentation are lactic-acid fermentation and alcoholic fermentation.

Lactic-Acid Fermentation

Lactic-acid fermentation is used to make certain foods such as yogurt and cheese. It also occurs in your muscles during strenuous exercise. As in cellular respiration, two molecules of ATP provide the energy to break down a glucose molecule into two molecules of pyruvate, which produces two molecules of ATP. However, during lactic-acid fermentation, the pyruvate is changed into lactic acid instead of more ATP molecules.

Alcoholic Fermentation

Alcoholic fermentation, which occurs in some single-celled organisms, is used to produce bread and beverages such as wine and beer. In alcoholic fermentation, glucose is changed into ethyl alcohol, or ethanol, two molecules of ATP, and carbon dioxide.

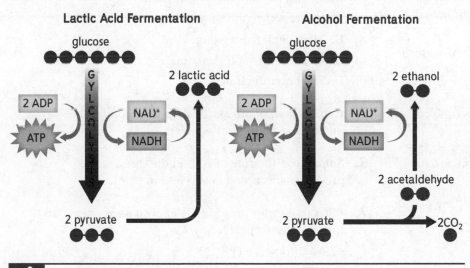

WORKPLACE SKILLS

Summarize Information in Workplace Graphics

In the sciences, as well as in many other careers, information is communicated through various graphic representations, including diagrams, tables, charts, and graphs. It is important to be able to interpret the graphic representations presented. Find a graphic in your workplace or in any public building. Describe the graphic and summarize the information it contains.

Think about Science

Directions: Answer the following questions.

1. What is the key difference between cellular respiration and fermentation?

   A. Fermentation does not produce ATP.
   B. Fermentation happens in the absence of oxygen.
   C. Fermentation does not involve pyruvate molecules.
   D. Fermentation is used to manufacture yogurt.

2. In which type of organism does alcoholic fermentation take place?

   A. plants
   B. animals
   C. single-celled organisms
   D. multicellular organisms

Vocabulary Review

apply   **cellular respiration**   **chlorophyll**

enzymes   **fermentation**   **photosynthesis**

1. The process in which glucose and other organic molecules are broken down to release energy in the presence of oxygen is called _____.

2. _____ are complex proteins that regulate chemical reactions in organisms.

3. _____ is the process by which organisms capture light energy and change it into chemical energy.

4. When you _____ what you have learned, you put it to use for a practical purpose.

5. The process that releases the energy stored in organic molecules in the absence of oxygen is called _____.

6. _____ is the pigment that gives plants their green color and allows plants to capture the energy of sunlight.

Skill Review

Directions: Answer the following questions.

1. Areas near the Earth's poles do not get any light for a portion of the year. Few plants grow in these areas. What characteristic might help a plant survive in those conditions?
   A. The ability to store large amounts of water
   B. More chloroplasts in the leaves
   C. More ATP synthase in the leaves
   D. The ability to store large amounts of food

2. Glucose, a simple sugar, is written as $C_6H_{12}O_6$ in a chemical equation. What elements are in glucose?
   A. carbon dioxide, hydrogen, oxygen
   B. chlorophyll, hydrogen, oxygen
   C. carbon, hydrogen, oxygen
   D. carotene, hydrogen, oxygen

3. Which of these is a product of the Calvin cycle?
   A. carbon dioxide
   B. sugar
   C. hydrogen
   D. oxygen

4. How do you think people get the oxygen necessary for cellular respiration?
   A. It enters through the skin.
   B. They get it from water.
   C. It enters through stomata.
   D. They breathe it in.

5. Explain why photosynthesis is important to life on Earth. Justify your answer.

6. Summarize the role of ATP in the three processes discussed in this lesson.

7. What molecules provide the energy necessary for the Calvin cycle?
   A. NADPH and ATP
   B. ATP and chlorophyll
   C. chlorophyll and sugar
   D. sugar and NADPH

Skill Practice

Directions: Answer the following questions.

1. Alcoholic fermentation is what causes bread that contains yeast to rise. When bread rises, it develops small pockets of gas. What gas is contained in these small pockets?

   A. hydrogen

   B. carbon dioxide

   C. oxygen

   D. nitrogen

2. During strenuous exercise, the cells in muscles may not receive enough oxygen. This causes a burning sensation in the muscles. What process most likely accounts for this burning sensation?

   A. photosynthesis

   B. cellular respiration

   C. lactic-acid fermentation

   D. alcoholic fermentation

3. From the information in the lesson about cellular respiration, what can we infer?

   A. Photosynthesis in plants must always precede cellular respiration.

   B. Cellular respiration occurs only in animals.

   C. Photosynthesis and cellular respiration share many processes.

   D. No relationship exists between photosynthesis and cellular respiration.

4. The rate of cellular respiration in humans can be measured by the amount of carbon dioxide exhaled. Which would you expect to be true about the rate of cellular respiration for a group of students who are the same age, height, and weight?

   A. Boys would have a higher rate of cellular respiration than girls.

   B. Girls would have a higher rate of cellular respiration than boys.

   C. Physically active people would have a higher rate of cellular respiration than people who are not physically active.

   D. People who are not physically active would have a higher rate of cellular respiration than physically active people.

5. Which of these is a likely result of large areas of forest being cut down?

   A. An increase in sugar production

   B. A decrease in lactic-acid fermentation

   C. An increase of oxygen in the atmosphere

   D. A decrease of oxygen in the atmosphere

6. What is the advantage of energy production in aerobic conditions? Justify your answer.

Directions: Use the diagram to answer questions 7–8.

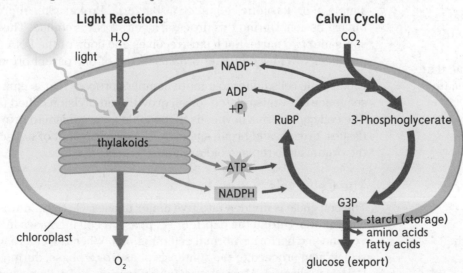

7. Based on the diagram, describe the process of photosynthesis.

8. According to the diagram, what is needed to carry out photosynthesis? What are some of the final products of photosynthesis?

Energy and Cells

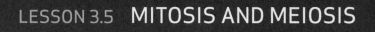

LESSON OBJECTIVES

- List the cell cycle stages
- Explain the processes involved during the different types of cell division
- Compare and contrast mitosis and meiosis

CORE SKILLS & PRACTICES

- Analyze Events and Ideas
- Understand and Explain Nontextual Scientific Presentations

Key Terms

cell cycle
the sequence of events that leads to cell growth and division

chromatid
one copy of a chromosome that is joined to its exact duplicate sister chromatid

chromosomes
structures where genes are located

meiosis
a type of cell division that produces gametes

mitosis
the process that divides the nucleus of a cell

Vocabulary

contrast
to show differences between

Key Concept

Cells divide through the process of mitosis or meiosis. Mitosis produces daughter cells that are identical to the parent cell. Meiosis produces sex cells that combine to produce offspring that are genetically different from parent cells.

Cell Growth and Division

Every organism is composed of one or more cells, which are units of life. A cell can grow larger to a certain extent. But at some point, instead of continuing to grow, the cell divides. The process by which one parent cell divides into two daughter cells is known as cell division, or cell reproduction.

The actual process of cell division depends on whether the cell is prokaryotic or eukaryotic. A prokaryotic cell lacks a nucleus or any other membrane-bound organelles. A eukaryotic cell is organized into membrane-bound organelles, such as the nucleus and mitochondria. Cell division is relatively simple in prokaryotic cells such as bacteria. Prokaryotes reproduce through binary fission. During this process, a cell's DNA is copied. The cell then splits into two parts. Each part receives one copy of the DNA. Binary fission produces two new daughter organisms out of one parent organism.

Eukaryotic cells undergo a more complex process that is part of a larger sequence of events related to cell growth and division called the **cell cycle**. The cell cycle forms new cells that enable an organism to grow and develop tissues, organs, and organ systems. The development of new cells also allows the organism to replace old or damaged cells.

The Cell Cycle

The cell cycle is divided into five major phases: G_1, S, G_2, mitosis, and cytokinesis. During the gap 1, or G_1, phase, a cell increases in size and volume and performs normal cell functions. When the cell reaches a certain size, it may proceed to the synthesis phase, or S phase, during which the cell's DNA is replicated. After successful replication, the cell proceeds to the gap 2 phase, or G_2. In G_2, the cell undergoes another phase of growth in which extra organelles and cytoplasm are produced in preparation for cell division.

The G_1, S, and G_2 phases are all considered part of a larger phase called interphase. After interphase, the cell is ready to divide.

During **mitosis**, or the M phase, the nucleus divides into two nuclei. Once mitosis is complete, the cell undergoes cytokinesis and divides into two daughter cells that are identical to the parent cell.

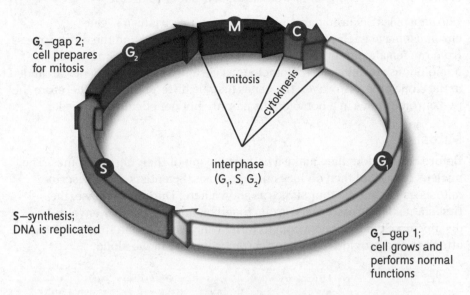

G_2—gap 2; cell prepares for mitosis

G_2

M

C

mitosis

cytokinesis

S

interphase
(G_1, S, G_2)

G_1

S—synthesis; DNA is replicated

G_1—gap 1; cell grows and performs normal functions

CORE SKILL

Analyze Events and Ideas

In order to better understand what you are reading, it is often necessary to analyze the ideas presented. Write a paragraph that gives a summary of the major events in the cell cycle. What are the main events that occur during the cell cycle? Why do the events occur in the order they do?

The cell must pass through a variety of checkpoints during the cell cycle. Each checkpoint is a stopping point that allows the cell to determine whether it is ready to move on to the next phase. These checkpoints occur during the G_1 and S phases and at the end of the G_2 and M phases. The checkpoint in the S phase, for example, evaluates whether the cell's DNA has been replicated properly. If it has not, the cell may not continue to prepare for division.

Think about Science

Directions: Answer the following questions.

1. Which of these happens to a cell during interphase?

   A. The nucleus of the parent cell divides.
   B. The cell becomes two daughter cells.
   C. The cell's DNA undergoes replication.
   D. The number of cell organelles decreases.

2. At which checkpoint in the cell cycle would a scientist evaluate whether the nucleus has divided properly?

   A. G_1 checkpoint
   B. S checkpoint
   C. G_2 checkpoint
   D. M checkpoint

Chromosomes and Cell Division

The nucleus of a eukaryotic cell divides during mitosis, or the M phase of the cell cycle. In other words, mitosis divides the genetic material in the cell. Genes are not located randomly in cells. Instead genes are lined up on structures called **chromosomes**. Each chromosome is made up of a combination of DNA wrapped with proteins and can contain thousands of genes.

Scientists often use nontextual materials in their presentations. Many people understand visual representations of concepts more easily than they understand text. Examine the diagram on this page showing the stages of mitosis. Why is it helpful to have a diagram that shows this process instead of just using text? Give at least one example of how the diagram helped you understand mitosis.

Most of the time, a chromosome is a structure that looks like a thin thread. Just before a cell divides, the chromosome shortens and takes on an X shape. Each side of an X-shaped chromosome is called a **chromatid**. The two chromatids, called sister chromatids, are exact copies of each other and are held together at a point called the centromere. Chromosomes can be seen clearly in a microscope only when the cell is about to divide.

Chromosomes occur in pairs in most eukaryotic organisms. One chromosome in each pair comes from the male parent, and the other comes from the female parent. The chromosomes in each pair are known as homologous chromosomes. Homologous chromosomes have genes arranged in the same order. However, the genes may be different forms. Therefore the two chromosomes in a homologous pair are not genetically identical.

Mitosis

Before cells divide, they make a complete copy of their chromosomes. The nucleus of the cell then divides during mitosis. Scientists often describe mitosis as having the four stages as shown here. During prophase, the first stage, the chromosomes group together, and the nuclear envelope disappears. Spindle fibers begin to form, which are protein fibers that can attach to and provides a path for chromosomes to move along.

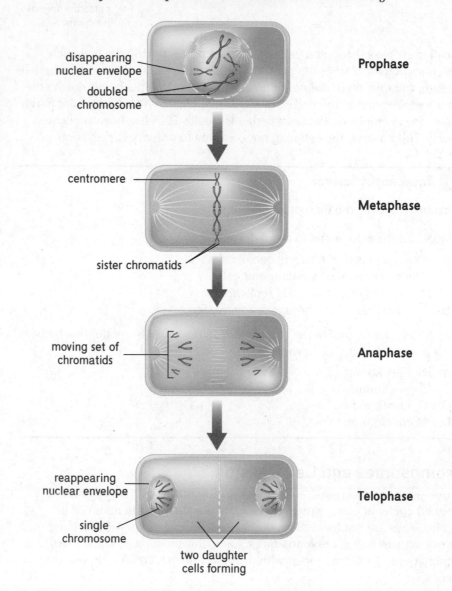

disappearing nuclear envelope

doubled chromosome

Prophase

centromere

sister chromatids

Metaphase

moving set of chromatids

Anaphase

reappearing nuclear envelope

single chromosome

two daughter cells forming

Telophase

In metaphase, the second stage, the chromosomes line up across the center of the cell. During anaphase, the third stage, spindle fibers shorten and split the centromeres apart. As the fibers continue to shorten, sister chromatids move to opposite ends of the cell. In telophase, the final stage, the cell membrane pinches in at the center of the cell. A nuclear envelope reappears around each group of now single chromosomes. Simultaneously, in the process called cytokinesis, the cell splits into two identical cells called daughter cells. Each new daughter cell has a complete set of chromosomes.

◁° Think about Science

Directions: Answer the following questions.

1. During which stage of mitosis does the nuclear envelope disappear?
   A. anaphase
   B. metaphase
   C. prophase
   D. telophase

2. What does the dividing cell look like during metaphase?
   A. Chromatids are being pulled to either side of the cell.
   B. Chromosomes are lined up down the center of the cell.
   C. Nuclear envelopes are forming around chromosomes.
   D. Chromosomes shorten and form X-shaped chromatids.

Sexual Reproduction

During sexual reproduction, two sex cells combine to form a cell that can develop into a new organism. However, if sex cells were like normal body cells, the cell resulting from their combination would have twice the number of chromosomes needed.

A cell cannot function properly if it has too few or too many chromosomes. This is why sexual reproduction involves **meiosis**, a form of cell division in which the nucleus divides twice to reduce the number of chromosomes by half. Cell division that involves meiosis occurs only in the production of male gametes (sperm) and female gametes (eggs). When a sperm cell combines with an egg cell, the zygote formed has a nucleus with the correct number of chromosomes. The zygote then divides using mitosis to form the many cells of a multicellular organism. The diagram on page 130 **contrasts**, or shows some differences, between the processes of the two phases of meiosis.

Meiosis

Meiosis occurs in two phases: meiosis I and meiosis II. Each phase of meiosis has four stages.

Meiosis I separates homologous chromosomes.

- During prophase I, homologous chromosomes pair up. Each of these chromosomes consists of two chromatids—replicated during S phase producing chromatids. Crossing over between chromatids occurs during prophase I, and genetic material is exchanged between the homologous chromosomes. The nuclear envelope breaks down, and spindle fibers form.

Some human disorders, such as Klinefelter's syndrome, are caused when chromosomes do not divide properly. Use the Internet to research Klinefelter's syndrome, its causes, and its effects.

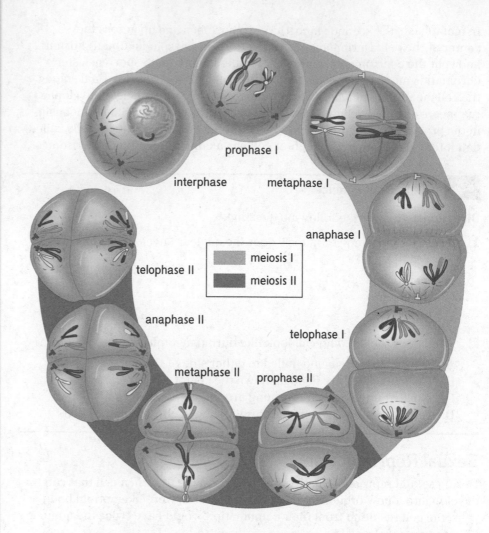

- During metaphase I, homologous chromosomes line up at the equator.
- During anaphase I, spindle fibers shorten and separate homologous chromosomes from each other, moving them to opposite sides of the cell.
- During telophase I, spindle fibers break down. Chromosomes uncoil, and nuclear envelopes form, creating two nuclei. The cell then divides.

Meiosis II splits sister chromatids.

- During prophase II, chromosomes condense, and spindle fibers form once again within each new cell.
- During metaphase II, the centromeres of the chromosomes line up randomly along the center of each new cell.
- During anaphase II, the centromeres split, and sister chromatids separate. Spindle fibers shorten and move these chromatids to opposite sides of each cell.
- During telophase II, spindle fibers break down. Nuclear envelopes form around chromosomes to form four nuclei. Each cell divides.

The end result of meiosis is four cells, each with half the number of chromosomes that are in a body cell of the organism.

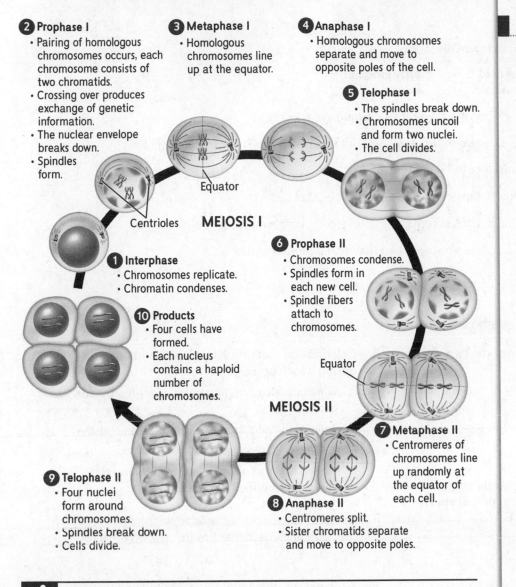

2 Prophase I
- Pairing of homologous chromosomes occurs, each chromosome consists of two chromatids.
- Crossing over produces exchange of genetic information.
- The nuclear envelope breaks down.
- Spindles form.

Centrioles

3 Metaphase I
- Homologous chromosomes line up at the equator.

Equator

MEIOSIS I

4 Anaphase I
- Homologous chromosomes separate and move to opposite poles of the cell.

5 Telophase I
- The spindles break down.
- Chromosomes uncoil and form two nuclei.
- The cell divides.

1 Interphase
- Chromosomes replicate.
- Chromatin condenses.

6 Prophase II
- Chromosomes condense.
- Spindles form in each new cell.
- Spindle fibers attach to chromosomes.

10 Products
- Four cells have formed.
- Each nucleus contains a haploid number of chromosomes.

Equator

MEIOSIS II

9 Telophase II
- Four nuclei form around chromosomes.
- Spindles break down.
- Cells divide.

8 Anaphase II
- Centromeres split.
- Sister chromatids separate and move to opposite poles.

7 Metaphase II
- Centromeres of chromosomes line up randomly at the equator of each cell.

Think about Science

Directions: Answer the following questions.

1. Which of these events occurs during meiosis I?
   A. Sister chromatids separate and move to opposite poles.
   B. Homologous chromosomes line up at the cell's center.
   C. Four nuclei form around the divided chromosomes.
   D. Centromeres holding sister chromatids together split

2. During which of these stages of meiosis does an exchange of genetic information take place between chromosomes?
   A. anaphase II
   B. telophase I
   C. prophase I
   D. metaphase II

Vocabulary Review

Directions: Write the missing term in the blank.

cell cycle	chromatid	chromosome
contrast	meiosis	mitosis

1. A _____ is one arm of an X-shaped chromosome.

2. When you _____ something, you point out its differences from something else.

3. There may be a thousand genes located on one _____.

4. Gametes are produced through the process of _____.

5. During the _____, DNA is replicated, and a cell gets ready to divide.

6. The process of _____ produces two identical daughter cells.

Skill Review

Directions: Answer the following questions.

1. During which stage of mitosis are the two nuclei for the daughter cells formed?

A. anaphase

B. metaphase

C. prophase

D. telophase

2. During which stage in meiosis would you see homologous chromosomes being pulled apart from each other?

A. anaphase I

B. telophase I

C. anaphase II

D. telophase II

3. During which stage do sister chromatids separate and move to opposite poles?

A. anaphase I

B. telophase I

C. anaphase II

D. telophase II

4. In which phase of the cell cycle would a growing but nondividing skin cell most likely be found?

A. G_1

B. G_2

C. M

D. S

5. Cell division that involves meiosis only occurs during which process?

A. when a male gamete combines with a female gamete

B. when male and female gametes are produced

C. when a zygote is formed

D. when the zygote divides to form many the cells of a multicellular organism

6. Explain why mitosis is defined as the division of the cell's nucleus instead of just the division of the cell.

7. Explain how one daughter cell could end up with extra genetic material through an error during mitosis.

8. Compare and contrast the processes of mitosis and meiosis.

Skill Practice

Directions: Use the diagram to answer questions 1–3.

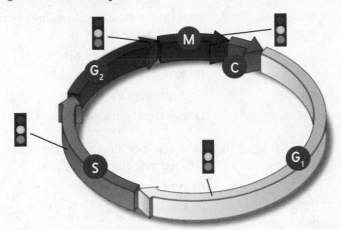

1. Which of these checkpoints allows the cell to leave interphase in the cell cycle?

   A. G_1 checkpoint

   B. S checkpoint

   C. G_2 checkpoint

   D. M checkpoint

2. DNA in a cell has been replicated, but the cell has not produced extra organelles in preparation for division. Which checkpoint would most likely stop the cell from progressing through the cell cycle?

   A. G_1 checkpoint

   B. S checkpoint

   C. G_2 checkpoint

   D. M checkpoint

3. Which of these events would stop a cell from progressing through the final checkpoint of the cell cycle?

   A. Sister chromatids do not separate on one chromosome.

   B. A resting cell does not increase in size or volume.

   C. The nuclear envelope disappears, and chromosomes double.

   D. Production of extra cytoplasm causes a cell to grow.

Directions: Answer the following questions.

4. Which of these stages in meiosis is most similar to metaphase in mitosis?

   A. anaphase I

   B. prophase II

   C. telophase I

   D. metaphase II

5. Explain how the process of meiosis increases genetic differences between offspring and parents.

6. Unregulated cell division and changes to genes are two aspects of cancer. Infer how cancer could be related to errors in the cell cycle.

Directions: Answer the following questions.

1. Which of the following provides evidence in support of the cell theory?

   A. a microscopic view of mitosis

   B. a microscopic view of a maggot

   C. a microscopic view of a protein molecule

   D. a microscopic view of cellular organelles

2. Which of the following describes the levels of organization of cells in the body, from simplest to most complex?

   A. body system → organ → tissue → cell

   B. cell → organ → tissue → body system

   C. cell → tissue → organ → body system

   D. body system → tissue→ cell → organ

3. Which organelle in the cell converts energy from a sandwich into molecules that provide energy to the cell?

   A. endoplasmic reticulum

   B. golgi

   C. lysososme

   D. mitochondria

4. How does the cell move a substance from an area of low concentration to an area of higher concentration?

   A. active transport

   B. diffusion

   C. gradient

   D. osmosis

5. What are the three basic organs that all plants have in common?

   A. leaves, roots, seeds

   B. leaves, roots, stem

   C. roots, stems, shoots

   D. flowers, leaves, roots

6. Which of the following explains how a fruit is formed on a flowering plant?

   A. a pollinated flower transforms into a fruit.

   B. The ovary surrounding a seed swells and forms a fruit.

   C. The protective coat falls of the seed and it grows into a fruit.

   D. Pollen grains collect around a seed and the seed becomes a fruit.

7. How does oxidative phosphorylation produce energy for the cell?

   A. glucose is broken down

   B. Kreb's cycle is activated

   C. hydrogen atoms split

   D. electron transport chain

8. In which specific part of the plant cell does the Calvin cycle function?

   A. root

   B. stem

   C. stroma

   D. vacuole

9. At which two checkpoints of the cell cycle is there twice the amount of DNA as in a normally active cell?

   A. G2 and M

   B. G1 and G2

   C. S and G2

   D. M and G1

10. Human body cells have 46 chromosomes. How many chromosomes are present in a sperm cell?

    A. 12 chromosomes

    B. 23 chromosomes

    C. 46 chromosomes

    D. 92 chromosomes

11. Explain why it is beneficial for many small cells to make up an organism as opposed to several larger cells?

12. How do ribosomes act to carry out genetic instructions in the cell?

13. Explain how vascular plants have adapted to live on land as opposed to in water environments.

14. Explain why photosynthesis is necessary for human life on Earth.

15. Plasmodial slime mold is an organism that is composed of a single large cytoplasm and many nuclei. Explain how this organism could form based on what you know about mitosis?

Directions: Use the diagram to answer questions 16–17.

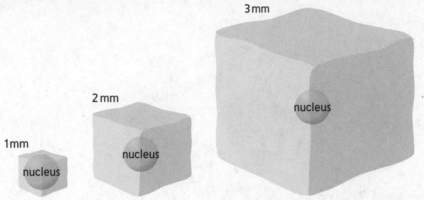

16. Based on the diagram above, which of the following explains why there is a limit to the volume of a cell?

    A. The cells will be larger than normal and so the organism will double in size.

    B. The cell will produce twice as many proteins and will function at twice the normal rate.

    C. The cells will not survive because there will not be enough organelles inside to support cell function.

    D. The cell will not survive because not enough materials will be able to pass through the cell's surface.

17. Assuming that a cell is a cube as shown in the image above. What is the surface area of a cell with a width of 3 mm? The area of each face of the cube is calculated using the equation:

    $$A = l \times w$$

    where A is the area, l is the length of the side, and w is the width of the side.

    A. 9 mm²

    B. 27 mm²

    C. 36 mm²

    D. 54 mm²

Directions: Read the passage and answer questions 18–20.

In 1859, a French chemist named Louis Pasteur designed an experiment to test spontaneous generation. He bent the neck of a flask into an S-shape. This made it possible for air to reach the broth inside, but any microorganisms in the air would get stuck in the neck of the flask and be unable to reach the broth. Since no microorganisms grew in this broth, Pasteur knew that spontaneous generation did not occur. To confirm that microorganisms came from the air, Pasteur then tilted the flasks, and microorganisms suddenly appeared in the broth. In this way, Pasteur showed that microorganisms exist in the air; they do not arise from nonliving matter.

18. Why was it necessary for Pasteur to bend the neck of the flask in his experiment?

    A. It prevented air from getting into the flask.

    B. It prevented microorganisms from escaping the flask.

    C. It prevented microorganisms from entering the flask.

    D. It prevented the broth from spilling out of the flask.

19. How did Pasteur's experiment provide evidence in support of the cell theory?

20. Which statement best explains why it was common for people in the 19th century to think that organisms arose from spontaneous generation?

    A. The microscope was not invented.

    B. Scientists did not know what cells were.

    C. Maggots were often found on rotting foods.

    D. People did not understand about reproduction.

Directions: Use the diagram to answer questions 21–22.

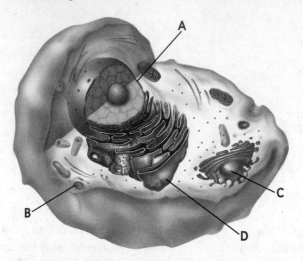

21. Which organelle is filled with enzymes that break down large organic molecules?

A. A

B. B

C. C

D. D

22. In which organelle is a protein modified before it is transported out of the cell?

A. A

B. B

C. C

D. D

Directions: Use the equation to answer questions 23–24.

$$\text{light energy} + 6CO_2 + 6H_2O \rightarrow C_6H_{12}O_6 + 6O_2$$

23. Based on the light reaction for photosynthesis shown above and what you know about the relationship between photosynthesis and cellular respiration, what is the overall reaction that occurs during cellular respiration?

A. $C_6 H_{12}O_6 + 6O_2 \rightarrow 6CO_2 + 6H_2O + \text{energy}$

B. $\text{energy} + C_6 H_{12}O_6 + 6O_2 \rightarrow 6CO_2 + 6H_2O$

C. $\text{energy} + 6CO_2 + 6H_2O \rightarrow C_6H_{12}O_6 + 6O_2$

D. $C_6 H_{12}O_6 + 6CO_2 \rightarrow 6H_2O + 6O_2 + \text{energy}$

24. Using the information in the equation for photosynthesis, explain why a plant cannot grow in the absence of sunlight?

Directions: Use the diagram to answer questions 25 and 26.

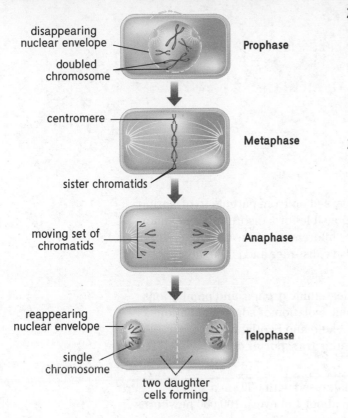

disappearing nuclear envelope

doubled chromosome

Prophase

centromere

Metaphase

sister chromatids

moving set of chromatids

Anaphase

reappearing nuclear envelope

Telophase

single chromosome

two daughter cells forming

25. At which phases of mitosis is the nuclear envelope absent?

A. anaphase and prophase

B. metaphase and anaphase

C. prophase and metaphase

D. telophase and anaphase

26. At which phase do the chromosomes split?

A. anaphase

B. metaphase

C. prophase

D. telophase

Check Your Understanding

On the following chart, circle the number of any item you answered incorrectly. Next to each group of item numbers, you will see the pages you can review to learn how to answer the items correctly.

Lesson	Item Number(s)	Review Page(s)
3.1: Cells: Basic Unit of Life	1, 2, 11, 18, 19, 20	98–101
3.2: Cell Structure and Function	3, 4, 12, 16, 17, 21, 22	104–107
3.3: Plant Structure and Function	5, 6, 13	110–115
3.4: Energy and Cells	7, 8, 14, 23, 24	118–123
3.5: Mitosis and Meiosis	9, 10, 15, 25, 26	126–131

Pass It On

Core Practices

- Cite specific textual evidence to support a finding or conclusion
- Express scientific information or findings visually

Question

How can a genetic disorder spread through a population?

Background Concepts

Genetic disorders involve chromosomal changes and can be passed on from parents to offspring. Sometimes a parent can carry a gene or a group of genes responsible for a disorder but not show signs of the disease. However, they can still pass it on to their children and some of their children may have the symptoms of the disorder. This is called a recessive disorder and is the most common type of human genetic disorder.

Most genetic disorders are not evenly distributed among gender, ethnic groups, and populations. The uneven distribution seen in many cases is due to geographic isolation of some populations. For example, on the isolated Faroe Islands located between Iceland and Scotland, there is a higher frequency of the recessive genetic disorder called carnitine transporter deficiency (CTD) than is found in the rest of the world.

On the Faroe Islands about 100 of the 48,000 residents were diagnosed with CTD in a single month during 2010. In comparison, throughout the world, only about 1 in every 100,000 newborns are diagnosed with this disease. Individuals with CTD have trouble using fat as an energy source for the body. Symptoms of this genetic disorder include extreme fatigue, muscle weakness, poor appetite, seizures, brain swelling, breathing problems, heart problems, and even death. An increase in movement of individuals in and out of isolated populations has been shown to decrease the frequency of some genetic disorders.

Hypothesis

Review the background information on the genetic disorder CTD and develop a hypothesis to address the question why the frequency of this disease is so much greater on the Faroe Islands compared to that in the rest of the world.

✔ Test-Taking Tip

On your exam, you may encounter a question that asks you to choose the best visual representation of a set of scientific data. For example, a multiple choice question may ask you to choose the graph that best represents the data or information presented in the question. When you face this type of question, it is important to remember that the answer is right in front of you, you just need to determine what the question is asking you, and then find the graph that provides the relevant information that you need. Read the question completely and then read all of the labels, titles, and axes on each graph given as an answer choice. Study the curve or set of points plotted on the graph carefully. A correct analysis of the graphs will lead you to choose the correct answer.

Investigation

After developing a hypothesis, the next step is to gather information and determine whether your hypothesis is supported or not. Research information about the Faroe Islands and CTD. Also research information about genetic disorders and remote populations. Cite specific evidence in these sources that relates to your hypothesis. Learn about the disease and how it is acquired. Information about the disease can be found on the website of the U.S. National Library of Medicine. Draw a diagram that explains how a heritable disease is passed on. The diagram should take the form of a pedigree. An example of a pedigree diagram is shown. In the diagram males are represented by a square, and females are represented by a circle. Parents are joined together by a horizontal line and offspring branch off and are connected to parents via a vertical line. Shapes that are fully shaded represent individuals with the disease and open shapes represent individuals that are not affected by the disease. Add a letter designation below the square or circle to represent the genotype of each individual in the pedigree.

Collect and Analyze Data

Collect information about heritable traits and remote populations. Cite specific textual evidence from the background information given and your research that is related to your hypothesis. Determine which information supports your hypothesis and which does not.

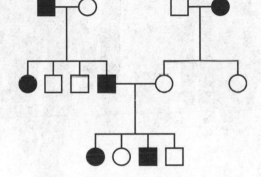

Interpretation

Summarize the information collected. Determine whether your hypothesis is valid based on the information you collected. Does the information you found call for a modification to your hypothesis?

When evaluating and interpreting the information or data you collected, ask yourself these questions:

- Does the defective gene need to be passed to offspring by both parents or only one parent?

- How does a heritable disorder spread through a population?

- Why is CTD so prevalent in the Faroe Islands?

Results

Discuss your results using evidence to support your conclusions. Discuss any observations about the information you gathered from reliable sources, possible sources of error, unexpected results, and any remaining questions. If your hypothesis was not supported, discuss your recommendations for formulating a new hypothesis or changes you would make to the investigation.

Consider these questions as you discuss your results:

- Why isn't the disease as common in other areas outside of the Faroe Islands?

- What factors determine whether an offspring inherits the disorder?

- Would increased immigration to the island influence the prevalence of CTD? How and why?

Chapter 4

Heredity and Evolution

Humans all have the same basic physical features but, with the exception of identical twins, everyone looks different. Every living organism has physical characteristics that set it apart from other individuals. All of these observable traits are passed down, or inherited, from a parent to its offspring. Although each species has unique characteristics, scientists have discovered that all living things share common ancestors. In fact, all life on Earth can be traced back to a single organism.

Tetra Images/Getty Images

Lesson 4.1
Basic Principles of Genetics

Genes are subunits of DNA, which is found in nearly every cell type in every living organism. Each gene or combination of genes contains a specific code that specifies the characteristics of a particular trait. Learn how genes are passed from parents to offspring, and how the combination of genes in each offspring is what makes it different from its parents.

Lesson 4.2
Probability of Traits

Scientists can look at two parent organisms and predict the characteristics of their offspring. Learn how to use a Punnett square to determine the probability that the offspring of two parents will inherit certain traits.

Lesson 4.3
Common Ancestry

Scientists group together, or classify, organisms according to how many traits they have in common. Learn how scientists have traced the evolution of species to see where they branched apart and developed unique traits.

Lesson 4.4
Heredity: Genetic Variations and Expression

Various factors can cause a change in physical and genetic traits that are passed from parent to offspring. Learn how DNA can be rearranged, or can have mutations that cause changes in traits from one generation to the next.

Lesson 4.5
Selection and Adaptation

Almost all species adapt to a changing environment through the process of natural selection. Learn how humans can mimic the process of natural selection by selectively breeding plants and animals with desired traits.

Goal Setting

You can gain an understanding of genetics by studying your own family. Are there any unique traits specific to one or more members of your family, such as eye color? Make a chart and list the members of your family. As you read, choose or investigate four traits that interest you. Compare each family member and describe that trait for each individual. Are there traits common to all family members? Are some traits unique to one individual?

LESSON 4.1 Basic Principles of Genetics

LESSON OBJECTIVES

- Describe how Mendel's research contributed to modern genetics
- Explain the link between chromosomes, genes, and alleles
- Relate meiosis to the inheritance of traits

CORE SKILLS & PRACTICES

- Describe a Data Set Statistically
- Apply Scientific Processes

Key Terms

allele
one of two or more forms of a gene

gene
a segment of DNA that contributes to the characteristics, or traits, of an organism

genetics
the field of biology devoted to studying heredity

heredity
the passing of traits from one generation to the next

trait
a heritable characteristic

Vocabulary

statistics
the field of study involving the collection and analysis of data

Key Concept

Some characteristics of organisms are passed from parents to offspring. How this occurs and characteristics of offspring can be studied on the molecular level.

Traits, Heredity, and Genetics

People tend to look like other members of their family because they share similar traits. A person's—or any other organism's—**traits** are their heritable characteristics. The color of your eyes, the shape of your nose, and the texture of your hair are just some of your many traits. Some traits are not visible. For example, your blood type is a trait, but not one you can see just by looking. Traits are different from learned characteristics. Learned characteristics, such as the ability to play an instrument or drive a car, are things you learn and are not heritable.

Traits are passed from parents to offspring. This passing of traits from one generation to the next is known as **heredity.** The field of biology devoted to studying heredity is called **genetics.** An understanding of genetics on a molecular level is relatively new because of the complex technology scientists needed to study structures as small as the DNA within cells. That does not mean the study of genetics is new, however. For thousands of years, people have been using their observations to breed plants and animals with specific traits.

Mendel and the History of Genetics

In the mid-nineteenth century, an Austrian monk named Gregor Mendel became one of the first people to diligently study genetics. For his studies, Mendel observed pea plants from his garden. Mendel could study how specific traits are inherited from one generation to the next generation. For example, he could observe the flower color in the plants produced when a plant with white flowers was bred with a plant with purple flowers. This type of controlled breeding is called cross-pollination.

Basic Principles of Genetics

Dominant and Recessive Traits

In one of his earliest experiments, Mendel crossed a short pea plant with a tall pea plant. The parent plants that are first crossed are known as the P_1 generation. Mendel planted the seeds that resulted from the cross. The offspring plants are called the F_1 generation. Mendel discovered that all the offspring in the F_1 generation grew to be tall. It was as if the shortness trait had disappeared.

Mendel then allowed the plants of the F_1 generation to self-pollinate. Again, he planted the seeds that were produced. In this generation, known as the F_2 generation, some plants were tall, and some were short. The shortness trait had reappeared. Mendel conducted similar crosses to test for other traits. He tested for seed shape, seed color, flower color, and flower position. In every case, Mendel discovered that one trait seemed to disappear in the F_1 generation and reappear in the F_2 generation. Mendel concluded that each trait is controlled by two factors. He called the form of a trait that appeared in the F_1 generation the dominant trait. He named the form of the trait that disappeared until the F_2 generation the recessive trait.

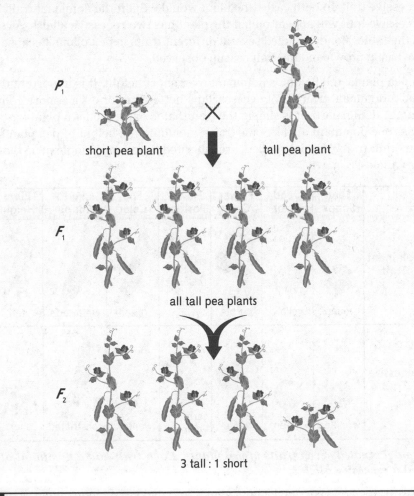

Think about Science

Directions: Fill in the blank.

1. In the pea-plant example, the tall form of the trait is the
   _____ trait.

2. The short form of the trait is the _____ trait.

Scientists who study genetics—as well as all subjects—collaborate with other scientists around the world. When interacting with others outside of one's own social or cultural group, it is helpful to be aware of social and cultural differences. Imagine that you are about to host a scientist from another country. What social or cultural practices in your life do you think the visiting scientist might not be familiar with?

Chromosomes, Genes, and Alleles

The factors Mendel described are now called genes. And it is now understood that a **gene** is a segment of DNA that contributes to the traits of an organism. Recall that DNA is an organic molecule that carries the information of heredity. One way of thinking about genes is that a gene determines a particular trait. The reality is much more complex, however. Genetics is a very active area of research, and scientists continue to find new evidence that helps explain how traits are inherited. A single organism can have tens of thousands of different genes. Genes are found within chromosomes, and a chromosome can contain thousands of genes.

Different forms of a gene are called **alleles.** Pea plants, for example, have two different alleles for the gene for height: one allele for tall height and one allele for short height. Mendel found that the tall trait in peas is dominant and the short trait is recessive. Each plant receives two alleles for a trait—one from each parent. The dominant trait will appear if the plant has at least one allele for the dominant trait. In other words, the plant could have two alleles for the dominant trait, or one allele for the dominant trait and one allele for the recessive trait. In both cases, the plant would exhibit the dominant trait. The recessive trait will appear only if the plant has two recessive alleles. As shown in the table, Mendel studied several different traits in pea plants because they are easily grown and the traits easily observed.

In pea plants, tall height is dominant over short height. It is important to note that a dominant trait is not necessarily a better trait or even a more common trait. A dominant trait is simply the trait that is expressed if a plant has at least one dominant allele. Some traits, including the height of pea plants and the other traits Mendel studied, are inherited based on a single gene that has two alleles.

	Seed Shape	Seed Color	Flower Color	Flower Position	Pod Color	Pod Shape	Plant Height
Dominant Trait	round	yellow	purple	axial (side)	green	inflated	tall
Recessive Trait	wrinkled	green	white	terminal (tips)	yellow	constricted	short

Mendel studied seven traits of pea plants. Each trait had a dominant allele and a recessive allele.

Most traits, however, have many alleles and depend on much more complex patterns of inheritance as well as on environmental factors. This is why most traits, including human height, have a continuous range of possibilities and not just two alternatives, such as tall or short.

Representing Alleles with Text

To describe alleles, scientists use an uppercase letter for the dominant allele. The lowercase version of the same letter is used for the recessive allele. The allele for tall height, therefore, is written as T, and the allele for short height is written as t. If an individual has a dominant allele and a recessive allele, the dominant allele is usually written before the recessive allele *(Tt)*.

Think again about Mendel's crosses. He selected true-breeding plants, which means that the plants had two copies of the same allele for a trait. The tall plants had two alleles for tall height *(TT)*, and the short plants had two alleles for short height *(tt)*. The plants in the F_1 generation received one allele from each parent. Therefore they received an allele for tall height from the tall parent and an allele for short height from the short parent. As a result, every plant in the F_1 generation had both types of alleles *(Tt)*. Because tall height is dominant over short height, all the plants were tall.

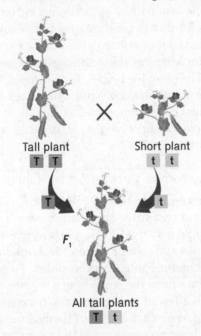

Representing Alleles on Chromosome Diagrams

Bacteria and other prokaryotes have a circular chromosome. Eukaryotes have linear chromosomes that occur in pairs called homologous chromosomes. For sexually reproducing organisms, one chromosome in each pair came from the male parent and the other came from the female parent.

The number of chromosomes is different from one organism to another. Humans, for example, have 23 pairs of chromosomes. Dogs have 39 pairs of chromosomes. Both chromosomes have genes for the same trait arranged in the same order. However, there may be different alleles for a gene on each chromosome. Therefore homologous chromosomes are not genetically identical.

CORE SKILL

Apply Scientific Processes

In the sciences, a prediction is a statement of what is expected to happen, given a particular set of conditions. Based on what you have read about dominant and recessive traits, what could you predict about the height of offspring of two parent pea plants that each had the alleles *Tt?*

Describe a Data Set Statistically

Statistics is the field of study involving the collection and analysis of data. Percentages are an important tool of descriptive statistics. A percentage tells the number of something expressed per 100. To calculate percentage, you divide a fraction and multiply it by 100. For example, $\frac{3}{4}$ expressed as a percentage is $0.75 \times 100 = 75$ percent.

Imagine you are studying a trait that is controlled by two alleles, Q and q. You are sampling a population to identify the alleles that individuals carry for this trait. There are 80 individuals in the population. There are 20 individuals that have the alleles qq. What percentage of the population has the alleles qq?

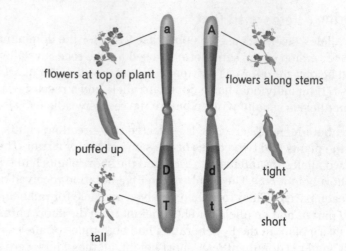

flowers at top of plant
flowers along stems
puffed up
tight
tall
short

The illustration above shows a pair of homologous chromosomes for a pea plant that carries genes for flower position, pea-pod shape, and height. In reality, there would be many more genes along these chromosomes, but this diagram is helpful for learning about the basics of genetics. The shaded areas represent genes. The gene for height, for example, is the shaded area at the bottom end of the chromosomes. Notice that each chromosome has a different allele for height. One chromosome has an allele for tall height (*T*), and the other has an allele for short height (*t*). In other words, the diagram shows visually what is meant by *Tt*.

Homologous Chromosomes Versus Sister Chromatids

Recall that chromosomes replicate before cell division. The replicated chromosome is made up of two sister chromatids, which are exact copies of one another. To understand genetics, it is important to distinguish between homologous chromosomes and sister chromatids. Look at the illustration. On the left you see a pair of homologous chromosomes. They are unreplicated. Homologous chromosomes have the same genes but are not identical, because they may carry different alleles for each gene. Both chromosomes in the homologous pair make exact copies of themselves during replication. After replication, each chromosome is made of two sister chromatids. The sister chromatids of a replicated chromosome are identical copies.

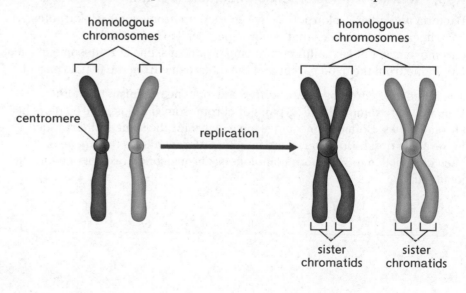

homologous chromosomes
homologous chromosomes
centromere
replication
sister chromatids
sister chromatids

Inheritance and Meiosis

Mendel's observations can be explained by the cellular process of meiosis. Recall that in sexually reproducing organisms, the process of meiosis produces gametes: sperm and eggs. Each gamete contains a unique genetic makeup. Fertilization occurs when sperm and egg combine, resulting in a zygote that divides through mitosis to eventually become a multicellular organism. The inheritance of traits occurs through the physical processes of meiosis and fertilization.

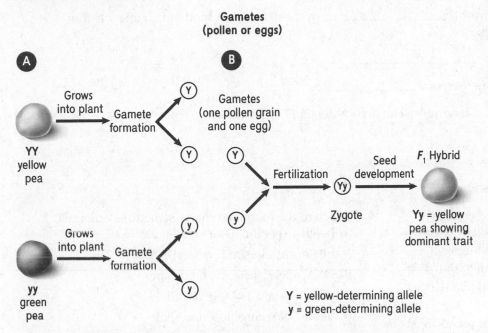

The diagram shows two peas and their color alleles. Each parent plant has two alleles, one on each chromosome within a homologous pair. Each chromosome replicates before meiosis. Meiosis separates each homologous pair and separates the sister chromatids. Only one of the original pair of homologous chromosomes ends up in a single gamete. The parent plant with yellow peas (YY) has Y alleles on both chromosomes; therefore, it only forms gametes with the Y allele. The parent plant with green peas (yy) has y alleles on both chromosomes; therefore, it only forms gametes with the y allele. The Y and y gametes join through fertilization, forming offspring with Yy alleles. All offspring plants have the dominant Y allele, so they will produce yellow peas. In this way, traits are passed from parent to offspring through chromosome movement.

Think about Science

Directions: Answer the following questions.

1. Which alleles does a plant that produces green peas have?

   A. YY C. yY

   B. Yy D. yy

2. Which alleles does a plant that produces yellow peas have?

   A. YY or Yy C. yY or yy

   B. Yy or yy D. yy or Yy

Vocabulary Review

Directions: Write the missing term in the blank.

allele   gene   genetics
heredity   trait   statistics

1. The dominant trait was expressed because the individual carried the dominant _____ .

2. Many scientists use _____ to organize their data.

3. Maria wondered about the patterns of _____ of the disease her mother had and whether Maria was at risk for the same disease.

4. Blood type is an example of a(n) _____ .

5. Most traits are influenced by more than one _____ .

6. Work in a(n) _____ laboratory can involve testing DNA samples.

Skill Review

Directions: Answer the following questions.

1. For Mendel's pea plants, yellow seed color is the dominant trait, and green seed color is the recessive trait. If a pea plant has yellow seed color, what can you infer about the parent plants?

  A. Both the male and female parent plants must have had green seeds.

  B. Both the male and female parent plants must have had yellow seeds.

  C. One parent plant must have had yellow seeds, and the other must have had green seeds.

  D. One parent plant must have had yellow seeds, and the other could have had green or yellow seeds.

2. Which of the following is a genetic trait?

  A. Speaking Spanish

  B. Having five fingers

  C. Having dyed blue hair

  D. The ability to play the piano

3. Compare and contrast homologous chromosomes and sister chromatids.

4. Which of the following shows structures ordered from most specific to most general?

  A. allele, chromosome, gene, DNA

  B. DNA, allele, gene, chromosome

  C. chromosome, DNA, gene, allele

  D. gene, DNA, chromosome, allele

5. Looking at the diagram on page 147, which alleles does a plant that produces yellow peas have?

  A. YY or Yy

  B. Yy or yy

  C. yY or yy

  D. yy or Yy

6. Consider a purple-flowered *(PP)* pea plant and a white-flowered *(pp)* pea plant. Explain how the representations PP and pp relate to genes, chromosomes, and alleles.

7. Consider a purple-flowered *(Pp)* pea plant. Which alleles could this plant pass to its offspring? Explain your answer in the context of meiosis.

Skill Practice

Directions: Use the information to answer questions 1–3.

Human body cells have 23 pairs of homologous chromosomes, for a total of 46 chromosomes. One pair is made of sex chromosomes that determine the sex (male or female) of an individual. The other 22 pairs of chromosomes are called autosomes. They determine traits other than sex. In females, sex chromosomes are described by the letters XX. Females have two X chromosomes. In males, sex chromosomes are described by the letters XY. Males have only one X chromosome and one Y chromosome.

1. Based on the passage, can you tell from which parent you inherited each of your sex chromosomes? Explain your answer.

2. Which statement in the passage explains the function of autosomes?

Directions: Answer the following questions.

3. For Mendel's pea plants, the allele for seed shape is either round *(W)* or wrinkled *(w)*. How would you use letters to represent the alleles of an individual plant that has round seeds? Explain your answer.

4. If you know the allele that is on one of a pair of homologous chromosomes for a particular gene is the allele for the dominant trait, can you tell which allele for the same gene is on the other chromosome in the pair? Explain your answer.

5. When Mendel crossed a tall pea plant with a short pea plant, he found that all the offspring were tall. How can this observation be explained based on today's understanding of genetics?

6. An organism that exhibits a dominant trait must have
   A. no alleles for the recessive trait.
   B. multiple genes for the dominant trait.
   C. one or more alleles for the dominant trait.
   D. no more than one gene for the recessive trait.

7. Seed shape was one of the traits Gregor Mendel studied in pea plants. Seed shape has two forms: round and wrinkled. Mendel crossed a plant with round seeds and a plant with wrinkled seeds. He found that the wrinkled form of the trait disappeared—none of the offspring had wrinkled seeds. How would he have characterized that form of the trait?
   A. as a learned trait
   B. as a heritable trait
   C. as a recessive trait
   D. as a dominant trait

LESSON 4.2 Probability of Traits

LESSON OBJECTIVES

- Identify traits and describe their relationship to alleles
- Analyze the probability of traits using Punnett squares
- Predict the traits of offspring based on the parents
- Analyze multiple traits and other patterns of heredity

CORE SKILLS & PRACTICES

- Use Percents
- Determine the Probability of Events

Key Terms

genotype
the genetic makeup of an organism

monohybrid cross
a mating between two parents that differ in only one trait

phenotype
observable traits in an organism

Punnett square
a chart used to predict the possible genotypes and phenotypes of offspring

Vocabulary

percent
part of one hundred

probability
the likelihood that a certain event will occur

Key Concept
Some traits are inherited. The probability of inheriting a trait can be calculated.

Inheriting Traits

Every person has a set of characteristics, or physical traits, that allows you to identify that person. Height and hair color are two of these traits. Specific examples of these physical traits, such as blond hair or short height, are called the **phenotype** of the person.

Alleles and Traits

The genetic makeup of an organism is called its **genotype.** This genetic makeup involves combinations of alleles, or different forms of a gene, that influence an organism's phenotype. Pairs of alleles make up the genotype that controls the expression of a trait. For example, a pea plant that has a tall phenotype could have the genotype *TT*. However, because the allele for tallness is dominant, the tall pea plant could also have one allele that codes for tallness *(T)* and another masked, or recessive, allele that codes for shortness *(t)*. In this case, the genotype of the pea plant would be *Tt*.

A pea plant that has a short phenotype must have two recessive alleles, so it would have the genotype *tt*. An organism with the same two alleles for a trait (for example, *TT* or *tt*) is homozygous for that trait. An organism with two different alleles for a trait (for example, *Tt*) is heterozygous for that trait.

Some human traits, such as the type of earwax a person has, are determined by just two alleles—one dominant and one recessive. However, most human traits are controlled by multiple alleles or by multiple genes. The color of hair you have, for example, is such a trait. Traits are also influenced by environmental conditions.

© Sam Edwards/age fotostock

Think about Science

Directions: Answer the following questions.

Dark purple flowers *(P)* are dominant in pea plants, and white flowers *(p)* are recessive.

1. What is the flower phenotype for a pea plant with the genotype *Pp?*

    A. All white flowers
    B. All dark purple flowers
    C. Flowers of both colors
    D. All light purple flowers

2. If a pea plant has dark purple flowers, what could be its genotype?

    A. *PP* only
    B. *Pp* only
    C. *pp* only
    D. *PP* or *Pp*

CORE SKILL

Use Percents

Construct a Punnett square that shows a cross between a pea plant with yellow seeds *(Yy)* and a pea plant with green seeds *(yy)*. Then use percents to examine the predictions from the Punnett square. What is the percent chance that an offspring will have yellow seeds? What is the percent chance that an offspring will have green seeds?

Punnett Squares

A **Punnett square** shows how the alleles for one or more traits could combine during a cross, or mating, of two parents to produce specific genotypes and phenotypes in the offspring, the individuals of the next generation. Punnett squares are useful for predicting the probabilities of genotypes for traits that have dominant-recessive inheritance.

Using Punnett Squares

To use a Punnett square for a **monohybrid cross,** a mating between two parents that differ in only one trait, draw a box with four squares in it. Place the genotype for one parent across the top. Place the genotype for the other parent down the side. Then fill in the boxes, placing the corresponding allele from each column and row in each box. The combinations of alleles in the boxes represent the possible genotypes of the offspring. The Punnett square here shows all possible genotypes for the offspring of a cross between two tall parent pea plants, each with the genotype *Tt*. The following symbols represent this cross: *Tt* × *Tt*. According to the Punnett square, the offspring from this cross could have the *TT*, *Tt*, or *tt* genotype. Those with the *TT* or *Tt* genotype would have the dominant phenotype, which is tall height. Those with the *tt* genotype would have the recessive phenotype, which is short height.

Cross Between Two Heterozygous Tall Pea Plants

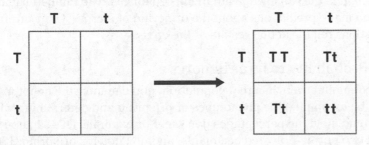

Percents

Once a Punnett square is completed, you know the possible genotypes of the offspring. You can then describe these genotypes using percents. A **percent** describes a part of 100. For example, 50 percent means 50 out of 100. In the Punnett square shown here, one out of four boxes has the *TT* genotype. Other ways to write "one out of four" are *one-fourth* and $\frac{1}{4}$. A fraction can be written as a percent. The fraction $\frac{1}{4}$ is equal to 25 percent, so you can predict that there is a 25 percent chance that an offspring will have the *TT* genotype.

Probability of Traits

Probability

You calculate probability the same way you calculate percentages. If a trait is predicted for one out of four offspring, you press $1 \div 4$ on your calculator and get 0.25. Then press $\times$ and 100 to find the percent probability, which is 25 percent. What is the probability of a trait that is predicted for three out of 16 offspring?

The same is true for the *tt* genotype. Half of the boxes, or two out of four, have the *Tt* genotype. The fraction $\frac{2}{4}$ is the same as the fraction $\frac{1}{2}$, and this fraction is equal to 50 percent.

Now think about the phenotypes of the offspring. A plant will be tall if it inherits one dominant allele. Three of the four boxes, written as a fraction as $\frac{3}{4}$, or 75 percent, include a dominant allele. Therefore, there is a 75 percent probability that an offspring will be tall and a 25 percent probability that an offspring will be short.

⤴ Think about Science

Directions: Answer the following questions.

1. Construct a Punnett square for a cross between a pea plant with purple flowers *(Pp)* and a pea plant with white flowers *(pp)*. How many boxes in the Punnett square show the genotype *pp?*

   A. 1 box   C. 3 boxes
   B. 2 boxes   D. 4 boxes

2. A pea plant with yellow seeds *(YY)* is crossed with a pea plant with green seeds *(yy)*. What is the percent chance that an offspring would have green seeds?

   A. 0 percent   C. 50 percent
   B. 25 percent   D. 100 percent

Predicting Traits

Do the percents you found mean that if two plants produce 100 offspring, exactly 25 will be short? No, they do not. Punnett squares help you predict the **probability**, which means the likelihood, that particular combinations of alleles will be produced. The actual outcome may be higher or lower than the predicted number. As an example, think about flipping a coin. When you flip a coin, it might land heads-up or tails-up. The probability that the coin will land heads-up is one out of two, which is 50 percent. You can predict that if you flip a coin 10 times, it will land heads-up 50 percent of the time, which is five times. If you then go ahead and flip a coin 10 times, it may land heads-up one time, four times, eight times, or even 10 times. The result is a matter of chance. It is the same way with living organisms. The Punnett square helps you make predictions about the offspring of a cross. Only careful observations tell the actual results of the cross.

Using Probability to Infer Genotype

When examining traits in a real population, you can infer the genotype of parents by examining the phenotypes of offspring and determining which cross would yield the percentages you see. For example, let's say you crossed two purple-flowered pea plants, and you got 462 offspring: 120 with white flowers and 342 with purple flowers. When you determine the percentage of each type of flower, you have 26 percent with white flowers and 74 percent with purple flowers. This is close to the 75 percent and 25 percent you predict when you cross two plants that are heterozygous for the trait. Therefore the genotypes of the parents are most likely *Pp* and *Pp*.

Multiple Traits and Other Patterns of Heredity

You can sometimes use a Punnett square to find the probability of multiple traits. In a dihybrid cross, two traits are crossed at the same time. You must use a larger Punnett square of 16 squares to accommodate all the possible combinations of the two traits. The Punnett square shown here predicts allele combinations in offspring for the human traits of freckles and earwax. Wet earwax *(W)* is associated with a dominant allele, as are freckles *(F)*.

	WF	Wf	wF	wf
WF	WWFF	WWFf	WwFF	WwFf
Wf	WWFf	WWff	WwFf	Wwff
wF	WwFF	WwFf	wwFF	wwFf
wf	WwFf	Wwff	wwFf	wwff

wet earwax, freckled: 9;
wet earwax, not freckled: 3;
dry earwax, freckled: 3;
dry earwax, not freckled: 1.
Ratio: 9:3:3:1

Sometimes traits are determined by genes on sex chromosomes, or the X and Y chromosomes that determine gender. Genetic females carry two X chromosomes. Genetic males carry one X and one Y chromosome. Traits that are determined by sex chromosomes are known as sex-linked traits.

One sex-linked trait is color blindness. People who are color blind cannot see the difference between certain colors such as red and green. Red-green color blindness is caused by a recessive allele carried on the X chromosome. Because it is a recessive trait, a female will be color-blind only if she receives the allele for color blindness from both parents. A female who carries an allele for a disorder but does not exhibit the disorder is considered to be a carrier of that disorder. Because males have only one X chromosome, if a male inherits the allele for color blindness on the X chromosome he receives from his mother, he will be color-blind.

Punnett squares can be used to predict the genotypes of offspring for traits that have multiple alleles. For example, the ABO blood group gene has three alleles—I^A, I^B, and i—that combine in pairs to form the different blood types A, AB, B, and O. Instead of three possible genotypes (as in dominant-recessive inheritance), the ABO blood-group inheritance has six possible genotypes: I^AI^A, I^AI^B, I^BI^B, I^Ai, I^Bi, and ii.

⌁ Think about Science

Directions: Answer the following question.

1. If two people with no freckles and dry earwax have a child, what is the probability that the child would have the same phenotype as the parents?

   A. 0 percent   C. 56 percent

   B. 25 percent   D. 100 percent

Determine the Probability of Events

Probability measures the likelihood that some event will occur. Geneticists use probability to determine how likely a person will inherit a specific disease or a trait like eye color. Look at the table that shows the dihybrid cross. Determine the probability of each of the phenotypes listed next to the table.

Vocabulary Review

Directions: Write the missing term in the blank.

genotype   monohybrid cross   percent

phenotype   probability   Punnett square

1. A _____ is part of 100.

2. The appearance of an organism is its _____ .

3. A _____ allows you to predict the percent chance of each genotype from a cross.

4. A dihybrid cross considers two traits, and a _____ considers one.

5. A _____ is a combination of alleles for a particular trait.

6. Males have a higher _____ for color blindness than females overall.

Skill Review

Directions: Answer the following questions.

1. How many boxes are in the Punnett square used for a monohybrid cross?

A. 4

B. 8

C. 16

D. 32

2. Smooth *(S)* and wrinkled *(s)* seeds are two phenotypes of pea plants. In a cross between two pea plants with wrinkled seeds *(ss)*, what is the probability that offspring will have smooth seeds?

A. 0 percent

B. 25 percent

C. 50 percent

D. 75 percent

3. Which option shows the possible genotype(s) in a cross between two smooth-seed pea plants, one with the *Ss* genotype and the other with the *SS* genotype?

A. *SS* only

B. *SS* and *Ss*

C. *Ss* only

D. *Ss* and *ss*

4. How are percent and probability related?

5. Use one of your own traits to describe how phenotype and genotype are related.

6. If a color-blind woman had a male child, why would you know that he would be color-blind?

7. A cross between a white-flowered pea plant *(pp)* and a purple-flowered pea plant *(Pp)* produces 145 offspring. What is the most likely number of white-flowered offspring produced, according to probability?

A. 31   C. 102

B. 69   D. 145

8. What is the probability that a male with normal vision and a female carrier for color blindness will have a male child that is color-blind?

A. 0 percent   C. 50 percent

B. 25 percent   D. 75 percent

9. What is the probability that you will get heads each time you flip a coin?

A. 25 percent   C. 75 percent

B. 50 percent   D. 100 percent

Skill Practice

Directions: Use the Punnett square to answer questions 1–4.

female parent

	B	b
B	**BB** brown offspring	**Bb** brown offspring
b	**Bb** brown offspring	**bb** blue offspring

male parent

1. What color of eyes does each parent represented by the chart have?

   A. Both have blue eyes.

   B. Both have brown eyes.

   C. Female has blue, and male has brown.

   D. Female has brown, and male has blue.

2. Suppose a child born to this couple has blue eyes. What gene pair must this child have received?

   A. *Bb*

   B. *bB*

   C. *BB*

   D. *bb*

3. Suppose the couple represented by the chart has four children. Which is the least likely possibility for eye color of the children?

   A. four brown

   B. three brown, one blue

   C. two brown, two blue

   D. one brown, three blue

4. What is the probability that a child of these parents will have the *Bb* genotype?

   A. 10 percent

   B. 25 percent

   C. 50 percent

   D. 75 percent

Directions: Answer the following questions.

5. What is the probability that a woman who is a carrier for color blindness and a man who is color-blind will have a daughter who is color-blind? Use a Punnett square to determine your answer.

6. A genetic counselor is talking to a couple about the different phenotypes that could occur if they have children. The counselor collects information from the couple about the occurrence of color blindness in their extended family. Why would the counselor need to know which family members were color-blind in order to determine the probability of this phenotype?

LESSON OBJECTIVES

- Describe Darwin's theory of evolution
- Discuss how cladograms help analyze specie relationships

CORE SKILLS & PRACTICES

- Make Inferences
- Evaluate Whether a Conclusion or Theory is Supported or Challenged by Particular Data or Evidence

Key Terms

ancestry
the lineage or bloodline of descendants

cladograms
diagrams that show the relationships of organisms

evolution
change in living organisms over long periods of time

Vocabulary

arrange
to move or organize into a particular order or position

fossil
the preserved remains of an organism

species
distinct group of organisms that can produce live offspring

Key Concept

The Theory of Universal Common Ancestry suggests that all organisms on Earth evolved from a single common ancestor. Scientists construct diagrams and charts to show how seemingly diverse species share common traits.

Darwin and Evolution

For centuries, scientists have been posing questions about the origin of life on Earth. In 1859, the English naturalist Charles Darwin published *On the Origin of Species,* which provided sound logic and evidence about how organisms change over time. Darwin proposed a theory that all forms of life developed gradually from different, and often much simpler, parent organisms. He proposed that weaker, or less adaptable, members of a population died without reproducing and that the strongest members of the population passed on traits to the next generation.

Scientists have since confirmed that each population of organisms undergoes changes over time, and this process is what scientists call **evolution.** Within a population, a small group of individuals can become isolated from the rest of the population. Over many generations, the isolated group may evolve different traits than those within the original population of organisms. If an isolated group becomes so different that it is no longer able to reproduce with the original population, it is then considered a new species. A **species** is a distinct group of organisms that can reproduce only with each other to produce live offspring. These ideas all became part of Darwin's famous theory of evolution by natural selection.

Fossils

Scientists are able to find evidence of evolution when examining fossils. A **fossil** is the preserved remains of an organism that was once living. When an organism dies, the soft parts of it decay, but the harder parts are left behind. Over many years, layers of sediment build up over the dead organism. As sediment builds up, pressure, along with chemical changes, causes the sediment to harden into rock. This type of rock forms layers that represent different geologic time periods and is known as sedimentary rock.

Other fossils formed when insects or small animals were trapped in tree sap or ice. A fossil can be part of the organism itself, such as bones, teeth, or shells, or it can also be a trace of an organism, such as an imprint of a leaf or a footprint. A fossil can even be something left behind by an organism, such as animal droppings.

Fossils provide a snapshot of life on Earth over time, and they reveal that life on Earth has changed over time. Fossil evidence showed scientists that new species appeared at different points in time, which strongly supported Darwin's theory of evolution.

Think about Science

Directions: Answer the following questions.

1. Two organisms that can produce live offspring are considered to be the same _____.

2. List two species that are similar and that you think may have evolved from a single species into two distinct species.

The Theory of Universal Common Ancestry

In Darwin's publication *On the Origin of Species*, he also proposed that all organisms that have ever lived on Earth descended from a single primitive ancestor. An ancestor is an organism that lived in the past and produced offspring. These offspring produced another generation of offspring, and this continues with every new generation. When we look at the **ancestry** of a person or an organism, we look at the whole line of descendants coming from a single parent. Thus, Darwin's theory became known as the Theory of Universal Common Ancestry (UCA). This theory was difficult for people to accept because it suggested that an oak tree, a caterpillar, a dog, and a human all originated from a common ancestor. During Darwin's lifetime, there was no clear way to test his theory.

Evaluate Whether a Conclusion or Theory is Supported or Challenged by Particular Data or Evidence

Scientific theories typically form over many decades and are based on the work of many scientists. A scientific theory is something that is widely accepted in the scientific community. New evidence can result in a modification of an existing theory, but most theories stand the test of time.

Research Darwin's voyage to the Galápagos Islands. Find information about the species he studied there and the evidence he gathered to formulate his ideas about evolution. Pose an argument in which you maintain that the evidence Darwin collected either supports or challenges the modern theory of evolution. Give at least three supporting facts in your argument.

Making Inferences

You make an inference when you use facts from a diagram or text and what you already know from your own experiences to make an educated guess about something not included in the text. Study the cladogram on the opposite page. Next, write a brief paragraph explaining the relationship between the species in the diagram. Include the traits that are the same and different and what might have happened to cause the species to diverge from one another.

It is easy to see how people in the same family are related or even how two different dog breeds might be related, but it is very difficult to see evidence that a human is related to bacteria. Long after Darwin's UCA theory was proposed, scientists developed a quantitative large-scale test for the relatedness of species. With this test, they have found that evidence in the natural world overwhelmingly supports UCA. Scientific evidence links all three domains of life: Eukarya (humans, animals, plants, yeast), Bacteria, and Archaea. Scientists can now link every known organism back to a single common ancestor. However, what this universal ancestor looks like and where it lived are still questions unanswered by scientists. The most current hypothesis is that the first form of life on Earth was a simple, single-celled organism that lived in water.

Think about Science

Directions: Answer the following questions.

1. The theory of Universal Common Ancestry states that

    A. all humans are related to each other.
    B. all life originated from a single organism.
    C. all life has slowly changed over time.
    D. all species that look similar are related to each other.

2. What evidence has scientists found to support UCA?

Cladograms

The evolutionary relationship of organisms can be studied using a method called cladistics. Cladistics is the systematic method for making and testing predictions about evolutionary relationships among organisms. Organisms are organized into groups, or clades, and every member of a clade shares the same evolutionary history. Therefore species in a clade have more in common with each other than they do with species of another clade. Also, the members of a clade share a unique group of characteristics that did not exist among their distant ancestors. This type of categorization of organisms assumes that new species arise when an existing species is split into two or more isolated groups. It also assumes that all organisms continue to change over time.

Scientist can describe the evolutionary relationship between species by using a diagram. These diagrams, called **cladograms,** show where traits diverge over time. To build a cladogram for a group of species, you need to rely on research and evidence collected by scientists about each species. To construct a cladogram, follow four simple steps:

- First, choose a group of organisms to compare. As an example, let's look at the relationship between the squid, the frog, the carp, the eagle, the whale, and the cow.
- Next, construct a table with the name of each organism across the top and some structural features you want to compare listed in the first column.

	Squid	Carp	Frog	Eagle	Whale	Cow
Produces eggs	X	X	X	X	X	X
Has a backbone		X	X	X	X	X
Has lungs			X	X	X	X
Warm-blooded				X	X	X
Gives birth to live young					X	X

- After the table is complete, group together the organisms that share the same traits within concentric circles as shown.

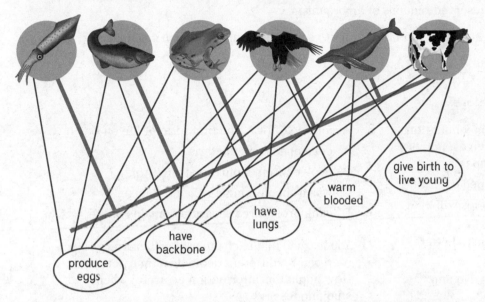

- Finally, now that you have an idea about how these species are the same and how they are different, draw a cladogram as follows.

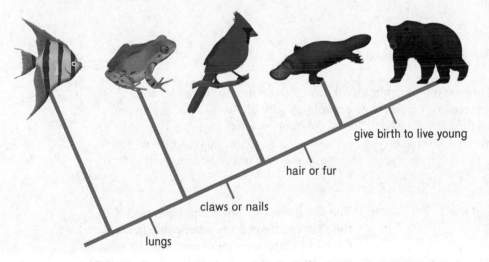

All the organisms that branch off to the right of a trait have that trait, and those that lie to the left of a trait do not have that trait. In this way, you can see where species diverge from one another. You can also see which species are more closely related to each other.

TECHNOLOGY SKILL

Use Internet Resources

It is important to have a focus when you begin researching a topic on the Internet. You also need to be aware of which types of sources are reliable. Always try to find other sources to validate the information you read.

Choose four different species to research on the Internet. Then choose five structural features and determine whether they are included in the organisms you have chosen to study. To **arrange** means to move things into a particular order or position. To organize the data you gather for each species, arrange it in a table similar to the one on this page. Then construct a cladogram to see how each species relates to the others.

Vocabulary Review

Directions: Write the missing term in the blank.

ancestry	arrange	cladogram
evolution	fossil	species

1. When we examine the _____ of an organism, we examine the whole line of descendants.

2. A(n) _____ is a diagram of the evolutionary relationship of organisms.

3. A group of organisms that produce live, fertile offspring is called a _____.

4. The theory of _____ was that living organisms will change over time.

5. A(n) _____ is a preserved remains of an organism.

6. It is useful to _____ data in a table in order to see relationships between organisms.

Skill Review

Directions: Answer the following questions.

1. If organisms in a population pass on a mutation that makes them better able to survive a hot, dry climate, which is most likely to happen?

   A. The species will remain unchanged over time.

   B. Only a few survivors of the species will live in hot, dry climates.

   C. The species will evolve over time to better survive in the desert.

   D. The species will evolve to survive in any climate.

2. Which two theories did Darwin develop that help scientists better understand the history of species?

3. According to UCA, the first form of life on Earth

   A. developed from bacteria.

   B. evolved from a universal ancestor.

   C. was a simple, single-celled organism.

   D. came from three separate domains of life.

4. You learned that each layer of sedimentary rock represents a different geological time period. How might this information be useful when studying fossils?

Directions: Use the information to answer questions 5 and 6.

The fossil record is not the only evidence that supports evolution. Scientists also consider the structures of the bodies of living things. For example, most animals with backbones have two pairs of limbs. Each kind of limb, such as forelimbs, has a different function. A whale uses its forelimbs to swim through the water. A crocodile uses them to swim and also to move on land. A bird uses its forelimbs to fly. Despite the different functions, the basic arrangement of bones is similar in each of these animals' forelimbs.

5. What do variations in the function of the forelimbs of each species suggest?

   A. The physical characteristics are a response to behavioral changes.

   B. Each organism has physically adapted to environmental challenges.

   C. All living things have the ability to alter their structure in order to survive.

   D. Surprising similarities exist among organisms at the early stages of development.

6. The forelimbs of each animal mentioned in the passage represents a heritable [genetic OR trait] variation due to mutation or sexual reproduction. Explain how these variations provide evidence that supports the theory of evolution.

Skill Practice

Directions: Answer the following questions.

1. Using the species and traits in the cladogram below, finish the cladogram according to what traits you think each organism possesses.

	Angelfish	Frog	Cardinal	Platypus	Brown bear
Lungs					
Claws or nails					
hair or fur					
Gives birth to live young					

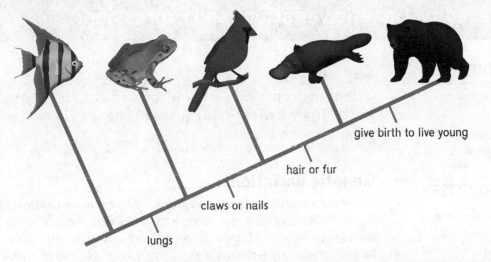

give birth to live young

hair or fur

claws or nails

lungs

2. The "blueprint" that provides the information for how all organisms look is found in a chemical in the body called DNA. DNA was discovered in 1953 by two scientists named Watson and Crick. How can the discovery of the genetic material DNA help scientists gather evidence for the Theory of Evolution?

3. An adaptation is a change in a species that makes it better suited for its environment. How do adaptations in a species help promote evolution? Explain your answer.

LESSON 4.4 Heredity: Genetic Variations and Expression

LESSON OBJECTIVES

- Identify sources of heritable genetic variation
- Explain how the environment affects genetic expression

CORE SKILLS & PRACTICES

- Make Predictions Based upon Data or Evidence
- Cite Textual Evidence

Key Terms

crossing over
the process in which DNA from the father and DNA from the mother are exchanged

DNA replication
the process in which an extra copy of DNA is made

epigenetics
the study of how the chemicals that are not part of the DNA sequence affect the expression of genes

genetic recombination
the redistribution of genes during meiosis

mutation
a random change that occurs in the DNA of a cell

Vocabulary

assess
to make a judgment about

Key Concept

Offspring from sexual reproduction have a unique set of traits. There are various causes of changes in traits from one generation to the next.

Genetic Variation

Think for a moment about the variation of human and animal species on Earth. Millions of different species as well as individuals within one species can show a variety of traits. Humans have different eye colors, hair colors, heights, and shapes. Animals also have a large variety of traits. Dogs, for example, can be very small like a Chihuahua or very large like a Great Dane. They have different fur colors, patterns, and shapes. This tremendous variation can be traced back to genes, the expression of genes, and the interaction of genes and the environment.

Mitosis and Meiosis

You learned about mitosis and meiosis in Chapter 3. Recall that mitosis is the process in which one cell divides into two cells with the same genetic information. These two cells have the same number of chromosomes as the original cell. Recall that meiosis is the process in which one cell is divided into four cells. These cells are gametes, sperm or egg cells. Gametes have half as many chromosomes as the original cell and have genetic information that is different from the original cell.

Crossing Over

Genetic recombination, or the redistribution of genes in cells, is what causes gametes to have different genetic information. An additional source of genetic variation occurs during Prophase I of meiosis, when DNA from the male parent and DNA from the female parent exchange parts of chromosomes in a process called **crossing over**. This process is shown in the illustration. Crossing over results in each gamete—egg cell or sperm cell—receiving new combinations of genes. Genetic recombination leads to an increase in the variety of traits within a population.

Crossing Over

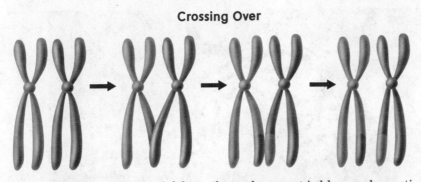

In this diagram, genetic material from the male parent is blue, and genetic material from the female parent is pink. When the two chromosomes cross over, genetic material from each parent detaches and then attaches to the opposite parent's chromosome. This gives each set of chromosomes a different combination of genes.

Replication

Before mitosis or meiosis occurs, an extra copy of DNA is made in a process called **DNA replication.** During DNA replication, the two strands of a DNA molecule separate from one another in a process that is similar to the unzipping of a zipper. The "teeth" of the zipper are nucleotides. DNA is made up of four different nucleotides defined by the following bases:

- adenine (A)
- guanine (G)
- cytosine (C)
- thymine (T)

These pair up with one another according to base pairing rules: A pairs with T, and C pairs with G. During replication, new bases attach to each separated strand of DNA, according to the base pairing rules. For example, if the base on the old strand was adenine (A), the rule requires the base thymine (T) to attach to it. The process results in two exact copies of the original DNA molecule. The key enzyme responsible for DNA replication is called DNA polymerase.

DNA Replication

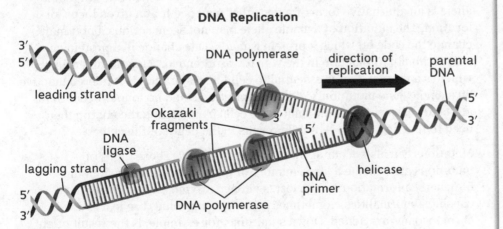

Mutation

A **mutation** is a random change that occurs in the genetic material of a cell. Mutations can be caused by errors that occur during replication, or other normal processes related to genetic material. Environmental sources, including electromagnetic radiation with high energy, such as ultraviolet light or x-rays; radiation of particles from radioactive materials or nuclear reactions; and chemicals that react readily also cause mutations.

21ST CENTURY SKILL

Communicate Information

Clear communication is important in any setting. How you communicate information affects whether others understand your message. Research a genetic disorder, such as cystic fibrosis, and think about how you might communicate what you learn to others. Consider that the way you communicate information could depend on your target audience. For example, you would communicate to a group of elementary school students in a different way than you would to a group of adults. Similarly you would explain the cystic fibrosis to a group of people who are familiar with genetics in a different way than you would to a group of people who are unfamiliar with genetics. What other factors might you consider when you communicate information?

Heredity: Genetic Variations and Expression

Make Predictions Based upon Data or Evidence

Search for data on the Internet or in a library about how gender and race affect the incidence of genetic mutations that cause red-green color blindness. Predict how many people in your community might be at risk for red-green color blindness.

A white tiger is a Bengal tiger that has a recessive mutation in the gene for color. The several hundred white tigers that exist today can be traced back to the same tiger caught years ago in India.

Mutations are copied during the process of replication and are passed down to daughter cells during mitosis. This means the number of cells that have the mutation will multiply. Cancer cells pass along mutated DNA in this way. Mutations occurring from mitotic division affect body cells, not gametes. Therefore they do not get passed to offspring.

Mutations can also occur in gametes—egg or sperm cells. If one of these cells is combined in a fertilized egg, all the cells of the new individual will have the mutated DNA. Mutations in the gametes often result in serious diseases, such as cystic fibrosis.

Mutations may occur in a single allele—one form of a gene. Recall that an allele is an alternative form of a gene that may occur at a given locus, or location. The mutation of a single allele may not seem serious, but it may change the code by which a protein is made. One change in a protein can stop its ability to function in the way it was intended. Suppose an enzyme, which is a protein, that is essential to cellular respiration is rendered inactive by a single gene mutation. Cellular respiration could no longer occur in the affected cells, which would inhibit the cells from getting the energy they need to function. This eventually results in the death of the cells.

Mutations can also occur at the chromosome level. These types of mutations can change a large number of genes at once. Large amounts of genetic information can be lost, switched around, or duplicated, causing abnormalities. Sometimes entire chromosomes are lost or extra chromosomes are added. Down syndrome, for example, is the result of an extra copy of chromosome 21.

Think about Science

Directions: Answer the following questions.

1. How does crossing over create genetic variation?
2. What are some things that cause mutations?

Heredity: Genetic Variations and Expression

Genetic Expression and the Environment

Having a particular gene does not always mean that gene will be expressed in that individual. Many cellular processes regulate gene expression. Some genes become active only under certain environmental conditions. For example, the color of the light a certain butterfly is exposed to as a caterpillar determines the intensity of the color of its wings as an adult.

Additionally characteristics of individuals are not simply the result of inheritance but may be strongly influenced by their environment. A person's body weight may be affected by his or her genetics. However, a diet and exercise can also influence a person's body weight. Although hair color may be inherited, it can also be changed through chemical processes and sunlight.

Chemical Environment

The chemical environment of the cell can have an effect on the cellular reactions in which DNA is involved, and, particularly, in the expression of genes. **Epigenetics** is the study of how the chemicals that are not part of the DNA sequence affect the expression of genes (phenotype). For example, the foods we eat, the things we do, and how we feel have an effect on the chemicals in our body. These chemicals can cause genes to be expressed and repress expression of genes. So, in a very direct way, our environment can affect our physical characteristics.

Genetic Testing

Genetic testing is a group of procedures performed on blood or other biological tissue to find genetic variations related to disease. Genetic testing may reveal the risk a person has of developing a particular disease, but not whether a person will actually develop the disease. Developing the actual disease often depends on environmental factors. One type of genetic test is used to determine if certain genes have mutations that increase the risk of breast cancer. Whether cancer actually develops depends on the interaction of genes with the environment.

As genetic testing becomes more common, people are faced with some difficult choices. Some couples may be faced with the decision of whether they should have children if there is a chance they could pass on a specific disease to them. Genetic counselors are medical professionals who help people understand their risks of heritable disease and help them consider their options when faced with these decisions.

⤨ Think about Science

Directions: Answer the following questions.

1. How can the food we eat affect genetic expression?
   A. It causes gene mutations.
   B. It causes replication errors.
   C. It changes when crossing over occurs.
   D. It changes the chemicals in our cells.

2. What is one benefit of genetic testing?
   A. You can find out if you will get a particular disease.
   B. You can find out how to prevent a particular disease.
   C. You can find out all the diseases you will get.
   D. You can find out if you are at risk for a particular disease.

Cite Textual Evidence

Find an article in a science magazine or an encyclopedia about a genetic mutation, such as fragile X syndrome. Write an essay to **assess,** or make a judgment about, whether the evidence given in the text supports the author's claim. Be sure to cite the textual evidence in your essay.

Vocabulary Review

Directions: Write the missing term in the blank.

assess	crossing over	epigenetics
genetic recombination	mutation	replication

1. The process in which DNA from the male parent and DNA from the female parent exchange chromosomes is called _____ .

2. A(n) _____ is a random change that occurs in the genetic material of a cell.

3. _____ is the redistribution of genes in a cell.

4. _____ is the study of how the chemicals that are not part of the DNA sequence affect the expression of genes.

5. You _____ when you make a judgment about something.

6. _____ is the process in which an extra copy of DNA is made.

Skill Review

Directions: Answer the following questions.

1. What are the results of replication?
   A. mutations
   B. a strand of RNA
   C. genetic variation
   D. two exact copies of DNA

2. Which is most likely the cause of one kind of faulty protein?
   A. crossing over
   B. a missing chromosome
   C. an additional chromosome
   D. mutation of a single gene

3. When does crossing over occur?
   A. during DNA replication
   B. during Prophase I of meiosis
   C. during Metaphase II of meiosis
   D. during Metaphase I of mitosis

4. Identical twins develop from a single zygote (a cell formed by the union of two gametes) and share the same genes. Suppose both carry the trait for skin cancer, yet only one develops skin cancer later in life. Explain this, using the ideas proposed by epigenetics.

5. One gene in a cell is mutated before replication occurs. This cell then goes through the process of meiosis. How many of the four resulting gametes will have the mutated gene?
   A. None of them.
   B. One of them.
   C. Half of them.
   D. All of them.

6. Which gene expression is best explained by epigenetics?
   A. eye color
   B. physical height
   C. reading disability
   D. childhood diabetes

Skill Practice

Directions: Answer the following questions.

1. Which disease is the result of an extra chromosome?

   A. cancer

   B. HIV

   C. sickle-cell anemia

   D. Down syndrome

2. Explain the different effects a mutation in a regular cell will have versus a mutation in a gamete (egg or sperm cell) and why one effect might be more serious than the other.

3. Why might people *not* want to be genetically tested?

   A. The test may change their DNA.

   B. They may not want to prevent disease.

   C. They may fear what they will find out.

   D. The test may change their phenotype.

4. Explain why crossing over is important.

5. The coloring of Siamese cats is the result of a mutation of an enzyme involved in the production of pigment. This mutation causes the enzyme not to function at temperatures equal to or higher than normal body temperature. Based on this information, what do you think are the coldest parts of a Siamese cat?

   A. body

   B. body and ears

   C. ears, nose, body, tail

   D. ears, tail, feet nose

Directions: Use the information to answer questions 6 and 7.

Scientists use cloning to alter the natural processes of heredity. Cloning involves one parent producing genetically identical offspring. To produce a clone of a mammal, scientists obtain an egg cell from a donor organism. They then remove the nucleus, and therefore the DNA, from the cell. The next step is to take a cell from the adult being cloned. The nucleus from this cell is fused into the egg cell. The result is a complete cell that can divide. Once the single cell divides into a ball of cells, it is placed inside a host mother. There it develops normally into an offspring that is genetically identical to the original.

6. Why might a clone be different from the original organism? Explain your reasoning.

7. What can scientists do to help ensure a clone is genetically identical to its parent? Justify your answer.

LESSON 4.5 Selection and Adaptation

LESSON OBJECTIVES

- Explain the process of natural selection and describe artificial selection
- Describe different types of adaptations

CORE SKILLS & PRACTICES

- Reconcile Multiple Findings, Conclusions, or Theories
- Draw Conclusions

Key Terms

adaptation
any trait that helps an organism survive and reproduce

artificial selection
the process by which humans breed other animals and plants for particular traits

natural selection
a process by which organisms that are best adapted to their environment tend to survive

speciation
the evolutionary process when new biological species arise

Vocabulary

example
an illustration of a rule, method, or topic

variations
different characteristics that can help a species survive

Key Concept

Through natural selection, adaptations evolve. Natural selection explains how species change over time and new species arise.

Natural Selection

Charles Darwin was a naturalist who, from 1831 to 1836, traveled around the world on the sailing ship the HMS *Beagle*. Throughout the trip he collected fossils and made detailed observations about the types of plants and animals he saw, as well as the habitats in which they lived.

Darwin's travels took him to a group of small islands off the west coast of South America known as the Galápagos Islands. Although the individual islands are relatively close to one another, they have different climates and different species of plants. Darwin observed that some islands were hot and dry with few plants, while others received more rainfall and had a larger variety of plants. Darwin collected information about many species of organisms. In particular, he made extensive observations of giant tortoises that lived on the islands. Darwin noticed that the shells of the tortoises were different on each island. For example, one type of tortoise, the saddleback tortoise, had a long neck and a curved shell, while a tortoise on a different island, the domed tortoise, had a shorter neck and a shell that looked like a dome.

In addition, Darwin observed 13 different species of finches, a type of small bird. Each species of finch had a different-shaped beak. The shape of the beak was related to the type of food available on the island where the bird lived.

geospiza parvula   certhidea olivacea   geospiza fortis   geospiza magnirostris

These are some of the finches Darwin observed on the Galápagos Islands. Notice how their beaks are different. The shape of the beak is related to the food available where each finch lives.

Lissa Harrison

Darwin's Theory

After returning to his home in England, Darwin spent many years trying to explain the observations he had made. In 1859, Darwin presented his theory called **natural selection** in a book titled *On the Origin of Species by Means of Natural Selection.* It is based on the idea that most organisms produce more offspring than are able to survive. The offspring must compete with each other for food, water, and space. Some offspring have **variations,** or traits, that will make them better able to survive. These variations can be inherited and are known as favorable variations. Organisms that inherit favorable variations are said to be more "fit" than others.

Those organisms that are fit are more likely to live to reproduce (this is sometimes known as survival of the fittest). When organisms survive to reproduce, they pass the favorable variations on to their offspring. Over time, the favorable variations are found in more and more members of the species. In this way, the traits of a species evolve. Sometimes the changes are so great that a new species is formed. This evolutionary process by which new biological species arise is called **speciation.** Natural selection can be used to explain changes in most species over time.

① In nature, organisms produce more offspring than can survive. Fishes, for example, can sometimes lay millions of eggs.

② In any population, individuals have variations. Fishes, for example, may differ in color, size, and speed.

③ Individuals with certain useful variations, such as speed, survive in their environment, passing those variations to the next generation.

④ Over time, offspring with certain variations make up most of the population and may look entirely different from their ancestors.

Artificial selection is the process by which humans breed other animals and plants for particular traits. In his book, Darwin discussed how selective breeding produces change over time, using examples of selective breeding of pigeons, cats, cattle, and dogs. Use of selective breeding to produce plant and animal strains is common in agriculture. Darwin used selective-breeding changes to support his theory of natural selection.

Think about Science

Directions: Answer the following question.

1. Why might farmers use artificial selection when they plant crops from one year to the next?

Reconcile Multiple Findings, Conclusions, or Theories

If several scientists are conducting research on the same question, they will sometimes obtain results that differ. To reconcile those findings, scientists will try to understand how two different facts or ideas can be true at the same time.

How do you think Darwin interpreted the 13 different types of beaks the finches had? How might a beak be different depending on the type of food a species of finch eats?

Adaptations

The theory of natural selection explains what Darwin observed about tortoises and finches. Darwin suggested, for example, that all the tortoises evolved from a common ancestor. The domed tortoise, which generally has a short neck and a shell that does not allow it to stretch its neck easily, was found on an island with plenty of plants. It didn't need to stretch its neck to reach food, so it thrived on this island.

The saddleback tortoise lived in a dry habitat with fewer plants. It needed to stretch to reach taller plants. In this environment, tortoises with long necks and shells that were open around the legs and neck were favored by natural selection. As a result, they were more likely to survive and reproduce. Over many generations, the adaptations—a saddleback shell and a long neck—increased within this species. An **adaptation** is any trait that helps an organism survive and reproduce in its environment. Eventually only saddleback tortoises could be found on the dry, sparsely vegetated islands.

The finches could be explained in a similar way. A single species of finch, which came from nearby South America, originally inhabited the islands. Each island provided a different source of food. Some birds needed a strong beak to crack open seeds. Others needed a narrow beak to reach into plants for food. Natural selection favored those birds with the variation that made them better able to obtain food on their island.

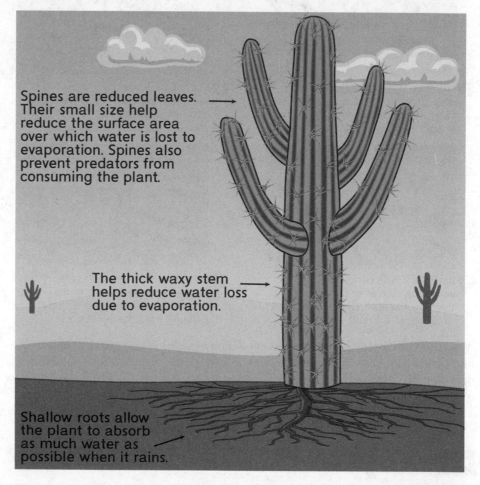

Spines are reduced leaves. Their small size help reduce the surface area over which water is lost to evaporation. Spines also prevent predators from consuming the plant.

The thick waxy stem helps reduce water loss due to evaporation.

Shallow roots allow the plant to absorb as much water as possible when it rains.

There are many examples of adaptations that help organisms survive in their environment. An **example** is something or someone that represents a whole group. A polar bear has thick fur and a layer of fat to keep it warm in its cold surroundings. The only heat a polar bear gives off comes from its breath.

Another adaptation the polar bear has is its large feet, which help the bear paddle through water and spread out the bear's weight so it can walk safely on ice while hunting seals.

Plants, too, have adaptations to help them survive. The saguaro cactus lives in the very dry environment of the desert. This plant can reach heights of up to 12 m and can live to be 200 years old. The cactus has a thick, waxy stem with ribs that can expand to store water. The roots of the cactus do not grow deep into the soil. This makes it possible for the cactus to take in as much water as it can when it rains. The plant then saves some water for periods when there is no rain.

Protection from Predators

It is a hot afternoon on the Serengeti. A hungry pride of female lions is watching a group of zebras. As the zebras move, their stripes blend together. It is difficult for the lions to pick out a single zebra because they cannot tell how many there are or exactly how far away they are. Unless one zebra strays from the crowd, the lions will go hungry—for now. Stripes on a zebra are an example, or illustration, of an adaptation. The mixture of stripes created when many zebras stand together is an adaptation that helps each zebra survive. Like a zebra's stripes, many adaptations protect an organism from predators. Some adaptations help organisms hide from predators, while others, such as strong odors, encourage predators to stay away. Still other adaptations, such as an antelope's fast speed, help prey escape from predators.

Camouflage

Some organisms blend in with their environment. For example, the color and slow movement of a stick insect might make it look like a twig on a tree. Camouflage is the ability to blend into the surroundings.

Mimicry

Mimicry is the ability of a harmless organism to look like a different, often more dangerous, organism. King snakes, which are harmless, and coral snakes, which are dangerous, have similar coloring. Because the king snake, shown on the left, looks similar to a coral snake, predators are less likely to try to consume it.

Protective Covering

Porcupines are one example of an animal with a protective covering. The pointy quills that cover its body protect it from predators. Some plants have sharp needles for the same reason.

CORE SKILL

Draw Conclusions

When you draw a conclusion, you form an opinion about something you have learned or read. Think of an animal you are familiar with and identify adaptations it has, such as fur, feathers, scales, sharp teeth, claws, or markings that allow it to blend in with its environment. Draw conclusions about the survival benefit of these adaptations. Write a paragraph to describe your conclusions.

Camouflage in Action

Flexibility and Adaptability

In everyday language, the word *adaptation* has a different meaning than its scientific meaning. In the workplace, to be adaptable means to be able to accommodate different circumstances. For example, one company may have a quiet, independent work style in which people arrive, go to their desk, and quietly work. Other companies may have a more collegial style, where people work together in large, open rooms, freely talking and asking questions. List personal qualities a worker might have that would make it easier for him or her to adapt to a particular working environment

Warning Colors

The bright blue poison arrow frog does not blend into its environment at all. In fact, its bright coloring invites predators to notice the frog. Like the poison arrow frog, many brightly colored organisms are poisonous, and the bright colors act as a warning to predators not to eat them.

Predator Adaptations

Like prey, predators have adaptations that help them survive. These include any traits that help them detect and catch their prey. Some predators, such as owls, have excellent vision, which helps them spot a tiny mouse among the leaves on the forest floor. Most species of owls have outstanding night vision as well. In addition, their feathers direct sound toward their highly sensitive ears, which helps them find prey that might otherwise stay hidden. Owls have sharp, powerful talons on their feet they use to grab and hold on to prey until it suffocates.

Female lions have a keen sense of smell to help them detect if prey is nearby. They also have excellent night vision, which they use to hunt for prey in the dark. Female lions can reach speeds of about 50 kilometers per hour for short distances, which helps them catch their prey. Once they do, they have large, sharp teeth to hold and kill the prey.

Other animals, such as Burmese pythons, have heat sensors in their top lips. Along with a keen sense of smell, the sensors help them find prey, such as warm-blooded mammals. They also have jaws with a loose hinge. Once a snake has captured its prey, this loose hinge makes it possible for the snake to open its mouth wide enough to fit the prey inside.

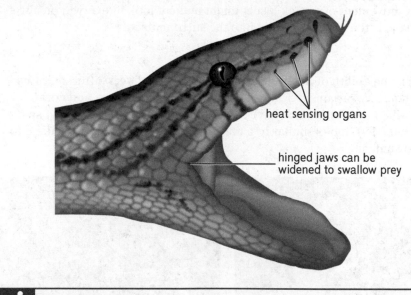

heat sensing organs

hinged jaws can be widened to swallow prey

Think about Science

Directions: Answer the following questions.

1. How could the adaptations of the giant tortoises of the Galápagos Islands be explained through natural selection?

2. What adaptations might an animal that lives in or near the water, such as a crocodile, have to help it survive?

3. What adaptations might birds have evolved to help them survive?

Speciation

The process by which a new species of organism arises from a parent population is called speciation. Speciation can occur in more than one way.

Allopatric Speciation

When populations of the same species become isolated from each other geographically, they can evolve distinct characteristics. During his time in the Galápagos Islands, Darwin noticed that finches varied from island to island. He later learned that each finch was a separate species that had evolved from a common ancestor. The birds had diversified to take advantage of different food sources on each island. This is called allopatric speciation. It is a process in which populations of organisms are impacted by natural selection and diversify rapidly into new forms when a change in an environment makes new resources available.

Sympatric Speciation

Sometimes new species arise from populations that are not geographically isolated. Even though the two groups have a range that overlap, they still evolve into distinct species. This is called sympatric speciation. The best-known examples of this are cichlid fishes in the lakes of East Africa. There are at least 800 species, all of which have diversified from a common ancestor. Each species occupies a distinct niche. In Lake Victoria, more than 300 species of cichlid fish from one parent species.

Adaptive Radiation

Darwin's finches, discussed earlier, are examples of adaptive radiation. The 13 different species of finches all evolved from a common ancestor and have adapted different beaks so that each of them is able to consume a different type of food. The marsupials in present-day Australia also evolved from a common ancestor. Kangaroos evolved powerful legs that allow them to travel over vast areas in search of food. Koalas' smaller size, centralized center of gravity, and climbing ability have allowed them to climb in order to reach the eucalyptus leaves they eat.

Cichlid Fishes

fish eater — zooplankton eater — snail eater — leaf eater — algae scraper

Think about Science

Directions: Answer the following questions.

1. What is speciation?
2. What is the main difference between allopatric speciation and sympatric speciation?

WORKPLACE SKILL

Understand the Purpose of Workplace Documents

User documentation in the workplace helps workers understand how to use equipment or follow procedures. Just as Darwin documented what he saw on his travels, user documentation can explain in great detail the different functions of a piece of equipment, such as a photocopier. There is variation in equipment, and no two brands work exactly the same. It is important to refer to the user documentation when you have a question, so you don't damage the equipment by guessing how it works.

Write user documentation that explains step by step how to use a piece of equipment you are familiar with, either at home or at work.

Vocabulary Review

Directions: Write the missing term in the blank.

natural selection   artificial selection   adaptation
speciation   variation   example

1. The process by which humans breed other animals and plants for particular traits is called
_____ .

2. _____ is the evolutionary process by which new biological species arise.

3. A(n) _____ is an illustration of a rule, method, or topic.

4. A(n) _____ is a difference or trait that, if favorable, can help a species better survive.

5. Charles Darwin's idea that some offspring have variations that will make them better able to survive is called _____ .

6. A(n) _____ is any trait that helps an organism survive and reproduce itself in its environment.

Skill Review

Directions: Answer the following questions.

1. Which of the following is evidence of speciation?
   A. Dogs and cats live within close proximity in a recently developed urban area.
   B. Frogs found in an area where a recent toxic spill occurred exhibit several types of limb deformities.
   C. A community of related humans unearthed during an archeological dig have similar bone structure.
   D. Separate squirrel populations that inhabit the north and south rims of Arizona's Grand Canyon cannot breed and produce fertile offspring.

2. Which conclusion can be made about artificial selection?
   A. It appears to support the theory of natural selection.
   B. Though widely used in agriculture, the results are largely negative.
   C. It must occur naturally as a result of mutations to be truly effective.
   D. Selective breeding cannot be used to alter the genetic makeup of organisms.

3. About the time of the Industrial Revolution in England, the surface of normally light gray trees turned black from soot that landed on the trees. Peppered moths that are white or black lived on these trees. Birds preyed upon the moths. Suggest how the change in tree color affected the population of these moths.

4. The South African burrowing bullfrog inflates its body like a balloon when it senses danger. Explain how this is an adaptation that helps the frog survive.

5. Why might a predator avoid eating a brightly colored grasshopper?

6. Which adaptation would be most useful for birds on a small island that is hit periodically by severe storms that kill most of the island's land animals?
   A. Longer claws, useful for carrying twigs
   B. A high-pitched cry, useful for mating
   C. Darker tail feathers, useful for camouflage
   D. A wider beak, useful for capturing fish

7. Which of these is the best definition of allopatric speciation?
   A. Allopatric speciation occurs when organisms become separated geographically and evolve different characteristics.
   B. Allopatric speciation occurs when organisms occupy the same range but evolve different characteristics.
   C. Allopatric speciation occurs when organisms are separated geographically but do not diversify in their environments.
   D. Allopatric speciation occurs when organisms evolve from a single ancestor but do not diversify into separate species.

Skill Practice

Directions: Use the illustration to answer questions 1 and 2.

A conclusion is a logical opinion formed after considering the known facts or evidence. An interesting question concerning the physical development of organisms is the discovery of vestigial structure. A vestigial structure is a body part that no longer serves its original purpose. An example of a vestigial structure is the presence of leg bones in a snake. These small bones have no apparent function in snakes that exist at the present time. One explanation of vestigial structures is that animals today evolved from ancestors who once needed these organs. According to this explanation, snakes inherited the genes that produce leg bones from an ancestral relative. These relatives were most likely ancient reptiles that did have legs.

1. Which phrase **best** describes a vestigial structure?
   A. Is small and easily identified
   B. Is present in all modern reptiles
   C. Is not inherited
   D. Is without a known use

2. Which of these is **not** a vestigial structure?
   A. Small leg bones in whales
   B. Wings of flightless birds, such as ostriches
   C. Ears of birds who use sound to fly at night
   D. Eyes of salamanders that live in pitch-black caves

Directions: Answer the following questions.

3. If variation exists among the puppies in a litter, what does that mean?

4. How might a mutation that produces a white tiger affect the tiger's survival?

5. Why is fast speed a useful variation for a fish?

6. How might a brightly colored fish be less fit than a fish that blends in with the ocean floor?

7. Plants that grow on the floor of a rain forest often have large, flat leaves. How is the structure of these leaves an adaptation that helps them survive?

Directions: Use the diagram to answer questions 8–9.

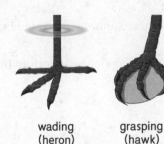 

| wading (heron) | grasping (hawk) | perching (warbler) | swimming (duck) | running (rhea) |

8. Which of the five birds represented is most suited to use its feet to pick up small animals?
   A. heron   D. duck
   B. hawk   E. rhea
   C. warbler

9. Explain how the different bird-foot structures shown are adaptations. How does natural selection explain the evolution of these adaptations?

Directions: Answer the following questions.

1. Which of the following explains how Mendel discovered that there are two copies of each gene that specifies a trait?

   A. A trait would disappear in the F_1 generation and reappear in the F_2 generation.

   B. A trait would be present in the F_1 generation and disappear in the F_2 generation.

   C. A trait would be present in the F_1 generation and also present in the F_2 generation.

   D. A trait would be present in F_1 and F_2 and then disappear in future generations.

2. Two things that are homologous have the similar structure and function. How is it possible that homologous chromosomes are not identical?

   A. One chromosome may not be able to replicate itself.

   B. One chromosome may be missing one or more genes.

   C. Each chromosome may have different allele for a single gene.

   D. Each chromosome may have unique genes but same structure.

3. A Punnett square is used in genetics to

   A. predict the phenotype of the two parents.

   B. predict the phenotype of the offspring.

   C. predict the genotype of the parents.

   D. predict the genotype of the offspring.

4. In the cross between two heterozygous individuals, what is the probability of an offspring that is homozygous for the recessive allele?

   A. 0%

   B. 25%

   C. 50%

   D. 75%

5. What can scientists use to support the idea that humans are related to E.*Coli* bacteria?

   A. Theory of Natural Selection

   B. Theory of Evolution

   C. Theory of UCA

   D. Theory of Adaption

6. A systematic method for studying evolutionary relationships is called

   A. cladistics

   B. Darwinism

   C. evolution

   D. ecology

7. Which cellular process is the cause of variation in the physical traits of offspring?

   A. replication

   B. recombination

   C. mitosis

   D. mutation

8. Which of the following is true about mutations in DNA?

   A. Mutations occur after DNA replication in the cell.

   B. Mutations are only caused by environmental factors.

   C. Mitotic mutations cannot be inherited by offspring.

   D. Meiotic mutations cannot be inherited by offspring.

9. Which of the following is an example of an adaptation in an organism?

   A. shallow roots of a cactus plant

   B. hunting instinct of lions

   C. selective breeding of pigeons

   D. inheritance of physical trait

10. The isolation of part of a population due to geographical constraints causes the development of new traits in the offspring of this sub population. Variation in these offspring can lead to

   A. adaptation

   B. infertility

   C. natural selection

   D. speciation

11. How can two plants with different genotypes for a particular trait have identical phenotypes?

12. Explain why a male is more likely to express a sex-linked recessive trait found on the X chromosome than a female.

13. In order to distinguish between a particular clade of mammals and other clades of mammals, why is hair not a useful characteristic to study?

14. Explain why a scientist who studies epigenetics would be interested in studying the composition of food.

15. Compare artificial selection and natural selection.

Directions: Use the diagram to answer questions 16–18.

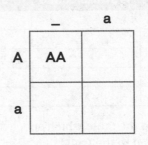

16. Fill in rest of the possible offspring for the cross represented in the Punnett square.

17 What percentage of the offspring will be homozygous recessive?

18. If a second cross is done between two offspring plants and 120 offspring are produced, what is likely the genotype of the parents if 62 offspring are homozygous recessive and 58 offspring are heterozygous?

   A. Aa × Aa

   B. Aa × aa

   C. AA × aa

   D. aa × aa

Directions: Use the table to answer questions 19–21.

	Fur	Warm-blooded	Bones	Lungs	Four-legged
Dog	X	X	X	X	X
Bee					
Frog			X	X	X
Fish			X	X	
Bear	X	X	X	X	X

19. Based on the data in the table which species is most distantly related to the frog?

A. bee

B. dog

C. fish

D. kangaroo

20. Which species is most closely related to the bear?

A. dog

B. fish

C. frog

D. kangaroo

21. Fill in the cladogram with the data from the table.

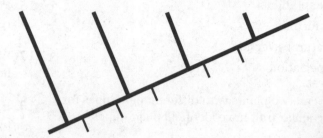

Directions: Read the passage and answer questions 22–23.

During DNA replication, the two strands of a DNA molecule separate from one another in a process that is similar to the unzipping of a zipper. The "teeth" of the zipper are nucleotides. DNA is made up of four different nucleotides with the bases: adenine (A), cytosine (C), guanine (G), and thymine (T). These structures are commonly called bases, and they pair up with one another according to base pairing rules: A pairs with T, and C pairs with G. During replication, new bases attach to each separated strand of DNA, according to the base pairing rules. After replication there are two identical double stranded DNA molecules.

22. What would be the DNA sequence of a newly replicated portion of a DNA strand during DNA replication if the existing strand has the sequence GATCCTG?

A. GATCCTG

B. AGCTTCA

C. CTAGGAC

D. TCGAAGT

23. How many newly synthesized double stranded DNA molecules would be produced after three rounds of DNA replication?

A. 2

B. 4

C. 6

D. 8

Heredity and Evolution

Directions: Read the passage and answer questions 24–26.

Darwin's travels took him to a group of small islands off the west coast of South America known as the Galápagos Islands. Although the individual islands are relatively close to one another, they have different climates and different species of plants. Darwin observed that some islands were hot and dry with few plants, while others received more rainfall and had a larger variety of plants. Darwin collected information about many species of organisms. In particular, he made extensive observations of giant tortoises that lived on the islands. Darwin noticed that the shells of the tortoises were different on each island. For example, one type of tortoise, the saddleback tortoise, had a long neck and a curved shell, while a tortoise on a different island, the domed tortoise, had a shorter neck and a shell that looked like a dome. In addition, Darwin observed 13 different species of finches, a type of small bird. Each species of finch had a different-shaped beak. The shape of the beak was related to the type of food available on the island where the bird lived.

24. The 13 different species of finch that Darwin collected from the Galápagos Islands are an example of

   A. adaptive radiation.

   B. flexibility.

   C. mimicry.

   D. sympatric speciation.

25. Explain how the tortoises Darwin observed supported his theory of natural selection.

26. Explain how climate can affect a species of plant or animal?

Directions: Answer the following questions

27. Which of the following is an accurate statement about a physical adaptation?

   A. Physical adaptation occurs randomly in all species.

   B. Physical adaptations occur without any genetic changes.

   C. All genetic variation causes a physical adaptation in a species.

   D. Genetic variation may cause a physical adaptation in a species.

28. Explain why an adaptation in a species will take place faster if the allele for the trait is dominant instead of recessive.

29. How does evidence of adaptation present a strong argument in favor of the theory of Universal Common Ancestry?

Check Your Understanding

On the following chart, circle the number of any item you answered incorrectly. Next to each group of item numbers, you will see the pages you can review to learn how to answer the items correctly.

Lesson	Item Number(s)	Review Page(s)
4.1: Basic Principles of Genetics	1, 2, 11, 28	142–147
4.2: Probability of Traits	3, 4, 12, 16, 17, 18	150–153
4.3: Common Ancestry	5, 6, 13, 19, 20, 21	156–159
4.4: Genetic Variations and Expression	7, 8, 13, 15, 25, 26	162–165
4.5: Selection and Adaption	9, 10, 15, 24, 25, 26, 27, 28	168–173

Genetically Modified Foods

Core Practices

- Cite specific textual evidence to support a finding or conclusion
- Reason from data or evidence to a conclusion

Question

How is genetic engineering replacing artificial selection in agriculture to alter food crops?

Background Concepts

Natural selection is a very slow process that occurs over many generations. Artificial selection can occur more rapidly over a few generations. Artificial selection, unlike natural selection, does not necessarily convey greater fitness of the species. Instead, artificially selected traits are based on what the person breeding the organism desires. In agriculture, farmers have been selectively breeding plants and animals to bring about changes in their features over the course of human history. For example, some vegetables such as broccoli, cauliflower, and kale were cultivated through changes made to the wild mustard plant. Farmers also selectively breed animals such as chicken or beef cattle so that the animals have less fat and more meat.

Genetically modified foods (GMOs) are developed from plant and animal DNA that has been modified to introduce changes in genes that do not occur naturally. This is a type of artificial selection because desired traits are introduced into an organism, and these organisms are selectively bred to pass on those traits to offspring. Modifications to plants, through the latest techniques in genetic engineering, include changes to improve crop yields by improving resistance to diseases or pests. Plant geneticists can isolate the gene responsible for drought resistance in one plant and insert that gene into another species of plant, making that plant's offspring drought resistant, too. Some other modifications increase the size of fruits or vegetables, while others increase their sugar content. According to the US Food and Drug Administration (FDA) and the US Department of Agriculture (USDA), there are more than 40 plant varieties that are now being genetically modified and 13 countries growing crops with GMOs.

In addition to making crops more hardy and fruits and vegetables more flavorful, there are some advantages and disadvantages to GMOs. Because the world's population has increased to over 6 billion people and is expected to rise to 12 billion in the next 50 years, GMOs can help increase the food supply to ensure food for the world's growing population. Some scientists and public-interest groups have argued that the use of GMOs will create unintended environmental hazards, causing harm to other organisms. Another concern is that GMOs will cross-breed with other plants in their surrounding environment, causing problems in ecosystems.

Hypothesis

A hypothesis is an explanation based on what evidence is available. It is a starting point for a scientific investigation that will prove to be either correct or false based on more evidence gathered. Develop a hypothesis to address an advantage or disadvantages associated with GMOs and their use in agriculture.

Investigation

After developing a hypothesis, the next step is to gather information and data to determine whether your hypothesis is supported. Research the topic of GMOs using the Internet or other reliable sources. When using the Internet as a source of information, search for government or academic sites to avoid sites that offer uninformed opinions. Gather as much information about GMOs as you can to support or refute your hypothesis. Determine how genetic engineering in plants has altered artificial selection practices.

Collect and Analyze Data

Collect data about GMOs and organize it into a two charts. The first chart should have three columns that compare natural selection, artificial selection, and GMOs in agricultural plants. The second chart should have two columns that list the advantages and disadvantages of genetic engineering in agricultural plants.

Interpretation

Summarize the data collected and interpret the evidence to determine if your hypothesis is supported.

When evaluating and interpreting the information or data you collected, ask yourself the following questions:

- How is the production of GMOs different from the traditional methods of artificial selection?

- What are the advantages of GMOs?

- What are the disadvantages of GMOs?

Results

Discuss your results using evidence to support your conclusions. Discuss any observations about the information you gathered from reliable sources, possible sources of error, unexpected results, and any remaining questions. If your hypothesis was not supported, discuss your recommendations for formulating a new hypothesis or changes you would make to the investigation.

Consider the following questions as you discuss your results.

- What do you think will be the potential advantages and disadvantages to incorporating GMO technology into the breeding of agricultural animals?

- Do you think GMOs can solve the world's hunger problems, or do you think they will result in too many negative consequences for other organisms, including humans?

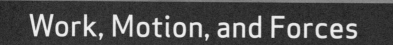

Chapter 5

Work, Motion, and Forces

Pushing a car that is stuck or is broken down may look like hard work. But, in the physical world, no work occurs unless the car moves. Work occurs when a force is applied to move an object over a distance. Understanding the physics behind motion, force, and work can help you to better understand how people and machines do work.

Glow Images

Lesson 5.1
Motion

We might think of motion as the movement of an object, such as a racecar speeding toward the finish line. In this lesson you will learn how scientists define motion in the physical world. Learn that in science, motion is described not only by how fast an object is moving, but also by which direction it is traveling, and by any change in direction or speed that may occur during movement.

Lesson 5.2
Forces and Newton's Laws of Motion

Motion is related to the force that is present between two objects. Newton's three laws of motion explain the relationship between the motion of an object and the forces acting on it. Learn how Newton's law of universal gravitation explains how our feet stay on the ground and how the planets in our solar system stay in orbit.

Lesson 5.3
Work and Simple Machines

Did you know that the knife you use to cut your food is a simple machine? When you use that knife to cut your food, you are doing work. In this lesson you will learn how scientists define work. You will also learn about six different types of simple machines and how these simple machines can be used together to create compound machines.

Goal Setting

You use simple machines at home and at work every day. A knife, a screwdriver, and a pair of scissors are all examples of simple machines. Even the system set up to easily lift a garage door is a simple machine. Most things that help to make a task easier can be thought of as simple machines.

Think of a task that you often do at home or at work that is difficult to perform and think of ways you can use a simple machine to make this task easier. Write down your ideas. After you have read this chapter, draw a sketch of a simple machine that might help with your task and explain how it will make the task easier.

LESSON OBJECTIVES

- Analyze motion in terms of speed, velocity, and acceleration
- Apply the concept of the law of conservation of momentum

CORE SKILLS & PRACTICES

- Express Scientific Information or Findings Numerically
- Interpret Graphs and Functions

Key Terms

acceleration
the rate of change of velocity

conservation of momentum
the total momentum of a system does not change during a collision

momentum
the product of the mass and the velocity of a moving object

speed
the distance an object travels per unit of time

velocity
the speed and direction of a moving object

Vocabulary

graph
a diagram that represents the change of a variable in comparison with other variables

Key Concept

Objects are in motion all around us. Motion can be described by speed, velocity, and acceleration. A moving object has momentum, which can be transferred between objects.

Describing Motion

An object is in motion when it changes position. When an object moves from one location to another, it is changing position in relation to a stationary point known as a reference point. Earth's surface, or something attached to it, are common reference points. The Sun, other stars, and the planets can be used as reference points to describe motion in the solar system and the universe. Earth is in constant motion relative to the Sun.

Speed

One measure of motion is **speed,** or the distance an object travels over time compared to a reference point. Speed can be calculated using the following equation.

$$\text{speed} = \frac{\text{distance}}{\text{time}}$$

Speed is always measured in a unit of distance per a unit of time, such as meters per second (m/s) or kilometers per hour (km/h). A falling rock, for example, might hit the ground at a speed of 10 m/s, while a car on the highway may travel at a speed of 100 km/h (about 60 mph).

Velocity

If you know a car is traveling at 100 km/h, you still do not have enough information to completely describe its motion. **Velocity** is a measure of both the speed and direction of an object's motion. If you have a compass in your car, you may be able to determine that your velocity is 100 km/h east. Meanwhile, the rock falling from a cliff is traveling at 10 m/s downward.

Like speed, velocity is measured relative to some reference point. Because velocity includes a direction component, velocities can combine either by adding together or subtracting from each other. For example, suppose a train is moving east at 200 km/h relative to the ground. A passenger walks toward the front of the train at 4 km/h relative to the people seated on the train. The passenger's overall velocity relative to the ground is 204 km/h east. As the same passenger walks back toward his seat at 4 km/h toward the back of the train, his overall velocity is 196 km/h east.

Acceleration

In common language, to accelerate means to go faster. Press the accelerator pedal on a car, and the car's speed increases. In physical science, however, an **acceleration** is the rate of change in velocity. Remember that velocity includes the speed and direction of an object. Therefore a change in velocity can be a change in either speed or direction. A car that is slowing down is accelerating in the opposite direction of its motion. This is sometimes called a deceleration. A moving object that changes direction is also undergoing an acceleration even if its speed does not change.

To determine the acceleration of an object, first calculate the change in velocity by subtracting the initial velocity from the final velocity. Then divide the change in velocity by the amount of time over which the change occurred.

$$\text{acceleration} = \frac{(\text{final velocity} - \text{initial velocity})}{\text{time}}$$

If the direction of motion does not change, the change in velocity is the same as the change in speed. The change in velocity is then the final speed minus the initial speed. The change in velocity is a unit of speed, such as m/s. Therefore the unit of acceleration is a unit of speed divided by a unit of time. Time is commonly measured in seconds, so acceleration is usually measured in meters per second per second, or m/s².

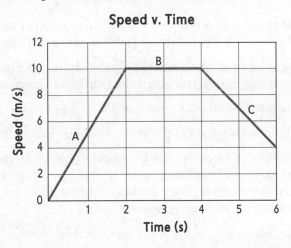

Speed v. Time

The acceleration of an object can be represented using a graph. Speed or velocity is plotted on the vertical axis, and time is plotted on the horizontal axis. For objects that are speeding up and slowing down, the slope of the line on a speed-time graph, such as the one above, is the acceleration. In section A, speed increases from 0 m/s to 10 m/s in 2 seconds for an acceleration of 5 m/s². The line in section A slopes upward, and the acceleration is positive. In section B, the line is flat, so the slope of the line is 0, indicating that the object is moving at a constant speed of 10 m/s. In section C, the object is slowing down from a speed of 10 m/s to 4 m/s in 2 seconds, an acceleration of –3 m/s².

CALCULATOR SKILL

Calculating an Average Speed

The speed of a moving object often varies. Think about traveling in a car that is speeding up to enter a highway, slowing down to make a turn, or coming to a stop at a red light. The average speed is the total distance traveled divided by the total time spent traveling. Average speed can be very different from the speed at any particular time.

A bus travels in a loop through town, stopping to pick up and drop off passengers. In one loop, the bus travels a total distance of 18 km. If it takes the bus 30 minutes to make a loop, what is its average speed?

CORE SKILL

Interpret Graphs and Functions

A **graph** is a diagram that represents the relationship between two variables. The word *graph* can also be used as a verb to describe the activity of creating a graph. For example, a speed-versus-time graph shows the speed at which an object is moving at any given time. In order to graph, or use a diagram to represent, the distance an object travels versus the time you know its speed, you follow these steps. Calculate the total distance traveled at several different times on the *y*-axis of a grid and then the points representing each time as a coordinate pair (time, distance) on the *x*-axis. Finally draw a line connecting each plotted point.

Graph the motion of an object traveling 12 m/s on a coordinate grid.

Work Effectively with Tools

When you use tools in the workplace, you must follow safety procedures, and you must also know how to use the tools effectively to accomplish a goal. Assume that you need to use a large hammer to loosen two heavy metal parts that have become stuck together over time. Hitting one of the parts with the hammer is likely to cause a dent due to the force applied at the point of contact. Suggest a way you can reduce the force caused by the momentum of the elastic collision between the hammer and the metal.

Think about Science

Directions: Answer the following questions.

1. A ball rolls 20 m across a parking lot in 4 s. What is the speed of the ball?

2. What does a horizontal line on a speed-time graph indicate about the acceleration of an object traveling in a straight line?

Momentum

To understand momentum, we first need to understand the relationship between mass (the amount of matter in an object) and force (a push or pull exerted on an object). Imagine a person struggling to push a piano. Then imagine the person using the same force to push a small book, which has a much smaller mass than the piano. While the piano might barely move, the book would move easily. **Momentum** is the product of velocity and mass. A bullet is small, but it has great momentum when it travels at high speeds. A heavy truck—even one that moves slowly—also has great momentum.

Calculating Momentum

Momentum is a property of a moving object that is equal to the mass of the object multiplied by the velocity of the object. Because velocity includes direction, momentum has a direction associated with it. An object's momentum is in the direction of its velocity. Momentum can be calculated as follows.

$$\text{momentum} = \text{mass} \times \text{velocity}$$

If mass is measured in kilograms, and velocity in meters per second, momentum has units of kilogram-meters per second, or kg · m/s.

The greater the velocity of an object, the greater the object's momentum. Consider, for example, a 12-kg bicycle at two different velocities.

2 m/s south: momentum = 12 kg × 2 m/s = 24 kg · m/s south

3 m/s south: momentum = 12 kg × 3 m/s = 36 kg · m/s south

The greater the mass of an object, the greater the object's momentum. Consider a cart moving at a velocity of 2 m/s west. Bricks can be added to the cart to change its mass. The calculations below show how the cart's momentum increases as its mass increases.

2 kg: momentum = 2 kg × 2 m/s = 4 kg · m/s west

5 kg: momentum = 5 kg × 2 m/s = 10 kg · m/s west

Law of Conservation of Momentum

When two objects collide, one object's momentum can be transferred to the other object. No momentum is created or lost in the process. The law of **conservation of momentum** states that if no other forces act on the objects, their total momentum remains the same after they interact.

Collisions of Objects

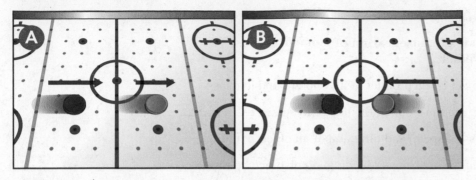

The amount of momentum that is transferred when two objects collide depends on the objects' initial motion. In graphic A, both pucks are moving toward the right. They have the same mass, but the puck on the left is moving faster. Its momentum is greater than the momentum of the puck on the right. After they collide, both pucks will continue to move in the same direction. The puck on the right will speed up, and the puck on the left will slow down. The momentum of each puck will change, but the total momentum of both pucks will be the same as it was before the collision.

In graphic B, the pucks are moving at the same speed toward each other. As a result, their momentum is equal in magnitude but opposite in direction. After they collide, each reverses direction. They again travel at the same speed but in opposite directions. Thus, their total momentum is the same before and after the collision.

Elastic Collisions

In an elastic collision, there is no loss of kinetic energy in the collision. For example, in the collision shown in B, the pucks move away at the same speed but at opposite directions from their original motion. Momentum and kinetic energy are both conserved in an elastic collision. When objects larger than molecules collide, there is always some energy change, so the collision is not perfectly elastic.

Inelastic Collisions

Some of the kinetic energy is changed to another form of energy in an inelastic collision. In a completely inelastic collision, the two objects stick together after the collision. Any real-world collision between objects converts some of the kinetic energy into some other form of energy such as heat, sound, or the motion of particles inside the objects.

For example, a bicycle helmet protects the rider in an accident by transmitting the energy of a collision with the ground into the padding of the helmet. As the protective foam collapses, it absorbs energy. Without the helmet, much more of the energy of the collision is transferred to the rider's head. Although energy is not conserved, momentum is conserved in an inelastic collision.

Think about Science

Directions: Fill in the blank.

1. A ball of wet clay thrown against a wall sticks to the wall in a(n) _____.

Express Scientific Information or Findings Numerically

When you express scientific information numerically, values generally have a number value and a unit. When you perform numerical calculations using scientific measurements, always pay close attention to both the number and the unit. Values can be added or subtracted only if they have the same units. For multiplication and division, the same operation applies to the number and to the units.

Consider a massive sculpture of a Newton's cradle with 2.0-kg balls. If one 2.0-kg ball moving at a velocity of 0.70 m/s strikes one end of the line, all the momentum is transferred to a 2.0-kg ball on the other side of the Newton's cradle, what is the velocity of that ball?

Vocabulary Review

Directions: Write the missing term in the blank.

acceleration   graph   law of conservation of momentum
momentum   speed   velocity

1. The _____ of an object is the product of its velocity and its mass.

2. On a speed-time _____, the slope of the line represents _____.

3. An object's _____ is the speed and direction of an object's motion.

4. A runner's _____ can be determined by dividing distance by time.

5. The _____ applies to any collision.

Skill Review

Directions: Answer the following questions.

1. What is the speed of a car that travels 1080 meters in 1 minute?
   A. 0.30 m/s
   B. 18 m/s
   C. 32 m/s
   D. 96 m/s

2. What is the acceleration of a runner who speeds up from the starting line to run at 3.6 m/s over a period of 2.0 seconds?
   A. 0.90 m/s^2
   B. 1.8 m/s^2
   C. 3.6 m/s^2
   D. 7.2 m/s^2

3. What is the momentum of a 45.0-kg dog running south at 9 meters per second?
   A. 5.00 kg • m/s south
   B. 45.0 kg • m/s south
   C. 405 kg • m/s south
   D. 3650 kg • m/s south

4. A Newton's cradle will continue moving for a long time, but it eventually stops. Use what you have learned about energy and collisions to explain why the motion stops after many collisions.

5. Explain how velocity and speed are alike and how they are different.

6. When eggs are in a box separated by thin wooden slats, many of the eggs break during shipping. Propose a way to keep the eggs from breaking during shipping, and explain how the proposed solution would affect momentum during collisions between the eggs and the box.

7. What is the momentum of a 0.060-kg tennis ball served east across the court at 45 meters per second?
   A. 0.27 kg • m/s east
   B. 0.75 kg • m/s east
   C. 2.7 kg • m/s east
   D. 7.5 kg • m/s east

8. What is the momentum of a 4.5-kg bowling ball rolling to the right in the ball return chute at 0.60 meters per second?
   A. 0.75 kg • m/s to the right
   B. 2.7 kg • m/s to the right
   C. 7.5 kg • m/s to the right
   D. 27 kg • m/s to the right

9. During an inelastic collision, some of the _____ energy is changed to other forms of energy.

Skill Practice

Directions: Use the diagram to answer questions 1–3.

The graph shows the rate at which the speed of an object increases as the object falls due to gravity. For example, an object dropped from a tall building reaches a speed of 29 m/s after falling for 3 seconds.

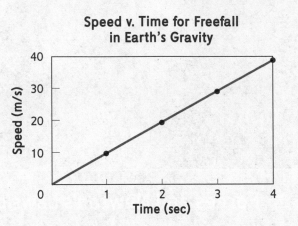

Speed v. Time for Freefall in Earth's Gravity

1. Under the action of gravity, how much does an object's speed increase each second it falls?

   A. 2.5 m/s

   B. 4.9 m/s

   C. 9.8 m/s

   D. 19.6 m/s

2. Acceleration is an object's change in speed over a given period of time. What is the acceleration of an object between 2 s and 3 s?

   A. 2.5 m/s²

   B. 9.8 m/s²

   C. 29 m/s²

   D. 33 m/s²

3. What is the speed of an object after 2 seconds of free fall?

   A. 4.9 m/s

   B. 7.3 m/s

   C. 9.8 m/s

   D. 19.6 m/s

Directions: Answer the following questions.

4. Which of these vehicles has the greatest momentum?

   A. A 1,000 kg car driving north at 100 km/h

   B. A 12,000-kg bulldozer driving north at 8 km/h

   C. A 15,000-kg dump truck driving north at 6 km/h

   D. A 2,000-kg truck driving north at 48 km/h

5. Calculate the acceleration of a person riding a bicycle in a straight line who speeds up from 4 m/s to 6 m/s in 5 s.

6. What is the momentum of a 50-kg dolphin swimming 10.4 m/s?

7. A rail car with a mass of 15,000 kg rolls down a track at 10 m/s. It collides with a second 15,000-kg car that is initially stationary. The two cars link together and continue moving in the initial direction of the first car. Calculate the initial and final momentums and the final velocities of the cars. Show your work.

8. A car begins from a stationary position and travels 15 kilometers north in 0.5 hour, stops for 0.5 hour, and then continues traveling north at 50 km/h for 2.0 hours. Draw a speed-time graph to show the motion of the car during its trip.

LESSON 5.2 Forces and Newton's Laws of Motion

■ LESSON OBJECTIVES

- Describe Newton's laws of motion
- Explain how the law of universal gravitation describes the force of gravity between two objects with mass

■ CORE SKILLS & PRACTICES

- Apply Formulas from Scientific Theories
- Solve Linear Equations

Key Terms

force
a push or pull

gravity
the attraction between two objects because of their mass

inertia
the tendency of an object to resist a change in motion

weight
a measure of the force of gravity on an object

Vocabulary

law
a statement that describes a relationship in nature that has been observed to always occur under certain conditions

state
to express in words

Key Concept

Newton's laws describe the motion of objects. Newton's law of universal gravitation relates the mass and distance between two objects to the force of gravity between two objects. These laws can be used to predict the motion of everyday objects.

Newton's Laws of Motion

The best pool players can predict how all the balls on the table will move once the cue ball is set into motion. They carefully control where and how hard they hit the cue ball so it moves where they want it to go. Pool balls move in predictable ways because, like all objects, they respond to forces in a certain ways.

Forces

A **force** is defined as a push or pull exerted between two objects that are interacting in some way. A pool player interacts with the pool stick when he or she pushes it forward. The pool stick interacts with the cue ball when it strikes the cue ball. The cue ball may interact with other balls when it hits them. It also interacts with the table as it rolls and even when it sits motionless.

Not all forces are the same. Forces in which the two interacting objects are physically touching each other are called contact forces. The force between the pool stick and the cue ball is a contact force because the cue ball must touch the ball to push it forward. Friction is also a contact force that resists the motion of an object. Friction is a result of the fact that surfaces are not perfectly smooth, even if it appears that they are. Friction between the rolling pool ball and the table causes the ball to slow down as it rolls. Friction occurs between any objects that are touching, whether the objects are stationary, sliding, or rolling.

Forces in which the two interacting objects are not physically touching each other are known as action-at-a-distance forces. When a magnet is brought near a paper clip, the magnet exerts a force on the paper clip without having to touch it. The Moon exerts a pull on Earth's oceans, even though the Moon is hundreds of thousands of kilometers away from Earth.

Gwengoat/E+/Getty Images

Newton's First Law

In the seventeenth century, Sir Isaac Newton published three laws that explain the motion of objects. A **law** is a statement that describes a relationship in nature that has been observed to always occur under certain conditions. The motions of pool balls, a paper clip, the Moon, and Earth are all described by Newton's laws of motion.

Newton's first law of motion states that an object at rest tends to stay at rest, and an object in motion tends to stay in motion with the same velocity, unless an unbalanced force acts on it. To **state** means "to declare," or "to express in words." The combination of all the forces acting on an object is the net force. Balanced forces cancel each other to produce a zero net force. Unbalanced forces do not cancel out. When a car is parked, the forces acting on it are balanced, and it does not move. It will stay at rest until an unbalanced force is exerted on it. The forces on the car are also balanced when it is in motion with a constant velocity. It will continue moving at this velocity until an unbalanced force acts on it.

The forces on a parked car are balanced until an unbalanced force is exerted on it.

Another way of thinking of the first law of motion is that an object tends to resist any change in its motion. **Inertia** is the tendency of an object to resist any change in its motion. The more mass an object has, the greater its inertia.

Newton's Second Law

According to Newton's second law of motion, an object acted upon by a net force will accelerate in the direction of the force. Acceleration can be determined by the following equation:

$$\text{acceleration} = \frac{\text{net force}}{\text{mass}} \qquad a = \frac{F_{net}}{m}$$

Acceleration is measured in m/s², net force is measured in N, and mass is measured in kg. According to the equation, the acceleration of an object produced by a net force is directly proportional to the magnitude of the net force, in the same direction as the net force, and inversely proportional to the mass of the object. This means that if two cars are acted on with the same force, the car with less mass car will have a larger acceleration. Similarly if the two cars with the same mass are acted on by two different forces, the car acted on by the larger force will have a greater acceleration.

CORE SKILL

Solve Linear Equations

You need to compare the masses of two objects. One accelerates at 5 m/s² when pulled with a net force of 30 N, and the second one accelerates at 3 m/s² when pulled with a net force of 18 N. To find the mass of each object, you need to rearrange the equation to isolate the variable for mass, m.

$$a = \frac{F_{net}}{m}$$

Start by multiplying both sides of the equation by m so that it is removed from the denominator and F_{net} is isolated.

$$m \times a = \frac{F_{net}}{m} \times m$$

$$ma = F_{net}$$

The variable m is still not alone, so divide both sides of the equation by a.

$$\frac{ma}{a} = \frac{F_{net}}{a}$$

$$m = \frac{F_{net}}{a}$$

Now you can solve for m by substituting the given values for force and acceleration into the equation.

$$m_2 = \frac{\frac{30\ kg}{m/s^2}}{5\ m/s^2} = 6\ kg$$

$$m_2 = \frac{\frac{18\ kg}{m/s^2}}{3\ m/s^2} = 6\ kg$$

The objects have the same mass, 6 kg, because the ratio of the force to the acceleration is the same.

Calculate and compare the force needed for a 50-kg person to accelerate at 1.5 m/s² and for a 65-kg person to accelerate at 1.2 m/s².

Apply Technology to a Task

Taking notes using a computer program can help you keep information organized. As long as you save the file using a logical name and folder structure, it will be easily accessible when you need it again.

If you don't already have one, make a computer folder to store your test-preparation work. Use a computer program to make a four-column table for a KWLH chart for this lesson as shown on page 448. Include information about each of Newton's laws and the law of universal gravitation. Pick a logical file name for your notes file and remember to save the file frequently as you work.

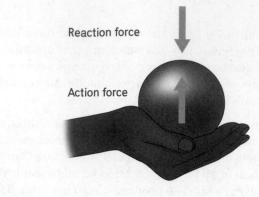

Reaction force

Action force

Newton's Third Law

According to Newton's third law of motion, when one object exerts a force on a second object, the second object exerts a force on the first object that is equal in strength and opposite in direction. These two forces are called action and reaction forces. Both forces are exerted at the same time, and either force can be considered the action force or the reaction force.

According to this law, whenever two objects interact with each other, they exert forces on each other. When you sit in a chair, your body exerts a downward force on the chair, and the chair exerts an upward force on your body. The action and reaction forces of this interaction are the force on the chair and the force on your body.

The magnitude of the force on the first object equals the magnitude of the force on the second object. The direction of the force on the first object is in the direction opposite of the force on the second object. When you hold a ball, you exert an upward force on the ball, while the ball exerts a force of equal magnitude downward on your hand.

If equal and opposite forces on an object cancel out, why don't action and reaction forces cancel out? Forces can cancel out only if they act on the same object. Action and reaction forces do not act on the same object. When a person takes a step, the person's foot exerts an action force on the ground. The ground, which is Earth, exerts a reaction force on the person's foot that pushes the person forward.

Think about Science

Directions: Answer the following questions.

1. Which is true, based on Newton's first law?
   A. A ball that is in motion has a tendency to come to a stop.
   B. A ball that is not moving has a tendency to stay stationary.
   C. The net force on any moving ball is not zero.
   D. A force must act on a ball to prevent it from moving.

2. A pushed box is accelerating at 3.0 m/s². If the force pushing the box is tripled, what is the acceleration of the box?
   A. 0.0 m/s²
   B. 1.0 m/s²
   C. 3.0 m/s²
   D. 9.0 m/s²

The Law of Universal Gravitation

Newton also developed the law of universal gravitation, which describes the force of gravity between any two objects that have mass. **Gravity** is a force of attraction between two objects because of their mass. Earth exerts gravitational force on everything on its surface. Everything on Earth's surface exerts gravitational force on Earth. The planets, their moons, and stars exert gravitational force on one another.

Newton determined that the force of gravity depends on the masses of the objects and the distance between them. He developed an equation to identify this relationship.

$$F = \frac{Gm_1m_2}{r^2}$$

In this equation, F represents the gravitational force, m_1 is the mass of one object, m_2 is the mass of the other object, and r is the distance between their centers. The letter G is the universal gravitational constant. Its accepted value is $G = 6.67 \times 10^{-11}$ N $\cdot$ m^2/kg^2. The equation shows that the attraction between two objects gets stronger as mass increases and gets weaker as mass decreases. It also shows that gravity decreases rapidly as the distance between the objects increases.

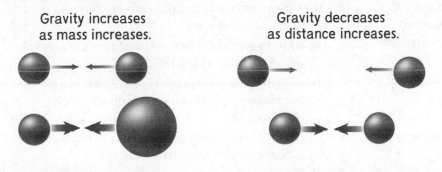

Gravity increases as mass increases.

Gravity decreases as distance increases.

Weight Versus Mass

When you step on a bathroom scale, the scale measures your weight. **Weight** is a measure of the force of gravity on an object. Although weight depends on mass, they are not the same quantity. Mass (m) is the amount of matter in an object. Weight (W) is a force equal to the mass of an object multiplied by the acceleration due to gravity (g), $W = mg$.

Near Earth's surface, the acceleration due to gravity is 9.8 m/s^2 for all objects. However, the acceleration due to gravity is different on other planets because the planets have different masses. For example, the acceleration due to gravity on Jupiter is 2.6 times more than it is on Earth. So, the same object on Jupiter would weigh 2.6 times more than it would on Earth, even though the object's mass remains the same.

Think about Science

Directions: Answer the following questions.

1. Doubling the mass of one object _____ the force of gravity, while doubling the distance between the two objects _____ the force of gravity by _____.

2. The weight of a person who has a mass of 50 kg is _____ N on Earth and would be _____ on Mars, where the acceleration due to gravity is smaller than it is on Earth.

Apply Formulas from Scientific Theories

Newton's law of universal gravitation explains why gravity decreases quickly as the distance between objects increases. Look at the equation for the force of gravity again. Notice that distance between the two objects, r, is squared. That means the distance is multiplied by itself.

Earth has a mass of about 6.0×10^{24} kg. Use the equation for the law of universal gravitation to explain how gravity changes when a 170-kg astronaut is 4 meters above Earth's surface in a building and 400,000 meters above Earth in the space station. (Recall that gravity is measured from the center of an object. The distance from the center of Earth to the surface is about 6,300,000 meters. Be sure to add this distance into your calculations.) Do your calculations support the idea that astronauts orbiting Earth are not pulled to Earth by gravity? Explain your answer.

Vocabulary Review

Directions: Write the missing term in the blank.

force	gravity	inertia
law	state	weight

1. The attraction between any two objects because of their mass is _____.

2. The force on an object due to gravity is _____.

3. A(n) _____ is a push or pull that may or may not cause an object to move.

4. An object tends not to move because of its _____.

5. A(n) _____ describes a relationship in nature that occurs under certain conditions.

6. To _____ means "to declare in words."

Skill Review

Directions: Answer the following questions.

1. Which does Newton's first law predict will happen to a passenger in a car after the car stops suddenly before another force acts on the passenger?

   A. The passenger will move backward.

   B. The passenger will continue to move forward.

   C. The passenger will move forward slightly before stopping.

   D. The passenger will stop with the car.

2. What is the average acceleration of a 20-kg box that is pushed with a net force of 7 N, 8 N, and 15 N of force?

   A. 0.4 m/s^2

   B. 0.5 m/s^2

   C. 2 m/s^2

   D. 200 m/s^2

3. Gravity pulls a falling apple to Earth. If this is the action force, what is the reaction force?

   A. The apple pulling up on Earth

   B. There is no reaction force for gravity.

   C. The air pushing up on the apple

   D. The apple pushing down on the air

4. How is the force of gravity related to the mass and distance of objects?

   A. Gravity is directly proportional to mass and inversely proportional to distance.

   B. Gravity is directly proportional to mass and inversely proportional to the square of the distance.

   C. Gravity is inversely proportional to mass and directly proportional to distance.

   D. Gravity is inversely proportional to the square of mass and directly proportional to distance.

5. When a pool stick hits a cue ball, what are the action and reaction forces?

   A. The pool player pushing on the stick, and the stick pushing on the ball

   B. The stick pushing on the ball, and the ball pushing on the table

   C. The stick pushing on the ball, and the ball pushing on the stick

   D. The ball pushing on the table, and the table pushing on the floor

6. For years, people believed it was the tendency of objects to return to rest because objects are observed to come to a stop. Explain whether this contradicts Newton's first law of motion and use evidence to support your argument.

7. When a rocket launches, it must overcome the force of gravity. When the fuel is ignited, the gas produced rushes out of the bottom of the rockets. Use Newton's third law to explain what causes a rocket to lift off.

Forces and Newton's Laws of Motion

Skill Practice

Directions: Use the diagram to answer questions 1–4.

Weight is a force, so it is measured in newtons. To find the weight of an object on Earth's surface, multiply the mass in kilograms by 9.8 m/s². For example, a person who has a mass of 60.0 kg will weigh 588 N.

$$W = 60.0 \text{ kg} \times 9.8 \text{ m/s}^2 = 588 \text{ kg} \cdot \text{m/s}^2 = 588 \text{ N}$$

An acceleration of 9.8 m/s² can be used when calculating weight on Earth. Remember that the acceleration due to gravity, however, varies from one planet to another. Therefore a person's weight would change on different planets. The table shows a 60.0-kg person's weight on other planets.

Planet	Weight (N)
Mercury	222
Venus	533
Earth	588
Mars	222
Jupiter	1,390
Saturn	629
Uranus	523
Neptune	662

1. What is the acceleration due to gravity on Venus?
   A. 0.11 m/s²
   B. 8.9 m/s²
   C. 9.8 m/s²
   D. 54.4 m/s²

2. How much greater is the acceleration due to gravity on Earth than on Mars?
   A. 0.17 times greater
   B. 2.6 times greater
   C. 6.1 times greater
   D. 366 times greater

3. What is the weight of a 75-kg person on Saturn?
   A. 539 N
   B. 654 N
   C. 786 N
   D. 735 N

4. The acceleration due to gravity depends on the mass of the planet and the distance between an object on the surface of planet and center of the planet, which is given by the radius of the planet. Which can explain the why the acceleration due to gravity of Mercury is the same as it is on Mars?
   A. Mars has less mass than and the same radius as Mercury.
   B. Mars has more mass and a larger radius than Mercury
   C. Mars has the same mass as and a larger radius than Mercury.
   D. Mars has more mass and a smaller radius than Mercury.

Directions: Answer the following questions.

5. Freefall occurs when a falling object experiences only the force of gravity. If a ball is dropped from a height of ten meters, on which planet will it be moving the fastest when it reaches the ground? Justify your answer using the data in the table above.

6. A tennis ball and a bowling ball are dropped from the roof of a building on Earth. Will they accelerate at the same rate if the only force acting on them is gravity? Combine the equations for Newton's second law and the law of universal gravitation to justify your answer.

LESSON 5.3 Work and Simple Machines

LESSON OBJECTIVES

- Calculate work and power
- Define and identify the need for machines
- Analyze the use of simple and complex machines

CORE SKILLS & PRACTICES

- Identify and Refine Hypotheses for Scientific Investigations
- Follow a Multistep Procedure and Analyze the Results

Key Terms

compound machines
machines made of more than one simple machine

mechanical advantage
the amount of mechanical help a machine provides

power
the rate at which work is done

simple machines
devices that make work easier—specifically a wedge, wheel and axle, lever, and pulley

work
occurs when a force moves an object

Vocabulary

revise
to make changes, especially to correct or improve

Key Concept

When forces move an object over a distance, work has been done. Simple machines are used to make work easier by reducing either the force or the distance. Compound machines are made of more than one simple machine.

Work and Power

In science, force and distance determine the amount of work done. Machines and technology help reduce the amount of work people have to do. For example, luggage movers deliver luggage to and from airplanes. They reduce the amount of work employees and passengers have to do.

Defining Work

In science, **work** is when a force moves an object in the same direction the force is being exerted. Work is done when a teacher lifts a chair, a horse pulls a wagon, and a dancer leaps into the air. However, not all forces result in work. In order for work to be done, two conditions must be met. First, a force must be exerted on an object that causes that object to move. Second, the force must be exerted in the same direction the object moves.

One student lifts a book from the floor to a shelf 1 meter above the ground. A second student lifts the same book to the same height and then carries it to a shelf across the room. Which student does more work on the book? The answer might surprise you because the answer is neither student. Both students do the same amount of work on the book.

Work is done only when a force causes an object to move in the same direction the force is being applied. Therefore work is done when an upward force is exerted to lift the book. If the force is exerted in a direction different from the direction in which the object moves, no work is done. This means no additional work is done when the book is carried across the room, because the force on the book is upward, and the direction of motion is horizontal.

Calculating Work

The amount of work done is shown by the equation:

$$\text{work} = \text{force} \times \text{distance, or } W = Fd.$$

When force is measured in newtons and distance is measured in meters, the unit of work is the newton·meter (N·m), which is also known as a joule (J), the SI unit for work.

The work done can be determined if the force and the distance are known. Suppose a weight lifter lifts a dumbbell weighing 70 N a distance of 1 m. How much work does he do? The force required to lift an object near Earth's surface is equal and opposite to the weight of the object, so the weight lifter must exert an upward force of 70 N to lift the dumbbell. The force moves the dumbbell a distance of 1 m.

$$W = 70 \text{ N} \times 1 \text{ m} = 70 \text{ N·m} = 70 \text{ J}$$

Because the second weight lifter raised the dumbbell twice as high, twice as much work was done. Finally the third weight lifter raised twice as much weight twice as high. This represents the greatest amount of work.

W = 70 N × 1 m = 70 J   **W** = 70 N × 2 m = 140 J   **W** = 140 N × 2 m = 280 J

Defining and Calculating Power

Power measures the rate at which work is done.

It can be calculated using the following equation:

$$\text{power} = \text{work} \div \text{time, or } p = \frac{W}{t}$$

When work is measured in joules, and time in seconds, the unit of power is the joule per second, which is the same as the SI unit watts (W). Power can be calculated if the work and time are known. For example, what is the power when a person does 140 J of work in 20 s?

$$p = \frac{140 \text{ J}}{20 \text{ s}} = 7 \text{ W}$$

If the time decreased to 10 s, the power would double.

$$p = \frac{140 \text{ J}}{10 \text{ s}} = 14 \text{ W}$$

Think about Science

Directions: Answer the following questions.

1. If 1250 J of work is done on an object that weighs 50 N, how far can that object be raised?

    A. 5 m
    B. 25 m
    C. 125 m
    D. 1200 m

2. A crane lifts a car that weighs 16,000 N 12 m in 5 s. What is the power of the crane?

    A. 267 W
    B. 6,667 W
    C. 38,400 W
    D. 960,000 W

Follow a Multistep Procedure and Analyze the Results

Sometimes the application of abstract scientific concepts to the real world requires a multiple-step procedure. After following each step, you will want to analyze your results. Try this investigation.

Find a set of stairs you can safely walk and run up. Measure the vertical height of the set of stairs in meters. Record how many seconds it takes you to first walk up the stairs and then run up the stairs. Calculate the work you did in walking and running up the stairs. (For force, multiply your weight in pounds by 4.4 newtons per pound to find your weight in newtons.) Calculate the power you needed to walk and run up the stairs.

Now analyze your results. How does the work you did in each situation compare? How does the power needed in each situation compare?

Machines

A machine is any device that makes doing work easier. For any type of machine, work is done on the machine and by the machine. The work that is done on the machine is the input work and the work that the machine does is the output work.

Work is a force exerted over some distance; therefore two forces are involved when a machine is used. The force exerted on a machine is called the input force, so the input work done on a machine is equal to the input force times the distance over which the input force is exerted. The force exerted by the machine is called the output force. So, the output work, or the work done by the machine, is equal to the output force times the distance over which the output force is exerted.

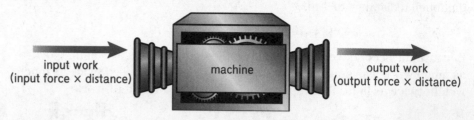

input work
(input force × distance)

machine

output work
(output force × distance)

Simple Machines

The most basic machines are called **simple machines,** which are machines that do work with only one movement of the machine. There are six basic types of simple machines: inclined plane, screw, wedge, lever, wheel, and axle.

Inclined Plane

Walking or driving straight up a steep incline is much more difficult than traveling along the winding, sloped path. A gentler slope reduces the amount of force needed to move an object. The simple machine that takes advantage of this principle is the inclined plane. An inclined plane is a flat surface set at an angle to a horizontal surface. A ramp is an example of an inclined plane.

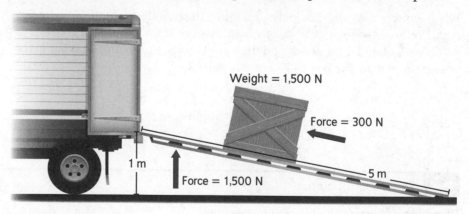

Weight = 1,500 N

Force = 300 N

1 m

Force = 1,500 N

5 m

The same amount of work is done to lift a box as is done to push that box up an inclined plane. To lift the box, the amount of work done is equal to the force of 1,500 N times the distance of 1 m, or $W = 1{,}500 \text{ N} \times 1 \text{ m} = 1{,}500 \text{ J}$. To push the box along the ramp, the amount of work done is equal to the force of 300 N times the distance of 5 m, or $W = 300 \text{ N} \times 5 \text{ m} = 1{,}500 \text{ J}$. The same amount of work is done to lift the box as is done to push that box up the ramp. The advantage of the inclined plane is that the plane enables the mover to use a smaller force. The trade-off is that the force must be exerted over a longer distance.

Screw

Some simple machines are modified versions of other simple machines. A screw is an inclined plane wrapped in a spiral around a central cylinder. The spirals, or threads, of the screws form small ramps that run upward from the tip. Unlike a ramp over which a person might push a box, the inclined plane of a screw moves through an object or material. Screws are found in many common devices, such as jar lids, light bulbs, and bolts.

Wedge

Like the screw, a wedge is a simple machine in which an inclined plane moves through or between objects. It is an inclined plane with one or two sloping sides. It is thick at one end and tapers to a thin edge. Wedges are generally used for separating objects or holding them in place. Knives, axes, and shovels are common examples. A wedge makes work easier by decreasing the required input force. In turn, the input force must be exerted over a longer distance. A wedge also changes the direction of the input force. As the carving tool is moved through the wood, the downward input force is changed into a horizontal force that pushes the wood apart.

Lever

A lever is a rigid bar that is free to rotate about a fixed point to lift something, known as the load. The fixed point the lever rotates about is the fulcrum. The part of the lever between the input force and the fulcrum is the input arm, and the part between the fulcrum and the output force is the output arm. Levers can be categorized into three classes.

A crowbar, a seesaw, and a boat oar are examples of first-class levers. In a first-class lever, the fulcrum is located between the input and output forces, and the fulcrum's position determines how easy it is to lift the load. The motion of the object being moved is in the direction opposite of the input force.

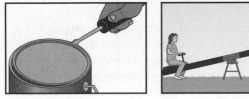

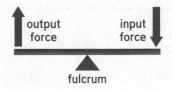
output force   input force
fulcrum

21ST CENTURY SKILL

Creativity and Innovation

Machines are the result of someone's innovation. People started with simple machines that helped them accomplish everyday tasks. Today we use both simple machines and compound machines.

Cleaning the floors of your home can be an exhausting and time-consuming chore, but today we have machines that can vacuum and mop our floors without our pushing them. They move around on the floor on their own and clean. When these machines bounce into the wall or furniture, they change direction. They can even return to their charging base on their own when they're finished.

Describe another example of how innovation and creativity has reduced work today.

A hypothesis is a tentative explanation based on insufficient evidence. Before scientists perform an investigation, they use their prior knowledge to predict what they think will happen. After the experiment is performed, they **revise,** or rewrite, the hypothesis for the next experiment based on what they learned. When scientists revise their work, they change it to improve it or correct it.

Try this activity. Tape ten pennies together in a stack. Place a pencil under a ruler at the six-inch mark. Place the pennies at the one-inch mark and push with one finger on the eleven-inch mark. Consider how much force it took to lift the pennies. Make a hypothesis about where you could put the pennies to make it harder or easier to lift the pennies and then test your hypothesis.

After you perform the investigation several times, revise your hypothesis based on the results. Use the idea of work and levers to explain your results.

A wheelbarrow and a bottle opener are examples of second-class levers. In this type of lever, the output force is located between the input force and the fulcrum.

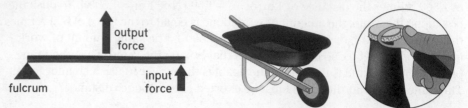

A fishing rod and a baseball bat are examples of third-class levers. A third-class lever's fulcrum is at the end of the lever, and the input force is exerted between the fulcrum and the output force. In addition, a third-class lever does not change the direction of the input force. A third-class lever exerts a smaller output force over a longer distance.

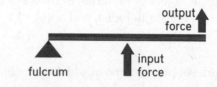

Pulley

A pulley is a grooved wheel with a rope, chain, or cable running along the groove, and it can be fixed or movable. A fixed pulley is attached to something that does not move, such as a ceiling or a wall, with the distance the rope is pulled down equaling the distance the load moves upward. For the input work to equal the output work, the input force on the rope must equal the output force on the load; therefore a fixed pulley does not change either force or distance. It changes only the direction of the input force.

A pulley attached to the object being moved is called a movable pulley. Unlike a fixed pulley, a movable pulley multiplies force; therefore the input force must be exerted over a greater distance. When fixed and movable pulleys are combined, a system of pulleys is formed.

Wheel and Axle

A wheel and axle is a simple machine consisting of two circular objects of different sizes. The axle, which is the smaller of the two objects, is attached to the center of a larger wheel. The wheel and axle rotate together. The input force can be applied to either the wheel or the axle. Doorknobs, screwdrivers, and faucet handles are examples of wheel and axles.

Compound Machines

Compound machines, like cars, are made up of more than one simple machine. Burning fuel in the cylinders of a car engine causes the pistons to move up and down. This makes the crankshaft rotate. The force exerted by the rotating crankshaft is transmitted to other parts of the car, such as the transmission and the differential. Both of these parts contain gears, which are wheel and axles. Cars also contain levers and pulleys.

Think about Science

Directions: Answer the following question.

1. A bicycle is a compound machine. Identify at least two simple machines that are used in a bicycle.

Mechanical Advantage

Work is the transfer of energy. Recall that energy is neither created nor destroyed—it is conserved. Therefore the output work cannot be greater than the input work for any machine. If a machine does not multiply work, how is it useful? A machine makes work easier by multiplying force or distance or changing the input force's direction.

The number of times a machine increases the input force is the **mechanical advantage** (MA) of the machine. The MA of a machine is the ratio of the output force to the input force. It can be calculated using the following equation:

$$\text{mechanical advantage} = \frac{\text{output force}}{\text{input force}}, \text{ or } MA = \frac{F_{out}}{F_{in}}$$

Both the input force and the output force are measured in newtons. As a result, the units cancel, and mechanical advantage does not have any units associated with it.

For a first-class lever, the closer the output force is to the fulcrum, the greater the mechanical advantage of the lever. Because a second-class lever multiplies force, its mechanical advantage is always greater than 1. For a third-class lever, however, $F_{out} < F_{in}$, so the mechanical advantage is always less than 1.

The mechanical advantage of a fixed pulley is 1. As shown below, a person needs to exert a force of 4 N to lift the 4-N weight. However, the person is able to pull downward instead of upward, which is easier.

The mechanical advantage of a movable pulley is greater than 1. It is equal to the number of rope segments holding up the load. Force is multiplied because the input force is exerted over twice the distance of the output force. A force of 2 N can be exerted to lift a load that weighs twice as much, which is 4 N.

CALCULATOR SKILL

Using Formulas

When given a problem that involves calculating the ideal mechanical advantage (IMA) of a simple machine, use the formula for that machine. Read the problem and identify the numbers needed for the formula. Replace the variables in the formula with the numbers, isolate the variable that you need to solve for, and use your calculator to solve. Use these formulas to solve the following problems. Show your work.

$$IMA_{\text{inclined plane}} = \frac{\text{length of inclined plane}}{\text{height of slope}}$$

$$IMA_{\text{lever}} = \frac{\text{length of input arm}}{\text{length of output arm}}$$

1. The IMA of a 4-m-long inclined plane is 10. What is the height of the inclined plane?

2. The IMA of a lever with a 0.5-m output arm is 6. What is the length of the input arm?

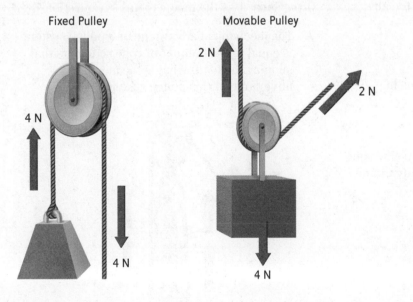

Fixed Pulley — 4 N, 4 N

Movable Pulley — 2 N, 2 N, 4 N

✺ Think about Science

Directions: Answer the following question.

1. How can you increase the mechanical advantage of a movable pulley?

Work and Simple Machines

Vocabulary Review

Directions: Write the missing term in the blank.

work   power   simple machine
compound machine   mechanical advantage   revise

1. A _____ is made of two or more of the six types of simple machines.

2. A _____ does work with only one movement of the machine.

3. By multiplying force by distance and then dividing by time, _____ can be calculated.

4. After the teacher reviewed my lab report, he asked me to _____ it to include more details.

5. _____ is done if a force is exerted on an object, and the object moves in the direction of that force.

6. If the input force is greater than the output force, the _____ is less than 1.

Skill Review

Directions: Answer the following questions.

1. What is the force a person exerts in pulling a wagon 20 m if 1,500 J of work are done?

   A. 15 N

   B. 75 N

   C. 750 N

   D. 30,000 N

2. Which of the following would guarantee an increase in the work done?

   A. A decrease in distance

   B. An decrease in force

   C. An increase in force and a decrease in distance

   D. An increase in force and distance

3. What is the force needed to lift a 1,950-N weight using a machine with a mechanical advantage of 15?

   A. 130 N

   B. 195 N

   C. 1,935 N

   D. 29,250 N

4. Which could be categorized as a screw?

   A. jar lid

   B. roller coaster

   C. plunger

   D. scissors

5. Two students are asked to unload identical boxes of books. One student completes the job in 10 minutes and the other takes 20 minutes. Compare the work and power of the two students.

6. Explain why machines cannot decrease the amount of work required to complete a task.

Directions: Use the image to answer question 7.

7. The mechanical advantage of a pulley system is equal to the number of rope segments that support the load. What is the mechanical advantage of this pulley system?

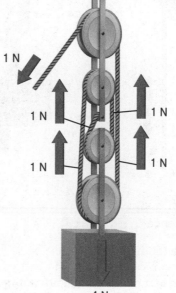

Skill Practice

Directions: Answer the following questions.

1. A person pushes down on a jack, which lifts a car. Which statement is true?

   A. The output force of the jack is much less than the input force of the person.

   B. The distance the person pushes down on the handle is shorter than the distance the jack lifts the car.

   C. The amount of work done increases.

   D. The car jack multiplies the force applied to it.

2. Use the formula $p = W/t$ to find a mathematical relationship between power and velocity.

   A. $p = F/v$

   B. $p = vW$

   C. $p = Fv$

   D. $p = W/v$

3. When a person twists a screw into a piece of wood, an input force is exerted on the screw. What must the threads of the screw do so that a force pulls the screw into the wood?

   A. Increase the distance over which the force is exerted

   B. Change the direction of the force

   C. Decrease the force exerted on the screw

   D. Increase the resulting number of watts

4. Use the formula below to find the IMA of a wheel and axle that has a wheel radius of 15 cm and an axle radius of 6 cm.

$$IMA_{\text{wheel and axle}} = \frac{\text{radius of wheel}}{\text{radius of axle}}$$

Directions: Use the information to answer questions 5–7.

Building the Pyramids

The Great Pyramid of Giza is made of 2.3 million blocks, each of which weighs more than 2 tons. Building a structure such as this would be an amazing feat today, with power tools to cut the blocks and cranes to move them into place. The Great Pyramid, however, was built about 4,500 years ago when its builders had only hand tools and the power of their own muscles. No one really knows how they did it; however, historians and archeologists know the types of tools the ancient Egyptians had and how these tools were probably used.

The Great Pyramid is constructed of several types of stone, including limestone and granite. Workers used copper chisels to cut out limestone blocks. They used quartz, the hardest of several minerals in granite, to slowly scrape cuts in the granite. Workers forced the blade of a saw down onto quartz particles on the rock's surface. The saw slowly cut into the rock.

Each block was put onto a wooden platform where workers secured the block and platform onto a track of wooden rollers. As the block was pushed and pulled, it rolled along on top of the track of rollers while hundreds of workers dragged the heavy blocks up the pyramid. Then workers used poles and ropes to get each block into its correct place.

5. Based on evidence from the passage, what type of simple machine was the copper chisel? Justify your answer.

6. How might an inclined plane have helped in the construction of the pyramids?

7. Why did the workers use poles and ropes to get the blocks in place? Use simple machines in your explanation.

Directions: Use the following sentence to answer questions 1 and 2.

> An airplane is flying east over the city of Chicago at 885 kilometers per hour (km/h).

1. Describe the airplane's position, speed, and velocity.

2. How long will it take the plane to reach New York City if New York is approximately 1125km from Chicago? Use the formula below to calculate the time in hours.

$$\text{speed} = \tfrac{\text{distance}}{\text{time}}$$

Directions: Answer the following questions.

3. A driver of a car travels 64 miles per hour and stops at a traffic light. He then resumes driving at 64 miles per hour when the light turns green. What has changed about the motion of the car during this entire process?
   A. The car has experienced a change in direction.
   B. The car has experienced an increase in velocity.
   C. The car has experienced a change in acceleration.
   D. The car has experienced a decrease in momentum.

4. Which of the following information is needed to calculate the momentum of a baseball travelling to home plate?
   A. mass and speed
   B. mass and velocity
   C. speed and direction
   D. distance and velocity

5. A rock with a mass of 30 kg is dropped from a cliff and hits the ground with an acceleration of 70 m/s². Use the formula below, where F is force, m is mass, and a is acceleration, to calculate how much force the rock exerts as it strikes the ground.

   $$F = \tfrac{m}{a}$$

   A. 2.3 kg · $\frac{m}{s^2}$
   B. 210 kg · $\frac{m}{s^2}$
   C. 430 kg · $\frac{m}{s^2}$
   D. 2,100 kg · $\frac{m}{s^2}$

6. Which of Newton's laws explains why it is safer to wear a seatbelt in a moving car?
   A. first law of motion
   B. second law of motion
   C. third law of motion
   D. law of universal gravitation

7. Which of Newton's laws explains why it is easier to stop a tennis ball from rolling than a bowling ball?
   A. first law of motion
   B. second law of motion
   C. third law of motion
   D. law of universal gravitation

8. Which of the following is an example of an action-at-a-distance force?
   A. a magnet attracting a paper clip
   B. a horse pulling a wagon full of hay
   C. a baseball bat hitting a ball into the air
   D. friction between a car tire and the road

9. Which of the following actions would decrease the gravitational force between two objects?
   A increasing the mass of one object
   C. increasing the weight of both objects
   B. increasing the distance between objects
   D. decreasing the distance between objects

10. If an object weighing 75 N is pushed uphill a vertical height of 56m, how much work is being done on the object? Use the formula below, where W is work, F is force, and d is distance, to find the correct answer.

    $$W = Fd$$

    A. 0.14 J
    B. 1.33 J
    C. 428 J
    D. 4,200 J

11. If a gas-powered motor does 10,000 J of work in 30 s, what is the power of the motor? Use the formula below, where W is work, and t is time, to find the correct answer.

$$P = \frac{W}{t}$$

A. 300,000 Js

B. 3,300 W

C. 333 W

D. 0.003 s/J

12. Which of the following is an example of a wheel and an axle?

A. a crowbar

B. a garage door

C. a screwdriver

D. a wheelbarrow

13. How does using a fixed pulley to lift a heavy object with a rope change the force applied to the rope?

A. It changes the force of the object on the rope.

B. It only decreases the force applied to the rope.

C. It only changes the direction of the input force.

D. It changes the direction and the amount of the input force.

14. Which of the following defines the mechanical advantage of a machine?

A. sum of the output force and the input force

B. product of the input force and the output force

C. division of the input force by the output force

D. division of the output force by the input force

Directions: Use the graph to answer questions 15–17.

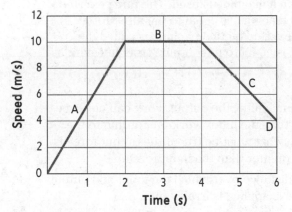

Speed v. Time

15. Between which points on the graph has the acceleration changed from 0 to -3 m/s^2?

A. Points A and B

B. Points B and C

C. Points A and C

D. Points C and D

16. In the portion of the graph near which point is the acceleration positive?

A. Point A

B. Point B

C. Point C

D. Point D

17. Explain what is occurring at point B in terms of the speed and acceleration of the object, assuming the object has not changed direction.

18. Which of the following best describes the difference between elastic and inelastic collisions?

A. In an elastic collision kinetic energy is transformed, but in an inelastic collision energy is not transformed.

B. In an elastic collision kinetic energy is not transformed, but in an inelastic collision kinetic energy is transformed.

C. In an elastic collision objects continuously collide and separate, but in an inelastic collision objects only collide once.

D. In an elastic collision, objects stick to one another on impact, but in an inelastic collision objects move away from each other after they collide.

19. Explain how momentum is conserved when two objects collide into one another.

20. Explain why action and reaction forces do not cancel each other out if it is known that equal and opposite forces result in a net force of zero?

21. Explain the difference between the weight and the mass of an object.

Directions: Use the passage to answer questions 22–23.

The word machine often brings to mind images of complex devices with intricate parts. While some machines fit this description, others are very simple, but a machine is any device that makes doing work easier. For any type of machine, work is done on the machine and by the machine. The work that is done on the machine is the input work, and the work that the machine does is the output work. Work is a force exerted over some distance; therefore, two forces are involved when a machine is used. The force exerted on a machine is called the input force, so the input work, done on a machine, is equal to the input force times the distance over which the input force is exerted. The force exerted by the machine is called the output force, so the output work, or the work done by the machine, is equal to the output force times the distance over which the output force is exerted.

22. According to the passage, if the input force of a machine is 60 N and this force is exerted over 25 cm, what is the work done on the machine to get it to function?

A. 1.5 J

B. 15 J

C. 150 J

D. 1,500 J

23. For any machine, the output work can never be greater than the input work. According to the passage what must be true if the output force is 3 times greater than the input force?

A. The distance over which the input and output force is applied is irrelevant.

B. The input force must be applied over a greater distance than the output force.

C. The output force must be applied over a greater distance than the input force.

D. The input force and the output force must be applied over the same distance.

A

B

24. Will one set of spheres have a greater gravitational pull on each other? Explain your answer.

25. What will happen to the gravitational force between the set of spheres labeled A if the mass of one sphere is doubled? Explain your answer.

Directions: Use image to answer question 26 and 27.

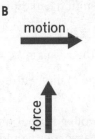

A

motion

force

B

motion

force

26. Which set of arrows, A or B, represents work being done on an object? Explain your answer.

27. What other information must be known to calculate how much work is done on an object?

A. acceleration

B. distance

C. mass

D. speed

Check Your Understanding

On the following chart, circle the number of any item you answered incorrectly. Next to each group of item numbers, you will see the pages you can review to learn how to answer the items correctly. Pay particular attention to reviewing those lessons in which you missed half or more of the questions.

Lesson	Item Number(s)	Review Page(s)
5.1: Motion	1, 2, 3, 4, 15, 16, 17, 18, 19	184–187
5.2: Forces and Newton's Laws of Motion	5, 6, 7, 8, 9, 20, 21, 24, 25	190–193
5.3: Work and Simple Machines	10, 11, 12, 13, 14, 22, 23, 26, 27	196–201

Collision and Impact

Core Practice

- Evaluate whether a conclusion or theory is supported or challenged by particular data or evidence

Question

How long an impact time is needed to stop an egg dropped from a height of 2 meters without breaking it?

Background Concepts

Momentum is described most simply as mass in motion. The momentum of a moving object is equal to the mass of the object multiplied by its velocity ($p = mv$, where p is momentum, m is mass, and v is velocity). When two objects collide, momentum is transferred between the two objects, but the total momentum between them is conserved.

As you learned, the equation for force is F = ma, where F is force, m is mass, and a is acceleration. We can modify this equation by substituting the definition of acceleration, $a = \frac{\Delta v}{t}$. The symbol Δ indicates change, so the change in velocity (final velocity $-$ initial velocity) is expressed by Δv. Therefore, $a = \frac{\Delta v}{t}$. The resulting equation is then:

$$F = m \left(\frac{\Delta v}{t} \right)$$

Multiply both sides of this equation by t and the result is $Ft = m\Delta v$.

Ft is known as impulse and $m\Delta v$ is the change in momentum. Therefore, impulse is equal to the change in momentum.

When force is exerted on an object during a collision, that object encounters an impulse. Without a car air bag, during a collision the passenger would collide with the hard surface of the dashboard in an inelastic collision. The impact time is short but the force is large and damaging. To protect passengers, airbags extend the impact time, or the time over which the force is exerted upon the passenger, so that they come to a stop more slowly. With increased time that the force is exerted, the same impulse is achieved with less force on the passenger. The amount of impulse required to stop the passenger is the same, but the manner in which the impulse is achieved is different with and without the airbag.

Hypothesis

A hypothesis is an explanation based on the evidence available. It is a starting point for a scientific investigation that will prove to be either correct, partially correct, or incorrect based on more evidence that is gathered.

A force acting on a egg when it is dropped from any height onto a hard surface will usually break the egg. How can the impact time be increased to prevent the egg from breaking? Develop a hypothesis that can be verified through testing to answer this question.

Investigation

After developing a hypothesis, the next step is to gather data to determine whether your hypothesis is supported or not.

Your task is to design and test a method to protect an egg from breaking when dropped from a height of 2 meters. This will test your hypothesis. Use the information you read in the Background Concepts section to determine how you can alter the impact of the collision by protecting the egg.

MATERIALS

Raw eggs   Plastic sandwich bag

Materials to protect the egg such as: plastic straws, string, tape, paper, plastic bags, paper towels, glue, plastic containers, foam, cardboard, recycled materials, etc.

Enclose an egg inside a plastic sandwich bag at the start of each trial, to prevent a mess if the egg breaks on impact. Create something that can decrease the force.

Conduct trials to test the effectiveness of your design. To begin, drop an unprotected egg from a height of 2 meters and record the results. Design a way to protect the egg, drop the egg from 2 meters, and record the results. You can modify your design between trials if needed.

Collect and Analyze Data

Record all of the data from each trial in a table. Include observations of the egg when it lands, and what you did to modify the impact. Also describe or sketch each design to protect the egg.

Interpretation

Summarize the data collected and interpret the evidence to determine if your hypothesis is supported. When evaluating data you collected, ask yourself these questions:

- Were you able to construct a design to protect the egg from breaking? Did you need to modify your design (hypothesis) during the investigation?

- How does this experiment illustrate the concepts of impact and momentum?

Results

Discuss your results using evidence to support your conclusions. Discuss any observations, possible sources of error, unexpected results, and any remaining questions. If your hypothesis was not supported, discuss your recommendations for formulating a new hypothesis or changes you would make to the investigation.

Consider these questions as you discuss your results:

- In what way will a collision of a moving object with a hard surface differ from the collision of the same object with a softer, more elastic surface?

- How does the principle applied in this investigation have a greater impact on design and engineering?

Chapter 6

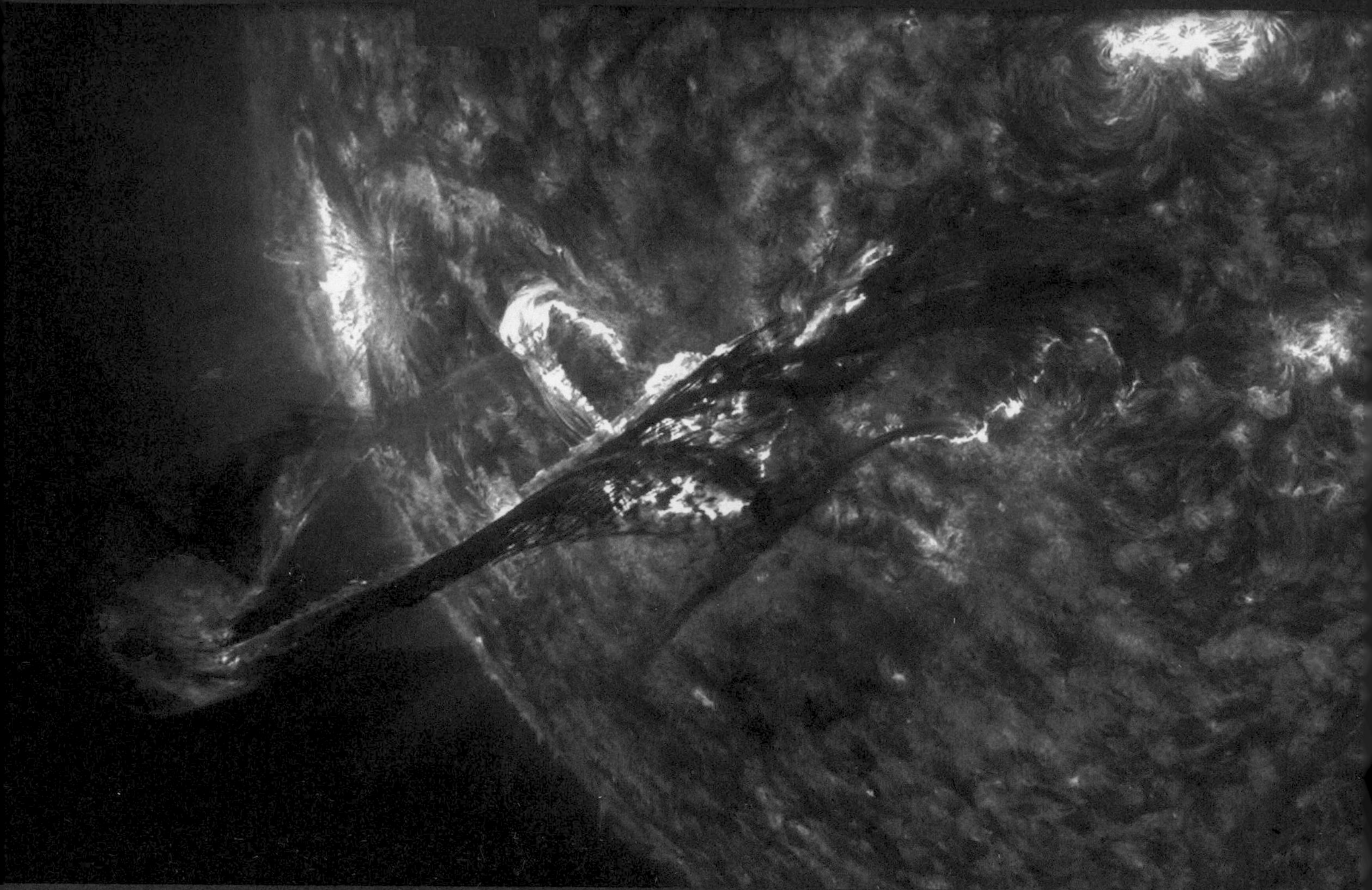

Energy

Just about everything around us uses energy. We use energy to light up our homes, make our motor vehicles run, and cook our food. Both you and your car need energy to move, but the energy required to move your body is in a different form and comes from different sources than the energy required to move your car. Humans take in fuel in the form of food, and this food provides energy for the maintenance of our body and for everyday activities. Cars take in fuel in the form of gasoline, and this fuel gives the car the power to operate properly. All sources of energy on Earth come from the Sun.

NASA/GSFC/SDO

Energy

Lesson 6.1
Types of Energy and Energy Transformations

There are many different types of potential and kinetic energy. Every action is connected to energy in one form or another. Learn that energy in the physical world can never be created or destroyed, but it can change from one type of energy to another.

Lesson 6.2
Sources of Energy

Different types of energy on Earth come from a variety of sources. Learn how some sources are replaced as quickly as they are consumed while other energy sources take millions of years to replace.

Lesson 6.3
Heat

The random motion of particles in a substance is a type of energy. This energy is transferred from one object to another in the form of heat. Learn how heat can transfer from one substance to another by three different methods: conduction, convection, and radiation.

Lesson 6.4
Waves

Some forms of energy such as sound and light, can travel in waves. In this lesson you will learn about the wave theory, the different types of waves, and their properties.

Goal Setting

Create a chart like the one at right. Think of an everyday example of the use of each of the types of energy listed in the chart. When you have completed this chapter, check your list to see if your examples were correct.

Type of Energy	Example
Electrical	Computer
Mechanical	
Radiant	
Chemical	
Nuclear	
Magnetic	
Thermal	

LESSON OBJECTIVES

- List how kinetic and potential energy act with matter
- Identify and compare various types of energy

CORE SKILLS & PRACTICES

- Identify the Strengths and Weaknesses of a Scientific Investigation
- Interpret Meaning of Mathematical Symbols

Key Terms

law of conservation of energy
states that energy cannot be created or destroyed

energy transformation
the change of one type of energy into another type of energy

kinetic energy
energy that results from motion

mechanical energy
the sum of an object's kinetic energy and its potential energy

potential energy
energy that is due to its position

Vocabulary

anticipate
to think of something that will or might happen in the future

Key Concept

There are many types of energy that cause changes in the world around us. Energy of one type can be transformed into energy of another type, but the total amount of energy cannot be changed.

What Is Energy?

A car races by. A light is switched on. Sound filters out from speakers. These are all forms of energy—motion, light, and sound. Energy is the ability to make things happen. Every action is connected to energy in one form or another. Objects can have energy due to their movement or their position.

Scientists measure energy in joules (J). It takes about one joule for a person to lift an apple one meter off the ground. Eating the apple provides the human body with about 250,000 J. Every form of energy, including movement, stored energy, heat, and light, can be measured in joules.

Kinetic Energy

Kinetic energy is the energy of an object's or particle's motion. The amount of kinetic energy depends on two things: the object's mass and how fast the object is moving. The amount of kinetic energy *(KE)* in joules that an object has is determined by the equation $KE = \frac{1}{2}mv^2$, where m equals the mass of the object in kilograms and v equals its velocity in meters per second. Energy can be expressed in units of joules, where 1 joule is 1 $(kg \cdot m^2)/s^2$.

If two objects have equal mass, the object that is moving faster has more kinetic energy. The diagram at the top of the next page shows calculations for the kinetic energy for three vehicles. Notice that Car B and Car C have equal mass, but Car C has more kinetic energy than Car B because it is moving faster. If two objects are moving at the same speed, the object with more mass has more kinetic energy than the object with less mass. As shown in the diagram, Truck A and Car B are traveling at the same speed. However, Truck A has more kinetic energy than Car B because Truck A has more mass. Notice that a change in speed affects energy more than a change in mass. If a car doubles its speed, its kinetic energy increases by a factor of four. A truck with four times the mass of a car has four times as much energy as the car when they travel at the same speed.

Kinetic Energy

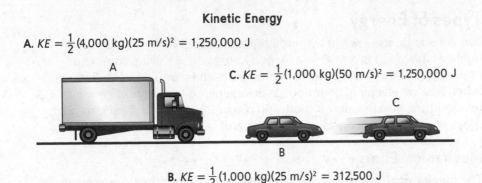

A. $KE = \frac{1}{2}(4{,}000 \text{ kg})(25 \text{ m/s})^2 = 1{,}250{,}000 \text{ J}$

C. $KE = \frac{1}{2}(1{,}000 \text{ kg})(50 \text{ m/s})^2 = 1{,}250{,}000 \text{ J}$

B. $KE = \frac{1}{2}(1{,}000 \text{ kg})(25 \text{ m/s})^2 = 312{,}500 \text{ J}$

Potential Energy

Potential energy is energy an object has due to its position. Potential energy does not involve motion, it is dependent on the interaction between two objects and the forces involved. This is considered stored energy.

Consider a book on a table. Together, the book and Earth have potential energy. Gravitational potential energy is the energy resulting from the gravitational forces between two objects. Raising an object above the ground increases the gravitational potential energy because work has been done on the object against the force of gravity. Gravity is a force that is described as a field, meaning there is a region in space that has this force at every point.

Gravitational potential energy *(GPE)* is related to the mass and height of the object, and acceleration due to the gravitational field. This can be expressed as $GPE = mgh$, where m is the mass of the object in kilograms, g is the acceleration due to gravity in meters per second squared (9.80 m/s^2 near Earth's surface), and h is the height the object is raised in meters.

If you lift a 2.00 kilogram book to a shelf 1.20 meters above the floor, what is the change in potential energy in joules? The gravitational field of the book is not considered because the field of an object only affects other objects.

$GPE = mgh$

$GPE = (2.00 \text{ kg})(9.80 \text{ m/s}^2)(1.20 \text{ m})$

$GPE = 23.5 \text{ (kg·m}^2)/\text{s}^2 = 23.5 \text{ J}$

The gravitational potential energy will increase by 23.5 J.

Potential energy can also be affected by other field forces between objects. For example, a magnetic field exerts a force on a paper clip that pulls the paper clip toward a magnet. The field forces around charged particles are called electrical fields. When a charged particle or object is moved a distance against the force of this field, its electric potential increases.

🔗 Think about Science

Directions: Answer the following questions.

1. A leaf falls from a tree to the ground. At what point is the gravitational potential energy the greatest?

   A. while the leaf is still attached to the branch
   B. after the leaf has fallen a short distance
   C. when the leaf is about half way to the ground
   D. when the leaf hits the ground

Scientific equations generally use abbreviations or symbols to represent variables used in the calculation. To **interpret,** which is to explain, the meaning of the symbols in an equation, look for descriptions and definitions in the surrounding text. If explanations cannot be found there, examine equations that were presented earlier in the text for the same symbols. The description will identify the variable represented by the symbol and its units. It is important to note the units and convert any values in a problem to the standard units of the equation.

Study the equations on these pages. Notice the symbols used to represent each variable. They are all italicized letters. On a separate piece of paper, write down each of the symbols shown here and their meanings. Include the units of the variable each symbol represents.

Identify the Strengths and Weaknesses of a Scientific Investigation

A well-designed experiment allows the investigator to obtain results that can be reproduced by repeating the experiment. Careful evaluation of the experimental design, keeping in mind the goal of the investigation, will allow you to determine how well the design matches those goals.

Consider the following design of an investigation into the amount of thermal energy needed to melt 10.0 grams of ice starting at a temperature of −4° C.

1. Add 100.0 grams of water to a clean, dry beaker.

2. Measure and record the temperature of the water.

3. Remove ice from a freezer held at −4° C.

4. Crush the ice and weigh 10.0 grams of ice.

5. Add the ice to the water.

6. When the water temperature becomes stable, measure and record the temperature of the water.

7. Calculate the amount of energy transferred from the water to the ice using the change in temperature and the mass of water.

Evaluate the experimental design. Can you suggest one or more changes to the design that would improve the accuracy of the experiment?

Types of Energy

You constantly use energy in your daily activities. When you turn on the lights or heat food in a microwave, you know you are using some type of energy. In other cases, your interactions with energy are less obvious. When you are sleeping, your body is using energy to maintain your internal temperature, breathe, digest food, and repair injured cells. There are many types of energy that constantly do work and cause changes around you.

Mechanical Energy

The **mechanical energy** of an object is the sum of its kinetic energy and its potential energy. As shown below, when the roller coaster is at the top of the hill, all of its energy is stored as gravitational potential energy. When the cars travel down the hill, their kinetic energy increases and the gravitational potential energy decreases by an equal amount. Not counting friction, the mechanical energy remains the same throughout the entire ride as the cars move up and down the hills of the roller coaster.

If you throw a ball in the air, the kinetic energy of its upward motion will decrease as gravitational potential energy increases. When the ball has reached its highest height, it has no kinetic energy at all. As the ball falls back to the ground, kinetic energy again increases and gravitational potential energy decreases by an equal amount. Overall the total amount of mechanical energy does not change as the ball moves from one position to another.

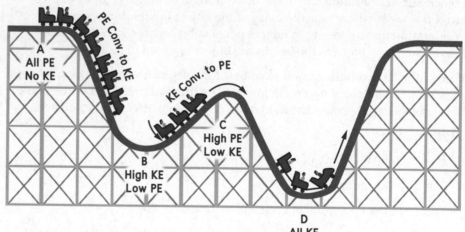

Thermal Energy

While it may not be obvious, every piece of matter around you is full of energy. The atoms and molecules that make up matter are always interacting. Liquid or gas particles flow from place to place, and even the molecules of a solid constantly vibrate. Thermal energy is the sum of the kinectic energy and the potential energy of the particles that make up matter.

Thermal energy can be detected when it flows from one object to another as heat. Faster-moving particles have more kinetic energy than slower-moving particles. When the particles collide, energy transfers from the faster particles to the slower particles. When you touch a hot pan, some of the energy of the rapidly vibrating metal atoms is transferred to your hand, in which atoms are moving more slowly. Wind is generated when heat is transferred from areas of the atmosphere with greater thermal energy to other regions with less thermal energy.

Types of Energy and Energy Transformations

Chemical Energy

When a match is struck, it emits light, sound, and thermal energy. All this energy had been stored in the match in the form of chemical energy. **Chemical energy** is the potential energy stored in the bonds between the atoms of a substance. The sources of this stored energy are the electromagnetic force fields of the charged particles that make up the atoms. Interactions among these fields provide energy that can be released during a chemical reaction.

Chemical energy is the source of most of the energy humans need to function. Plants store chemical energy in carbohydrates formed during photosynthesis. Humans release this chemical energy during digestion and use it to power systems inside the body.

Nuclear Energy

The nuclei of atoms contain a tremendous amount of potential energy. Energy stored in the nucleus of an atom is called nuclear energy. Nuclear energy holds the particles of the nucleus together. It can be released when nuclei are combined, which occurs in reactions in the Sun. Nuclear energy can also be released when nuclei are split apart, which occurs in nuclear reactors on Earth. One kilogram of uranium used as fuel in a nuclear power plant produces the same amount of energy as 14,000 kilograms of coal burned in a coal-fired power plant.

Radiant Energy

Radiant energy is emitted from a source as waves. These waves carry energy from the Sun through the vacuum of space to Earth. Radiant energy is a form of kinetic energy. In addition to the light we can see, radiant energy includes radio waves, microwaves, infrared radiation, ultraviolet radiation, gamma rays, and X-rays.

Think about Science

Directions: Fill in the blank.

1. Turning on a flashlight releases _____ energy.

2. Thermal energy is the sum of the _____ and potential energy of the particles in an object.

3. Energy stored in the nucleus of an atom is _____ energy.

4. Chemical energy is a type of potential energy stored in

   _____.

Electrical Energy and Magnetic Energy

Some objects can affect other objects from a distance due to a force field that exists around the them. A force field is a push or pull exerted in a region around the object producing it. Electrical energy and magnetic energy are both the result of fields. These forms of energy are related to one another.

Understand and Apply Basic and Multistep Instructions

When you perform an experiment or operate a machine, you usually follow a written instruction sheet or operator's manual that contains illustrations and numbered steps to guide you through the process.

Illustrations may include detailed drawings of how parts fit together. Directions are generally arranged in small blocks that are numbered to indicate the correct order in which operations are performed. You must follow these directions carefully to obtain the desired result. Performing the steps in the wrong order can change the results, make a machine operate incorrectly, or cause a hazardous condition.

Why do you think it is important to follow directions precisely in a laboratory or work setting? Explain your reasoning.

Electrical Energy

You may have experienced a shock after walking across a carpet and then touching a metal object, such as a doorknob. The shock comes from a transfer of electric charge. There are two types of electric charge: positive and negative. Two charges that are alike repel one another, and two charges that are different attract one another. Electrons are negatively charged atomic particles that naturally repel each other through the interaction of the electric fields that surround each electron. Electrical potential energy is the result of the positions of the charged particles within the electric fields. The friction of shuffling feet on a carpet rubs electrons from the carpet onto the feet. This buildup of charge generates electrical potential energy. Potential energy becomes kinetic energy when a static shock carries the charges toward positive charges located on the doorknob. It would be reasonable to expect, or **anticipate**, a static shock when you shuffle your feet on a carpet.

Electrons in a circuit have both kinetic and potential energy. When the electrons travel through a closed path, or electric circuit, some of its kinetic and potential energy can be changed to other forms of energy, such as light, thermal energy, or sound. Electrical energy powers many appliances and machines at home and at work.

Magnetic Energy

A magnet produces a force that can attract or repel other magnets and can attract certain other substances. You can feel this by holding two magnets near each other. Depending on how you hold the magnets, you can feel them push or pull on each other. This push or pull is due to the force of a magnetic field. The field is produced by moving electrons as in atoms. The magnetic field is exerted in a region surrounding the magnet, and it is strongest close to the magnet. The magnetic field stretches between two magnetic poles, which are regions where the magnetic field exerted by a magnet is the strongest. The north and south poles are at opposite ends of a bar magnet.

When two magnets are brought close together, their magnetic fields interact with each other. As shown here, the north pole of one magnet will repel the north pole of another magnet. South poles also repel each other. The north pole of one magnet and the south pole of another magnet, however, attract each other and stick together.

Magnetic Fields

Two north poles repel

Two south poles repel

Opposite poles attract

Think about Science

Directions: Answer the following question.

1. Earth has a magnetic field that extends from its North and South Magnetic Poles. When a compass is allowed to line up with Earth's magnetic field, the end labeled with an N points toward the magnetic North Pole. Based on this observation, if Earth's North Pole were a labeled magnet, should it be labeled as N or as S?

Conservation of Energy

People often talk about energy as if it were used up or lost during an activity. However, the energy still exists, just in a form that may not be obvious. The **law of conservation of energy** states that energy can be changed in form but it cannot be created or destroyed.

Types of Energy and Energy Transformations

It can take some detective work to follow the path of energy as it changes forms. For example, it takes a lot of energy to run a race. After the race, the runner's body has less energy than it had before. The chemical energy used to power muscles has been converted into kinetic energy and thermal energy. The total amount of energy in the universe is the same after the race as it was before.

Energy Transformation

We observe changes in energy all the time. For example, when an object moves against gravity, some of its kinetic energy is transformed to potential energy. An electric circuit that includes a light bulb transforms electrical energy into radiant energy and thermal energy. The change of one form of energy to another form of energy is called **energy transformation.**

Energy can change forms in many different ways. Energy conversions occur continually in living things. The human body provides many examples of energy transformations. The body takes in chemical potential energy in the form of food. The food is transformed into other chemicals in the digestive system. Sugars provide chemical energy for bodily functions, and fats store potential energy for future use. The heart and other muscles convert chemical energy to kinetic energy as blood circulates and the body moves. Some of the body's energy is transformed to sound. The body releases thermal energy in the form of heat. Nerves use electrical energy to communicate within the body.

Plants transform radiant energy into chemical energy. Electric eels transform chemical energy into electrical energy. Running deer transform chemical energy into kinetic energy. The table includes more examples of energy transformations.

Examples of Energy Transformations

Initial Energy Type	Final Energy Type	Example
Chemical	Electrical	Battery discharge
Chemical	Kinetic	Muscle movement
Chemical	Radiant and thermal	Combustion
Electrical	Kinetic	Electric motor
Electrical	Magnetic	Electromagnet
Radiant	Electrical	Solar cell
Radiant	Thermal	Absorption of sunlight
Thermal energy	Kinetic energy	Steam turbine

Think about Science

Directions: Answer the following question.

1. What energy transformation occurs in a toaster?
   A. kinetic energy to electrical energy
   B. electrical energy to thermal energy
   C. magnetic energy to electrical energy
   D. potential energy to kinetic energy

CALCULATOR SKILL
The Equal Sign

When you use a calculator to perform a mathematical operation, you generally finish the calculation by tapping the equal sign (=). Because this is often the final step, it may seem that the number that appears after tapping the equal sign is the final answer, but the sign actually only indicates the relationship between two sides of an equation. Be sure to return to your original problem to verify that the number you obtain when you evaluate the equation is, in fact, the answer to the question that has been posed. It may be an intermediate result.

Express, in words, the relationship between x and y in the following equation: $x = y - 2$.

Vocabulary Review

Directions: Write the missing term in the blank.

law of conservation of energy   anticipate   kinetic energy
mechanical energy   potential energy   energy transformation

1. Energy that is stored in an object or substance is its _____.

2. When an acorn falls from a tree, its _____ does not change.

3. During a(n) _____, one type of energy is changed into another type of energy.

4. If you walked to the store, you would _____ that chemical energy from food you ate would be transformed into kinetic energy as you move.

5. _____ states that energy cannot be created or destroyed.

6. As an automobile accelerates, its _____ increases.

Skill Review

Directions: Answer the following questions.

1. Which factor defines the difference between the kinetic energy and potential energy of an object such as a ball?
   A. The size of the object
   B. The motion of the object
   C. The mass of the object
   D. The nature of the object

2. Which term could be substituted for the term *potential energy?*
   A. heat energy
   B. rotational energy
   C. stored energy
   D. vibrational energy

3. Analyze the table on page 217. Which type of energy transformation does not appear among the examples?
   A. kinetic energy → kinetic energy
   B. kinetic energy → potential energy
   C. potential energy → kinetic energy
   D. potential energy → potential energy

4. Which action would increase potential energy?
   A. Turning on a flashlight
   B. Lighting a candle with a match
   C. Rolling a ball so that it falls off a shelf to the floor
   D. Placing similar poles of two magnets closer together

5. What energy transformation is necessary to regulate your body temperature on a cold day?
   A. kinetic energy to thermal energy
   B. electromagnetic radiation to chemical energy
   C. electrical energy to kinetic energy
   D. chemical energy to thermal energy

6. In a hydroelectric power plant, falling water turns a turbine that causes a copper coil to spin inside a strong magnetic field. The power plant transforms _____ and _____ into a _____.

Skill Practice

Directions: Use the diagram to answer questions 1–3.

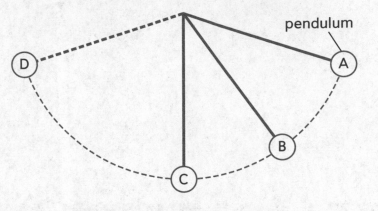

The pendulum is released at point A and swings to point D before returning.

1. Which statement is true when the pendulum reaches point C?

   A. $KE = (1/2)GPE$

   B. $GPE = 0$

   C. $KE = GPE$

   D. $KE = 0$

2. Which statement is true when the pendulum reaches point D?

   A. $KE = (1/2)GPE$

   B. $GPE = 0$

   C. $KE = GPE$

   D. $KE = 0$

3. Which two factors determine the maximum gravitational potential energy of the pendulum?

Directions: Answer the following questions.

4. Using the formula $KE = 1/2mv^2$, what is the kinetic energy of a 12.5 kg dog running across a field at 3.50 m/s?

   A. 3.57 J

   B. 43.8 J

   C. 76.6 J

   D. 153 J

5. Which energy transformation occurs when an ice cube melts on a sunny windowsill?

   A. radiant energy → potential energy

   B. potential energy → thermal energy

   C. radiant energy → thermal energy

   D. kinetic energy → potential energy

6. A walnut falls from a tree to the ground. If you know the mass of the walnut and the original height of the walnut above the ground, explain how you could calculate its velocity at the end of its fall.

7. Make a sketch to indicate how the energy of electrons can be potential energy in some circumstances or kinetic energy in other circumstances.

Directions: Use the illustration to answer question 8.

8. Label the two circles of the Venn diagram as *Kinetic Energy* and *Potential Energy*. Then sort the following terms in the Venn diagram.

   Electric current   **Chemical energy**

   Heat   **Mechanical energy**

   Magnetic energy

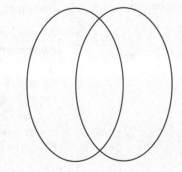

Types of Energy and Energy Transformations

LESSON 6.2 Sources of Energy

LESSON OBJECTIVES

- Identify various sources of energy
- Describe nonrenewable and renewable resources
- Explain the factors that influence why people choose one energy source over another

CORE SKILLS & PRACTICES

- Distinguish between Cause and Effect
- Understand and Explain Textual Scientific Presentations

Key Terms

fossil fuel
a fuel formed from the remains of ancient organisms

nonrenewable resource
a resource that can be used up

nuclear fission
the splitting of a nucleus into two smaller nuclei

renewable resource
a natural energy resource that can be replaced

Vocabulary

classify
to group into categories based on similar characteristics

energy resource
a natural material people use to meet their energy needs

Key Concept

There are many sources of energy. Which type of energy source people choose to use depends on each source's advantages and disadvantages.

Sources of Energy

You use energy in many different ways. A car engine transforms the energy stored in gasoline to kinetic energy as you drive. The buildings in which you live and work use electricity for lighting, heating, and operating equipment. The electricity and fuels you use are produced from different energy sources, each having advantages and disadvantages.

Resources are anything on Earth people use to meet their needs, such as minerals, water, soil, and air. You use energy when you turn on a light, cook dinner, turn on the air conditioner, or drive a car. This energy is usually in the form of electricity produced at a power plant or from fuels that are burned.

An **energy resource** is a natural material people use to meet their energy needs. Energy resources include coal, oil, natural gas, the Sun, and the wind, among others. Most energy resources contain potential energy, often in the form of chemical energy. A power plant transforms the potential energy into electricity. Power plants use coal, water, or another resource to generate that electricity. In most power plants, the potential energy is converted to the kinetic energy of a moving turbine, which is connected to a generator that transforms kinetic energy into electricity.

All energy resources may be classified as renewable or nonrenewable. A **nonrenewable resource** cannot be quickly replaced after it is used and, therefore, has the potential to be used up. Fossil fuels, such as coal, or the uranium used in nuclear reactions, are nonrenewable energy resources. The supply of these fossil fuels in the world is shrinking. A **renewable resource** can be replenished. Sunlight, geothermal energy, biomass, wind, and water are renewable energy resources. The Sun's energy is considered renewable because it can not be used up by humans.

Fossil Fuels

Nonrenewable energy resources must be extracted from the ground so they can be turned into usable fuels. **Fossil fuels** are fuels that formed from the remains of ancient organisms over millions of years. Fossil fuels include coal, oil, and natural gas. They may be found close to Earth's surface or kilometers underground. Fossil fuels each have distinct advantages and disadvantages, including the ways they can be used, the types of pollution they produce, and how long their supplies are expected to last.

The energy in fossil fuels originally came from sunlight. Photosynthetic organisms that lived in the past used energy from the Sun to produce organic substances that store energy. These organisms died, decomposed, and were covered with layers of rock over millions of years. Under conditions of extreme heat and pressure, the fossil fuels we use today were formed. Today, energy companies may drill several kilometers underground to reach deposits of fossil fuels.

Sources of Energy Used in United States in 2012*

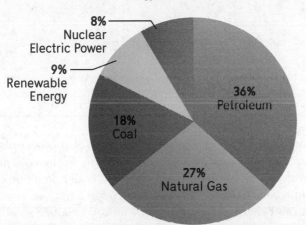

- 8% Nuclear Electric Power
- 9% Renewable Energy
- 18% Coal
- 36% Petroleum
- 27% Natural Gas

*Does not add to 100 due to rounding.

Coal is a solid material formed from the remains of dead plants. Today, most coal is burned in power plants. Oil and natural gas formed from the remains of microscopic marine organisms. Oil is a complex liquid mixture that needs to be separated and converted into useable fuels at oil refineries. Gasoline, propane, kerosene, and jet fuel are all components of crude oil. The relatively recent process of hydraulic fracturing, or fracking, is used to extract, or remove, natural gas that is trapped in rock. Natural gas is used in gas stoves and home furnaces, as well as in some vehicles, such as certain buses.

When fossil fuels are burned, their stored energy is converted to thermal energy, which may then be converted to other types of energy. Fossil fuels are easy to transport and inexpensive compared to other sources of energy. However, burning fossil fuels produces carbon dioxide and other pollutants that may be released into the air.

Nuclear Energy

Radioactive atoms are the source of energy in nuclear power plants. The process of splitting a nucleus into two smaller nuclei is called **nuclear fission.** A large amount of energy is released during the nuclear fission of very small amounts of elements such as uranium. The energy and particles released during fission, called radioactivity, can generate energy, but it can also harm living organisms.

Sources of Energy

Use Prior Knowledge

You already know some information about energy resources from your everyday experiences. For example, gasoline is burned in most cars, and natural gas or propane is often used to heat homes. You can use this prior knowledge to help you answer questions on a test. However, be careful to distinguish between facts you know and opinions you may have. For example, it is a fact that gasoline is burned in a car engine. It is an opinion that energy produced by fossil fuels is better than energy produced by nuclear fuels. Use only facts you may already know to support or eliminate an answer choice.

Review the Think About Science questions on this page. For each question, write down a fact you know that could help you answer the question.

There are different types of uranium atoms, called isotopes. Uranium-235 (U-235) is an isotope used as fuel in nuclear power plants. While U-235 is nonrenewable, there is enough of it to last for thousands of years. U-235 atoms split apart, or decay, when hit by high-speed neutrons in a nuclear reactor. When they undergo nuclear fission, that process produces two more stable atoms and subatomic particles called neutrons. The produced neutrons hit other uranium atoms, causing a chain reaction that must be carefully controlled. Some of the released energy is in the form of thermal energy that is converted to electricity in the nuclear power plant.

Nuclear Fission of a U-235 Nucleus

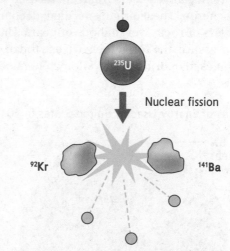

A nuclear power plant operates much the same way as a coal power plant. In each, thermal energy is used to produce electrical energy. In the coal plant, thermal energy is produced by the burning of coal in a boiler. In a nuclear plant, thermal energy comes from the fission of nuclei in a nuclear reactor. In each plant, the thermal energy is used to boil water to produce steam. The steam turns a turbine connected to an electric generator. The generator produces electrical power, which then flows down electric power lines.

The use of nuclear energy does not release carbon dioxide or other pollution into the atmosphere. Another advantage of nuclear energy is that a small amount of uranium can produce a large amount of energy. One disadvantage of nuclear energy is that the waste material produced is highly radioactive and must be stored safely.

Think about Science

Directions: Answer the following questions.

1. All fossil fuels and nuclear energy share which characteristic?
    A. They can be replaced quickly.
    B. They produce carbon dioxide.
    C. They can release thermal energy.
    D. They are burned in automobiles.

2. What is a potential advantage of fossil fuels over nuclear fuels?
    A. Fossil fuels do not produce pollution.
    B. There are vast supplies of fossil fuels.
    C. Fossil fuels can be easily transported.
    D. Fossil fuels are used by many people.

Renewable Energy Resources

Some renewable energy resources, such as the Sun, geothermal energy, and wind, are inexhaustible, meaning they cannot be used up. Others, such as biomass, need to be actively replaced in order for them to be renewable.

Solar Energy

Most of the energy on Earth originally comes from the Sun. People can use sunlight directly to produce electricity using solar cells. Solar cells contain materials that absorb sunlight, similar to the function of chlorophyll in plants. This absorbed light is converted to electricity inside the solar cell. Solar cells may be small, such as those used to charge the batteries in solar flashlights. They may also be combined into large modules placed on the roofs of buildings or into very large arrays used at solar power plants. Solar thermal power plants use sunlight to heat fluids that produce steam, which is then used to generate electricity similar to coal or nuclear power plants. Sunlight may also be used to heat water for homes.

Unlike fossil fuels, solar energy does not produce pollution. However, energy cannot be produced at night ,and less energy is produced on cloudy days. Also, the cost of solar panels may be too high for many people.

Geothermal Energy

Geothermal energy comes from the heat generated inside Earth. The temperature and pressure deep inside Earth are hot enough to melt rock. Some areas near Earth's surface, called hot spots, are so hot they can transform water pumped underground into steam. Hot spots are good locations for geothermal power plants. Cool water from Earth's surface is pumped underground and heated by Earth's interior until it changes to steam. The steam turns a turbine that powers a generator. The generator produces electrical energy. Iceland and the United States are two countries that use geothermal energy. Because geothermal power plants do not burn fuels, they do not release carbon dioxide or particulates into the atmosphere. The major limit on the use of geothermal energy is the number of locations where hot rocks are close to Earth's surface.

CORE PRACTICE

Understand and Explain Textual Scientific Presentations

In order to understand scientific text, it is often necessary to **classify** information. When you classify information, you organize it according to specific features. In this lesson, we have discussed *renewable* and *nonrenewable* resources. To extract the information needed to compare and contrast topics, you should pick out key words or phrases that could help you classify the sources of energy discussed in this lesson into renewable and nonrenewable resources.

Read each of the topics on these two pages again. Which key words or phrases can you use to classify the topics? Use a graphic organizer, such as the Venn diagram below, to organize the information in a way that will help you classify the information. Identifying and organizing information in this way can help you synthesize the information you read.

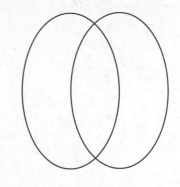

Geothermal Power Plant

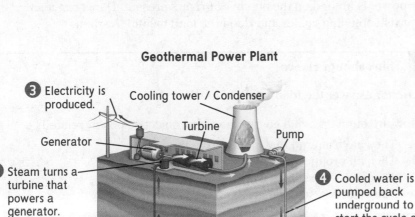

❸ Electricity is produced.

Cooling tower / Condenser

Turbine

Pump

Generator

❷ Steam turns a turbine that powers a generator.

❹ Cooled water is pumped back underground to start the cycle all over again.

❶ Water heated by Earth's interior changes to steam.

Fractures in rock

Steam

Magma

Science texts that explain processes often include a cause and its resulting effects. In this section, the cause of wind was explained, as well as the process of how solar cells, wind turbines, and hydropower plants produce electricity. Words or phrases may help you distinguish between the cause and its effects. For example, the part of the sentence that comes before *results in* or *causes* is a cause, and the part of the sentence that comes after is an effect. The sequence of events presented in a paragraph also gives clues that help distinguish between cause and effect.

Examine the paragraph about wind energy. Use the graphic organizer at the back of the text to write the causes on the left side of the page and effects on the right side of the page. Use an arrow to connect each cause to its effect. Remember, an effect of one cause may be the cause of another effect.

Biomass

Biomass is matter from living organisms, which means that the ultimate energy source of biomass is the Sun. Corn, soybeans, switchgrass, and other crops are grown as biomass to produce fuels. Biomass also includes waste products, such as wood chips from lumber mills and unused leftovers from crops. Biomass, such as wood, may be burned in homes as a source of heat. It is also used in some power plants to produce heat used to generate electricity. Some biomass, such as corn and soybeans, are converted into biodiesel fuel or ethanol. Unlike fossil fuels, biomass can be replaced quickly. However, burning biomass is similar to burning fossil fuels because it releases carbon dioxide and other pollutants into the air.

Wind Energy

Wind is also the result of energy from the Sun, as winds are caused by temperature differences in the air. For centuries, people have been using windmills to harness the energy of the wind to pump water or grind grain. Today, wind turbines convert the energy of the wind into electricity. Similar to power plants, each wind turbine uses a generator to produce electricity. However, instead of steam, wind pushes on the blades of the turbine to turn it. Wind energy does not release pollution and it is only efficient in areas with strong, steady winds.

Energy from Water

The Sun drives the water cycle and is a main source of the energy of moving water. Water also has gravitational potential energy that is transformed to kinetic energy as water flows downhill. People have been using energy from water for centuries to grind grain, saw wood, and run textile mills. Modern hydroelectric power plants generate electricity when flowing water turns turbines beneath dams. All dams in rivers store water to be released as it is needed, but only a few are used in the production of hydroelectric power. New ways of generating hydroelectric power, such as using the energy of tides and waves, are also currently being used.

Hydroelectric power is very efficient and creates no pollution. However, water power is limited by the number of rivers present. Dams can also disrupt fish breeding cycles and flood the land behind the dam.

Think about Science

Directions: Answer the following questions.

1. How are biomass, wind energy, and hydroelectric power related?
   A. They have energy that comes from the Sun.
   B. They all produce pollution.
   C. They must be replaced as they are used.
   D. They can be used to meet any energy need.

2. Which is a use of energy from biomass but not from geothermal energy?
   A. producing heat
   B. producing electricity
   C. powering cars
   D. recharging batteries

Choosing Sources of Energy

Many factors determine the energy sources people use, including availability, cost, and environmental impact. Worldwide, fossil fuels provide the majority of the energy used for electricity, heating, and transportation. The current supplies of fossil fuels allow producers to meet demands, making them comparatively cheap. Although advancements are being made with renewable energy resources, the technology is already in place to drill or mine and refine fossil fuels. Fossil fuels also release a large amount of energy when burned and have the advantage that they can be stored and used when needed. This makes them an important energy resource for transportation.

Energy Sources Used to Generate Electricity in United States*

5%
Other Renewables
(Biomass 1.42%,
Geothermal 0.41%,
Solar 0.11%,
Wind 3.46%,
Petroleum 1%,
Other Gases < 1%)

7% — Hydropower

37% Coal

19% Nuclear

30% Natural Gas

*Does not add to 100 due to rounding.

Fossil fuels also have disadvantages as their extraction can cause environmental damage. The carbon dioxide they produce when burned contributes to climate change, and the other pollutants released can cause smog and acid rain.

A large amount of nuclear energy is produced from little fuel and does not produce carbon dioxide, but it does produce radioactive waste. This waste must be stored safely for long periods of time. While accidents at nuclear power plants are rare, they can have devastating consequences.

Geothermal, wind, and water energy resources are available only in certain places. For example, wind can produce electricity only in places where the wind is strong enough to turn the blades of the turbines. Geothermal energy can be generated in areas where there are hot springs. It is currently more expensive to generate electricity by using wind and solar energy than it is by using fossil fuels, however costs are decreasing.

Think about Science

Directions: Answer the following questions.

1. Which is a disadvantage of biomass but not of hydroelectric power?

   A. radioactive waste
   B. pollution in the atmosphere
   C. availability at any location
   D. inability to be replaced

2. Which could cause the cost of natural gas to increase but is not likely to affect solar power?

   A. decrease in supply
   B. improvements in technology
   C. out-of-date technology
   D. increase in supply

WORKPLACE SKILL

Understand Business Fundamentals

Even the smallest business has overhead costs that need to be paid in order to operate the business. Overhead costs include rent, office supplies, advertising, insurance, Internet service, and utilities. Minimizing overhead costs helps maximize the profitability of a business. The overhead cost for gas and electrical energy depends on the amount of energy used by a business. Depending on the nature of the business, energy costs can be a large portion of the overall overhead.

Think of a business you would be interested in starting and briefly describe your business. Then list the top five uses of energy that would contribute to your business overhead costs and identify the energy resources you would be most likely to use. Describe at least two ways you could conserve energy to reduce overhead costs. Finally evaluate the possible choices of energy resources for your business. For example, you may or may not have a choice of the energy resources the utility company uses to generate electricity, but you might consider adding solar panels. Explain how your choice of energy resources for your business is influenced by the potential overhead expenses.

Vocabulary Review

Directions: Write the missing term in the blank.

classify   energy resource   fossil fuel
nonrenewable resource   nuclear fission   renewable resource

1. Any natural material people use as fuel is a(n) _____.

2. During _____, a large atom splits apart into two smaller atoms.

3. A(n) _____ cannot be replaced as quickly as it is used.

4. To organize examples into groups based on their qualities is to _____ them.

5. A(n) _____ can be replaced as it is used.

6. A(n) _____ came from the remains of organisms that died millions of years ago.

Skill Review

Directions: Answer the following questions.

1. Which is a justification for using renewable energy resources?

   A. Their costs are likely to decrease rather than increase.

   B. They do not contribute to global warming.

   C. They do not cause environmental damage.

   D. They are readily available in all areas.

2. Which explains why biomass is a renewable energy resource?

   A. Biomass does not produce pollution.

   B. Biomass's energy comes from the Sun.

   C. There is more biomass on Earth than people can use.

   D. Biomass can be replaced within a few years of being used.

3. The eastern United States does not have any hot spots. Which type of power plant is unlikely to be found in the eastern United States due to the availability of the energy resource?

   A. a coal power plant

   B. a biomass power plant

   C. a geothermal power plant

   D. a nuclear power plant

4. Which energy resources originally got their energy from sunlight that is absorbed by living organisms?

   A. soybeans and wind

   B. soybeans and coal

   C. oil and uranium

   D. wind and coal

5. Fossil fuels and nuclear power each have advantages and disadvantages. Compare and contrast these energy resources. Based on this comparison, choose which energy resources you would use to generate electricity and justify your response.

Directions: Use the graph to answer question 6.

6. The graph shows how the price of energy from coal, fuel oil, and natural gas for manufacturers has changed from 1998 to 2010. Based on this graph, explain how the energy usage by manufacturers of these three energy sources has most likely changed from 2002 to 2010.

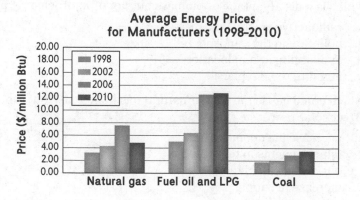

Average Energy Prices for Manufacturers (1998–2010)

Sources of Energy

Skill Practice

Directions: Use the information to answer questions 1–3.

Most communities are far away from the power plants where their electricity is generated. Once the power plant generates electricity, it can be sent over wires to where it is used. Still, different communities may use different amounts of each energy resource, based on the resources they have available. Power companies in areas where there are mountains with large rivers may be able to generate more of their electricity from hydropower. Power companies in areas with a reliable amount of sunlight year-round are starting to build power plants that produce electricity using solar cells.

However, even renewable energy is not without impacts. Dams built to hold water can affect fish populations and the water supply in rivers and streams below the dam. Solar power plants require a large amount of space, so building them may affect local animal populations. People are continuing to search for a balance between meeting our energy needs and environmental impacts.

1. Which of these best explains why mountainous areas may be good locations to produce hydropower?
   A. The rock underneath mountains is usually very warm.
   B. Water in mountains tends to be cleaner than in other places.
   C. Water flows down mountains and can be collected in dams.
   D. Mountains tend to be windy, producing waves on lakes.

2. Which energy resource is most likely to be the best renewable energy resource to generate electricity in the desert?
   A. natural gas
   B. hydropower
   C. solar energy
   D. nuclear energy

3. Building both dams and large solar power plants can affect local animal populations. Which of these is a possible way that wind turbines could negatively affect animal populations?
   A. Wind turbines could affect bird populations if birds run into the blades while migrating.
   B. Wind turbines reduce the amount of land that can be used by grazing animals.
   C. Wind turbines destroy the natural beauty of the landscape.
   D. Wind turbines use wind that would otherwise help disperse atmospheric pollutants.

Directions: Answer the following questions.

4. After hydroelectric dams are built, the amount of water in the river decreases, and the river runs more slowly. Distinguish between the cause and effect and identify subsequent effects.

5. Explain why people would choose to build power plants that use renewable energy resources instead of increasing the percentage of electricity produced from nonrenewable energy resources.

6. What are some possible positive and negative effects of building solar power plants? How would you plan a solar power plant to minimize the negative effects? Provide a justification for your response.

7. Compare and contrast hydroelectric power and wind power in terms of their benefits, limitations, and potential disadvantages. Explain the situations in which each type of energy resource would be best used.

LESSON 6.3   Heat

▉ LESSON OBJECTIVES

- Describe the difference between temperature and heat
- Explain how energy is uniformly distributed between substances
- Describe the methods of heat transfer
- Recognize that friction converts kinetic energy to heat

▉ CORE SKILLS & PRACTICES

- Express Scientific Information or Findings Verbally
- Evaluate Evidence

Key Terms

heat
the transfer of thermal energy

radiation
the transfer of thermal energy as electromagnetic waves

temperature
the measure of the average kinetic energy in a substance

Vocabulary

compare
to determine how two things are alike or different

conduction
the transfer of thermal energy between particles that collide

convection
the transfer of thermal energy by the movement of particles

Key Concept

When thermal energy is added to a substance, there is an increased movement of the particles that make up the substance. More movement of the particles means an increased kinetic energy. This increased kinetic energy can be transferred to other parts of the substance and to other substances.

Principles of Heat

People refer to temperature when they describe the weather or food. Scientists, however, would define **temperature** as a measure of the average kinetic energy of the particles in a substance.

The SI unit for temperature is Kelvin, but degrees Celsius is also used. You may also be familiar with the Fahrenheit temperature scale, but it is not often used in science. When the temperature of a substance goes up, the kinetic energy of its particles increases. This energy, combined with its potential energy, is called thermal energy.

Particles not only have thermal energy, they also transfer energy to their surroundings. A person who stands in the sunlight or takes a warm shower can feel the thermal energy from the Sun or water. The transfer of thermal energy is called **heat,** which is measured using the SI unit joule (J), the same unit that is used for all other forms of energy. Thermal energy is a form of energy that is transferred as heat.

Heat is the flow of thermal energy between substances at different temperatures. The direction of heat flow is always from hotter to colder substances. The hotter substance cools as it warms the cooler substance. Heating continues until the energy is distributed uniformly throughout both substances and both substances are at the same temperature. Heat can also cause change in the state of a substance—it can cause a solid to change to a liquid or a liquid to change to a gas. In each case, the kinetic energy of the particles increases.

Early scientists and philosophers thought heat was a substance that flowed from one substance to another. Later observations and experiments showed that heat results from the movement of particles. Scientists observed that the source of heat does not determine the effect heat has on its surroundings. Whether from chemical reactions, friction, nuclear reactions, or electricity, heat has the same effect.

⚛ Think about Science

Directions: Answer the following questions.

1. _____ measures the average kinetic energy of the particles in a substance.

2. _____ is the flow of energy that warms a person standing next to a campfire.

3. Which unit listed below describes the amount of thermal energy transferred from one substance to another?

   A. degrees Fahrenheit
   B. Kelvin
   C. joules
   D. degrees Celsius

4. One kilogram of which of these substances will have the lowest average thermal energy?

   A. tap water
   B. ice
   C. ice water
   D. steam

Kinetic Energy Transfer

Kinetic energy is transferred as heat by three methods: conduction, convection, and radiation. You may have experienced conduction if you have ever been burned by a hot substance, such as the handle of a heated pan. You can observe convection by adding hot water to one end of a full bathtub and noticing that the water in the entire tub becomes warmer, not just the water near the faucet. You can feel heat transferred by radiation by putting your hands near a radiator or a fire.

Conduction

Conduction is the transfer of thermal energy between particles that collide with each other. When these particles make contact, the particle with more kinetic energy passes some energy to the particle with less energy. For example, electric stove burners transfer thermal energy by conduction to the bottom of a pan of water. The hot pan's particles transfer their energy to the cooler water in the pan. Another example occurs when heat is conducted from your hand to a cold snowball. In scientific terms, the snow does not make your hand cold. Instead, your hand warms the snow, and because the thermal energy is transferred, your hand feels cooler. In all cases of conduction, thermal energy is transferred by the collisions between particles resulting from contact.

CORE PRACTICE

Express Scientific Information or Findings Verbally

Thermal energy cannot normally be seen, but infrared images can detect it. Temperature differences in different parts of this person show up as different colors, with the yellow-orange to white parts being the warmest.

While these colors are like a code to scientists, this information can also be expressed verbally. You might say that the most heat being transmitted by radiation is occurring in the brain, and the least amount of heat is being radiated from the shoulders..

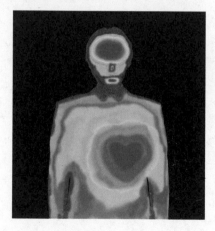

Try this activity:

Make a colored ice cube by adding food coloring to the water before freezing. Fill a tall, clear container with room-temperature water, let it settle two minutes, and then carefully add the colored ice cube. Observe the convection currents in the container by looking at it from the side.

How would you describe your findings verbally? Be sure to include enough detail so someone can understand what you saw.

Convection

Unlike particles in solids, particles in liquids and gases can mix and flow past one another. This allows heat to be transferred within the substance as particles with more thermal energy move and mix with particles with less thermal energy. The transfer of thermal energy by the movement and mixing of particles is called **convection.** Convection occurs in gases and liquids.

Particles with more thermal energy move faster and tend to spread apart. When thermal energy increases in a fluid, the fluid expands. When the fluid expands, the density of the warmer fluid is less than the density of the cooler fluid that surrounds it. Think about how an electric burner conducts heat to a pan of water. The water being warmed at the bottom of the pan becomes less dense than the cooler water above it. The cool, dense water sinks, pushing the warm water upward. That warm water then cools and sinks to the bottom of the pan, and the process continues. The rising and sinking action of the water is a convection current.

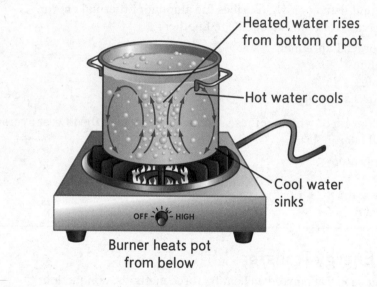

Heated water rises from bottom of pot

Hot water cools

Cool water sinks

Burner heats pot from below

Radiation

Thermal energy is transferred through the air to your hand when you put your hand near a radiator or fireplace. This energy is transferred by **radiation,** which is thermal energy transferred as waves. Unlike conduction and convection, radiation does not need matter to travel through, so it can travel through empty space. The Sun's energy radiates through space to Earth 150 million kilometers away.

✺ Think about Science

Directions: Fill in the blank.

1. An ice cube in a cup of water is another example of _____. Cold water melting from the ice cube _____. As the cooler, denser water sinks, it pushes the warm water to the _____ where it cools and continues the cycle.

2. You walk across the sand on the beach. The heat from the sand is transferred to your feet by _____. Your skin feels warm as the Sun heats it by _____.

Energy Conversions Involving Heat

What happens when you rub a piece of wood with a cloth compared to when you rub the same piece of wood with sandpaper? The amount of friction produced when a cloth is rubbed across a piece of wood is much less than it is when sandpaper is used. This is because the friction between two surfaces depends on the types of surfaces involved and how hard the surfaces are pressed together. When a larger force is pushing two substances together, particles on the surfaces that would not normally come into contact do so, creating more friction between the substances.

If you continue to rub the cloth or sandpaper against the piece of wood, your hand would start to feel warm because friction converts the kinetic energy of rubbing to heat. Which would heat up faster, the cloth or the sandpaper? Because the sandpaper produces more friction, sanding the wood will produce more heat.

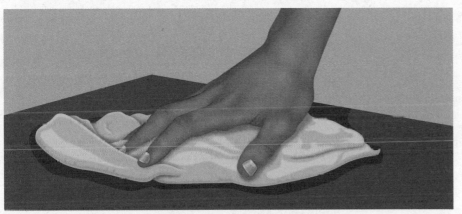

Heat is generated by rubbing a cloth against a piece of wood.

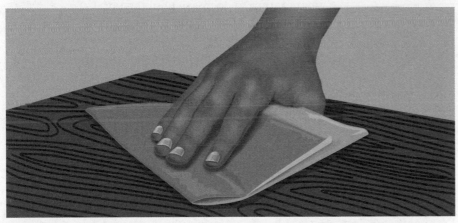

Rubbing sandpaper against a piece of wood creates more friction and produces more heat.

Think about Science

Directions: Answer the following questions.

1. Why does snow melt when you walk on it?
2. Why does a spacecraft get very hot as it reenters the atmosphere?
3. You erase a mistake on your paper. Why is your paper warm?

Vocabulary Review

Directions: Write the missing term in the blank.

compare   conduction   convection
heat   radiation   temperature

1. When we _____ our results, we find that your readings are much more accurate than mine.

2. _____ occurs when heat is transferred from one location to another by the movement and mixing of molecules.

3. Because of _____, I could feel heat when I held my hand over the flame.

4. The _____ of a substance is the measure of the average kinetic energy of its particles.

5. The transfer of _____ can occur in three ways.

6. The spoon that was in the soup bowl was extremely hot because the heat from the soup had been transferred by _____.

Skill Review

Directions: Answer the following questions.

1. What does heating a substance cause the motion of the particles in the substance to do?

    A. decrease

    B. increase

    C. stay the same

    D. stop

2. Which transfers heat through contact?

    A. radiation

    B. convection

    C. reduction

    D. conduction

3. You are roasting a marshmallow by holding it beside a campfire. How is heat transferred to the marshmallow?

    A. radiation

    B. convection

    C. reduction

    D. conduction

4. Explain why a person might rub two sticks together to start a fire.

5. You pour some cold milk into your hot chocolate. Which is the best description of what happens next?

    A. Friction causes the hot chocolate's temperature to decrease until the hot chocolate and the milk have less thermal energy than before.

    B. Friction causes the milk's temperature to increase until it has more thermal energy than the hot chocolate.

    C. Thermal energy is transferred from the hot chocolate to the milk until the hot chocolate and milk have the same temperature.

    D. Thermal energy is transferred from the milk to the hot chocolate until the hot chocolate has less thermal energy than the milk.

6. Explain the relationship between heat and temperature.

Skill Practice

Directions: Use the graph to answer questions 1 and 2.

State Changes of Water

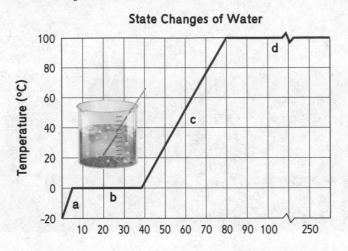

1. At which part of the graph does the water have the highest average kinetic energy?

   A. a

   B. b

   C. c

   D. d

2. At which part of the graph do the water molecules have the least motion?

   A. a

   B. b

   C. c

   D. d

Directions: Answer the following questions.

3. The temperature of a beaker of water is 15° C. The water is poured into a second beaker of water. What should the temperature of the water in the second beaker be so that the molecules of the mixed water will have the greatest motion?

   A. 0° C

   B. 10° C

   C. 25° C

   D. 50° C

4. You have a beaker of ice water. Use what you know about heat to plan an investigation that shows how convection affects the temperature of the water. Describe an experiment you could conduct, and explain the results you would expect to see.

5. Use what you know about thermal energy to explain what happens to food when you put it in the refrigerator.

6. Explain how each of the following examples shows conduction, convection, or radiation: light reflected from the Moon reaches Earth; steam from a factory rises into the sky; a cold penny warms from being held.

7. Explain why energy from the Sun does not reach Earth by conduction or convection.

8. The car in front of you stops suddenly. You must slam on your brakes to avoid a wreck. It smells like your tires are burning. Explain why.

LESSON OBJECTIVES

- Explain the nature of waves and its relationship with matter and energy
- Identify mechanical, electromagnetic, transverse, and mechanical waves
- Analyze the waves in the electromagnetic spectrum

CORE SKILLS & PRACTICES

- Use Data or Evidence to Form a Conclusion
- Determine Details

Key Terms

electromagnetic waves
waves created by vibrating electrical charges that can travel through matter or space

radiation
transfer of energy by electromagnetic waves

wave
a repeating disturbance that transfers energy as it travels through matter or space

Vocabulary

discriminate
to notice that one thing is different from another thing

medium
the matter through which a wave travels

Key Concept

Waves carry energy that spreads out as the wave travels. There are different types of waves that all exhibit properties of wavelength, frequency, and amplitude.

The Nature of Waves

A **wave** is a repeating disturbance that transfers energy as it travels through matter or space. The world around you is full of many different types of waves. Sound waves, ocean waves, light waves, and radio waves are all types of waves.

When something vibrates, it moves back and forth. The way an object vibrates demonstrates the properties of that vibration and is directly related to the properties of the wave that forms. The ripples traveling across the surface of a pond, for example, are vibrations produced when a leaf disturbs the surface of the water. The swinging motion of a giant pendulum is another example of a vibration. So, too, is the flapping of a bird's wings and the rhythmic jolts of Earth's crust during an earthquake.

Waves, Matter, and Energy

An important property of waves is that they transfer energy, but not matter, from place to place. For example, you can create a wave using a length of rope and a table, as shown in the diagram on the next page. Hold on to one end of the rope and then flick your wrist to send a wave moving along the rope away from you. The wave does not carry matter (the rope) along with it. Although the wave moves the rope up off the table, there is no additional rope at the other end of the rope after the wave passes.

Waves do not transfer matter from place to place—they only transfer, or transmit, energy. In the rope example, the wave, not the rope, moves away from the wrist, which is the source of the wave. The same is true for water waves. The disturbance, or wave, moves away from the source, but the water—the matter—does not. When waves splash onto a beach over and over again, the same water is oscillating to bring energy, not water, to the shore.

©Thinkstock

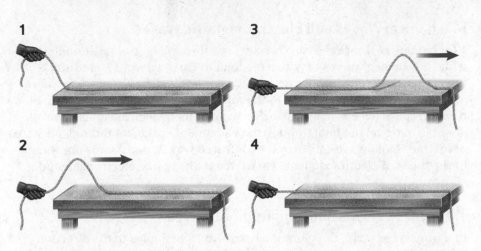

1   **2**   **3**   **4**

CORE SKILL

Determine Details

As you read, look for headings, boldfaced words, key phrases, and other clues that support the main idea. The main idea of this section is that waves are disturbances that transmit energy. Look at the paragraphs of this section again. Identify 2-3 phrases that directly support the main idea. Then find a phrase that provides interesting information but is not necessarily supportive.

A wave's movement continues as long as the wave has energy to carry. This energy has the ability to do work. When a wave encounters an object along its path, it does work on the object. For example, a resting boat will be set into motion by a passing water wave. As work is done on the boat, the wave loses energy. Waves lose energy as they do work. Sea cliffs are formed in part because energy-carrying waves erode the rock below them.

Waves transmit energy in various ways and through all phases of matter. An example of a solid transmitting wave energy is the seismic wave produced by an earthquake that takes place when rocks are under pressure and snap or slide into new positions. Waves that are felt and seen in water are examples of a liquid medium transmitting wave energy. Gases also transmit wave energy, as in an explosion, when heat and sound waves are generated.

Think about Science

Directions. Answer the following questions.

1. In a stadium wave, a section of fans stands up with their arms raised and then sit back down. When executed in succession from one section to the next a visual wave is created that spreads around a circular stadium. Which part of a stadium wave represents the source of the disturbance?

    A. The stadium
    B. The fans in the stadium
    C. A fan standing up and down
    D. The motion of the wave around the stadium

2. A boat is about half a kilometer offshore. A strong wind begins to blow. Which of the following best describes the transfer of energy that will take place between the wind, the boat, and the water?

    A. Energy in the wind will be transferred to the boat and the water.
    B. Energy in the boat will be transferred to the wind and the water.
    C. Energy from the water will be transferred to the wind and the boat.
    D. Energy from the boat will be transferred to the shoreline.

Wave Types and Their Properties

You can **discriminate,** or tell apart, one type of wave from another by understanding the types and properties of waves. Waves can be divided into two major categories—mechanical and electromagnetic—based on whether they require matter to travel. Waves can also be categorized based on the direction of the vibration relative to the direction of the wave velocity.

Mechanical Waves and Electromagnetic Waves

Electromagnetic waves can carry energy through matter or through space, while mechanical waves require a medium to carry energy. A **medium** is the matter through which waves travel. Longitudinal and transverse waves are types of mechanical waves. Although mechanical waves cannot travel through space, electromagnetic waves can. In fact, electromagnetic waves are able to travel not only through the vacuum of space but through all states of matter. Radio waves, microwaves, infrared waves, and X-rays are some of the types of electromagnetic waves that make up the electromagnetic spectrum.

Transverse Waves and Longitudinal Waves

In a transverse wave, the vibration occurs at right angles to the direction in which the wave travels. Some mechanical waves, such as water waves, are also transverse waves. In the example using the rope on the table, when flicked, the rope moved up and down, whereas the wave moved parallel to the top of the table. The two motions are at right angles to each other. The peaks, or crests, and valleys, or troughs, in the rope match the up-and-down motion of the flicking hand. If the hand moves up and down at a constant rate, the crests and troughs will be spaced at equal intervals. Like the wave in the rope, the direction of a water wave, an example of a transverse wave, is at a right angle to the movement of the water.

The second type of mechanical wave is a longitudinal, or compression, wave. In a longitudinal wave, such as a sound wave or a seismic wave, the medium moves back and forth parallel to the direction in which the wave travels. You can create a longitudinal wave by squeezing together several coils of a stretched-out spring and releasing them. You will observe that the vibration of the medium, the coil, is parallel to the wave's motion.

Parts and Properties of Waves

All waves can be identified by their characteristics and properties. Transverse waves are characterized by a repeating pattern of crests and troughs. The rest position represents the medium when a wave is not traveling through it. In longitudinal waves, a repeating pattern of compressed and noncompressed sections is produced. The more compressed areas are areas of compression, while the less compressed areas are areas of rarefaction, which are areas of reduced pressure or density.

Wavelength

Wavelength is the distance between a point on a wave and the next identical point. For a transverse wave, this means from the top of one crest to the top of the next crest, or from the bottom of one trough to the bottom of the next trough. In a longitudinal wave, wavelength is measured from the center of one compression to the center of the next compression, or from the center of one rarefaction to the center of the next rarefaction. Waves vary in wavelengths. Ocean waves have wavelengths measured in meters (m), whereas light waves are measured in billionths of a meter (0.000000001 m), or nanometers.

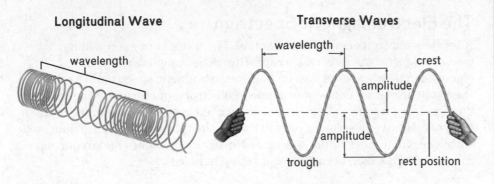

Longitudinal Wave

wavelength

Transverse Waves

wavelength

crest

amplitude

amplitude

trough

rest position

Frequency

The frequency of a wave is the number of wavelengths that pass a given point in one second (1 s) and is measured in units of hertz (Hz). One hertz is equal to one complete cycle, or wavelength, per second. Thus, if 5 wavelengths pass each second, the wave has a frequency of 5 cycles/s, which is expressed as 5 Hz. The frequency of waves can vary widely. For example, the frequency of ocean waves is less than 1 Hz, while the frequency of visible light is about 1,000,000,000,000,000 Hz (10^{15} Hz).

Speed

If a wave's frequency and wavelength are known, the wave's speed can be calculated by using the following equation: speed = frequency × wavelength. This equation can also be written using the symbol v for speed, the symbol f for frequency, and the Greek letter lambda (λ) for wavelength, or $v = f \times \lambda$.

The speed of a wave is dependent upon the medium through which it travels. Sound waves, for example, travel at approximately 340 m/s through air, at more than 1,400 m/s in water, and at an estimated 5,800 m/s in steel. Light waves are also affected by the medium through which they travel. In the vacuum of space, the speed of light is 9.0×10^8 m/s. The speed slows in gases, and it slows more in liquids and solids. Temperature also affects wave speed. The speed of sound in air is increased at higher air temperatures.

Amplitude

The amplitude of a wave is related to the amount of energy it carries. The greater the energy a wave has, the greater its amplitude. The amplitude of any transverse wave is the distance from the rest position to either a crest or a trough. In longitudinal waves, the amplitude depends on how tightly the medium is squeezed together in its regions of compression. Using a coil as a model, imagine areas of a wave that are squeezed together. When compressions are more tightly squeezed, the wave has a higher amplitude.

⸰ Think about Science

Directions: Answer the following questions.

1. Based on the formula $v = f \times \lambda$, which of the following is true for a sound wave whose velocity is 340 m/s?

    A. As the frequency of a wave increases, its wavelength decreases.
    B. As the frequency of a wave increases, its wavelength increases.
    C. As the frequency of a wave increases, its wavelength stays the same.
    D. As the frequency of a wave increases, its wavelength increases twice as quickly.

Speed of Light	
Medium	Speed (km/s)
vacuum	300,000
air	< 300,000
liquid water	226,000
glass	200,000
diamond	124,000

The speed of light in a vacuum is an incredibly fast 3.00 × 10[8] m/s, or 300,000 km/s. Using the information in the table, what conclusion can you make about how the speed of light is affected by solid, liquid, and gas mediums?

The Electromagnetic Spectrum

All waves transmit energy as they travel. The transfer of energy along electromagnetic waves is called **radiation.** The complete range of electromagnetic waves makes up the electromagnetic spectrum. The spectrum displays a continuous range of electromagnetic waves arranged by increasing frequency and decreasing wavelength. Waves with the highest frequencies have the highest energy levels. The types of waves are indicated within certain ranges of the spectrum. However, the names and frequency ranges are not exact, because they overlap in places.

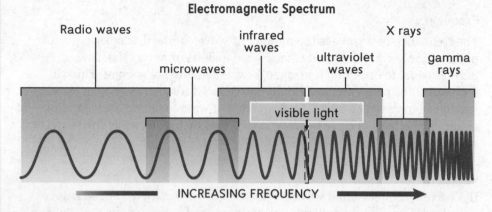

Electromagnetic Spectrum

Radio waves — microwaves — infrared waves — visible light — ultraviolet waves — X rays — gamma rays

INCREASING FREQUENCY

Radio Waves and Microwaves

Like all electromagnetic waves, radio waves are produced when electric charges vibrate. Radio waves are the longest in the spectrum with wavelengths that range from the length of a football to longer than a football field. Radio waves also have the lowest frequencies and carry the least amunt of energy of all electromagnetic waves. Televisions, radios, and cellular phones use radio waves. Radio waves with the highest energy are microwaves. Microwave ovens and cellular phones use these higher-frequency radio waves.

Infrared Waves

The warm sensation you feel when sunlight is absorbed by your skin is the result of electromagnetic waves called infrared waves. The wavelength of infrared waves is shorter than that of radio waves but longer than that of visible light. Infrared, or IR, waves are approximately 0.00075 mm to 1 mm in length. Television remote controls, orbiting satellites, and even some animals use infrared wavelengths.

Visible Light

Visible light is the part of the electromagnetic spectrum humans can see. These visible rays of the spectrum are recognized by the human eye as color. In order of long wavelength to short wavelength, the colors are red, orange, yellow, green, blue, indigo (deep blue), and violet. When all the colors of the visible spectrum are present, the light appears white. Nearly all things are visible because they reflect light given off by the Sun or another source, such as a light bulb. Visible light is extremely important to Earth's organisms because plants use the red and blue bands of the spectrum to create food in a process called photosynthesis.

Two theories about the nature of light focus on different properties of light. According to the Wave Theory of Light, light is a luminous energy emitted by a light source and travels through space as a transverse wave. According to the Particle Theory of Light, light energy is both radiated (transmitted) and absorbed as tiny packets, or bundles, and not as continuous waves.

Ultraviolet Waves

Ultraviolet, or UV, waves have higher frequencies than visible light waves. Wavelengths for UV light range between 10 billionths and 400 billionths of a meter long. The waves damage living cells and cause sunburn, and too much exposure to UV waves can lead to skin cancer. Ultraviolet waves, along with all other electromagnetic waves, are emitted by the Sun.

Short exposures to ultraviolet waves have several beneficial effects. The human body uses the ultraviolet energy to produce vitamin D, a necessary nutrient. Hospitals use UV waves to disinfect surgical equipment. Some materials fluoresce, or emit visible light, when struck by ultraviolet waves. Police detectives sometimes use fluorescent powder and an ultraviolet light source to look for fingerprints.

X-Rays and Gamma Rays

X-rays are high-energy electromagnetic waves with wavelengths shorter than those of ultraviolet waves. Gamma rays have the shortest wavelength and highest energy of the electromagnetic waves. Whereas ultraviolet waves can penetrate the top layer of a person's skin, X-rays have enough energy to pass through skin and muscle. X-rays and gamma rays have important uses in medicine. Images are formed when X-rays are beamed through a person's body. The rays strike a film plate or an electronic sensor, creating an image of internal structures such as bones. Gamma rays are used to treat some cancers. Exposing a cancerous tumor to a highly focused beam of gamma rays can kill the cancerous cells.

Think about Science

Directions: Select the correct answer to the following questions.

1. Which statement accurately describes the organization of waves on the electromagnetic spectrum in terms of frequency, velocity, and wavelength?

    A. Frequency and velocity increase; wavelength decreases.
    B. Frequency increases; velocity and wavelength decrease.
    C. Frequency decreases; wavelength decreases.
    D. Frequency decreases; wavelength increases.

2. What is the disturbance that produces an electromagnetic wave?

    A. Nuclear explosions
    B. Heat
    C. Wind
    D. Vibrating electrons

Vocabulary Review

Directions: Write the missing term in the blank.

wave   electromagnetic waves   radiation
medium   discriminate

1. Understanding wave properties helps you _____ one type of wave from another.

2. A(n) _____ is a disturbance that transfers energy from place to place.

3. The speed of a wave depends on the _____ through which it travels.

4. Another term for radiant energy is _____.

5. Infrared and ultraviolet are two types of _____.

Skill Review

Directions: Answer the following questions.

1. Which of these are properties, or parts, of a sound wave?

   A. crest, trough, amplitude

   B. compression, crest, trough

   C. trough, frequency, rarefaction

   D. compression, rarefaction, amplitude

2. What are the two categories of mechanical waves based on the direction of the vibration relative to the direction of the wave?

   A. Amplitude waves and energy waves

   B. Electromagnetic waves and mechanical waves

   C. Frequency waves and velocity waves

   D. Transverse waves and longitudinal waves

3. You move a length of rope to demonstrate transverse waves. There is a piece of red tape on one part of the rope. After the wave trough goes through the tape, in what direction does the piece of tape move?

   A. up

   B. down

   C. sideways

   D. It will stop where it is.

4. Which describes electromagnetic waves in order of increasing frequency?

   A. microwaves → X-rays → radio waves → visible light →gamma rays → UV waves

   B. radio waves → gamma rays → X-rays → microwaves → UV waves → visible light

   C. radio waves → microwaves → visible light → UV waves → X-rays → gamma rays

   D. visible light → radio waves → microwaves → gamma rays → X-rays → UV waves

5. Two sound waves with the same wavelength are compared. The frequency and wave speed of one wave are twice that of the other wave. How can you explain this difference?

6. Compare the longitudinal wave properties demonstrated by a coil at rest and a coil that is compressed.

7. Look at the diagram on page 238. Which types of electromagnetic waves have the most similar frequencies?

   A radio waves and gamma rays

   B. microwaves and infrared waves

   C. UV waves and radio waves

   D. X-rays and microwaves

Skill Practice

Directions: Use the information to answer questions 1 and 2.

The electric eye, or photoelectric cell, is a mechanism used to open and close a garage door when a beam of light is activated or broken. The principle of the electric eye is based on the photoelectric effect. The photoelectric effect occurs when a beam of light strikes certain metals, causing electrons to be knocked out of the metal, producing an electric current. This is how it happens: Light falling on the inside of a bulb coated with an active substance causes electrons to be emitted. The electrons are attracted to a positively charged electrode positioned in the center of the bulb as a filament. An electric current results when the electrons (negatively charged particles) are attracted to the positively charged particles of the electrode. It is observed that electrons are knocked loose only when a certain light energy is reached. The current can then be controlled by changes in light intensity. It appears that electrons are able to absorb only a certain amount of light at one time. When light shines on the electric eye, a current is established, and the door moves. When the beam of light is broken, the door stops.

1. How does the principle of the electric eye relate to the theories of the nature of light?
   A. It contradicts the idea that light is generated only in a star.
   B. It complements the idea that light acts like particles in a wave.
   C. It disputes the belief that all light exists only as a continuous wave.
   D. It supports the theory that light comes only from a luminous source.

2. In an electric garage door opener, what is the source of the disturbance?
   A. An electric current is produced.
   B. Light causes electrons to be emitted.
   C. Electrons are attracted to a filament.
   D. The garage door opens or closes.

Directions: Answer the following questions.

3. Which statement explains most accurately why sound cannot travel from Mars to Earth?
   A. Sound waves are classified as transverse waves.
   B. The distance between Mars and Earth is too great.
   C. Space has no matter and is considered a vacuum.
   D. Longitudinal waves cannot travel through space.

4. Imagine a small rubber ball floating in a pond. Describe the physical motion of the ball as a transverse wave moves along the surface of the water.

5. Discuss how the properties of frequency and wavelength are related.

6. During a thunderstorm, thunder and lightning are produced at the same time. You see the lightning before you hear the thunder. Use what you know about waves and wave properties to explain your answer.

7. Think about mechanical and electromagnetic waves. What is probably the biggest difference between them?
   A. Mechanical waves can travel through space.
   B. Electromagnetic waves can not carry energy through matter.
   C. Electromagnetic waves require a medium to carry energy.
   D. Mechanical waves require a medium to carry energy.

Directions: Answer the following questions.

1. A diver standing on the edge of a 30 meter platform has greater _____ energy than _____ energy.

2. The water molecules in a mug of hot water have _____ kinetic energy than water molecules in a glass of ice water.

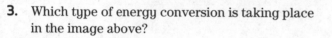

3. Which type of energy conversion is taking place in the image above?

   A. thermal → radiant

   B. radiant → thermal

   C. radiant → chemical

   D. chemical → radiant

4. Energy stored in the bonds between atoms of molecules is

   A. radiant energy

   B. nuclear energy

   C. thermal energy

   D. chemical energy

5. Which two types of energy are a result of field forces such that objects are affected at a distance?

   A. nuclear and thermal

   B. radiant and magnetic

   C. nuclear and electrical

   D. electrical and magnetic

6. Which renewable energy source has a similar effect on the environment as burning coal?

   A. biomass

   B. water

   C. wind

   D. geothermal

7. Which of the following transfers thermal energy as heat by conduction?

   A. iron skillet

   B. microwave

   C. solar cooker

   D. boiling water

8. When our hands are cold we often rub them together quickly to generate heat and warm them up. Which of the following best describes what is causing the energy conversion from mechanical energy to thermal energy that warms your hands?

   A. conduction

   B. convection

   C. friction

   D. radiation

9. Which of the following are high-energy electromagnetic waves?

   A. gamma rays and infrared rays

   B. radio waves and X-rays

   C. gamma rays and X-rays

   D. microwaves and radio waves

10. Which two wavelengths of visible light are essential for survival of organisms on Earth?

   A. red and blue

   B. yellow and red

   C. blue and green

   D. yellow and green

11. To calculate the speed a wave travels, what two values must be known?

   A. distance and time

   B. frequency and distance

   C. wavelength and distance

   D. frequency and wavelength

12. A longitudinal wave can be modeled by a(n)

   A. vibrating spring

   B. coiled spring

   C. ocean wave

   D. jump rope

13. _____ waves can transfer energy through empty space, but _____ waves require a medium to transfer energy.

14. To calculate the kinetic energy of an object, you must know its _____ and _____ .

15. Energy from water, wind energy, and biomass have energy from _____ as their source.

16. _____ always flows from hotter to cooler substances.

17. Compare coal and wind as energy sources. What are some advantages and disadvantages of each energy source?

18. Explain why nuclear fission can be both helpful and harmful to humans.

19. "Most of the energy on Earth originally comes from the Sun." Give three examples to support this statement and explain how each of these sources of energy are converted from the Sun's radiant energy to a beneficial use.

20. When two objects of different temperatures are in contact with each other, over time both objects will be about the same temperature. Explain why this happens in terms of heat and thermal energy.

21. Explain why the transfer of thermal energy by convection occurs in gases and liquids, but not in solids.

22. Explain how ultraviolet waves can be both harmful and beneficial to humans.

23. Which of the following is true about light waves?

    A. Energy travels in light waves from one position to another.

    B. Matter travels in light waves from one position to another.

    C. Neither energy nor matter travels via light waves.

    D. Matter in the atmosphere is needed for light waves to travel.

24. Which of the following best explains how coal obtains energy?

    A. Animals and plants take in energy from the Sun → organisms die and decay → buried for millions of years → energy is trapped underground and slowly forms into coal

    B. Energy is transferred from plants to rocks → rocks get buried under many layers of soil → pressure from soil increases the energy in the rock → coal is formed over time

    C. Plants get energy from the Sun → Animals eat plants → organisms die and decay → buried deep in soil → extreme heat and pressure trap energy → coal is formed over time

    D. Animals take in energy from plants → animal waste contains excess energy → animal waste is buried under soil for millions of years → waste forms coal that contain trapped energy

Directions: Use the following chart to answer questions 25–26.

Energy Sources Used to Generate Electricity in United States in 2012*

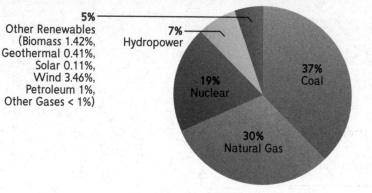

5% Other Renewables (Biomass 1.42%, Geothermal 0.41%, Solar 0.11%, Wind 3.46%, Petroleum 1%, Other Gases < 1%)

7% Hydropower

37% Coal

19% Nuclear

30% Natural Gas

*Does not add to 100 due to rounding.

25. Which renewable energy source is available in almost all regions of the U.S., but was underutilized in 2012?

    A. Sun

    B. wind

    C. water

    D. nuclear

26. If energy use were based solely on cost effectiveness, which was the least expensive form of energy used in 2012?

    A. coal

    B. solar energy

    C. petroleum

    D. natural gas

Directions: Use the following passage to answer questions 27–29.

> Thermal energy is related to heat but the two terms have different meanings. Atoms and molecules within matter are constantly moving, rotating, and vibrating. The sum of their kinetic and potential energies is called the thermal energy of the object. The temperature of the object is a measure of the average thermal energy per atom or molecule. Heat is energy that normally flows from an object at higher temperature to one at a lower temperature. If a hot piece of iron is placed in a bucket or water, it cools. The iron atoms have more energy than the water molecules and transfer some of their energy to the water in the form of heat. The transfer continues until the average thermal energy per iron atom equals the average thermal energy per water molecule.

27. Based on this passage, what is the relationship between the heat and temperature of an object?

A. The temperature difference between objects determines the direction of flow of heat.

B. The flow of heat from an object is not related to temperature difference.

C. The flow of heat from an object is a measure of its kinetic energy.

D. The flow of heat from an object is greater for objects with lower temperature.

28. Explain why a substance with greater average kinetic energy can heat the air around it more than a substance with lower average kinetic energy.

29. Explain how radiant energy from the Sun can raise the temperature of the air.

Check Your Understanding

On the following chart, circle the number of any item you answered incorrectly. Next to each group of item numbers, you will see the pages you can review to learn how to answer the items correctly

Lesson	Item Number(s)	Review Page(s)
6.1: Types of Energy and Energy Transformations	1, 2, 3, 4, 5, 14	212–217
6.2: Sources of Energy	6, 15, 17, 18, 19, 24, 25, 26	220–225
6.3: Heat	7, 8, 16, 20, 21, 27, 28, 29	228–231
6.4: Waves	9, 10, 11, 12, 13, 22, 23	234–239

Go With the Flow

Core Practices

- Reason from data or evidence to form a conclusion

Question

Is the statement, "close the refrigerator door, you're letting the cold air out" an accurate statement based on the principles of energy flow?

Background Concepts

Temperature is the measure of the average kinetic energy of the particles in a substance. We all have an idea of what a particular temperature "feels" like. When it is 20°F outside, we know it will feel very cold when we go outside. When we first grasp a mug of hot tea or coffee, it feels very hot in our hand, but after a few minutes, it doesn't feel so hot. This happens because thermal energy is transferred to other objects or the surroundings, heating them.

Hot coffee transfers thermal energy to the mug, our hand, and the surroundings until thermal energy is distributed evenly between the coffee and its surroundings and their temperatures are the same.

To do this, energy is transferred by conduction, convection, or radiation from an object of higher temperature to an object of lower temperature until both objects reach the same temperature. The direction of the flow of heat is always from a warmer to a colder substance.

Hypothesis

A hypothesis is a explanation based on what evidence is available. It is a starting point for a scientific investigation that will either be confirmed, need to be revised, or be shown to be incorrect based on more evidence gathered. If you leave the refrigerator door open, someone may yell out, "close the door you're letting the cold air out!" Develop a hypothesis that will argue for or against the validity of the statement, "you're letting the cold air out." Explain your reasoning to support or refute this statement.

Investigation

After developing a hypothesis, the next step is to gather information and data to determine whether your hypothesis is supported or not.

Set up an experiment to test the direction of the flow of heat.

MATERIALS

shallow baking dish, glass or metal

water

glitter

food coloring

2 thermometers

heat source: burner, small hot plate, canned heat or stove top if using a metal pan (DO NOT place glass baking dish directly on stovetop or over flame.)

PROCEDURE

1. Fill the baking dish with enough water to cover the bottom of the dish.

2. Place the center of the dish over the heat source to heat the water. Make sure that only the center of the dish is being heated and that the heat source is low enough to slowly heat the water.

3. Add a small amount of glitter and food coloring to the water in the center of the dish. Measure the temperature of the water in the center of the dish that is over the heat source and at the edge of the dish, which is not over the heat source.

4. Measure and record the two temperatures every 2 minutes for 30 minutes. Be sure to measure the temperature in the same two spots each time.

5. Observe the movement of the water containing the glitter and the food coloring.

Collect and Analyze Data

Make a table to record all the temperature data. Make a bar graph of the temperature change for each location over time. Analyze the graph to look for a trend in the data.

Record any observations that you made about the flow of colored water and glitter through the dish.

Interpretation

Summarize the data collected and interpret the evidence to determine if your hypothesis is supported.

When evaluating and interpreting the information or data you collected, ask yourself these questions:

- In which direction did the thermal energy flow through the baking dish as the water in the center was heated?

- Did the water in the dish move or remain still as it was heated? How did you know?

- What type of thermal energy transfer occurred in this experiment?

Results

Discuss your results using evidence to support your conclusions. Discuss any observations about the information you gathered, possible sources of error, unexpected results, and any remaining questions. If your hypothesis was not supported, discuss your recommendations for formulating a new hypothesis or changes you would make to the investigation.

Consider these questions as you discuss your results:

- Does the cold air from inside of the refrigerator flow out?

- What happens to particles as energy is transferred from one substance to another?

- Based on what you have learned about the flow of thermal energy between objects, why do you think thermal equilibrium is always established over time?

Chapter 7

Matter

Mix flour, eggs butter and sugar in a bowl. Would you eat this mixture of food? Probably not! But, if you mix all of these ingredients together and then bake the mixture in the oven you would have a delicious cake! This is an example of chemistry taking place in your kitchen. Chemistry is simply the study of matter and how it can change forms. Changes in matter are illustrated by following a simple recipe, or by studying complex reactions that take place in a laboratory.

Tom Merton/OJO Images/Getty Images

Lesson 7.1
The Structure of Matter

Matter is made up of very tiny particles called atoms. An element is a pure chemical substance consisting of one type of atom. In this lesson you will learn about atoms and elements, and how elements are organized into the Periodic Table of Elements.

Lesson 7.2
Physical and Chemical Properties of Matter

Matter can be described by texture, color, and hardness. Matter also has physical properties that can be measured such as mass, volume or density. Learn how matter can be described by its chemical properties, such as how it reacts to oxygen or water, or by its ability to burn.

Lesson 7.3
Chemical Reactions

Chemical reactions take place all around us every day—in the kitchen, and even in our gardens. In this lesson you will learn that when two or more types of matter interact with each other in a chemical reaction, atoms from each element combine to form a different substance.

Lesson 7.4
Solutions

Solutions can consist of any state of matter. When you mix a glass of instant ice tea you are making a solution of water and powdered tea mix. In this lesson you will learn about different types of solutions and their properties.

Goal Setting

Choose a relatively simple recipe that involves combining several ingredients and also requires cooking on the stove or in the oven. Write each step of the recipe in a table like the one shown at right. Next, predict whether a chemical or physical change takes place, if a chemical reaction occurs, or a solution is formed at each step. You can check more than one. After you read this chapter, come back to this chart and change your answers if necessary.

Recipe Step	Physical Change	Chemical Change	Chemical Reaction	Solution Formed
Example: heating water and sugar on the stovetop.				

LESSON 7.1 The Structure of Matter

▎LESSON OBJECTIVES

- Describe the structure of matter
- Understand how elements are organized in the periodic table
- Describe how atoms form molecules

▎CORE SKILLS & PRACTICES

- Apply Scientific Models
- Understand and Explain Textual Scientific Presentations

Key Terms

atom
the smallest particle of an element that has the properties of that element

element
a substance in which all the atoms are the same

matter
anything that has mass and takes up space

Vocabulary

chemical bond
a force that holds together two atoms in a compound

label
to name or describe something in a specified way

periodic table
an organized list of all known elements

Key Concept

All matter is made of atoms. Atoms of different elements have unique properties that determine the properties of the substance they make up.

The Structure of Matter

Think about icebergs floating in an arctic ocean under a sky of puffy white clouds, and you see a variety of shapes and textures. The chunks of icebergs are icy blue and made of frozen water. The ocean is liquid water. The clouds in the sky are puffs of water vapor. The ice, the ocean, and the clouds are all examples of **matter**, which is anything that has mass and takes up space. It is important to understand that not all matter is visible. For example, air is matter, even though it cannot be seen.

To decide whether something is matter, consider the definition of the term: *anything that has mass and takes up space.* The light waves that enable you to see the colors of the icebergs, the water, or the clouds do not have mass or take up space. Therefore, they are not matter. For this same reason, heat and sounds are also not matter. Different kinds of matter can be described in different ways. However, let's first discuss the structure of matter.

Atoms and Elements

All matter is made up of one or more elements, and each element is made up of atoms. An **element** is a substance in which all the atoms are the same. Nearly 100 fundamental elements occur in nature. Elements are represented by chemical symbols made up of one or two letters. The first letter is always capitalized and, if there is one, the second letter lowercase. The letters of the symbol are often an abbreviation of the element's name in English. For example, the symbol for carbon is C, and the symbol for helium is He.

An **atom** is the smallest particle of an element that has the properties of that element. Every atom is made up of even smaller particles called protons, neutrons, and electrons. Two of these particles, the protons and neutrons, are found in the nucleus—which is located in the center of an atom. A cloud of particles, called an electron cloud, surrounds the nucleus.

Every kind of atom has a different number of protons. But all the atoms of an element have the same number of protons. Protons have a positive electrical charge, electrons have a negative electrical charge, and neutrons are electrically neutral.

Periodic Table of the Elements

In the early nineteenth century, only a few elements were known to exist. In 1869, the Russian chemist Dmitri Mendeleev compared various properties of individual elements, including color, atomic mass, density, melting point, and boiling point. Mendeleev concluded that the elements should be arranged in order of increasing atomic mass. In 1913, Henry Moseley, a physicist, arranged the elements according to increasing atomic number instead of atomic mass. Immediately some of the inconsistencies associated with Mendeleev's table were eliminated. The patterns identified by Mendeleev, Moseley, and others serve as the foundation of periodic law. The resulting arrangement of elements has become known as the **periodic table.** Each square has a **label** that includes the element's name and its properties (see page 452).

Organization of the Periodic Table

Each horizontal row of the periodic table is called a period. For example, the row from sodium (Na) to argon (Ar) is Period 3. Each of the 18 vertical columns of the periodic table is called a group. The elements in a group generally have similar chemical and physical properties. A group is sometimes called a family. The changing patterns of the periodic table are referred to as periodic trends. Certain periodic trends can be identified from left to right across periods and down groups.

Atomic Number and Atomic Mass

All atoms of an element have the same atomic number, which equals the number of protons in the nucleus. For example, every atom of the element oxygen has 8 protons; therefore, the atomic number for oxygen is 8. Elements are arranged in order of increasing atomic number. Because the number of electrons is equal to the number of protons, both the number of protons and the number of electrons increase across a period and down a group.

Because electrons have negligible mass relative to protons and neutrons, most of an atom's mass is in its nucleus. The atomic mass of an atom is expressed as the mass number, the total number of protons and neutrons in the nucleus. Each element in the periodic table has its own square, which includes the element's name, chemical symbol, atomic number, atomic mass, and natural state. Each square shows the atomic number above the element symbol, and the atomic mass below the symbol.

Atomic Radius

The atomic radius is essentially the distance from the nucleus to the outermost electrons of an atom. As you move across a period, one electron and one proton are added to each element. The increased attraction between positively charged protons in the nucleus and negatively charged electrons in the energy levels pulls the electrons closer to the nucleus. Electrons exist within levels in the atom. Thus, atomic radius decreases across a period. Moving down a group, new energy levels in the electron clouds of the elements are added to accommodate additional electrons. Atomic radius therefore increases down a group.

CORE PRACTICE

Understand and Explain Textual Scientific Presentations

A summary of an investigation about rust formation is shown below. Read the passage and then answer the question.

> The compound iron oxide, or rust, is the result of a chemical reaction between iron and oxygen. The reaction is enhanced by the presence of water. In this investigation, the effect of salinity on rust formation in three different experimental conditions was measured and compared. Three iron nails were tested. Nail X was placed into a test tube with room-temperature distilled water. Nail Y was placed into a test tube with a room-temperature saltwater solution. Nail Z was placed into a test tube with no water. The mass of each nail was 0.50 gram before being placed in the test tube. After one week, the mass of each nail was measured. Nail X measured 0.71 gram, Nail Y measured 0.90 gram, and Nail Z measured 0.64 gram.

What conclusion about rust formation can you infer based on the information presented?

Apply Scientific Models

Over the years, our understanding of atomic structure has changed as new information and technologies have developed and as different scientists have investigated the topic and proposed new models. In the early 1900s, Niels Bohr proposed the model shown below. In Bohr's model, electrons travel along orbits that are at fixed distances from the nucleus.

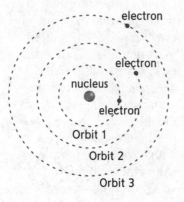

In 1927, the Bohr model was revised based on suggestions made by German scientist Werner Heisenberg. The model proposed by Heisenberg is called the electron cloud model.

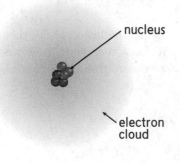

Which of the two models relates to the statement *Scientists can describe only a possible area where the electrons could be located at any specific time?* Explain your choice.

Metals, Nonmetals, and Metalloids

Elements are classified into three general categories: metals, nonmetals, and metalloids. On the periodic table, notice the zigzag section toward the right side. This section serves to identify metals, nonmetals, and metalloids. Most elements in the periodic table are metals—malleable, shiny, conductive, ductile elements—and are to the left of the zigzag section.

With the exception of hydrogen, the nonmetals are found to the right of the zigzag section on the periodic table. More than half of the nonmetals are gases at room temperature. The properties of nonmetals are essentially the opposite of the properties of metals—dull, brittle, and poor conductors.

Metalloids, the elements that form the zigzag section between the metals and nonmetals, have some of the properties of metals. All metalloids are solids at room temperature. They can be shiny or dull, malleable or brittle. Metalloids typically conduct heat and electricity better than nonmetals do, but not as well as metals. Whether a metalloid acts as a conductor depends on conditions such as temperature, light, and exposure to other elements.

Groups of Elements

All the elements in a group of the periodic table share certain properties because they have the same number of electrons in the outermost energy level. As a result, they are likely to behave in similar ways to obtain a complete set of electrons in the outermost energy level. Groups 1 and 2, along with Groups 13 through 18, are known as the representative elements, or main group elements. The behavior of representative elements is generally predictable. For example, sodium always reacts with chlorine to form sodium chloride.

Group 1 elements are known as the alkali metals. Alkali metals are soft enough to be cut with a knife. They are usually silver in color, shiny, and have low densities. The elements in Group 2 are the alkaline earth metals. These elements are generally hard, gray-white, and good conductors of electricity. The elements in Groups 3 through 12 are known as transition elements, or transition metals. The behavior of transition elements is less predictable. For example, iron might react with oxygen to form FeO or Fe2O3, depending on the amount of oxygen available.

Think about Science

Directions: Fill in the blank.

1. _____ are good conductors of electricity.

2. _____ are solid at room temperature.

3. An element with the atomic number of 16 has _____ protons in its nucleus.

4. The total number of _____ make up an atom's mass number.

Compounds

Atoms in our bodies, in the environment, and in space are constantly coming together to form new substances. When the atoms of two or more different elements combine chemically, they form a compound. Many elements in nature are combined into compounds. Examples of compounds include carbon dioxide, ammonia, table salt, and rust. A molecule is the smallest part of a compound that can exist by itself.

Chemical Bonds

When atoms combine to form compounds, a bond is formed between the atoms. A **chemical bond** is a force that holds together two atoms. This bond forms between electrons in the outermost energy level of an atom's electron cloud. An atom will bond with another atom to gain a complete set of electrons in its outer level by either transferring or sharing electrons. An atom that has 8 electrons in its outer shell does not form chemical bonds. Elements that are likely to transfer or share electrons with other elements are described as being reactive. Because all the elements in a group on the periodic table have the same number of electrons in the outermost energy level, they are likely to behave in similar ways to obtain a complete set of electrons in the outermost energy level.

Chemical Formulas

Just as elements can be represented by chemical symbols, compounds can be represented by chemical formulas. A chemical formula shows the elements in a compound and the ratio of their atoms. The elements in a compound always combine in a specific ratio. For example, water is a compound in which two atoms of hydrogen combine with one atom of oxygen. No matter where on Earth you find the water, or whether the water is ice, water vapor, or liquid water, every water molecule always exists in this ratio of two hydrogen atoms to one oxygen atom.

The chemical formula for the compound known as carbon dioxide is CO_2. The formula includes the chemical symbol for carbon, C, and the chemical symbol for oxygen, O—the two elements that make up the compound. The number 2 below the symbol for oxygen is called a subscript. A subscript below an element's symbol indicates the number of atoms of that element present in each molecule of the compound. The subscript below the symbol for oxygen indicates that there are two atoms of oxygen. If there is no subscript, as in the case of the carbon atom, it is understood that there is one atom of that element. So, the ratio of oxygen to carbon in every molecule of carbon dioxide is 2 to 1.

Think about Science

Directions: Answer the following questions.

1. What is represented by the number *3* in the chemical formula for rust, Fe_2O_3?
   - A. The number of iron atoms in one molecule
   - B. The total number of atoms in each molecule
   - C. The number of oxygen atoms in one molecule
   - D. The number of electrons shared between iron and oxygen

2. Atoms combine to form compounds by sharing
   - A. protons.
   - B. neutrons.
   - C. electrons.
   - D. molecules.

Vocabulary Review

Directions: Write the missing term in the blank.

atoms   chemical bond   matter
elements   periodic table   label

1. _____ is anything that has mass and takes up space.

2. A molecule is formed when two or more _____ combine.

3. The atoms that form a molecule are held together by a _____.

4. A compound is formed when the _____ of two or more _____ combine.

5. The arrangement of elements in the _____ is in order of increasing atomic number.

6. Each square on the periodic table has a _____ with the element's chemical symbol.

Skill Review

Directions: Answer the following questions.

1. An atom of carbon has six protons in its nucleus. Where on the periodic table would you find the element with seven protons?

   A. above it

   B. below it

   C. to the right of it

   D. to the left of it

2. The ratio of elements in a molecule of ammonia is one nitrogen atom to three hydrogen atoms. Which is the chemical formula for ammonia?

   A. $3NH_3$

   B. NH_3

   C. N_3H

   D. N_3H_3

3. Which property determines the charge of an atom's nucleus?

   A. the number of protons

   B. the number of neutrons

   C. the number of electrons

   D. the total number of shells

4. When the compound chalk, $CaCO_3$, is heated, it decomposes into the products lime, CaO, and carbon dioxide, CO_2. How would you classify these two products?

   A. atoms

   B. elements

   C. neutrons

   D. compounds

5. A sample of gold cannot have atoms with different numbers of protons. Why?

6. Water, H_2O, is often referred to as a universal solvent because of its ability to dissolve the molecules of so many compounds. Table sugar is a solid compound of carbon, hydrogen, and oxygen. Describe an experiment in which you compare the solvent properties of water and oil on the forces holding together the molecules of a sugar cube, $C_{12}H_{22}O_{12}$.

Skill Practice

Directions: Use the diagram to answer questions 1 and 2.

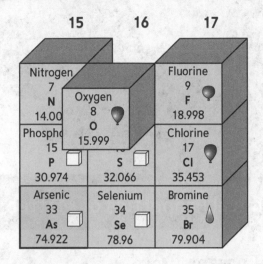

1. Of the elements shown, which are in the same group as oxygen?

   A. nitrogen and fluorine

   B. sulfur and selenium

   C. phosphorous and chlorine

   D. arsenic and bromine

2. The element arsenic is a metalloid. Based on the organization of metals, nonmetals, and metalloids on the periodic table, how would you classify chlorine and bromine?

   A. Chlorine is a metalloid; bromine is a nonmetal.

   B. Chlorine is a nonmetal; bromine is a metalloid.

   C. Chlorine and bromine are both nonmetals.

   D. Chlorine and bromine are both metals.

Directions: Answer the following questions.

3. Four elements are examined. Element A is in group 2, period 6. Element B is in group 4, period 4. Element C is in group 10, period 7. Element D is in group 11, period 3. Which element should have the greatest atomic mass?

   A. Element A

   B. Element B

   C. Element C

   D. Element D

4. The chemical formula for carbon monoxide is CO. The formula for carbon dioxide is CO_2. The formula for water is H_2O. The formula for hydrogen peroxide is H_2O_2. Which chemical name could be used to describe water?

   A. hydrogen peroxide

   B. dihydrogen monoxide

   C. hydrogen dioxide

   D. dihydrogen pentoxide

5. How could you conduct an investigation to examine the interaction between water and three metals from the periodic table?

6. Using the periodic table on pages 452–453, create a Venn diagram comparing the elements germanium and arsenic.

7. Which of these is the defining characteristic of an atom?

   A. It has all the properties of an element.

   B. It carries a positive electrical charge.

   C. It exists as a particle and as a wave.

   D. It can exist naturally or be manmade.

8. Which diagram represents the increasing structural relationship between elements, protons, and atoms?

   A. protons→atoms→elements

   B. elements→protons→atoms

   C. protons→elements→atoms

   D. atoms→elements→protons

LESSON OBJECTIVES

- Compare the physical and chemical properties of matter
- Relate the properties of elements to their position in the periodic table

CORE SKILLS & PRACTICES

- Cite Textual Evidence
- Evaluate Conclusions

Key Terms

chemical property
the ability or inability of a substance to react with or change into a new substance

physical property
a characteristic of matter that can be observed without changing its chemical properties

states of matter
the physical forms in which all matter exists

sublimation
the change of state from a solid to a gas

Vocabulary

evaluate
to determine the quality of

melting point
the temperature at which a substance changes from solid to liquid

Key Concept

Matter can be described by its physical properties and chemical properties. The properties of elements are similar within groups on the periodic table.

Properties of Matter

You use characteristics to identify and classify everything around you. When you are grocery shopping, you can tell the difference between a carrot and potato simply by looking at them. You could even tell the difference between an orange and apple without seeing them simply by the way their skin feels. Properties can be used to identify any type of matter.

Physical Properties

Color, shape, and size are physical properties of matter. A **physical property** of matter is a characteristic that can be observed without changing the matter into a different substance. Each substance has a unique set of physical properties that distinguishes it from all other substances. Some physical properties, such as texture and hardness, describe how an object feels. These properties are observed by looking at or touching an object. You can observe whether matter is smooth or rough and hard or soft.

Some physical properties, such mass and volume, are determined by making measurements. Mass is the amount of matter in an object, and volume is the amount of space matter takes up. The mass and volume of an object can be used to find another physical property—density. Density is the amount of mass in a given volume, and it is a unique property of matter that is useful in separating and identifying substances.

Physical properties can be used classify and identify matter, but some properties are more helpful than others. Physical properties such as density, temperature, and color do not change when the amount of matter changes. Some of these properties, such as density, are characteristic of a substance. For example, a single drop of pure water and five gallons of pure water both have a density 1.0 g/mL. Other physical properties, such as mass and volume, do change when the amount of matter changes. A full glass of water has a greater volume and mass than half a glass of water.

Glow Images

Chemical Properties

Over time, the surface of a shiny silver spoon will become dull and black because silver tarnishes when exposed to air. The ability to tarnish is a chemical property of some types of matter. A **chemical property** is the ability or inability of a substance to react with or change into one or more new substances.

Like physical properties, chemical properties are used to classify substances. Unlike physical properties, however, chemical properties occur only when the composition of a substance changes. This means that a new substance must be formed. Chemical properties cannot be determined by looking at or feeling the substance or by taking measurements.

Have you ever seen a rusty old car, tractor, or set of tools? All these objects may develop rust, a flaky, reddish-brown substance that can form on some metals when the metals are exposed to air. The ability to rust is a chemical property of iron and metals that contain iron. When iron combines with oxygen and water in air, rust forms. Rust has a different chemical composition than that of the iron from which it formed. You can determine if a substance has the ability to rust only by observing the formation of rust.

Another chemical property is flammability, which is the ability to burn. Paper and wood are examples of matter that have the ability to burn. Matter that is described as flammable, such as paper, wood, gasoline, and many cleaning products, can burn easily and quickly. As with physical properties, every substance has a certain set of chemical properties. Silver can tarnish, but it does not rust or burn. Iron can rust, but it is less flammable and does not tarnish.

Physical Properties That Depend on Amount	Physical Properties That Do Not Depend on Amount	Chemical Properties
mass	boiling point	ability to tarnish
volume	color	ability to rust
size	density	ability to burn (flammability)
	hardness	ability to react with oxygen
	melting point	
	temperature	
	texture	
	shape	

Think about Science

Directions: Answer the following questions.

1. Which physical property would be most useful when trying to identify a substance?

   A. density
   B. flammability
   C. mass
   D. shape

2. Which property can be observed only by the formation of a new substance?

   A. ability to rust
   B. color
   C. melting point
   D. texture

After a very cold night, Trevor observes frost on the grass outside. He concludes that water from the air must have condensed into liquid overnight, and then the liquid froze to form the frost. **Evaluate,** or determine the quality of, this conclusion. Use information from the diagram on this page to explain your evaluation.

Changes of State

A glass of ice water sits in front of you on the table. It is obvious the water in the glass is both a solid, which is the ice, and a liquid. There is also water vapor in the air, which is a gas. Solid, liquid, and gas are all **states of matter,** which are the physical forms in which all matter exists. The state of matter is a physical property that depends on temperature and pressure. A change of state is the conversion of a substance from one physical form to another. The composition of a substance does not change as the substance is converted from one state to another. When ice cream melts on a warm day, it changes from a solid to a liquid. Although they look different, both the solid ice cream and the melted ice cream contain the same molecules.

When matter changes from one state to another, thermal energy is absorbed or released. When matter is heated, it absorbs thermal energy. Matter releases thermal energy as it cools. Substances need to be heated or cooled to a certain temperature to change state. The temperatures at which a substance changes from one state to another do not depend on the amount of the substance. The **melting point** is the temperature at which a solid changes into a liquid. The boiling point is the temperature at which a liquid changes into a gas. The melting and boiling points of water are the same whether there are two or twenty liters of water.

Melting

The change from the solid state to the liquid state is called melting. A substance must absorb thermal energy to melt. The particles in a solid vibrate more vigorously as the thermal energy and the temperature of the solid increase. At the melting point, the particles vibrate so intensely that the attractive forces between them are overcome, and the particles begin to move past one another. The temperature of the substance stays constant while the solid changes to a liquid. A substance has a characteristic melting point that can help identify it. For example, the melting point of water is 0°C, whereas the melting point of table salt is 801°C.

Freezing

The change of state from a liquid to a solid is called freezing. Freezing is the reverse of melting, so the freezing point of a substance is the same as its melting point. However, to change a liquid into a solid, the liquid must be cooled. As a liquid is cooled, it loses thermal energy, and its particles slow down and come closer together. At the freezing point, the attraction between the particles overcomes their motion. The temperature stops decreasing as the liquid becomes a solid.

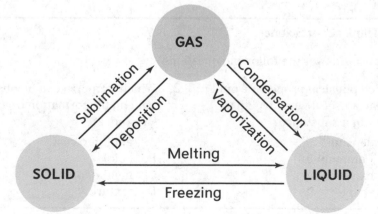

Vaporization

The change of state from a liquid to a gas is called vaporization. A substance needs to absorb thermal energy to change from a liquid to a gas. There are two ways vaporization occurs: boiling and evaporation.

Vaporization that occurs throughout a liquid is called boiling. When a liquid boils, gas bubbles form within the liquid and rise to the surface. A liquid boils only when its temperature reaches its boiling point. At that temperature, the particles have enough energy to overcome the attractive forces between them. The particles are free to spread apart, and the liquid changes into a gas. Like the melting point, the boiling point can be used to identify a substance. The boiling point of water is 100°C at sea level.

A puddle formed during a rainstorm disappears as sunlight shines on it because of evaporation. Evaporation is vaporization that occurs only at the surface of a liquid and at temperatures below the boiling point of a substance. The water molecules on the surface of the puddle absorb energy from the Sun. Once they have absorbed enough energy, the particles spread apart, and the liquid water changes into water vapor. The water molecules become dissolved in the air.

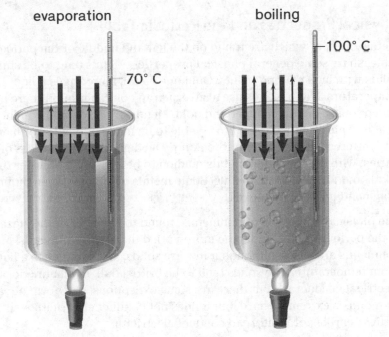

Condensation

Droplets of water form on glass when water vapor cools and condenses. The change of state from a gas to a liquid is called condensation. Condensation is the reverse of boiling and occurs when a gas cools. As a gas releases thermal energy, its particles slow down, and its temperature drops. When the particles slow down enough for the forces of attraction to pull them together, the gas changes into a liquid.

Sublimation

Under certain conditions, matter can change from a solid directly to a gas. The change of state in which a solid changes directly to a gas is called **sublimation.** During sublimation, the particles of a solid absorb enough energy so that they change from being held very close together to being very far apart. You may have seen fog for special effects made by the sublimation of dry ice, which is solid carbon dioxide.

Physical and Chemical Properties of Matter

Directions: Answer the following questions.

1. Which is a change of state from a gas to a liquid?
   A. boiling   C. freezing
   B. condensation   D. sublimation

2. During which change do the particles in a substance gain enough energy to begin moving past one another?
   A. boiling   C. freezing
   B. evaporation   D. melting

Predicting Properties

You can use the periodic table to predict the physical and chemical properties of elements. Knowing whether an element is a nonmetal, metal, or metalloid can help you predict several general physical properties. Knowing the group of an element can help you predict its chemical properties.

Physical Properties and the Periodic Table

Metals, most of which are found on the left and middle of the periodic table, share some general physical properties. Metals tend to be shiny solids with high melting points. Only one metal, mercury, is a liquid at room temperature. Many metals are a silvery gray color, although there are some exceptions, including copper and gold. Metals are also good conductors of heat and electricity and tend to be able to be made into wires or hammered into different shapes without breaking. The density and hardness of metals varies, with the transition metals tending to be denser and harder than the alkali and alkaline earth metals. Some metals are magnetic, including cobalt, iron, neodymium, and nickel.

The physical properties of nonmetals, found to the right of the zigzag line in the periodic table, tend to be more varied than those of metals. Many nonmetals are gases, although a few are solids, and bromine is a liquid at room temperature. The solids tend to be brittle, dull, nonmagnetic, and poor electrical conductors, but there are some exceptions. One form of carbon, diamond, is extremely hard, but it does not conduct electricity well. Another form of carbon, graphite, can conduct electricity.

The seven metalloids, located between the metals and nonmetals in the periodic table, have properties of both. All metalloids are solids at room temperature. They can be shiny or dull, brittle or able to be shaped. Metalloids typically conduct heat and electricity better than nonmetals but not as well as metals. Whether a metalloid acts as a conductor depends on conditions such as temperature, light, and whether it's mixed with other certain elements.

The group of an element can sometimes be helpful in predicting physical properties. For example, the elements in group 1 and group 2 are softer and less dense than the transition metals found in groups 3 through 12. The noble gases in group 18 are all colorless gases. However, groups 13 through 17 contain metals, nonmetals, and metalloids, so, for these groups, the group does give not a good indication of expected physical properties.

Metal

Nonmetal

Chemical Properties and the Periodic Table

As you have learned, the ability of an element to form bonds depends on the outermost electrons in the atoms of that element. This and other chemical properties of elements vary in a regular way within the groups of the periodic table. Elements in the same group have similar chemical properties because they have the same number of electrons in their outermost electron shell. The outermost electron shell is the highest electron shell that contains electrons. The electrons in this shell are the only electrons that are shared or exchanged to form chemical bonds.

The chemical properties of elements can also be predicted by the location of an element in a period of the periodic table. Chemical properties change regularly across a period because the number of outermost electrons increases across a period. The group number indicates the number of valance electrons. For example, all the elements in group 1 have one outermost electron, and elements in group 2 have two outermost electrons. For groups 13 through 18, the number of electrons in the outermost energy level is the group number minus ten.

The metals in group 1 are slightly more reactive than those in group 2. However, both groups of elements are very reactive because they can transfer one or two electrons to another element to have a full outermost energy level. None of these elements are found alone in nature because they combine so readily with other elements. The transition metals, found in groups 3 through 12, are less reactive, although many still have the ability to react with oxygen and other nonmetals. A few transitions metals, such as gold, rarely react. The halogens, group 17, are nonmetals and are very reactive because they need to gain only a single electron to have a full outermost energy level. On the other hand, the noble gases, group 18, are inert, which means they are very unreactive. They have a full outermost energy level and are found as uncombined atoms in nature.

Properties of Materials

Very few of the materials around you are made of a single element. Some materials are compounds, but most are complex mixtures. The chemical composition of a compound can help you predict the properties of a compound because the properties are the result of interactions between the atoms, ions, or molecules that make up the compound. By understanding these interactions, scientists and engineers can design materials that have specific properties. For example, they can make steel that is stronger than pure iron or polymers that are rigid or flexible.

Think about Science

Directions: Answer the following questions.

1. Based on its position in the periodic table, which element would you expect to conduct electricity?
   - A. chlorine (Cl)
   - B. nitrogen (N)
   - C. phosphorus (P)
   - D. silver (Ag)

2. Based on its position in the periodic table, which element would you expect to be the most reactive?
   - A. argon (Ar)
   - B. cobalt (Co)
   - C. magnesium (Mg)
   - D. silicon (Si)

CORE PRACTICE

Cite Textual Evidence

A person tests an element that is a liquid at room temperature and finds that the element does not conduct electricity, but it readily undergoes chemical reactions. Based on these results, the person concludes that the element can be found in group 1 of the periodic table. Evaluate this conclusion by citing evidence from the text on these two pages.

Vocabulary Review

Directions: Write the missing term in the blank.

chemical property   evaluate   melting point
physical property   states of matter   sublimation

1. Density is a(n) _____ .

2. A property that can be observed only when a new substance forms is a(n) _____ .

3. Solids, liquids, and gases are _____ .

4. During _____ , a solid changes directly to gas.

5. To make a judgment about the quality of a conclusion is to _____ the conclusion.

6. Ice changes to liquid water at the _____ of water.

Skill Review

Directions: Answer the following questions.

1. Which of these properties could be the same for samples of sulfur and potassium?

   A. boiling point

   B. density

   C. mass

   D. melting point

2. Over the course of a week, the water left in the bottom of a cup sitting on a desk disappears. Which change happened to the water?

   A. It boiled.

   B. It evaporated.

   C. It melted.

   D. It sublimed.

Directions: Use the table to answer questions 3–6.

3. Which two elements would have the most similar chemical properties?

   A. aluminum (Al) and arsenic (As)

   B. carbon (C) and nitrogen (N)

   C. carbon (C) and silicon (Si)

   D. silicon (Si) and arsenic (As)

4. Predict the physical properties of aluminum, silicon, and phosphorus. Justify your predictions.

5. Predict which element is most likely to have the properties most similar to gallium. Justify your prediction based on the way the elements are organized in the periodic table and the atomic structure of the atoms.

6. Design a procedure to distinguish between samples of aluminum and silicon based on at least two physical properties.

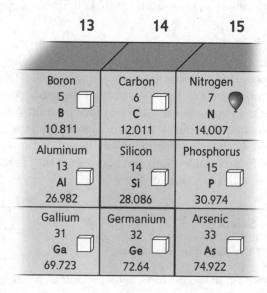

Skill Practice

Directions: Use the graph to answer questions 1–7.

The graph below shows how the temperature of water changes as the water is heated and changes state. This type of graph is called a heating curve.

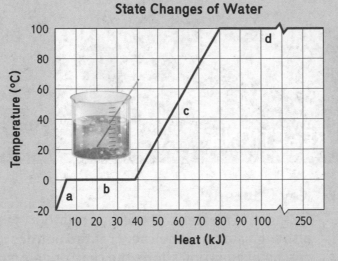

State Changes of Water

The graph shows that as heat is added, the temperature increases until the water reaches its melting or boiling point. The temperature does not change as the water undergoes a change of state, because the energy absorbed by the water goes into overcoming the attractive forces between the particles. Once the change of state is complete, heating the water causes its temperature to rise once again.

1. If heat is being added to the water, which change occurs in region **b**?

   A. boiling

   B. freezing

   C. melting

   D. subliming

2. Which states(s) of water are present in region **c** of the graph?

   A. gas only

   B. gas and liquid

   C. liquid only

   D. liquid and solid

3. How much heat is added in region **c** of the graph?

   A. 0 kJ

   B. 40 kJ

   C. 80 kJ

   D. 100 kJ

4. What is not included on the graph?

   A. The region where condensation occurs

   B. The region where freezing occurs

   C. The region where the temperature of gas increases

   D. The region where the temperature of a solid increases

5. What happens in region **d** as the water is heated and cooled? Explain your reasoning.

6. Pure ethanol has a melting point of –114°C and a boiling point of 78°C. Explain how the heating curve of ethanol would differ from the heating curve shown for water.

7. A new heating curve is made using twice the volume of water used to make the heating curve shown. How will this new heating curve compare to the heating curve shown? Justify your response.

LESSON OBJECTIVES

- Explain how matter is conserved during a chemical reaction
- Use balanced chemical equations to represent chemical reactions
- Classify chemical reactions based on energy changes

CORE SKILLS & PRACTICES

- Identify and Reduce Sources of Error
- Determine Central Ideas

Key Terms

chemical reaction
the process in which substances are changed into new substances

endothermic reactions
reactions that require the addition of energy to proceed

exothermic reactions
reactions that release energy as the reaction proceeds

law of conservation of mass
the combined mass of all the reactants is equal to the combined mass of all the products.

Vocabulary

develop
to create or produce something over a period of time

Key Concept

Changes in matter and energy occur during a chemical reaction, although matter is neither created nor destroyed. A balanced chemical equation shows the rearrangement of atoms and describes a chemical reaction.

What Happens During a Chemical Reaction?

Recall that during a physical change, such as melting or freezing of a substance, the physical properties of the substance change, but its chemical properties do not. In contrast, a chemical change occurs when the chemical properties of matter change as new substances form. Rusting is an example of a chemical change. When iron rusts, metallic iron reacts with oxygen and a substance made up of iron and oxygen atoms forms. That substance is rust. The chemical properties of rust are different from those of the pure iron. The physical properties of rust, such as its color and hardness, are also different from those of iron. When matter changes chemically, both its physical properties and its chemical properties change.

Changes in Matter

How do chemical changes occur? The process by which one or more substances change into new substances is called a **chemical reaction**. In a chemical reaction, the atoms of the reactants—the substance or substances that existed before the reaction—are rearranged and form products—the substance or substances that exist after the reaction is completed. A forest fire is an example of chemical reactions on a very large scale. Molecules that make up trees and other organic matter in the forest combine with oxygen in the atmosphere and produce carbon dioxide, water vapor, and other compounds. At the same time, the chemical reaction releases a lot of energy as heat.

When a chemical reaction takes place, atoms rearrange as the chemical bonds between some atoms are broken and new chemical bonds form between other atoms. This rearrangement of atoms causes new substances to form.

Masterfile

The rearrangement of the atoms of hydrogen molecules and oxygen molecules is illustrated here. The models to the left of the arrow show the bonds that exist between hydrogen atoms and between oxygen atoms. To the right of the arrow, each new bond connects two hydrogen atoms to an oxygen atom. The chemical and physical properties of water are very different from those of hydrogen or oxygen.

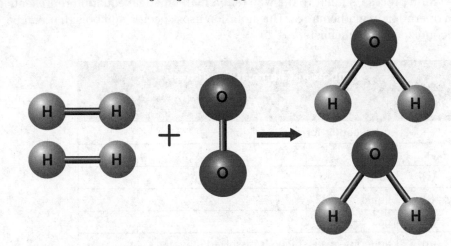

Law of Conservation of Mass

Atoms do not appear or disappear during a chemical reaction. All the atoms in the reactants will be in the products in exactly the same numbers as before the reaction, but they will be in a different arrangement. This idea is expressed in one of the most important laws of chemistry, the **law of conservation of mass**, which states that in a chemical reaction, the combined mass of all the reactants is equal to the combined mass of all the products. Matter is conserved; it is neither created nor destroyed.

The illustration of the formation of water shows that two molecules of hydrogen react with each molecule of oxygen and form two molecules of water. You can see that the reactants must react in these proportions to follow the law of conservation of mass. What would happen if the ratio of hydrogen and oxygen molecules in the reaction mixture were equal—for example, 50 molecules of hydrogen and 50 molecules of oxygen? In this case, some of the molecules cannot react. After 25 molecules of oxygen have reacted, forming 50 molecules of water, no hydrogen molecules remain.

In this situation, hydrogen is called the limiting reactant, which is the reactant that is completely consumed when the reaction goes to completion and limits the amount of product formed. The final mixture will contain 50 molecules of water and 25 molecules of unreacted oxygen. The actual numbers of molecules involved in a reaction would be many orders of magnitude higher. These numbers are used only for demonstration.

Think about Science

Directions: Answer the following questions.

1. What change always indicates that a chemical reaction has occurred?
2. What is the limiting reactant when 2,000 molecules of hydrogen and 750 molecules of oxygen are available for the formation of water?

How Are Chemical Reactions Represented?

Hydrogen and oxygen molecules react to form water. That is one way to describe the chemical reaction that occurs between hydrogen and oxygen. Chemists do not explain chemical processes in sentences. They use a form of notation that represents the reactants and the products and shows the reaction process, similar to the way that a mathematical equation represents an operation in mathematics. This notation uses specific symbols that can be recognized by all chemists.

Symbols in Chemical Equations	
Symbol	**Meaning**
$\rightarrow$	produced or forms
+	plus
(s)	solid
(l)	liquid
(g)	gas
(aq)	aqueous—a substance is dissolved in water
$\xrightarrow{heat}$	the reactants are heated
$\xrightarrow{light}$	the reactants are exposed to light
$\xrightarrow{elec.}$	an electric current is passed through the reactants
$\xrightarrow{0°C}$	the reaction is carried out at 0°C

Chemical Equations

A chemical equation is a form of notation that shows the reactants and products involved in a chemical reaction. The reactants are shown on the left, and the products are shown on the right, with an arrow between to indicate the direction in which the reaction proceeds. The arrow indicates that something is produced or formed. Words above the arrow can describe the conditions under which the reaction takes place. They can show, for example, if the reaction requires heat to occur. Each reactant is separated in the equation by a plus sign (+), as shown in the equation below. If there are two or more products, each product is also separated by a plus sign. The equation for the formation of water is written as follows:

$$2H_2 \text{ (g)} + O_2 \text{ (g)} \rightarrow 2H_2O \text{ (l)}$$

Notice that in this equation, a number appears in front of some of the chemical formulas. These numbers, called coefficients, indicate how many molecules of each substance are involved in the reaction. If there is no coefficient in front of a formula, the coefficient is assumed to be 1. The coefficient shows the ratio of molecules in a reaction. In this reaction, the ratio is two hydrogen atoms to one oxygen atom, so two hydrogen molecules will react with one oxygen molecule and produce two water molecules.

Balancing Chemical Equations

Look at the following chemical equation written without coefficients:

$$H_2 (g) + O_2 (g) \rightarrow H_2O (l)$$

Count the number of atoms on each side of the equation. Recall that the subscripts indicate the number of atoms in one molecule of a compound. There are two hydrogen atoms and two oxygen atoms on the reactant side of the equation. There are two hydrogen atoms but only one oxygen atom on the product side of the equation. The number of atoms on each side of the equation is not the same. This means that the reaction as written cannot take place, because it violates the law of conservation of mass.

Coefficients are used to write a balanced chemical equation, which is an equation with the same number of atoms on both sides of the arrow. Adding coefficients to a chemical equation does not change the reactants or products. It simply shows the ratios of substances involved in the reaction. Balancing a chemical equation is often a trial-and-error process.

To balance the equation, place the coefficient 2 in front of the formula for water. This signifies that two molecules of water are produced for every one molecule of oxygen that reacts.

$$H_2 (g) + O_2 (g) \rightarrow 2H_2O (l)$$

Notice that oxygen is now balanced in the equation. There are two oxygen atoms on the left side of the equation and two on the right. Hydrogen, however, is now unbalanced. To balance hydrogen, place the coefficient 2 in front of hydrogen on the reactant side of the equation.

$$2H_2 (g) + O_2 (g) \rightarrow 2H_2O (l)$$

The number of atoms of each element on the left is now equal to the number of atoms of that element on the right. The equation is balanced.

How to Balance a Chemical Equation	
Step 1	Identify the reactants and products and write their chemical formulas on the appropriate sides of the equation.
Step 2	Count the number of atoms of each element on each side of the equation. If you need to, use a table to keep track of the numbers.
Step 3	Try coefficients that will balance the equation. Start with elements that appear in only one molecule on each side of the equation, if possible. Never change the subscripts in a chemical formula to balance an equation. That changes the identity of the substances.
Step 4	Check to be sure that you have the same number of atoms of each element on both sides of the equation.

Think about Science

Directions: Write balanced equations for the chemical reactions.

1. $CH_4 + O_2 \rightarrow CO_2 + H_2O$
2. $KOH + H_2SO_4 \rightarrow K_2SO_4 + H_2O$

WORKPLACE SKILLS

Organize Information

The first step in solving a problem, either in a textbook or in the workplace, is to organize the information needed to find the solution. For example, in order to balance a chemical equation, you must first identify the reactants and the products of the reaction. Then you organize this information by writing an unbalanced chemical equation that shows how substances change during the chemical reaction. This allows you to confirm that the same elements appear on both sides of the reaction arrow. After the information is organized in the correct format, it is possible to determine the ratios of all the substances involved. How are the reactants and the products separated in this organizational format?

Many computerized instruments and tools include dedicated computer programs that control their operations or analyze the data they generate. In addition to these specialized programs, there are common programs that can be applied to many different workplace tasks. For example, word-processing programs are used to write and edit reports, databases organize information about inventories and ordering, and spreadsheet applications can be used to calculate numerical results and track financial information. Which type of computer program do you think would be most useful for balancing chemical equations? Explain your answer.

Energy Changes in Chemical Reactions

What causes the bonds between hydrogen atoms in a hydrogen molecule and between the oxygen atoms in an oxygen molecule to break at the start of the chemical reaction that forms water? It takes energy to break the chemical bonds between atoms or ions in a compound. This means that all chemical reactions require some energy to get started. The minimum amount of energy required for a chemical reaction to occur is called activation energy. Different reactions require different amounts of this energy to get started. Light, heat, and electricity are some common sources of activation energy.

Exothermic Reactions

While energy can be released in the form of light, motion, or electricity, in most chemical reactions, energy is released in the form of heat. Reactions that release heat are called **exothermic reactions**. The energy given off in a chemical reaction comes from the original bonds that are broken (the reactant bonds) and the new bonds that are formed (the product bonds) during the reaction. Although all reactions require activation energy, some reactions give off energy once they are started. If the products of a reaction are more stable—that is, their bonds require less energy—than the reactants, energy will be released as the products are formed. Think of logs burning in a campfire or fireplace. Logs do not start burning spontaneously. It takes energy to get them to start burning. Once burning, however, they give off a great deal of energy in the form of light and heat. All combustion reactions are exothermic and involve a release of energy as heat.

Endothermic Reactions

Some chemical reactions require not only activation energy but also a continuous supply of energy in order for the reaction to continue. Such reactions stop when that energy source is removed. The reactants no longer react, and the products no longer form. Overall these reactions absorb more energy than they give off. Reactions that absorb heat are described as **endothermic reactions**. Chemical reactions involved in baking cookies, for example, are endothermic reactions driven by thermal energy. In this case, the heat is from the oven. Reactions absorb energy when the products formed are less stable—their bonds require more energy—than the reactants.

Representing Energy Changes

The energy changes that occur during a chemical reaction can be modeled on a graph plotting the energy stored in chemical bonds against the progress of the reaction. These diagrams show that the products of an endothermic reaction have more chemical energy than the reactants, while the products of an exothermic reaction have less energy than the reactants.

Endothermic Reaction

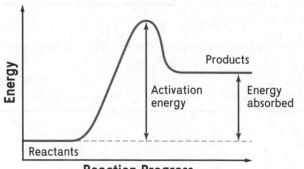

Exothermic Reaction

Think about Science

Directions: Fill in the blank.

1. When vinegar and a solution of baking soda are mixed, the final solution is colder than either of the original solutions. This observation indicates that the reaction between vinegar and baking soda is an _____ reaction.

2. The thermal energy released by a forest fire indicates that combustion is an _____ reaction.

Chemical-Reaction Rate

Some reactions happen very quickly in just fractions of a second. Others take hours or even years to complete. A reaction's rate depends on the nature of the substances involved. It also depends on how often the particles of those substances collide with one another. The more the particles collide, the more likely the substances are to react, and the faster the reaction will be.

Effect of Temperature on Reaction Rate

Heating a substance increases the speed at which the particles move. The faster the particles move, the more frequently they will collide with the particles of other substances. Adding heat to most reactions will cause the reactions to occur more quickly. Cooling reactions tends to cause them to occur more slowly.

Effect of Concentration on Reaction Rate

Concentration describes how much of a substance is in a given unit of volume. For example, if 20 g of sodium chloride is dissolved in 1 l of water, the solution contains 20 g of salt per liter of solution. If an additional 20 g of salt is added to the solution, the change in volume is too small to notice. The concentration of the solution is 40 g of salt per liter of solution.

A high concentration of reactants means there are a great many particles per unit volume. There are more reactant particles available for collisions. More collisions occur, and more product is formed in a certain amount of time. A low concentration of reactants means there are fewer particles per unit volume. With fewer reactant particles available, there will be fewer collisions. Less product will form in a certain amount of time.

CORE PRACTICE

Identify and Reduce Sources of Error

In any investigation, there are steps in which errors can affect the results or observations. To **develop**, or create, ways to obtain the best possible data, you should examine each step of the investigation. Identify possible sources of error and make changes to minimize errors. Consider an investigation to determine the effect of concentration on reaction rate when two solutions are mixed. Based on information in this section, identify an action to avoid errors in measuring the reaction rate.

Vocabulary Review

Directions: Write the missing term in the blank.

chemical reaction   develop   law of conservation of mass
exothermic reaction   endothermic reaction

1. Rapid cooling of the liquid when two solutions are mixed is evidence of a(n) _____ reaction.

2. In order to write a chemical equation, you need to identify all the reactants and all the products of a(n) _____.

3. A(n) _____ indicates the proportions of all the substances involved in a reaction.

4. In order to _____ an effective investigation, examine each step for possible errors.

5. Heat is produced during a(n) _____.

Skill Review

Directions: Answer the following questions.

1. Which of the following always occurs when a chemical reaction has taken place?
   A. Release of thermal energy
   B. Formation of a new substance
   C. Change of state from liquid to gas
   D. Increase in the volume of material

2. Which of these is a balanced chemical equation?
   A. $C_2H_6 + 5O_2 \rightarrow 2CO_2 + 3H_2O$
   B. $C_2H_6 + 7O_2 \rightarrow 2CO_2 + 3H_2O$
   C. $2C_2H_6 + 5O_2 \rightarrow 2CO_2 + 6H_2O$
   D. $2C_2H_6 + 7O_2 \rightarrow 4CO_2 + 6H_2O$

3. What energy changes occur during an endothermic chemical reaction?
   A. Thermal energy is released to the environment as new bonds form.
   B. Energy from the environment is absorbed to form new chemical bonds.
   C. Energy from chemical bonds is released to the environment as new bonds form.
   D. Energy is absorbed by the reactants and is released to the environment as heat.

4. Explain how increasing the temperature of a reaction mixture causes the reaction rate to increase.

5. Write a balanced chemical equation for the chemical reaction in which carbon disulfide (CS_2) and oxygen (O_2) react and form carbon dioxide (CO_2) and sulfur dioxide (SO_2).

6. In a lab demonstration, lithium metal is burned inside a closed container according to the equation $4Li(s) + O_2(g) \rightarrow 2Li_2O(s)$. If the ratio of lithium atoms to oxygen molecules in the container is 9:2, what is the limiting reagent?

7. Magnesium metal ($Mg(s)$) and oxygen gas ($O_2(g)$) react and form magnesium oxide ($MgO(s)$). Write a balanced equation for this reaction and determine how many grams of magnesium oxide will be formed when 24.3 g of magnesium reacts with 16.0 g of oxygen.

Skill Practice

Directions: Use the diagram to answer questions 1–3.

Energy vs. Reaction Progress

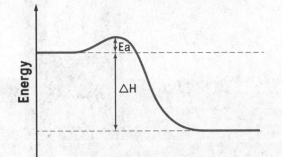

1. What does the symbol ΔH on the graph represent?

   A. Activation energy of the chemical reaction

   B. Energy stored in the chemical bonds of the reactants

   C. Change in energy as products are formed from reactants

   D. Total chemical energy added to the reaction mixture during the reaction

2. What is the source of activation energy needed for this chemical reaction?

   A. Energy absorbed from the environment

   B. Energy transferred to the environment

   C. Chemical energy stored in product chemical bonds

   D. Chemical energy stored in reactant chemical bonds

3. How can the chemical reaction shown on the graph be classified?

   A. balanced reaction

   B. unbalanced reaction

   C. endothermic reaction

   D. exothermic reaction

Directions: Answer the following questions.

4. Which of these is a balanced chemical equation?

   A. $AgNO_3(aq) + 2Na_2S(aq) \rightarrow Ag_2S(aq) + 4NaNO3(aq)$

   B. $2AgNO_3(aq) + 2Na_2S(aq) \rightarrow Ag_2S(aq) + 2NaNO_3(aq)$

   C. $2AgNO_3(aq) + Na_2S(aq) \rightarrow Ag_2S(aq) + 2NaNO_3(aq)$

   D. $3AgNO_3(aq) + 2Na_2S(aq) \rightarrow 2Ag_2S(aq) + 3NaNO_3(aq)$

5. Consider the chemical reaction represented by the equation $NiCl_2(s) + 3O_2(g) \rightarrow NiO(s) + Cl_2O_5(g)$. What is the limiting reagent if the reaction mixture starts with the ratio of 3 $NiCl_2(s)$ to 10 $O_2(g)$?

   A. $NiCl_2$ (s)

   B. O_2 (g)

   C. NiO (s)

   D. Cl_2O_5 (g)

6. Write a balanced chemical equation for the chemical reaction in which hydrogen (H_2) and nitrogen (N_2) react and form ammonia (NH_3). Do not include the state of the substances.

7. Many chemical reactions will sustain themselves after activation energy is added to the reaction mixture, meaning that no more energy needs to be added to keep the reaction going. Determine whether such self-sustaining reactions are endothermic reactions or exothermic reactions. Explain your answer.

LESSON 7.4 Solutions

■ LESSON OBJECTIVES

- Describe solutions and how they form
- Compare acids and bases

■ CORE SKILLS & PRACTICES

- Identify and Interpret Independent and Dependent Variables in Scientific Investigations
- Determine Hypotheses

Key Terms

acid
a chemical that forms a salt when mixed with a base

base
a chemical that forms a salt when mixed with acid

concentration
the amount of solute that is dissolved in a quantity of solvent

solubility
the amount of a substance that will dissolve in a given amount of another substance

solution
when one substance is completely dissolved in another

Vocabulary

saturation
the state of being combined until there is no further tendency to combine

Key Concept

A solution forms when one or more pure substances dissolve in another pure substance. A solution can be a gas, a liquid, or a solid.

Nature of Solutions

What happens when sugar is poured into a cup of hot water? Gradually, the sugar seems to disappear. The sugar dissolves, or breaks apart, in the water. The molecules of sugar separate and mix with the water molecules. In time, they become uniformly mixed into a solution of water and sugar.

A **solution** is a mixture in which one substance is completely and evenly dissolved in another. In contrast to heterogeneous mixtures, where substances do not combine, homogeneous solutions have substances that are evenly distributed so every drop or granule of the mixture is exactly the same as the others. Solutions do not settle into layers, as water and sand might, and they are usually transparent or evenly colored. They often look like single, pure substances, a characteristic that makes them difficult to recognize. However, if you tasted a solution of water and sugar, or water and salt, you would notice at once that it was a solution because of the sweet or salty taste.

Although many common solutions are liquids, solutions can exist as all three states of matter: solids, liquids, and gases, or some combination thereof. A teardrop is a solution of water, salt, and other compounds. A steel bridge is a solution of iron, carbon, and other elements. Air is a gaseous solution made up of 78 percent nitrogen, 21 percent oxygen, and 1 percent other trace gases. Brass is a type of solid solution called an alloy that is made from a mixture of copper, zinc, and other materials. An alloy is a solid solution in which the atoms of two or more metals are uniformly mixed.

The Parts of a Solution

Every solution consists of two parts—a solute and a solvent. The solute is the substance that is dissolved in a solution, such as sugar or salt. The solvent is the substance that does the dissolving in a solution, such as water or another liquid. The solvent makes up the larger amount of a solution.

Solutions

PhotoAlto/Alamy

When sugar is dissolved in water, sugar is the solute and water is the solvent. In a solution of air nitrogen is the solvent and oxygen is the solute.

Solutions form as a result of the interactions between the particles of a solvent and the particles of a solute. The solvent breaks apart the particles of the solute to make the solution. In order for a solution to form, solute particles must separate from one another, and the solute and solvent particles must mix.

Aqueous Solutions

When the solvent in a solution is water, the solution is called an aqueous solution. The word *aqueous* means "related to water." Fruit punch, tea, contact lens solution, liquid soap, and vinegar are examples of aqueous solutions. Water is the solvent in many solutions. Because many different kinds of substances can dissolve in water, it is known as the "universal solvent."

Think about Science

Directions: Answer the following questions.

1. In sweet tea, which of these are the solutes?
    A. Natural flavors
    B. Water and sugar
    C. Particles from tea leaves and sugar
    D. Water and particles from tea leaves

The Solution Process and Solubility

The solution process involves the dissolving of a solute in a solvent. Water will form a solution with two different types of compounds: ionic compounds or polar covalent compounds. Ionic compounds, such as salt, are made of a positive and a negative ion held together. Polar covalent compounds, such as sugar, consist of atoms held together by the sharing of electrons. Because of the way the electrons are shared in polar covalent compounds, the molecules have two sides with opposite charges, positive and negative.

Dissolving Ionic Compounds

Water itself is made up of polar molecules that attract charged particles. In a solution of saltwater, the positively charged ions of salt (Na^+) are attracted to the partially negative oxygen atoms of the water molecules. The negatively charged ions of salt (Cl^-) are attracted to the partially positive hydrogen atoms of the water molecules. As the ions are pulled toward the oppositely charged ends of the water molecules, the force that holds them weakens. The compound dissociates, or splits, into its individual ions that mix uniformly with the water, making saltwater.

Dissolving Covalent Compounds

When water dissolves polar covalent compounds, the compounds generally do not dissociate, as do ionic compounds. They become separated from one another. For example, when polar molecules such as sugar dissolve in water, the molecules do not split. The molecules are pulled from one another, surrounded by water molecules, and then evenly distributed in the water.

Rate of Dissolving

Different solutes dissolve in different solvents at different rates. Some solutes dissolve quickly and others slowly. Rate of dissolving is a measurement that

Determine Hypotheses

A hypothesis is a tentative explanation of an observation or a natural event based on research and background knowledge but insufficient evidence. Example: *Saber-toothed tigers became extinct because of the sudden occurrence of an ice age.*

An experiment's procedure instructs you to set up a hot-water bath and an ice bath, and put salt into a test tube with water. Next, you warm the test tube in the hot-water bath until the salt dissolves. Finally you move the test tube to the ice bath and note the temperature at which ice crystals first appear.

Give two examples of hypotheses related to this investigation.

Solutions

Identify and Interpret Independent and Dependent Variables in Scientific Investigations

In a controlled experiment, scientists change only one variable at a time. The independent variable is the variable that is changed. The variable that is observed to find out if it changes is called the dependent variable. Working with a group, design, or plan from start to finish, an experiment to observe and measure how temperature or the concentration of sugar affects the rate at which sugar dissolves in water. Identify the independent and dependent variables in your experiment.

Perform the experiment and record your observations. Draw conclusions about how the rate at which sugar dissolves can be changed. Be sure to include the interpretation of both the independent and dependent variables.

describes how quickly a solute dissolves in a given solvent. The rate at which a solute dissolves is affected by several factors: the type of solvent involved, stirring, surface area, and temperature.

Type of Solvent

Polar solutes and ionic solutes dissolve in polar solvents. Nonpolar solutes dissolve in nonpolar solvents. This general rule can be summarized as "like dissolves like." Recall that salt and sugar can dissolve in water because they are "like" water—they are polar. However, oil, which is nonpolar, will not be able to dissolve in water, a polar solvent. These are "unlike."

Stirring

Shaking or stirring a solution helps the solute dissolve more quickly and increases the rate of dissolving. Moving the molecules around helps bring fresh solvent in contact with a solute. That is why stirring iced tea after you put sugar into it will sweeten the tea faster.

Surface Area

Breaking a solid into smaller pieces will increase the rate of dissolving in the same way that it increases its rate of reaction. Dissolving occurs at the surface of a solid. Breaking up a solid increases the solid's surface area, which increases the amount of solute that comes into contact with the solvent. This causes the solute to dissolve more quickly. For example, if you drop a sugar cube into iced tea, it will take a while for it to dissolve. You can sweeten the tea more quickly by using an equal amount of granular sugar. The pieces are much smaller, so a much greater number of sugar molecules will be in direct contact with the water molecules of the tea.

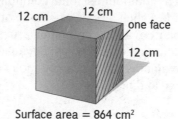

Surface area = 864 cm²

A face of a cube is the outer surface that has four edges. A cube has six faces.

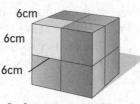

Surface area = 1,728 cm²

The cube can be pulled apart into smaller cubes of equal size. Here there are eight cubes and 48 faces.

Temperature

Increasing the temperature of the solvent will increase the rate of dissolving. The increased temperature causes both the solute and solvent particles to come in contact with one another more quickly and more frequently. The particles move around and interact with one another at a faster rate, helping bring fresh solvent in contact with the solute.

Solubility

Some substances will not form a solution no matter how much they are stirred, shaken, or heated. Such a substance is insoluble in that solvent. Vinegar is insoluble in oil, and oil is insoluble in water. When a substance can dissolve in a solvent, the substance is soluble. Sugar, salt, some vitamins, and minerals are soluble in water.

Solubility is the maximum amount of a solute that can dissolve in a given amount of a solvent under a given set of conditions, like temperature or pressure. If a solute has a high solubility, a large amount of the solute can dissolve under given conditions. If a solute has a low solubility, only a small amount of the solute can dissolve under the conditions. When a solute has an extremely low solubility, it is considered insoluble. Solubility is usually expressed in grams of solute per 100 g of solvent as shown in the table.

Solubility of Substances in Water at 20°C

Substance	Solubility in g/100 g of Water
Solid Substances	
salt (sodium chloride)	35.9
baking soda (sodium bicarbonate)	9.6
sugar (sucrose)	203.9
Gaseous Substances*	
oxygen	0.0005
carbon dioxide	0.16

*at normal atmospheric pressure

Rules of Solubility

Conditions such as temperature and pressure can affect the solubility of a substance by either increasing or decreasing its solubility. For example, the solubility of liquids and solids increases as temperature increases. In contrast, the solubility of gases in liquid solvents decreases as temperature increases. Although pressure has no effect on liquid and solid solutes, it can affect the solubility of gaseous solutes in liquid solvents. Increasing pressure causes the solubility of gases in liquid solvents to increase, and decreasing pressure causes the solubility to decrease. For example, carbonated beverages are bottled under pressure to keep carbon-dioxide gas in solution. When a bottle is opened, the pressure is released and the gas bubbles out of the solution.

Describing Solutions

A solution can contain different proportions of solute and solvent. For example, a glass of lemonade may be sour or sweet. For this reason, scientists use concentration and solubility to describe solutions more precisely.

Using Concentration

Concentration is the amount of solute that is dissolved in a quantity of solvent. If there is a little solute in a solution, the solution is dilute. If there is a lot of solute in a solution, the solution is said to be concentrated.

Concentration can be described more precisely by providing the proportions of the substances in the solution. A solution of cranberry juice, for example, might have 100 percent juice or only 10 percent juice.

Using Solubility

Scientists use solubility to describe how much solute is in a solution. **Saturation** is when a solution contains the maximum amount of dissolved solute it can hold at a given temperature. If more solute is added to a saturated solution, the solute will not dissolve. For example, when adding sugar to tea, there will come a time when the sugar starts to accumulate at the bottom of the glass rather than dissolve. The tea is saturated.

When a solution contains less than the maximum amount of solute it can hold at a given temperature, the solution is unsaturated. More solute will dissolve if it is added to the solution under the existing conditions. When a solution contains more dissolved solute than a saturated solution under the same conditions it is supersaturated, or is "more than saturated."

Think about Science

Directions: Fill in the blank.

1. _____ and _____ are two factors that can affect solubility.

2. Scientists describe solutions using either _____ or _____ .

3. When a solution contains more dissolved solute than a saturated solution, the solution is called _____ .

Acids and Bases

There are different definitions of acids and bases, but in all cases, acidic and basic solutes have specific results when they form solutions in water. In aqueous solutions, acids increase the hydrogen (H^+) concentration, and bases increase the hydroxide (OH^-) concentration.

Acids

An acid is a compound that, when dissolved in water, will produce positively charged hydrogen ions (H^+). Acids taste sour, are highly reactive, and can corrode metals. Vinegar, orange juice, lemon juice, batteries, and the body's digestive fluids all contain acids. The strength of an acid is determined by the degree to which the acid dissociates in solution. An acid is considered strong if nearly all the molecules are converted into ions in water. An acid is considered weak if only a small fraction of the molecules dissociate in water.

Bases

When dissolved in water, a **base** forms hydroxide ions (OH^-), a negatively charged compound made of one oxygen atom and one hydrogen atom. Bases are able to take a proton from an acid or to give up an unshared pair of electrons to an acid. Bases are described as alkaline and they dissolve in water and have a slippery feel. Many hydroxides are bases. Household cleaning agents such as ammonia, borax, lye, and detergents are common examples of bases. When an acid combines with a base, a salt forms, and water is released because the metal found in the base replaces the hydrogen contained in the acid. Inorganic acids, bases, and inorganic salts can conduct electricity when dissolved in water.

Chemists apply a litmus test to a substance to determine whether it is an acid or a base. An acid turns blue litmus paper red, and a base turns red litmus paper blue. When you combine acids and bases, they neutralize each other.

pH Level

Acids and bases vary in strength, as do solutions containing acids and bases. Some solutions might have a high concentration of hydrogen ions and thus would be very acidic, whereas others might have only a small concentration of hydrogen ions and thus would be much less acidic. To determine how acidic or alkaline (basic) a solution is, scientists use a measurement called pH. The pH of a solution is a measure of the concentration of hydrogen ions in the solution. The greater the hydrogen-ion concentration, the more acidic the solution, and the lower the pH level. The lower the hydrogen-ion concentration, the more alkaline the solution and the higher the pH level. To indicate the pH level, scientists use a pH scale that ranges from 0 to 14. If a solution has a pH less than 7, it is considered acidic, and if a solution has a pH greater than 7, it is considered alkaline. If a solution has a pH of exactly 7, it is considered neutral, which means it is neither acidic nor alkaline because it has an equal number of hydrogen and hydroxide ions. Pure water is neutral.

Acid-Base Reactions

Acids and bases can react with each other. When an acid is added to a base solution, their hydroxide ions and hydrogen ions combine to form molecules of water. The other ions combine to form a salt. A salt is an ionic compound formed from the negative ions of an acid and the positive ions of a base.

The reaction of an acid with a base is called a neutralization reaction. This is because the products formed are neutral—they are neither acids nor bases. The general formula for an acid-base reaction is:

$$\text{Acid} + \text{base} \rightarrow \text{salt} + \text{water}$$

Here is an example.

$$\text{HCL (aq)} + \text{NaOH} \rightarrow \text{NaCL (aq)} + H_2O$$

This example shows the formation of table salt. Although people often think only of table salt when they hear the term salt, there are hundreds of different salts that can form when an acid reacts with a base.

Think about Science

Directions: Answer the following questions.

1. What could be the pH level of an alkaline solution?
   A. 2
   B. 5
   C. 7
   D. 13

2. What is a solution that has excess hydrogen ions?
   A. acid
   B. base
   C. neutral
   D. saturated

Apply Workplace Policies and Procedures

Many workplaces use chemicals for cleaning and maintenance or for manufacturing. Many chemicals can be dangerous if handled improperly or mixed with other chemicals. Because of this, workplace policies and procedures are in place to ensure workers handle chemicals safely.

Identify one workplace policy or procedure an employer might enforce to ensure workers are safe when handling chemicals. Explain the reasoning for why this policy is enforced.

Vocabulary Review

Directions: Write the missing term in the blank.

acid	**base**	**concentration**
saturation	**solubility**	**solution**

1. The _____ level made it impossible for more sugar to dissolve in the tea.

2. Because the _____ of baking soda is low, only a small amount will dissolve in 100 g of water.

3. Fruit juice tastes sour because it is a(n) _____.

4. A solution of steel may contain a _____ of 2 grams of carbon to every 98 grams of iron.

5. The red litmus paper turned blue, so we knew the substance was a(n) _____.

6. Brass is a(n) _____ made of zinc and copper.

Skill Review

Directions: Answer the following questions.

1. Which of these is the solvent in a bottle of shampoo?
   A. soap
   B. fragrance
   C. water
   D. chlorine

2. Formic acid is found in some ant vernoms. Which substance would you apply to an ant bite to relieve some of the pain?
   A. baking soda
   B. orange juice
   C. distilled water
   D. vinegar

3. What is the basic principle of the solution process?
   A. Like dissolves like.
   B. Unlike dissolves unlike.
   C. Polar solvents dissolve nonpolar solutes.
   D. Nonpolar solvents dissolve polar solutes.

4. Water and alcohol cannot mix to become a solution. Which best describes them?
   A. soluble
   B. insoluble
   C. solution
   D. homogeneous

5. What is a characteristic of a solution?
   A. It will settle into layers.
   B. Every part is exactly the same.
   C. It is only solid or liquid.
   D. It has variation in color throughout.

6. A medical condition known as decompression sickness, or "the bends," sometimes occurs in deep-sea divers as they rise to the surface quickly. It is caused by nitrogen gas coming out of the diver's organs in a manner similar to the way gas comes out of a soda can that has been shaken. Based on what you know about solubility, explain why this condition might occur.

7. You place a sugar cube in a glass of cold water and measure how long it takes for the cube to completely dissolve. You have learned ways to increase the rate at which a solute is dissolved. Use this knowledge to develop a hypothesis about how you could most effectively increase the dissolving rate of the sugar cube.

8. Which of these is a solution?
   A. aluminum
   B. trail mix
   C. table salt dissolved in water
   D. oatmeal cookie

Skill Practice

Directions: Answer the following questions.

1. Sodium carbonate has a pH of 11.5. What could it be mixed with to form a neutral solution?

   A. bleach (pH 12)

   B. toothpaste (pH 9)

   C. distilled water (pH 7)

   D. sparkling orange drink (pH 4.5)

2. How do you know that water and sand do not form a solution?

   A. Sand is heavier than water.

   B. Sand does not stay mixed evenly in the water.

   C. Sand is not a liquid.

   D. Sand makes the water muddy.

3. Hand warmers contain a supersaturated solution of sodium acetate and an activator strip. When the hand warmer is bent back and forth, crystals begin to form. The reaction releases heat energy, which warms your hands. You want to conduct an experiment for how long the hand warmers will produce heat. Identify your independent and dependent variables.

Directions: Use the graphic to answer question 4.

4. Scientists use graphs called solubility curves to show how temperature affects a substance's solubility. Each point on a solubility curve shows the maximum amount of solute that can dissolve in an amount of solvent at a given temperature. Look at the graph. The solubility of sodium chlorate at 50° C is about _____ g/100 g of water. How does the solubility of sodium chlorate change as the temperature increases?

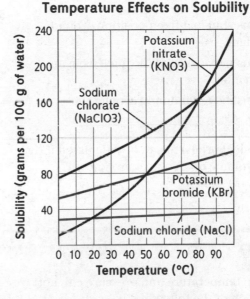

Temperature Effects on Solubility

Directions: Use the passage to answer questions 5 and 6.

A solution can become supersaturated if it is saturated at a high temperature and then cooled very slowly. The slow cooling allows all the solute to remain dissolved, although the solution is holding more solute than it normally could hold at the lower temperature. Supersaturated solutions are unstable. If they are disturbed, the excess solute comes out of the solution. Rock candy is made by taking a supersaturated sugar solution and adding seed crystals, which causes the sugar to crystallize onto a string and then be eaten.

5. Based on evidence from the passage, what conditions must exist for a solution to become supersaturated?

   A. The solute must be dissolved with a string in it.

   B. There must be a seed crystal added after lowering the temperature.

   C. It must be saturated at a high temperature and then cooled slowly.

   D. The temperature must rise quickly and fall slowly.

6. What evidence is there that the supersaturated solution that makes rock candy is unstable?

Directions: Answer the following questions.

1. The atomic number of an element gives you information about
   A. the number of electrons in the atom
   B. the number of protons in the atom
   C. the number of protons and electrons in the atom
   D. the number of neutrons and electrons in the atom

2. Which of the following is the most accurate statement about the electrons in an atom?
   A. Electrons all travel in the same orbit around the nucleus.
   B. Electrons stay in a fixed position around the nucleus.
   C. Electrons move around the nucleus in an electron cloud.
   D. Electrons move randomly around the nucleus.

3. Which physical property can be calculated if the mass and volume of an object are known?
   A. density
   B. reactivity
   C. temperature
   D. velocity

4. A change in temperature and pressure can not change which of the following?
   A. boiling point
   B. melting point
   C. state of matter
   D. mass

5. When vaporization occurs at the surface of a liquid, the phenomenon is called
   A. boiling
   B. condensation
   C. evaporation
   D. sublimation

6. Which of the following will have the fastest reaction rate?
   A. 10 g Na + 0.005 g Cl_2 at 20°C
   B. 10 g Na + 0.005 g Cl_2 at 40°C
   C. 10 g Na + 0.025 g Cl_2 at 20°C
   D. 10 g Na + 0.025 g Cl_2 at 40°C

7. What specific type of reaction takes place when a greater amount of energy is released as bonds of the reactants are broken than what is needed for bonds of the products to form?
   A. chemical reaction
   B. endothermic reaction
   C. exothermic reaction
   D. physical reaction

8. If 2.5 g of reactants undergo a chemical reaction, what is the total mass of the products produced?
   A. 2.5 g
   B. 5.0 g
   C. It depends on how many products form.
   D. It depends on how many reactants there are.

9. Which of the following is a solution?
   A. cereal and milk
   B. salt water
   C. chlorine
   D. trail mix

10. Which of the following will increase the rate at which a solid solute dissolves in a liquid solvent?
    A. density of the solute
    B. mass of the solvent
    C. increased surface area of the solute
    D. decreased surface area of the solute

11. Which of the following is a chemical property of a substance?
    A. density
    B. hardness
    C. boiling point
    D. flammability

12. What can be said about a solution that is at a point where the addition of one more microgram of solute will not dissolve at a given temperature?
    A. The solute is insoluble.
    B. It is a saturated solution.
    C. It is an unsaturated solution.
    D. It is a supersaturated solution.

13. Which of the following takes place during a chemical reaction?

A. Elements change into new elements.

B. New matter is created as products form.

C. Chemical bonds break and new bonds form new substances.

D. The mass of the reactants is greater than the mass of the products

14. What information can be obtained from the chemical formula of a compound?

15. Explain why H_2 is the limiting molecule in the chemical reaction between H_2 and O_2 if there are the same number of molecules of each.

16. Explain the statement, "like dissolves like."

Directions: Use the Periodic Table below or on pages 452–453 to answer questions 17–19.

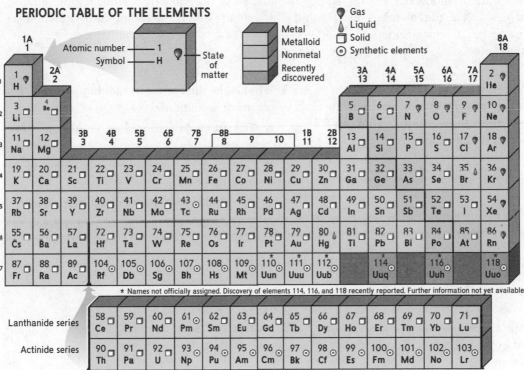

17. Which is the third element of period 2 on the periodic table?

A. aluminum

B. boron

C. calcium

D. scandium

18. Which of the following has the smallest atomic radius?

A. chlorine

B. iodine

C. potassium

D. sodium

19. Which of the following is a nonmetal element?

A. beryllium

B. fluorine

C. magnesium

D. silicon

20. How can the periodic table be used to determine the number of valence electrons in an oxygen atom?

21. Which of the following describes most of the known elements on Earth?

A. Most known elements on Earth are metals.

B. Most known elements on Earth are metalloids.

C. Most known elements on Earth are nonmetals.

D. Most known elements on Earth are organic.

Directions: Read the passage and answer questions 22–23.

When matter changes from one state to another, thermal energy is absorbed or released. When matter is heated, it absorbs thermal energy. Matter releases thermal energy as it cools. Substances need to be heated or cooled to a certain temperature to change state. The temperatures at which a substance changes from one state to another do not depend on the amount of the substance. The melting point is the temperature at which a solid changes into a liquid. The boiling point is the temperature at which a liquid changes into a gas. The melting and boiling points of water are the same whether there are two or twenty liters of water.

22. The freezing point of water is 0°C. What occurs in a sample of water at at this temperature if the sample is cooled from a higher temperature and heated from a lower temperature?

23. What is the difference in melting point of 10 grams of sodium and 0.1 gram of sodium?

A. Ten grams of sodium has a higher melting point.

B. One-tenth of a gram of sodium has a higher melting point.

C. They both have the same melting point.

D. There is not enough information to tell.

Directions: Use the chemical equation to answer questions 24–26.

$$KClO_3 \rightarrow KCl + O_2$$

24. Identify the number of atoms of each element in the products and in the reactants. Record your answers in the table.

Reactants	Products
K =	K =
Cl =	Cl =
O =	O =

25. Is this a balanced chemical equation? Explain your answer.

26. Write a balanced equation for the chemical decomposition of potassium chlorate. Check your equation by counting the number of each atom on each side of the equation.

Directions: Read the passage and answer questions 27 and 28.

To determine how acidic or alkaline (basic) a solution is, scientists use a measurement called pH. The pH of a solution is a measure of the concentration of hydrogen ions in the solution. The greater the hydrogen-ion concentration, the more acidic the solution and the lower the pH level. The lower the hydrogen-ion concentration, the more alkaline the solution and the higher the pH level. To indicate the pH level, scientists use a pH scale that ranges from 0 to 14. If a solution has a pH less than 7, it is considered acidic, and if a solution has a pH greater than 7, it is considered alkaline. If a solution has a pH of exactly 7, it is considered neutral, which means it is neither acidic nor alkaline because it has an equal number of hydrogen and hydroxide ions. Pure water is neutral.

27. Explain how adding vinegar to water will change the pH of the water.

28. Why is pH a property of a solution?

Check Your Understanding

On the following chart, circle the number of any item you answered incorrectly. Next to each group of item numbers, you will see the pages you can review to learn how to answer the items correctly.

Lesson	Item Number(s)	Review Page(s)
7.1: The Structure of Matter	1, 2, 14, 17, 18, 19, 21	250–253
7.2: Physical and Chemical Properties of Matter	3, 4, 5, 11, 20, 22, 23	256–261
7.3: Chemical Reactions	6, 7, 8, 13, 15, 24, 25, 26	264–269
7.4: Solutions	9, 10, 12, 16, 27, 28	272–277

Energy in Chemical Reactions

Core Practices

- Identify and interpret independent and dependent variables in scientific investigations
- Identify possible sources of error and alter the design of an investigation to ameliorate that error

Question

How can you determine whether a chemical reaction is exothermic or endothermic?

Background Concepts

A chemical reaction involves the breaking of bonds in the reactants and the formation of bonds in the products. All chemical reactions require an activation energy to begin. But reactions can be exothermic or endothermic, depending whether the reaction releases or absorbs energy as it proceeds.

Chemical reactions can occur between ordinary ingredients that you have in your kitchen. Baking soda, which is sodium bicarbonate, can react with vinegar, which is acetic acid. This reaction can be summarized by the following equation:

$$NaHCO_3(s) \ + \ CH_3COOH(l) \ \rightarrow \ CO_2(g) \ + \ H_2O(l) \ + \ Na^+(aq) \ + \ CH_3COO^-(aq)$$

sodium bicarbonate   acetic acid   carbon dioxide   water   sodium ion   acetate ion

In this reaction, more energy is required to break the bonds in the reactants than is released by the formation of products. This is also a spontaneous reaction, which means that it proceeds without outside intervention, such as heating.

Hypothesis

A hypothesis is a explanation based on what evidence is available. It is a starting point for a scientific investigation that will either be confirmed, need to be revised, or be shown to be incorrect based on more evidence gathered. Based on the information given and your knowledge of chemical reactions, form a hypothesis about whether the reaction between baking soda and vinegar is exothermic or endothermic.

Investigation

After developing a hypothesis, the next step is to gather information and data to determine whether your hypothesis is supported or not. Perform the following experiment to determine the type of reaction that occurs between sodium bicarbonate and acetic acid.

MATERIALS

Vinegar	Baking soda
Thermometer	Glass or beaker, 250 mL

PROCEDURE

Place about 10 milliliters of vinegar in the cup. Place the thermometer in the cup and measure the temperature of the vinegar. This will be the temperature at time 0 of the experiment. Keep the thermometer in the cup and add about $\frac{1}{2}$ teaspoon baking soda. Watch the thermometer and record any change in temperature every 15 seconds. Repeat this experiment two more times, so that you have three trials and three sets of data.

Collect and Analyze Data

Record the change in temperature once every 15 seconds until the temperature remains constant for three readings. Use a table to record the data from all three trials. Make a graph of temperature vs. time and plot each data point on the graph. Time should be on the x-axis and temperature should be on the y-axis. Make note of the trend observed in the graph. Is it a straight line or a curve? Does it increase or decrease? Think about what the trend means in terms of whether the reaction is exothermic or endothermic.

Interpretation

Summarize the data collected and interpret the evidence to determine if your hypothesis is supported and why.

When evaluating and interpreting the information or data you collected, ask yourself these questions:

- What did you expect to happen to the temperature of this reaction based on your hypothesis? Is this the result you obtained? Was your hypothesis supported by the experiment or not?

- This reaction occurs spontaneously. Where did the energy come from so that the reaction could proceed? What evidence do you have?

- Were there any differences in your results for the three trials? Explain your answer.

Results

Discuss your results using evidence from your data to support your hypothesis. Discuss any observations made during the reaction. What happened when the baking soda was added to the vinegar? When you placed your hand on the outside of the cup, how did it feel, cold or warm? Also, discuss any possible sources of error, or unexpected results. If your hypothesis was not supported, discuss your recommendations for formulating a new hypothesis or changes you would make to the investigation that may make the results of the experiment more reliable.

Consider these questions as you discuss your results:

- What are the independent and dependent variables in this experiment?

- Identify any possible sources of error in your experiment that may have led to inaccuracies or variability in your results. What changes can you make to your experiment to eliminate these sources of error?

- What do you think would happen if you doubled the amount of baking soda added to the vinegar? How would it affect the temperature of the reaction?

Chapter 8

The Earth

Earth looks calm and unchanging from space. In reality, many things are happening on Earth's surface, in the atmosphere, and beneath Earth's crust. There is so much happening on Earth, that scientists have devoted a whole field of study to the Earth and its components. Earth science is the study of the elements that make up our planet, how those elements interact, and how everything on Earth affects the organisms that live on it.

NASA/NOAA/GSFC/Suomi NPP/VIIRS/Norman Kuring

Lesson 8.1
The Atmosphere

The characteristics of the atmosphere are unique to this planet and are what make life on Earth possible. In this lesson you will learn about the components of the atmosphere and how changes in these components can lead to climate change which affects all living organisms.

Lesson 8.2
The Oceans

Seventy-one percent of the Earth's surface is covered by oceans. Learn how the oceans have a great impact on Earth's climate and on the many organisms that live both in the water and on land.

Lesson 8.3
Earth's Structure, Composition, and Landforms

Scientists who study the Earth's structure are called geologists. Geologists study the structure, composition and processes at and below the Earth's surface. This lesson will help you to understand how Earth's structures form and change over time.

Lesson 8.4
Earth's Resources

Humans and other organisms depend on many of the natural resources available on Earth as a source of food and energy. Learn about natural resources that are found both at the Earth's surface and below the crust.

Lesson 8.5
Interactions Between Earth's Systems

Various systems on Earth regulate its structures and composition. In this lesson you will learn about different types of weathering that occur to Earth's rocks and landforms and how they bring change to Earth's structure and composition.

Goal Setting

Use a concept web like the one on page 447 to help you keep track of what you learn about Earth. Begin by placing Earth in the center of the web and draw circles all around it. As you complete each lesson, add to the concept web by recording important ideas and details about each component of Earth, including the atmosphere, the oceans, Earth's crust and inner layers, and its resources.

LESSON OBJECTIVES

- Describe the characteristics of Earth's atmosphere
- Characterize the effects of gases in the atmosphere
- Explain the causes and effects of climate change

CORE SKILLS & PRACTICES

- Describe Data Sets Statistically
- Interpret Graphs

Key Terms

atmosphere
the layer of gases that surrounds Earth

climate change
a persistent and noticeable change in weather patterns over a long period of time

greenhouse effect
the natural heating of Earth's surface by atmospheric gases

ozone
atmospheric gas that helps block harmful rays from the Sun

Vocabulary

gas
particles that vibrate and move freely and quickly

tabulate
to arrange in an organized manner for study purposes

Key Concept

The characteristics of the atmosphere make life on Earth possible. Changes in the types and amounts of gases in the atmosphere cause climate change, which affects organisms.

The Composition of the Atmosphere

What is in the air you breathe? Air includes **gases,** which are made of particles that vibrate and move freely at high speeds. The main gases in the atmosphere are nitrogen and oxygen. Air also includes solid particles, such as ice crystals, dust, and salt. These gases and particles form Earth's **atmosphere,** which extends from the Earth's surface to outer space.

The atmosphere plays several important roles in making life possible on Earth. The atmosphere provides the three gases necessary for life: oxygen, nitrogen, and carbon dioxide. It protects Earth's inhabitants from most of the Sun's ultraviolet light and it helps keep the planet at a temperature suitable for life. The atmosphere also continually replenishes our freshwater supply through precipitation.

Gases in the Atmosphere

So how, exactly, does the atmosphere accomplish all these feats? To answer this question, we must examine the composition of the atmosphere and how certain gases interact with energy.

Most of the atmosphere is composed of two gases: nitrogen (78 percent) and oxygen (21 percent). The remaining 1 percent is a mixture of other gases, including argon, carbon dioxide, water vapor, and other gases.

Together, nitrogen (N_2) and oxygen (O_2) make up about 99 percent of the total gases in Earth's atmosphere. Animals and plants require these gases to perform important life functions. Most organisms on Earth need oxygen to breathe. And, nitrogen is an element organisms need to produce proteins and is essential for plant growth.

Water vapor is the gaseous form of water (H_2O). It is the source of clouds, rain, and snow. It absorbs heat and plays a critical role in regulating, or controlling, the amount of energy the atmosphere absorbs.

NASA

Like water vapor, carbon dioxide (CO_2) absorbs heat and helps regulate the amount of energy in the atmosphere. Carbon dioxide is also vital for plant growth and is involved in the process of photosynthesis. During photosynthesis, green plants and algae convert carbon dioxide and water into carbohydrates and oxygen.

Ozone (O_3), a gas formed by the addition of an oxygen atom to an oxygen molecule, blocks harmful ultraviolet radiation from the Sun before it reaches Earth's surface. Ozone concentration is highest at about 20 km above the Earth's surface. This is called the ozone layer. If ozone did not absorb this radiation, many organisms could not tolerate exposure to the Sun.

Interaction of Gases with Solar Energy

Water vapor and carbon dioxide play an important role in regulating the amount of energy the atmosphere absorbs and emits. These gases, along with methane and nitrous oxide, occur naturally in the atmosphere and moderate the balance between the energy received by the Sun and the energy emitted by Earth. They keep Earth from becoming too hot or too cold to support life.

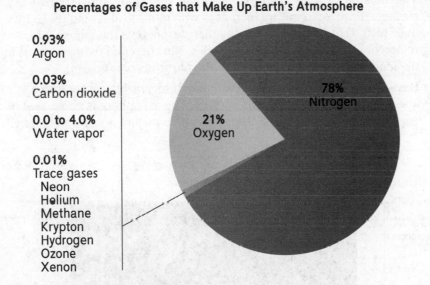

Percentages of Gases that Make Up Earth's Atmosphere

0.93%
Argon

0.03%
Carbon dioxide

0.0 to 4.0%
Water vapor

0.01%
Trace gases
Neon
Helium
Methane
Krypton
Hydrogen
Ozone
Xenon

78%
Nitrogen

21%
Oxygen

Particles in the Atmosphere

In addition to gases, the atmosphere also contains tiny solid particles, including dust, sea salt, ice crystals, and ash. They provide a surface on which water vapor can condense into liquid or solid droplets, allowing clouds to form. Precipitation such as rain and snow falls from clouds. Without it, plants could not grow, and our freshwater drinking supplies would run dry.

Think about Science

Directions: Answer the following questions.

1. Which two gases make up most of Earth's atmosphere?
   A. oxygen and nitrogen
   B. carbon dioxide and water vapor
   C. argon and methane
   D. ozone and nitrous oxide

Apply Technology to a Task

In addition to the gases and particles you've read about, the atmosphere can contain substances that are considered pollutants. Ozone near Earth's surface, for example, is produced when gases emitted by vehicles react chemically with sunlight. Ground-level ozone has been linked to increased rates of asthma in children and can affect adults with existing lung conditions.

The Environmental Protection Agency works with state and local agencies to monitor and release data about air quality. They publish a daily Air Quality Index (AQI). Use the Internet to research the AQI for your area. Research past AQI as well to determine if air quality changes with the seasons. **Tabulate,** or organize, your findings in a spreadsheet. Calculate the percentage of days in an average month that have poor air quality. How might air quality in your area affect your ability to do daily tasks, such as working or exercising?

The Layers of the Atmosphere

The atmosphere extends from Earth's surface to outer space and is composed of five different layers. Scientists distinguish between these layers by comparing the layers' composition and the way air temperatures change with altitude.

- **Troposphere** This layer is closest to the ground and is where most weather takes place. It extends to about 12 km above Earth's surface and contains almost all of the atmosphere's mass. Earth's surface temperature is regulated by carbon dioxide in the troposphere.

- **Stratosphere** This layer extends from the top of the troposphere to about 50 km. Temperatures in the stratosphere generally rise with increasing altitude because the upper stratosphere contains a concentrated ozone layer that absorbs ultraviolet radiation.

- **Mesosphere** This layer is the middle layer of the atmosphere between 50 km and 85 km above Earth's surface. It is the coldest part of the atmosphere because very little solar radiation is absorbed in this layer.

- **Thermosphere** This layer extends to about 500 km above Earth's surface. Here, temperature increases with altitude and may reach more than 1000° C at the top. Within the thermosphere is the ionosphere, a region of electrically charged particles. Nitrogen and oxygen atoms in the ionosphere also absorb potentially harmful solar energy.

- **Exosphere** This is the outermost layer. It blends into outer space at about 10,000 km above Earth's surface. The exosphere is composed of very light gases, such as hydrogen and helium, and is extremely thin.

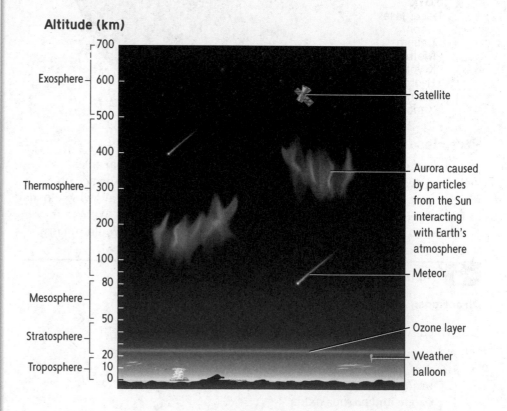

Altitude (km)

Exosphere — 600
— 500
Thermosphere — 300
— 200
— 100
Mesosphere — 80
— 50
Stratosphere — 20
Troposphere — 10
— 0

Satellite

Aurora caused by particles from the Sun interacting with Earth's atmosphere

Meteor

Ozone layer

Weather balloon

The Atmosphere

Energy in Earth's Atmosphere

Earth's surface temperature must stay in a range in which organisms can live—not too hot and not too cold. The mild temperature range presently found on Earth's surface results from two effects: the heating of the surface from sunlight, and the insulating and warming properties of the atmosphere.

Solar Radiation and Heat

The Sun is the source of most energy on Earth. About 30 percent of energy from the Sun is reflected back into space by the atmosphere, the clouds, and Earth's surface. About half of solar energy is absorbed by Earth's surface, and the remaining 20 percent is absorbed by the atmosphere and clouds.

There is a balance between the amount of solar radiation absorbed by Earth and the amount of solar radiation sent back into space. The balance between incoming radiation and outgoing heat is called the radiation balance. Over the course of one year, the amount of energy Earth loses to space is approximately equal to the amount of energy it receives from the Sun. This ensures that our planet has a relatively stable climate. For Earth to remain livable, the amount of energy received from the Sun and the amount of heat energy returned to space must remain equal.

Solar Radiation

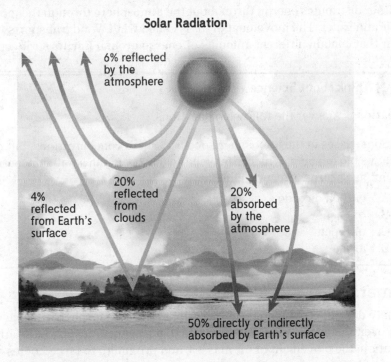

6% reflected by the atmosphere

4% reflected from Earth's surface

20% reflected from clouds

20% absorbed by the atmosphere

50% directly or indirectly absorbed by Earth's surface

The Greenhouse Effect

The Earth's surface absorbs about 50% of the solar radiation that comes to Earth. Then, Earth's surface radiates a portion of that energy outward as thermal infrared radiation. Greenhouse gases, such as carbon dioxide and methane, absorb some of that infrared radiation by transforming it into energy. The greenhouse gases emit energy as infrared energy in all directions. Some of this energy escapes to space, some is absorbed by other molecules of greenhouse gas, and some of it warms Earth. This additional heating of Earth from the greenhouse gases is the greenhouse effect.

Without greenhouse gases and the greenhouse effect, Earth's average temperature whould be much colder. Recently scientists have become concerned with the enhanced impact of the greenhouse effect due to rising concentrations of greenhouse gases in the atmosphere.

The Atmosphere

CORE PRACTICE

Describe Data Sets Statistically

Research indicates that the increase in greenhouse gases in the atmosphere is related to the increased use of fossil fuels in industrialized and developing countries. This growth in greenhouse gas emissions is expected to continue to increase as the global population rises. The world's population has doubled since 1965, and studies indicate that it will double again by the year 2100.

Research greenhouse gas emissions in the United States. Determine what percentage of that amount results from the use of electricity and transportation.

Write a persuasive essay that describes your data and suggests three ways Americans could reduce their greenhouse-gas emissions. Support your argument by using statistics and scientific reasoning.

Transfer of Energy

Half of the incoming energy from the Sun is absorbed by Earth's surface, warming the ground. The heat generated is then transferred to, and distributed throughout, the atmosphere through the processes of conduction and convection.

Conduction is the transfer of energy between objects that come into direct contact with one another. It occurs when molecules collide. The warm surface of Earth transfers heat to the layer of atmosphere directly above it through conduction. Convection, on the other hand, is the transfer of energy by the flow of a heated substance, such as a liquid or gas. During convection, the rising and sinking of air sets up a circulation pattern that transfers heat from Earth's surface to higher layers of the atmosphere. This circular movement of air is called a convection current.

Weather

Energy from the Sun does not heat Earth evenly. This uneven distribution of energy sets in motion convection currents that cause weather. Weather is the condition of the atmosphere at a particular place and time. Weather varies from day to day, from hour to hour, and also from place to place on Earth.

Weather distributes energy throughout the atmosphere through the movement of air and water. The movement of air is called wind. Wind transports masses of air that contain different amounts of energy around Earth's surface.

Think about Science

Directions: Answer the following questions.

1. Some gases in the atmosphere occur in small concentrations, but can have big impacts. Which atmospheric gas occurs in small concentrations, but has a large affect on climate?

    A. carbon dioxide
    B. oxygen
    C. nitrogen
    D. argon

Climate

Climate describes the long-term conditions of the atmosphere in a particular area over a long period of time. Factors that affect climate include latitude, elevation, the movement of air masses, and proximity to large bodies of water. Climate can be changed by both natural events and human activities.

Climate Change

Climate change is a persistent and noticeable change in local or global weather patterns over a long period of time. During ice ages, for example, large sheets of ice, called glaciers, covered much of our planet's surface. These glaciers have mostly receded and only cover a few parts of Earth's surface now. At other times, Earth's average temperature has been much higher than it is today.

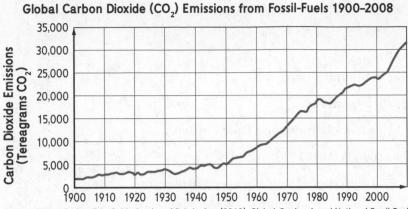

Global Carbon Dioxide (CO₂) Emissions from Fossil-Fuels 1900–2008

Source of data: Boden, T.A., G. Marland, and R.J. Andres (2010). Global, Regional, and National Fossil-Fuel CO2 Emissions. Carbon Dioxide Information Analysis Center, Oak Ridge National Laboratory, U.S. Department of Energy, Oak Ridge, Tenn., U.S.A. doi 10.3334/CDIAC/00001_V2010.

Natural Causes of Climate Change

Many natural processes or events can affect Earth's climate. For example, volcanic eruptions can release gases and dust into the atmosphere, where they block incoming solar radiation. This can lower global temperatures for several years. Changes in the shape of Earth's orbit or in the intensity of incoming solar radiation can also cause Earth's climate to change.

Impact of Human Activities

Human activities also play a role in climate change. Humans began burning fossil fuels such as coal and oil for energy around the Industrial Revolution. Fossil fuels contain carbon, so burning them releases carbon dioxide into the atmosphere. Recall that carbon dioxide is a greenhouse gas. Rising levels of greenhouse gases can cause an increase in the greenhouse effect. An increase in the greenhouse effect could result in a gradual rise in Earth's surface temperature

Effects of Climate Change

Climate change can involve global warming, or a slow rise in Earth's average temperatures. This may not seem like something to worry about, but, if left unchecked, this process could negatively affect Earth's organisms, including humans. Rising temperatures speed up the melting of glaciers and ice caps. This, in turn, causes the sea level to rise and increases submergence of low-lying areas.

In addition, changing precipitation patterns caused by climate change might cause severe droughts or floods. Both droughts and floods could result in the loss of lives and property. Climate change could also alter ecosystems as species unable to survive warmer temperatures die or migrate to cooler climates.

Think about Science

Directions: Answer the following questions.

1. Identify one activity you do each day that involves using fossil fuels. Then describe how you could change that activity to ensure that it does not add carbon dioxide to the atmosphere.

2. According to chart above, the amount of CO₂ emissions increased by approximately _____ Tereagrams CO₂ between 1950 and 2000.

CORE SKILL

Interpret Graphs

Examine the graph on this page that shows changing levels of atmospheric carbon dioxide over time. Briefly describe the overall trend in the graph. Predict how a graph of fossil-fuel consumption would look over the same time period. Research use of fossil fuels from 1900 to 2008 and construct a graph to better compare your data to your prediction. Predict how changes in the consumption of fossil fuels would affect levels of atmospheric carbon dioxide.

Vocabulary Review

Directions: Write the missing term in the blank.

| atmosphere | climate change | gas |
| greenhouse effect | ozone | tabulate |

1. You can use a table to _____ data as you study.

2. _____ in Earth's atmosphere helps block harmful rays from the Sun.

3. _____ is the layer of air that surrounds Earth.

4. Gases that are part of the _____ absorb energy and help keep Earth warm.

5. Nitrogen is the main _____ in Earth's atmosphere.

6. A change in the long-term weather patterns of an area is called _____.

Skill Review

Directions: Answer the following questions.

1. Which of these best describes the pathway a rocket would follow when launched from Earth?

   A. troposphere → stratosphere → mesosphere → thermosphere → exosphere

   B. stratosphere → thermosphere → exosphere → troposphere → mesosphere

   C. exosphere → thermosphere → mesosphere → stratosphere → troposphere

   D. thermosphere → troposphere → stratosphere → mesosphere → exosphere

2. The concentration of gases in the atmosphere decreases with height from Earth's surface. A low concentration of which gas high in the atmosphere would explain why this part of the atmosphere is inhospitable to animal life?

   A. water vapor

   B. oxygen

   C. nitrogen

   D. ozone

Directions: Use the passage to answer questions 3 and 4.

Plants absorb carbon dioxide from the atmosphere for use in photosynthesis. As a byproduct, plants release oxygen gas to the atmosphere. When large areas of tropical rain forests are cleared for logging or other purposes, an increase in the usual level of carbon dioxide in the atmosphere may result. Because of this, tropical rain forests have long played a role in maintaining Earth's present temperature range.

3. How do tropical rain forests play a role in helping maintain Earth's normal temperature range?

   A By decreasing the amount of all gases in the atmosphere

   B By increasing the level of carbon dioxide in the atmosphere

   C By providing cleared areas of land to absorb radiation from the Sun

   D By helping to reduce excess carbon-dioxide gas in the atmosphere

4. Which of the following is implied by this passage?

   A. The cutting of tropical rain forests could cause the greenhouse effect.

   B. The cutting of tropical rain forests could lead to an increase in climate change.

   C. The cutting of tropical rain forests could lead to a decrease in climate change.

   D. The cutting of tropical rain forests could lead to an increase in oxygen levels.

Skill Practice

Directions: Use the passage to answer questions 1 and 2.

You might think that the planet Venus, a close neighbor of Earth, is a planet where organisms could develop and grow. Venus is similar in size to Earth, and, like Earth, Venus has both a solid surface of minerals and an atmosphere. However, the surface temperature of Venus is about 482° C—much too hot for any form of life we know. The composition of Venus's atmosphere also differs from Earth's. The atmosphere on Venus has an extremely high level of carbon-dioxide gas. On Earth, excess heat energy is released back into space. However, on Venus, the atmosphere does not allow the energy trapped by the atmosphere to be released.

1. Identify the process that causes Venus's surface temperature to remain so high, and explain how this process differs on Earth.

2. Design a model that compares the flow of heat energy on Venus and on Earth. Present your model to the class and briefly explain how variations in the flow of energy can change climate.

Directions: Answer the following questions.

3. In your own words, state the cause-and-effect relationship between burning fossil fuels and climate change.

4. Which statement explains why ozone is an important gas in Earth's atmosphere?
   A. It provides a surface for water vapor to condense to form clouds.
   B. All plants need it to perform photosynthesis.
   C. It prevents harmful radiation from reaching Earth's surface.
   D. It forms when three oxygen atoms combine.

5. If you were to launch a satellite to collect data about weather and the ozone layer, in which layer would you want your satellite to orbit? Explain your answer.

6. Air pressure is a measure of the weight of air pressing down on an area of Earth's surface. Which layer of the atmosphere has the highest air pressure? Explain your answer.

7. Thick clouds form over an area. Predict what will occur in that area.
   A. The radiation balance will not be affected.
   B. More solar radiation will reach the surface.
   C. The atmosphere will absorb more solar radiation.
   D. More solar radiation will be reflected into space.

8. A student examines a graph that shows how levels of atmospheric carbon dioxide have increased over the past 150 years. The student concludes that the increase is caused by an increase in the human population on Earth. How would you respond to this conclusion?

9. Synthetically produced chemicals called chlorofluorocarbons (CFCs) have been banned from use as propellants (in aerosol sprays such as hair sprays) and as refrigerants. Evidence suggests that these chemicals get into the atmosphere and damage the ozone layer. How might CFCs indirectly affect organisms on Earth's surface?

10. How are greenhouse gases related to Earth's temperature?

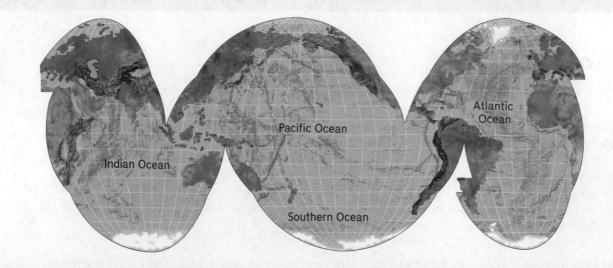

Indian Ocean

Pacific Ocean

Atlantic Ocean

Southern Ocean

LESSON OBJECTIVES

- Compare and contrast the sources and properties of saltwater and freshwater
- Summarize the characteristics and movements of oceans
- Describe how oceans affect and interact with Earth's climate and organisms

CORE SKILLS & PRACTICES

- Apply Scientific Models
- Identify and Interpret Variables in Scientific Investigations

Key Terms

oceans
large bodies of water that contain dissolved salts

salinity
measure of dissolved salts in a solution

water cycle
the continuous movement of water from Earth's surface to its atmosphere and back again

Vocabulary

characteristics
properties or traits that can be used to identify an object or event

draw conclusions
to interpret or make inferences based on the results of an investigation

Key Concept

Oceans have a great impact on Earth's climate and organisms. The movement and characteristics of ocean water differ with depth and distance from the equator.

Water on Earth

Earth is often called "the blue planet" because much of its surface is covered by water. **Oceans** are vast bodies of saltwater that cover 71 percent of Earth's surface. They contain about 97 percent of Earth's total water supply. The remaining 3 percent of Earth's water supply is made up of freshwater sources, such as rivers, lakes, ponds, and streams. Most freshwater, however, is frozen in polar ice caps or large, slow-moving sheets of ice called glaciers. Freshwater is also found underground in spaces between rocks. This water is called groundwater.

Unlike ocean water, freshwater contains very little dissolved salts. The lack of salts gives freshwater a lower density than saltwater. Recall that density is the amount of mass in a given volume of a substance. Freshwater and saltwater also differ in other ways. Freshwater freezes at a higher temperature than saltwater, and it boils at a lower temperature than saltwater. The presence of salt in water affects the temperature at which water changes state.

The Water Cycle

Water moves continuously from Earth's surface to its atmosphere in the **water cycle.** Heat from the Sun drives the water cycle. The heat causes water to evaporate, or change to a gas called water vapor. When water evaporates from the surface of the ocean, the salts are left behind.

As water evaporates, it rises into the air. Because air temperature tends to decrease with altitude in the lower atmosphere, the water vapor cools as it rises. Cooling causes the water vapor to change back into tiny drops of liquid water during the process of condensation. Millions of these droplets combine to form clouds. Some of the tiny droplets can combine to form larger droplets that fall back to Earth's surface as precipitation in the form of rain, snow, or hail. Precipitation is always freshwater.

Directions: Answer the following questions.

1. Compare and contrast saltwater and freshwater.
2. You are given a sample of freshwater. What would happen to the density of the water if you added salts and stirred?

The World's Oceans

Typically three major oceans are identified on Earth: the Pacific Ocean, the Atlantic Ocean, and the Indian Ocean. Two smaller oceans, the Arctic Ocean and the Southern Ocean, are located near Earth's poles. In many places, the continents serve as natural boundaries between two oceans. Yet all the oceans are interconnected and thus form one global ocean. Water flows freely throughout the global ocean. Because of this, oceans share certain **characteristics,** or traits, and movements.

Ocean Characteristics

If you've even accidentally gulped ocean water, you know it is salty. The salt content of ocean water is one of its characteristics, along with temperature and density.

Salinity

The measure of the concentration of dissolved salts in ocean water is called **salinity.** Much of the salt comes from rocks on land that have been broken down and dissolved and then transferred to the sea. Smaller amounts of salts come from fertilizer and other substances that run off the land. Scientists measure salinity in units called parts per thousand (ppt). One part per thousand equals one gram of salt per thousand grams, or 1 kg, of water. On average, ocean water has a salinity of 35 ppt, or 3.5 percent. The remaining 96.5 percent is water.

Salinity varies by location. In the warm subtropics, the rate of precipitation, which adds freshwater to the ocean, is lower than the rate of evaporation from the surface of the ocean. There, salinity may reach concentrations of 37 ppt. In tropical waters near the equator where precipitation is abundant, salinity is lower. In regions where freshwater mixes steadily with ocean water, such as the mouth of a river or the leading edge of a melting glacier, salinity may decrease to 32 ppt.

Temperature

Just as salinity can vary slightly throughout the global ocean, so too does the temperature of ocean water. The uppermost surface layer of the ocean, about 100 m thick, is the brightest and warmest layer. The thermocline layer lies below the surface layer and above the colder, dark bottom layer of ocean water. Within the thermocline layer, water temperature decreases rapidly with depth. The temperature in the ocean's bottom layer is fairly uniform and is near freezing, even in tropical waters, where surface temperatures are warm.

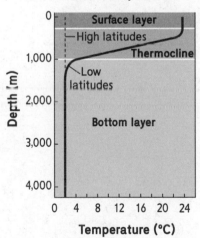

Ocean Water Temperatures

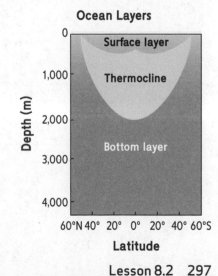

Ocean Layers

Apply Scientific Models

Use common materials, such as a large rectangular plastic container, modeling clay, a fan, and water, to model how continents affect the shape, size, speed, and direction of surface currents. Write down each step of your procedure before you carry out your investigation. Make sure the steps are in logical order. You may want to work with a partner to complete your model. Afterward, compare and contrast your observations with those of another pair of students. Did you obtain the same results? What might account for any differences in your observations?

Density

The density of water varies with differences in salinity and temperature. The salts in seawater add to the overall mass of the water; therefore seawater is denser than freshwater, and density increases with salinity. Warm water is less dense than cold water, so it rises above the cold water and spreads out. For this reason, ocean layers tend to remain more or less separate from one another.

Ocean Movements

Similar to winds moving in the atmosphere, water flows in the ocean. These movements of ocean water include surface currents, density currents, waves, and tides.

Surface Currents

A surface current is a wind-driven movement of ocean water that affects the top several hundred meters of the ocean's surface. Global winds drive surface currents, however, they are also influenced by the Coriolis effect and continents. The Coriolis effect is a result of Earth's rotation on its axis. It causes currents in the Northern Hemisphere to deflect to the right and currents in the Southern Hemisphere to deflect to the left. Continents interact with and change the shape, size, speed, and direction of surface currents.

Density Currents

Winds are not the only source of ocean currents. A density current forms when ocean waters with different temperatures and salinities meet and interact. Density currents move cold, salty water along the bottom portion of the ocean. The dense water travels slowly but steadily along the ocean bottom toward the equator. There, the waters become warmer and intermix, causing their salinity to decrease. With fewer salts and a warmer temperature, the water is less dense, so it rises and flows back toward the poles to replace the sinking water.

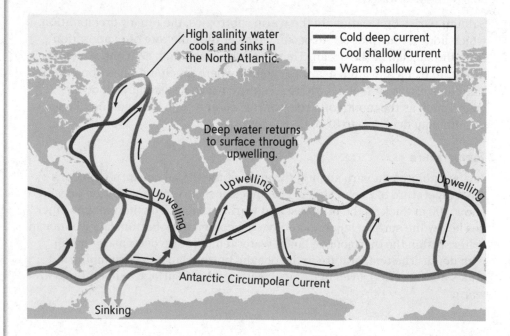

The Oceans

Waves

The ocean surface rises and falls into moving crests and troughs called waves. A wave is a rhythmic movement that carries energy through space or matter—in this case, ocean water. Winds skimming over the surface of the water are the main causes of ocean waves.

As shown in the diagram, waves move water a short distance in a circular path. The highest point of a wave is the crest, and the lowest point is the trough. The distance between two adjacent crests or two adjacent troughs is the wavelength. Typically the wavelength increases as wind speed increases.

Other wave characteristics include wave height, or the vertical distance between a crest and a trough. Wave height depends on three factors: wind speed, wind duration, and fetch. In oceanography, fetch is the distance a wind blows over water. As a wave nears shore, friction between the ocean floor and the water causes the wave to lose energy and change shape. The wavelength decreases and the wave becomes taller and steeper, finally breaking on the shore.

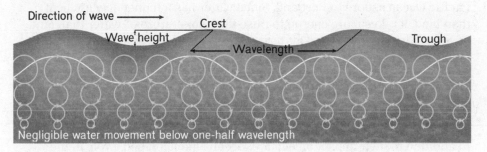

Direction of wave

Crest

Wave height

Wavelength

Trough

Negligible water movement below one-half wavelength

Tides

Tides are the periodic rise and fall of sea level that occurs twice a day in most coastal areas. They form because of the pull of gravity from both the Moon and the Sun. Because the Moon is so much closer to Earth than the Sun, its influence on Earth's tides is greater. As the Moon moves through its orbit, its gravity pulls on Earth. The water on the side of Earth that faces the Moon bulges out in the direction of the Moon.

The water on the opposite side of Earth from the Moon is not affected as strongly. However, as the Moon's gravity pulls on Earth, Earth moves ever so slightly toward the Moon. In effect, Earth moves away from the water on the opposite side of Earth from the Moon. The result is two bulges of water— one being formed by the Moon's gravity, and one being formed by Earth's movement away from the water on its side farthest from the Moon. These bulges of water, called high tides, shift position as Earth rotates on its axis, which is why tides repeat in a daily cycle.

⚛ Think about Science

Directions: Answer the following question.

1. The salinity of ocean water in an area is 35 ppt. Predict what would happen to the salinity of the water if rates of precipitation increased.

    A. It would decrease.
    B. It would double.
    C. It would increase slightly.
    D. It would remain the same.

Identify and Interpret Variables in Scientific Investigations

In this section, you learn that saltwater and freshwater have different properties. Saltwater and freshwater mix at the mouths of rivers, which are called estuaries. Design an experiment to investigate the layering that occurs when ocean water and freshwater mix at estuaries.

1. Begin your experiment by formulating a hypothesis.

2. Write a step-by-step procedure for your investigation, including any safety measures you will take and which materials and technology you will need. Identify the independent and dependent variables in your investigation.

3. Carry out your experiment and record your results. You may want to conduct multiple trials or measurements to reduce the possibility of error.

4. Analyze how the independent variable affected the dependent variable. Then draw a conclusion about how the salinity affects the layering of water. When you **draw conclusions,** you interpret or make inferences based on results of an investigation.

Impact of Oceans

Oceans are home to countless organisms, ranging from microscopic bacteria to huge whales. In addition, oceans moderate Earth's climate and keep surface temperatures within a range that supports life. Without this moderating effect, many living things could not survive. Oceans affect climate and living things and, in turn, are affected by climate changes and human activities.

Effects on Climate

How do oceans help regulate Earth's surface temperatures? They absorb solar energy more slowly and retain it longer than dry land does. If the oceans quickly absorbed and released the Sun's energy, Earth's average temperature would range from above 100° C during the day to below –100° C at night. With heat being exchanged this quickly between the atmosphere and Earth's surface, violent weather patterns would occur.

The relatively warm winters and cool summers of Portland, Oregon compared to Minneapolis is due to the wind moving oceanic air from the Pacific Ocean ashore to Portland. Since water has a higher specific heat than land, it takes more energy to raise the temperature of water than land. So, ocean temperatures and air termperatures over oceans do not vary as much as temperatures over land. Gyres help moderate variations in Earth's temperature. As water circulates through a gyre, it warms near the equator and cools in higher latitudes.

Interactions with Living Things

In addition to their impact on climate, oceans likely played a role in the origin of life. Scientists believe that life originated in water. Over the course of billions of years, oceans have continued to nurture life by providing shelter for organisms and food for many more, including humans. However, recent human activities have the potential to adversely affect ocean environments and, by extension, all life on Earth.

Ocean Habitats

Most ocean life lives in the upper sunlit part of the ocean, where light for photosynthesis can occur. Algae and plants form the base of the food supply of ocean animals, just as they do for land animals. Marine algae produce most of the oxygen that people and most other organisms need to survive.

Even so, many living things survive in the ocean's darkest, deepest waters. These organisms have adapted to a cold, low-light, low-oxygen environment. Typically these organisms survive on nutrients and dead plant and animal matter that sink from the water above.

Some ocean habitats are home to a wide variety of organisms. Coral reefs, for example, are sources of shelter and food for numerous living things. The reefs are made of colonies of colorful living organisms—corals—that thrive in warm, shallow ocean waters. The corals secrete a hard substance that over time forms a structure called a coral reef. Many small fish and other organisms shelter in or near the reefs, while larger fish such as sharks use the reefs as hunting grounds.

Unfortunately coral reefs around the world are suffering. Coral bleaching is the whitening of coral colonies due to the death of the algae that live within healthy corals. Without these algae, the coral colony slowly starves to death. Scientists believe that coral bleaching is caused by the quality of ocean water. Possible factors include rising water temperatures caused by climate change, water pollution, changes in water pH, and silt runoff from coastal areas.

Sea Level

The height of the surface of the oceans, called sea level, has changed many times during Earth's geologic past. When sea level is low, more land is exposed, and organisms that live on land can expand their habitats. When sea level is high, less land is exposed, and land habitats can be underwater.

Climate change caused by burning fossil fuels is linked to a current rise in sea level. When fossil fuels are burned, carbon dioxide is released into the atmosphere. Carbon dioxide is one of the gases that help regulate Earth's climate. Too much carbon dioxide in the atmosphere can cause climate change.

Changes in climate related to human activities and other factors have increased the melting of ice caps and glaciers. This has caused a rise in sea level. Scientists estimate that the global sea level has risen by approximately 17 cm since the early 1900s. Although this may seem like a small amount, it can have grave consequences if left unchecked. Coastal cities could end up partially underwater. Many coastal habitats might be lost.

Food Sources

For thousands of years, oceans have provided humans and other living things with food in the form of marine organisms. Scientists estimate that marine organisms are the main source of protein for 2.6 billion people.

Today, however, overfishing is causing the populations of many marine species to rapidly decline in number. Overfishing occurs when too many fish or other marine animals are harvested. This decreases the overall populations of these species and reduces the amount of food available for humans and other species. The graph below shows the decline in codfish harvested due to overfishing.

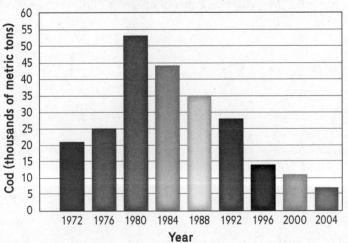

U.S. Atlantic Cod Harvest (1972 to 2004)

WORKPLACE SKILL

Make Decisions Based on Workplace Graphic

The population of Atlantic cod decreased substantially in the mid 1990s. In hopes of restoring the population, the fishing industry in New England proposed limits on the amount of commercial fishing ships allowed to harvest cod.

Analyze the graph on this page and describe the pattern you observe in the harvest of Atlantic cod since 1972. What inferences can you make based on the data? What additional measures might be taken to help the fishing industry recover?

Vocabulary Review

Directions: Write the missing term in the blank.

characteristic   draw conclusions   ocean
salinity   water cycle

1. When you _____, you make inferences based on the results of an investigation.

2. Water evaporates from the surface of the ocean as part of the _____.

3. Temperature is a(n) _____ of ocean water.

4. The _____ of ocean water would increase with distance from freshwater sources.

5. A(n) _____ contains saltwater, and a river contains freshwater.

Skill Review

Directions: Answer the following questions.

1. Surface currents generally affect the top 400 m of ocean water. At which depth would you expect the speed of surface currents to be greatest?

   A. 100 m
   B. 200 m
   C. 300 m
   D. 400 m

2. An oceanographer is measuring the height of waves in a portion of the ocean. The wave heights are steadily increasing. Which factor is most likely causing wave heights to increase?

   A. a decrease in fetch
   B. an increase in wind duration
   C. a decrease in wind speed
   D. an increase in wavelength

3. A scientist has a sample of ocean water in the lab. He wants to increase the salinity of the water by modeling natural processes. Which model would increase the water's salinity?

   A. Put the water in a shady, relatively cool area.
   B. Put the water under a heat lamp.
   C. Use a bottle sprayer to add "precipitation" to the water.
   D. Put the water in a sheltered area away from strong winds.

4. An ocean is located at a latitude that experiences four distinct seasons. During which season would you expect rates of evaporation to be lowest?

   A. winter
   B. spring
   C. summer
   D. fall

5. Describe a way to determine if a sample of water comes from the ocean or from a river.

6. Predict what might happen to tides if the Moon were farther from Earth. Explain your answer.

7. Give an example of how a surface current can affect coastal climates.

8. Identify two consequences of climate change.

Skill Practice

Directions: Use the information to answer questions 1 and 2.

Temperature of Ocean Water	
Sample 1	6° C
Sample 2	0° C
Sample 3	18° C
Sample 4	8° C

1. A scientist is taking samples of ocean water at different depths. His results are shown in the table above. Which sample most likely came from a density current?

   A. Sample 1

   B. Sample 2

   C. Sample 3

   D. Sample 4

2. Microscopic marine organisms called phytoplankton require sunlight to make their own food during photosynthesis. Which sample of ocean water likely contained the most phytoplankton?

   A. Sample 1

   B. Sample 2

   C. Sample 3

   D. Sample 4

Directions: Answer the following questions.

3. What basic motion does water follow as a wave passes?

   A. forward

   B. backward

   C. up and down

   D. circular

4. Which would have the greatest impact on global ocean water density?

   A. strong winds

   B. increase in daylight hours

   C. long-term increase in air temperature

   D. thunderstorm with heavy rainfall

5. Evaluate the importance of oceans to life on Earth, citing evidence to support your evaluation.

6. Design an experiment to investigate the effect of temperature on the layering of ocean water. Describe the steps you would take and the tools you would use.

7. Summarize the properties (temperature, salinity, density) you would expect to find at different depths of the ocean.

8. According to the US Environmental Protection Agency, average temperatures in Alaska have risen by about 2° C (3.4° F) over the past five decades. Scientists estimate that this trend will continue into the future and may even accelerate. Predict how the rising temperatures will affect humans and other organisms that live near coastal regions in Alaska.

9. Explain how it is possible that pollution in the Indian Ocean could negatively affect marine organisms that inhabit the Pacific Ocean.

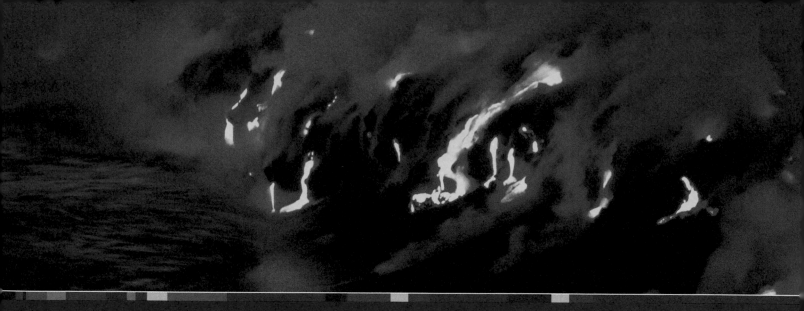

LESSON OBJECTIVES

- State the theory of plate tectonics and plate movement
- Describe minerals, rocks, soil, and the rock cycle

CORE SKILLS & PRACTICES

- Understand and Apply Scientific Models, Theories, and Processes
- Draw Conclusions

Key Terms

erosion
the transport of weathered materials from one place to another

mineral
a naturally occurring, inorganic solid with a specific chemical composition and crystalline structure

plate tectonics
the slow movement of sections of Earth's crust and mantle

rock cycle
the continuous changing and remaking of rocks over time

weathering
the natural breakdown of rock into smaller pieces

Vocabulary

theory
a set of ideas intended to explain facts or events

Key Concept

Earth is divided into three layers with different compositions. Interactions between Earth's tectonic plates cause most of Earth's volcanoes, earthquakes, and mountains. Minerals, rocks, and soil can be formed or changed during the rock cycle.

Earth's Structure

Scientists know that Earth is made up of a number of different layers. These layers can be defined in two ways. One way is to differentiate the layers by their compositions, or what they are made of. The other way is by their physical properties such as temperature, rigidity, or whether the layer is solid or liquid. Earth can be divided into three layers based on their compositions. These layers are called the crust, the mantle, and the core.

- The crust forms the outer layer of Earth. There are two types of crust—continental crust and oceanic crust. Continental crust is generally thicker and less dense than oceanic crust.

- The mantle is the layer of Earth beneath the crust. It ranges in temperature from 100°C to 4000°C—much warmer than the temperatures found in Earth's crust. The mantle is divided into two main zones: the upper mantle and the lower mantle. Both the upper mantle and lower mantle are solid. However, part of the upper mantle, the asthenosphere, can slowly flow. It responds to heat like a piece of plastic left outside on a hot, sunny day. Even though the hot plastic is still solid, it can be easily bent.

- The core is the central part of Earth and is divided into two parts: an outer liquid core and a inner solid core. Temperatures here may be as high as 7000°C, but high pressure causes the inner core to remain solid.

Think about Science

Directions: Answer the following questions.

1. Compare continental crust with oceanic crust.

2. What parts of Earth's interior layers are solid, and which parts can flow?

Digital Vision/Getty Images

Earth's Composition

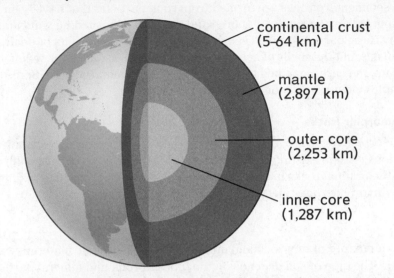

continental crust
(5–64 km)

mantle
(2,897 km)

outer core
(2,253 km)

inner core
(1,287 km)

CORE PRACTICE

Understand and Apply Scientific Models, Theories, and Processes

Scientists often use models to make difficult concepts easier to understand. In this lesson, a model is used to explain Earth's interior structure. If you were asked to use a physical model to represent the interior structure of Earth, what would you choose? Explain your reasoning.

Scientists think that Earth first consisted of hot, molten magma. As it cooled, the heaviest elements sank toward the center and the lighter elements remained closer to the surface. Thus, Earth's crust, mantle, and core are made up of different materials. The core is primarily composed of the heaviest elements, iron and nickel. The mantle contains large amounts of the elements iron and magnesium. Earth's crust contains mostly light elements, such as silicon and oxygen.

Minerals

One or more elements may form a **mineral,** which is a naturally occurring, inorganic solid that has a specific chemical composition and a definite crystalline structure. Earth's crust is composed of about 3,000 minerals. Some examples of minerals are gold, pyrite, and quartz.

All minerals are inorganic—that is, they do not contain any plant or animal matter—and they are solid. In addition, each type of mineral has a specific chemical composition, which is written as a chemical formula. For example, the mineral hematite contains two iron (Fe) atoms for every three oxygen (O) atoms. Its chemical formula is Fe_2O_3. You could break hematite into many pieces, but each piece would still have the same ratio of iron atoms to oxygen atoms. Finally all minerals have a definite crystalline structure, which means the atoms are arranged in a specific repeating pattern. Sometimes the crystal structure can be observed by looking at the mineral itself. Other times, the individual crystals are so small they can be seen only with magnification.

Igneous, Sedimentary, and Metamorphic Rocks

Minerals combine to form rock, which is a naturally occurring solid mixture of one or more minerals. The structure and composition of rocks provide clues to the processes that formed them. The three main types of rocks are igneous, sedimentary, and metamorphic.

Igneous Rocks

The temperature and pressure inside Earth's mantle can be high enough to cause rocks to melt and become magma. Rocks that form when this magma cools and crystallizes are called igneous rocks. Examples of igneous rocks include granite, diorite, and basalt.

Sedimentary Rocks

Most sedimentary rocks are formed from rock particles that have been transported away from their source and then are deposited by wind and water. These particles, called sediment, might also include bits of dead organisms and the shells of sea animals. Over time, as layers of sediment build up, they are cemented together to form sedimentary rocks. Some examples include sandstone, shale, and limestone.

Metamorphic Rocks

Metamorphic rocks are formed when extreme heat, pressure, or chemical reactions change existing rocks into new rocks. The new rocks usually differ from the original rocks in their physical and chemical properties. Examples of metamorphic rocks include quartzite, gneiss, and marble.

Soil

Soil is a mixture of tiny rock and mineral particles, organic material, water, and air. The type of soil depends on the types of rock and mineral particles as well as the types and amount of organic materials. Some soils are rich in nutrients that plants need to grow. The organic matter in soil may come from decaying leaves and other plant material. Animals also contribute to the organic matter in soil with their decaying bodies and wastes. This matter is called humus.

The Rock Cycle

Rocks can change from one type to another. The continuous changing and remaking of rocks is called the **rock cycle.** It may take thousands or millions of years for rocks to complete the cycle.

The cycle begins as rock is exposed to and transformed by natural forces. For example, **weathering**, which is the breakdown of rock into smaller pieces by natural processes, wears away rock, as does erosion. **Erosion** is the transport of weathered materials from one place to another by water, ice, wind, or gravity.

Weathering and erosion break rock into sediment. From here, deposition occurs, which means eroded materials are dropped or deposited. The sediment is buried, and lithification occurs. Lithification is the conversion of soft sediment into hard, sedimentary rock.

For example, pieces of an igneous rock might break apart and wash away into streams as grains of sand. Over many years the sandy sediment deepens, and the pressure on the layers increases. Minerals dissolved in the water precipitate between the grains of sand to cement them together. Heat and pressure cause the formation of metamorphic rock. Cooling and crystallization of magma form igneous rock. The stages of the rock cycle occur both beneath and above Earth's surface.

Think about Science

Directions: Answer the following question.

1. Predict whether soil in a desert would be good for growing plants. Explain your reasoning.

The Theory of Plate Tectonics

Evidence suggests that about 225 million years ago, the continents were one large land mass named Pangaea. Over time, pieces of the land mass moved apart. For many years, scientists could not explain why the continents drifted apart. The work of many scientists contributed to a theory that the crust and upper mantle are made up of about 20 sections, or plates. A scientific **theory** is a widely accepted explanation of something in the natural world based on knowledge that has been repeatedly confirmed through observation and experimentation.

According to the theory of **plate tectonics,** these plates "float" on the heavier material below. These plates are composed of the lithosphere, which includes the crust and the upper-most mantle. The plates move because currents of partially molten rock in the mantle carry them along. They move very slowly—about half an inch to four inches a year.

One type of evidence that supports this theory is the spreading of the seafloor. The Mid-Atlantic Ridge is a long underwater mountain range that sits about halfway between the continents on either side of it. Scientists believe that the seafloor is spreading outward along this ridge. The spreading seems to be caused by the continual flow of magma from cracks in Earth's crust and from eruptions in volcanoes along this mountain chain. Because the seafloor is spreading, North and South America are slowly moving farther from Europe and Africa. Sea-floor spreading explains the continued widening of the Atlantic Ocean over the past 180 million years.

Divergent Boundaries

Mid-ocean ridges are examples of divergent boundaries, or boundaries between two tectonic plates that are moving apart from each other. Most of Earth's divergent boundaries are on the ocean floor. When a divergent boundary occurs in an ocean, an ocean ridge is formed. It is along divergent boundaries at mid-ocean ridges that seafloor spreading occurs. The formation of new ocean crust at divergent boundaries often leads to volcanic activity and earthquakes. Although most divergent boundaries form ridges on the ocean floor, there are some divergent boundaries on continents. When continental crust starts to separate, it stretches and forms a long narrow valley called a rift valley.

Convergent Boundaries

When two tectonic plates push into each other, the boundary where they meet is a convergent boundary. Remember that there are two types of crust: oceanic crust and continental crust. When these two types of crust collide, they can form three types of convergent boundaries: oceanic-oceanic, oceanic-continental, and continental-continental.

Oceanic-oceanic convergent boundaries occur when oceanic crust collides with oceanic crust. The cooler and denser of the two plates slides under the other plate in a process called subduction. The plate that is subducted sinks into the mantle where it melts into magma. Some of the magma is forced back to Earth's surface and causes volcanic eruptions. These eruptions form chains of volcanic islands, called island arcs that run alongside the ocean trench. This type of convergent boundary is shown on the top of page 308.

CORE SKILL

Draw Conclusions

When you draw conclusions, you make a judgment after considering the information you have read. Reread the paragraphs about plate tectonics, and ask yourself, "If the continents once fit together, but now have moved apart, can I conclude that the continents are still moving? What will the planet look like in the future? Write several sentences to describe your conclusions.

You want to start a construction business that builds homes that can withstand strong earthquakes. Research the frequencies of earthquakes in the United States. Which part of the United States would be the best region in which to start your business, and why? What type of construction materials might you use that you would not use in less earthquake prone regions?

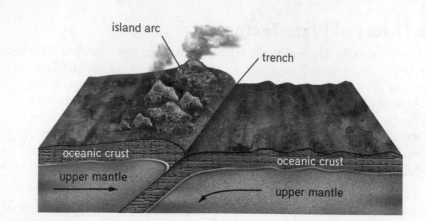

When a continental plate converges with an oceanic plate, subduction also occurs. An oceanic plate is always denser than the continental plate, so the oceanic plate is always subducted. This type of convergent boundary also creates an ocean trench and a chain of volcanoes. However, the volcanoes form under the continental plate to make a mountain range that has many volcanoes.

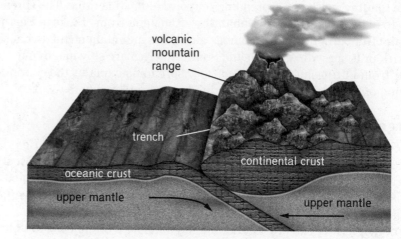

The third type of convergent boundary is formed when two continental plates collide. Because both plates have nearly the same density, the two edges are pushed together and lifted up, forming a high mountain range.

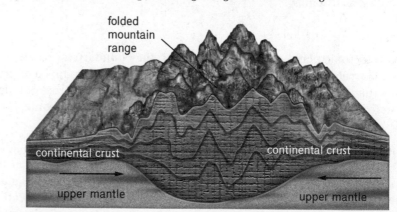

Transform Boundaries

A transform boundary occurs when two tectonic plates slide horizontally past each other and crust changes shape or is broken. Transform boundaries have long cracks that run along them, sometimes for kilometers. These cracks are called faults. Earthquakes often take place along these faults.

Volcanoes and Earthquakes

Most earthquakes occur at plate boundaries along faults in the Earth's crust. The pushing, pulling, and scraping of Earth's tectonic plates against one another causes stress to build up along faults near the plates' edges. However, there is a limit to how much stress a rock can withstand before it breaks. The movements of plates can build up enough stress to fracture rock. When the rocks on each side of a fracture move past each other, it is called a fault. Earthquakes are caused when large amounts of energy are released by rocks breaking and moving. The larger the fault and movement, the larger the earthquake. The energy released is what causes earthquakes.

Recall that most land volcanoes form at convergent boundaries. Volcanoes also form where two oceanic plates diverge. However, not all volcanoes form along plate boundaries. Some of Earth's most well-known volcanoes form at hot spots. A hot spot is a break in Earth's crust through which magma erupts. These are unusually hot regions of the mantle where columns, or plumes, of magma rise toward Earth's surface. The magma then melts the crust and flows out onto the surface, forming a volcano.

Mountain Building

When tectonic plates move and collide with each other, they create great amounts of stress on rocks. These stresses can cause folding and faulting. Often the stress causes the land near the plate boundaries to change. Huge amounts of stress can result in the formation of mountain ranges. The four types of mountains are folded mountains, fault-block mountains, dome mountains, and volcanic mountains.

- **Folded mountains** are formed when rock layers are pushed together and fold upward. The highest mountains on Earth, the Himalayas in Asia, are an example of a folded mountain range. Folded mountains often occur along continental-continental convergent plate boundaries.
- **Fault-block mountains** occur when land on one side of a fault drops down relative to the land on the other side. When mountains are formed in this way, they are called fault-block mountains. Fault-block mountains can occur along normal faults at divergent plate boundaries. They can also form where the land is under tensional stress. The Grand Tetons in Wyoming are an example of fault-block mountains.
- **Dome mountains** are formed when Earth's crust heaves upward without folding or faulting occurring. These mountains are the result of massive amounts of magma pushing upward. The Adirondack Mountains of New York State and the Black Hills of South Dakota are examples of dome mountains. Dome mountains do not have to form at plate boundaries.
- **Volcanic mountains** form when magma erupts onto Earth's surface and forms mountains. Recall that most volcanic mountains form over convergent boundaries at subduction zones. Many of the mountains in the Cascade Range, which runs from Washington State to California, are volcanic mountains.

Think about Science

Directions: Answer the following question.

1. When magma flows out onto Earth's surface,
   A. mountains can form.
   B. earthquakes can occur.
   C. midocean ridges can form.
   D. volcanoes can form.

Understand Data in Different Formats

A scientist measures the width of an ocean trench every year. His data show how much wider it becomes every year.

Year 1: Base measurement

Year 2: Trench is 5 cm wider than Year 1.

Year 3: Trench is 10.1 cm wider than Year 1.

Year 4: Trench is 14.9 cm wider than Year 1.

Year 5: Trench is 20 cm wider than Year 1.

Make a bar graph or data table to represent these results.

Earth's Structure, Composition, and Landforms

Vocabulary Review

Directions: Write the missing term in the blank.

plate tectonics   mineral   rock cycle
weathering   erosion   theory

1. _____ is the breaking down of rock into smaller pieces by natural processes.

2. A(n) _____ is a naturally occurring, inorganic solid that has a specific chemical composition and a definite crystalline structure.

3. _____ describes the slow movement of sections of Earth's crust and upper mantle.

4. The _____ is the continuous changing and remaking of rocks over time.

5. A(n) _____ is the explanation of some aspect of the natural world based on knowledge that has been repeatedly confirmed through observation and experimentation.

6. _____ is the transport of weathered materials from one place to another by water, ice, wind, or gravity.

Skill Review

Directions: Use the diagram to answer questions 1 and 2.

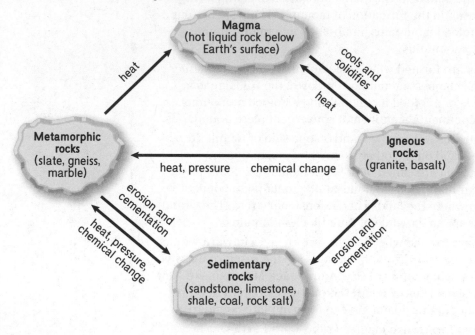

1. When granite is heated, which type of rock does it start out as, and what does it change to?

    A. igneous rock to magma

    B. metamorphic rock to igneous rock

    C. igneous rock to sedimentary rock

    D. sedimentary rock to magma

2. Which of the following are needed to change sedimentary rock into metamorphic rock?

    A. cooling and a chemical change

    B. heat and erosion

    C. heat and a chemical change

    D. erosion and a chemical change

Directions: Answer the following questions.

3. Based on what you know about minerals, which of the following is not a mineral?

   A. quartz

   B. amber

   C. mica

   D. calcite

4. Which of the following is *not* true about tectonic plates?

   A. Tectonic plates can melt if they are subducted at plate boundaries.

   B. Tectonic plates are more dense than the material below them, so they sink down.

   C. Tectonic plates ride on fluid material that moves by convection.

   D. Tectonic plates are less dense than the material below them, so they "float" on top.

Skill Practice

Directions: Answer the following questions.

1. What is likely the cause of the seafloor spreading at the Mid-Atlantic Ridge?

   A. The movement of continents, followed by underwater earthquakes

   B. The formation of mountain ranges due to faults in underwater land formations

   C. The moving apart of tectonic plates with an outpouring of magma

   D. The eruption of underwater volcanoes with an outpouring of lava

2. What is the best evidence that seafloor spreading occurs at about the same rate on both sides of the Mid-Atlantic Ridge?

   A. The shape of South America is similar to the shape of Africa.

   B. The continents to the east and west of the ridge are about the same distance from the ridge.

   C. The seafloor to the west of the ridge contains the same types of minerals as the seafloor to the east.

   D. Many types of minerals found in South America are also found in Africa.

3. Using what you know about plate tectonics, where is new crust being formed on Earth?

4. Describe how a volcanic mountain range might form on the edge of a continent where two plates converge. Then describe how a volcanic mountain range might form under the ocean where two oceanic plates diverge.

5. Explain how the rock cycle is affected by plate tectonics.

LESSON 8.4 Earth Resources

LESSON OBJECTIVES

- Identify Earth's living and nonliving resources
- Discuss fossil fuels and the impact of using nonrenewable energy resources
- Summarize the advantages and disadvantages of renewable energy resources

CORE SKILLS & PRACTICES

- Express Scientific Information or Findings Verbally
- Interpret Graphics

Key Terms

fossil fuels
energy resources that form over millions of years from the remains of once-living organisms

natural resources
resources provided by Earth, including organisms, nutrients, rocks, water, and minerals

Vocabulary

demonstrate
to clearly show a process or explain a concept

sustainability
the ability to maintain resources at levels that allow them to be available for future use

Key Concept

Earth supplies a wide variety of natural resources. All organisms on Earth, including humans, use resources provided by the environment. The use of resources has both advantages and disadvantages.

Natural Resources

You and every other living organism on Earth must have certain resources to grow, maintain life processes, and reproduce. The resources that Earth provides are called **natural resources** and include Earth's organisms, nutrients, rocks, water, and minerals. Natural resources provide us with food and the materials and energy we need to build and heat our homes. All items you use every day come from natural resources.

Living Things

Picture a breakfast menu of eggs, toast, bacon, sausage, milk, butter, pancakes, and maple syrup. These foods come from living things. Living things can also be used for other purposes. Trees are used to build homes and make furniture and paper products. Horses are used for transportation and recreation.

In addition to serving as a source of food, green plants provide the oxygen we need to survive through the process of photosynthesis. During this process, green plants use sunlight, water, and carbon dioxide to produce sugars and oxygen. Without green plants and other producers, Earth's atmosphere would not contain the oxygen that we breathe.

Nonliving Things

Fresh air and water, fertile soil, and elements that cycle through Earth's systems such as nitrogen, carbon, and phosphorus are examples of nonliving natural resources. These are elements that animals and plants need to live.

Freshwater has unique properties that make it ideal for the transport of nutrients throughout the body. Freshwater is also used by people for farming and recreation. Farms could not grow crops without fertile soil. It contains the nutrients plants need to thrive.

Earth Resources

Some natural resources are found within Earth. Metals such as copper, gold, and silver are present in small amounts in Earth's crust. Gold and silver are also used for electronics because they are good conductors of electricity. Copper is often used to make pipes and electrical wires.

⚛ Think about Science

Directions: Answer the following questions.

1. Give three examples of how people use living things to meet their needs.

2. What materials are used during photosynthesis to provide oxygen in the air?

Nonrenewable Energy Resources

Every time someone takes a hot shower, watches television, or does research on a computer, they use energy. Energy resources are natural resources that provide the power for these activities. Nonrenewable energy resources are resources that cannot be replaced or that can be replaced only by natural processes over millions of years. They include fossil fuels and nuclear energy.

Fossil Fuels

Energy sources that formed over geologic time as a result of the compression and incomplete decomposition of plants and other organic matter are called **fossil fuels.** Like many nonrenewable resources, they are often obtained through extraction, which means removing them with effort or force by mining, drilling, or other processes.

The high concentration of carbon and hydrogen in fossil fuels makes them efficient energy sources. Fossil fuels include coal, petroleum, and natural gas. These resources are not evenly distributed around the world. Instead some countries have ample reserves, while other countries have few if any fossil fuels; they must import fossil fuels or rely on other resources to meet their energy needs.

Coal

The most commonly used and most abundant fossil fuel is coal. Coal is a solid brownish black rock formed from plants that lived millions of years ago. Coal was once used to power trains and heat homes. Today more than 90 percent of the coal used in the United States generates electricity for homes and industries, including the steel, cement, and paper industries.

Petroleum

Liquid fossil fuels such as petroleum are still commonly used to heat homes and run engines. Petroleum, also known as crude oil, is found underground in certain areas where conditions were right for it to accumulate after it formed. It is refined to make common energy resources that include jet fuel, gasoline for cars, fuel oil for home heaters, and other fuels such as kerosene and propane. Petroleum is also used to make plastics, waxes, and the oil and asphalt used to pave roads.

Scientists often present
their findings to their peers
and to the public in press
conferences, seminars, and
other meetings. Research more
about air pollution related to the
burning of fossil fuels. Present
your findings in a brief oral
presentation before the class.
Your presentation should clearly
define each type of pollution,
explain how it forms, and
describe its effects.

Natural Gas

The third major type of fossil fuel is natural gas. Natural gas is a mixture of
gases that accumulate underground. It is often found with petroleum and
coal deposits. Like the other fossil fuels, natural gas is used to generate
electricity and heat buildings. It is also used as a cooking fuel; stoves in many
homes burn natural gas. In recent years, some cars and buses have been
designed to run on natural gas, mainly because it is the cleanest burning
fossil fuel.

Consequences of Using Fossil Fuels

Fossil fuels are the primary sources of energy in the United States because
they are fairly efficient and are relatively inexpensive to extract. However,
there are consequences associated with their extraction and use.

Habitat Destruction

Fossil fuels are most often found underground, so mining or drilling is
necessary to extract the resources. These processes can destroy or disrupt
habitats. In the United States, land must be reclaimed, or restored to a
suitable habitat, following mining and drilling operations. However, living
things are still displaced by the extraction of fossil fuels, and the land cannot
be restored completely. It can take many years for the habitat to recover.

Pollution

Using fossil fuels can also affect water, land, and air quality. Drainage from
mines or accidental oil spills can pollute land and water. Air pollution occurs
from particles that are released when fossil fuels are burned for energy.
Smog is a type of air pollution that forms when emissions from vehicles that
burn fossil fuels react with sunlight. Acid rain is another type of pollution
that forms when emissions from burning fossil fuels react with water and
gases in the atmosphere to increase significantly the acidity of rain. Both
types of pollution can harm ecosystems and cause health problems.

Climate Change

Burning fossil fuels is also associated with climate change. To better
understand the relationship between fossil fuels and climate change, you
must first understand the carbon cycle. Recall that the carbon cycle is
the series of processes by which carbon is exchanged between living and
nonliving things on Earth. Fossil fuels store carbon; when these fuels are
burned, carbon dioxide is released into the atmosphere. Atmospheric carbon
dioxide helps moderate temperatures on Earth. An increase in carbon
dioxide, however, increases the greenhouse effect and causes the Earth's
temperature to rise. This process is known as climate change.

Measurements show that the amount of carbon dioxide in Earth's atmosphere
has increased 28 percent in the last hundred years. At this rate, the level
could rise another 40 percent by the end of the 21st century. Recall that
consequences of climate change include the melting of glacial ice and the
resulting rise in sea level. Coastal cities, such as San Francisco and New
York, could become partially submerged.

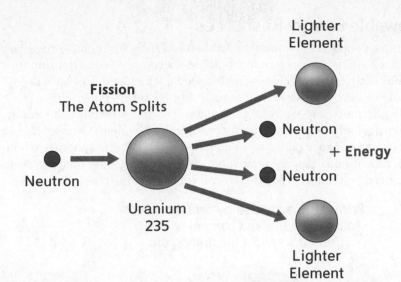

**Fission
The Atom Splits**

Neutron

Uranium
235

Lighter
Element

Neutron

+ **Energy**

Neutron

Lighter
Element

Nuclear Energy

Energy associated with changes in the nucleus of an atom is called nuclear energy. Most nuclear energy is produced by a process called fission. During fission, the nuclei of atoms are split, and a large amount of energy is released. Radioactive elements consist of atoms that have a natural tendency to undergo nuclear fission. Uranium is one radioactive element commonly used in the production of nuclear energy. This energy is used to heat water to produce the steam that powers electric generators. While the process of fission is inexhaustible, radioactive elements cannot be replaced. Therefore nuclear energy is considered a nonrenewable resource.

Consequences of Using Nuclear Power

Nuclear power has some advantages. It can produce electricity at relatively low costs, and it does not pollute the air. However, nuclear power plants produce dangerous radioactive wastes. These wastes must be stored properly for thousands of years so that radiation cannot escape into the environment. Nuclear accidents, such as the 1979 incident at Three Mile Island in Pennsylvania and the 1986 explosion at Chernobyl in Ukraine, alerted people to the hazards of nuclear power plants. Public concern about the safety of nuclear power plants has slowed the increase of their use throughout the world.

Think about Science

Directions: Answer the following questions.

1. Why are fossil fuels considered nonrenewable?
   A. They are limited.
   B. They generate energy.
   C. They produce pollution.
   D. They cause climate change.

2. Which disadvantage is associated with the use of nuclear power?
   A. air pollution
   B. climate change
   C. radioactive wastes
   D. habitat disruption

21ST CENTURY SKILL

Civic Literacy

An energy company is proposing a nuclear power plant in your area. The state is holding public meetings to allow local residents to express their opinions on this matter. As a concerned citizen, you are planning on attending the meeting and expressing your thoughts. You want to support your opinions with scientific data.

Research the history of nuclear power plants in the United States, focusing on positive impacts (for example, job creation) and negative impacts (for example, environmental contamination). Use your research to write a brief statement you would present at the meeting.

Renewable Energy Resources

Today most people rely on nonrenewable fossil fuels for their energy needs. People are looking for ways to meet global energy needs and to promote **sustainability.** Sustainability is a principle by which resources are used in such a way as to preserve their availability for future generations. Possible alternatives to nonrenewable energy sources include solar energy, wind energy, hydropower, geothermal power, and biomass. Most of these resources do not cause pollution or increase levels of atmospheric carbon dioxide. In addition, they are renewable resources, meaning they can be used and replaced by natural processes over a relatively short period of time.

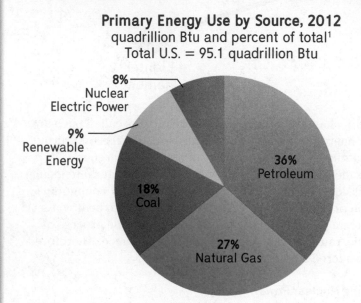

Primary Energy Use by Source, 2012
quadrillion Btu and percent of total[1]
Total U.S. = 95.1 quadrillion Btu

- 8% Nuclear Electric Power
- 9% Renewable Energy
- 18% Coal
- 36% Petroleum
- 27% Natural Gas

[1]Does not add to 100 due to independent rounding.
Source: U.S. Energy Information Administration, *Monthly Energy Review*, Table 1.3 (April 2013), preliminary 2012 data.

Solar Energy

Solar energy is the energy from the Sun that warms Earth and gives us light. It can be used to heat buildings, make electricity, and charge batteries. Buildings may be heated by passive solar heating or by active solar heating. Passive solar heating captures sunlight directly and converts it into heat. Active solar heating requires collectors, such as solar panels, to absorb solar energy. Unlike the burning of fossil fuels, the use of solar energy does not create any pollution. However, the technology used to generate large-scale solar power can be expensive. In addition, scientists are still working on developing an efficient way to store large amounts of solar energy for long periods of time.

Hydropower

Hydropower is electricity produced by free-falling or free-flowing water. Often dams are built across rivers to create reservoirs of stored water. As this water flows through pipes at controlled rates, it causes turbines to spin and produce electricity. The energy of ocean waves through the ebb and flow of tides can also be captured to generate electricity. Today about 10 percent of the electricity used in the United States is generated by water. While hydropower does not pollute the environment, there can be negative consequences. The building of dams, for example, changes the natural patterns of water flow and can destroy wildlife habitats and interrupt the migration routes of fish. The large areas that become flooded when dams are built can even force people to move from their homes.

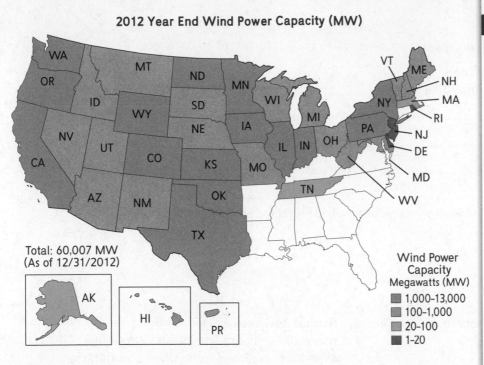

2012 Year End Wind Power Capacity (MW)

Total: 60,007 MW
(As of 12/31/2012)

Wind Power
Capacity
Megawatts (MW)
- 1,000–13,000
- 100–1,000
- 20–100
- 1–20

CORE SKILL

Interpret Graphics

Imagine that you work for a state agency concerned with developing a plan for future energy resources. Locate your state on the map showing wind-power capacity on this page. Use the map to write a brief recommendation for your state about how much time and resources it should invest in wind energy in the future. Refer to the data to support your recommendation.

Afterward, exchange your recommendation with a partner and analyze your partner's reasoning. What was the overall goal of his or her recommendation? Do you agree with the recommendation? Explain the reasoning behind your evaluation.

Wind Energy

Wind energy is captured by wind turbines that look something like traditional windmills. The wind turns the blades of the turbines. The energy of the movement of the blades is then used to produce electricity. There are many benefits to using wind power. Wind is an unlimited resource that does not pollute the environment. The land underneath wind turbines can also continue to be used for other purposes, such as farming. As a result, wind energy is one of the least expensive ways to produce electricity. The major disadvantage of using wind energy is that it is economical to build wind turbines only in areas with steady winds. Most of the wind farms in the United States are located in California and Hawaii.

Geothermal Energy

Geothermal energy is produced by naturally occurring steam and hot water beneath Earth's crust. Water trapped underground in rock fractures or in porous rock is heated by Earth's internal heat. Some of this water becomes steam and usually escapes at continental-plate boundaries. Many geothermal power plants use this steam to generate electricity. In Reykjavik, Iceland, for example, geothermal energy is so plentiful that almost 80 percent of the buildings are heated directly by water from geothermal wells. Geothermal energy is abundant, and it does not cause pollution. A disadvantage, however, is that it can be used only on a large scale near tectonically active sites.

Biomass

Organic matter can be used as fuel to provide power or heat. The total amount of plant or animal matter on Earth that could be converted to fuel is called biomass. Fuels that come from living things are called biomass fuels. Examples of biomass fuels include wood and field crops. Solid waste from animals, which often contains bits of plants, can also be used for fuel.

In addition to being burned directly for heat, biomass fuels are now being converted into gas and alcohol fuels. Biomass is readily available, but like fossil fuels, it can add pollutants to the air when burned.

Vocabulary Review

Directions: Write the missing term in the blank.

> **demonstrate**   **fossil fuels**
> **natural resources**   **sustainability**

1. I used research to _____ that nuclear power can be dangerous.

2. Plants are examples of living _____.

3. Coal is one of the _____ that has been linked to a rising level of atmospheric carbon dioxide.

4. _____ involves making sure resources are around for future generations to use.

Skill Review

Directions: Answer the following questions.

1. Why are fossil fuels the primary source of energy in the United States?

   A. They don't cause pollution.

   B. They are renewable.

   C. They are easily obtained.

   D. They are found near tectonic activity.

2. Which solution would likely be the most effective in reducing the levels of atmospheric carbon dioxide?

   A. Building more geothermal power plants

   B. Placing restrictions on nuclear power plants

   C. Developing cars that get high mileage

   D. Placing higher taxes on fossil fuels

3. Demonstrators are protesting against a proposed hydropower plant in their area. Which group is most likely to be involved in the demonstration?

   A. Citizens United to Protect Habitats

   B. Citizens Against Air Pollution

   C. Citizens Against the Release of Toxic Substances

   D. Citizens Concerned About Climate Change

4. Natural resources can be classified as renewable or nonrenewable. However, like all matter, they can be classified according to other characteristics. Brainstorm one way you could classify natural resources. Then create a table showing your classification scheme.

5. In your own words, define a renewable resource and a nonrenewable resource.

6. A lumber company is trying to practice sustainability. Describe one way the company can achieve its goal.

7. An opinion piece in the newspaper argues that the best energy plan involves expanding the use of fossil fuels. Write a brief rebuttal to this article. Be sure to include a rationale for your position.

8. Identify one advantage and one disadvantage of using solar power.

9. Compare geothermal energy and biomass.

Skill Skill Practice

Directions: Use the passage to answer questions 1 and 2.

Three Mile Island in Pennsylvania is the location of a nuclear power plant that on March 28, 1979, had a partial core meltdown—the overheating and melting of the core of a nuclear reactor. The accident occurred over a five-day period. Government officials frantically tried to decide whether a complete evacuation of nearby communities was necessary. The fear was that radioactive gas would escape into the air and that radioactive waste might find its way to groundwater.

Luckily the reactor was finally brought under control. Although no injuries or deaths were reported, the dangers of nuclear power plants remain in many people's minds.

1. Which of the following was most likely true when nuclear power was first developed?

   A. Scientists believed that disasters such as a core meltdown could be prevented.

   B. Scientists believed that a core meltdown in a nuclear power plant was impossible.

   C. Scientists did not know that nuclear power plants would create radioactive waste.

   D. Scientists did not know that radioactive waste was terribly toxic to humans.

2. Why are many people so concerned about nuclear power, even though no injuries or deaths were reported at Three Mile Island?

   A. If not contained, radioactive wastes can cause instant death.

   B. A core meltdown can cause an explosion that can level an entire community.

   C. Radioactive wastes can cause long-term, serious health problems.

   D. Radioactive gases are the biggest contributors to climate change.

Directions: Answer the following questions.

3. Which energy resources, or combination of energy resources, would be most appropriate for your area? Explain your choices.

4. According to the US Energy Information Administration, oil use for the production of electricity has stayed approximately the same since 1982. Make an inference to explain this.

5. Classify the resources you have used today as renewable or nonrenewable. Then identify at least three ways you could have reduced your use of nonrenewable resources.

6. Review the charts in this lesson that show the location of fossil-fuel reserves around the world. Which fossil fuel would best meet future energy needs in the United States based only on local availability? Explain your answer.

7. Scientists sometimes point out that many energy sources can be traced back to the Sun. Use one example of an energy resource to explain why this statement is true. Then provide an example of an energy source that does not come from the Sun.

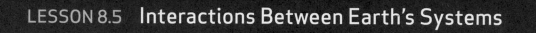

LESSON 8.5 Interactions Between Earth's Systems

LESSON OBJECTIVES

- Describe Earth's weather systems
- Compare weathering with erosion and deposition
- Describe different natural hazards

CORE SKILLS & PRACTICES

- Use Sampling Techniques to Answer Scientific Questions
- Follow a Multistep Procedure
- Evaluate Multiple Sources

Key Terms

deposition
the process by which material is either laid on the ground or sinks to the bottom of a body of water

natural hazard
the natural forces that can result in a serious threat to life

weather
the condition of the atmosphere at a particular place and time

weather systems
when an air mass remains over the same area for days or weeks

Vocabulary

experiment
a scientific investigation carried out with the goal of solving a scientific question

Key Concept

Earth's systems interact, resulting in a variety of effects, some of which are disastrous.

Weather

Weather is something you likely think about and talk about daily. From the scientific perspective, **weather** is the condition of the atmosphere at a particular place and time.

Water in the Atmosphere

Water is constantly moving between Earth's surface and the atmosphere in the water cycle. At any one time, only a small percentage of Earth's freshwater is present in the atmosphere as water vapor. This small percentage of water, however, greatly affects Earth's weather.

Humidity

Humidity refers to the amount of water vapor present in the air. The ability of air to hold water vapor is related to its temperature. Warmer air can hold more water vapor than cooler air. Clouds form when warm, moist air rises into the atmosphere and cools. As the air cools to a temperature at which the air is completely saturated, water vapor condenses around small particles in the atmosphere, such as dust or sea salt, and forms tiny water droplets or ice particles. A cloud is a collection of millions of these tiny water droplets or ice particles.

Precipitation

Precipitation is any solid or liquid form of water that falls from clouds. For example, rain is liquid water that forms from clouds. Snow forms when water vapor in clouds changes directly into a solid due to low temperatures. Sleet forms as rain falls through a layer of freezing air, producing falling ice. Hail consists of balls of ice that form in clouds as warm updrafts of air carry raindrops upward, where they freeze; as the frozen raindrops fall again, they combine with water, and the ball of ice grows. Eventually the hail becomes heavy enough to fall to Earth's surface.

Weather Systems

Changes in weather are caused by the movements and interactions of air masses. An air mass is a large body of air that takes on the temperature and moisture characteristics of the area over which it forms. **Weather systems** form when air remains over the same area, called the source region, for days or weeks. During this period, the temperature and humidity of the air mass become similar to that of the source region. For example, an air mass that develops over the Gulf of Mexico will likely be warm and wet. This is because the Gulf area is warm and has a lot of water evaporating into the air.

At Earth's middle latitudes, weather systems with different characteristics sometimes meet. The boundary that forms between them is called a front. A front is a narrow region separating two air masses of different densities. Differences in temperature, pressure, and humidity cause these densities. Fronts are usually associated with weather in the middle latitudes, where there are both warm and cold air masses. Fronts do not occur in the tropics, because only warm air masses exist there. The arrival of a front indicates a change in weather.

A cold front forms when a cold air mass meets and displaces a warm air mass. Because the cold air is denser than the warm air, it moves under the warm air. This causes the warm air to rise. As the warm air rises, it cools, and the water vapor in it condenses. Cold fronts can produce clouds, thunderstorms, heavy rain, or snow. Cooler weather usually follows a cold front because the warm air is pushed away from Earth's surface.

A warm front forms when a warm air mass meets and overrides a cold air mass. The warm, less dense air moves over the cold, denser air and gradually replaces it. The air ahead of a warm front develops a front boundary that is less steep than the boundary ahead of a cold front. Warm fronts usually bring extensive cloudiness and drizzly rain. After a warm front passes, weather conditions are generally warm and clear.

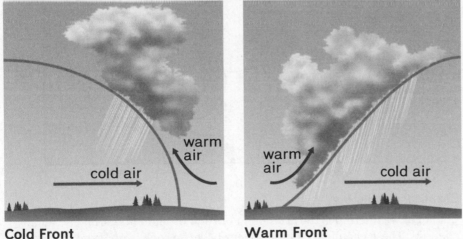

Cold Front   **Warm Front**

Think about Science

Directions: Answer the following questions.

1. How does air temperature affect humidity?

2. How does the temperature and humidity of an air mass compare to that of its source region?

3. What kind of front forms when a cold air mass displaces a warm air mass?

CORE SKILL

Evaluate Multiple Sources

Read a weather report online or in a newspaper. Then watch a video weather report or weather channel. How are air masses and fronts shown in each source? What did you learn from the video that was different from the printed information? Write a paragraph to describe your conclusions.

CORE PRACTICE

Use Sampling Techniques to Answer Scientific Questions

Conduct an **experiment,** which is a scientific investigation, by collecting data. Record the high and low temperatures in your community for a week. What conclusions can you draw about the temperature range in your community for the week you collected data?

Earth's Changing Surface

At first glance, land on Earth's surface looks solid and unchanging. But Earth's surface is constantly changing. Sometimes the changes are rapid and violent such as earthquakes. Other times, the changes take place slowly and gently, such as weathering.

Weathering

Recall that weathering is the breaking down of rock into smaller pieces by natural processes. Weathering helps produce soil, which is a mixture of tiny rock fragments and organic materials produced by living things. Most organic materials in soil are the decaying remains of plants and animals. Weathering may bring about both physical and chemical changes in rock.

Mechanical Weathering

Mechanical weathering breaks rocks apart, causing physical changes without changing the chemicals within the rocks. Mechanical weathering occurs when ice, water, wind, gravity, pressure, plants, or animals cause rocks to break into smaller pieces.

One type of mechanical weathering is caused by the action of freezing water. Water from rain, rivers, or streams flows over a rock and fills any small cracks in the rock's surface. During cold weather, the water freezes and expands as it turns to ice. The force of the expansion widens the cracks and can eventually split the rock into pieces.

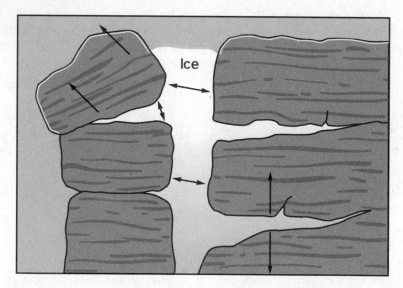

Chemical Weathering

Chemical weathering is the crumbling of rock brought about by chemical changes. These chemical changes occur because rock is exposed to water and atmospheric gases. For example, when the iron in a rock is exposed to water, the iron changes to rust. The rust is formed from the chemical reaction of iron in rock, water, and oxygen gas. The most common agents of chemical weathering are water, carbon dioxide, acids, and oxygen.

Plants and Animals

Plants and animals contribute to both physical and chemical weathering. For example, roots growing in small cracks will increase in size and split rocks. Chemicals present in the roots bring about chemical changes that dissolve rock. Burrowing animals, such as gophers and worms, create tunnels that allow water and atmospheric gases to penetrate more easily into surface soil, exposing buried rocks to weathering.

Erosion and Deposition

Recall that erosion is the transport of weathered materials from one place to another by water, ice, wind, or gravity. **Deposition** is the process by which the eroded material is either laid on the ground or sinks to the bottom of a body of water. Erosion and deposition complement each other because all eroded material is deposited somewhere. Together, these two processes are responsible for creating many of the landforms that surround us. The three main agents of erosion are gravity, wind, and water.

Gravity

Gravity erosion is the falling of rock fragments due to gravity. If small rock pieces break from solid rock high on a cliff, they fall until other rocks stop them. Hillsides covered with loose rocks are often the result of the gravity erosion of weathered rocks higher up.

Wind

Wind erosion is the movement of materials by wind. This type of erosion acts mainly on small rock fragments and loose soil and sand. Strong winds often carry fine rock particles. Wind erosion is common in dry locations where there is loose, sandy soil and in areas with strong winds. Wind causes dunes to migrate by moving sand grains from the windward side of the dune and transporting them to the leeward side. As this process continues, the dune migrates downwind.

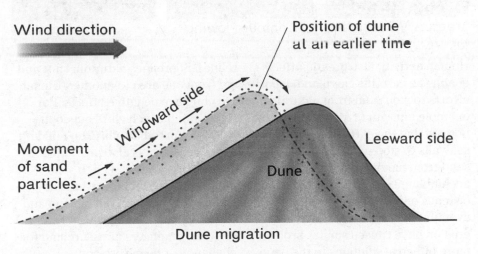

Wind direction

Position of dune at an earlier time

Windward side

Leeward side

Movement of sand particles

Dune

Dune migration

Water

Water erosion is the most powerful of all types of erosion. Rivers cause the breakup of rocks and move rock fragments along the direction of the river's flow. The Grand Canyon was created, in great part, by the water-erosion effects of the Colorado River. Although water is a powerful source of erosion, water erosion usually happens gradually.

Use Data Effectively

Look at precipitation and temperature data for your community. Which month is the rainiest month, on average? Which month is the driest month? When is your area most likely to get snow or sleet? Explain how you drew your conclusions.

Erosion and People

Erosion has proven to be one of farmers' worst fears. In the 1930s, many farmers of the central plains of the United States overused their land; this meant that the nutrient content had no time to recover. The crops grown in such soil were weak; thus, when an extended drought struck, crops quickly died. With no plant roots to hold the soil, high winds blew much of the topsoil away from this farming region, which became known as the Dust Bowl.

The US government started programs to financially assist farmers and to teach soil-conservation techniques that would prevent this crisis from happening in the future. Some techniques used to prevent erosion include planting trees for windbreak barricades, using contour plowing so the flowing water cannot pick up speed downhill to carry soil away, or terracing or making flat fields along hillsides. Other agricultural practices, including using cover crops, strip cropping, and crop rotation, can help conserve soil and prevent erosion.

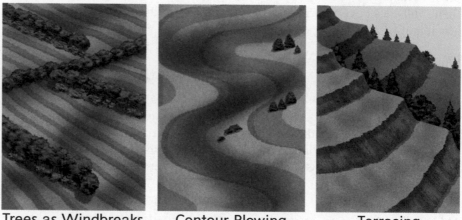

Trees as Windbreaks   Contour Plowing   Terracing

Human activity also greatly affects shorelines. Shorelines naturally shift and change as currents carry and deposit sand from one area to another. Human efforts to stop sand from naturally moving can have negative effects. For example, the city of Miami Beach built hotels along beach cliffs but soon noticed that the cliffs were eroding. The city reinforced the cliffs by building seawalls to stop waves from reaching them. The seawalls also prevented sand from moving naturally along the shoreline. As a result, beach sand accumulated along the seawalls on the sides that were hit by waves. The beaches on the other sides of the walls, however, were deprived of sand and eventually disappeared. Other structures built by humans to prevent beach erosion have caused similar problems. Shoreline engineers are searching for more effective solutions to the ongoing challenge of beach erosion.

Think about Science

Directions: Answer the following questions.

1. Describe how erosion and deposition are related. Then draw a diagram to show this relationship.
2. Give one example each of wind erosion, water erosion, and erosion by gravity.

Extreme Weather Systems

A **natural hazard** results from the interaction of natural forces at work within Earth's interior or Earth's atmosphere and can pose a serious threat to the life and health of local residents as well as other organisms in the area. When Earth's weather systems interact, they can sometimes create dangerous situations. Thunderstorms, tornadoes, and hurricanes are all natural hazards caused by weather patterns. Other natural hazards, such as earthquakes and volcanoes, are the result of the movement of Earth's tectonic plates.

Thunderstorms

Thunderstorms are small, intense weather systems that produce heavy rain, strong winds, lightning, and thunder. They can develop when the air near Earth's surface is warm and moist. As the warm air moves upward, it cools, condenses, and forms clouds. Eventually water droplets fall back to Earth's surface. As the water droplets fall, they cool the surrounding air, which becomes denser. The dense air sinks quickly, creating a downdraft that causes strong winds.

Severe thunderstorms may result in strong winds, hail, flooding, and tornadoes—all of which can cause property damage and loss of human life. Hail associated with thunderstorms can cause great damage to crops by destroying plants. When rain from thunderstorms falls faster than the ground can absorb it, flooding may occur. Lightning strikes during thunderstorms are the cause of approximately 7,500 forest fires each year in the United States.

Tornadoes

A tornado is a violent, rotating column of air that is in contact with the ground below and a cloud above. When the conditions are right, the air near Earth's surface may begin to rotate horizontally. If this rotating cylinder of air is close enough to a thunderstorm's upward-moving winds, it might be tilted from a horizontal to a vertical position. Rain and hail helps lower the rotating air to the ground. A lower layer of dense air collides with a less-dense upper layer. The air between two colliding air masses rotates horizontally. The rotation diameter decreases and wind speed increases. The difference in pressure between the center and outer portion of the tornado produces violent winds.

Few tornadoes are larger than 200 m in diameter, and most tornadoes last only a few minutes. They can, however, be extremely destructive to plants, buildings, and humans.

Hurricanes

A hurricane is a large, rotating, low-pressure storm that forms over warm tropical waters. Hurricanes need two conditions to form: a large supply of very warm ocean water and some sort of disturbance to lift warm air up and to keep it rising. Usually a hurricane begins as a group of thunderstorms moving over tropical ocean waters. As a hurricane intensifies, more warm air moves to replace air that has risen. Heat energy is released into the atmosphere through the cooling and condensing of water vapor in rising air. This release of heat energy produces powerful winds.

Hurricane winds can cause massive destruction, especially to communities along shorelines. Storm surge, which occurs when strong winds drive ocean water onto land, can also cause severe flooding.

Interactions Between Earth's Systems

CORE PRACTICE

Follow a Multistep Procedure

Put some sand or soil in a basin or tub. Drizzle water over the soil to re-create patterns of erosion and deposition of sand or soil. Next, use small sticks or pieces of wood to create terraces or seawalls. Demonstrate how people can both prevent erosion and make erosion worse.

21ST CENTURY SKILL

Leadership and Responsibility

How do emergency responders prepare for an impending natural disaster? Conduct research and then give a short presentation that describes your results.

Vocabulary Review

Directions: Write the missing term in the blank.

deposition   experiment   natural hazard
weather   weather system

1. The condition of the atmosphere at a particular place and time is called _____ .

2. A(n) _____ forms when an air mass remains over the same area, called the source region, for days or weeks.

3. A(n) _____ is the natural forces at work within Earth's interior or atmosphere that can result in a serious threat to the life and health of people and other organisms in the area.

4. A scientific investigation carried out with the goal of solving a scientific question is called a(n) _____ .

5. _____ is the process by which material is either laid on the ground or sinks to the bottom of a body of water.

Skill Review

Directions: Answer the following questions.

1. When ocean waves move sand from the north end of a beach to the south end, what process is occurring most?

A. mechanical weathering

B. chemical weathering

C. wind erosion

D. water erosion

2. Acidic rain falling on a limestone headstone and dissolving the limestone by releasing calcium and bicarbonate into water. Which process is occuring here?

A. mechanical weathering

B. chemical weathering

C. wind erosion

D. water erosion

Directions: Use the illustration to answer questions 3 and 4.

3. Would a hurricane originating in the Gulf of Mexico likely hit the west coast of Africa? Why or why not?

4. Identify the oceans in which hurricanes do not form. Explain why this is the case.

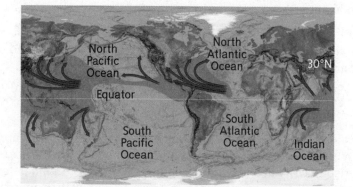

Interactions Between Earth's Systems

Skill Practice

Directions: Use the passage to answer questions 1 and 2.

When a river goes around a bend, the river tends to erode the outside curve more than the inside curve. Because of this, a river that contains a slight bend can actually create a small lake that ends up cut off from the river. The small lake that is formed is called an oxbow lake because its U shape resembles the shape of an oxbow. In the illustration, the four steps in the formation of an oxbow lake are not arranged in order.

1. In what order should the drawings be placed to show how a lake might develop from a slight bend in a river?

   A. A, C, B, D

   B. C, B, A, D

   C. B, A, C, D

   D. C, A, B, D

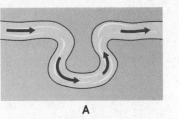

A

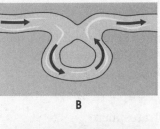

B

2. Explain how fish might have come to be living in the lake in D. Can the fish ever get back to the river?

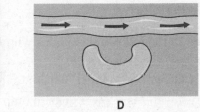

C

D

Directions: Answer the following questions.

3. Water vapor is invisible to the unaided eye. Which type of moisture in the air is water vapor?

   A. fog

   B. mist

   C. clouds

   D. moist air

4. Compare and contrast thunderstorms, tornadoes, and hurricanes.

5. Write whether each of the following is most likely caused by wind erosion, water erosion, or erosion from gravity.

   A. Large boulders that tumble down the slope of a hill or cliff _____

   B. Sand dunes that move and change location in the desert _____

   C. A deep canyon cut into a rocky landscape in the southwestern United States.

   _____

   D. A flood-plain area that has the top soil layer removed during heavy rains

   _____

6. Which technique used by a farmer is not related directly to preventing erosion?

   A. Planting trees as windbreaks

   B. Terracing

   C. Contour plowing around a hill

   D. Planting more seeds than are needed

7. How does wind abrasion make rocks smoother?

8. Explain what causes dunes to move over time.

9. How might the sediment at the bottom of a stream indicate the speed of the water that deposited it?

Directions: Answer the following questions.

1. Which of the following gases is present in the greatest concentration in the Earth's atmosphere?

   A. carbon dioxide

   B. nitrogen

   C. oxygen

   D. ozone

2. In which layer of the atmosphere would you expect to find electrically charged particles?

   A. exosphere

   B. mesosphere

   C. stratosphere

   D. thermosphere

3. Which of the following explains why freshwater can float on top of seawater?

   A. freshwater is a higher density than seawater

   B. freshwater is a lower density than seawater

   C. freshwater is a higher temperature than seawater

   D. freshwater is a lower temperature than seawater

4. Which of the following is the main cause of wave formation in oceans?

   A. the moon

   B. the Sun

   C. tides

   D. wind

5. What are the two layers in Earth's structure in which particles can flow past one another?

   A. lower mantle, outer core

   B. lower mantle, inner core

   C. upper mantle, outer core

   D. upper mantle, inner core

6. Which type of rock is most likely to contain the fossils of dead organisms?

   A. igneous

   B. metamorphic

   C. sedimentary

   D. magma

7. What natural resource provides us with oxygen and energy to live?

   A. atmosphere

   B. coal

   C. green plants

   D. water

8. Which fossil fuel is most easily obtained and the most commonly used energy source?

   A. biomass

   B. coal

   C. natural gas

   D. petroleum

9. Which of the following explains why the Atlantic Ocean is continually getting wider over time?

   A. convergent boundaries

   B. divergent boundaries

   C. transform boundaries

   D. continental boundaries

10. Under which of the following conditions does a cold front form?

    A. warm, less dense air moves over colder air

    B. cold air mass displaces a warm air mass

    C. warm air mass overrides a cold air mass

    D. increase in humidity and decrease in temperature

11. Which of the following is an example of chemical weathering?

    A. ice formation during low temperature

    B. pressure due to sedimentary layers

    C. the formation of rust on an iron gate

    D. water running through a streambed

12. What would be the consequence if all dust, ash, and salt crystals were removed from the atmosphere?

13. Compare the two types of currents that cause movement of water in the ocean.

14. Order the events that occur in the formation of sedimentary rocks as bedrock is exposed to wind and rain.

   A. weathering, transportation (erosion), deposition, lithification

   B. deposition, weathering, transportation (erosion), lithification.

   C. lithification, transportation (erosion), weathering, deposition

   D. transportation (erosion), weathering, lithification, deposition

15. What is the cause of acid rain and what is one consequence to ecosystems?

16. What is a likely outcome if a fast moving thunderstorm off the coast of the Island of St. Lucia, located in the Caribbean Sea, if the storm heads northwest right into another thunderstorm further north and off the coast of the Turks and Caicos Islands, which lie to the east of Cuba? Explain your answer.

Directions: Read the passage and answer questions 17 and 18.

Climate change can involve global warming, which is a slow rise in Earth's average temperatures. This may not seem like something to worry about, but if left unchecked, this process could negatively affect Earth's organisms, including humans. Rising temperatures speed up the melting of glaciers and ice caps. This, in turn, causes the sea level to rise and increases submergence of low-lying areas.

In addition, changing precipitation patterns caused by climate change might cause severe droughts or floods. Both droughts and floods could result in the loss of lives and property. Climate change could also alter ecosystems as species unable to survive warmer temperatures die or migrate to cooler climates.

17. An increase in the amount of greenhouse gases in the atmosphere increases Earth's temperature. According to the passage, how might greenhouse gases affect animals that live in arctic regions?

18. How might a climate change in Earth's polar regions affect the entire planet?

   A. It will cause a rise in sea level and could destroy many land areas.

   B. It will increase the concentration of greenhouse gases in the atmosphere.

   C. It will cause an increase in temperature in other regions close to the equator.

   D. It will decrease the temperature of ocean waters and may kill some marine life.

Directions: Use the diagram to answer questions 19–20.

Ocean Water Temperatures

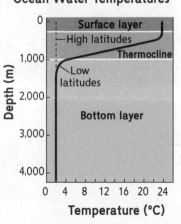

19. In which region of the ocean is there the greatest variability in temperature?

   A. bottom layer

   B. ocean floor

   C. surface layer

   D. thermocline

20. What might account for the near freezing temperatures of the ocean's bottom layer?

Directions: Use the graph to answer questions 21–23.

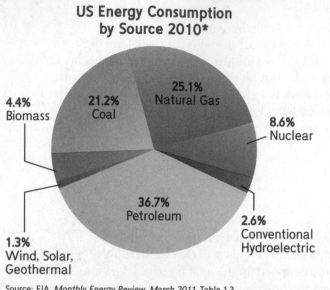

US Energy Consumption by Source 2010*

25.1% Natural Gas

21.2% Coal

4.4% Biomass

8.6% Nuclear

36.7% Petroleum

2.6% Conventional Hydroelectric

1.3% Wind, Solar, Geothermal

Source: EIA, *Monthly Energy Review, March 2011*, Table 1.3 Primary Energy Consumption by source (Quadrillion BTU), 7, *Does not add to 100 due to rounding.

21. Which resource is the most used renewable energy source in the United States?

A. biomass

B. natural gas

C. petroleum

D. solar energy

22. Which non-renewable energy source is likely the cause for the most pollution on Earth?

A. biomass

B. coal

C. nuclear

D. petroleum

23. Why is solar energy used so infrequently when it is such a readily available source of renewable energy on Earth?

Directions: Use the graph to answer questions 24 and 25.

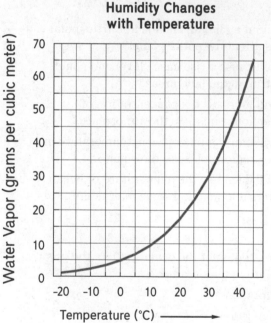

Humidity Changes with Temperature

Water Vapor (grams per cubic meter)

Temperature (°C)

24. How much more water vapor can the air hold at 40°C as compared to 25°C?

A. $10 \frac{g}{m^3}$

B. $25 \frac{g}{m^3}$

C. $40 \frac{g}{m^3}$

D. $50 \frac{g}{m^3}$

25. Explain how the amount of water vapor in the air changes with temperature.

Check Your Understanding

On the following chart, circle the number of any item you answered incorrectly. Next to each group of item numbers, you will see the pages you can review to learn how to answer the items correctly.

Lesson	Item Number(s)	Review Page(s)
8.1: The Atmosphere	1, 2, 12, 17, 18	288–293
8.2: The Oceans	3, 4, 13, 19, 20	296–301
8.3: Earth's Structure, Composition, and Landforms	5, 6, 14	304–309
8.4: Earth Resources	7, 8, 15, 21, 22, 23	312–317
8.5: Interactions Between Earth's Systems	9, 11, 16, 24, 25	320–325

The Effects of Climate Change

Core Practices

- Understand and apply scientific models, theories, and processes
- Identify possible sources of error and alter the design of an investigation to correct that error

Question

How might a change in climate affect Earth's water cycle?

Background Concepts

Water as solid, liquid, and gas is in continuous movement on, above, and below the surface of Earth through the water cycle. The movement of water on Earth is affected by climate changes. Among the most serious and environmental issues confronting Earth today are the potential changes to Earth's water cycle as a result of climate change. There is evidence that Earth's climate is undergoing changes in response to an increase in greenhouse gases and environmental pollution, causing changes in the atmosphere that alter Earth's response to radiation from the Sun. Scientists agree that these changes may profoundly affect the concentration of water vapor in the atmosphere, the formation of clouds, precipitation patterns, and freshwater runoff patterns. For example, as the temperature of the lower atmosphere on Earth becomes warmer, there is an increase in the rate of evaporation from oceans and freshwater sources. This increases the water vapor in the atmosphere, leading to more intense precipitation and storms over land areas.

Hypothesis

A hypothesis is an explanation based on available evidence. It is a starting point for a scientific investigation that will be confirmed, revised, or shown to be incorrect based on more evidence gathered. Develop a hypothesis about the effect of climate on precipitation and the water cycle.

Investigation

Once you have formed your hypothesis, you will want to test it. To explore the water cycle and the effects of changing climate conditions further, design and build a model to simulate essential elements of the water cycle on Earth. When designing a model to observe the water cycle, you need to make sure it is a closed system, so that evaporated water stays in. Use the materials and the procedure below to create your system.

MATERIALS

Clear plastic shoe box with cover (or aquarium if available)

Plastic dish such as a Petri dish or plastic bowl

Modeling clay

2–3 lamps, with a 100 watt or higher bulb; use a heat lamp if available

Water

Blue food coloring

Crushed ice pieces

PROCEDURE

1. Shape a mountain out of modeling clay. Make your mountain about 2 inches shorter than the height of the shoebox. Place the clay mountain in the shoe box, off to one side. Be sure that the sloped side faces the center of the shoe box.

2. Fill the bottom of the shoe box with enough water to cover about $\frac{1}{4}$ of the "mountain" slope. Add 3–4 drops of blue food coloring to the water. This is your "ocean."

3. Place the lid on top of the shoebox.

4. Place the plastic dish on top of the shoebox above the "mountain." Place the crushed ice in the dish.

5. Position one lamp over the "ocean," and turn it on.

6. To better see the circulation of water through the system, add some smoke to the shoebox. To add smoke, light 2 matches and blow them out. Partially open the lid to the box, quickly drop the smoking matches into the water and close the lid.

7. Once you have recorded observations of your system, add a second lamp to the area over the ocean. Record observations. You can add a third lamp if it is available.

Collect and Analyze Data

Observe any movement of water that you see happening inside the box and make note of it. Determine where there is condensation, evaporation, and precipitation if observed. Also note any elements of the water cycle that are not represented in your closed system. Compare your observations when one lamp is positioned over the "ocean" as compared to two or three lamps. Compare what you observe in your closed system to how water circulates on our planet.

Determine how accurate a representation your model is, and make note of any possible sources of error or ways to improve the system. Also observe any changes to the "land" areas in your system. Research the topic of the water cycle and climate change to gather information on the changes in precipitation that are observed due to an increase in average global temperature.

Interpretation

Summarize the data collected and interpret the evidence to determine if your hypothesis is supported. Use a table to record your observations.

When evaluating and interpreting the information or data you collected, ask yourself these questions:

- Where in the system did you observe condensation? Where did you observe evaporation? Where did you observe precipitation?

- What processes of the water cycle are not represented in this system? How could you represent these processes in your system?

- What are some possible errors in this system? How could you alter the design to make the experiment better?

Results

Discuss your results using evidence to support your conclusions. Discuss any observations about the information you gathered from reliable sources, possible sources of error, unexpected results, and any remaining questions. If your hypothesis was not supported, discuss your recommendations for formulating a new hypothesis or changes you would make to the investigation.

Consider these questions as you discuss your results:

- What happened when more lamps were added to the system? How did this change affect the precipitation in the system?

- Why might scientists use models to study how changes in climate affect the water system?

- How might changes in precipitation affect human activity on Earth?

Chapter 9

The Cosmos

Mankind has studied the universe for thousands of years. Early astronomers studied the stars and Galileo discovered that all planets revolve around the Sun. Over the centuries, astronomers, astrophysicists, and other scientists have come to understand more and more about the Earth and its relation to our solar system, the galaxy, and the universe.

NASA/JPL-Caltech/Cornell University and University of Leiden

Lesson 9.1
Structures in the Universe

The structure of our universe is massive and it includes billions of stars, solar systems, and galaxies. It can be organized in a hierarchical arrangement of least complex to most complex. In this lesson, you will learn about theories that have been formed to explain how the universe began. You will also learn about the different types of stars and galaxies that populate our universe.

Lesson 9.2
Structures in the Solar System

Our solar system is just one of many in the vast universe. Our own solar system includes the Sun, eight planets, many moons, asteroids, comets, and stars. All of the planets in our solar system revolve around the Sun, and moons revolve around a specific planet. In this lesson, you will learn about the different characteristics of the planets and other structures in our solar system. You will also learn how scientists can determine the age of Earth and different structures found on our planet.

Goal Setting

Use a K-W-L-H Chart like the one shown at right and located on page 448 to help you track what you know and what to learn about the solar system. Before you read this chapter, write down some things that you know about Earth, the moon, the solar system and the universe in the first column of the chart. Next, write down some questions that you would like to find the answers to in the second column. As you read, fill in the third column with information that you have learned. Finally, think of ways that you can learn more about each topic that interests you.

What I Know	What I Want to Know	What I Learned	How Can I Learn More

LESSON OBJECTIVES

- Describe the hierarchical structure of the universe
- Summarize evidence in support of the Big Bang theory
- Compare the structures of different types of galaxies

CORE SKILLS & PRACTICES

- Identify the Strengths and Weaknesses of One or More Experimental Designs
- Analyze Structures

Key Terms

constellations
recognizable patterns formed by groups of stars in the night sky

galaxy
a large group of stars, dust, and gases held together by gravity

stars
hot, glowing balls of gas that generate their own light

universe
everything that exists throughout space

Vocabulary

estimate
an approximate calculation

structure
an object with form, composition, or arrangement

Key Concept

The universe is billions of years old and contains stars, solar systems, galaxies, and all the matter that exists within them.

The Universe

The **universe** consists of everything that exists throughout space including the solar system, stars, galaxies, and all matter and energy. The universe is massive—so massive that it stretches beyond our comprehension of everything we know. Let's begin by examining some of the objects that make up the universe.

Structures in the Universe

A **structure** is an object with a characteristic form, composition, or arrangement. As such, the structures of the universe include the solar system, stars, galaxies, and everything contained within them. Earth, for example, is part of a solar system that includes the Sun, the planets, moons, comets, and other objects that move in a path around the Sun. The solar system is one of many solar systems found in the Milky Way galaxy and throughout other galaxies. Likewise, the Milky Way galaxy is one of billions of galaxies in the universe. Galaxies often occur in groups called clusters and in even larger groups called superclusters. Superclusters form first by matter spreading throughout the expanding universe and then by gravity pulling the matter together into clumps and strands. Areas dense with matter are called filaments. Filaments form thin threadlike structures through space and are the largest structures in the universe.

Comparison of Structures in the Universe

Structure	Diameter (km)
Earth	12,742
Sun	1,391,000
Earth's Solar System	11,827,040,000
Milky Way Galaxy	1,000,000,000,000,000,000

Robert Llewellyn/Corbis

The Big Bang Theory

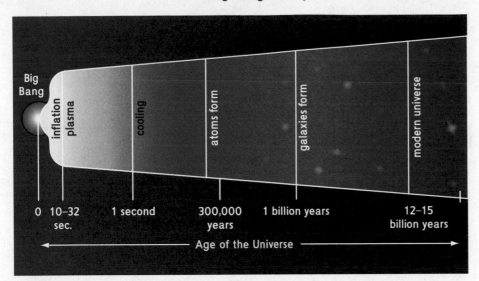

Analyze Structures

Reread the text under the heading *Structures in the Universe* and note how the author arranges the information. This arrangement is a type of structure that follows a certain pattern. In your own words, describe this pattern and explain how it helped you better understand the information presented in the text. Then identify a different type of text structure used in this lesson and compare the two approaches.

Big Bang Theory

The Big Bang theory states that the universe began from a dense speck of energy and matter, smaller than a grain of sand. This tiny point rapidly expanded due to extremely high pressure and temperatures. It is a misconception that the universe actually exploded into existence. The Big Bang is more accurately described as a rapid expansion. As the expansion continued, the universe cooled to a temperature of about 2.7 K (–270°C), a temperature it still is today. Earth is now part of this vast, much cooler cosmos. Many questions about the Big Bang are still left unanswered, and some of them may never be answered. No one really knows why the universe expanded and what existed before the Big Bang. The theory does, however, fit well with scientific observations.

Radiation

One piece of evidence supporting the Big Bang is the existence of radiation. Through scientific investigation, scientists have concluded that the original, extremely hot and dense speck of matter and energy would have emitted a lot of radiation, which is now spread throughout the universe. In 1965, scientists discovered the radiation when they detected weak background noise while using a radio antenna. The noise was due to cosmic background radiation, or low-level radiation from space. The radiation corresponded to a temperature of about 2.7 K (–270°C), which closely matched the temperature of the universe today as predicted by the Big Bang theory.

Universe Expansion

Another piece of evidence comes from the American astronomer Edwin Hubble. Through his observations, Hubble concluded that the universe was expanding because all galaxies were moving away from Earth. Hubble discovered that the farther away a galaxy was, the faster it moved away. According to Hubble, this evidence showed that the universe was once squeezed together and is now expanding. These conclusions raised more questions. For example, if the universe is expanding, what is it expanding from? If scientists traced the expanding universe back in time, it goes back to a single point. The existence of this single point corresponded to the beginning of the universe and led to the formation of the Big Bang theory.

Structures in the Universe

Identify the Strengths and Weaknesses of One or More Experimental Designs

Astronomers have developed methods to **estimate,** or give an approximate value for, the number of stars in the sky. Research and test one method for estimating star numbers. Then evaluate how well that method worked. What are the strengths and weaknesses of the method you chose? How could you revise the method to improve your estimation?

Our Aging Universe

Astronomers have used different methods to estimate the age of the universe. One estimate is based on the mass of the oldest known stars. This star mass-based estimate places the universe between 11 and 18 billion years old. Another estimate is based on the expansion rate and cosmic radiation levels. According to this estimate, the universe is about 13.7 billion years old. In comparison, humans have lived on Earth for less than 100,000 years.

Think about Science

Directions: Answer the following questions.

1. Look back at the diagram of the Big Bang. Why does the diagram become wider over time?

2. A scale model shows the relative proportions of an object as it appears in real life. Examples include scale airplane models and scale train sets. Look at the table on page 336 that shows the diameters of different structures in the universe. Could you build a scale model that includes all these structures? Why or why not?

The Stars

Stars are most visible on clear nights, far from the lights of a city or town. From the scientific perspective, **stars** are hot, glowing balls of gases that generate their own light.

Stars can be classified into groups according to their mass, luminosity (energy output in terms of light), temperature, age, and diameter. The Hertzsprung-Russell diagram (H-R diagram) is a graph that shows the relationships among different groups of stars. Luminosity is plotted along the vertical axis of the graph, and star-surface temperature is plotted along the horizontal axis.

Notice the diagonal pattern of stars that runs from the top left to the bottom right of the diagram. This is the main sequence. Stars spend most of their lifetime as main-sequence stars. As more hydrogen is converted to helium, stars change into one of the other types of stars shown. The Sun is located in the middle of the main sequence. It is an average star in terms of brightness and temperature.

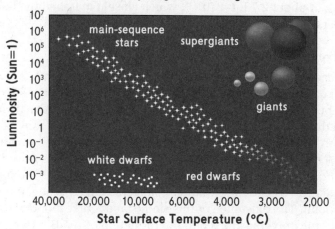

Hertzsprung-Russell Diagram

Birth of a Star

All stars, including average stars and massive stars, begin as a cloud of gas and dust called a nebula. The nebula's gravity causes the cloud of dust and gas to contract and collapse on itself. At the same time, the rotation of the cloud causes it to form the shape of a disk. The hot, glowing center of condensed dust and gas is called a protostar.

Eventually the hot protostar becomes dense enough and hot enough for fusion to take place. Fusion occurs when two or more nuclei collide to form a heavier nuclei. In a star's core, or center, helium is the product of the fusion of hydrogen nuclei. The helium that forms has a mass that is less than the mass of the combined hydrogen nuclei. This means that the mass lost during the fusion of hydrogen to helium is converted to energy—a tremendous amount of energy. The process of fusion powers the Sun and all stars and produces the heat and light that generate from stars.

Once the protostar begins to give off light and heat, it has become a stable star. The star's life cycle from this point on is determined by its mass.

Life Cycle of a Star

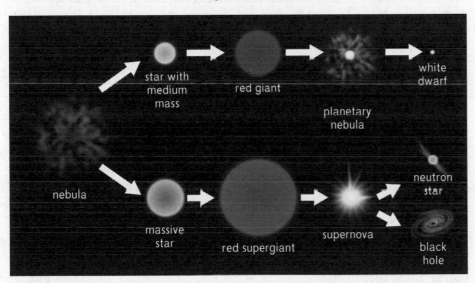

Death of a Star

A star with medium mass such as the Sun continues to fuse hydrogen into helium for the first few billion years of its life. As the star ages, it uses up its supply of hydrogen. Now the star's core is mostly helium, and it begins to shrink while its outer shell expands, cools, and turns red. The star is now considered a red giant.

Red Giant

A red giant is relatively cool on its surface but continues to get hotter in its helium core until the helium atoms fuse into carbon atoms, and the star begins to die. Then, the surface gases blow away, forming a planetary nebula, and only the hot core is left. This tiny, dense star, with its matter packed tightly together, is called a white dwarf. It finally dies when all its energy has been burned up. Most likely, this will happen to the Sun in about five billion years.

Supernovas

A massive star may not lose enough mass to become a white dwarf and thus becomes a red giant or a larger supergiant as it ages. However, after it runs out of hydrogen and fuses helium atoms into carbon, its massive core is so hot that the carbon atoms fuse into iron. This iron core absorbs energy until it collapses. The entire outer portion of the star explodes, causing a supernova. A supernova explosion can light up the sky more brightly than the Sun for a short period of time.

A supernova explosion produces heavy elements such as silver, gold, and lead. These elements and gases from the star blow into space and create a new nebula, out of which another star may eventually form, along with new planets.

Black Holes

When a large star dies during a supernova explosion, what happens to leftover materials from the core? If stars are one and a half to four times larger than the Sun, they will become neutron stars. A neutron star is only about 20 km in diameter, but it is extremely dense.

Stars with masses greater than 20 times that of the Sun are too massive to form neutron stars. Instead the core of a very massive star that has exploded will collapse on itself forever. This continuous collapsing compacts the core of the star into an increasingly smaller volume. The extremely dense object that remains is called a black hole. The gravitational force of a black hole is so strong that not even light can escape.

Constellations

Groups of recognizable star patterns, such as animals, common objects, or mythical characters, are called **constellations.** Ursa Major is a familiar constellation; it contains the Big Dipper. Other familiar constellations include Orion the Hunter and Leo the Lion. Most of the star constellations were first identified by the ancient Greeks. Today scientists recognize 88 constellations. The stars in constellations may appear close together from our point of view on Earth, but the stars in most constellations are separated by vast distances.

Think about Science

Directions: Answer the following questions.

1. Number the steps in star formation in correct sequence.

   _____ Temperatures in the core become high enough for fusion to begin.

   _____ The nebula becomes compressed because of gravitational forces.

   _____ A protostar begins to give off heat and light.

   _____ A cloud of dust and gas forms.

2. The core of a massive star collapsing on itself forms a(n) _____ .

3. As stars age, they use up their supplies of _____ .

4. Ursa Major is an example of a(n) _____ .

| Spiral Galaxy | Elliptical Galaxy | Irregular Galaxy |

Types of Galaxies

A **galaxy** is a large group of stars, dust, and gases held together by gravity. Galaxies have different sizes and shapes. A dwarf galaxy might contain a few million stars, whereas a giant galaxy might contain more than a trillion stars. Earth and our solar system is part of the Milky Way galaxy, which contains nearly 100 billion stars. Galaxies are often named according to their shape. The most common types of galaxies known at this time are spiral, elliptical, and irregular.

Spiral Galaxies

Most galaxies are spiral galaxies, including our own, the Milky Way. Spiral galaxies have long arms that extend outward and bend around a large central bulge. The arms form a flattened disk-like shape. The galaxy's central bulge contains mostly older stars. Younger stars, along with dust and gases, are contained in the spiral arms.

Elliptical Galaxies

Smooth, regularly shaped galaxies without spiral arms are called elliptical galaxies. These galaxies are tightly packed groups of stars that contain relatively little dust or gas. Elliptical galaxies are more three-dimensional in shape than are spiral galaxies. Elliptical galaxies are typically shaped like spheres or footballs. They have bright centers and contain mainly old stars. Elliptical galaxies and the stars within them are generally older than spiral galaxies. This is why they have relatively little dust and gas—most of this matter has been used up in star formation. The sizes of elliptical galaxies vary greatly.

Irregular Galaxies

Galaxies that are not spiral or elliptical are called irregular galaxies. As the name suggests, irregular galaxies do not have normal, uniform, or symmetrical shapes. They are generally the youngest galaxies. They are irregular shaped because there has not been enough time for gravitational forces to form spiral or elliptical galaxies.

Think about Science

Directions: Answer the following questions.

1. What do all galaxies have in common?

   A. same shape   C. same contents

   B. same age   D. same number of stars

Vocabulary Review

Directions: Write the missing term in the blank.

constellation	estimate	galaxy
star	structure	universe

1. You and everything around you are part of the _____ .

2. Astronomers use different methods to _____ the total number of stars in the night sky.

3. A filament is the largest _____ in the universe.

4. The Sun is the _____ that provides Earth with heat and light.

5. A(n) _____ is smaller than a galactic cluster but larger than a star.

6. The Big Dipper is part of the _____ Ursa Major.

Skill Review

Directions: Answer the following questions.

1. Which statement best summarizes the relationship between luminosity and temperature for main-sequence stars in the H-R diagram?

  A. As luminosity decreases, temperature decreases.

  B. As luminosity increases, temperature decreases.

  C. As luminosity decreases, temperature remains the same.

  D. As luminosity holds steady, temperature increases.

2. While researching galaxies, a student comes across information about a newly discovered galaxy. The information states that the galaxy contains a mixture of about 100 billion new stars and old stars. The student can find no other information about this galaxy and decides to classify it as irregular. Is the student correct?

  A. No, because spiral galaxies contain mixtures of new stars and old stars.

  B. No, because irregular galaxies contain mainly old stars and little dust or gas.

  C. Yes, because irregular galaxies contain approximately 100 billion stars.

  D. Yes, because irregular galaxies are called irregular because of their mix of star ages.

Directions: Use the passage to answer questions 3 and 4.

One of the strangest objects in the universe is known as a black hole. A black hole is believed to be the very dense remains of a large star that, due to gravitational force, has collapsed to a fraction of its previous size. The gravitational field of a black hole is so strong that even light cannot escape.

A black hole is surrounded by a spherical boundary called a horizon. Light can enter the horizon but can never escape. Therefore a black hole appears totally black, its outer radius extending to its horizon.

3. What can you infer from this passage?

  A. Light is destroyed when it enters a black hole.

  B. Black holes are bigger than the stars from which they formed.

  C. Light can not escape the gravitational field of a black hole.

  D. Black holes are relatively rare throughout the universe.

4. If black holes appear totally dark, how might astronomers locate them?

Skill Practice

Directions: Answer the following questions.

1. A star is no longer contracting. What can you infer about the star?

   A. It is dying and will soon explode.

   B. It has consumed all its hydrogen.

   C. It has just begun nuclear fusion.

   D. It is no longer generating energy.

2. Research additional evidence either in support of or against the Big Bang theory. Evaluate the theory based on the evidence in this lesson and the additional evidence you find.

3. Some power plants use nuclear power to generate electricity. The process involves fission, or the splitting of heavy atoms into lighter atoms. Stars also generate energy by nuclear power. They use fusion, which involves combining light nuclei into heavier nuclei. Infer why fusion is not used as an energy source on Earth.

4. When discussing the origin of the universe, a student explains that the Big Bang theory is called the "Big Bang" because the universe began with a big explosion in space. What would you say to the student?

5. Look back at the table on page 336 that compares the sizes of structures in the universe. Astronomers often use units other than kilometers to describe some of these structures. For example, the diameter of the Milky Way galaxy is often given as 100,000 light-years. One light-year is equal to about 10 trillion kilometers. Why do you think astronomers use units other than kilometers to describe certain structures in the universe?

6. Compare the life cycle of a star with medium mass to a star with high mass. Use a graphic organizer to summarize how the life cycles of the two stars differ.

Directions: Use the passage below to answer questions 7–8.

1) For centuries scientists investigated the night sky. They began by studying the moon, Sun, and the planets. The Greeks watched the stars and saw patterns, or constellations, among the stars. Over time, the stars in constellations such as the Big Dipper appeared to spread out. The stars were moving away from each other; the universe was increasing in size.

2) Scientists have observed that the universe is still expanding and cooling. Recent research suggests that it is expanding at an accelerated rate rather than the constant rate associated with the Big Bang theory. No one knows if this expansion will continue. Scientists have developed three models of what may happen eventually. No one is sure which, if any, of these models is correct. Scientists can only estimate the changes that will occur to the universe.

3) • **Open universe** – An open universe has no limits. It will continue to expand forever.

4) • **Flat universe** – At some point in the future, a flat universe will reach a certain size and then remain at that size.

5) • **Closed universe** – It is suggested that at some future time, a closed universe will begin to contract and eventually collapse to its original state as a small, dense, hot mass.

7. Scientists jokingly use the phrase "the big crunch" to refer to one of the models of the universe. Which paragraph suggests the possibility of a "crunched" universe?

   A. Paragraph 2

   B. Paragraph 3

   C. Paragraph 4

   D. Paragraph 5

8. Which definition best matches the use of the word **estimate** in paragraph 2?

   A. an unquestioned fact

   B. an accurate calculation

   C. a statement of certainty

   D. an approximate prediction

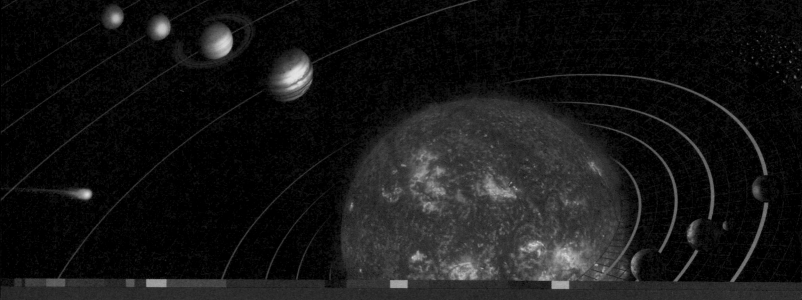

LESSON OBJECTIVES

- Identify and compare structures within Earth's solar system
- Explain how scientists determine the age of Earth

CORE SKILLS & PRACTICES

- Cite Specific Textual Evidence to Support a Finding or Conclusion
- Use Ratio and Rate Reasoning

Key Terms

planetesimals
solid particles that form the building blocks of planets

solar system
the Sun, planets, and objects that orbit it

Vocabulary

asteroids
small bodies that orbit the Sun

comets
small bodies left over from the solar system formation

construct
to create something by organizing ideas or objects

relative dating
determining the age of events by comparing to others

satellites
objects that orbit larger objects

Key Concept

Earth is part of the solar system and interacts with other parts of the solar system.

Earth's Solar System

Our **solar system** has a gaseous Sun at its center. Four gaseous planets, four terrestrial planets, many moons, and other small objects such as asteroids and comets, orbit around our central Sun. The orbital paths are shaped like a slightly squashed circle, or ellipse. Astronomers believe our solar system first formed from huge clouds of gas and dust called nebulas.

Nebulas

In the previous lesson, you read that all stars begin as nebulas. Nebulas exist in vast regions of space between the stars and consist mainly of hydrogen and helium gas. When a nebula condenses, its gravitational force becomes stronger. This causes the nebula to collapse inward toward its center and become much denser. If the nebula is rotating, it will spin faster as it collapses to resemble a flattened, rotating disk. Eventually the dense concentration of gas at the center of this rotating disk becomes a star. When nebulas begin to condense and form stars, they are called planetary nebulas. The nebula that formed into our own solar system is called the solar nebula.

Planets and Moons

As the solar nebula collapsed, tiny grains of condensed matter began to stick together as they collided. These solid particles, called **planetesimals,** formed the building blocks of planets. These planetesimals continued to grow in size, collide, and join together. Eventually they formed the planets of the solar system. A planet is a nearly round object in space that orbits a star. Many planets also have natural **satellites,** or moons that orbit them.

The Inner Planets: Terrestrial

Astronomers believe the Sun's strong gravity may have pulled in the gases surrounding the inner planets as they formed. Heavier elements, such as iron and nickel, were left behind. These elements and others eventually combined to form rocky and dense planets. These inner, or terrestrial, planets, in order from closest to farthest from the Sun, are Mercury, Venus, Earth, and Mars.

Planet	Distance from Sun (AU)	Orbital Period (Earth Days)	Period of Rotation (Earth Days)	Mass (kg)	Diameter (km)	Average Temperature (°C)
Mercury	0.39	87.96	58.7	3.3×10^{23}	4,878	167
Venus	0.723	224.68	243	4.87×10^{24}	12,104	464
Earth	1	365.26	1	5.98×10^{24}	12,756	15
Mars	1.524	686.98	1.026	6.42×10^{23}	6,787	−65

Mercury is the closest planet to the Sun and is the smallest of all the planets. It has no moons and is only about one-third the size of Earth. Mercury rotates very slowly on its axis. As a result, one day on Mercury, or Mercury's period of rotation, is 59 Earth days long.

Venus is the hottest planet in the solar system. It is so hot that liquid water cannot exist on its surface. In contrast to Earth's clouds, which are made of water vapor, Venus's thick clouds are made of sulfuric acid.

Earth is the third planet from the Sun and the fifth largest in the solar system. It is the only planet known to support life.

Mars is the fourth planet from the Sun, and it is sometimes called the red planet. This is because its soil has a high iron content that gives it a reddish color. The composition of Mars's atmosphere is similar to that of Venus. Yet the density and pressure of Mars's atmosphere is much less than that of Venus. Although there is no liquid water on the surface of Mars today, there is evidence that liquid water was present in the past.

The Outer Planets: Gas Giants

The planets that formed in the outer solar system had gravities strong enough to attract the gases, dust, and the planetesimals surrounding them. As a result, they grew into large planets called gas giants. These planets do not have solid surfaces and are larger than the terrestrial planets. The interiors of the gas giants are made up of either gas or liquid.

The gas giants include the planets Jupiter, Saturn, Uranus, and Neptune. All the gas-giant planets have rings made of icy particles. Because these planets make up the outer solar system, they are farthest from the Sun and thus are very cold planets. Many of the planets have moons orbiting them, and Jupiter has more moons than any other planet—63 have been discovered so far.

Jupiter, the fifth planet from the Sun, is by far the largest of the planets. Gaseous Jupiter is more than 300 times more massive than solid Earth. Jupiter has a very short period of rotation—its day is only ten Earth hours long.

Saturn is the second largest planet in the solar system. It has the largest and most visible ring system. Like Jupiter, Saturn rotates very quickly. Because Saturn spins so rapidly, the winds at its equator are extremely strong, causing violent storms.

CALCULATOR SKILL

Solving Equations

Mercury rotates on its axis every 58.7 Earth days. Write an equation in which × = the number of times Mercury rotates on its axis. Use your equation to calculate how many times Mercury rotates in one Earth year. Solve the equation and show your work.

Cite Specific Textual Evidence to Support a Finding or Conclusion

Citing textual evidence is a way to clarify or support an idea or conclusion. When you are asked to cite evidence from a passage or text, find the specific information that supports the idea or conclusion.

Reread the section about Pluto. Cite textual evidence that supports the conclusion that Pluto was reclassified due to its small size.

WORKPLACE SKILL

Schedule and Coordinate

A standard system of time zones was established in 1884. The prime meridian, an invisible line that runs through Greenwich, England, was selected as 0 degrees longitude. The rest of the world is divided into 24 time zones, each separated by one hour.

A supervisor is managing a project involving three remote employees, one on the West Coast of the United States and two on the East Coast. What would be the best East-Coast times for the East Coast employees to call the West Coast employees during their normal workday (8 am to 5 p.m.)?

While Uranus is much smaller than Jupiter or Saturn, it is four times larger than Earth and contains almost 15 times more mass. The rotational axis of Uranus is tilted almost 90 degrees making its axis almost parallel to the plane of the solar system and so it looks like it is lying on its side. Neptune and Uranus are sometimes called the twin giants because of their similar colors, sizes, masses, and temperatures. Neptune's atmosphere is similar to that of Uranus. It contains mainly hydrogen and helium, with a small amount of methane.

Pluto

Pluto was discovered in 1930 and was originally classified as the ninth planet from the Sun. However, it could not be classified as a gas giant, because of its composition and small size, nor could it be considered a terrestrial planet because of its low density and, again, its small size. So, in 2006, Pluto was reclassified as a dwarf planet.

Asteroids and Comets

Asteroids are small, rocky bodies that orbit the Sun. Most asteroids orbit the Sun in a wide area between Jupiter and Mars. This area is called the asteroid belt. It is thought that asteroids are pieces of planetesimals left over from the time when the solar system formed. A fragment of an asteroid or any material that falls from space toward Earth and enters Earth's atmosphere is called a meteoroid. When a meteoroid enters Earth's atmosphere, it burns up and produces a streak of light. This light is visible from Earth and is called a meteor. If the meteor does not completely burn up, the remaining part hits Earth and is then called a meteorite.

Comets are also leftovers from the formation of the solar system. They are small bodies made of ice and rock. On average, comets range in size from one to ten km in diameter. Occasionally they are larger. When Earth intersects with a comet's orbit, particles from the comet burn up when they enter Earth's upper atmosphere, producing a meteor shower. People often describe these burning particles as falling or shooting stars.

Think about Science

Directions: Answer the following questions.

1. Which characteristic applies to all eight planets in our solar system?
   A. Layers of gas and liquid
   B. Rocky surface and molten core
   C. One or more moons
   D. Elliptical orbit

2. Which inference logically follows the fact that nebulas are mostly made up of hydrogen and helium?
   A. All the helium in our solar system will eventually condense.
   B. Hydrogen and helium are the primary gases that make up the Sun.
   C. The atmospheres of all planets must be made mostly of helium.
   D. Hydrogen and helium gases are found only on the gaseous planets.

Earth's Movement and the Moon

As the Earth spins on its axis and orbits the Sun, we experience day and night, the seasons, and other natural events. Earth makes one revolution around the Sun every 365.25 days (one year). It rotates on its axis every 23 hours and 56 minutes (one day). The extra 0.25 days from each revolution are collected every four years into a leap day on February 29. Earth's axis is an imaginary line that travels from the North Pole to the South Pole. The axis is tilted 23.5 degrees and points in the same direction throughout Earth's journey around the Sun. As a result, at one point in its orbit, Earth's northern hemisphere tilts toward the Sun. Then, six months later, the northern hemisphere tilts away from the Sun. Earth's tilt and its orbital motion around the Sun create the seasons.

The Moon has only a little over 1 percent of Earth's mass and has only one-sixth of Earth's gravity. Its diameter is about one-quarter of Earth's diameter. In fact, fifty Moons could fit inside Earth. The Moon's periods of orbit and rotation are both 27 days, 7 hours, and 43 minutes. The Moon rotates exactly one time each time it travels around Earth. As a result, as the Moon orbits Earth, the same side is always facing our planet.

The Earth, Moon, and Tides

The gravitational force of the Moon is the primary driving force that causes tides. As the Moon travels around Earth, its gravity pulls at the side of the Earth that is closest to it, causing the water to "bulge." This bulge is called high tide. This gravitational pull repeats in a daily cycle as Earth rotates on its axis.

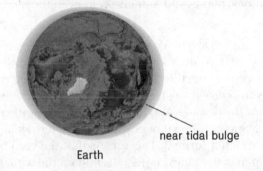

near tidal bulge

Earth

Moon

Lunar and Solar Eclipses

A solar eclipse occurs when the Moon passes directly between the Earth and the Sun. Though the Sun is much larger than the Moon, the apparent sizes of the Moon and the Sun as viewed from Earth are similar. For this reason, during a total solar eclipse, the Moon can completely block the Sun. The only light visible during a total solar eclipse comes from the dimly lit outer gaseous layers of the Sun called the corona. When a solar eclipse happens, the Moon casts a shadow on Earth that is made up of an inner and outer region. People who witness a solar eclipse from the inner region of the Moon's shadow see a total solar eclipse, while people who witness the event from the outer region see only a partial solar eclipse.

A lunar eclipse occurs when the Moon, Earth, and Sun are in a line. The Moon does not produce its own light. It appears to glow only because it reflects some of the sunlight that strikes it. When Earth's shadow blocks that sunlight, the Moon experiences a lunar eclipse and becomes almost dark. A lunar eclipse occurs one to two times per year and is much more common than a total solar eclipse.

Sometimes test items provide
information that is not
necessary for completing
the item.

Read the passage below.
Then, identify the information
that is not needed to answer
the question at the end of the
passage.

Asteroids are rocky bodies
that orbit the Sun. They
range in size from a few
kilometers to about 1,000
km in diameter. When
asteroids break up, the
fragments fall from space
and can enter Earth's
atmosphere as meteoroids.
When a meteoroid does
not completely burn up,
small fragments hit Earth's
surface and are called
meteorites. How would
you compare meteoroids
and meteorites?

Think about Science

Directions: Fill in the blank.

1. The seasons are caused by _____ on its axis and its
   movement around the Sun.

2. The _____ are primarily the result of the Moon's
   gravitational pull on Earth.

3. A(n) _____ results when the Moon lines up between
   Earth and the Sun.

Earth's Age

Scientists have determined that the Earth formed about 4.6 billion years
ago and has experienced considerable changes since then. Scientists have
constructed, or made, a geologic time scale to organize Earth's long history.
The geologic time scale is divided into segments of time that are designated
as eons, eras, periods, and epochs.

Relative Dating

Scientists learn about Earth's past by studying rocks and fossils. They
also apply other knowledge, including studies of weather and climate,
earthquakes and volcanoes, plants and animals, and even the atoms that
make up matter.

The walls of the Grand Canyon are made of distinct rock layers of mostly
sedimentary rock that were deposited long before the Colorado River began
flowing. Rock layers often become tilted or bent over time. They rarely
remain horizontal, as is the case at the Grand Canyon. It is possible to
determine which layer of the Grand Canyon is the oldest. Scientists conclude
that in an undisturbed sequence of sedimentary rock, each rock layer lies
just above the layer on which it formed. This means that the very bottom
layer of the Grand Canyon is the oldest layer. Moving up the wall, the layers
become younger.

When describing rocks as *older* and *younger,* the concept of relative dating
is being used. **Relative dating** means dating by comparing two objects.
Relative dating does not tell the numeric age of a rock layer, only that it is
older or younger than layers around it.

Relative dating applies not only to rocks, but to fossils as well. Remember
that fossils, are deposited at the same time that the surrounding sediment
was deposited. This means that the fossils are the same age as the
sedimentary rock that surrounds them. In a pile of undisturbed layers of
rocks, the fossils in the lower layers are older than the fossils in the upper
layers. Scientists discovered that the stacked layers of rock contain a unique
sequence of fossils from the bottom to the top.

Useful fossils for relative dating are abundant and easy to recognize. They
are also found over large regions, but are constrained to short periods of
time. These fossils can serve as index fossils and are used by scientists to
date the rock layers in which the fossils occur. An index fossil that lies in
a rock layer beneath a different index fossil means that lower index fossil
is older. Recording the sequence of fossils in the rock record enabled
geologists to construct the relative geologic time scale.

When scientists find rock layers that are geographically separated, but contain the same index fossil, they know that those layers were deposited at the same time. Scientists call this matching of fossils in rock layers time correlation. By comparing rock sequences from widely separated areas, scientists have unraveled and documented the history of the earth

Absolute Dating

To determine the numerical age of a layer of rock or a fossil, scientists must rely on absolute or numerical dating. Numerical dating is the process of establishing the age of an object by determining the number of years it has existed.

One way to determine the absolute age of a fossil is by measuring the amount of radioactive carbon it contains. Carbon is a very common element in living things. One type of carbon is called carbon-14 and is not as stable as other types. Atoms of carbon-14 slowly decay, or break apart, by radiating particles from their nuclei. Once an organism dies, it no longer takes in radioactive carbon-14 atoms. After 5,730 years, an organism's remains contain only half of its original supply of carbon-14. This time span is called the half-life of carbon-14. The half-life is the time it takes for half of a radioactive sample to decay. In numerical dating, the half-life of carbon-14 is used to determine a fossil's age.

This type of dating is called radiocarbon dating, which is a type of radiometric dating. Radiometric dating methods are those that measure the half-lives of decaying elements to determine the absolute age of a sample. Although radiocarbon dating is useful, it has some limits. A sample of carbon-14 decays almost entirely in about 60,000 years. Because of this, it is not useful for dating fossils older than 60,000 years. It is also not useful for dating objects that do not contain carbon. To date Earth's oldest fossils and rocks, scientists must use radioisotopes of elements with longer half-lives. For example, potassium-40 has a half-life of 1.26 billion years. Scientists have used these isotopes to date rocks that are over three billion years old.

Other numerical-dating methods rely on data that is easier to observe. The age of a tree can be determined by counting the rings in its wood. Trees grow more during the summer than during any other season. Wider rings indicate a good growing season and an agreeable climate. In this way, tree rings also serve as records of Earth's climate.

Think about Science

Directions: Answer the following questions.

1. What is the difference between numerical dating and relative dating?

CORE SKILL

Use Ratio and Rate Reasoning

The table below shows the rate of decay of carbon-14. Provide information that would go on a row of data added at the bottom of the table.

Half-Life of Carbon-14

Age	Half-Lives	Percent of Remaining Carbon-14, Compared to the Original Supply
0	0	100%
5,730 years	1	50%
11,460 years	2	25%
17,190 years	3	12.5%
22,920 years	4	6.25%
28,650 years	5	3.125%

Vocabulary Review

Directions: Write the missing term in the blank.

construct   comets   satellite
planetesimals   relative dating   solar system

1. Scientists _____ models to help them visualize the solar system.

2. Small bodies of ice and rock called _____ are left over from the formation of the solar system.

3. Our moon is an example of a natural _____ .

4. Scientists use _____ to compare the ages of different rocks.

5. Our _____ is made up of the Sun and the planets and other bodies that travel around it.

6. _____ are solid particles that form the building blocks of planets.

Skill Review

Directions: Use the passage to answer questions 1 and 2.

In 1992, another small Pluto-like body was discovered in the far reaches of the solar system, as were several hundred more within the next few years. In August 2006, the International Astronomical Union voted to change the definition of a planet. According to the new definition, for an object to be classified as a planet, it must (1) orbit the Sun, (2) be large enough so that its gravity pulls it into a nearly round shape, and (3) be dominant enough in its orbit to clear away other objects. To be considered a dwarf planet, an object must meet two of the criteria of a planet: (1) orbit the Sun and (2) have a nearly round shape.

1. Which criteria is the determining factor in Pluto's reclassification as a dwarf planet instead of a planet?

   A. A planet revolves around the Sun following an elliptical orbit.

   B. A planet is massive enough to clear other objects from its orbit.

   C. A planet's gravity causes its shape to be nearly round.

   D. A planet has a molten core and at least one moon.

2. Based on the passage, what can you infer is the cause of a planet's shape?

   A. the Sun's orbit

   B. the Sun's gravity

   C. the planet's gravity

   D. the planet's orbit

Directions: Answer the following questions.

3. Which phrase describes what you see when you view a lunar eclipse?

   A. Earth's shadow blocking sunlight from hitting the Moon

   B. The Moon blocking our view of the Sun

   C. The Moon's shadow blocking sunlight from hitting Earth

   D. The Sun blocking our view of the Moon

4. What would be one result if Moon's gravity increased?

   A. High tides would be more frequent.

   B. High tides would be higher.

   C. High tides would be less frequent.

   D. High tides would be lower.

Skill Practice

Directions: Use the passage to answer questions 1 and 2.

Scientists have a hypothesis about how the solar nebula began its collapse. They believe that a disturbance, possibly from a nearby supernova, sent shock waves through the nebula. These shock waves caused much of the gas and dust in the nebula to be pushed toward the center of the nebula. As the nebula compressed, the gravitational forces overcame the internal pressure of the nebula's hot gases and collapsed. This resulted in a spinning pancake shape of hot gas with a bulge in the middle. The dense, hot center portion would become the Sun. The heavy, rocky material pulled in strongly by gravity stayed near the central bulge. This heavy material would become the inner planets. The lighter elements, mainly hydrogen, stayed near the outer edge and would become the outer planets.

1. According to the passage, what does the proposed hypothesis for the formation of the solar system try to explain?
   A. Why inner planets are made of heavy elements and outer planets are gaseous
   B. Why inner planets are gaseous and outer planets are made of heavy elements
   C. Why outer planets have only a few moons and inner planets have many moons
   D. Why outer planets have many moons and inner planets have only a few moons

2. What made it possible for the solar nebula to collapse?
   A. Gas pressure overcoming gravity
   B. Gravity overcoming gas pressure
   C. Gas pressure overcoming electrical force
   D. Nuclear force overcoming gas pressure

Directions: Answer the following questions.

3. Which statement about Earth's tilt on its axis is true?
   A. Earth's tilt decreases during the spring.
   B. Earth's tilt increases during the winter.
   C. Earth's tilt stays the same as it orbits the Sun.
   D. Earth's tilt changes only during summer and winter.

4. Which of the following best summarizes a comparison between the time span of human history to that of geologic time?
   A. Human history makes up most of geologic time.
   B. Human history makes up about half of geologic time.
   C. Human history makes up only a fraction of geologic time.
   D. Human history makes up about a quarter of geologic time.

5. A new solar body, Object X, is discovered orbiting the Sun in the area between Saturn and Jupiter. The object has an elliptical orbit, contains no other objects in its orbit, and is roughly triangular in shape. How would scientists most likely classify Object X? Explain your answer.

6. Earth's axis is tilted at a 23.5-degree angle from vertical. Predict how conditions on Earth would change if that angle increased to 30 degrees. Provide a rationale for your prediction.

7. The half-life of carbon-14 is 5,730 years. What can be concluded about the carbon-14 content of a fossilized organism that is approximately 22,000 years old?

Directions: Answer the following questions.

1. Which force is essential for the formation of a supercluster such as the Milky Way?

   A. centrifugal

   B. electromagnetic

   C. friction

   D. gravity

2. Which of the following supports the Big Bang theory?

   A. collisions and temperature

   B. radiation and energy

   C. radiation and expansion

   D. collisions and expansion

3. What are astronomers able to estimate based on the mass of the oldest known star?

   A. the age of the universe

   B. the shape of the star

   C. the rate of expansion

   D. the beginning of life

4. What chemical conversion takes place as a star transforms from a main-sequence star to another type of star?

   A. helium → hydrogen

   B. hydrogen → helium

   C. helium → oxygen

   D. oxygen → hydrogen

5. Which of the following is a characteristic common to both spiral and elliptical galaxies?

   A. the oldest stars are at the center

   B. they are flattened and disk-like

   C. the oldest stars are at the outer edge

   D. they both contain large amounts of dust

6. Which of the following best explains how our solar system formed?

   A. the solar nebula condensed to form stars and planets

   B. the solar nebula expanded to form stars and planets

   C. meteoroids collided to form rocky planets and gaseous stars

   D. a decrease in gravitational force led to formation of many planets and stars

7. What do the four planets closest to the Sun have in common?

   A. They are all gaseous planets.

   B. They are all rocky and dense.

   C. They are all orbited by a moon.

   D. They are all about the same temperature.

8. Which of the following describes the rotation of Jupiter and Saturn around their axes?

   A. They rotate in the opposite direction from Earth.

   B. They both rotate more slowly than Earth.

   C. They both rotate much more quickly than Earth.

   D. They both follow an elliptical rotation pattern.

9. What movement of the planet Earth determines the length of one year?

   A. rotation around its axis

   B. tilt of Earth on its axis

   C. rotation around the Sun

   D. revolution around the Sun

10. What is the cause of the ocean's high tide on Earth?

    A. rotation of Earth on its own axis

    B. revolution of earth around the Sun

    C. strong gravitational force causes the water to "bulge"

    D. weak gravitational force causes water level to rise

11. Stars can be organized in a Hertzsprung-Russell diagram according to which properties?

    A. size and color

    B. distance from Earth

    C. surface temperature and luminosity

    D. age and surface temperature

12. Why does a black hole appear to have an absence of light?

    A. As the star exploded, forming a black hole, the light energy traveled through space.

    B. The gravitational force of a black hole is so strong that light cannot escape.

    C. They are located so far away from the Sun that no light reflects off black holes.

    D. There is an absence of burning hydrogen gas, so no light is produced.

13. How do you think the Sun would appear from Earth if Earth left its orbit and traveled about 4 light years away from the Sun? Explain you answer.

14. Explain why astronomers can sometimes find traces of gold and silver in space.

15. How can scientists use the Grand Canyon to determine the relative age of rock layers?

16. If a fossil is found in a layer of rock, how can the absolute date of the fossil be determined without any other available information?

Directions: Read the passage and answer questions 17–19.

One piece of evidence supporting the Big Bang is the existence of radiation. Through scientific investigation, scientists have concluded that the original, extremely hot and dense speck of matter and energy would have emitted a lot of radiation, which is still spread throughout the universe. In 1965, scientists discovered such radiation when they detected weak background noise while using a radio antenna. The noise was due to low-level radiation from space. The radiation corresponded to a temperature of about 2.7 K (-270°C), which closely matches the temperature of the universe today as predicted by the Big Bang theory.

Another piece of evidence comes from the American astronomer Edwin Hubble. Through his observations, Hubble concluded that the universe was expanding because all galaxies were moving away from Earth. Hubble discovered that the farther away a galaxy was, the faster it moved away. According to Hubble, this evidence showed that the universe was once squeezed together and is now expanding. These conclusions raised more questions. For example, if the universe is expanding, what is it expanding from? If scientists traced the expanding universe back in time, it goes back to a single point. The existence of this single point corresponds to the beginning of the universe and led to the formation of the Big Bang theory.

17 What evidence did Hubble find in support of the Big Bang theory?

A. There is radiation in space.

B. The universe is continually expanding.

C. The universe is continually shrinking.

D. There are tiny energy particles scattered in space.

18. How does the temperature of the universe today support the Big Bang theory?

19. How did Hubble's work support the idea that the universe began as a small speck of matter and energy?

A. Hubble detected radiation from a single point in space.

B. Hubble found evidence of an explosion many light years away.

C. Scientists can trace the expanding universe back to a single point.

D. The Hubble telescope detected a small piece of matter with a large amount of energy.

Directions: Use the passage to answer questions 20–23.

As the Earth spins on its axis and orbits the Sun, we experience day and night, the seasons, and other natural events. Earth makes one revolution around the Sun every 365.25 days (one year). It rotates on its axis every 23 hours and 56 minutes (one day). The extra 0.25 days from each revolution are collected every four years into a leap day on February 29. Earth's axis is an imaginary line that travels from the North Pole to the South Pole. The axis is tilted 23.5 degrees and points in the same direction throughout Earth's journey around the Sun. As a result, at one point in its orbit, Earth's northern hemisphere tilts toward the Sun. Then, six months later, the northern hemisphere tilts away from the Sun. Earth's tilt and its orbital motion around the Sun create the seasons.

The Moon has only a little over 1 percent of Earth's mass and has only one-sixth of Earth's gravity. Its diameter is about one-quarter of Earth's diameter. In fact, fifty Moons could fit inside Earth. The Moon's periods of orbit and rotation are both 27 days, 7 hours, and 43 minutes. The Moon rotates exactly one time each time it travels around Earth.

20. How does the motion of Earth contribute to the seasonal changes experienced over most of the Earth?

21. If the moon rotates on its axis only once for every time it revolves around Earth, what can you determine about how much of the moon we can see from Earth?

22. If gravitational force pulls objects toward a body, and the weight of an object is dependent on its mass and the gravitational force, according to the passage, why would we weigh less on the moon than on Earth?

23. Regions of Earth experience seasonal climate changes because of the _____ of Earth's _____.

Check Your Understanding

On the following chart, circle the number of any item you answered incorrectly. Next to each group of item numbers, you will see the pages you can review to learn how to answer the items correctly.

Lesson	Item Number(s)	Review Page(s)
9.1: Structures in the Universe	1, 2, 3, 4, 5, 11, 12, 13, 14, 17, 18, 19	336–341
9.2: Structures in the Solar System	6, 7, 8, 9, 10, 15, 16, 20, 21, 22, 23	344–349

Kepler's Laws and Satellite Launch

Core Practices

- Cite specific textual evidence to support a finding or conclusion
- Reason from data or evidence to form a conclusion

Question

How do Kepler's Laws help scientists when launching a satellite?

Background Concepts

In the 1600s, German astronomer Johannes Kepler published three laws of planetary motions. While Kepler's laws are written for planets, they apply to any object in orbit, including the Moon orbiting Earth or a satellite orbiting any body in space.

Kepler's first law of planetary motion states that the orbit of each planet around the Sun follows an elliptical path with the Sun at one focus. An ellipse is a shape that has two foci (plural for focus), which are points within the ellipse that depend on its shape. This means that a planet orbiting around the Sun will be closer to the Sun during parts of its orbit and farther from the Sun during other parts of its orbit.

Kepler's second law of planetary motion states that as a planet moves around its orbit, it sweeps out equal areas in equal amounts of time. This means that the planets speed is not constant. A planet moves faster when it is closer to the Sun than it does when farther away.

The amount of time it takes for a planet to complete one full orbit around the Sun is called a period. Kepler's third law of planetary motion states that the square of the ratio of the orbital periods of two planets is equal to the cube of the ratio of their average distances from the Sun. So, this law relates the orbital period of satellites to their distance from the Sun. A more distant planet has a longer path, and it also travels slower because there is also less gravitational pull from the Sun. Unlike the other two laws, this law compares two orbits.

When a satellite is launched into space to orbit Earth, if it has sufficient speed it falls to Earth at the same rate that Earth curves. Instead of falling to Earth, the satellite stays the same height above Earth and orbits it in an elliptical path, much the same way that Earth orbits the Sun. In fact, astrophysicists use Kepler's laws to launch satellites into space and determine their orbital path and speed. The space telescope Kepler is named after the scientist and orbits Earth in search of habitable planets.

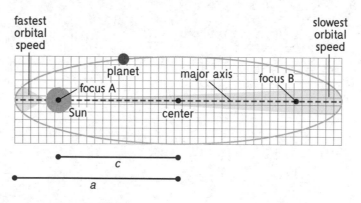

To better understand Kepler's laws, see the Smithsonian National Air and Space Museum and NASA websites.

Hypothesis

A hypothesis is an explanation based on what evidence is available. It is a starting point for a scientific investigation that will be confirmed, revised, or shown to be incorrect based on more evidence gathered. Develop a hypothesis that explains how Kepler's laws might be used when launching a satellite into orbit around a planet in our solar system. Site specific textual evidence from the background information in your hypothesis.

Investigation

After developing a hypothesis, the next step is to gather information and data to determine whether your hypothesis is supported or not. To better understand how Kepler's laws of orbital motion are used when launching satellites, answer the following question:

- What calculations about the expected orbit of a satellite would be needed before a satellite is launched?

Collect and Analyze Data

Gather information from various reliable websites about how satellites are launched into orbit and how their orbital path is calculated.

Construct a two-column table to record the information you gather. Label the first column "Kepler's Laws" and list each of the three laws there. Label the second column "My Hypothesis" and include how you think the law is used when launching satellites. Label the third column "How Law Is Used" and include information you have collected about how the law applies to an orbiting satellite and its launch. Be sure to cite specific evidence gathered from websites.

Interpretation

Summarize the data collected and interpret it to determine if your hypothesis is supported. Since Kepler's laws apply to planets and satellites, you can use information you gathered to better understand how satellites are set in motion to orbit Earth and other planets. Use specific evidence gathered from websites and the data calculated for known planetary orbits to predict how satellites are sent out to orbit bodies in space. When evaluating and interpreting the information or data you collected, ask yourself these questions:

- How does an object's distance from the body it orbits affect its orbital shape and period?
- What information did you find about how the speed of an orbit affects a satellite's launch?
- What other information did you find about launching satellites?
- Did the information you find support your hypothesis? Do you need to revise your hypothesis based on information and data gathered? Explain your reasoning.

Results

Discuss your results, citing evidence to support your conclusions. Discuss the information you gathered from reliable sources about satellite launches and how they are dependent on Kepler's laws. If your hypothesis was not supported by the information you gathered, discuss your recommendations for formulating a new hypothesis or changes you would make to the investigation.

Consider these questions as you discuss your results:

- What information can you cite to support the claim that Kepler's laws help scientists to determine launch paths of satellites into space?
- What are some potential problems that scientists may encounter when launching a satellite into orbit?
- How can the data about a planet's orbital shape and period help scientists launch satellites into orbit?

Directions: Use the diagram to answer questions 1 and 2.

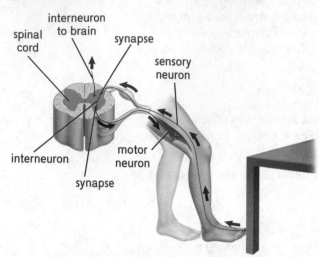

1. According to the diagram, what part of the nervous system sends a message to your spinal cord if you stub your toe?

   A. brain
   B. synapse
   C. motor neuron
   D. sensory neuron

2. According to this diagram, what do motor neurons do?

Directions: Fill in the blank with the word that best fits.

artery   capillary   vein

3. If you cut yourself, and blood flows slowly, you have most likely injured a(n) _____.
   A(n) _____ is a microscopic vessel that connects larger vessels. If an accident victim is losing blood so rapidly a tourniquet is needed, a(n) _____ has likely been damaged.

Directions: Chose the best answer for each question.

4. Diabetes is a condition in which glucose from digested food builds up in the bloodstream. Cells need glucose, but glucose cannot enter cells without insulin to move the glucose from the bloodstream into cells. Once glucose enters cells, the blood sugar levels drop. Which of the following explains what might happen to homeostasis in the body if the pancreas were damaged or diseased?

   A. Insulin may not be released and the positive feedback mechanism controlling blood glucose levels would be affected.
   B. Glucose would not be processed properly in the pancreas and too much glucose in the body would be harmful or fatal.
   C. The release of insulin would be affected and the negative feedback mechanism controlling blood glucose levels would be disrupted.
   D. Damage to the pancreas would not affect the blood glucose levels of the body. They would continue to rise and fall based on the type of food ingested.

5. The hypothalamus responds to both internal and external stimuli. Based on this information, which of the following best explains what causes your body to know when to stop eating?

   A. Stress arising from a full stomach
   B. Olfactory stimuli, such as food aromas
   C. Blood-borne stimuli, including insulin and glucose levels
   D. Neurally transmitted information arising from the stomach

6. Which of the following types of fats would probably have the most health benefits?

   A. fats found in beef
   B. fats found in seeds
   C. fats found in margarine
   D. fats found processed cookies

7. Which of the following is NOT a way that an infectious disease can spread?

   A. rubbing eyes
   B. improper nutrition
   C. sharing eating utensils
   D. cleaning cat litter boxes

8. Ermines often live in underground burrows. They have dark brown fur in the summer, but white fur in the winter. In which type of land biome would you most likely find ermines?

   A. taiga
   B. tundra
   C. tropical rain forest
   D. temperate rain forest

9. Which biome covers most of Earth's surface?

   A. desert biome
   B. marine biome
   C. grassland biome
   D. freshwater biome

Directions: Use the diagram to answer questions 10 and 11.

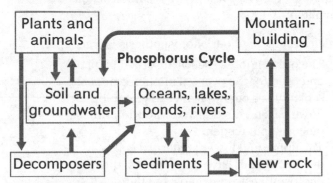

Phosphorus Cycle

10. According to the diagram, when an animal dies, what could happen to the phosphorous in its body?

    A. Decomposers return the phosphorous from the animal's body to the soil and groundwater.
    B. The phosphorous in the animal's body forms new rock, which helps in mountain building.
    C. The phosphorous moves directly from the dead organism to oceans, lakes, ponds, and rivers.
    D. Decomposers return the phosphorous from the animal's body to sediments that form new rock.

11. In lakes, excess phosphorous is a pollutant. According to the diagram, what is the most direct way that excess phosphorous enters lakes?

    A. From new rock
    B. From dead leaves
    C. From groundwater
    D. From animal waste

Directions: Chose the best answer for the following questions.

12. What effect could the removal of a top predator, such as a wolf, have on the carrying capacity of an ecosystem?

    A. The carrying capacity of food of prey populations, such as grasses, will increase.
    B. Many new top predators will move into the area, decreasing the carrying capacity for top predators.
    C. The carrying capacity of populations that wolves had preyed upon, such as rabbits, will increase temporarily.
    D. The carrying capacity of animals that were preyed on by wolves will increase as these animals become top predators.

13. Oak trees produce acorns (seeds) in great numbers every other year. What is one explanation for this?

14. Some ecosystems rely on naturally occurring fires to regulate growth, but some ecosystems in the American southwest endure too many fires, which upsets the natural cycles. For example, some invasive species, which are highly flammable grow rapidly after fires in these regions. Which of the following is likely to be a consequence of this growth?

    A. decreased fire frequency
    B. decreased growth of nonnative weeds
    C. increased production of animal homes
    D. increased destruction of native species

Directions: Fill in the blank with the word that best fits.

   biodiversity   carbon dioxide
   extinction   parasites

15. While global temperatures have changed naturally during the history of the Earth, most scientists agree that the release of _____ into the atmosphere from the burning of fossil fuels contributes to this rise in temperature. Sea levels have risen as polar ice caps melt. Animals, such as polar bears, that depend on the arctic ice are likely to become in danger of _____ as their habitats melt away. Some species, especially _____, may be able to expand their ranges, but overall _____ will decrease.

Directions: Answer the following questions about spontaneous generation.

16. Explain how Francisco Redi used controls in his experiment and what his results indicated about spontaneous generation.

17. What did Pasteur do that Redi didn't, which helped prove spontaneous generation did not occur?

   A. After no microorganisms appeared in the broth, Pasteur put cheesecloth over the opening to keep maggots out.

   B. Pasteur knew that if microorganisms could live in the air, they could live in other nonliving matter, which proved spontaneous generation.

   C. After no microorganisms grew in the broth, Pasteur then allowed air to reach the broth, which allowed microorganisms to grow in the broth.

   D. Pasteur tilted his flasks so that air reached the broth, and still no microorganisms grew in the broth, which proved that spontaneous generation did not occur.

Directions: Fill in the blank with the word that best fits.

   cytoplasm   endoplasmic reticulum
   nucleus   organelles   ribosomes

18. Cells are like small machines. Just as a machine has many parts that work together, a cell needs _____ to carry out the cell processes. The _____ is the central organelle that contains the genetic material in the form of deoxyribonucleic acid (DNA). The _____ surrounds the nucleus. All other organelles are found in the cytoplasm. It is a jellylike substance made of water, amino acids, carbohydrates, fats, and nucleic acids. _____ are organelles in which amino acids assemble to form proteins according to instructions in DNA. The cell contains a system of membranes and sacs known as the _____. The endoplasmic reticulum acts like a highway along which molecules can move from one part of the cell to another.

   Golgi apparatus   lysosomes
   mitochondria   vacuoles

19. In the cell's cytoplasm, the _____ modifies and packages proteins for use in the cell or for transport. Cells also have energy generators called _____, which convert energy stored in organic molecules into compounds the cell can use. _____ are small organelles filled with enzymes that digest organic molecules such as carbohydrates, lipids, and proteins. Many cells have saclike organelles called _____ that store materials for the cell.

Directions: Answer the following questions.

20. Even though vascular plants often have woody structures, they can wilt in dry weather. Why is this likely?

21. Which statement about photosynthesis is true?

   A. The green light we see is absorbed by plants and used for the process of photosynthesis.

   B. A plant uses energy from sunlight to break down carbon dioxide and water to produce glucose and oxygen.

   C. The upper and lower epidermal cells in a leaf do not have chloroplasts, thus photosynthesis mostly occurs there.

   D. In hot, dry weather, plants close their stomata to lessen water evaporation from leaves. Once the CO_2 in plant leaves reaches a low level, they begin the process of photosynthesis.

Directions: Use the diagram to answer questions 22 and 23.

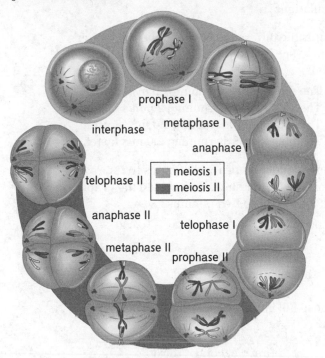

prophase I

interphase

metaphase I

anaphase I

telophase II

meiosis I
meiosis II

anaphase II

telophase I

metaphase II

prophase II

22. Why does sexual reproduction involve the nucleus dividing twice, instead of once like other cells do?

A. Cells copy their chromosomes before they divide. During sexual reproduction cells copy their chromosomes twice, so they need to divide twice.

B. The nucleus of the cell divides during mitosis. But in sexual reproduction, the nucleus divides twice so it will have half the number of chromosomes.

C. A sperm cell combines with an egg cell during sexual reproduction to form a single cell. In one cell division, the daughter cells would have twice the number of chromosomes.

D. A sperm cell combines with an egg cell during sexual reproduction. It needs to divide twice in order to make one complete copy of its chromosomes. If it divided once, it would not make a complete copy.

23. According to the diagram, what happens during prophase I?

A. Homologous chromosomes pair up. Crossing over occurs, and genetic material is exchanged. Spindle fibers form.

B. Spindle fibers shorten and separate homologous chromosomes from each other, moving them to opposite sides of the cell.

C. Spindle fibers break down. Chromosomes uncoil and nuclear envelopes form, creating two nuclei. The cell then divides.

D. Spindle fibers lengthen and attach to chromosome centromeres in the cell. Homologous chromosomes line up at the equator.

Directions: Use the Punnett square diagram to answer questions 24 and 25.

	RA	Ra	rA	ra
RA	RRAA		RrAA	
Ra		RRaa		Rraa
rA	RrAA	RrAa		RA
ra		rrAa		

24. Look at the Punnett square. It shows a dihybrid cross of pea plants. *R* represents the dominant allele for shape (round); *r* represents the recessive allele (wrinkled). *A* represents the dominant allele for color (yellow); *a* represents the recessive allele (green). Complete the rest of the Punnett square.

25. How many combinations of offspring are round and yellow?

A. 1
B. 3
C. 6
D. 9

Directions: Choose the best answer for each question.

26. If organisms in a population pass on a mutation that makes them better able to survive a hot, dry climate, which is **least** likely to happen if the climate becomes cool and wet?

A. Only a few survivors of the species will live in cool, wet climates.

B. The species will evolve over time to better survive in the cool, wet climate.

C. The species will evolve to survive in hot and dry as well as cool and wet climates.

D. A species better suited to the wet climate will outcompete them, and the species with the mutation will die out.

27. One gene in a cell is mutated before replication occurs. This cell then goes through meiosis. How many of the four resulting gametes will have the mutated gene?

A. none of them
B. one of them
C. half of them
D. all of them

28. Which adaptation would be most useful for small birds that live in a shady forest?

A. long claws, useful for capturing fish
B. dark feathers, useful for camouflage
C. a flat beak, useful for scraping rocks
D. long legs, useful for standing in shallow water

Directions: Use the graph to answer questions 29–31.

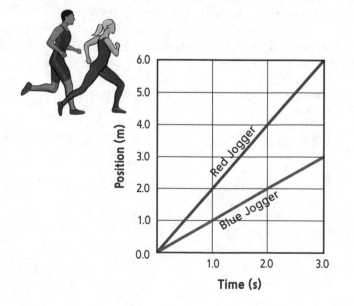

29. Explain how you can use the graph to tell which jogger is running faster without completing any calculations?

30. What is the difference between the red jogger's average speed and the blue jogger's average speed?

A. The red jogger is running 1.0 m/s faster.
B. The blue jogger is running 2.0 m/s faster.
C. The red jogger is running 1.0 m/s slower.
D. The blue jogger is running 2.0 m/s faster.

31. The red jogger stops for 2 minutes to fix a problem with her shoe. How would the graph look during these two minutes?

A. no line
B. a vertical line
C. a horizontal line
D. a line slanting downward

Directions: Fill in the blank with the word that best fits.

first   second   third

32. Newton's _____ law of motion explains why a crash-test dummy hits into the windshield when a car brakes suddenly.

Directions: Choose the best answer for each question.

33. A shopping cart with a mass of 40 kg is pushed with a net force of 8 N. How does its acceleration change if the mass of the shopping cart is increased to 80 kg?

Force = mass × acceleration

$$F = ma$$

A. It decreases from 0.2 m/s^2 to 0.1 m/s^2.
B. It decreases from 2.0 m/s^2 to 1.0 m/s^2.
C. It increases from 5.0 m/s^2 to 10.0 m/s^2.
D. It increases from 0.5 m/s^2 to 5.0 m/s^2.

34. A backhoe does 40,000 J of work to lift a boulder 5.0 m. What force did the backhoe apply to the boulder?

Work = Force × distance

$$W = Fd$$

A. 1,300 N
B. 8,000 N
C. 45,000 N
D. 200,000 N

35. A student hypothesizes that if she runs up a ramp as she pushes a heavy object she will do less work than if she walks up the ramp as she pushes the object. Which procedure should she follow to decide if she needs to revise her hypothesis?

A. She should measure the time it takes her to lift the object by running and by walking.
B. She should measure the force she needs to exert when running and walking.
C. She should measure the distance the object moves when she pushes it up the ramp and when she lifts it vertically.
D. She should measure the speed of the object when the runs and when she walks.

36. A mountain climber lifts a 6.00-kg pack. What is the gravitational potential energy of the pack at 7.00 m above the base of the cliff? Use the equation for gravitational potential energy to answer the question. Remember that g is the acceleration due to gravity, which is 9.8 m/s².

Gravitational Potential Energy =
mass × acceleration due to gravity × height

$$GPE = mgh$$

A. 42.0 J
B. 252 J
C. 412 J
D. 1,340 J

Directions: Fill in the blank with the word that best fits.

radiant   thermal   magnetic   nuclear

37. A hair dryer transforms electrical energy to
_____ energy.

Directions: Use the passage to answer questions 38 and 39.

Most communities are far away from the power plants where their electricity is generated. Once the power plant generates electricity, it can be sent over wires to where it is used. Still, different communities may use different amounts of each energy resource, based on the resources they have available. Power companies in areas where there are mountains with large rivers may be able to generate more of their electricity from hydropower. Power companies in areas with a reliable amount of sunlight year-round are starting to build power plants that produce electricity using solar cells.

However, even renewable energy is not without impacts. Dams built to hold water can affect fish populations and the water supply in rivers and streams below the dam. Solar power plants require a large amount of space, so building them may affect local animal populations. People are continuing to search for a balance between meeting our energy needs and environmental impacts.

38. Which title would best describe the passage?
A. Alternate Energy Resources are the Way of the Future
B. Headache-Free Energy Resources
C. Choosing the Best Resources
D. Turn Away from Fossil Fuels and Look to the Sun

39. Tidal power uses energy associated with high and low ocean tides to produce electricity. Describe conditions where tidal power might be most useful along with obstacles to using tidal power.

Directions: Use the information to answer questions 40 and 41.

A student sets up an investigation by placing in ice cube in each of three containers. The student then places all three containers in a tub of hot water and records the time it takes for each of the ice cubes to melt.

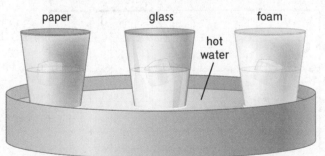

Container	Time for ice to melt (min)
Paper	3.2
Glass	4.1
Foam	9.8

40. What is the independent variable in the investigation?

A. the type of container
B. the time it takes each ice cube to melt
C. the temperature of the water
D. the number of containers

41. Which conclusion is valid based on the data?

A. Ice in a paper container remains solid longer than in the other containers.
B. Foam slows the flow of heat better than the other containers.
C. Hot water cools when containers of ice are placed in it.
D. The temperature of ice in a glass container changes more than ice in other containers.

Directions: Answer the following questions.

42. The chemical formula for glucose is $C_6H_{12}O_6$. What does the number *12* represent?

A. The total number of atoms in a molecule
B. The number of atoms of hydrogen
C. The number of bonds with hydrogen atoms
D. The number of protons in a hydrogen atom

43. When Mendeleev was first developing the periodic table, he predicted the existence of elements that had not yet been discovered. Explain what properties he might have used to make such predictions.

Directions: Use the graph to answer questions 44 and 45.

State Changes of Water

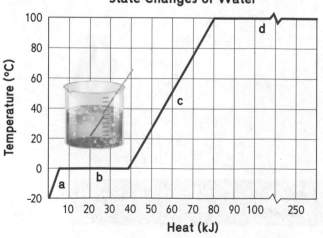

44. Why does temperature remain constant in region **b** of the graph, but increase in region **c**?

45. Which region of the graph represents matter in the solid state?

A. region **a**
B. region **b**
C. region **c**
D. region **d**

Directions: Answer the following questions.

46. A teacher is demonstrating a reaction by dissolving ammonium chloride in water. Which observation would be a clue that indicates an endothermic reaction is occurring?

A. The solution changes color.
B. All of the ammonium chloride dissolves.
C. The container in which the reaction takes place feels cold.
D. Some of the ammonium chloride sinks to the bottom of the container.

47. A student drops a sugar cube in 100 g of water at 30°C, stirs, and measures how long it takes for the sugar to dissolve. The student then crushes a sugar cube and repeats the procedure. What is the independent variable in the investigation?

A. the solute used
B. the temperature of the water
C. the surface area of the solute
D. the time it takes for the solute to dissolve

48. A scientist is investigating pollution and determines that a sample of rainwater is acidic. Which observation might lead the scientist to this conclusion?

A. It has a pH of 4.8.
B. Its volume increases when it is frozen.
C. It can dissolve table salt that is added to it.
D. It can undergo a reaction to form hydrogen and oxygen.

Directions: Use the data table to answer questions 49 and 50.

COMPOSITION OF SEVERAL TYPES OF COAL				
	Lignite	Subbituminous	Bituminous	Anthracite
Carbon, %	37	51	75	86
Hydrogen, %	7	6	5	3
Oxygen, %	48	35	9	4
Moisture, %	43	26	3	2
Nitrogen, %	0.7	1.0	1.5	0.9
Sulfur, %	0.6	0.3	0.9	0.6
Energy Value, (kcal/kg)	3,488	4,784	7,441	7,683

49. One of the elements that makes up coal is directly related to the energy value of coal. Based on the pattern you observe in the chart, which element is most responsible for the energy value of coal?

A. carbon
B. oxygen
C. nitrogen
D. hydrogen

50. For what purpose is the information in the table most likely used?

A. the abundance of each type of coal
B. the selling price of each type of coal
C. the region in which each type of coal is found
D. the estimated total reserves of each type of coal

Directions: Answer the following questions.

51. A student is using two blocks of clay to model the movement of tectonic plates. She pushes the blocks of clay together and observes how they change. What can you conclude about the student's model?

A. She is modeling ridge formation at divergent boundaries.
B. She is modeling earthquake activity at transform boundaries.
C. She is modeling mountain building at convergent boundaries.
D. She is modeling subduction at oceanic-continental boundaries.

52. Design an experiment to investigate the effect of changing ocean temperatures on coral reefs. Describe your procedure, and identify your dependent and independent variables.

Directions: Fill in the blank with the word that best fits.

mesosphere   stratosphere
thermosphere   troposphere

53. The _____ is the layer of Earth's atmosphere that is closest to the surface and contains most of the air that we breathe.

Directions: Use the passage to answer questions 54 and 55.

Hurricanes have high-speed winds that blow circularly around a low-pressure area known as the "eye." The diameter of the area of destructive winds may exceed 240 kilometers, with lesser winds extending out twice that distance. The speed of the circular winds ranges between 119 kilometers per hour (for category 1) to more than 250 kilometers per hour (for category 5). Along with strong winds, hurricanes are characterized by heavy rainfall and violent ocean waves.

Hurricanes move along a curving path at a speed of between 40 and 80 kilometers per hour—a speed much slower than that of their circulating winds. Just north of the equator, hurricanes tend to move in a northwesterly direction. As they move farther north, hurricanes begin to move more directly north or northeasterly.

54. What is one effect of a hurricane?

A. hail damage
B. heavy snows
C. strong winds
D. cold temperatures

55. Suppose a hurricane is 640 km off the east coast of the United States and is headed toward the shore of North Carolina. If a hurricane warning is now issued, about how much preparation time do people have before the hurricane may hit land?

A. between 2 hours and 6 hours
B. between 8 hours and 16 hours
C. between 2 days and 4 days
D. between 5 days and 7 days

Directions: Use the information and the diagram to answer questions 56 and 57.

As far back as 1100 B.C., ancient astronomers drew patterns of stars, called *constellations*, that they believed had special importance. They thought that stars were part of the surface of a large sphere in which Earth stood at the center. They pointed out that the stars in a constellation had the shape of a particular figure or design. *The Big Dipper* and *Orion* are well-known constellations seen in the Northern Hemisphere today.

Perhaps not surprisingly, different cultures have perceived many of the same stars of constellations in different ways. For example, in Greek culture the stars of Orion were seen as a hunter, while many of these same stars were seen in Japanese culture as a set of drums.

As science advanced, astronomers discovered that stars are different distances from Earth. In fact, constellations are formed by stars that are not even near one another. However, all stars in the constellations that we see in the night sky are found in the same galaxy—the Milky Way.

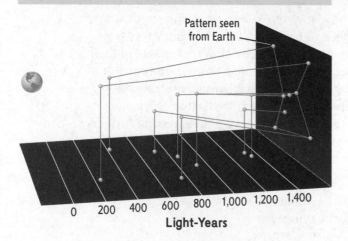

Pattern seen from Earth

0   200   400   600   800   1,000   1,200   1,400
Light-Years

56. Which series ranks the structures discussed in the reading passage from smallest to largest?

A. star, constellation, galaxy
B. constellation, star, galaxy
C. galaxy, star, constellation
D. galaxy, constellation, star

57. The Sun is the closest star to Earth. All other stars are vast distances away. In the group of stars in the constellation Orion, about what distance is the star that is closest to Earth from the star that is farthest from Earth?

A. 250 light-years
B. 500 light-years
C. 1,100 light-years
D. 2,250 light-years

Directions: Choose the best answer for each question.

58. Scientists estimate that Earth is approximately how old?

A. 1.2 million
B. 9.7 million
C. 4.6 billion
D. 13.8 billion

59. A scientist finds a fossil and determines that its carbon-14 content is about 25% of its original supply. Carbon-14 has a half-life of 5,730 years. Approximately how old is the fossil?

A. 2,865 years
B. 5,730 years
C. 11,460 years
D. 17,190 years

60. What would happen if the Moon rotated twice as quickly as it does now?

A. Seasons on Earth would be less extreme.
B. The frequency of lunar eclipses would increase.
C. All sides of the Moon would be visible from Earth.
D. High tides would be higher and low tides would be lower.

61. What factor best explains why Jupiter has more identified moons than any other planet?

A. Jupiter has a ring system.
B. Jupiter is the biggest planet.
C. Jupiter is made mainly of gas.
D. Jupiter is farthest from the Sun.

62. Write an address for yourself starting with your street that uses structures of progressively increasing size to describe your location in the universe.

1. **D** A sensory neuron sends a message to your spinal cord and then onto the brain if you stub your toe. So although the brain and the spinal cord are involved in processing the message it travels from the foot to these areas via sensory neurons.

2. Motor neurons receive messages from the spinal cord, which, in this case, cause the leg muscles to move to react to the pain of stubbing a toe.

3. If you cut yourself, and blood flows slowly, you have most likely injured a [vein]. A [capillary] is a microscopic vessel that connects larger vessels. If an accident victim is losing blood so rapidly a tourniquet is needed, an [artery] has likely been damaged.

4. **C** The pancreas releases the hormone insulin. Insulin is required to maintain the negative feedback mechanism that controls blood glucose levels in the body. If the pancreas does not release insulin, or if it releases insulin uncontrollably, then normal blood glucose levels cannot be maintained and homeostasis is disrupted.

5. **D** You can infer that information transmitted via sensory receptors in the stomach causes the hypothalamus to secrete hormones that make the body no longer feel hungry.

6. **B** The fats in nuts and seeds reduce inflammation and improve cholesterol levels, so these would be a healthy source of fat. Fats found in margarine or cookies are often trans fats, which have been shown to be harmful to people. Saturated fats found in red meat and trans fats found in snack foods contribute to heart disease.

7. **B** While improper nutrition can cause diseases, improper nutrition would not cause a disease that others can catch. Rubbing your eyes, especially after touching doorknobs or other surfaces with viruses; sharing eating utensils, and cleaning litter boxes can all cause the spread of infectious disease.

8. **A** The taiga is most likely to have winter animals with thick fur that burrow underground to stay warm. Although the tundra is very cold, and many animals have a thick coat of fur to keep them warm, the ground is permanently frozen in a tundra biome, and an animal cannot easily burrow underground. Tropical and temperate rain forests have much warmer climates that would make these adaptations unnecessary.

9. **B** About 75 percent of Earth's surface is covered by water, and most of that is saltwater oceans. Marine biomes are those regions covered by salt water. The land biome that covers the most land surface is the taiga biome, not the desert or grassland biome.

10. **A** Plants and animals that die are broken down in nature by decomposers. Decomposers return the phosphorous from the animal's body to the soil and groundwater, and also to oceans, lakes, ponds, and rivers. While the phosphorous may eventually become part of sediment or new rock, it is first releases into soil and water through the process of decomposition.

11. C Most excess phosphorous enters lakes through groundwater runoff of fertilizers, sewage, and industrial wastes. Dead leaves and animal waste are first broken down by decomposers before they contribute phosphorous to lakes, rivers, ponds and oceans.

12. C. Populations that wolves preyed upon, such as rabbits, will increase until they reach some other limiting factor, such as lack of food. A new top predator will likely move into the area eventually, but it would most likely be only one species, not many. However, prey such as rabbits are herbivores and will not become predators in the wolves place.

13. Sample answer: If there are more acorns than are needed to reach the carrying capacity of acorn-eating squirrels, for example, not all of the acorns will be eaten and therefore, some of the acorns will grow into new oaks. Oak trees produce small numbers of acorns one year, to reduce the number of squirrels. The following year, they produce large number of acorns, so there will be excess acorns to grow into oak trees.

14. D The introduction of flammable invasive species can increase the risk of fires and further destroy native growth.

15. While global temperatures have changed naturally during the history of the Earth, most scientists agree that the release of [carbon dioxide] into the atmosphere from the burning of fossil fuels contributes to this rise in temperature. Sea levels have risen as polar ice caps melt. Animals, such as polar bears, that depend on the arctic ice are likely to become in danger of [extinction] as their habitats melt away. Some species, especially [parasites], may be able to expand their ranges, but overall [biodiversity] will decrease.

16. Francesco Redi's experiment tested the hypothesis of spontaneous generation. In his experiment, Redi placed a piece of meat in several jars. In his experiment, some of the jars were open to air and, as a control, some were covered with cheesecloth. All other conditions were kept the same for both types of jar. Redi found that maggots appeared only in the jars that were open to the air and could be entered by flies. This led many to doubt spontaneous generation and Redi is credited with having performed the first controlled scientific experiment.

17. C After no microorganisms grew in the broth, Pasteur then allowed air to reach the broth by tilting the flasks. Microorganisms grew when the broth was exposed to air, which confirmed that microorganisms came from the air, and did not arise from spontaneous generation.

18. Cells are like small machines. Just as a machine has many parts that work together, a cell needs [organelles] to carry out the cell processes. The [nucleus] is the central organelle that contains the genetic material in the form of deoxyribonucleic acid (DNA). The [cytoplasm] surrounds the nucleus. All other organelles are found in the cytoplasm. It is a jellylike substance made of water, amino acids, carbohydrates, fats, and nucleic acids. [Ribosomes] are organelles that use amino acids to assemble proteins according to instructions in DNA. The cell contains a system of membranes and sacs known as the [endoplasmic reticulum]. The endoplasmic reticulum acts like a highway along which molecules can move from one part of the cell to another.

19. In the cell's cytoplasm, the [Golgi apparatus] modifies and packages proteins for use in the cell or for transport. Cells also have energy generators called [mitochondria], which convert energy stored in organic molecules into compounds the cell can use. [Lysosomes] are small organelles filled with enzymes that digest organic molecules such as carbohydrates, lipids, and proteins. Many cells have saclike organelles called [vacuoles] that store materials for the cell.

20. Sample answer: Vascular plants transport water and dissolved minerals through the roots to the rest of the plant. Lignin, a hard substance in xylem, helps give structure to the plant. In dry weather, it is likely the plant does not get enough water, so even though it has a woody structure, the plant wilts from lack of water.

21. B A plant uses energy from sunlight to break down carbon dioxide and water to produce glucose and oxygen. Both water and carbon dioxide are needed for the process of photosynthesis, and glucose is the product formed during photosynthesis. The plant uses glucose as an energy source.

22. C A sperm cell combines with an egg cell during sexual reproduction to form a single cell. In one cell division, the resulting daughter cells would have twice as many chromosomes as a normal cell. To reduce the number of chromosomes to the correct number, the nucleus divides twice during meiosis.

23. A During prophase I, homologous chromosomes pair up. Crossing over occurs, and genetic material is exchanged. Spindle fibers form.

24.

	RA	Ra	rA	ra
RA	RRAA	RRAa	RrAA	RrAa
Ra	RRAa	RRaa	RrAa	Rraa
rA	RrAA	RrAa	rrAA	RA
ra	RrAa	Rraa	rrAa	rraa

25. D There are nine combinations that have the phenotype round yellow, three that are round green, three that are wrinkled yellow, and one that is wrinkled green. The ratio 9:3:3:1 is typical for a dihybrid cross

26. C The least likely possibility is that the species will evolve to survive in both hot and dry and cold and wet climates. A species usually adapts to changing conditions over time, but it will not adapt to survive in all conditions. It is much more likely that only a few members will survive, that the species will adapt to the new climate conditions, or another species may present strong enough competition for food or shelter that the species will die out.

27. C Since the cell undergoes meiosis, it must be a gamete, or sex cell. Therefore, a mutation can be passed on from parent to offspring. Since two sex cells combine during fertilization, and then undergo two divisions during meiosis, half of the daughter cells will carry the mutated gene.

28. B Dark feathers might increase the chance of survival in a shady forest, since dark feathers might make it easier for birds to hide from predators.

29. Sample answer: The slopes of the lines indicate the average speeds of the joggers. The red jogger's slope is greater so she is running at the greater average speed.

30. A The average speed is determined by choosing two points on the line and finding the slope. The red jogger's average speed is 2.0 m/s and the blue jogger's average speed is 1.0 m/s. Therefore, the red jogger is running 1.0 m/s faster.

31. C In a time vs distance graph, if the jogger stops moving, the distance will not change for some period of time. Since distance is plotted on the vertical axis, constant distance is represented by a horizontal line.

32. Newton's [first] law of motion explain why a crash-test dummy hits into the windshield when a car brakes suddenly. According to Newton's first law of motion, an object at rest tends to stay at rest, and an object in motion tends to stay in motion with the same speed and in the same direction, unless an unbalanced force acts on it.

33. A Acceleration equals force divided by mass. The initial acceleration is $8 \text{ N} \div 40 \text{ kg} = 0.2 \text{ m/s}^2$. The final acceleration is $8 \text{ N} \div 80 \text{ kg} = 0.1 \text{ m/s}^2$.

34. B If $W = Fd$, then $F = \frac{W}{d}$.
So $F = \frac{40,000 \text{ J}}{5.0 \text{ m}} = 8000 N$.

35. B To compare the amount of work done in both cases, the student would have to measure the force exerted and the distance over which it is exerted. She would find that the work done is the same in both cases. Running only changes the speed at which work is done.

36. C If $GPE = mgh$, then GPE of the pack is $6.00 \text{ kg} \times 9.8 \text{ m/s}^2 \times 7.00 \text{ m}$, or 412 J.

37. A hair dryer transforms electrical energy to [thermal] energy.

38. C The passage discusses hydroelectric power and solar power in terms of the advantages and disadvantages. The best title would indicate that each source has to be evaluated based on its advantages and disadvantages.

39. Sample answer: Tidal power would be most useful in regions along coastlines. Although the electricity can be transmitted to inland regions, it would be most efficient along the coast. Not every coastline, however, would be suitable for tidal power plants. The conditions would have to make it possible to construct the turbines necessary to convert the energy to a usable form.

40. A The independent variable is the factor that the student changes. In this investigation, the student changes the type of container.

41. B The data show that the time required for all the ice to melt increased from paper to glass to foam. This means that the ice cube melted at the slowest rate in the foam cup, so the foam must have slowed the transfer of heat from the water more than the other containers.

42. B The 12 is a subscript next to the H. H is the chemical symbol for hydrogen and the subscript indicates the number of atoms of hydrogen in one molecule of glucose.

43. Sample answer: The periodic table groups elements together according to their properties. Medeleev arranged the elements in order, but he also arranged them in vertical groups in such as way that properties would repeat after a specific number of groups. That arrangement is now shown as vertical groups. In the current table, elements are arranged in order of atomic number and, ignoring the transition metals, properties repeat every eight groups. Where gaps existed in the table, Mendeleev could predict the properties of an unknown element that could fill that gap in the table.

44. During region **b**, the graph is horizontal. This indicates that energy in the form of heat is being absorbed, but the temperature is not changing. The absorption of heat without an increase in temperature occurs when a substance is changing state. The energy changes the arrangement of molecules. This change of state occurs at 0°C which is the melting, temperature of water, so it must representing melting. In region **c**, the molecules maintain the structure of a liquid. The absorbed energy causes the molecules to move faster, which increases their average kinetic energy. Because average kinetic energy is measured by temperature, the absorbed energy results in an increase in temperature in region **c**.

45. A Region A of the graph represents matter in the solid state because it is the region that is below the melting point.

46. D An endothermic reaction absorbs heat from its surroundings. The loss of heat would make the container in which the reaction occurs feel cold.

47. C The independent variable is the factor being changed. The student changes the surface area of the sugar, which is the solute, by using it whole and then crushing it. The crushed sugar cube will have greater surface area than the whole sugar cube.

48. A An acid is a substance with a pH that is less than 7.0. The other choices are characteristics of water, whether or not it is acidic.

49. A According to the table, as the carbon content of coal increases, its energy value increases.

50. B The information in the table would be used to determine the price of coal according to its energy value. Coal with a low energy value would cost less than coal with a high energy value.

51. C The student is modeling a convergent boundary, wherein two tectonic plates collide. When two tectonic plates push into each other, the boundary where they meet is a convergent boundary. Mountains can form along these boundaries.

52. Answers may vary; sample answer: I would fill two aquariums with saltwater and add corals. I would keep the saltwater in one aquarium at the optimal temperature for corals. I would use a heat lamp to increase the temperature of the saltwater in the second aquarium. I would observe the health of the corals over several days. My dependent variable is the health of the corals; my independent variable is saltwater temperature.

53. The [troposphere] is the layer of Earth's atmosphere that is closest to the surface and contains most of the air that we breathe.

54. C A hurricane is characterized by strong winds, heavy rainfall, and violent ocean waves. Heavy snows and cold temperatures are characteristic of blizzards.

55. B Hurricanes move at speeds of 40 to 80 kilometers per hour. If the hurricane is 640 km off the east coast of the United States, people have about 8 to 16 hours to prepare for the storm (640 km ÷ 80 km/hr = 8 hr; 640 ÷ 40 km/hr = 16 hr).

56. A A star is a single entity. It is smaller than a constellation, which is made up of multiple stars. A constellation is smaller than a galaxy, which is made up of billions of stars.

57. C The closest star to Earth in the constellation Orion is about 250 light-years away. The farthest star is about 1,350 light-years away; 1,350 light-years − 250 light-years = 1,100 light-years.

58. C Scientists estimate that Earth is approximately 4.6 billion years old. The universe may be approximately 13 to 14 billion years old.

59. C If the fossil contains 25% of its original supply of carbon-14, then two half-lives have passed since the organism began decaying; 5,730 years/half-life × 2 half-lives = 11,460 years.

60. C The Moon rotates exactly one time as it revolves around Earth. Because of this, the same side of the Moon always faces Earth. If the Moon rotated more quickly, all sides of the Moon would be visible to an observer on Earth.

61. B Jupiter is the biggest planet and therefore has the strongest gravity. Its strong gravity keeps many moons in orbit around the planet.

62. Sample answer: My address is 10 Oak Street; Cleveland, Ohio; the United States; North America; Earth; the Solar System; the Milky Way Galaxy; the Universe.

Check Your Understanding

On the following chart, circle any items you missed. This helps you determine which areas you need to study the most. If you missed any of the questions go back and review the reference pages.

Item #	Reference	Item #	Reference	Item #	Reference	Item #	Reference
1	p. 18	17	p. 99	33	p. 193	49	p. 288
2	p. 18	18	p. 105	34	p. 197	50	p. 288
3	p. 27	19	p. 106	35	p. 199	51	p. 307
4	p. 31	20	p. 110	36	p. 213	52	p. 297
5	p. 37	21	p. 118	37	p. 214	53	p. 290
6	p. 43	22	p. 131	38	p. 223	54	p. 325
7	p. 50	23	p. 131	39	p. 223	55	p. 325
8	p. 66	24	p. 151	40	p. 228	56	p. 325
9	p. 66	25	p. 151	41	p. 228	57	p. 345
10	p. 75	26	p. 163	42	p. 251	58	p. 336
11	p. 75	27	p. 164	43	p. 251	59	p. 348
12	p. 81	28	p. 168	44	p. 258	60	p. 347
13	p. 81	29	p. 185	45	p. 258	61	p. 345
14	p. 84	30	p. 185	46	p. 268	62	p. 338
15	p. 87	31	p. 185	47	p. 274		
16	p. 98	32	p. 191	48	p. 276		

Lesson 1.1

Think about Science, page 16

1. **C** Cartilage is strong and flexible, but can wear down as people grow older.

2. **A** Ribs form a cage-like bone structure that surrounds and protect the lungs

Core Practice, page 17

Sample answer: You could use your own arm as a physical model to feel and observe how the muscles contract and stretch. You could find videos of the movement of skeletal muscle to integrate with information you gathered from text, diagrams, and your physical model.

Think about Science, page 17

1. biceps

2. hinge

Core Skill, page 18

Sample answer: graphic organizer would include "Neuron" in central oval with the following in ovals attached to the central oval: "Dendrites receive messages."; "Cell body contains the nucleus."; "Axon transports electrical signal."; "Synapse is empty space between neurons."

Think about Science, page 19

1. parietal lobe

2. cerebellum

3. spinal cord

4. frontal lobe

21st Century Skill, page 19

Sample answer: Damage to certain parts of the brain could prevent it from receiving or sending signals to the rest of the body. Damage to the spinal cord could block messages that would usually travel from the brain down the spinal cord and out to the body, or from the body, through the spinal cord, and up to the brain. Safety measures to protect the nervous system could include wearing a helmet to protect the brain, driving a car with safety features such as air bags, and driving carefully and following all safety laws.

Vocabulary Review, page 20

1. cartilage

2. joint

3. muscle

4. tendon

5. integrate

6. neuron

Skill Review, page 20

1. **D** A major function of the bone marrow is the production of blood cells.

2. **A** A nerve impulse begins at the hand with the detection of heat. A message is sent along nerve cells in the hand, to the arm, and then to the spinal cord. From the spinal cord the message is sent to the brain, where the information is processed. A signal is then sent from the brain along the same route, back to the hand so that it reacts and moves away from the hot surface. This whole process happens almost instantaneously.

3. **B** A synapse is most like a joint in the skeletal system because it connects one nerve cell to another.

4. **C** Dancing to music would be most likely to activate the cerebellum rather than another portion of the brain because the cerebellum controls coordination, posture and balance, all of which are incorporated into dancing.

5. Sample answer: As the batter waits for the pitch, her arms are bent, which means her biceps are contracted. Tendons in the arms connect the arm muscles to the major bones in the arm. When the ball approaches the bat, the batter straightens her arms to swing the bat. This causes her triceps to contract. The triceps remain contracted as she drives the ball into left field.

6. Sample answer: The reflex response allows humans to respond to potential dangers more quickly than they would without the response. For example, the reflex response allows you to move your body away from heat, fire, or sharp objects in order to minimize the risk of injury.

Skill Practice, page 21

1. **D** A man who sustains an injury to his brain that causes him to become temporarily blinded and unable to stand or walk without falling has most likely damaged his cerebellum and occipital lobe. The cerebellum controls balance and coordination required for walking and the occipital lobe of the cerebrum controls sight.

2. **C** A concussion causing swelling in the frontal lobe might affect short-term memory loss and loss of coordination since the frontal lobe regulates voluntary movement and decision making and problem solving.

3. **C** Smooth muscle helps you when you swallow by contracting the esophagus to move the food down into the stomach.

4. **A** A ligament has a function that is most similar to the function of a tendon because ligaments connect bones together at most joints in the body and tendons connect muscles to bones.

5. Sample answer: If cardiac muscle were voluntary, the heart would beat only when you were conscious, and you would have to think about it to make it beat even when you were asleep. However, in order for you to stay alive, the heart must beat constantly. The beating heart keeps blood flowing throughout the body so that nutrients and oxygen can be delivered to cells and wastes can be removed. Therefore, it is critical that cardiac muscle is involuntary muscle.

6. Sample answer: Because the myelin sheath provides insulation that keeps the nerve impulse within the axon, the sheath would allow the nerve impulse to pass down each axon quickly and efficiently, thereby moving a signal quickly and efficiently through the nervous system. Without the myelin sheath, the nerve impulse could jump between axons, causing other nerves to be activated and interfering with the signal being sent from the brain or the body.

7. Sample answer: The knees must bend so you can sit down, and they must also be able to bend to propel you forward when you are walking or running. The ankles must allow you to change direction quickly as you are moving. Therefore, ankle joints must allow for more range of motion than knee joints. Gliding joints found in the ankles do allow for more range of motion than the hinge joints found in the knees.

Lesson 1.2

Core Practice, page 23

1. Sample answer: Yes, this is supported by the evidence. The evidence shows that digestion takes different amounts of time. It is reasonable that this variation is the result of a variety of factors and not simply because of one particular difference. There are so many variables involved—for example, a person's size, type of meal eaten, or the particular differences between the organs of different individuals.

2. No. Although the data are consistent with this statement, this is too broad of a conclusion to draw from just six measurements. The data show that there is quite a bit of variation in digestion times and it is quite likely that if the digestion times of more people were included, some might have digestion times greater than 60 hours.

Think about Science, page 23

1. small intestine

2. mouth

3. liver

4. stomach

21st Century Skill: Business Literacy, page 24

Student responses should offer reflections on the challenges and opportunities of in-home caregiving (e.g. being responsible for additional people outside of one's own family; building relationships and helping others) and provide a statement, with explanation, about whether or not the student would enjoy that type of work.

Core Skill, page 25

Responses will vary. A student might use a photo or illustration of the mouth and describe how chewing helps in the physical breakdown of food while saliva contributes to the chemical breakdown of food.

Think about Science, page 25

1. sweating

2. kidney

3. urethra

Think about Science, page 26

1. Sample answer: gas exchange; oxygen diffuses into the bloodstream and carbon dioxide diffuses out

2. Sample answer: The main organs of the respiratory system are the lungs, which are made up of many small air sacs called alveoli.

Eliminate Unnecessary Information, page 27

The first two sentences are not needed to answer the question. These sentences tell facts about the digestive system that are not necessary to answer the actual question. Crossing out these sentences and focusing on the third sentence—the actual question in this case—can help in answering the question. The answer is the small intestine.

Vocabulary Review, page 28

1. arteries

2. esophagus

3. veins

4. capillaries

5. alveoli

Skill Review, page 28

1. **C** The circulatory and excretory systems interact most directly to produce urine. Blood from the circulatory system enters the kidneys, which are part of the excretory system, and waste is filtered out. The material that the body needs is returned to the blood and blood continues through the circulatory system and other materials are excreted as waste.

2. **B** The alveoli are responsible for the actual exchange of oxygen and carbon dioxide. The gases move from areas of higher concentration to areas of lower concentration inside the alveoli. Oxygen moves into the bloodstream because there is more oxygen in the alveoli than there is in the blood. Carbon dioxide leaves the bloodstream because there is more carbon dioxide in the blood than in the alveoli.

3. **B** If gallstones block the duct through which bile passes, the breakdown of fats in the small intestine will be most affected because bile is required to break down fats in the small intestine and this bile comes from the pancreas where it is stored.

4. **D** The respiratory system works with the circulatory system to provide oxygen to all body cells. Oxygen enters the lungs and travels through the body via the bloodstream.

5. **A** The digestive system with the circulatory system to provide nutrients to all body cells. Nutrients pass through the walls of the small intestine and into the bloodstream so they can travel through the body to the location where they are needed.

6. **D** Carbon dioxide is removed from your body through the lungs when you breathe.

Skill Review, page 29

7. Sample answer: The small lines where the red and blue vessels come together are the capillaries. Capillaries are small, so they are represented by these networks of lines. They are also the place where gas exchange occurs, which is why the red and blue colors change at the capillaries.

8. Sample answer: Capillaries have to be thin because this is where oxygen and other materials move from the bloodstream into the rest of the body.

Skill Practice, page 29

1. Sample answer: The excretory system works with the respiratory system to remove carbon dioxide gas from the body.

2. **C** One similarity between the digestive system and the respiratory system is that both rely on the circulatory system to transport materials throughout the body. The circulatory system transport oxygen and nutrients throughout the body.

3. Responses should include a reasonable hypothesis that describes an interaction between two body systems and a description of a reasonable approach to testing the hypothesis. Sample answer: High sugar intake increases heart rate for the time period that the body is digesting the sugary food; I could test this by having a group of people each drink a large glass of juice and then measure their heart rates every 5 minutes for one hour.

4. Responses should provide accurate scientific information about the body system and a reasonable rationale for why the body system was chosen. Students should eliminate the digestive system (unless they give an example related to choking and consider that digestive-system-related). Sample answer: The EMTs would need to determine if the victim was breathing and if the victim's heart was working properly. Either of these problems would be life-threatening because the circulatory system delivers oxygen from the respiratory system to all parts of the body. Without a constant circulation of oxygenated blood, life is at risk.

5. Responses should describe the process accurately and in detail. Sample answer: When you eat, the food gets digested by your digestive system. After you chew your food, it goes down your esophagus and into your stomach. From there, it moves into the small intestine, which is a tube-like structure. In the small intestine, sugar and other nutrients pass into the bloodstream. This happens by diffusion. The sugar is carried away in your blood to all parts of the body.

Lesson 1.3

Think about Science, page 31

1. **C** Hormones travel throughout the bloodstream to various parts of the body. The other statements are not true.

2. **B** An increase in how fast the heart beats is an example of a hormone effect on the muscular system because the heart consists of involuntary cardiac muscle. The heart rate is increased when the hormone epinephrine is released into the bloodstream in response to fear or anxiety.

Core Practice, page 31

Sample answer: The pancreas releases hormones, so it is part of the endocrine system. The hormones released by the pancreas are related to the management of sugar concentrations in the bloodstream, so this organ is also involved with the digestive system.

Workplace Skills, page 32

Student outline should include the key points from the section on the male reproductive system.

Core Skill, page 33

Sample answer: The pituitary glands, testes, and ovaries should be in the overlapping area. The other glands mentioned in the endocrine system section should be listed in the part of the diagram only under the *Endocrine System* heading. The other structures mentioned in the reproductive system section should be listed in the part of the diagram only under the *Reproductive System* heading.

Vocabulary Review, page 34

1. reconcile
2. fetus
3. gametes
4. placenta
5. hormones
6. glands

Skill Review, page 34

1. **B** The testes produce sperm cells, which are sex cells that are able to fertilize an egg.

2. **D** Facial hair is a secondary male sex characteristic that is controlled by the hormone testosterone.

3. **A** The parathyroid gland regulates levels of calcium in the bloodstream.

4. **C** The ovaries in the female reproductive are most similar to the testes in the male reproductive system. Both the ovaries and the testes contain the sex cells.

5. **D** After ejaculation, millions of sperm are likely to be present in the scrotum 24 hours later.

6. **B** Endometriosis can result in infertility.

7. Sample answer: In order for a hormone to trigger a specific body reaction, only specific cells can be activated. If there were no specific target cells, and the hormone could interact with all cells, all cells would respond.

8. Sample answer: Both the male and female reproductive systems produce sex cells that move through the system. Both are controlled by hormones.

9. Sample answer: During labor, hormones are released that cause the uterus to contract and relax, which moves the baby from the uterus, down the birth canal, and out of the vagina.

Skill Practice, page 35

1. adrenal
2. thymus
3. pineal
4. pituitary
5. thyroid
6. reproductive

7. **A** If disease caused progesterone levels to remain at their peak throughout an affected woman's menstrual cycle, the uterine lining would thicken without being shed. Estrogen would still act to cause thickening of the uterine lining, but after if an egg is not fertilized, the progesterone levels would not drop with the estrogen levels and so the uterine lining would not break down and shed through the vagina.

8. **A** Cells in the ovaries have receptors for follicle-stimulating hormone since eggs mature inside follicles in the ovaries.

9. **B** About 274 cycles. A 28-day cycle occurs 13 times per year and the woman went through 13 menstrual cycles per year for 21 years. $21 \times 13 = 273$, so the closest answer would be 274 cycles.

10. Sample answer: Step 1: The body senses a dangerous situation; Step 2: The pituitary gland is stimulated to release ACTH; Step 3: ACTH stimulates the pituitary gland to release epinephrine; Step 4: Epinephrine stimulates a stress response from heart and skeletal muscles.

11. Sample answer: Yoga and meditation can reduce the secretion of hormones that trigger stress reactions and potentially increase the secretion of hormones that trigger a relaxation response.

12. Sample answer: The fallopian tubes cannot expand enough to accommodate a developing fetus. If the pregnancy is not terminated, the developing embryo can rupture the fallopian tube, causing bleeding and possible death to the mother.

Lesson 1.4

Think about Science, page 37

1. **C** The nervous system is essential for maintaining all conditions of homeostasis throughout the human body. The nervous system controls internal and external sensory receptors that are essential for maintaining homeostasis.

2. **A** Shivering is an example of a response to an external stimulus of a cold external temperature relative to the body's temperature.

Core Skill, page 37

Sample answer: Humans are affected by external conditions, and these external conditions change depending on the environment we are in. Certain body conditions can fluctuate depending on the environment, such as body temperature, heart rate, the condition of the eyes' pupils, and hydration levels. Evidence:

- Body temperature is dependent on the external temperature. An increase or decrease in temperature can increase or decrease our internal body temperature.

- The degree of pupil dilation is dependent on light conditions. Bright light causes pupils to contract and get smaller, and decreased light conditions cause pupils to dilate and grow larger.

- Hydration levels are dependent on the environment. If it is very hot, and the body sweats, the body loses water on the skin's surface. This causes us to feel thirsty because the body is less hydrated.

Core Practice, page 38

Sample answer: Low blood pressure detected → signal sent to hypothalamus → hypothalamus sends signal to circulatory system → heart rate increases, and blood vessels constrict → pressure increases in blood vessels → overall blood pressure increases

Think about Science, page 39

1. negative-feedback mechanism
2. negative-feedback mechanism
3. positive-feedback mechanism

Workplace Skill, page 39

Sample answer: Students may notice that individuals who are more active have a lower resting heart rate. Individuals who exercise more intensely return to their resting heart rate more quickly after exercise than those who do not exercise. This may indicate that the heart is healthier and able to function more efficiently in individuals who exercise regularly. More efficient functioning of the heart means it can return to its resting heart rate more quickly, and homeostasis can be more easily maintained.

Vocabulary Review, page 40

1. negative-feedback mechanism
2. positive-feedback mechanism
3. homeostasis
4. infer
5. stimuli
6. response

Skill Review, page 40

1. sweat

2. **B** The sequence of events that will lead to a response when the body experiences an increase in blood pressure is as follows: first, internal sensors detect increased pressure in blood vessels; next, a signal travels through the nervous system to the brain; then a signal is sent from the brain to the circulatory system; that signal triggers blood vessels to dilate; finally, blood pressure decreases

3. **A** Low blood pressure is an internal stimuli that can decrease heart rate. A low body temperature can also lower heart rate, but the change in body temperature is due to an external stimuli.

4. **C** Smaller animals have less surface area than larger animals. This means that there is less area for heat to escape the body, which makes them better suited to maintain homeostasis than humans. They can also curl up more than humans to further reduce the amount of surface area exposed to the external environment.

5. Sample answer: Hunger is a response that occurs due to cues from within the body. An empty stomach, which is an internal stimuli, will trigger a hunger response. This response elicits the behavior of eating a snack or a meal to alleviate the feeling of hunger. This helps maintain homeostasis because it helps keep blood glucose levels at a normal level and it helps keep cellular metabolism functioning at a normal rate.

6. Sample answer: When a meal is eaten, there is an increase in blood glucose levels in the body. Insulin is produced and released to lower blood glucose levels back to the set point value. Because the release of insulin acts to reverse the rise in blood glucose levels, this is an example of a negative-feedback mechanism.

7. Sample answer: A fever increases body temperature as part of a positive-feedback mechanism to kill the infecting agent in the body. Because a positive-feedback mechanism acts to accelerate a change rather than reverse conditions back to a set value, it has the potential to be harmful rather than helpful. If a viral or bacterial infection continues to spread through the body, despite the increase in body temperature, the feedback mechanism could continue to increase the internal temperature to a harmful level in an effort to try to kill the infecting agent. Above a certain temperature, there are harmful effects to the brain and other body parts, and extreme temperatures can lead to death.

Skill Practice, page 41

1. **B** By interpreting the data in the graph, you can determine that the heart rate of an individual is 60 bpm when homeostasis is maintained.

2. Sample answer: Both external and internal stimuli can act on the body and cause the heart rate to deviate from its resting heart rate.

3. Sample answer: When not enough light is present in the external environment, the eye compensates for this by the relaxation of muscles that allow the pupil to expand. This reverse from a constricted pupil to a relaxed one represents a negative-feedback mechanism because the relaxation of the pupil helps bring more light into the eye when light is lacking in the environment. The change in pupil size restores the normal function of the eye. In addition, the release of pigment also helps restore normal vision when light conditions are low.

4. Sample answer: In the presence of bright light, the muscles around the pupil contract, causing the pupil size to decrease. A decreased pupil size is necessary so that too much light does not enter the eye. If these muscles do not function properly, the pupil will not contract and will let in too much light. If too much light enters the eye and reaches the retina, it could burn or damage the rods and cones in this part of the eye. If rods and cones are damaged, this will affect the eye's ability to see color in bright light and also black and white in dim light.

5. Sample answer: When light enters the eye, a signal is sent to the brain, and the brain processes the information from the signal to determine whether the external light is intense or dim. This means the nervous system is involved in maintaining homeostasis in the eye. In addition, the brain sends a signal back to the eye so the muscles around the pupil contract in bright light and relax in low light. This indicates that the muscular system is involved in maintaining homeostasis.

Lesson 1.5

21st Century Skill, page 43

Answers may vary; Sample answer: Students should include an argument based on their knowledge of how nutrition and sugar affects health and whether they feel their consumption of certain items should be controlled.

Think about Science, page 45

1. **B** Protein is responsible for building and maintaining muscle tissues. There are nine essential amino acids that are required for maintaining muscles, skin and hair.

Core Skill, page 45

Sample answer: Sarah will lose weight on her new wellness plan. She needs to have a minimum of 1620 calories to maintain her current weight. The amount of calories she is eating per day, 1800, subtracted by the amount of calories burned by the increased activity, 430, is equal to 1370 calories. Since this is 250 less calories than is needed to maintain her weight, she will lose weight on this plan.

Vocabulary Review, page 46

1. nutrients

2. minerals

3. calories

4. vitamins

5. nutrition

Skill Review, page 46

1. **A** Meats provide the most protein compared to vegetables, grains, and nuts. Protein from meat contains all 20 amino acids, so meat is considered a complete protein source.

2. **D** Broccoli contains carbohydrates, vitamins, and fiber. Vegatables are a source of carbohydrates and they also contain fiber and essential vitamins.

3. **B** According to the vitamin and mineral tables, vitamin D and calcium are important for bone health. Vitamin D is essential for bone formation and the absorption of calcium, and calcium is plays an essential role in maintaining healthy bones.

4. Sample answer: Sweating may increase during exercise, resulting in more water loss than usual. This lost water needs to be replaced.

5. fat

6. **B** Excess cholesterol can clog arteries and lead to heart disease.

7. **C** unsaturated fats

Skill Practice, page 47

1. **D** Although the pork chops will provide the better source of complete protein, since John is a vegetarian, the peanut butter will provide a healthy protein source needed to build muscle. The other options are carbohydrates and will not provide John with a protein source.

2. **C** Baked chicken with broccoli and brown rice contains lean proteins, unsaturated fats, and vegetables. Brown rice is rice that has not been processed or refined, so it is more healthful than white rice.

3. **A** Vitamin A is important for eye function.

4. $1900 + 0.3 \times 1900 = 2470$ calories. She now needs about 2470 calories daily.

5. Answers may vary; sample answers: Yes, because John is getting a good amount of protein, and he is eating vegetables.

6. Answers may vary; sample answer: John is eating a variety of nutrient-rich foods but he is not getting enough complex carbohydrates or water, and his diet contains too many fats.

7. Answers may vary; sample answer: I would suggest that John limit his intake of fats, eat more complex carbohydrates with his meals, and eat more fruits. John should drink water in place of soda.

Lesson 1.6

Think about Science, page 49

1. **B** Skin is a nonspecific defense. It acts as a barrier to keep many infectious agents out of the body and is nonspecific because it cannot target specific pathogens. The immune system and its components can target a specific pathogen.

2. **D** Antigens trigger the body's defenses against specific pathogens. Antigens are proteins located on the cell wall of a pathogen and trigger an immune response.

3. Sample answer: Both infectious and noninfectious diseases disrupt the normal functioning of the body. However, only infectious diseases are caused by pathogens.

4. Sample answer: Noninfectious diseases can be caused by improper nutrition, lack of exercise, smoking, and alcoholism. Genetics can also be a cause of noninfectious disease.

Core Skills, page 49

Sample answer: Skin causes pathogens to die because the dry, acidic environment does not allow pathogens to get what they need to live. The effect on the body is that many pathogens do not get past the skin, so the body stays healthy.

Calculator Skill, page 50

443.30 cases per 100,000 people

Think about Science, page 51

1. Sample answer: Some people cannot afford to pay for the vaccine, do not have health insurance to cover vaccines, or do not get vaccinated because of religious beliefs or cultural customs.

2. Sample answer: When a knife used for cutting poultry, or a surface where poultry was prepared for cooking is not properly cleaned before using it to cut or prepare another type of food, salmonella may be spread to other foods.

3. Sample answer: Vaccines are made of dead or weakened pathogens because the immune system can create antibodies for the pathogen, but the pathogen cannot infect the body.

4. Sample answer: High temperatures can kill most pathogens that live in uncooked foods.

Core Practice, page 51

Sample answer: I think the CDC should concentrate on *Campylobacter* and *Vibrio* because the percentage of cases of these two disease agents is on the rise. I feel it is most important to stop the problem from growing.

Vocabulary Review, page 52

1. vaccine

2. epidemic

3. disease

4. immunity

5. pathogen

6. analyze

Skill Review, page 52

1. **D** Infectious diseases are caused by the transmission of pathogens, which is not true of noninfectious diseases.

2. **D** Vaccines will not work unless they get past the skin, because they need to be recognized by the immune system. So, they are often injected.

3. **B** Cancer cells are different from other body cells, so the immune system attacks them. The immune system attacks any unrecognizable cells that are in the body.

4. **C** *E. coli* may cause symptoms that are worse, or more recognizable than *Vibrio*, so it is diagnosed more often.

5. Sample answer: Officials can use the data presented to identify diseases that are most prevalent and concentrate their efforts on preventing those diseases.

Skill Practice, page 53

1. **D** Hepatitis could most likely be transmitted from mother to baby since it is transmitted through blood.

2. **A** Both antibiotics and vaccines fight infectious disease by preventing the pathogen cell from surviving and dividing.

3. **B** B cells produce antibodies that recognize specific antigens and mark the cells as a target for killer T cells.

4. **A** Hepatitis, and AIDS can be transmitted during a blood transfusion if the blood is not properly tested because these are blood-borne pathogens.

5. **C** Administering a vaccine to as many people as possible would be the most effective in preventing an epidemic. Educating people on how to prevent the spread of air-borne illness can also help to prevent an epidemic.

6. Sample answer: Many people travel to and from the United States. They may have contracted the disease in other areas of the world. The disease may then spread to people in the US. My reasoning for this is that the malaria had to come from outside the US because the disease is eradicated here.

7. Sample answer: I work with children on a daily basis. Because many young children have not learned basic health habits, they are prone to infectious diseases. As a result, I should wash my hands more often than I currently do. I can also have the children wash their hands often.

8. Sample answer: Because 90 percent of the deaths occur in people 65 years and older, flu-associated deaths of people 65 years and older in the United States between 1976 and 2007 range from about 2,700 to about 44,100.

9. Sample answer: Wash hands regularly, eat a healthful diet, get sufficient sleep, and get a flu vaccination.

Chapter 1 Review

1. **D** The skeletal body is made up of bones that are hard and strong. These bones provide a structural framework for the body.

2. marrow

3. Red blood cells transport oxygen throughout the body. White blood cells help to fight infection when pathogens enter the body.

4. **C** The ankle can rotate in almost all directions because it is attached the leg at a gliding joint. Gliding joints allow for limited movement in many directions, where as pivot and hinge joints allow for a limited range of motion. Ball and socket joints also allow from movement in most directions. They connect the larger bones of the shoulder and hip.

5. Sample answer: Muscles can only contract and relax to cause movement. Every joint is controlled by opposing muscles. In the leg, the muscles at the back of the thigh contract and the muscles in the front relax to bend the knee. To straighten the leg, the muscles in the front contract and the muscles in the back relax.

6. **A** A neuron consists of three main parts: dendrites, a cell body, and axons. Axons send an electrical signal to other neurons or different cell types. The axons of nerve cells have an insulating coating that increases the speed at which a signal travels.

7. cerebrum

8. **B** Oxygen is carried in the bloodstream. Blood rich in oxygen is carried away from the heart via arteries and oxygen-poor blood is carried back towards the heart via veins. Arteries and veins are connected by tiny capillaries.

9. **C** Oxygen is breathed into the lungs and deposited into alveoli which are surrounded by tiny blood vessels. Oxygen passes through the alveoli into the bloodstream via the process of diffusion. Diffusion is the movement of particles from an area of higher concentration to an area of lower concentration. Alveoli have a higher concentration of oxygen than the blood so oxygen diffuses into the blood stream.

10. Sample answer: Blood passes through the kidneys and the kidneys extract a fluid containing water, urea, and valuable nutrients. Waste products are carried from the kidneys and are excreted as urine. Water and valuable nutrients are returned to the blood.

11. hormones

12. **D** The parathyroid gland releases hormones to help regulate the amount of calcium in the bloodstream. The thyroid releases he hormone thyroxine which regulates the process by which cells break down chemicals to obtain energy.

13. **C** A developing fetus grows inside the uterus. Once an embryo has been fertilized and it starts to divide and develop, some cells differentiate to form the placenta. The placenta is an organ that allows nutrients and oxygen to pass between the mother and the fetus.

14. C The menstrual cycle takes about 28 days. During this time, a egg is released and starts to mature inside the ovaries. Estrogen is released from the follicle which causes the uterine lining to thicken. In about 14 days, the egg is released from the follicle in a process called ovulation. The empty follicle continues to release estrogen and also begins to release another hormone, progesterone. These two hormones cause the uterine lining to grow even thicker. If the egg is not fertilized as it travels down the fallopian tube, it dies, and disintegrates. Estrogen and progesterone levels drop, and the lining of the uterus breaks down and is shed through the vagina as menstrual blood.

15. Sample answer: 1)Water is involved in every cellular process; 2) Brain function is slowed down without water because neurotransmitters do not function properly. 3) The human body can only survive a few days without water, but can go weeks without food.

16. D In general, unsaturated fats are considered more healthful than saturated fats. Some types of unsaturated fats have been shown to improve blood cholesterol levels, decreasing the risk of heart disease. Unsaturated fats come from plants, nuts and seeds. Most fish also contain unsaturated fats.

17. D Studies reported by the CDC (Center for Disease Control) have provided evidence that the most effective way to prevent the spread of pathogens from one person to another is by the act of frequent hand-washing.

18. Sample answer: In order for a T cell to destroy an infected cell, it needs to be tagged by an antibody made by B cells in the body. If the antigens of a particular pathogen are not yet recognized by any antibody produced in the body, the infected cell will not bind with the antibody. Without the antibody tag, killer T cells will not recognize the infected cell and it will not be destroyed.

19. Sample answer: In a person with an autoimmune disorder, the immune system cannot distinguish normal body cells from pathogens. Therefore, in these individuals, the immune system will attack the body's own cells, in other words, its "self."

20. vaccine

21. Sample answer: The body uses a negative or a positive feedback mechanism to maintain homeostasis. For example, if the pH of blood rises above the normal level, a negative feedback mechanism will be triggered to lower the pH to its normal level. Once the pH has returned to its normal level, the negative feedback mechanism shuts off.

22. Sample answer: When all systems in the body are functioning properly and all body conditions are at their normal level, the body can be considered to be in balance. When a variable such as internal body temperature deviates from its normal range, homeostasis is disrupted and the body systems are imbalanced. Systems in the body are constantly working to keep all conditions in the normal range. Returning any fluctuating values to normal can be considered a balancing act.

23. C Excess bile is stored by the gallbladder.

24. A The enzymes produced by the pancreas break down nutrients.

25. Sample answer: Chewed food travels through the esophagus and into the stomach. Enzymes and digestive liquids in the stomach help digest food into a nutrient-rich mixture of small particles and liquid. This mixture passes from the stomach into the small intestine. Nutrients can pass through the wall of the small intestine into the blood stream. Once they enter the circulatory system, nutrients can reach cells throughout the body.

Lesson 2.1

Think about Science, page 64

1. abiotic, biotic

2. Answers may vary; sample answer: squirrels, rabbits, deer

3. **C** A puddle is the most likely habitat for a mosquito. A mosquito lays its eggs in water, so the puddle would provide the best place for a mosquito to reproduce.

Core Practice, page 65

Sample answer: A plant growing in climate A is used to a more tropical climate. It is close to the equator, which has high average temperatures and a lot of precipitation during the year. This plant grows at a low elevation and is close to the coast. Transporting this plant to climate B may be a shock that could kill the plant. Climate B appears to be a more temperate climate almost equidistant from the equator and the poles. If the plant is transplanted during summer months, it will probably survive if there is enough rainfall. But, as the temperatures drop and the chance of frost increases, the plant will most likely die.

21st Century Skill, page 66

Answers may vary. Student reports should identify the population being studied, the questions being explored, and the findings of the research.

Think about Science, page 67

1. temperature, precipitation

2. **B** Taiga and temperate rain forest biomes are dominated by evergreen trees. The taiga is an evergreen forest that covers more area on Earth than any other biome, and the temperate rain forest is a cool, wet, evergreen forest biome.

Vocabulary Review, page 68

1. ecosystems

2. organize

3. biotic

4. abiotic

5. biome

6. niche

Skill Review, page 68

1. **B** A community is all the interacting biotic factors in an environment. Organisms form a population and these interacting populations form a community.

2. **B** An ecologist focused on ecosystem ecology might study global warming because global warming will have an effect on all of the biotic and abiotc factors in an ecosystem.

3. Sample answer: trees, lake, ocean, lakeshore, dead tree

4. Sample answer: water, rock, sand, air

Skill Practice, page 69

1. **C** Population → community → ecosystem organizes the environment from the most basic relationships to the most complex. A population consists of a single species and a community consists of all the populations in an ecosystem. An ecosystem includes the community and all of the abiotic factors in the environment.

2. **B** An arctic region and a mountaintop region likely have similar climates. Both the arctic region and many mountaintops are a tundra biome, so they would experience similar climate.

3. Sample answer: Plants live in the shallow waters of wetlands, ponds, lakes, rivers and streams. These plants gain energy from the Sun. This energy is passed to organisms that eat the plants and then is passed from those organisms to other organisms that feed off them.

4. **B** A region of Earth in which trees lose their leaves in October and bud and flower in April is likely located between the north pole and the equator. The biomes that fits this description is the deciduous forest biome which is located between the equator and the north pole.

5. **A** The brittle bush plant is best adapted for a desert biome. Desert biomes experience extreme hot in the day and extreme cold at night. There is also very little precipitation is the desert. The brittle brush plant is well adapted to these conditions.

6. **D** You would expect to find a tundra biome in both A and D.

7. **D** All four regions contain grasslands.

Lesson 2.2

Core Skills, page 71

Sample answer: The simplest model of the flow of matter and energy in an ecosystem is called a food chain. Each step in a food chain is called a trophic level. Autotrophs are plants. Organisms that eat plants are called heterotrophs. Complex feeding pathways can be shown on a food web.

Think about Science, page 72

1. energy pyramid

2. trophic

Core Practice, page 74

Answers may vary; sample answer: Plants in a drought would die because they cannot get the water they need to survive. To test this hypothesis, I could grow grass in two cups of soil. I could water the grass in one cup and let the other cup dry out to simulate a drought. I could see what happens over time to the grass experiencing a drought. One way I could refine this hypothesis is to say that some plants do not need large amounts of water to survive.

Workplace Skill, page 75

1. 10 kilograms

2. Sample answer: There are fewer and fewer organisms as you move to higher trophic levels.

Think about Science, page 75

1. oxygen

2. Carbon

3. water cycle

4. nitrogen

5. phosphorous

Vocabulary Review, page 76

1. Heterotrophs

2. trophic level

3. Biomass

4. biogeochemical cycles

5. Eutrophication

6. Autotrophs

Skill Review, pages 76-77

1. **C** Phosphorous is an element that is mostly found in the form of phosphates and it cycles through Earth in a biogeochemical cycle

2. **B** Garden fertilizer would you most likely contain phosphates because plants absorb phosphates from soil to help them grow.

3. **A** Death and decay of both plants and animals releases phosphates back into soil and water. Phosphates are carried back to the ocean through weathering and runoff and on land, phosphates in the can be incorporated into rock over time.

4. **D** Sunshine is the source of energy that drives the water cycle. Radiant energy from the Sun causes evaporation of water from Earth's surface. Evaporation is one part of the water cycle.

5. B Mountain lions are carnivores and they are tertiary consumers in most ecosystems, meaning they eat both primary and secondary consumers. If mountain lions were reintroduced to the ecosystem some of the cattle and deer would be eaten by mountain lions.

6. D To prevent overgrazing by deer in an ecosystem, the deer population needs to be controlled. Introducing a predator, such as the wolf, from higher tropic levels, would reduce the deer population and prevent overgrazing.

7. Sample answer: Only 10 percent of the energy in a trophic level is passed to the next level. Ninety percent of the energy at each level is used for metabolic proceses or lost as heat to the environment. Because there is less energy available at each level, fewer animals can survive at each higher level. This explains why an energy pyramid is shaped like it is, and not like a cube.

Skill Practice, page 77

1. Sample answer: If an ecosystem had no decomposers, waste and dead organisms would not be broken down into nutrients. Plants would not get the nutrients in the soil they need to grow. Herbivores would not have enough to eat, and carnivores that eat herbivores would not have enough to eat either. The ecosystem would no longer be in balance. Populations would all decrease, and everything would eventually die.

2. Sample answer: Plants take in energy from the Sun to grow. As herbivores eat plants, the plant energy is passed on to the herbivores. As carnivores eat herbivores, energy from the herbivores is passed on through the ecosystem. Finally energy is passed to decomposers as they break down waste and dead material from organisms at all trophic levels.

3. C Calcium carbonate is contained in limestone, marble, and chalk. Each of these store carbon in the form of calcium carbonate, and the carbon in these rocks comes from marine organisms that decayed millions of years ago.

4. A The water cycle is the biogeochemical cycle that reacts with calcium carbonate, resulting in the release of carbon dioxide. As limestone, marble, and chalk go through weathering processes, calcium carbonate chemically reacts with water. Through this process carbon is released to the atmosphere, to oceans, and to lakes.

5. Sample answer: Nitrogen dissolves in water and can be washed into lakes, where it causes excess plant growth, which can kill fish.

6. Sample answer: Matter constantly cycles through biogeochemical systems. Water that was once in any of these animals could have evaporated into the atmosphere, traveled within the atmosphere, come back to Earth through precipitation, moved through surface and/or groundwater, and then eventually ended up in my water glass and become part of my body.

Lesson 2.3

Core Skills, page 79

Sample answer: Cutting down trees in this location would reduce the numbers of nesting places for a particular bird. Reducing the population of the bird would significantly increase the number of parasitic insects in the area. these insects have the capability of spreading blood-borne diseases. A study presented last year shows that cutting down trees in this forest is not a good idea.

Think about Science, page 80

1. **D** One organism is harmed while another benefits in a parasitic relationship.

Test-taking Skills, page 80

Students should produce an outline with main topics that match the main headings in this lesson, and all its subsections. Relevant details should be included for each subsection.

Think about Science, page 81

1. **D** A dragonfly and a fish are most likely to be in a predator-prey relationship.

Core Practice, page 81

Approximately 253 individuals; $1266 \div 5 = 253.2$

Vocabulary Review, page 82

1. Mutualism
2. Symbiosis
3. commensalism
4. carrying capacity
5. parasitism
6. Predation

Skill Review, page 82

1. **A** Mutualism describes the relationship between a flower and its pollinator. This relationship is mutualistic because both species benefit from the relationship. The flower benefits because the pollinator such as a bee or butterfly will transfer pollen from one flower to another assisting in the flower's reproductive process. The pollinator benefits because the flower is a food source.

2. **A** Space would likely be the most limiting factor for a barnacle population on a boat because the surface area of the boat is more limiting than the open ocean, the coast or a vast beach environment.

3. **D** A deer and a rabbit are most likely to compete for food resources because both of these species are herbivores and will compete for the same food source.

4. Sample answer: Prairie dogs could be limited by competition with each other for food or space within burrows. During a severe drought, they could be limited by water and food. Predators could limit the population, as could disease.

5. Sample answer: Removal of a top predator would reduce competition for food among other predators, allowing those populations to increase. It would also remove a predator population from the area, allowing prey population a greater chance of survival.

6. Sample answer: The death of the host would also kill the parasite, unless the parasite could move to a new host.

7. **A** When food, water, and space are abundant, the mosquito population is likely to have the greatest number of individuals.

8. **A** The remora and shark have a commensalism relationship.

9. **C** After the removal of wolf populations in the United States, crop-plant populations decreased.

Skill Practice, page 83

1. **B** Based on the data in the table, approximate carrying capacity is calculated to be about 190 individuals.

2. Sample answer: There may have been less food available, an increase in prey population, or a disease.

3. C Based on the data presented in the graph, the approximate carrying capacity for this population of paramecium is 275 paramecia.

4. Sample answer: The paramecium population was affected by a different limiting factor than food. In a lab, space would probably be limiting to population growth.

5. C A mutualism relationship was interrupted when the researcher transferred the plants because the researcher removed the plants from a beneficial relationship with another species in its ecosystem, it could no longer survive.

6. Sample answer: Competition between wolves and moose for food and space would limit the populations. Disease could limit the populations if the populations became too large.

Lesson 2.4

Think about Science, page 85

1. B Fires and floods be beneficial to ecosystems by providing nutrients for soils. Wildfires can benefit an ecosystem by clearing out dead and dying vegetation allowing for more light to reach new growth. Ash and charcoal from burned plants and trees can add nutrients to the soil. flooding can also deposit nutrient-rich soil as sediment settles along the banks of rivers and streams.

2. B After a volcanic eruption, grasses would be the first plants to re-inhabit the disrupted ecosystem. Trees would take several years to grow back, and once enough plant life was present as an energy source, animals could re-inhabit the area.

21st Century Skill, page 85

Sample answer: Some sources could include scientific research papers on honeybee decline. They can include journal or scientific magazine articles summarizing current research done on the topic. Some information that can help validate the research can include the date of the source. Recent studies are likely more valid as outdated information is proven false. In addition, the name of the group or the scientist presenting the information may be helpful in proving validity of the research. For example, a research paper presented by a university scientist may be more valid than information presented on a group website that can be edited by anyone using the site.

Core Skill, page 86

Answers may vary. Both proposed solutions introduce new problems, and neither problem solves the issue of soil erosion. Responses should identify a proposed solution and any problems that may result from that proposed solution. Students should support their answers with information from the lesson or independent research. Accept all reasonable answers.

Think about Science, page 87

1. habitat destruction

2. fossil fuels

Core Practice, page 87

Sample answer: The human population has grown exponentially in the past 400 years. This has occurred as humans have developed technology to control nature, grow more food, and keep people healthy. It is likely that the exponential human-population growth is connected to the increase in extinctions. Increased pollution and habitat destruction as populations shift and expand cause disruptions in ecosystems, killing off sensitive species.

1. habitat destruction

2. Invasive species

3. pollution

4. Extinction

5. valid

6. Biodiversity

Skill Review, page 88

1. **A** Goats shipped to Australia in the 1700s, causing vegetation loss would most likely be considered an invasive species since these goats were not native to Australia.

2. **A** Fertilizer is considered a human disruption to an ecosystem because it pollutes water by changing the pH of the water, causing algae blooms, and limiting the oxygen content of the water.

3. organisms, environment

4. habitat destruction

5. Sample answer: Weather systems like hurricanes deposit large amounts of rain, which can cause severe flooding, the drowning of plants, and soil erosion. Drought could cause vulnerable plants and animals to die, changing the food web. Long periods of drought may also cause the land to be susceptible to wildfire.

6. Sample answer: Increased human population results in habitat destruction and the use of more resources. Building and mining the land destroys habitats.

7. Sample answer: Air pollution causes acid rain, which can change the pH of soil and of the water, thereby changing the ability of things to live or grow.

Skill Practice, page 89

1. **C** Ash and coal help add nutrients to depleted soils.

2. **B** Habitat destruction occurs when one habitat is removed and replaced with another.

3. Answers may vary; sample answer: Builders might try to avoid clear-cutting when building a new community. People could set up wildlife preserves to relocate displaced wildlife. These are both ways to preserve some of the existing ecosystem for the species that live there.

4. Sample answer: The extinction of one animal can alter the food chain, which can cause other species of animal or plants to increase in population. This change in dynamics can diminish resources for other species.

5. Sample answer: Seeds of grasses and other small plants will start to take root. Some seeds adapted to fire may also start to grow. As the plants start to grow, animals will return and eat the plants. Over time, larger plants, including trees, will grow. Succession can take many years.

6. Answers may vary; sample answer: Both. Humans changed the ecosystem by eliminating a threat. This caused deer to become overpopulated. Natural rain caused the soil to wash away after the land was stripped of vegetation.

7. Sample answer: Removing this predator meant that the population of their prey, deer, increased. The increase in herbivore population put heavy stress on vegetation.

Chapter 2 Review

1. **B** A ecosystem includes all biotic and abiotc factors in an environment. Populations form a community in an ecosystem and the place where a population lives within an ecosystem is its habitat.

2. **C** Primary consumers are herbivores that only eat plants in an ecosystem. A secondary consumer eats primary consumers, and may, like the black bear, also eat plants.

3. D   A parasite feeds off its host often by attaching to the host and drinking its blood. Parasites such as mosquitoes and ticks can spread disease through the contact with the host's blood, causing harm to the host.

4. B   Within almost every food web, the Sun provides the necessary energy for organisms to live. Plants take in the Sun's energy and it is passed on to consumers as they eat plants or other consumers.

5. A   The populations of organisms decrease with increasing trophic levels in an ecosystem. Therefore, if there are 100 primary consumers in an ecosystem, the total number of secondary consumers would be less than 100.

6. A   The carrying capacity is the maximum size of a population that a specific environment can sustain over time. Carrying capacity and population growth can be influenced by interactions among populations which includes how efficiently and regularly a population can reproduce.

7. D   Wildfires can be destructive to an ecosystem, but there can also be some benefits associated with them. In some cases, a fire will clear out layers of dead matter and tree overgrowth in a forest. This allows for more sunlight to reach the forest floor, so new growth can take place.

8. C   Technology includes factories, automobiles, electricity, and many other pollution-causing activities. Pollution generated by the use of technology is harmful to surrounding ecosystems. For example, a power plant can generate electricity for daily use, but will release pollutants in the atmosphere and waterways.

9. A   Ecologists that study communities in an ecosystem investigate the factors that contribute to the diversity of populations in an area. Ecologists studying a community may look at the relationships between predators and prey, the ways in which different species compete for the same kinds of food, or how the presence of one species may benefit or harm another species.

10. C   The taiga includes an evergreen forest that covers more area on Earth than any other biome. Winter is still long and cold, but during the short summer, temperatures are milder. The precipitation in the taiga is mostly snow. Animals that stay active in the winter adapt by growing thick coats and living in burrows to keep warm.

11. A   Mountain ranges near the coast also affect climate. The climate between the ocean and the mountain will be warmer and wetter, while the climate beyond the mountain will be hotter and drier. These factors influence the communities that develop in a particular region. Therefore, the regions beyond the mountain are likely have characteristics of a desert biome and will be able to support cactus growth.

12. C   If excess nitrogen enters aquatic (water) ecosystems, algae may grow uncontrollably. Eventually exploding algae populations use up the oxygen in the water, and other organisms suffocate. In lakes, excessive phosphorus is a pollutant. Phosphate stimulates the growth of algae, which consume large amounts of dissolved oxygen. Lack of oxygen suffocates fish and other marine animals, as well as blocks sunlight to bottom-dwelling organisms.

13. Sample answer: A natural disaster like a fire or volcanic eruption will wipe out all plant life in an ecosystem. A few surviving seeds of hardy plants may begin to sprout over time, birds flying over the ecosystem may drop seeds or plants to the ground, or other animals may leave dropping that contains seeds of plants from near-by ecosystems. If the soil has enough nutrients to support plant growth, these seeds can germinate and grow new plants in the ecosystem.

14. Sample answer: Some limiting factors for a population of freshwater fish can be the oxygen content of the water, the availability of food sources such as plants and insects, the amount of nutrients in the water, and the size of a predator population.

15. Sample answer: Many species are threatened by extinction because of habitat destruction caused by human development. When humans develop land for new housing or farmland, it is no longer suitable for the organisms that lived there originally. Human activity to develop land can include draining wetlands, flooding land by building dams, strip-mining, and building new structures.

16. Sample answer: Wetlands are found in a freshwater biome. In a wetlands environment the soil is saturated with freshwater. The soil holds so much water that it can support the growth of aquatic plants.

17. B   Limiting factors are those that set an upper limit on the growth rate of a population. Such factors include reproduction, natural resources, space and nesting sites, competition, and waste and disease. In the passage, wolves are an example of a limiting factor because they are predators and top competitors in the ecosystem.

18. A   The relationships in the ecosystem described in the passage were disrupted by the human activity of hunting. If humans had not hunted and killed off all of the wolves, there would still be a natural balance in the ecosystem.

19. B   A commensal relationship is one in which one organism benefits and the other is not affected. Commensal species adapt by seeking partners that will provide the full benefit of the relationship.

20. C   The arrows in the diagram represent the flow of energy from one species to another. In this diagram energy flows from one of the plant species to the jackrabbit and from the jackrabbit to the wolf. This indicates that the jackrabbit eats the plant and the wolf eats the rabbit. Therefore, both species would be directly affected by the disappearance of the jackrabbit, but each species in the food web would be affected indirectly.

21. Sample answer: The ringnose rattle snake, long-tailed weasel, and the coyote are all competing for the kangaroo rat as a food source.

22. Sample answer: Kudzu is an invasive species, so it can come into an ecosystem and take up the resources needed for the growth and health of plants that are native to that ecosystem. Kudzu essentially kills off native plants and grows in their place.

23. Sample answer: Farmers and horticulturists often want to prevent damage to an ecosystem by introducing a new plant species. However, the introduction of a new species very often has adverse effects instead. The ecosystem is not capable of sustaining another species, or perhaps the conditions of the ecosystem cause the plant to grow extremely rapidly so that it limits the growth of native species. In this way the plant ends up disrupting the balance of the ecosystem instead of helping to preserve it.

24. 1935

25. C Carrying capacity can be affected by a limited food supply. If not enough food is available to support a population, the population size will be reduced.

26. D The carrying capacity can be determined at the position where the graph levels off. According to the graph the carrying capacity of the seal population is about 10,000.

Lesson 3.1

Core Skill, page 99

Sample answer: The author's purpose is to inform the reader about the experiments conducted to prove or disprove spontaneous generation. Pasteur's experiments with broth proved that spontaneous generation did not occur.

Think about Science, page 100

1. did not

2. did

3. did not

Core Practice, page 100

Sample answer:
1665: Robert Hooke designed the compound microscope.
1678: Antonie van Leeuwenhoek observed living cells in pond water.
1745: John Needham boiled broth and put it in a sealed flask. Organisms grew. He concluded that spontaneous generation does occur.
1768 Lazzaro Spallanzani repeated Needham's experiment but removed the air. No microorganisms grew. He concluded that spontaneous generation did not occur.
1838: Matthias Schleiden concluded that all plants are made of cells and that plants grow because new cells are produced.
1839: Theodor Schwann concluded that all animals are made of cells and that animals grow because new cells are produced.
1855: Rudolf Virchow presented the cell theory.
1859: Louis Pasteur used flasks with S-shaped necks to prove that spontaneous generation does not occur.

Think about Science, page 101

1. C Surface area determines how much material can enter a cell because it is the exposed surface of the cell. The larger the surface area, the more material can enter.

Calculator Skill, page 101

Volume =

1^3 mm = 1 mm^3

2^3 mm = 8 mm^3

4^3 = 64 mm^3

The volume is multiplied by 8.

Surface area =

1^2 mm × 6 = 6 mm^2

2^2 mm × 6 = 24 mm^2

4^2 mm × 6 = 96 mm^2

The surface area is multiplied by 4.

Surface-area-to-volume ratio =

6:1

3:1

1.5: 1

Vocabulary Review, page 102

1. Spontaneous generation

2. subdivide

3. Cell theory

4. cell

Skill Review, page 102

1. B Redi's experiment showed that maggots did not appear out of nowhere because maggots did not appear in the covered flasks, so it provided proof that microorganisms could not be produced by spontaneous generation.

2. B In Needham's experiment, microorganisms grew in boiled broth in a sealed flask, but Needham's experiment did not provide to completely prevent microorganism from reaching the broth if air got inside the sealed flask.

3. Sample answer: Specialized cells are organized into tissues, such as muscle tissue. A group of tissues can work together to form an organ, such as a heart. Organs that work together to perform a set of related tasks form a body system, such as the circulatory system. Various organ systems work together make up a complete organism, such as a human or a dog.

4. Sample answer: The ratio of a cell's surface area to its volume limits its size. If the cell is too large, it will require more materials than can pass through its surface area. Therefore a cell cannot grow larger than the size it needs to be to obtain all required materials through its surface.

5. **C** Pasteur used flasks with an S-shaped curve in the neck so that microorganisms would get trapped as air entered the flask. When the flask was tilted, the microorganisms were no longer trapped.

6. **A** The invention of the microscope allowed Robert Hooke to observe cork at a high enough magnitude to see that its structure consisted of many tiny units, or cells.

Skill Practice, page 103

1. **C** Pasteur's experiment improved upon John Needham's experiment because a criticism of Needham's experiment was that microorganisms in air could have contaminated his broth. Pasteur's experiment prevented microorganisms in air from getting into the broth because Pasteur used special flasks with a curved neck that could trap any microorganisms before they reached the broth.

2. **C** Muscle tissue is least likely to be found in the brain because the brain is not a muscle. It is likely to have nerve cells, blood cells, epithelial cells, and special cells called glial cells.

3. Sample answer: Cells divide so that they do not get too large. A cell's volume increases faster than its surface area. If a cell is too large, it cannot take in enough needed nutrients through its surface to survive.

4. **C** The amount of space a cell takes up is known as its volume.

5. **D** Redi placed cloth over the jar to prevent flies from laying eggs on the meat in the control jar.

6. **A** Redi should have been most careful that all the pieces of meat used in his experiment were free of fly eggs.

Lesson 3.2

Core Skill, page 105

Sample answer: I learned in the lesson that DNA holds instructions for making proteins. I know proteins are made up of amino acids. The DNA might provide information for how the amino acids should be organized to make a specific protein.

Think about Science, page 106

1. Ribosomes assemble proteins according to instructions found in DNA.

2. Sample answer: Plants cells generally have one large vacuole, while animal cells may have several small vacuoles.

3. Sample answer: The rigid outer layer of the cell wall makes it difficult for foreign substances to enter the cell and provides structure for the plant. The pores in the cell wall allow necessary materials to enter and leave the cell.

4. Sample answer: A prokaryotic cell is simpler than a eukaryotic cell. Unlike a eukaryotic cell, a prokaryotic cell has no nucleus and contains no membrane-bound organelles.

Workplace Skill, page 106

Sample answer: A scientific definition for the word *energy* is a fundamental entity of nature that is transferred between parts of a system in the production of physical change within the system. One everyday definition for *energy* is enthusiasm.

Think about Science, page 107

1. C Active cellular transport moves material from areas of lower concentration to areas of higher concentration. If a membrane is selectively permeable, some substances can move through it, and others cannot. Diffusion is the movement of molecules from an area of high concentration to an area of low concentration. Diffusion of water across a selectively permeable membrane, such as a cell membrane, is called osmosis.

2. A Diffusion moves molecules from an area of high concentration to an area of low concentration. Active transport moves material from areas of lower concentration to areas of higher concentration. Energy production and protein synthesis are not methods of transport.

Core Practice, page 107

Answer: Diffusion is the movement of molecules from an area of high concentration to an area of low concentration.

Vocabulary Review, page 108

1. osmosis

2. prokaryotic cell

3. organelle

4. eukaryotic cell

5. differentiate

6. nucleus

Skill Review, page 108

1. B Active transport accounts for this phenomenon because active transport moves material from areas of lower concentration to areas of higher concentration. Because materials oppose the natural flow to areas of lower concentration, carrier proteins in the cell membrane pick up and transport materials. This work requires energy.

2. C Bacteria are prokaryotic because they do not have a nucleus or membrane-bound organelles.

3. D In plant cells, chloroplasts are active in photosynthesis, the chemical process required to make food. Animal cells have no chloroplasts; therefore, animal cells do not make their own food through photosynthesis, but rather eat other organisms for food.

4. A Lysosomes are important to the health of a cell because they break down large molecules into parts the cell can reuse. Lysosomes are the recycling centers of cells, and help to prevent the buildup of cellular waste.

5. Answers may vary; sample answer: Vacuoles in plants provide support to the cell when the vacuoles are filled with water. If the plant does not get enough water, the vacuoles do not put enough pressure on the cell walls to support the plant.

6. Sample answer: The nucleolus inside the nucleus is where ribosomes are produced. Ribosomes use the information in DNA from the nucleus and amino acids in the cytoplasm to produce proteins and other molecules. Many ribosomes are attached to rough ER. ER transports the proteins made by the ribosomes. These proteins are transported to the Golgi apparatus where they are packaged for storage or sent outside of the cell.

Skill Practice, page 109

1. D Some cells have more mitochondria than other cells because they need more energy than other cells, and mitochondria are the energy generators of cells.

2. A It might be important for some organelles to be surrounded by membranes because membranes can regulate what goes in and out of an organelle. For example, digestive enzymes must be bounded by a membrane to protect the normal biomolecules of the cell within the cytoplasm.

3. C Mitrochondria are most like a power plant because they are the energy generators of cells.

4. **C** Since ribosomes are organelles that use amino acids to assemble proteins according to instructions in DNA, if a cell stopped producing ribosomes, the cell may not be able to repair itself because of lack of proteins.

5. Sample answer: Similarities: Both the nucleus and the brain are control centers that govern the activities in their respective spheres. Differences: The brain is much larger and more complex than the nucleus.

6. Answers may vary; sample answer: Objects have a specific structure that helps them perform their function. For example, the endoplasmic reticulum is structured with layers of membranes, which provide a path for transporting materials.

7. Answers may vary; sample answer: Descriptions should compare each and every cell part mentioned in this lesson and compare them to a process that goes on in a factory; for example, the Golgi apparatus could be compared to a packaging center, and the rough ER could be compared to an assembly line.

8. Sample answer: Both facilitated diffusion and active transport allow certain substances to cross a cell membrane. Both processes involve proteins embedded in the cell membrane. However, facilitated diffusion transports items from an area of high concentration to an area of low concentration, while active transport does the opposite.

9. Sample answer: The text is divided into three sections: one on cells, one on cellular transport, and one on types of cells. The subheads can tell you what parts are only in animal cells and what parts are only in plant cells. This helps me understand the difference between these two types of cells.

Lesson 3.3

Think about Science, page 111

1. **D** Vascular plants have tube-like tissue that transports water and other substances. They are able to survive on land because they have evolved to grow independent of wet environments, unlike nonvascular plants.

2. **C** Both gymnosperms and angiosperms produce seeds; gymnosperms often in cones, while angiosperms are flowering plants that produce seeds in fruits.

Core Practice, page 111

Sample answer: Responses should include a question, a hypothesis, a procedure, recorded observations, and conclusions based on those observations.

21st Century Skills, page 112

Sample answer: Students should give an outline of an article related to how plants are used in medicine.

Core Skill, page 113

Sample answer: The arrangement of the tissue in the epidermis is clear from the diagram but is not described in detail in the text.

Think about Science, page 115

1. Sample answer. Leaves capture the energy of sunlight, make organic molecules, and exchange gases with the environment.

2. Sample answer: The many string-like roots maximize the surface area exposed so the plant can absorb more water.

3. sepals, petals, stamen, pistil

4. Germination is when a seed begins to grow.

Vocabulary Review, page 116

1. Pollination

2. Phloem

3. Xylem

4. outline

5. Vascular plants

6. Transpiration

Skill Review, page 116

1. **D** The saguaro cactus is a tall flowering vascular plant that grows in the desert. It is a vascular plant because it has evolved to survive independent of wet environments.

2. **C** Roots are the first part of a plant to grow because roots hold the plant in place and absorb water from the soil. Water is one of the most important components of life and is necessary for the survival of all plants.

3. **C** The purpose of the sticky fluid at the end of the pistil is to help pollen grains stick to the pistil. The transfer of pollen grains from the stamen to the pistil, pollination, must take place before seeds can form. Pollination is the transfer of pollen grains from stamen to pistil. With few exceptions, pollination must take place before seeds can form. Pollen grains can be carried by wind, water, gravity, insects, or other animals.

4. **A** The most likely reason seeds would have hooks would be to help disperse the seeds when the hooks on the seeds attach to animals, which carry them away, where they can grow in a new area.

5. Answers may vary; sample answer: The diagram should include germination, growth, flower production, pollination, seed development, and seed dispersal.

6. Sample answer: Nonvascular plants must grow in places that are damp because they get water through osmosis. As a plant gets taller, it no longer touches the water available on the ground. Vascular plants contain xylem, which help plants pull water up from the roots. In this way, vascular plants can grow to be much taller than nonvascular plants.

7. Sample answer: The most significant difference between gymnosperms and angiosperms is the fact that angiosperms develop fruit around the seeds. I think this is the most significant difference because other differences, such as the fact that many gymnosperms are evergreens, are secondary and not true of all gymnosperms.

Skill Practice, page 117

1. **C** Cherry seeds are surrounded by a sweet fruit, which would likely be eaten by animals; therefore the method of seed dispersal most likely to scatter cherry seeds are animals, which would eat the seeds and disperse them through their droppings.

2. **C** Colony-collapse disorder might affect plants in an area because fewer flowers will be pollinated if a hive of bees is killed, as bees transfer pollen grains from stamen to pistil in the process of pollination.

3. **B** A plant with a woody stem might survive better in a windy environment than a plant with an herbaceous stem because woody stems are rigid and can withstand high winds better than nonrigid plants, which will be flattened by wind.

4. **D** Xylem and phloem are located in so many parts of a plant because all parts of a plant need the water and food xylem and phloem transport. Xylem transports water and dissolved minerals through the roots to the rest of the plant, while phloem transports organic molecules from the leaves throughout the plant.

5. **C** Transpiration is an important process because water would not circulate through the plant without transpiration. Water that exits the pores by transpiration actually "pulls" water up from the roots.

6. Sample answer: Gravitropism is the growth of plants toward Earth due to the pull of gravity.

7. Sample answer: The lower epidermis contains small pores called stomata that allow molecules in and out of the leaf.

8. palisade; spongy

Lesson 3.4

Core Practice, page 120

Answers may vary. Students should be able to clearly identify which information in their research is accepted fact and which is speculation.

Think about Science, page 121

1. **D** Since water (H_2O) is made of hydrogen and oxygen molecules, hydrogen ions, oxygen molecules, and electrons would result from the splitting of water molecules during photosynthesis.

Core Skill, page 121

$2H_2O \backslash 4H^+ + O_2$

Think about Science, page 122

1. The process of glycolysis breaks down a sugar molecule into two pyruvate molecules.

2. The main function of ATP is to store energy for use in the cell.

3. The inner membrane of a mitochondrion is where the Krebs cycle and oxidative phosphorylation occur.

4. Cellular respiration and photosynthesis are related processes in that one is the reverse process of the other.

21st Century Skill, page 122

Answers may vary; sample answer: Student models should begin with glucose and the process of glycolysis and include the following: the addition of oxygen and the transfer into the mitochondrion, the Krebs cycle, the production of ATP and carbon dioxide, oxidative phosphorylation with the electron-transport chain, and the production of water.

Workplace Skill, page 123

Sample answer: There is a small map of stairways and exits that is near the elevator at my workplace. It shows how people should exit the building in case of a fire or other emergency.

Think about Science, page 123

1. **B** Fermentation happens in the absence of oxygen, while cellular respiration is aerobic and requires oxygen.

2. **C** Alcoholic fermentation occurs in some single-celled organisms, and is used to produce bread and beverages such as wine and beer. In alcoholic fermentation, glucose is changed into ethyl alcohol, or ethanol, two molecules of ATP, and carbon dioxide.

Vocabulary Review, page 124

1. cellular respiration

2. Enzymes

3. Photosynthesis

4. apply

5. fermentation

6. Chlorophyll

Skill Review, page 124

1. **D** The ability to store large amounts of food might help a plant survive in areas that do not get light for a portion of the year because light is needed for the plants to make food during the process of photosynthesis.

2. **C** Carbon, hydrogen, oxygen are found in glucose, which is written as $C_6H_{12}O_6$. There are six carbon atoms, 12 hydrogen atoms, and six oxygen atoms in a glucose molecule.

3. **B** The Calvin cycle combines the hydrogen ions and electrons with carbon dioxide from the air to form sugars and other carbohydrates.

4. **D** People breathe in the oxygen they need. Unlike fish, they cannot get oxygen from water, and unlike plants they do not have stomata. Oxygen does not enter through the skin. Plants produce oxygen that is released in the atmosphere, and humans breathe in oxygen as air flows into their lungs.

5. Sample answer: Photosynthesis uses energy from sunlight to produce food. Both plants and animals need food for energy. Oxygen is a product of photosynthesis and is an essential material in cellular respiration. So, without the process of photosynthesis, most life on Earth could not exist.

6. Sample answer: ATP is an important molecule because it stores energy. This stored energy is used to provide energy in many chemical reactions that take place during photosynthesis, cellular respiration, and fermentation. ATP is also a product of cellular respiration and fermentation.

7. **A** NADPH and ATP provide the energy necessary for the Calvin cycle. This light-independent reaction combines the hydrogen ions and electrons with carbon dioxide from the air to form sugars and other carbohydrates.

Skill Practice, page 125

1. **B** In alcoholic fermentation, glucose is changed into ethyl alcohol, or ethanol, two molecules of ATP, and carbon dioxide. When bread rises, it develops small pockets of carbon dioxide gas.

2. **C** During strenuous exercise, the cells in muscles may not receive enough oxygen. This causes a burning sensation in the muscles, caused by lactic-acid fermentation. Two molecules of ATP provide the energy to break down a glucose molecule into two molecules of pyruvate, which produces two molecules of ATP. However, during lactic-acid fermentation, the pyruvate is changed into lactic acid instead of more ATP molecules.

3. **A** We can infer that photosynthesis in plants must always precede cellular respiration because photosynthesis is producing sugars, while cellular respiration is breaking down those sugars to release energy in the presence of oxygen.

4. **C** We can infer that physically active people would have a higher rate of cellular respiration than people who are not physically active because the active people expend more energy in a given time and would therefore, need to produce energy more quickly so their cells continuously function.

5. **D** A decrease of oxygen in the atmosphere is a likely result of large areas of forest being cut down because trees, like all plants, provide oxygen to the atmosphere.

6. Sample answer: Cellular respiration occurs in aerobic conditions. Fermentation does not. Cellular respiration produces considerably more ATP than fermentation, providing more energy to the organism.

7. Sample answer: During photosynthesis, light and water enter the thylakoids in chloroplasts, and a reaction takes place. In this reaction, oxygen is released, and NADPH and ATP are produced. The NADPH and ATP provide energy to change a substance from the Calvin cycle to RuBP. Carbon dioxide reacts with RuBP to produce 3-Phosphoglycerate, which goes through more reactions, producing G3P. From G3P starch, amino acids, fatty acids, and sugar are formed. The cycle then begins again.

8. Sample answer: Light energy, water, and carbon dioxide are needed to carry out photosynthesis. Glucose and oxygen are the final products of photosynthesis.

Lesson 3.5

Think about Science, page 127

1. **C** During interphase the cell's DNA undergoes replication. After interphase, the cell is ready to divide. During interphase the number of cell organelles increases, not decreases, in preparation for cell division.

2. **D** During mitosis, or the M phase, the nucleus divides into two nuclei. At the M checkpoint, therefore, a scientist would evaluate whether the nucleus has divided properly.

Core Skills, page 127

Answers will vary. Student responses should give a detailed explanation of how each phase in the cell cycle prepares the cell for the next phase.

Core Practice, page 128

Answers may vary; sample answer: A diagram is useful to show a process that can be observed visually because you can see how all the parts interact to complete the process. The diagram helped me understand what was meant by the textual descriptions, such as how the chromosomes "line up" in the center of the cell.

21st Century Skills, page 129

Sample answer: Klinefelter's syndrome occurs through nondisjunction, which means that homologous chromosomes fail to separate during meiosis. A person with Klinefelter's syndrome has two X chromosomes and one Y chromosome. The person is sterile, with male sex organs and some female characteristics, such as enlarged breasts.

Think about Science, page 129

1. **C** During prophase the chromosomes group together, and the nuclear envelope disappears.

2. **B** During metaphase, the dividing cell looks like chromosomes are lined up down the center of the cell. Spindle fibers lengthen and attach to centromeres of the chromosomes.

Think about Science, page 131

1. **B** During meiosis I, homologous chromosomes line up at the cell's center.

2. **C** During prophase I an exchange of genetic information takes place between chromosomes. Chromosomes condense, and spindle fibers form once again within each new cell.

Test-taking Skill, page 131

Answers may vary. Students should discuss the benefits of taking time to read and understand the question.

Vocabulary Review, page 132

1. chromatid
2. contrast
3. chromosome
4. meiosis
5. cell cycle
6. mitosis

Skill Review, page 132

1. **D** During telophase the two nuclei for the daughter cells are formed, the cell membrane pinches in at the center of the cell. A nuclear envelope reappears around each group of now single chromosomes.

2. **A** During anaphase I you would see homologous chromosomes being pulled apart from each other as spindle fibers shorten and separate homologous chromosomes from each other, moving them to opposite sides of the cell.

3. **C** During anaphase II, the centromeres split, and sister chromatids separate.

4. **A** In G_1 phase of the cell cycle a growing but nondividing skin cell will most likely be found, since during the G_1 phase, a cell increases in size and volume and performs normal cell functions.

5. **B** Cell division that involves meiosis occurs only in the production of male gametes (sperm) and female gametes (eggs).

6. Sample answer: Mitosis is the process that splits replicated chromosomes apart and forms new daughter-cell nuclei. Cytokinesis then divides the rest of the cell apart.

7. Sample answer: Sister chromatids could fail to divide during anaphase, so one doubled chromosome could be pulled into one of the new daughter cells.

8. Sample answer: Both processes divide genetic material and produce new cells. Mitosis produces identical daughter cells. Meiosis produces sex cells with half the genetic material of the original cell. The process of meiosis also produces new genetic combinations in daughter cells.

Skill Practice, page 133

1. **C** The G_2 checkpoint allows the cell to leave interphase, as the cell is ready to enter the M phase and divide.

2. **C** In G_2, the cell undergoes another phase of growth in which extra organelles and cytoplasm are produced in preparation for cell division. G_2 occurs after the S phase and DNA replication. The G_2 checkpoint would halt the process if the cell has not produced extra organelles in preparation for division.

3. **A** If sister chromatids did not separate on one chromosome, a cell would stop progressing through the final checkpoint of the cell cycle.

4. D   Metaphase II is most similar to metaphase in mitosis.

5. D   During metaphase II, spindle fibers lengthen and attach to centromeres. The centromeres of the chromosomes line up randomly along the center of each new cell. This is most similar to metaphase in mitosis in which chromosomes line up on the metaphase plate.

6.   Sample answer: Cancer could occur when a checkpoint fails and allows a cell with DNA-replication errors or other issues to continue to divide.

Chapter 3 Review

1. A   Before the invention of the microscope scientists could only observe organisms and materials with the naked eye. Once the microscope was invented they were able to see everything magnified so greatly that Robert Hooke was able to see the individual cell that made up the sample of cork he was studying.

2. C   Within any living organism the smallest unit is the cell. A group of the same type of cell makes up tissue. For example, skin cells join together to form such as skin tissue and muscle cells join together to form muscle tissue. Organs in the body are composed of tissue. For example, the heart is composed of muscle tissue and other types of tissue, too. Organs work together as a body system. For example, the heart is part of the circulatory system that pumps blood through the body.

3. D   The mitochondria is the organelle that processes molecules such as those from the foods we eat, into usable energy that body cells can use. The mitochondria is often referred to as the powerhouse of the cell.

4. A   Usually a substance will flow from a region of higher concentration to a region of lower concentration through the process of diffusion. When a substance moves in the opposite way, from lower to higher concentration it is called active transport.

5. B   There are two different types of plants: vascular plants and nonvascular plants. Among Vascular plants there are seed plants, gymnosperms, and angiosperms. Every type of plant has leaves, roots and stems. Other parts such as seeds or flowers vary depending on the type of plant.

6. B   During the process of fertilization in a flowering plant, the resulting fertilized egg develops into a seed in the ovary of the plant. The ovary surrounding the seed swells and forms a fruit.

7. D   The last stage of cellular respiration is oxidative phosphorylation. The high energy containing hydrogen atoms that are produced by the Kreb's cycle are split into protons and high-energy electrons. Electrons are passed down an electron-transport chain providing energy for the production of ATP.

8. C   One type of reaction that takes place during photosynthesis is the Calvin cycle. The Calvin Cycle is independent of light and takes place inside the chloroplast in the stroma.

9. C   After replication, but before a cell divides, there is twice as much DNA in the cell than there should be. Therefore, after the S phase, in which DNA replication takes place, there is twice as much DNA. Also, prior to mitosis, but after DNA replication, the cell with have twice as much DNA. This would be at the G_2 checkpoint.

10. B   There are 23 pairs of chromosomes in normal human body cells. The gametes, or egg and sperm cells each contribute one chromosome to each pair. Sperm and egg join together during fertilization so each gamete has only half the number of chromosomes as a normal cell.

11.   Sample answer: When a cell grows, its volume increases at a faster rate than its surface area. If a cell grows too large, it will require more proteins and other materials than can pass through the outer membrane. Therefore, there is a limit to the size a cell can grow and still function properly.

12. Sample answer: Ribosomes are responsible for the synthesis of proteins according to the instruction or code of a certain type of RNA. This RNA, called messenger RNA, is a component of ribosomes. Messenger RNA gets its instructions from DNA in the nucleus. DNA is the genetic material of the cell.

13. Sample answer: Vascular plants are true land plants because they are able to move water from their surroundings through their bodies via vascular tissue. They can move water from the ground, up through their roots and stem to all leaves and flowers.

14. Sample answer: The substances needed for cellular respiration, glucose and oxygen, are produced by the process of photosynthesis in plants. Cellular respiration is a basic process of survival.

15. Sample answer: If mitosis occurs repeatedly in the cell, the nucleus will divide. However, if cytokinesis does not occur after telophase, then the cell will never divide. Therefore, there will be a single cell with more than one nucleus.

16. **B** The cell will produce twice as many proteins and will function at twice the normal rate.

17. **A** The surface area would be 9 μm^2.

18. **C** Previous experiments were done in a straight neck flask. There was no way to ensure that microorganisms were not falling from the air into the broth. By bending the neck of the flask, Pasteur was able to trap any microorganisms that entered the flask when it was exposed to air. This way he could prove that microorganisms were in the air, and that spontaneous generation did not occur.

19. Sample answer: Pasteur's experiment proved that new cells or organisms did not arise spontaneously in or on non-living matter, in this case broth. This provides evidence in favor of the part of the cell theory that states that new cells are produced from existing cells.

20. **C** In the 18th century there was no refrigeration methods, so food, especially meat, rotted much more quickly than it does today. Flies were attracted to rotted meat and laid their eggs on it. People did not understand where the maggots came from and thought they arose spontaneously on the meat.

21. **B** On the diagram, the organelle labeled "B" is a lysosome. Lysosomes contain enzymes that digest, or break down, organic molecules such as carbohydrates, lipids, and proteins.

22. **C** Within the cell, proteins are modified in the Golgi apparatus so they can be used by the cell or transported out of the cell. Label C corresponds to the Golgi.

23. **A** The reverse reaction of photosynthesis is the reaction for cellular respiration, and so the products of photosynthesis are the reactants for cellular respiration.

24. Sample answer: Photosynthesis provides energy for the plant to grow and live. For photosynthesis to occur in plant cells, sunlight is required. Sunlight provides the energy needed to start the reaction between CO_2 and H_2O. This reaction produces sugar, which is the energy source that plants use to grow.

25. **B** The nuclear envelop breaks into fragments and disappears during the prometaphase of mitosis. In metaphase and anaphase, there is no nuclear envelope.

26. **B** The spindle fibers are longest during metaphase when the chromatid line up along the center of the cell and the spindle fibers lengthen and attach to the centromeres of the chromosomes.

Lesson 4.1

Think about Science, page 143

1. dominant

2. recessive

21st Century Skills, page 144

Answers may vary; sample answer: Student answers should reflect on their own particular social and cultural practices.

Core Skill, page 145

Sample answer: Each parent plant could pass a *T* or a *t* allele to the offspring. Therefore the offspring could have the alleles *TT, Tt,* or *tt.* Offspring that had *TT* and *Tt* alleles would be tall, so most of the offspring would be tall. The offspring with the alleles *tt* would be short.

Core Practice, page 146

Answer: $20/80 = .25 \times 100 = 25$ percent

Think about Science, page 147

1. **D** *yy* since these alleles not dominant. If the pea had even one *Y* allele, it would be yellow.

2. **A** To produce yellow peas, a plant must have at least one dominant *Y* allele. So it can have either *YY* or *Yy,* and still be yellow.

Vocabulary Review, page 148

1. allele

2. statistics

3. heredity

4. trait

5. gene

6. genetics

Skill Review, page 148

1. **D** You can infer that one parent plant must have had yellow seeds, and the other could have had green or yellow seeds if a pea plant has yellow seed color. Since yellow is the dominant trait, the plant only needs to inherit one copy of the yellow allele.

2. **B** Having five fingers is a heritable trait. The others are all learned behaviors.

3. Sample answer: Both are related to an organism's chromosomes, and both have two parts. Homologous chromosomes are pairs of chromosomes, one from each parent, that have the same genes but can have different alleles for each gene. Sister chromatids are exact copies of each other and make up a replicated chromosome. Because they are exact copies, they have the same alleles for each gene.

4. **B** From most specific to most general, the structures would be ordered as follows: DNA, allele, gene, chromosome. DNA contains sequences that code for a specific gene. More specifically a gene can have a slightly different sequence called an allele. All DNA is packaged in to chromosomes.

5. **A** A plant that produces yellow peas should have Y alleles on both cxhromosomes and so have YY or Yy.

6. Sample answer: Each letter (*P* or *p*) represents an allele. *P* represents the allele for purple flowers, and *p* represents the allele for white flowers. These are alleles for the gene for flower color. Each plant's alleles are represented by two letters (*PP* or *pp*) because each individual has two alleles for each trait, one on each of a homologous pair of chromosomes.

7. Sample answer: This plant could pass on either a *P* allele or a *p* allele. This is because these alleles are on homologous chromosomes that are separated during meiosis. Either allele would end up in any single gamete.

Skill Practice, page 149

1. Answer: Females (XX) cannot tell from which parent each X was inherited. Males (XY) must have inherited the Y from the male parent and the X from the female parent.

2. *They determine traits other than sex.*

3. *WW* or *Ww;* individuals with either of these pairs of alleles would have round seeds because *W* is the dominant allele, represented by the capital letter.

4. Sample answer: No, you can't tell which allele is on the other chromosome of the homologous pair. There will be an allele for the same gene, but homologous chromosomes are not identical, and one may have a different allele than the other.

5. Sample answer: The tall pea plant was *TT*, and the short was *tt*. The offspring were all *Tt*. In other words, the offspring all had one allele for tall height and one allele for short height. The tall allele was dominant, and the short allele was recessive, so the offspring all expressed the tall trait.

6. **C** An organism that exhibits a dominant trait must have one or more alleles for the dominant trait.

7. **C** The trait would have been characterized as recessive.

Lesson 4.2

Think about Science, page 151

1. **B** Dark purple flowers *(P)* are dominant in pea plants, and white flowers *(p)* are recessive. The flower phenotype for a pea plant with the genotype *Pp* is all dark purple flowers.

2. **D** *PP* or *Pp*, because purple *(P)* is dominant, and the organism, therefore, must have at least one *P*.

Core Skill, page 151

Sample answer: The student should construct a Punnett square for the following cross:

Yy × *yy*. From this cross, there is a 50 percent chance that an offspring will have yellow seeds and 50 percent chance an offspring will have green seeds.

Think about Science, page 152

1. **B** 2 boxes in a Punnett square for a cross between a pea plant with purple flowers *(Pp)* and a pea plant with white flowers *(pp)* would show the genotype *pp*, since the percentage of the genotypes in a cross between these parents would be 50 percent *Pp* and 50 percent *pp*.

2. **A** 0 percent because all of the offspring would have a dominant *Y* allele.

Calculator Skill, page 152

The probability of a trait is that is predicted for three out of 16 offspring is about 18.75 percent, which is rounded up to 19 percent. (3/16 = 0.1875)

Think about Science, page 153

1. **D** If two people with no freckles and dry earwax have a child, the probability that the child would have the same phenotype as the parents is 100 percent. Since freckles and wet earwax are both dominant, the both parents must have only the recessive genes.

Core Practice, page 153

Answer: Wet earwax and freckles: 56.25 percent; wet earwax and no freckles: 18.75 percent; dry earwax and freckles: 18.75 percent; dry earwax and no freckles: 6.25 percent

Vocabulary Review, page 154

1. percent
2. phenotype
3. Punnett square
4. monohybrid cross
5. genotype
6. probability

Skill Review, page 154

1. **A** Monohybrid cross Punnett squares have only 4 boxes, as each of the two parents has two alleles, so there is one box for each combination of alleles.

2. **A** 0 percent—since both pea plants have wrinkled seeds *(ss)*, which are recessive, none of the offspring will have smooth seeds.

3. **B** In a cross between two smooth-seed pea plants, one with the *Ss* genotype and the other with the *SS* genotype, the possible genotypes are *SS* and *Ss*.

4. Sample answer: When you determine the probability of a particular trait in offspring, you find the predicted percent of offspring that might have the trait.

5. Answers may vary; sample answer: I have no freckles, so my phenotype is nonfreckled, and my genotype is *ff*.

6. Sample answer: A color-blind woman has the two recessive sex-linked alleles for color blindness. Because a male child always receives his X chromosome from his mother, he would always receive the recessive sex-linked allele for color blindness.

7. **B** The most likely number of white-flowered offspring produced in a cross between a white-flowered pea plant (*pp*) and a purple-flowered pea plant (*Pp*) that produces 145 offspring is 69 because approximately 50 percent of the offspring will have white flowers, and 69 is the closest number to half of 145.

8. **B** The probability is 25 percent.

9. **B** The probability that you will get heads each time you flip a coin is 50 percent each time you toss it. Even if you have gotten heads 10 times in a row, the probability is still 50 percent on the eleventh throw.

Skill Practice, page 155

1. **B** According to the chart, both parents have brown eyes. The male parent has a dominant (B) and a recessive b, as does the female parent. So both parents have one dominant allele for brown eyes, and both parents therefore have brown eyes.

2. **D** If the child of brown-eyed parents has blue eyes, the child must have inherited two recessive genes for blue eyes: *bb*.

3. **D** According to the chart, the least likely possibility is one brown, three blue.

4. **C** According to the chart, the probability that a child of these parents will have the *Bb* genotype is 50 percent.

5. Sample answer: Because color blindness is recessive, the woman could be a carrier for the condition without knowing it. By examining her family history, the counselor could determine whether she might have the color-blindness

allele. This would be important to know because the condition is sex-linked, so any son would have a 50 percent chance of being color-blind if she were a carrier.

6. Sample answer: The probability of the offspring being both female and color-blind is 25 percent. There is a 50 percent chance for a girl child (XX). And a 50 percent chance that that girl child would be color blind (XCXC), as shown in the Punnett square below.

		Female Carrier	
		X^C	X^c
Male Carrier	X^C	$X^C X^C$	$X^C X^c$
	Y	$X^C Y$	$X^c Y$

Lesson 4.3

Think about Science, page 157

1. species

2. Sample answer: wolves, dogs

Core Practice, page 157

Sample answer: Argument can include evidence Darwin gathered about finches and their beak size, mockingbirds, iguanas, or giant tortoises.

Think about Science, page 158

1. **B** The theory of Universal Common Ancestry states that all life originated from a single organism. For example, that an oak tree, a caterpillar, a dog, and a human all originated from one single prehistoric ancestor.

2. Scientists have found a great deal of evidence in support of UCA.

Core Skill, page 158

Sample answer: All the species listed produce eggs, most have a backbone, a few are warm-blooded, and only two produce live young. The simplest form is the squid because it has the least amount of traits in common with any of the other species; therefore, it is likely that the other species evolved from the squid. There may have been incidents over time of geographical isolation that separated small populations. These populations then adapted to fit into their new environments, and those that were best able to survive passed on traits to the next generation. Over time, these isolated populations evolved into new species. If this process continues over millions of years, it will result in many different species that don't look alike.

Technology Skill, page 159

Answers may vary. The table and cladogram should be modeled after the images on the page.

Vocabulary Review, page 160

1. ancestry
2. cladogram
3. species
4. evolution
5. fossil
6. arrange

Skill Review, page 160

1. **C** If organisms in a population pass on a mutation that makes them better able to survive a hot, dry climate, the species will evolve over time to better survive in the desert. This occurs because the organisms with the mutation live to reproduce more than organisms without the mutation.

2. Theory of Evolution, Theory of Universal Common Ancestry

3. **B** According to UCA, the first form of life on Earth evolved from a universal ancestor.

4. Sample answer: Because fossils are found trapped in layers of sedimentary rock, knowing the geological age of each layer can help determine the age of the fossil and the time period in which the particular organism lived.

5. **B** Each organism has physically adapted to environmental challenges.

6. Answers will vary. The basic arrangement of bones is similar in each of the species but the differing functions of the forelimbs by each animal is evidence of evolution.

Skill Practice, page 161

1. The table should be completed as follows:

	Angelfish	Frog	Cardinal	Platypus	Brown bear
Lungs		X	X	X	X
Claws or nails			X	X	X
Hair or fur				X	X
Gives birth to live young					X

2. Sample answer: DNA from various species can be studied, and similarities can be found between species. Similarities in DNA can help support the theory of evolution because they provide more scientific evidence proving that species that seem unrelated have genetic similarities and therefore may have diverged from one species in the past.

3. Sample answer: An adaptation can help promote evolution because it increases an individual's chances for survival. Those individuals who have adapted will survive and reproduce and pass on the adapted trait to their offspring. In this way, a species changes over time.

Lesson 4.4

21st Century Skills, page 163

Sample answer: I would consider whether the communication is informal or formal, or whether visuals would help me communicate my message to a particular audience.

Think about Science, page 164

1. Sample answer: Crossing over makes it so that offspring have a different combination of genes than either parent.

2. Sample answer: radiation, chemicals, disrupted cellular process, mistake during DNA replication

Core Practice, page 164

Sample answer: Red-green color blindness is caused by a recessive gene on the X chromosome, so it is more likely to occur in males than in females. There does not appear to be any evidence that race plays a role in the incidence of color blindness.

Core Skill, page 165

Sample answer: Students should choose an article about a genetic mutation in any species. They should identify the claims the article makes and assess whether the author's claims are supported in the text. Students should include examples from the text to support their ideas.

Think about Science, page 165

1. **D** Food we eat can affect genetic expression by changing the chemicals in our cells, which could make certain genes become active.

2. **D** One benefit of genetic testing is that you can find out if you are at risk for a particular disease, but you cannot tell for certain that you will get a disease. If you know you are at risk for a disease, you can get tested for the disease more often, or you can alter risk factors that can affect the disease (such as smoking, amount of exercise, staying thin, and so on).

Vocabulary Review, page 166

1. crossing over
2. mutation
3. Genetic recombination
4. Epigenetics
5. assess
6. Replication

Skill Review, page 166

1. **D** Under normal circumstances, replication results in two exact copies of DNA. During DNA replication, the two strands of a DNA molecule separate from one another in a process that is similar to the unzipping of a zipper.

2. **D** The most likely cause of one kind of faulty protein is mutation of a single gene. . One change in a protein can stop its ability to function in the way it was intended.

3. **B** Crossing over occurs during Metaphase I of meiosis when DNA from the male parent and DNA from the female parent exchange parts of chromosomes. Crossing over results in each gamete—egg cell or sperm cell—receiving new combinations of genes. Genetic recombination encourages the increase in the variety of traits within a population.

4. Sample answer: Beneficial mutations allow some individuals to survive better than others. This means the mutated gene will more likely be passed on to the next generation.

5. **C** If one gene in a cell is mutated before replication occurs, and this cell then goes through meiosis, half of the resulting gametes will have the mutated gene. Mutations are copied during the process of replication and are passed down to daughter cells. This means the number of cells that have the mutation will multiply.

6. **D** Childhood diabetes is best explained by epigenetics. The foods we eat, the things we do, and how we feel have an effect on the chemicals in our body. These chemicals can cause genes to be expressed and repress expression of genes. So, in a very direct way, our environment can affect our physical characteristics.

Skill Practice, page 167

1. **D** Mutations can also occur at the chromosome level. These types of mutations can change a large number of genes at once. Large amounts of genetic information can be lost, switched around, or duplicated, causing abnormalities. Sometimes entire chromosomes are lost or extra chromosomes are added. Down syndrome is the result of an extra chromosome 21.

2. Sample answer: Mutations in regular cells are passed on only to daughter cells, so affect only the individual in which the mutation exists. Mutations in gametes are passed on to an offspring that inherits the mutated DNA . Mutations in gametes are heritable, and those in regular cells are not.

3. **C** People might *not* want to be genetically tested because they may fear what they will find out, especially if they are testing for something for which there is no cure.

4. Answers may vary; sample answer: Crossing over provides new combinations of alleles, resulting in greater variety among individuals. Students should give their own ideas as to why variety may be beneficial.

5. **D** Since the pigment enzyme in Siamese cats does not function at temperatures equal to or higher than normal body temperature, the coldest parts of Siamese cats must be ears, tail, feet, nose because these are the parts of the cat that are colored.

6. Sample answer: Mutations may have occurred as the cells replicated. Changes in the environment may have caused changes in the chemicals of the cell, turning certain genes on or off.

7. Sample answer: Scientists would need to limit exposure to environmental factors that cause mutations, such as high-energy radiation and particle radiation. Scientists would also need to create an environment for the clone similar to the environment of the parent so that its epigenetic makeup would remain as similar as possible.

Lesson 4.5

Think about Science, page 169

1. Sample answer: If farmers breed new plants using seeds from plants that survived well or produced fruit with desirable qualities, they can continue to improve their crops.

Core Practice, page 169

Sample answer: If a finch eats hard seeds, it might need a large, strong beak to crack the seeds open. If it eats small seeds or insects, it might not need a large beak.

Core Skill, page 171

Sample answer: Students should realize that adaptations help an organism survive in their natural environment. For example, a dog may have teeth for eating meat, fur to keep warm outdoors, and claws to dig in the ground after rodents.

Think about Science, page 172

1 Sample answer: The tortoises that had a variation for a long neck were able to reach plants more successfully and survive to reproduce. They passed on that variation to their offspring. After many generations, the variation became an adaptation.

2. Sample answer: A crocodile might be able to stay underwater for a long time. It blends in well. It has sharp teeth for eating and capturing prey.

3. Sample answer: Birds have light bones and feathers to help them fly. They have beaks adapted to eat food available in their habitat. They have claws that help them perch or catch prey.

21st Century Skill, page 172

Sample answer: A person who is used to working alone might need to adapt to a new job in a noisy office environment. He or she might have to learn to tune out the surrounding noise. Sometimes people bring their own music to work to help them tune out surrounding noise.

Think about Science, page 173

1. Sample answer: Speciation is the process by which a new species of organisms arises from a parent organism.

2. Sample answer: Allopatric speciation occurs when groups are isolated geographically and they evolve into a new species to take advantage of different resources in each area. Sympatric speciation occurs in the same range, but two species evolve to occupy a different niche.

Workplace Skill, page 173

Sample answer: To use my music player, I first have to push the ON button in the bottom center. Then I have to type in my four-digit passcode. Then I tap the MUSIC icon. Last, I tap the song or artist I want to hear.

Vocabulary Review, page 174

1. artificial selection

2. Speciation

3. example

4. variation

5. natural selection

6. adaptation

Skill Review, page 174

1. **B** Speciation is the process by which a new species arises.

2. **A** It appears to support the theory of natural selection.

3. Sample answer: The change in color probably gave the black moths an advantage, as they were not as easy for predators to see as the white moths. The number of white moths in the population likely decreased over time.

4. Sample answer: This adaptation makes the frog look bigger, and predators might decide it is safer not to approach it.

5. Sample answer: This adaptation makes the predator think the grasshopper is poisonous and therefore they avoid eating it.

6. **D** A wider beak, useful for capturing fish, would be most useful for birds on a small island that is hit periodically by severe storms that kill most of the island's land animals. This is a useful adaptation if the bird can capture fish when no other food is available.

7. **A** Allopatric speciation occurs when organisms become separated geographically and evolve different characteristics. Most often, the different characteristics evolve because a food source is different in the two locations.

Skill Practice, page 175

1. **D** According to the passage, a vestigial structure is one without a known use, such as a tail bone in humans.

2. **C** Ears of birds who use sound to fly at night are *not* vestigial structures because their ears are used for navigation.

3. Sample answer: The puppies are all a little different. They may be different colors, different sizes, have different temperaments, and so on.

4. Sample answer: A white tiger might not be able to survive well if it cannot blend in with its environment. A white tiger that lives in a snowy area might survive well, but a white tiger that lives in a region where it does not snow may stick out, making it easily recognizable by its prey.

5. Sample answer: Being fast can help a fish escape from slower predators; it may also help the fish react to dangerous situations more quickly.

6. Sample answer: A brightly colored fish might be easier for predators to see than a fish that blends in with its surroundings.

7. Sample answer: Large, flat leaves help the plants capture the little sunlight that filters through to the forest floor.

8. **B** According to the diagram, a hawk is the bird most suited to use its feet to pick up small animals because it has large claws for holding prey.

9. Sample answer: Each structure is an adaptation that helps the particular species survive in its environment. For example, the duck-foot structure is an adaptation that helps it swim. Natural selection explains that organisms have variations in traits and that variations that help an organism survive and reproduce will be passed on to offspring and become adaptations.

Chapter 4 Review

1. **A** Mendel performed experiments where he bred pea plants and studied the traits of the plants that grew in each generation. Mendel observed that all of the offspring in the first generation, F_1, of plants were tall, but in the second generation, F_2, some plants were tall and some were short.

2. **C**   A gene usually has more than one allele, and each allele is slightly different so that is can code for a different version of a trait. Two chromosomes will be homologous in that they are for example, both chromosome 13, but their alleles make them different in their DNA sequence.

3. **D**   When you know the genotype of two parents, you can arrange them in a grid, or Punnett square, so that you can predict the genotypes and phenotypes of the offspring. In each square of the grid, you place a different combination of alleles from both parents.

4. **B**   When each parent has one copy of each allele of a gene, there is a 50 percent chance that the offspring will be heterozygous, a 25 percent chance that they will be homozygous dominant, and a 25 percent chance that they will be homozygous recessive. You can use a Punnett square to check this answer.

5. **C**   Darwin's theory of Universal Common Ancestor states that all species on Earth are related and can be traced back to a single common ancestor.

6. **A**   Cladistics is the systematic method for making and testing predictions about evolutionary relationships among organisms. Organisms are organized into groups, or clades, and every member of a clade shares the same evolutionary history. Therefore species in a clade have more in common with each other than they do with species of another clade.

7. **B**   Genetic recombination, or the redistribution of genes in cells, is what causes gametes to have different genetic information. An additional source of genetic variation occurs during Metaphase I of meiosis, when DNA from the male parent and DNA from the female parent exchange parts of chromosomes in a process called crossing over.

8. **C**   Mitosis involves the division or normal body cells. A mutation in this type of cell only affects the individual because only DNA in sex cells is passed down to offspring.

9. **A**   An adaptation is any trait that helps an organism survive and reproduce in its environment. The shallow roots of a cactus help it to survive in dry conditions with very little precipitation.

10. **D**   The process by which a new species of organism arises from a parent organism is called speciation. Speciation can occur in more than one way. When populations of the same species become isolated from each other geographically, they can evolve distinct characteristics. Sometimes new species arise from a single ancestor, but the species are not geographically isolated. Even though the two groups have a range that overlap, they still evolve into distinct species.

11. One plant could have two copies of the dominant allele and the other plant have one copy of the dominant allele and one copy of the recessive allele. This plant would still have the dominant phenotype.

12. Sample answer: A trait that is determined by a gene on a sex chromosome, X chromosome is a sex-linked trait. If the trait is recessive, then there must be two copies of the recessive allele for the individual to have the trait. Females have two copies of the X chromosome, so they must have the recessive allele on both X chromosomes in order to have the trait. Males only have one copy of the X chromosome, so if they have just one copy of the recessive allele, they will have that trait.

13. Sample answer: To distinguish between different clades, scientists look for a characteristic that is unique to one clade or a set of clades. All organisms classified as mammals have hair, so that would not be a distinguishing characteristic of one clade.

14. Sample answer: Epigenetics is the study of how different chemicals not associated with our DNA affect the phenotype of a specific gene. The food we eat introduces certain chemicals into our diet can affect the expression of certain genes.

15. Sample answer: In artificial selection, human choose the traits they would like to see in an organism and they only breed organisms that have those desired traits. In natural selection, the environment plays a role in selecting the traits that are passed on to offspring. Individuals in a population that are more fit or able to survive than others, will mate and produce offspring with similar traits.

16.

	A	a
A	AA	Aa
a	Aa	aa

17. 25%

18. B Since about 50 percent of the offspring are homozygous recessive and about 50 percent are heterozygous, you know that one parent has have two copies of the recessive allele and one parent has to have one copy of each allele. Set up a Punnett square to confirm your answer.

19. A Since the bee has no traits in common with the frog, it is the most distantly related to it. Species that share a common trait more recently diverged into two species.

20. A Since the dog has the most traits in common with the bear, they share all five traits, they are the most closely related in the group of species presented.

21.

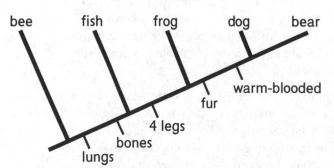

22. C If the existing strand has the sequence GATCCTG, , then the complementary strand that is replicated is CTAGGAC because each base can only pair with its complement: G pairs with C and A pairs with T.

23. D Each round of DNA replication produces two new daughter strands, one is synthesized using the coding DNA strand, and the other is synthesized on the non-coding strand. During one round of replication there are two new strands. After the next round the total would be double, or four new strands, and after the third round the total would double once more to eight.

24. A Darwin's finches are examples of adaptive radiation. The 13 different species of finches all evolved from a common ancestor and have adapted different beaks so that each of them is able to consume a different type of food.

25. Sample answer: Since the environmental conditions were different on each island, on each island different traits enabled the tortoise to obtain food and survive. Therefore, on different islands, different variations were more fit, so those traits were passed on to the next generation. Over time, the tortoises on each island looked very different from each other. Nature was responsible for the selection of traits.

26. The climate can affect the amount of sunlight and precipitation and therefore the food sources available to a species. A species may be able to adapt to survive in the new climate.

27. D Genetic variation can lead to the expression of a physical trait that makes an individual better suited, or adapted, to its environment.

28. Sample answer: An offspring only needs one copy of a dominant allele to express the physical characteristics of the trait that is the adaptation. Therefore, a dominant trait will be passed to offspring at a higher frequency than a recessive trait.

29. Sample answer: When a species adapts to its environment it undergoes changes in physical traits. These changes can be traced by studying fossils of a species and scientists can also see that new species evolve when adaptations occur. This argues that there was likely one species on Earth originally that underwent adaptations under different environmental conditions and these adaptations led to new species forming. In time, there were multiple species that continued to evolve forming new and different species.

Lesson 5.1

Calculator Skill, p. 185

18 km ÷ 0.50 h = 36 km/h

Core Skill, p. 185

Speed v. Time

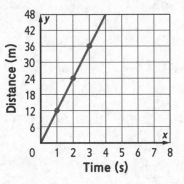

Think about Science, p. 186

1. 5 m/s

2. Sample answer: The object is traveling at a constant speed, and its acceleration is 0 m/s².

Workplace Skill, p. 186

Sample answer: Place a block of wood between the hammer and the metal part.

Core Practice, p. 187

0.70 m/s to the left

Think about Science, p. 187

1. collision

Vocabulary Review, p. 188

1. momentum

2. graph; acceleration

3. velocity

4. speed

5. law of conservation of momentum

Skill Review, p. 188

1. **B** Notice that the choices are given in meters per second. Convert the 1 minute in the question to 60 seconds to get a speed of 1080 m/60 s, and then simplify by dividing the numerator by 60. The speed is equal to 1080 m/60s = 18m/s.

2. **B** Acceleration = (final velocity - initial velocity)/time, where velocity equals speed if there is no change in direction of motion. The runner begins from rest so the change in speed is 3.6 m/s and the change in time is 2.0 s. So 3.6 m/s ÷ 2.0 s = 1.8 m/s².

3. **C** Momentum = mass × velocity. The mass is 45.0 kg and the velocity is 9.0 m/s south. So momentum is 45.0 kg × 9.0 m/s, which is 405 kg · m/s south.

4. Sample answer: The collisions are not completely elastic, so some of the kinetic energy is changed to other forms of energy during each collision.

5. Sample answer: Both velocity and speed are measures of distance per unit of time, but velocity includes a direction component, and speed does not.

6. Answers may vary; sample answer: Replace the wooden slat with corrugated cardboard. The collisions will be more inelastic as energy is transferred to bending paper layers.

7. **C** The momentum of a 0.060-kg tennis ball served east across the court at 45 meters per second is 2.7 kg • m/s east.

8. **B** The momentum of a 4.5-kg bowling ball rolling to the right in the ball-return chute at 0.60 meters per second is 2.7 kg • m/s to the right.

9. During an inelastic collision, some of the kinetic energy is changed to other forms of energy

Skill Practice, p. 189

1. **C** The acceleration due to gravity is 9.8 m/s².

2. **B** A falling object accelerates at the same rate during each second of its fall. The acceleration between 2 and 3 seconds is 9.8 m/s².

3. **D** After the first second, the object accelerates to 9.8 m/s. During the next second, its speed increases again by 9.8 m/s, giving a total speed of 19.6 m/s.

4. **A** Momentum = mass × velocity. The greatest combination of mass and velocity is the 1,000-kg car driving at 100 km/h.

5. Answer: 0.4 m/s²

6. 520 kg · m/s

7. Initial momentum:

Car 1: 15,000 kg × 10 m/s = 150,000 kg · m/s

Car 2: 15,000 kg × 0 m/s = 0 kg · m/s

Total initial momentum = 150,000 kg · m/s

Final momentum:

150,000 kg · m/s because momentum is conserved

Final velocity = final momentum ÷ mass = 150,000 kg · m/s ÷ 30,000 kg = 5 m/s]

8.

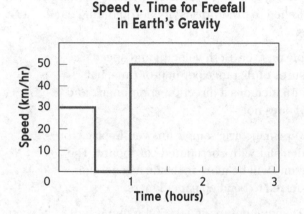

Speed v. Time for Freefall in Earth's Gravity

Lesson 5.2

Core Skill, p. 191

Rearrange the equation to find $F_{net} = ma$; 50 kg × 1.5 m/s² = 75 N and 65 kg × 1.2 m/s² = 78 N; the force needed is greater for the 65-kg person.

Think about Science, p. 192

1. B According to Newton's first law of motion, an object at rest tends to remain at rest. Objects resist a change in their motion.

2. D Force is directly proportional to acceleration, so if the force is tripled so is the acceleration. Therefore, the acceleration is 9.0 m/s²

Think about Science, p. 193

1. doubles; decreases; one-fourth

2. 490; less

Core Practice, p. 193

Sample answer: 1.72×10^3 N at 4 m; 1.51×10^3 N at 400,000 m; the force of gravity on Earth is greater than on the space station, but astronauts are still pulled to Earth by gravity, so the calculation does not support the idea.

Vocabulary Review, p. 194

1. gravity

2. weight

3. force

4. inertia

5. law

6. state

Skill Review, p. 194

1. B According to Newton's first law, an object in motion will continue to move with constant motion unless a force acts against it. In this case, the passenger will move forward until a seatbelt or windshield exerts a force.

2. B Force equals mass times acceleration, $F = ma$. This equation can be rearranged to solve for acceleration, $a = F/m$. The mass is 20 kg and three different forces are given. The acceleration for a force of 7 N, is $a = $ 7 N/20 kg, or 0.35 m/s². The acceleration for a force of 8 N, is $a = $ 8 N/20 kg, or 0.40 m/s². And the acceleration for a force of 15 N, is $a = $ 15 N/20 kg, or 0.75 m/s². To find the average of .35 m/s², 0.40 m/s², and 0.75 m/s², add them to find the total and then divide by 3 to get 0.5 m/s².

3. A Earth pulls the apple downward. The reaction force must be equal in magnitude and opposite in direction. So the reaction force would be exerted by the apple upward on Earth.

4. B Gravity decreases as the square of the distance decreases.

5. **C** When a pool stick hits a cue ball, the action and reaction forces are the stick pushing on the ball, and the ball pushing on the stick.

6. Sample answer: This idea does contradict Newton's first law because the law states that objects tend to stay in motion if they are in motion unless acted on by a force. The force that causes objects to come to a stop can be friction. The effects of friction can be seen when an object comes to a stop on a surface with only the surface to stop it. Objects stop more quickly on a rougher surface if the same amount of force is used to make them move because the force of friction is greater on rough surfaces.

7. Sample answer: The force of the gases being pushed out of the rocket is the action force. The reaction force is the gases pushing back on the rocket. The reaction force pushes the rocket upward.

Skill Practice, p. 195

1. **B** Weight is mass times the acceleration due to gravity, $W = mg$. This equation can be rearranged to solve for acceleration, $g = W/m$. On Venus, on 60.0-kg object weighs 533 N. So $g = 533$ N/60.0 kg $= 8.9$ m/s^2.

2. **B** Dividing the weight of an object on Earth by the weight of the same object on Mars gives a value 2.6 times greater.

3. **C** One way to solve the problem is to use the given weight to find the acceleration due to gravity on Saturn. Weight is mass times the acceleration due to gravity, $W = mg$. This equation can be rearranged to solve for acceleration, $g = W/m$.

4. **B** A larger mass would lead to an increase in the acceleration due to gravity, but an increased radius would lead to a decrease in the acceleration due to gravity. Therefore, it can be the same on Mars as on Mercury.

5. Sample answer: The ball will be going the fastest on Jupiter. The weight of the 60-kg person is the greatest on Jupiter. Therefore, the acceleration due to gravity is the greatest on Jupiter. The object moves the same distance on each planet, so its final velocity depends only on its acceleration.

6. Sample answer: The objects will accelerate at the same rate if only gravity is acting on the objects because acceleration due to gravity does not depend on the mass of the object. Combining the equations for the force on an object due to gravity and the law of universal gravitation shows that the mass of an object cancels out, and acceleration due to gravity depends only on the mass of Earth.

Lesson 5.3

Think About Science, p. 197

1. **B** Work is equal to force times distance, $W = F \times d$. The equation can be rearranged to solve for distance, $d = W/F$. In this situation, the force is the weight so $d = 1250$ J/50 N, which is 25 J/m. A joule is a N $\cdot$ m, so Newtons cancel and the final answer is 25m.

2. **C** Power = work/time = force $\times$ distance/time.

Core Skill, p. 198

Sample answer: For a body weight of 130 pounds and a vertical height of 3.5 meters, $W = 4.4$ N/lb $\times$ 130 lbs $\times$ 3.5 m $= 2002$ N−m, or 2002 J. The work is the same in each situation. If it took 7 s to walk the stairs, the power to walk the steps is 286 W. If it took 4 s to run the stairs, the power to run the stairs is 500.5 W. The power increases when it takes less time.

21st Century Skill, p. 199

Answers may vary: Responses should describe an invention and the human need that prompted its creation. They should explain the conditions under which the need might arise, the work required to complete a task with and without the invention, and possible further improvements that might make the invention even more useful.

Core Practice, p. 200

Sample answer: There is an inverse relationship between the distance and the force. The work stays the same for each situation. So, when the distance from the pencil, or the fulcrum, is less, the force needed to raise the pennies is greater. When the distance from the pencil, or fulcrum, is greater, the force needed to raise the pennies is less.

Think About Science, p. 200

1. Sample answer: The wheel is a wheel and axle, and the pedals are attached to levers that turn a pulley. Hand brakes and gearshifts are also levers.

Think about Science, p. 201

1. Sample answer: Increase the number of rope segments holding up the load.

Calculator Skill, p. 201

1. $15 \div 6 = 2.5$

2. $4 \div 10 = 0.4$ m

Vocabulary Review, p. 202

1. compound machine

2. simple machine

3. power

4. revise

5. Work

6. mechanical advantage

Skill Review, p. 202

1. **B** Work is equal to force times distance, $W = F \times d$. The equation can be rearranged to solve for force, $F = W/d$. In this case, 1,500 J/20 m = 75 N.

2. **D** Work is equal to force times distance. If force increases but distance decreases, work may remain the same. Similarly, if distance increases but force decreases work may also remain the same. The only guarantee that work increases is an increase in both force and distance.

3. **A** Mechanical advantage equals output force divided by input force. MA = output force/input force. The equation can be rearranged to solve for input force, input force = output force/MA. Therefore, input force = 1950 N/15, which is 130 N.

4. **A** The inside of a jar lid has threads like a screw.

5. Sample answer: The work is the same because the forces and the distances are the same. But more power is needed to do the work more quickly.

6. Sample answer: The amount of work is constant because the force and the distance do not change for a particular event. Machines can decrease the amount of work people have to do, but something—the machine—has to make up the difference in work.

7. There are four ropes so the mechanical advantage is 4.

Skill Practice, p. 203

1. **D** The person exerts a smaller force than is needed to lift the car. The jack multiplies the force applied to lift up the car.

2. **C** Work equals force times distance. Velocity equals distance divided by time, so time must equal distance divided by velocity. So rewrite the power equation as $p = \frac{F \times d}{\frac{d}{v}}$. Simplify to $p = Fv$.

3. **A** If the person exerts a smaller force than is needed to do work, that force must be exerted over a longer distance than the output force is.

4. Answer: $15 \div 6 = 2.5$

5. Sample answer: The copper chisel was a wedge because it is used to separate objects. It cut out limestone blocks.

6. Sample answer: Workers used ramps (inclined planes) to push the blocks into place. The ramps were extended as the pyramid rose higher.

7. Sample answer: The pole acted as a lever, and the ropes might have been pulleys. The pole would have been used to lift the block up, and the ropes could have been used to change the direction of the force as the workers positioned the blocks.

Chapter 5 Review

1. Sample answer: The position of the plane is over Chicago. The speed of the plane is 885 km/h. The velocity of this plane can be described as 885 km/h traveling east.

2. time = distance/speed, time = 1.27 hours

3. **C** An **acceleration** is the rate of change in velocity. A car that slows to a stop and then speed up again is first accelerating in a negative direction, or decelerating, and when the car speeds up again it is accelerating in a positive direction.

4. **B** Momentum is the product of velocity and mass. Therefore, you must know the mass of an object and the speed and direction it is traveling to calculate its momentum.

5. **D** Use the formula, $F = ma$ to calculate the force exerted by the rock. From the information given in the problem you know that the mass of the rock is 30 kg and its acceleration is 70 m/s². So, the force is equal to $F = (30 \text{ kg})(70 \text{ m/s}^2) = 2100 \text{ kg} \cdot \text{m/s}^2$.

6. **A** Newton's first law of motion states that an object at rest tends to stay at rest, and an object in motion tends to stay in motion with the same velocity, unless an unbalanced force acts on it. Therefore, if you wear a seat belt it will prevent your body from continuing to move forward when the car comes to a sudden stop.

7. **B** Newton's second law of motion states that an object acted upon by a force will accelerate in the direction of the force. The equation that explains this law is:

   $$\text{acceleration} = \frac{\text{net force}}{\text{mass}} \qquad a = \frac{F_{net}}{m}$$

   Therefore, since the bowling ball has a greater mass, it takes more force to stop it.

8. **A** Forces in which the two interacting objects are not physically touching each other are known as action-at-a-distance forces. When a magnet is brought near a paper clip, the magnet exerts a force on the paper clip without having to touch it. The Moon exerts a pull on Earth's oceans, even though the Moon is hundreds of thousands of kilometers away from Earth.

9. **C** The gravitational force between two objects is dependent on distance as shown in the equation:

   $$F = \frac{Gm_1m_2}{r^2}$$

   where r is the distance between the center of two objects. It also shows that gravity decreases rapidly as the distance between the objects increases.

10. **D** Using the formula and the weight and distance given in the equation for work, you can solve this problem:

    $$W = Fd$$
    $$W = 75\text{N} \times 56\text{m} = 4200 \text{ N·m} = 4200\text{J}$$

11. **C** Using the formula and the information given, the power of the motor is:

    $$p = \frac{W}{t}$$
    $$p = \frac{10{,}000\text{J}}{30\text{s}} = 333 \text{ Watts}$$

12. **C** The axle is attached to the center of a larger wheel, and the wheel and axle rotate together. The input force can be applied to either the wheel or the axle. A screwdriver (axle) acting on a screw (wheel) is an example of this type of simple machine.

13. **C** Lifting an object with a fixed pulley requires the same amount of force as lifting it by hand, but the pulley changes the direction of the input force, making easier to lift the object.

14. **D** The mechanical advantage of a machine is the ratio of the output force to the input force. It can be calculated using the following equation: mechanical advantage = output force / input force, written as $MA = F_{out} / F_{in}$.

15. **B** The acceleration has decreased from point B to point C. This can be determined by calculating the slope of the line between 4 seconds and 6 seconds.

16. **A** An increase in acceleration is indicated by a positive slope of the line. The curve exhibits a positive slope in the region of A.

17. Sample answer: At point B the slope of the line is zero. The object is moving at a constant rate of 10 m/s. Since the speed is constant, the acceleration at this point is zero.

18. **B** In an elastic collision, there is no loss of kinetic energy, or the energy of motion, in the collision. When two objects collide they will move apart at the same speed bu opposite direction with which they approached each other. In an inelastic collision, there is a change in kinetic energy, so the objects will not move apart with the same speed.

19. Sample answer: When two objects collide, momentum remains the same. However, the momentum of one object can be transferred to the other object during the collision. If no other forces act on the two colliding objects, the total momentum of the two objects remains constant.

20. Sample answer: Equal and opposite forces acting on the same object will cancel each other out for a net force of zero. However, although an action and a reaction force are equal and opposite forces, they do not act on the same object and do not therefore, cancel each other out.

21. Sample answer: Weight is the force of gravity acting on the object. Mass is the measurement of the amount of matter in an object. Weight and mass are related since weight is dependent on mass.

22. **B** Since $W = Fd$, the work done to get the machine to function is:

$$W = Fd$$
$$W = 60N \times 0.25m = 15J$$

23. **B** Since the output work of a machine is always less than the input work, the only way that the output force can be 3 times greater than the input force is if the input force is exerted over a greater distance. Since $W = Fd$, you can see that an increase in distance will give the same result as an increase in force.

24. Sample answer: The set of spheres that are closer together will have a greater gravitational force on each other. Since gravitational force is represented by the equation,

$$F = \frac{Gm_1m_2}{r^2}$$

this shows that gravitational force will increase as the distance between the objects, r, decreases.

25. Sample answer: If the mass of one sphere is doubled, the gravitational force will double. By using the equation,

$$F = \frac{Gm_1m_2}{r^2}$$

you can see that as the mass of either sphere increases, the force, F, will also increase.

26. Sample answer: Force and motion must be in the same direction for work to be done on an object, therefore work is being done in A, not B.

27. **B** Since work is equal to the force of an object times the distance over which the force is applied, the only relevant measurement is distance. Force is not directly dependent on acceleration, mass or speed.

Lesson 6.1

Think About Science, p. 213

1. **A** The gravitational potential energy is greatest while the leaf is still attached to the branch.

Core Skill, p. 213

Answers will vary.

Core Practice, p. 214

Answers may vary. Responses should explain how the suggested change would improve the accuracy of the results of the investigation.

Think About Science, p. 215

1. radiant

2. kinetic

3. nuclear

4. chemical bonds

Workplace Skill, p. 215

Sample answer: Scientists often test the validity of their hypotheses by whether the results of an investigation can be duplicated. If you don't follow the directions, your results might be different.

Think About Science, p. 216

1. The compass is labeled as S for South because if it is attracted to Earth's magnetic north pole, the end of the compass needle must be a magnet south pole.

Think About Science, p. 217

1. **B** A toaster converts the electrical energy supplied to it through the wire into thermal energy that heats the bread to make toast.

Calculator Skill, p. 217

The value of x is 2 less than the value of y.

Vocabulary Review, p. 218

1. potential energy

2. mechanical energy

3. energy transformation

4. anticipate

5. Law of conservation of energy

6. kinetic energy

Skill Review, p. 218

1. **B** Kinetic energy is energy associated with motion whereas potential energy is stored energy.

2. **C** An object stores potential energy as a result of its position or condition.

3. **D** Kinetic energy can be transformed into potential energy and vice versa. And kinetic energy can also transform into another form of kinetic energy, but potential energy is always converted into kinetic energy, not potential energy.

4. **D** If two similar magnetic poles are pushed together, they gain more energy that has the potential to move them apart when released.

5. **D** The transfer of chemical energy to thermal energy is necessary to regulate your body temperature on a cold day.

6. kinetic energy; magnetic energy; electric energy

Skill Practice, p. 219

1. **B** GPE increases with height. At point C, the pendulum is at its lowest height so its GPE is zero.

2. **D** When the pendulum reaches its highest point, it stops instantaneously and changes direction. At this point, it is not moving so its kinetic energy is zero.

3. The mass of the pendulum and the maximum height above the lowest point of the swing.

4. **C** Kinetic energy depends on mass and velocity. So KE $= \frac{1}{2}mv^2 = \frac{1}{2}(12.5 \text{ kg})(3.50 \text{ m/s})^2 = 76.6$ J.

5. **C** When an ice cube melts, it absorbs radiant energy from sunlight and transforms it into thermal energy as the water particles increase in speed.

6. You can calculate its gravitational potential energy from its mass and height. $GPE = mgh$. Then, you know that as the walnut falls, its gravitational potential energy is converted to kinetic energy. So just before it lands, its kinetic energy is equal to the gravitational potential energy it had before it fell. You can therefore set the kinetic energy equation equal to the gravitational potential energy $KE = \frac{1}{2}mv^2$ so GPE $= \frac{1}{2}mv^2$. Then you can rearrange the equation to solve for v; $v = \sqrt{\frac{2GPE}{m}}$.

7. Answers may vary; sketches should show that a stationary electron is surrounded by a field and that moving electrons in a circuit have both kinetic and potential energy.

8. Venn diagrams should show Kinetic Energy: Electrical current and Heat; Potential Energy: Chemical Energy, Magnetic Energy, and Both: Mechanical Energy.

Lesson 6.2

Think About Science, p. 222

1. C All energy sources can release thermal energy. Not all energy sources can be replaced, produce carbon dioxide, or can be burned.

2. C The dangers associated with handling nuclear fuels makes them difficult to transport, whereas fossil fuels can be easily transported.

Core Practice. p. 223

You might label one circle of the diagram as **Nonrenewable Resources** and the other as **Renewable Resources**. In the circle for Nonrenewable Resources, you might write fossil fuels and nuclear energy. In the circle for Renewable Resources, you might write solar energy, geothermal energy, biomass, wind energy, and energy from water.

Think About Science, p. 224

1. A Biomass, wind energy, and hydroelectric power are all ultimately driven by the Sun. The Sun, for example, heats the atmosphere unevenly, which causes wind. The Sun also heats water, causing it to evaporate, thereby driving the water cycle.

2. C Geothermal energy comes from inside Earth. This source of the energy cannot be transported and therefore cannot be used in cars, but biomass is abundant and readily accessible.

Core Skill, p. 224

Sample answers:

temperature differences → wind

wind → turns a windmill

windmill → pumps water or grind grain

wind turbines → electricity

wind → pushes turbine blades

Think About Science, p. 225

1. B Hydroelectric power does not release pollution into the air. Biomass, because it involves burning, does.

2. A Solar power is considered an inexhaustible energy source, meaning that it is constantly being produced so it will not decrease in supply like natural gas can since it is a nonrenewable resource.

Workplace Skill, p. 225

Be sure to consider the type of building your business might require and where is might be located. Think about what energy resources are available, and how each one will ultimately affect your overhead expenses. Look for ways to reduce your expenses by making different choices when it comes to energy resources.

Vocabulary Review, p. 226

1. energy resource

2. nuclear fission

3. nonrenewable resource

4. classify

5. renewable resource

6. fossil fuel

Skill Review, p. 226

1. A Renewable energy resources are continuously produced in nature. Their costs are likely to decrease over time as opposed to nonrenewable resources.

2. D Biomass is produced in nature at a rate that is close to the rate at which it is used.

3. C Hot spots are associated with geothermal energy, so this energy resource could not be used in the eastern United States.

4. B Plants absorb the energy of sunlight during photosynthesis. It is stored in foods, such as soybeans. Coal is formed from the remains of plants so it stores energy that originally came from the sunlight.

5. Answers may vary; sample answer: Fossil fuels and nuclear energy are nonrenewable and may run out someday. Fossil fuels are relatively inexpensive and can be used to meet a variety of energy needs, including electricity, heating, and transportation. Fossil fuels release carbon dioxide and other pollutants into the atmosphere. Nuclear energy does not produce carbon dioxide, but it does produce radioactive waste that must be stored for a long time. The locations of power plants that use either fossil fuels or nuclear energy are not limited by resource availability. Given the choice, I would choose to get my electricity from a power plant that uses nuclear energy because nuclear energy does not produce carbon dioxide.

6. Sample answer: The graph shows that the price of natural gas decreased significantly from 2006, while the cost of fuel oil and coal both increased. However, the price of coal is still less than natural gas. It is likely that the decrease in the cost of natural gas has increased its use, especially if the choice was between natural gas and fuel oil. If price is the only factor, the use of coal most likely did not change much, because its price is low compared to the other two sources of energy.

Skill Practice, p. 227

1. **C** Hydropower requires that water fall from one height to another.

2. **C** Solar energy is most useful in regions that receive a lot of sunlight throughout the year, such as in the desert.

3. **A** The blades of wind turbines can turn very quickly. They are generally high in the air where birds might fly into them.

4. Sample answer: The cause is the construction of the dam to produce electricity, and the effect is a decrease in the amount of water that flows through the river. Because there is less water, the river runs more slowly. Because the flow of the river is altered, fish populations could be harmed.

5. Sample answer: Fossil fuels are the primary nonrenewable energy resource, and they may run out. As a result, these fuels are likely to become more expensive in the future. Power plants that use nonrenewable energy resources do not have that problem. As the technology for using renewable resources improves, power plants that use these resources are likely to be able to reduce their cost of generating electricity. Additionally power plants that use fossil fuels produce carbon dioxide, and those that use nuclear energy produce radioactive waste. With the exception of biomass, power plants that use renewable energy resources do not produce those pollutants.

6. Sample answer: Solar power plants have the benefits of not producing pollution and of using energy from the Sun, which cannot be used up. As more solar power plants are constructed, the cost of generating electricity using solar power is likely to decrease. However, solar power plants can generate electricity only when the Sun is shining. Also, the solar panels needed to generate the electricity take up a lot of space, which could have a negative impact on animals and plants that live where the power plant is constructed. To minimize the negative effects, I would plan to construct a solar power plant in an area that receives a large amount of sunlight. I would also look for a location that has few plants and animals and study the impact of the power plant on those organisms.

7. Sample answer: Both hydroelectric power and wind power are produced from renewable resources and produce little pollution. However, they are also both limited in their availability. Wind power is available only in regions where there is sufficient wind, and hydroelectric power is available only where dams can be built in rivers. The dams needed for hydroelectric power can adversely affect fish populations downstream of the dam. Both types of power are used only for electricity generation. Unlike biomass, they cannot be burned in homes to produce heat or in cars to power engines. Both wind and hydropower would be best used to generate electricity in places where those resources are available.

Lesson 6.3

Think about Science, p. 229

1. Temperature

2. Heat

3. **C** Thermal energy is measured in joules.

4. **B** Temperature is a measure of the thermal energy of a substance. Ice is the coldest substance listed, so it will have the lowest average thermal energy per particle. It is also a solid and the particles in a solid will move more slowly than those in a liquid, which will move more slowly than those in a gas.

Core Skill, p. 229

Sample answer: Thermal energy is the amount of energy contained in a system, and it is measured in joules. Temperature is a measure of the amount of average thermal energy per particle in a substance. It is measured by Kelvins or degrees.

Think about Science, p. 230

1. convection; sinks; top

2. conduction; radiation

Core Practice, p. 230

Sample answer: As the ice cube melts, the water around it cools and sinks. As it sinks it pushes the water from the bottom of the container to the top.

Think about Science, p. 231

1. Sample answer: The friction between your shoes and the snow generates heat that melts the snow.

2. Sample answer: A large amount of thermal energy is generated by friction during the high speed reentry.

3. Sample answer: Rubbing the eraser on the paper results in friction, which generates heat.

21st Century Skill, p. 231

Sample answer: If a machine has been running, friction has probably caused part of the machine to heat up. Wearing gloves may prevent me from getting burned. Employee safety is the rationale behind this policy, and it convinces me to wear the gloves.

Vocabulary Review, p. 232

1. compare

2. Convection

3. radiation

4. temperature

5. heat

6. conduction

Skill Review, p. 232

1. **B** When a substance is heated, its particles absorb energy. This causes them to move faster and farther apart.

2. **D** Conduction involves the transfer of thermal energy between objects that are in direct contact.

3. **A** Thermal energy is transferred to the marshmellow by radiation.

4. Sample answer: The act of rubbing the sticks together is kinetic energy. The friction from the sticks rubbing together converts the kinetic energy into thermal energy, and the temperature of the sticks rises.

5. **C** Thermal energy is transferred from warmer substances to cooler substances.

6. Sample answer: Temperature measures of the average thermal energy of the particles in a substance. Temperature tells how active the particles are. This thermal energy is transferred as heat. Heat is the transfer of thermal energy in matter. The temperature determines in which direction the heat flows, because heat normally moves from a substance of higher temperature to a substance of lower temperature.

Skill Practice, p. 233

1. **D** The average thermal energy is highest when the temperature is highest. Temperature increases from bottom to top along this graph.

2. **A** Particles have the least motion when the water is in the solid state. This occurs at the bottom left of the graph.

3. D The motion of particles will be greatest at the highest temperature. Pouring the cooler water into the warmest water will result in the greatest motion.

4. Sample answer: I would get another beaker of hot water and take the temperature of both beakers of water. I would then pour the warm water into the ice water. I would measure the temperature of the water at regular intervals. I know that the thermal energy in the hot water is transferred as heat through convection to the ice water. The process continues until the ice water warms and the hot water cools to the same temperature. Once they reach the same temperature, the temperature will stop changing.

5. Sample answer: The food is warmer than the air in the refrigerator. When the food is placed in the refrigerator, heat flows from the food to the air of the refrigerator until they are the same temperature.

6. Sample answer: The light reflected from the Moon is an example of radiation as it travels to Earth in waves. The steam rising from a factory is an example of convection because the steam is hotter than the air around it and rises; the steam is less dense than the cooler air. When a cold penny is held, heat flows from the hand to the penny by conduction, and the penny is warmed.

7. Sample answer: Because the Sun and Earth are not in contact, the heat from the Sun cannot be transferred to Earth by conduction. The space between the Sun and Earth does not have either a liquid or a gas through which convection can occur.

8. Sample answer: The friction between your tires and the road is great when you slam on the brakes. The heat generated caused the tires to burn.

Lesson 6.4

Think about Science, p. 235

1. C The disturbance is the event that starts the wave. In this case, it would be the first fan who stood up and down.

2. A Energy of wind blows on water to create waves. It also pushes against the boat.

Core Skill, p. 235

Sample answer: Supportive phrases: *repeating disturbance; transfers energy through matter or space.* Interesting phrases: *sound waves, radio waves, ocean waves; the swinging of a giant pendulum.*

Think about Science, p. 237

1. B Frequency is directly related to velocity, so as one increases so does the other.

Calculator Skill, p. 237

Answer: 341 m/s

Think about Science, p. 237

1. A When the velocity of a wave remains the same, frequency and wavelength are inversely proportional. So, when frequency increases, the wavelength will decrease.

Core Practice, p. 238

Sample answer: The speed of light is slower in air, slower in liquid water, and even slower in solids like glass and diamonds than it is in a vacuum.

21st Century Skill, p. 239

1. When frequencies overlap, the amplitude of the wave increases.

2. Crossing the bridge in several small groups produces smaller-amplitude vibrations. These smaller waves are less likely to match the natural wave frequencies of the bridge, produce a large-amplitude wave, and cause the bridge to collapse.

Think about Science, p. 239

1. D As frequency decreases, the wavelength increases.

2 A Nuclear explosions are the disturbance that produces electromagnetic waves.

Vocabulary Review, p. 240

1. discriminate

2. wave

3. medium

4. radiation

5. electromagnetic waves

Skill Review, p. 240

1. **D** Sound waves are longitudinal waves. They can be described by compressions, rarefactions, and amplitude.

2. Both **C** and **D** are correct. Frequency and velocity waves, and transverse and longitudinal waves.

3. **A** The piece of tape moves upward as the wave moves along the rope.

4. **C** The electromagnetic spectrum is arranged in a given order by frequency. Radio waves have the lowest frequencies and gamma rays have the highest frequencies.

5. Sample answer: Because sound travels faster through water than through air, the wave with the higher wave speed could be traveling through water, while the other wave would be traveling through a slower medium, such as air.

6. Sample answer: The coil at rest would have no wave traveling along it, so it would have no compressions or rarefactions.

7. **B** Microwaves and infrared waves have similar frequencies.

Skill Practice, p. 241

1. **C** It disputes the belief that all light exists only as a continuous wave.

2. **B** Light causes electrons to be emitted.

3. **D** Sound waves, which are longitudinal, require a medium such as air in order to travel. There is no atmosphere between Earth and Mars so sound waves cannot travel through space.

4. Sample answer: The ball would rise and then fall as the energy is transferred along the surface of the water in the wave.

5. Frequency describes the number of times per second a point in the medium moves up and down. Wavelength describes the distance between two troughs on the wave. Frequency and wavelength are related by the wave velocity of the medium.

6. Sample answer: In air, light travels faster than sound. The light waves of the lightning travel faster than the sound waves of the thunder. Therefore, we see the lightning before we hear the thunder.

Chapter 6 Review

1. potential, kinetic

2. more

3. **B** When ice is melted by the Sun, radiant energy from the Sun increases the temperature of the ice, because the radiant energy is transformed into thermal energy.

4. **D** When the electrons in atoms interact to form a chemical bond, the energy that is stored in this bond is chemical energy. The sources of this stored energy are the electromagnetic force fields of the charged particles that make up the atoms.

5. **D** Some objects can affect other objects from a distance due to a field that exists around the them. A force is a push or pull exerted in an area around the object producing it. Electrical energy and magnetic forces are both the result of fields.

6. **A** Biomass is burned to produce energy and this releases pollutants into the atmosphere in much the same way that burning coal introduces carbon dioxide and other pollutants into the air.

7. **A** Conduction is the transfer of thermal energy between particles that collide with each other. When these particles make contact in a collision, the particle with more kinetic energy passes some energy to the particle with less energy. When an iron skillet is heated over a flame there is a transfer thermal energy by convection and radiation to the bottom of a skillet; then the thermal energy is conducted from the skillet to the food that is cooking inside of it.

8. **C** Friction between two objects converts kinetic, or mechanical energy to thermal energy in the form of heat.

9. **C** Within the electromagnetic spectrum, waves with the highest frequency have the highest energy level. Both gamma rays and X-rays have a high frequency and therefore, are both high energy waves.

10. **A** Within the visible light provided by the Sun, plants use the red and blue bands of the spectrum to create food in the process of photosynthesis. Plants appear green because they absorb red and blue light, but reflect the green light.

11. **D** A wave's speed can be calculated by using the following equation:

speed = frequency × wavelength.

12. **A** A longitudinal wave can also be called a compression wave. In a longitudinal wave, such as a sound wave or a seismic wave, the medium moves back and forth parallel to the direction in which the wave travels. You can create a longitudinal wave by squeezing together several coils of a stretched-out spring and releasing them.

13. electromagnetic, mechanical

14. mass, velocity

15. the Sun

16. Heat

17. Sample answer: Coal is a nonrenewable source of energy formed from dead plants that decayed millions of years ago and were covered with layers of rock. The heat and pressure under the many layers forms coal over time. Coal supplies are limited, but it is a readily available and inexpensive resource that is widely used in power plants to generate electricity. Another disadvantage is that burning coal generates pollution and excess carbon dioxide in the atmosphere. Wind power is a renewable energy source that can be used to turn large turbines and generate electricity. This is a clean source of energy that does not generate pollutants, but it takes a lot of land to put up enough wind turbines to generate electricity for a given population.

18. Sample answer: Nuclear fission is the source of energy in an nuclear power plant. The splitting of the nucleus of a uranium atom can produce a large amount of energy that is used to generate electricity. While there is enough uranium stored in the Earth to provide energy for thousands of years, the process of fission produces more radioactive particles. Radioactivity in high doses is harmful to humans, animals, and plants.

19. Sample answer: 1) fossil fuels: The energy provided to the plants and animals that died millions of years ago to form fossil fuels came either directly from the Sun, or the sun's energy was transferred from plants to animals that ate those plants. 2) wind energy: Wind is caused by temperature differences in the air and the Sun causes air to be warmer in some areas than others. 3) energy from water: Water moves through the Earth and the atmosphere in the water cycle. The Sun is the driving force behind the water cycle and is the source of energy of moving water.

20. Sample answer: Heat is the flow of thermal energy between substances at different temperatures and always flows from an object of higher temperature to an object of lower temperature. When a hot substance is in contact with a colder substance, energy will flow from the hotter object toward the cooler object so that over time both substances will be the same temperature and heat will no longer flow from one to the other.

21. Sample answer: Convection is the transfer of thermal energy generated by the movement and mixing of particles in a substance. In a gas or a liquid, particles can move past one another, but in a solid, the particles can only vibrate and cannot move around to cause the transfer of energy.

22. Sample answer: Ultraviolet waves have a high enough energy level that they can cause burns to the skin if exposed to them for too long. Excessive exposure can lead to sunburn or even skin cancer. However, short exposure to ultraviolet waves can have health benefits. UV waves produce vitamin D in the body. UV waves can also be used to kill pathogens in hospitals and laboratories. Also, police use UV lights to search a crime scene for fingerprints or body fluids.

23. A An important property of all waves that you should remember is that they transfer energy, but not matter, from one place to another.

24. C The energy that is released when coal is burned, originated from the Sun and passed from plants to animals in a food web. When plants and animals died millions of years ago, their bodies decayed and were buried under layers of soil. Due to intense pressure and extreme heat below Earth's surface, rock formed, trapping the energy of these decaying organisms inside. This rock is the coal extracted from the Earth and burned for its high energy content.

25. A According to the chart, only 0.11 percent of the energy used in the U.S. in 2012 came from Solar power. The Sun is an available energy source in just about all regions of the U.S.

26. A Coal was the most abundantly used energy source in the U.S. in 2012, so you can infer that it was also the cheapest form of energy.

27. A Temperature measures the average thermal energy per particle in an object. Heat is the flow of energy from one object to another. Heat flows from teh higher temperature object to the lower temperature object.

28. Sample answer: For an object to heat the air, it must transfer thermal energy from itself to the air. A higher temperature means greater average kinetic energy of particles in a substance and that means that the molecules in a substance of higher temperature are moving faster than those of a cooler temperature. Faster moving particles transfer more thermal energy than those that are moving more slowly. Therefore, substances with greater average kinetic energy can transfer more thermal energy to the surroundings.

29. Sample answer: Radiant energy from the Sun can be absorbed by gas molecules and increase their movement. The increase in movement causes an increase in kinetic energy. Increased kinetic energy results in an increase in the temperature of the air.

Lesson 7.1

Core Practice, p. 251

Sample answer: Rust forms more readily in saltwater than it does in distilled water or in air alone.

Think about Science, p. 252

1. Alkaline earth metals

2. Metalloids

3. 16

4. protons and neutrons

Core Skill, p. 252

Sample answer: Bohr's model suggests that an electron's specific orbit can be described, so this model applies to the statement in a limited way. The Heisenberg model shows electrons in a possible area, or "cloud." The statement applies more to this model.

Think about Science, p. 253

1. **C** A subscript is written down and to the right of the symbol for the element in describes. The *3* is to the right of the symbol O so it indicates 3 atoms of oxygen.

2. **C** Atoms can transfer or share electrons in order to form a bond between each other.

Workplace Skill, p. 253

Sample answer: This symbol appears when a danger to the eyes exists and when safety goggles should be worn.

Vocabulary Review, p. 254

1. Matter

2. atoms

3. chemical bond

4. atoms; elements

5. periodic table

Skill Review, p. 254

1. **C** Elements are arranged in order of atomic number on the periodic table. The atomic number is the number of protons so the element with 7 protons comes to the right element with 6 protons.

2. **B** The subscript shows the number of atoms. If no subscript is written, it is assumed to be 1. So the formula with NH_3 shows 1 atoms of nitrogen and 3 atoms of hydrogen.

3. **A** The atomic nucleus consists of protons and neutrons. Only protons carry an electric charge.

4. **D** Both products are made up of different elements, so they are compounds.

5. Sample answer: The atoms that make up an element are all the same and have the same properties, including the atomic number.

6. Answers may vary; sample answer: The experiment should include using water and some other liquid to dissolve a sugar cube. A possible liquid could be oil. One small beaker could contain 50 mL of room-temperature water. Another beaker could contain 50 mL of room-temperature oil. A sugar cube would then be placed in each beaker, and the time it takes for each sugar cube to dissolve would be timed. Times would be compared to demonstrate that water is the more effective solvent.

Skill Practice, p. 255

1. **B** A group is a vertical column of the periodic table.

2. **C** Nonmetals are to the right of the metalloids.

3. **C** Atomic mass increases down a group so the element in the highest period will have the greatest atomic mass.

4. **B** The prefix *di-* means two, so dihydride means 2 hydrogen atoms. The prefix *mono-* means one, so monoxide means 1 oxygen atom.

5. Answers may vary; sample answer: In the investigation, a few drops of water might be combined with a piece of pure silver (Ag), a square of aluminum foil (Al), and an iron nail (Fe). Every day for a week, a few drops could be added to each sample, and any observed changes recorded.

6. Sample answer: Diagrams should show one circle labeled *Germanium* and the other circle labeled *Arsenic*. The overlapping area should list the following: *both metalloids, both in the same period, both are solid at room temperature.* The germanium circle should list the following: *Group 14.* The arsenic circle should list the following: *Group 15.* The circles could also list the different atomic numbers.

7. **A** The defining characteristic of an atom is that it has all the properties of an element.

8. **D** The structural relationship is atoms to elements to protons.

Lesson 7.2

Think about Science, p. 257

1. **A** Unlike the other physical properties listed, which can be common to many substances, density is unique to a substance.

2. **A** Chemical properties can be observed only as the composition of the matter changes. The ability to rust, for example, is observed as the iron reacts with oxygen to form iron oxide.

Workplace Skill, p. 257

Iodine: 4.93 g/cm³, iron: 7.87 g/cm³, silicon: 2.33 g/cm³, sodium: 0.97 g/cm³.

Core Skill, p. 258

Sample answer: It is possible that the water in the air condensed and then froze, as the diagram shows that a gas changes to a liquid when it condenses and a liquid changes to a solid when it freezes. However, the diagram also shows that it is possible that the gas could have changed directly to a solid through the process of deposition.

Think about Science, p. 260

1. **B** Water vapor loses energy and becomes a liquid during condensation.

2. **D** The particles in a solid are held rigidly in fixed positions. They can slide past one another in the liquid state.

Think about Science, p. 261

1. **D** Metals can conduct electricity. Transition metals are found across the center of the table. Silver is a transition metal.

2. **C** Elements in Groups 1 and 2, as well as Group 7 are highly reactive. Magnesium is in group 2.

Core Practice, p. 261

Sample answer: The conclusion is not valid. The text states that elements in group 1 are reactive, but it also states that they are metals. According to the text, all metals except mercury are solids, and all metals conduct electricity, but the tested element was a nonconductive liquid. It is more likely that the element is a reactive nonmetal, such as the elements in group 17.

Vocabulary Review, p. 262

1. physical property

2. chemical property

3. states of matter

4. sublimation

5. evaluate

6. melting point

Skill Review, p. 262

1. **C** Different elements have different melting and boiling points, as well as different densities. They can, however, have the same mass.

2. **B** Water can absorb energy from the air or from sunlight to change from a liquid to a gas. This process is known as evaporation.

3. **C** Elements in the same group of the periodic table tend to share similar chemical properties. Carbon and silicon are in the same group.

4. Sample answer: Aluminum is a metal and it is a shiny, conductive, and relatively hard solid. Silicon is a metalloid and could be a shiny or dull solid. It is likely to be brittle and conductive under certain conditions. Phosphorus is a nonmetal and could be solid or a gas. If it is a solid, it will be brittle and nonconductive.

5. Sample answer: The properties of aluminum are likely to be the most similar to gallium. Aluminum and gallium are in the same group, so they have the same number of outermost electrons, which should give them similar chemical properties. They are also both metals, which means they should be shiny, conductive solids at room temperature. Although boron is in the same group, it is a metalloid and will have different properties than aluminum and gallium.

6. Sample answer: Aluminum is a metal, and silicon is a metalloid. To distinguish between the elements, I could test the electrical conductivity of the samples. Aluminum is likely to be more conductive than silicon, and I could look up known values to evaluate my results. I could also test the samples to determine whether they are brittle. Silicon is a metalloid, so it is likely to be brittle. Aluminum is a metal, so it would be malleable.

Skill Practice, p. 263

1. **C** The region represents a change from a solid to a liquid if energy is being added. This change is known as melting.

2. **C** The water is not changing state in this region of the graph. It is liquid only.

3. **B** The amount of heat is shown across the bottom of the graph. The difference from the beginning of the region to the end is 40 kJ.

4. **C** The graph stops once the gas is formed. It does not show a line representing the increase in the temperature of the gas.

5. Sample answer: As water is heated in region **d**, it boils because it is at 100°C, the boiling point of water. The temperature does not change, because the energy added is used to overcome the attractions between the water particles. If the heat is removed, the water will cool and condense because condensation happens at the boiling point as energy is transferred to the environment.

6. Sample answer: The melting and boiling points of ethanol are lower than those for water, so the straight lines labeled **b** and **d** will be at different temperatures. The straight line labeled **b** will be at −114° C because melting and freezing occur in this region of the graph. The straight line labeled **d** will be at 78°C because boiling and condensation occur in this region. The amount of heat that needs to be added in regions **a** and **c** will also be different.

7. Sample answer: In the heating curve made using twice the volume of water, the water will still melt at 0°C and boil at 100°C because melting point and boiling point are properties that do not depend on mass or volume. Therefore, regions **a** and **d** will occur at the same temperature as the curve shown. More energy will be needed to heat the water and to overcome the attractions between the particles as water changes states, so the new graph will show that more heat is added in each region.

Lesson 7.3

Think about Science, p. 265

1. Sample answer: A new substance is formed.

2. Oxygen

Core Skill, p. 265

Answers may vary; sample answer: During a chemical reaction, atoms are rearranged to form new substances, but the total number and types of atoms does not change. Yes, all examples of balanced chemical reactions support this central idea.

Think about Science, p. 267

1. $CH_4 + 2O_2 \rightarrow CO_2 + 2H_2O$

2. $2KOH + H_2SO_4 \rightarrow K_2SO_4 + 2H_2O$

Workplace Skill, p. 267

Sample answer: They are separated by an arrow that points from the reactants to the products.

21st Century Skill, p. 268

Answers may vary. Responses should explain why a particular type of program would be effective. Accept all reasonable answers.

Think about Science, p. 269

1. endothermic

2. exothermic

Core Practice, p. 269

Answers may vary; sample answer: The temperatures of the solutions must be kept constant.

Vocabulary Review, p. 270

1. endothermic

2. chemical reaction

3. balanced chemical equation

4. develop

5. exothermic reaction

Skill Review, p. 270

1. **B** During a chemical reaction, bonds are broken, atoms are rearranged, and new bonds are formed. As a result, a new substance or substances are always formed.

2. **D** A balanced chemical equation shows the same number of each type of atom on both sides of the equation. This equation shows 4 carbon atoms, 12 hydrogen atoms, and 14 oxygen atoms on both side of the equation.

3. **B** The prefix *endo-* means "into." Energy is absorbed from the environment during an endothermic chemical reaction.

4. Sample answer: Increasing temperature causes atoms or molecules to move faster, causing them to collide and react more frequently.

5. Answer: $CS_2 + 3O_2 \rightarrow CO_2 + 2SO_2$

6. Answer: Oxygen molecules

7. Answer: $2Mg(s) + O_2(g) \rightarrow 2MgO(s)$; 40.3 grams

Skill Practice, p. 271

1. **C** The symbol delta Δ is used to represent a change in some quantity. The letter H is used to represent the energy of a chemical reaction.

2. **A** Activation energy is the energy required for the reaction to proceed. It is absorbed from the environment.

3. **D** An exothermic reaction releases energy. As a result, the energy of the products is less than that of the reactants.

4. C A balanced chemical equation shows the same number of each type of atom on both sides of the equation. This equation shows 2 Ag atoms, 2 N atoms, 6 O atoms, 2 Na atoms, and 1 S atom on each side of the equation.

5. A The ratio in the equation of $NiCl_2(s)$ to $O_2(g)$ is 1:3. If the reaction mixture starts with $3\ NiCl_2(s)$ to $10\ O_2(g)$, the ratio is 1:10 so $NiCl_2(s)$ is the limiting reagent.

6. Answer: $3H_2 + N_2 \rightarrow 2NH_3$

7. Sample answer: Exothermic reactions can sustain themselves. In an exothermic reaction, there is a net gain in energy. Some of the energy released as one reactant is converted to products and used to start another reaction. Endothermic reactions use energy, so they cannot be sustained without more energy being added.

Lesson 7.4

Think about Science, p. 273

1. C The solvent is the substance that does the dissolving. In sweet tea, particles from tea leaves and sugar are the solutes and water is the solvent.

Core Skill, p. 273

Sample answer: Ice crystals will form at 0°C because that is the temperature at which water freezes. Ice crystals will form at a temperature below 0°C because salt water freezes at a lower temperature than pure water.

Core Practice, p. 274

Sample answer: The independent variable is the temperature of the water. The dependent variable is the time it takes for the sugar to completely dissolve. The experiment will include 1 cup of water at different temperatures and 1 tablespoon of sugar. I will time how fast the sugar dissolves in the water. My hypothesis is that the sugar will dissolve faster in warmer water. I observed that the sugar dissolved faster as the water temperature increased. After conducting the experiment, my results confirm my hypothesis. As the temperature increases, the time it takes for sugar to dissolve decreases.

Think about Science, p. 276

1. Heat; pressure

2. saturated; unsaturated

3. supersaturated

Think about Science, p. 277

1. D The term *alkaline* indicates a base. The pH of bases is above 7.

2. A An acid releases hydrogen ions in solution.

21st Century Skill, p. 277

Answers may vary; sample answer: Most workplaces require employees to wear safety glasses and gloves while handling chemicals. This policy ensures that workers' eyes and hands are protected from spills or splashes.

Vocabulary Review, p. 278

1. saturation

2. solubility

3. acid

4. design

5. base

6. solution

Skill Review, p. 278

1. C The solvent is the substance in which the other substances are dissolved. In shampoo, the solvent is water.

2. A You would apply a base. The only base listed is baking soda.

3. A Substances dissolve other substances with similar properties.

4. B A substance that does not dissolve in another substance is said to be insoluble. Polar solutes and ionic solutes dissolve in polar solvents and nonpolar solutes dissolve in nonpolar solvents.

5. B A solution is a homogenous mixture. That means that the mixture is uniform throughout, or example the same in every part.

6. Sample answer: The body can absorb more nitrogen gas as the pressure underwater increases when the diver goes deeper. When the diver returns to the surface, the nitrogen comes out of the solution, but if it happens too quickly, it will not get removed from the body, and it will form bubbles inside the diver's body.

7. Sample answer: Heating the water, crushing the cube, and stirring the water will result in the fastest rate of dissolving.

8. **C** A solution is a homogeneous mixture of one substance in another. Table salt dissolved in water is a solution.

Skill Practice, p. 279

1. **D** A pH of 11.5 indicates a strong base. It would have to be mixed with an acid to form a neutral solution. The only acid listed is sparkling orange drink because it has a pH that is less than 7.

2. **B** A solution forms when a solute becomes evenly mixed throughout. Sand would sink in water rather than dissolving.

3. Sample answer: The independent variable is the amount of sodium acetate in the solution or the size of the activator strip. The dependent variable is the time it takes to produce heat.

4. The solubility of sodium chlorate at 50° C is about 120 g/100 g of water.

5. **C** The solubility of some substances increases with temperature. If a solution at a higher temperature is saturated and then slowly cooled, the additional solute may remain in solution. As a result, the solution becomes supersaturated.

6. Sample answer: A seed crystal causes the sugar to crystallize on the string.

Chapter 7 Review

1. **B** Every atom is made up of protons, neutrons and electrons. The atomic number of any atom of the same element is given by the number of protons in its nucleus.

2. **C** In an atom, protons and neutrons are localized in the nucleus of the atom, and the electrons move about the nucleus in a region scientists call an electron cloud. Electrons are situated based on their energy levels and can move from one energy level to another depending on the state of the atom.

3. **A** Density is the amount of mass of a substance in a given volume and is calculated using the formula $d = \frac{m}{v}$, where m is mass and v is volume.

4. **D** Temperature and pressure can change the state of matter, boiling point and melting point of an object, but not its mass.

5. **C** When the particles at the surface of a liquid change from a liquid to a vapor, this process is called evaporation. Molecules on the surface of the substance absorb thermal energy and when the energy is at a great enough amount, the molecules will escape from the surface of the liquid.

6. **D** Temperature and concentration have an effect on the reaction rate of a chemical reaction. Rate will increase with increasing temperature and increasing concentration. The formation of sodium chloride will be faster if the temperature is 40°C instead of 20°C, and in a reaction with a greater amount of chlorine gas in the reaction chamber, the rate will also increase.

7. C Reactions that release heat are called exothermic reactions. The energy given off in a chemical reaction comes from the bonds that are broken in the reactants and the new bonds that are formed in the products. If the products of a reaction are more stable—that is, their bonds require less energy—than the reactants, energy will be released as the products are formed.

8. A The law of conservation of mass states that mass can neither be created or destroyed in a reaction. Therefore, even though changes to matter occur in a chemical reaction, the total mass of all of the products is equal to the total mass of all the reactants.

9. B Salt dissolved in water forms a solution. A solution forms when a solute completely dissolves in a solvent.

10. C Certain factors can increase the rate at which a solute dissolves. The rate of dissolving is affected by the type of solvent, the amount of stirring, the temperature, and the surface area of the solute. An increase in the surface area of the solute will increase the dissolving rate because it increases the amount of solute that comes into contact with the solvent.

11. D Flammability is a chemical property of a substance.

12. B A saturated solution is a solution that is at a point where the addition of one more microgram of solute will not dissolve at a given temperature.

13. C Chemical bonds break and new bonds form new substances.

14. A chemical formula gives information about which elements are in the compound and their ratios.

15. Sample answer: The reaction between H_2 and O_2 results in the formation of water, H_2O. Since there are twice as many hydrogen atoms as oxygen atoms in the final water molecule, the hydrogen molecules are used up twice as fast as the oxygen molecules. Therefore, the hydrogen molecule is the limiting factor in this chemical reaction.

16. Sample answer: Polar solutes and ionic solutes will dissolve more easily in a polar solute such as water. Nonpolar solutes will dissolve more easily in a nonpolar solvent.

17. B When you look at the periodic table the periods are arranged in rows moving across the table. In the second row, boron, B is the third element.

18. A The atomic radius is essentially the distance from the nucleus to the outermost electrons of an atom. Atomic radius decreases across a period. Moving down a group, new energy levels in the electron clouds of the elements are added to accommodate additional electrons. Atomic radius therefore increases down a group.

19. B Most elements in the periodic table are metals, and are to the left of the zigzag section, towards the right side of the table. With the exception of hydrogen, the nonmetals are found to the right of the zigzag section on the periodic table.

20. Sample answer: Oxygen is an element found in group 16 of the periodic table. The group number can be used to determine the number of electrons in the outermost or valence shell. In the case of groups 13 through 18, the number of valence electrons is equal to the group number minus 10. Therefore, the number of valence electrons in an oxygen atom is 6.

21. A Most of the known elements on Earth are metals.

22. At this temperature water is undergoing a change of state from a solid to a liquid as it is heated from a lower temperature or from a liquid to a solid as it is cooled.

23. C The melting point is a physical property of matter that does not change with a change in mass or volume of a substance.

24.

Reactants	Products
K = 1	K = 1
Cl = 1	Cl = 1
O = 3	O = 2

25. This chemical equation is not balanced because there are 3 atoms of oxygen in the reactants and only 2 atoms of oxygen in the products.

26. $2KClO_3 \rightarrow 2KCl + 3O_2$

Reactants	Products
K = 2	K = 2
Cl = 2	Cl = 2
O = 6	O = 6

27. Vinegar is an acid and so it has a lower pH than water which is neutral. An acid will lower the pH of a solution. pH is a measure of the hydrogen ion concentration in solution. An acid dissolved in water will add to the hydrogen ion concentration of the solution. Adding hydrogen to the solution will lower the pH value. So, adding vinegar to water will lower the pH of the solution to below 7.

28. To determine the pH of a solution, is it necessary to measure the concentration of hydrogen ions. Hydrogen ions will only dissociate from a substance when it is dissolved. So, it is necessary to have a solution to measure pH.

Lesson 8.1

Think about Science, page 289

1. A Nitrogen makes up about 78 percent of Earth's atmosphere. Oxygen makes up about 21 percent. The remaining 1 percent is a mixture of gases that includes argon, carbon dioxide, water vapor, and trace amounts of other gases.

Workplace Skill, page 289

Your answer will depend on air quality in your area. A sample answer might include the following information: About 30 percent of the days have poor air quality. When air quality is poor, I can't walk to work or jog after work. I tend to stay inside.

Core Practice, page 291

Keep in mind that a persuasive essay attempts to persuade the reader to support a particular point of view. Sample answer: According to the EPA, the generation of electricity accounts for approximately 33 percent of America's greenhouse-gas emissions, and transportation accounts for 28 percent. So electricity and transportation together account for 61 percent of Americans' greenhouse-gas emissions. Three ways Americans could significantly reduce their greenhouse-gas emissions include using public transportation, using human-powered transportation (walking or biking), or finding ways to reduce use of electricity.

Think about Science, page 292

1. A Carbon dioxide occurs in small concentrations in Earth's atmosphere, but as a greenhouse gas, it has a large impact on Earth's climate. Argon does not affect climate.

Think about Science, page 293

1. Your answer should mention some daily activity that uses fossil fuels, such as driving. You may suggest biking to work to reduce the amount of carbon dioxide added to the atmosphere.

2. 19,000

Core Skill, page 293

As you examine the graph, focus on the overall trend, rather than small fluctuations. Sample answer: The graph shows that levels of atmospheric carbon dioxide have risen over the past 100 years. A graph of fossil-fuel consumption would show the same trend. Burning more fossils fuels would cause an increase in levels of atmospheric carbon dioxide; conversely, burning fewer fossil fuels would cause a decrease in levels of atmospheric carbon dioxide.

Vocabulary Review, page 294

1. tabulate

2. ozone

3. atmosphere

4. greenhouse effect

5. gas

6. climate change

Skill Review, page 294

1. **A** The rocket would travel through the layers of the atmosphere in order from closest to Earth's surface to farthest from Earth's surface. The troposphere is the closest layer to Earth's surface, followed by the stratosphere, the mesosphere, the thermosphere, and the exosphere.

2. **B** Most living things need oxygen to survive. The concentration of oxygen decreases with altitude in the atmosphere, making the upper atmosphere inhospitable for life.

3. **D** Tropical rain forests play a role in helping maintain Earth's normal temperature range by helping to reduce excess carbon dioxide gas in the atmosphere.

4. **B** The cutting of tropical rain forests could lead to an increase in climate change.

Skill Practice, page 295

1. On Earth, the balance of incoming radiation roughly equals the amount of radiation released. The process that maintains this balance is called the greenhouse effect and is controlled by greenhouse gases such as carbon dioxide. Because Venus has an extremely high level of carbon dioxide, the greenhouse effect on Venus is likely much more severe than it is on Earth. Thus, an intense greenhouse effect would explain the difference between the surface temperatures of Earth and Venus.

2. Models may vary and can be two-dimensional (i.e. drawings) or three-dimensional (i.e. structures). You may suggest using terrariums to model the difference in the flow of heat energy on Venus and Earth. You may refer to increases or decreases in atmospheric carbon dioxide when explaining how variations in the flow of energy lead to climate change.

3. Sample answer: Fossil fuels are made of carbon. When they are burned, this carbon is released into the atmosphere as carbon dioxide. Levels of atmospheric carbon dioxide increase. Atmospheric carbon dioxide functions as a greenhouse gas. Increases in the concentration of carbon dioxide cause Earth's temperatures to increase, which leads to climate change.

4. **C** Ozone is an important gas in Earth's atmosphere because it prevents harmful radiation from reaching Earth's surface.

5. Sample answer: I would want my satellite to orbit in the exosphere so it would be above both the troposphere, where weather occurs, and the stratosphere, which contains the ozone layer. Also, the exosphere is very thin and would best allow for a smooth orbit without interference from air currents.

6 Sample answer: The troposphere has the highest air pressure because it is the layer closest to the Earth. Air pressure decreases with altitude as the mass of the air above you decreases.

7. **D** More solar radiation will be reflected into space when thick clouds form over an area.

8. Answers may vary; sample answer: I would agree that the human population has increased. However, I would point out that our use of fossil fuels has increased dramatically over the past 150 years, and that burning fossil fuels plays a major role in increasing levels of atmospheric carbon dioxide.

9. Sample answer: If chlorofluorocarbons destroy the ozone layer, less harmful ultraviolet radiation is absorbed in the upper atmosphere, and more of this harmful radiation reaches Earth's surface. If this harmful radiation reaches humans and other organisms, they could get sick or die.

10. Greenhouse gases warm the surface of the Earth. An increase in the concentration of greenhouse gases, such as carbon dioxide, leads to an increase of Earth's temperature.

Lesson 8.2

Think about Science, page 297

1. Saltwater contains dissolved salts; freshwater contains minimal small amounts of dissolved salts; saltwater is denser than freshwater.

2. The density of the water would increase.

Core Skill, page 298

Look over the list of materials and determine how you can use them to model how continents affect surface currents. You may fill the container with water to create a model global ocean. You can use the clay to create model continents throughout the ocean. You may place the fan near one end of the container and turn it on to model wind. You will likely observe that the model continents change the shape and direction of surface currents, often decreasing their size and speed. Differences in observations may be a result of differences in the number or size of model landforms or differences in wind speed.

Think about Science, page 299

1. **A** Precipitation is always freshwater. Adding freshwater to ocean water would cause the salinity of the ocean water to decrease.

Core Practice, page 300

Recall that the independent variable is the factor that changes in an investigation. The dependent variable is the factor that responds to changes in

the independent variable. Sample answer: Students will likely use a freshwater sample and a saltwater sample. They may add food coloring to the samples to distinguish them. Then they will likely mix the samples to observe layering. The independent variable is salinity. The dependent variable is layering. Students should conclude that water with high salinity sinks under water with little or no salinity because saltwater is denser than freshwater.

Workplace Skill, page 301

Make sure you are correctly interpreting the bar graph. The year is labeled at the bottom of each bar. The top of each bar corresponds to the cod harvested in any one particular year. Sample answer: The cod harvest has decreased since 1980. This could mean that the population of cod has decreased or that the fishing industry's efforts to limit the cod harvest have been successful. Additional measures may include restocking cod populations.

Vocabulary Review, page 302

1. draw conclusions

2. water cycle

3. characteristic

4. salinity

5. ocean

Skill Review, page 302

1. **A** Winds drive surface currents. The top layer of the ocean is exposed to wind, so the speed of surface currents would be greater at a depth of 100 m than it would at deeper depths.

2. **B** Wave height depends on wind duration, wind speed, and fetch. An increase in any of these factors would tend to increase wave height. Conversely, a decrease in any of these factors would tend to decrease wave height.

3. **B** If the ocean water were placed under a heat lamp, water would evaporate and leave the salts behind. This would increase the salinity of the remaining water.

4. **A** Evaporation from the surface of the ocean is caused by energy from the Sun. In latitudes that experience four distinct seasons, the intensity of sunlight would be lowest during winter. Therefore, rates of evaporation would be lowest during winter.

5. Sample answers: Taste the water, determine the density of the water, evaporate the water to see if salts remain behind.

6. The tides would not be as pronounced, because the Moon's gravitational pull is the main cause of tides, and if the Moon were farther away, its gravitational pull would decrease.

7. Sample answer: The California Current is a cold surface current that flows past the western coast of North America. It has a cooling effect on the regions it passes.

8. Sample answer: rising sea level; coral bleaching

Skill Practice, page 303

1. **B** Sample 2 has the coldest temperature, indicating that it came from deeper parts of the ocean where density currents flow.

2. **C** Sample 3 has the highest temperature and is most likely warmed by sunlight. Sunlight is needed by phytoplankton during photosynthesis.

3. **D** The basic motion water follows as a wave passes is a circular motion.

4. **C** Long-term increase in air temperature would have the greatest impact on global ocean water density.

5. Sample answer: Oceans are very important to life. They are a source of food and shelter to living things. They also moderate Earth's climate, keeping temperatures at an optimal level for life, and provide water that falls to Earth's surface as precipitation. Without precipitation, crops cannot grow.

6. Sample answer: Designs likely will involve using a sample of hot saltwater and a sample of cold saltwater. Food coloring can be added to the samples to distinguish them. The samples can be mixed, and the resulting layering observed.

7. You would expect salinity to be lower near the shore where freshwater sources flow into oceans. You would also expect water

temperatures to be higher in the shallow parts of the ocean and then decrease with depth as you move to the open ocean. Density depends on temperature and salinity, so ocean water near the shore would not be as dense as deep ocean water. You would expect to find high salinity and low temperatures along the bottom of the ocean where density currents flow.

8. Sample answer: A rise in sea level would adversely affect humans and other organisms along coastal regions in Alaska. Melting ice would reduce land habitats; rising temperatures would make the area unsuitable for some species. Homes and other structures might be damaged.

9. Sample answer: The oceans are interconnected, and water flows freely throughout the oceans. So, pollution in the Indian Ocean could eventually make its way to the Pacific Ocean and harm marine organisms there.

Lesson 8.3

Think about Science, page 304

1. Continental crust is usually thicker and lighter than ocean crust, which is thinner and denser.

2. The lower mantle and the inner core are solid. The outer core is liquid. Part of the upper mantle can flow slowly like soft plastic.

Core Practice, page 305

Visualize Earth's interior before you attempt to answer the question. Sample answer: I would use an avocado as a physical model of Earth's interior. The skin could represent Earth's crust, the flesh of the fruit could represent the mantle, and the pit could represent the core. This would be a good model because the skin is very thin, just as the crust of Earth is very thin, relative to the other layers. The pit is solid, just as Earth's inner core is solid (although Earth's core is solid only because of the immense pressure). In general, the different compositions of each part of the avocado represent the different compositions of each layer of Earth.

Think about Science, page 306

1. Desert soil would not be good for growing plants, because there would not be much organic material in the soil, as there are not many plants and animals in a desert.

Core Skill, page 307

Use information from the text as well as your own prior knowledge to draw conclusions. Sample answer: The continents are still moving because the plates are still moving. In the future, some continents will continue moving farther apart. In some places continents may ram into other continents.

21st Century Skill, page 308

Focus on regions that experience frequent earthquakes, and consider the physical and chemical properties of the materials used to construct buildings. Sample answer: The West Coast, perhaps along the San Andreas Fault, might be the best region in which to market this type of construction. Earthquakes are common along this fault, so buildings must be able to withstand the large amount of earthquake activity. Building materials should be flexible, such as types of metal or wood. Inflexible materials that will break, such as brick or stone, should be avoided.

Think about Science, page 309

1. **D** When heat and pressure force magma up through Earth's crust, volcanoes can form.

Workplace Skill, page 309

Sample Data Table:

Year	How Much Wider Trench Is Than First Measurement (cm)
Year 1	0
Year 2	5
Year 3	10.1
Year 4	14.9
Year 5	20

Vocabulary Review, page 310

1. Weathering
2. mineral
3. Plate tectonics
4. rock cycle
5. theory
6. Erosion

Skill Review, page 310

1. **A** Granite is an igneous rock. When it is heated, it changes into magma, or melted rock material.

2. **C** Metamorphic rocks form when rocks are subjected to intense heat, pressure, or chemical reactions.

3. **B** Amber is an organic material. Minerals are inorganic materials.

4. **B** The part of Earth that lies below tectonic plates is dense and flows like melted plastic. Less dense tectonic plates "float" on top of this fluid layer.

Skill Practice, page 311

1. **C** The Mid-Atlantic Ridge is a midocean ridge. This type of feature forms at divergent boundaries where tectonic plates move apart. Magma rises up through the resulting cracks.

2. **B** If seafloor spreading did not occur at equal rates on both sides of the ridge, the continents on either side of the ridge would be different distances from the ridge.

3. Sample answer: New crust is being formed wherever magma comes to the surface in volcanoes or cracks in Earth's crust, such as midocean ridges.

4. Sample answer: A volcanic mountain range might form where two plates collide, making the land rise to form a mountain range. One plate slides under the other, where it melts, and the magma is forced up into the volcanic mountains. A volcanic mountain range could also form where two plates diverge, such as at ocean ridges. The magma escapes where the plates diverge, forming a volcanic mountain range.

5. Sample answer: Plate tectonics force molten material from Earth's interior upward toward the surface, where it cools as igneous rock. Heat and pressure at plate boundaries can turn rock into metamorphic rock.

Lesson 8.4

Think about Science, page 313

1. Answers may vary; sample answer: People use trees to make furniture. They eat animals. They use horses for recreation, transportation, and farming.

2. Sunlight, water vapor, and carbon dioxide are used during photosynthesis to provide oxygen in the air.

Core Practice, page 314

You may find it helpful to view brief examples of scientific oral presentations on the Internet. Sample answer: Smog is a type of air pollution that forms when emissions from vehicles that burn fossil fuels react with sunlight. It can cause respiratory health problems. Acid precipitation is precipitation that is more acidic than normal. It forms when emissions from burning fossil fuels react with water and other gases in the air. Acid precipitation can damage aquatic ecosystems and harm trees. It can also chemically weather human-made structures, particularly those made of limestone.

Think about Science, page 315

1. **A** Fossil fuels are nonrenewable resources. Therefore, their supply is limited and may run out in the future.

2. **C** Nuclear power does not cause pollution, habitat disruption, or climate change. However, it does generate radioactive wastes that remain dangerous for many thousands of years. These wastes must be safely stored so that they do not contaminate the environment.

21st Century Skill, page 315

Remember to use reputable Internet sources for your research. Sites that end in .gov and .edu are good choices. Sample answer: One essay might support a nuclear power plant using data showing the number of jobs created, the amount of energy produced, and how advances in technology have lessened the threat of contamination from nuclear wastes.

Workplace Skill, page 316

Think about your audience before you begin your brochure. What is your customer base and what information is most likely to appeal to this base? Brochures will vary but should stress that solar energy is nonpolluting, so using it helps reduce the amount of carbon dioxide released into the atmosphere. Brochures should be organized in a logical manner and include graphics with captions and labels, as needed.

Core Skill, page 317

Be respectful when critiquing the work of other students. Point out potential issues in a constructive manner. Sample answer: My state of Ohio has a wind-power capacity of about 426 MW. This is below average compared to states such as Texas and California, which have wind-power capacities of 12,212 MW and 5,549 MW, respectively. While wind energy will never meet all of our state's energy needs, it still shows promise for some energy generation. In addition, it will help reduce our state's carbon-dioxide emissions. My recommendation is to research which parts of the state have the highest wind-power capacities and invest time and resources in developing wind energy in those areas.

Vocabulary Review, page 318

1. demonstrate

2. natural resources

3. fossil fuels

4. Sustainability

Skill Review, page 318

1. **C** Fossil fuels are easy to obtain and relatively inexpensive compared to other energy resources. They do cause pollution, however, and are nonrenewable.

2. **D** Placing higher taxes on fossil fuels would encourage people to conserve their use of these energy resources and so reduce the amount of carbon dioxide released into the atmosphere when fossil fuels are burned.

3. **A** A dam is required to generate hydropower on a large scale. Dams can disrupt habitats. This is one major disadvantage of hydropower.

4. Sample answer: Minerals, biomass, soil, and coal would be solids. Petroleum and water would be liquids. Wind, natural gas, and air would be gases.

5. Sample answer: A renewable resource can be used and replaced by natural processes over a relatively short period of time. A nonrenewable resource cannot be replaced or can be replaced only by natural processes over millions of years.

6. Answers may vary. Sample answer: The company can plant a new tree each time it cuts down an existing tree.

7. Answers may vary. Sample answer: Student rebuttals should summarize the disadvantages of using fossil fuels. They may mention that fossil fuels are nonrenewable and cause pollution and habitat disruption. In addition, they are associated with climate change. Students may also discuss the problems associated with basing an energy plan on energy sources that will someday run out.

8. Sample answer: Solar power is nonpolluting. The technology to generate solar energy on a large scale is expensive.

9. Geothermal energy is produced by naturally occurring steam and hot water beneath Earth's crust. Geothermal energy is abundant, and it does not cause pollution. A disadvantage, however, is that it can be used only on a large scale near tectonically active sites. Biomass is the total amount of plant or animal matter on Earth that could be converted to fuel. It is readily available, but it can add pollutants to the air when burned.

Skill Practice, page 319

1. **A** Nuclear power plants have safeguards to prevent a core meltdown. Scientists did not realize that these safeguards could fail.

2. **C** Radioactive wastes can remain in the environment for thousands of years. Exposure to these wastes can cause serious health problems that often appear years or even decades later.

3. Sample answer: Solar power is most appropriate, given that my area experiences many sunny days each year. I suggest that fossil fuels be used until an infrastructure for solar energy can be constructed.

4. Sample answer: Given that oil is limited, oil-producing countries are controlling how much oil is sold, and people are shifting their demand for oil to alternative energy resources.

5. Answers may vary. Sample answer: I have used resources including food, energy, air, minerals, and water. Ways to reduce use of nonrenewable resources include turning off appliances when they are not in use, reusing a container rather than throwing it away, and carpooling to work.

6. Sample answer: Coal would best meet future energy needs in the United States because we have the highest reserves of coal and many years of extraction remaining. Our proven reserves of natural gas are much lower, and we are not on the list of top countries for petroleum reserves.

7. Answers may vary. Sample answer: Biomass includes matter from plants. Plants get their energy from the Sun during photosynthesis. They store some of this energy in stems and other plant parts. When you burn plant matter, you are releasing energy that first came from the Sun. Nuclear energy involves the nuclear fission of radioactive elements and does not come from nor require the Sun's energy.

Lesson 8.5

Think about Science, page 321

1. Warmer air can hold more water vapor than cooler air.

2. Over time, the temperature and humidity of an air mass take on the temperature and humidity of the source region.

3. A cold front forms.

Core Skill, page 321

You may want to take notes as you read and view the weather reports. This will make it easier to compare the formats. Sample answer: The printed information stays visible for as long as I want to examine it, while the video continues on. The video shows damage caused by past storms, while the printed forecast describes the future.

Core Practice, page 322

Be sure to record your data soon after you take measurements to reduce the chance of error. Sample answer: The temperatures were higher during the day and lower at night. The difference between the highest high and the lowest low was about 40 degrees, but daily fluctuations were more commonly about 20 degrees.

Think about Science, page 324

1. Erosion carries away rock, and deposition deposits the rock somewhere else. Diagrams should reflect this relationship.

2. Sample answer: wind erosion: the formation of sand dunes; water erosion: the formation of canyons; erosion by gravity: rock slides

Workplace Skill, page 324

Answers will vary.

Core Practice, page 325

Use a spray bottle to create patterns of erosion and deposition. Keep in mind that one action, such as building seawalls, can have both positive and negative effects. Sample answer: The water moves the sand from one location to another. The sticks can keep the water from eroding some of the sand, but this also causes sand to be eroded in other places, which might be an unintended consequence of terraces or seawalls.

21st Century Skills, page 325

It may be helpful to focus on one particular group of emergency responders, such as a public organization or a agency. Sample answer: Emergency responders may do any of the following: staging emergency supplies; warning the public; shutting down public transportation; closing roads; asking people to evacuate from unsafe areas; sandbagging areas prone to flooding; stockpiling batteries, flashlights, food, and drinking water; rescuing people from dangerous situations caused by the natural disaster.

Vocabulary Review, page 326

1. weather

2. weather system

3. natural hazard

4. experiment

5. Deposition

Skill Review, page 326

1. D   The movement of sand by ocean waves is caused by water erosion.

2. B   Chemical weathering changes the composition of rock, causing it to weaken and crumble. This can occur when chemicals in rock react with water or oxygen in the air.

3. Sample answer: No, because winds and currents take the hurricane west and then north toward North America. Once away from warm, tropical water, the storm loses its energy source. The arrows show that hurricanes dissipate before crossing the northern part of the Atlantic Ocean.

4. Sample answer: North Pacific Ocean, North Atlantic Ocean, South Pacific Ocean, South Atlantic Ocean; the water is too cold in these areas to provide energy for a hurricane to form.

Skill Practice, page 327

1. D   The order should be C, A, B, D.

2. Sample answer: Fish might have been in the river, and over time, as the lake formed, they became trapped and could no longer get back to the river. The fish might be able to get back to the river if there are heavy rains or flooding that cause the lake to reconnect with the river.

3. D   Water vapor is part of moist air. Fog, clouds, and mist are all visible forms of liquid water droplets.

4. Sample answer: Hurricanes begin as small thunderstorms over warm, tropical water, but they can become large. They intensify as more warm air moves up into the atmosphere.

5. A.   gravity

   B.   wind

   C.   water

   D   water

6. **D** Planting more seeds than are needed is a technique used by a farmer that is not directly related to preventing erosion.

7. Sample answer: Wind causes grains of sand to blow, which over time can cause the rock to gradually become smoother as little pieces erode.

8. Sample answer: Wind removes sand grains from the windward side of the dune and transports them to the leeward side. As this process continues, the dune migrates downward.

9. Sample answer: Fast moving water can transport larger particles (gravel) than slow moving water. So, a stream bed that contains course gravel indicates a faster flowing river than a river that has only fine-grained sand in the channel.

Chapter 8 Review

1. **B** Most of the atmosphere is composed of two gases: nitrogen (78 percent) and oxygen (21 percent). The remaining 1 percent is a mixture of other gases, including argon, carbon dioxide, water vapor, and trace amounts of other gases.

2. **D** Within the thermosphere is the ionosphere, a region of electrically charged particles. Nitrogen and oxygen atoms in the ionosphere also absorb potentially harmful solar energy.

3. **B** Substances of greater density will sink beneath substances of a lower density. Freshwater has less salts and particles in it than ocean water, so it has a lower density than salt water found in the ocean. Therefore, freshwater will stay on top of saltwater when they are mixed.

4. **D** Waves form as a result of wind acting on the water's surface. A wave is a rhythmic movement that carries energy through space or matter—in this case, ocean water. Winds skimming over the surface of the water are the main causes of ocean waves.

5. **C** The mantle is the layer of Earth beneath the crust. It ranges in temperature from 100°C to 4000°C. Although the mantle is solid, the asthenosphere can platically deform and flow, like shaping modeling clay with your hands. The core is the central part of Earth

and is divided into two parts: an outer liquid core and a inner solid core. Particles in the liquid outer core can flow past each other.

6. **C** The Earth's sediment includes bits of dead organisms and the shells of sea animals. Over time, as layers of sediment build up, they are cemented together to form sedimentary rocks. Metamorphic rock forms under extreme heat and pressure, and igneous rock forms when magma cools.

7. **C** The process of photosynthesis in plants uses sunlight, water, and carbon dioxide from the atmosphere to produce organic materials and oxygen. All humans and animals depend on this oxygen for survival.

8. **B** Coal is the easiest fossil fuel to extract from the ground through mining techniques. It is the most readily available and cheapest form of fossil fuel to obtain; therefore, it is the most widely used energy source.

9. **B** Divergent boundaries explains why the Atlantic Ocean is continually getting wider over time.

10. **B** A cold front forms when cold air mass displaces a warm air mass.

11. **C** The formation of rust on an iron gate is an example of chemical weathering of a substance.

12. Sample answer: This would reduce the amount of solid particles in the atmosphere and therefore would reduce cloud formation. Solid particles such as ice, dust, salt, and ash provide a surface on which water vapor can condense. The condensation of water vapor in the atmosphere causes the formation of clouds. Clouds are necessary for precipitation, and precipitation is essential for life on Earth. Freshwater supplies are dependent on precipitation, and plants require precipitation for growth.

13. Sample answer: A surface current is caused by global winds blowing over the oceans' surface. The winds cause movement of the water at the surface in the same direction as the wind is flowing. A density current is caused by the mixing of ocean waters with different temperatures and salinities. Density currents move cold, salty water along the bottom portion of the ocean.

14. B Weathering causes rock to break into smaller pieces called sediment. This sediment is transported, deposited, and then buried by other sediments. The transformation of these sediments into rock is called lithification, which includes compaction and cementation.

15. Sample answer: When fossil fuels are burned as an energy source, by-products are released into the air and react with water and atmospheric gases. This causes the formation of acid rain. When this acid rain falls onto trees, if the acid content is high enough, the trees can be damaged and eventually die. Without trees, the balance of the ecosystem is disrupted.

16. Sample answer: The likely result is the formation of a hurricane. When multiple thunderstorms converge over the warm tropical waters of the Caribbean Sea, a hurricane can form.

17. Sample answer: An increase in greenhouse gases can cause an increase in temperatures. Therefore, an increase in greenhouse gases can lead to global warming. As the passage suggests, global warming speeds up the melting of glaciers and ice caps. This would lead to the destruction of the ecosystems in arctic regions and would negatively affect organisms such as the polar bear. Melting glaciers means there is less of a stable habitat for polar bears. Less habitable space may lead to more competition among species.

18. A A change in climate in Earth's polar regions that results in an increase in temperatures will melt the polar ice caps of this region. The melting ice will cause a rise in the sea level which can affect the coast of continents.

19. D The thermocline layer lies below the surface layer and above the colder, dark bottom layer of ocean water. Within the thermocline layer, water temperature decreases rapidly with depth.

20. Sample answer: The bottom layer of the ocean begins at depths greater than 1,000 meters below the surface. Sunlight cannot reach this depth of water, so any radiant energy provided by the Sun cannot reach this far to warm the water temperature. Therefore, the temperature is very low in the ocean's bottom layer.

21. A Biomass is organic matter that can be used as fuel. Since organic matter is readily available and abundant in most regions of Earth, it is the most used renewable resource.

22. D According to the chart, petroleum is the most widely used nonrenewable energy source, so it would be likely to contribute the greatest amount of pollution to the environment.

23. Sample answer: A large amount of energy is used daily and as of now, solar energy is more expensive than other sources to harvest and convert to usable sources. Also, there is not an efficient way to store solar energy for long periods of time.

24. B $25g/m^3$. At 40°C air can hold $50g/m^3$, and at 25°C air can hold up to $25g/m^3$.

25. Sample answer: The amount of water vapor in the air can change. Warmer air can hold more water vapor than cool air. Increasing air temperature enables the air to hold more water vapor. Rising temperatures also lead to increased evaporation, which increases the amount of water vapor in the air.

Lesson 9.1

Core Skill, page 337

Text can exhibit a number of different structures, such as chronological structure, problem/solution, compare/contrast, and cause and effect. A writer often lets content guide the type of structure used for the text. Sample answer: Under the heading *Structures in the Universe*, the author begins by describing the smallest entity, Earth, and then describing increasingly larger entities, such as the Sun, the solar system, galaxies, galactic clusters, superclusters, and filaments. This helped me better understand the scale of each entity. Under the heading, *The Big Bang Theory*, the author presented a problem—how did the universe begin?—and then presented information about how that problem is being solved.

Think about Science, page 338

1. The universe is still expanding; the increasing wideness represents the continued expansion.

2. Sample answer: No, I could not, because the Milky Way is so much larger than Earth. I could not find a usable scale.

Core Practice, page 338

You will first have to test the technique before you can evaluate it. Sample answer: You can divide the night sky into equal quadrants and count the number of stars in one quadrant. Then you can multiply this number by the total number of quadrants to get an estimate of the number of stars in the night sky. The strength of this method is that it allows you to focus on just one part of the sky, rather than on the entire sky. The weakness is that you can lose count, or your quadrants may be too large. To improve the method, it may be helpful to divide the sky into smaller sections.

Think about Science, page 340

1. 3, 2, 4, 1

2. black hole

3. hydrogen

4. constellation

Think about Science, page 341

1. **C** Galaxies have different shapes and ages, but all contain stars, dust, and gases held together by gravity.

Workplace Skill, page 341

You can find information online about how to use a computer-graphics program to develop a slide presentation. You can include both text and visuals on the slides. Be sure to arrange the slides in logical order. Presentations should focus on the hierarchical nature of the universe. They should describe and compare celestial structures in terms of size and composition.

Vocabulary Review, page 342

1. universe

2. estimate

3. structure

4. star

5. galaxy

6. constellation

Skill Review, page 342

1. **A** The higher the luminosity of a main-sequence star, the greater its temperature. Therefore, if the luminosity of the star decreased, its temperature would decrease as well.

2. **A** Irregular galaxies are relatively young and so contain mainly new stars. In contrast, spiral galaxies contain a mix of young and old stars, and elliptical galaxies contain many old stars.

3. **C** Light cannot escape the gravitational field of a black hole. This is a distinguishing characteristic of a black hole.

4. Sample answer: An astronomer might look for a darker-than-normal void in the night sky surrounded by a spherical horizon.

Skill Practice, page 343

1. **C** A protostar becomes a star when it no longer contracts upon itself and temperatures become hot enough for nuclear fusion to begin.

2. Answers may vary; sample answer: Evidence may include light spectra, the motion of distant galaxies, and the composition of matter in the universe. Evaluations may state that the Big Bang theory is the best explanation for the origin of the universe thus far, but that it still leaves many questions unanswered.

3. Sample answer: Theoretically, fusion would make a great energy resource in that it generates a lot of energy. However, given the high temperatures and pressures needed to fuse nuclei to generate energy, the technology does not yet exist to use fusion as an energy resource on a large scale.

4. Sample answer: Your interpretation is incorrect. The universe did not begin with a huge explosion in space. Instead it began from a tiny point that expanded at an incredible rate and created space.

5. Sample answer: Some of these structures are incredibly large. Their diameters, when given in kilometers, include too many digits to remember or to record without error. It's easier to use larger units when describing large structures in space.

6. Answers may vary; sample answer: Graphic organizers and summaries should indicate that all stars begin as nebulae that contract, due to gravity, to form protostars. A star with medium mass becomes a main-sequence star. When it uses up its supply of hydrogen, it becomes a red giant. The star begins to die when helium is fused into carbon and its outer surface gases blow away to form a planetary nebula. The hot, dense core that remains is called a white dwarf. A massive star may become a red giant or a Red supergiant as it ages. When carbon fuses into iron in its core, the iron core eventually collapses, and the outer portion of the star explodes in a supernova. The leftover materials from the core become neutron stars or black holes, depending on their mass.

7. **D** Paragraph 5 suggests the possibility of a "crunched" universe.

8. **D** An approximate prediction

Lesson 9.2

Calculator Skill, page 345

Show your work as you complete each step of the equation; $x = 365/58.7$ $x = 6.22$ rotations in one Earth year (365 days).

Think about Science, page 346

1. **D** All eight planets in our solar system have elliptical orbits. The outer planets are gaseous, and the inner planets are rocky. All of the outer planets and two of the inner planets have moons.

2. **B** Stars form from nebula, so the Sun, a star, is made of the same materials that make up a nebula: hydrogen and helium.

Core Practice, page 346

Look for sentences in the text that explain why Pluto was reclassified. Text evidence would include the following: *It could not be classified as a gas giant, because of its . . . small size, nor could it be considered a terrestrial planet because of its . . . small size.*

Workplace Skill, page 346

You will need to research and examine a map of time zones to answer this question. Sample answer: Scheduling the call early in the morning for the East Coast employees would be very early and likely not during business hours for the West Coast employees. Scheduling the call late in the afternoon may be too late for East Coast employees, as they have left work for the day. To accommodate the employees on both coasts, the best time would be in the middle of the day.

Think about Science, page 348

1. Earth's tilt

2. tides

3. solar eclipse

Test-taking Skill, page 348

Begin by identifying the information needed to answer the question. Other information in the paragraph can be eliminated. Sample answer: Because the question asks for a comparison of meteoroids and meteorites, the information about the size and orbit of asteroids is not needed.

Think about Science, page 349

1. Absolute dating determines the numerical age of an object by determining the number of years it has existed. Relative dating is used to determine the age of an object by comparing it to the age of other objects.

Core Skill, page 349

Note that the age and the number of half-lives in the table increase down each row, as the percent of remaining carbon-14 decreases. Use this information to determine the data needed in the bottom row: Age: 34,380 years; Half-Lives: 6; Percent of Remaining Carbon-14: 1.563%.

1. construct

2. comets

3. satellite

4. relative dating

5. solar system

6. planetesimals

Skill Review, page 350

1. **B** Like planets, Pluto orbits the Sun and has a nearly round shape. Unlike planets, Pluto is not massive enough to clear other objects from its orbit. For this reason, it was reclassified as a dwarf planet.

2. **C** The definition of a planet explains that gravity plays a role in giving a planet its nearly round shape.

3. **A** Asteroids and comets are small, rocky bodies that orbit the Sun. When materials from comets or asteroids enter Earth's atmosphere, they are called meteoroids.

4. **A** A lunar eclipse occurs when the Sun, Earth, and the Moon are in a line. Earth blocks sunlight from reaching the Moon and casts its shadow on the Moon.

Skill Practice, page 351

1. **A** The proposed model describes how gravity affected materials in the solar nebula; these materials later formed the objects in Earth's solar system. Gravity pulled strongly on heavy materials, keeping them closer to the Sun and eventually forming the inner planets. Gravitational pull was less strong on lighter materials, which eventually came together to form the outer planets.

2. **B** The solar nebula did not collapse until gravity overcame the internal pressure of the nebula's hot gases.

3. **C** Earth's axis remains at a tilt of 23.5° and points in the same direction throughout its revolution around the Sun.

4. **C** The Earth is approximately 4.6 billion years old, and the earliest evidence of humans dates back less than half a million years.

5. Sample answer: Scientists would probably classify Object X as a planetesimal since it satisfies only three of the criteria to be defined as a planet. Object X orbits the Sun, and it is dominant enough to clear objects from its orbit, but it is not nearly round in shape.

6. Sample answer: If Earth's tilt was increased, the seasons would become more extreme—winters would be colder, and summers would be hotter. Days during winter would be shorter and nights longer than they are now. Days during summer would be longer and nights shorter than they are now.

7. Sample answer: About four half-lives have passed since the organism began decaying. The fossil contains about 6.25% of its original amount of carbon-14.

Chapter 9 Review

1. **D** Galaxies can be found in large groups called clusters or superclusters. Superclusters form first by matter spreading throughout the expanding universe and then by gravity pulling the matter together into clumps and strands.

2. **C** The Big Bang theory states that the universe began from a dense speck of energy and matter, smaller than a grain of sand. This tiny speck then underwent rapid expansion. This hot, dense speck of matter emitted a lot of radiation as it expanded.

3. **A** The star-mass based estimate places the universe between 11 and 18 billion years old, which means the universe is about the same age.

4. B Stars spend most of their life as a main-sequence star, but as more hydrogen gas in converted into helium gas, the star can change into another type.

5. A In both an elliptical and spiral galaxy, the oldest stars are found in the center. In an elliptical galaxy, the bright center contains mostly old stars and the stars in its center are older than those found in a spiral galaxy. In a spiral galaxy, the central bulge contains mostly older stars and younger stars are found in the spiral's arms.

6. A Astronomers believe our solar system first formed from huge clouds of gas and dust called nebulas. When a nebula condenses, its gravitational force becomes stronger. This causes the nebula to collapse inward toward its center and become much denser. If the nebula is rotating, it will spin faster as it collapses to resemble a flattened, rotating disk. Eventually the dense concentration of gas at the center of this rotating disk becomes a star. When nebulas begin to condense and form stars and star systems, they are called planetary nebulas. The nebula that formed into our own solar system is called the solar nebula.

7. B The four inner planets are those closest to the Sun: Mercury, Venus, Earth, and Mars. Astronomers believe that the Sun's gravitational force may have pulled away the gases surrounding these planets as they formed. All four planets have characteristic rocky and dense composition due to the heavier elements left behind such as iron and nickel.

8. C The rotation of Jupiter around the Sun is much faster than that of Earth. It only takes Jupiter 10 Earth hours to rotate around the Sun. Saturn also rotates very quickly around the Sun as compared to Earth.

9. D The movements of the Earth determine the length of days, seasons and a full year. One revolution of the Earth around the Sun represents an Earth year, which is 365.25 days.

10. C The tides of the ocean are caused by the gravitational pull of the Moon on Earth. As the Moon travels around Earth its gravity pulls at the side of the Earth that is closest to it, causing the water to "bulge." This bulge is called high tide.

11. C Stars can be organized in a Hertzsprung-Russell diagram according to surface temperature and luminosity.

12. B The gravitational force of a black hole is so strong that light cannot escape. That is why it appears to have an absence of light.

13. Sample answer: If Earth traveled four light years from the Sun it would appear much smaller when viewed from Earth. In fact, it would look just like any other star in the sky. The Sun is classified as a star of medium brightness, but because it is the closest star to Earth, it appears brightest.

14. Sample answer: When a massive star gets older and runs out of hydrogen, it fuses helium atoms into carbon and because of the intense heat, carbon at the star's core fuses into iron. The iron core absorbs energy until the core collapses and there is a huge explosion called a supernova. The explosion produces heavy elements such as gold, silver, and lead. These elements blow into space when a supernova explosion occurs.

15. Sample answer: The Grand Canyon is composed of distinct rock layers that have remained in a horizontally stacked position over time. In this undisturbed sequence of sedimentary rocks scientists have determined that the rocks are layered from oldest to youngest, starting from the bottom layer. The formation does not indicate the exact age of each layer, but the age can be determined relative to the other layers of rock surrounding it.

16. Sample answer: Measuring the amount of radioactivity in the rock layer can help to determine the numerical age of the rock. Each radioactive element has a specific half-life. A half-life is the amount of time it takes for half of the total amount of radioactivity in a sample to decay. The number of half-lives that the layer has undergone can determine how long the layer has been in place.

17. **B** Hubble concluded that the universe was expanding because all galaxies were moving away from Earth. This conclusion was in support of the Big Bang theory.

18. Sample answer: In 1965 scientists discovered radiation in space that corresponded to a temperature of 2.7K, the temperature predicted by the Big Bang theory and the temperature of the universe today.

19. **C** Hubble concluded that the universe was expanding because all galaxies were moving away from Earth. Scientists traced the expanding universe back and found it converged on a single point.

20. Sample answer: Every 6 months one hemisphere is tilted toward the Sun and one hemisphere is tilted away from the Sun. The hemisphere pointed toward the Sun will experience spring and summer and the hemisphere tilted away will experience fall and winter. This is due to the fact that the part of Earth pointed away from the Sun will not be receiving the same amount of radiant energy from the Sun as the other half.

21. Sample answer: The Moon's periods of orbit and rotation are both 27 days, 7 hours, and 43 minutes. The Moon rotates exactly one time each time it travels around Earth. As a result, as the Moon orbits Earth, the same side of the moon is always facing our planet.

22. Since the Moon only has one-sixth of the Earth's gravitational force, we would not be pulled to the Moon with the same force that we are pulled toward Earth. If there is less gravitational force, our weight will be less on the Moon than on Earth.

23. tilt; axis

Name _____ **Date** _____ **Class** _____

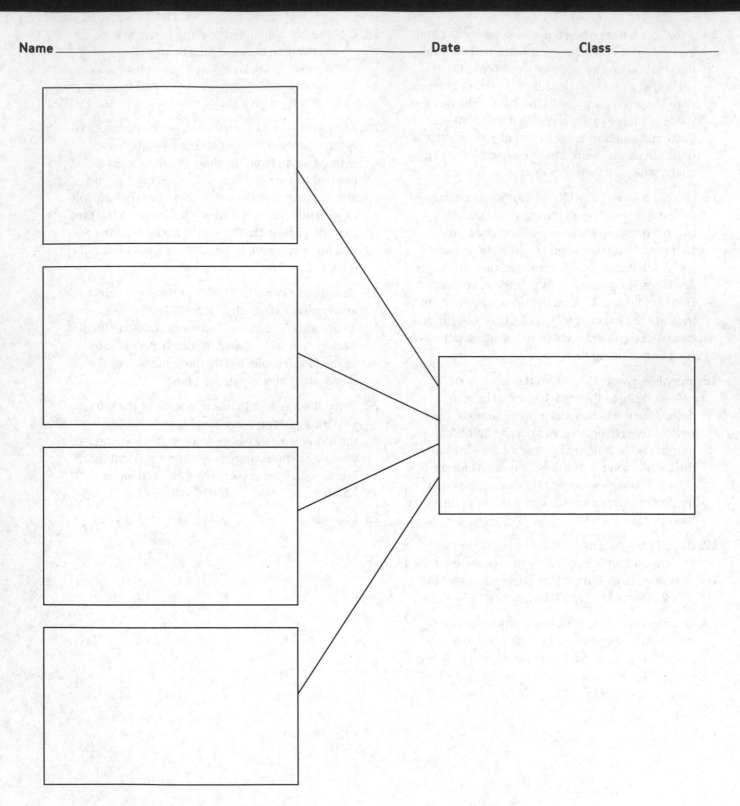

Name _____ **Date** _____ **Class** _____

Name_____ **Date**_____ **Class**_____

What I Know	What I Want to Know	What I Learned	How Can I Learn More

Name _____ **Date** _____ **Class** _____

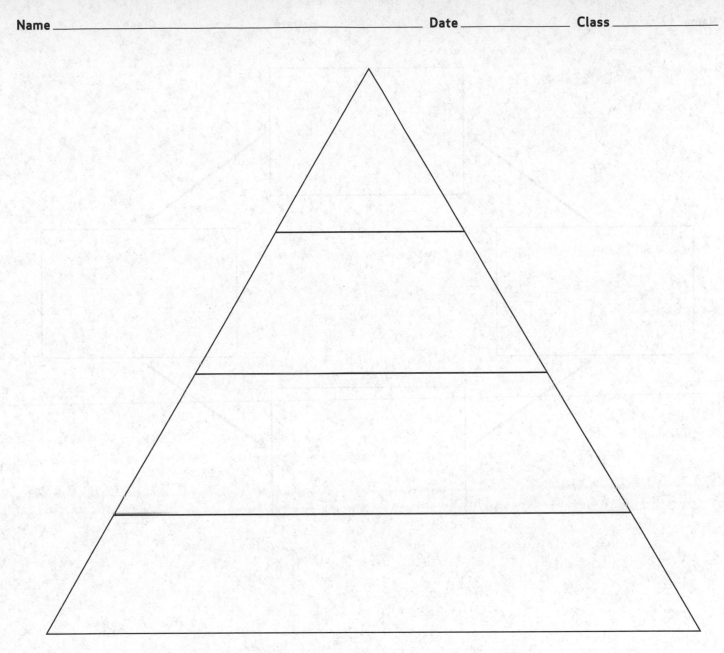

Name _____ **Date** _____ **Class** _____

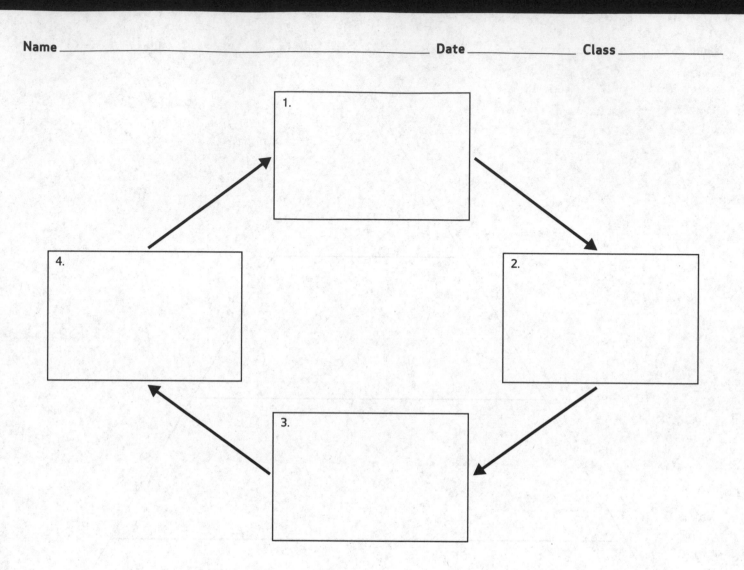

Name _____ **Date** _____ **Class** _____

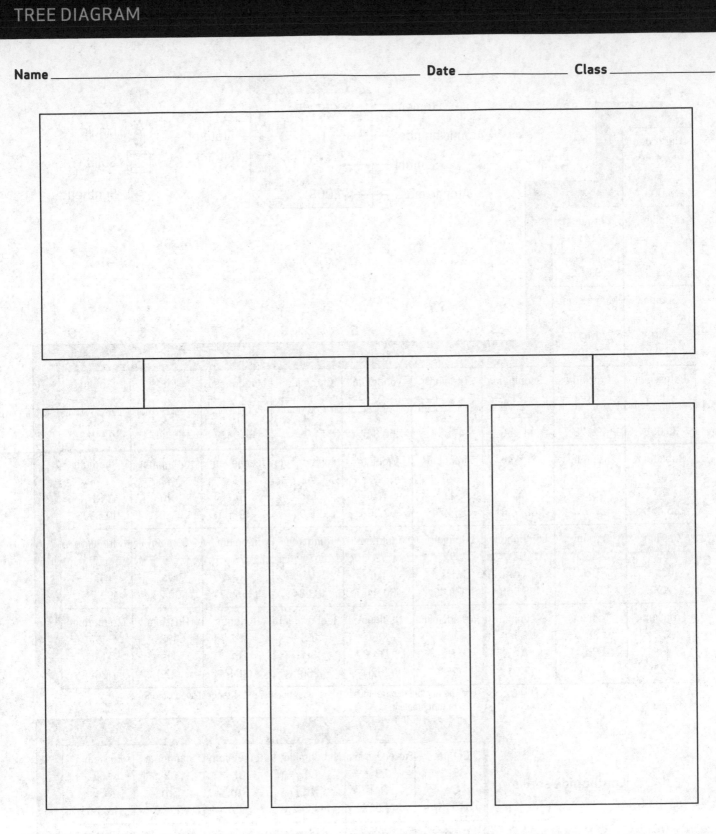

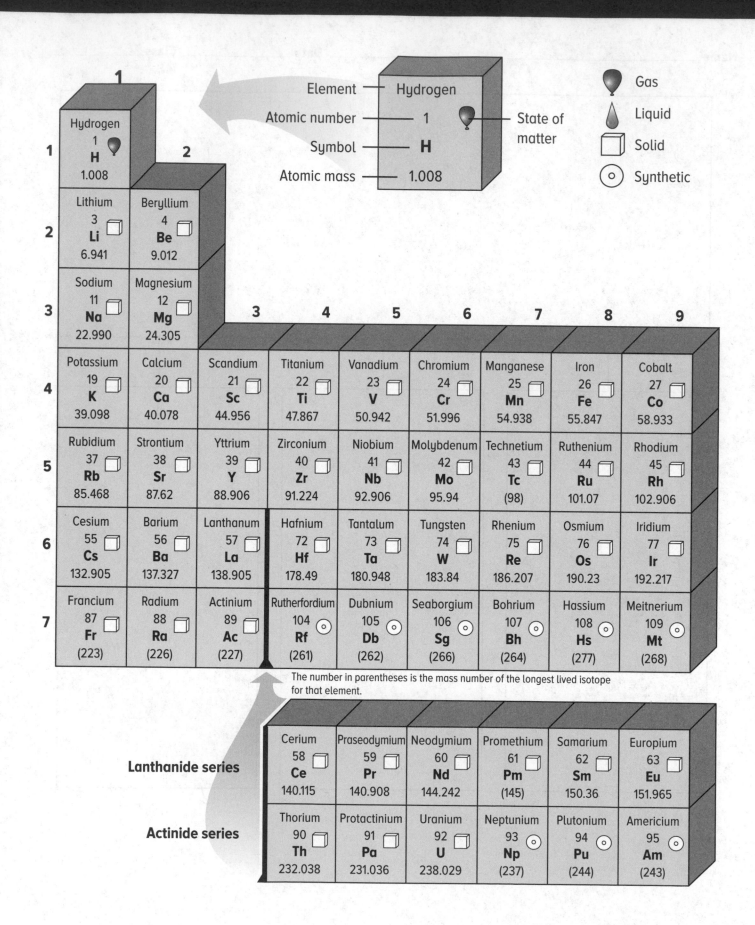

The number in parentheses is the mass number of the longest lived isotope for that element.

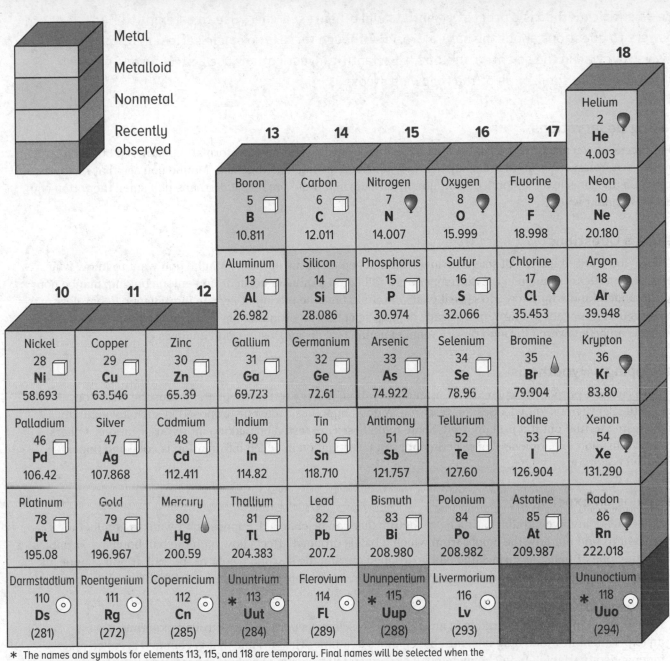

Metal

Metalloid

Nonmetal

Recently observed

10	11	12	13	14	15	16	17	18
								Helium 2 **He** 4.003
			Boron 5 **B** 10.811	Carbon 6 **C** 12.011	Nitrogen 7 **N** 14.007	Oxygen 8 **O** 15.999	Fluorine 9 **F** 18.998	Neon 10 **Ne** 20.180
			Aluminum 13 **Al** 26.982	Silicon 14 **Si** 28.086	Phosphorus 15 **P** 30.974	Sulfur 16 **S** 32.066	Chlorine 17 **Cl** 35.453	Argon 18 **Ar** 39.948
Nickel 28 **Ni** 58.693	Copper 29 **Cu** 63.546	Zinc 30 **Zn** 65.39	Gallium 31 **Ga** 69.723	Germanium 32 **Ge** 72.61	Arsenic 33 **As** 74.922	Selenium 34 **Se** 78.96	Bromine 35 **Br** 79.904	Krypton 36 **Kr** 83.80
Palladium 46 **Pd** 106.42	Silver 47 **Ag** 107.868	Cadmium 48 **Cd** 112.411	Indium 49 **In** 114.82	Tin 50 **Sn** 118.710	Antimony 51 **Sb** 121.757	Tellurium 52 **Te** 127.60	Iodine 53 **I** 126.904	Xenon 54 **Xe** 131.290
Platinum 78 **Pt** 195.08	Gold 79 **Au** 196.967	Mercury 80 **Hg** 200.59	Thallium 81 **Tl** 204.383	Lead 82 **Pb** 207.2	Bismuth 83 **Bi** 208.980	Polonium 84 **Po** 208.982	Astatine 85 **At** 209.987	Radon 86 **Rn** 222.018
Darmstadtium 110 **Ds** (281)	Roentgenium 111 **Rg** (272)	Copernicium 112 **Cn** (285)	Ununtrium * 113 **Uut** (284)	Flerovium 114 **Fl** (289)	Ununpentium * 115 **Uup** (288)	Livermorium 116 **Lv** (293)		Ununoctium * 118 **Uuo** (294)

* The names and symbols for elements 113, 115, and 118 are temporary. Final names will be selected when the elements' discoveries are verified.

Gadolinium 64 **Gd** 157.25	Terbium 65 **Tb** 158.925	Dysprosium 66 **Dy** 162.50	Holmium 67 **Ho** 164.930	Erbium 68 **Er** 167.259	Thulium 69 **Tm** 168.934	Ytterbium 70 **Yb** 173.04	Lutetium 71 **Lu** 174.967
Curium 96 **Cm** (247)	Berkelium 97 **Bk** (247)	Californium 98 **Cf** (251)	Einsteinium 99 **Es** (252)	Fermium 100 **Fm** (257)	Mendelevium 101 **Md** (258)	Nobelium 102 **No** (259)	Lawrencium 103 **Lr** (262)

The **scientific method** is a process scientists and other researchers use to attempt to find answers to questions about the natural world. Although there is no single series of steps that is always followed in the scientific method, all scientific investigations use a structured approach that may include some or all of the following steps.

Making Observations

The process of science often begins with an observation. An observation is information gathered by using your senses. Your senses involve seeing, hearing, smelling, tasting, and touching. Maybe you see that rust has formed on an iron shovel. It could be that you hear static in a radio broadcast. Perhaps you smell the rotten-egg odor of stagnant water.

Asking a Questions

What do you want to learn? All scientific investigation begins with a question. Maybe you want to know why there is a significant change in the air temperature following a thunderstorm. If you enjoy cooking, maybe you want to understand why the world's great chefs carefully time the mixing of certain ingredients. Regardless of what it is that you want to know, you always begin a scientific investigation by asking a question. A scientific question can be answered through observation, experimental design, testing, and analysis.

Developing a Hypothesis

A hypothesis is a proposed explanation for an observation. It is not a random guess. It must be based on observations, previous knowledge, and research. A good hypothesis must be proposed in such a way that it can be tested to find out if it is supported. Some hypotheses are tested by making more observations. Others are tested through experiments. An experiment is an investigation in which information is collected under controlled conditions.

Designing an Experiment

All experiments involve variables, which are factors that can be changed. Suppose you want to conduct an experiment to find out how the height from which a ball is dropped affects how high the ball bounces. Variables include the type of ball, the surface the ball is dropped on, and the starting height of the ball. If you change all the variables throughout the experiment, you will not be able to determine which variable affected the bounce.

Controlled Experiment

Instead of changing each variable in an experiment, scientists perform a controlled experiment, or an experiment in which only one variable changes at a time. The variable that is changed is called an independent variable. In the bouncing ball experiment, the starting height is the independent variable. Something that is independent does not rely on other factors. Every time you drop the ball, it is called a trial. The starting height changes during each trial.

The variable that is observed to find out if it changes is called the dependent variable. Something that is dependent relies on other factors. How high the ball bounces is the dependent variable. All the other variables remain unchanged. That means you need to drop the same type of ball onto the same surface under the same conditions.

Control Group and Experimental Group

Some experiments are performed with two groups of variables. In the control group, all the variables are kept the same. In the experimental group, the independent variable is changed. These groups are tested at the same time. The control group is used for comparison. It shows what would have happened if nothing was changed. Having information from the control group makes it easier to see the effects of changing an independent variable.

Collecting and Analyzing Data

The information obtained through observation is called data. Some investigations produce huge amounts of data. To make sense of all the information, scientists organize the data into forms that are easier to read and analyze. Data is often organized in tables or graphs. Line graphs are best for data that change continuously. Circle graphs are best for describing data that is divided into parts of a whole. Bar graphs are especially useful for comparing data.

Drawing Conclusions

Once the experiment is conducted and the data collected, a scientist tries to determine if the hypothesis is supported. A conclusion is a statement that uses evidence to indicate whether the hypothesis is supported. The evidence is derived from the data collected.

A conclusion is not necessarily the end of the investigation. If the conclusion indicates that the hypothesis is not supported, the scientist may develop a new hypothesis and design a new experiment to test it. If the conclusion indicates that the hypothesis is supported, the scientist needs to repeat the experiment many times to make sure the conclusion is the same and therefore valid. The scientist also needs to share his or her results with the scientific community. In this way, scientists can repeat the experiment to confirm the results.

Communicating the Results

Throughout the experiment, a scientist should keep careful records that describe everything about the research. These records include not only the data, but also information about the experiment's design, possible sources of error, unexpected results, and any remaining questions.

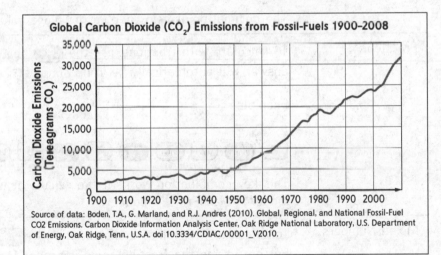

Global Carbon Dioxide (CO$_2$) Emissions from Fossil-Fuels 1900–2008

Source of data: Boden, T.A., G. Marland, and R.J. Andres (2010). Global, Regional, and National Fossil-Fuel CO2 Emissions. Carbon Dioxide Information Analysis Center, Oak Ridge National Laboratory, U.S. Department of Energy, Oak Ridge, Tenn., U.S.A. doi 10.3334/CDIAC/00001_V2010.

Scientists share their results with one another by communicating through written reports and journal articles, as well as through oral presentations. Sharing information in this way not only adds to the body of scientific knowledge, it also gives other scientists an opportunity to repeat the experiment. The results of an investigation can only be considered valid if they are achieved during repeated trials of the same procedure.

Order of Operations	The TI-30XS MultiView™ automatically evaluates numerical expressions using the Order of Operations based on how the expression is entered.	The correct answer is 23.
	Example $12 \div 2 \times 3 + 5 =$ [1] [2] [÷] [2] [×] [3] [+] [5] (enter) Note that the 2 is **not** multiplied by the 3 before division occurs.	
Decimals	To calculate with decimals, enter the whole number, then [.], then the fractional part.	The correct answer is 17.016.
	Example $11.526 + 5.89 - 0.4 =$ [1] [1] [.] [5] [2] [6] [+] [5] [.] [8] [9] [−] [0] [.] [4] (enter) The decimal point helps line up the place value.	
Fractions	To calculate with fractions, use the (n/d) button. The answer will automatically be in its simplest form.	The correct answer is $\frac{15}{28}$.
	Example $\frac{3}{7} \div \frac{4}{5} =$ [3] (n/d) [7] (enter) [÷] [4] (n/d) [5] (enter) This key combination works if the calculator is in Classic mode or MathPrint™ mode.	
Mixed Numbers	To calculate with mixed numbers, use the (2nd) (n/d) button. To see the fraction as an improper fraction, don't press the (2nd) (x10ⁿ) buttons in sequence below.	The correct answer is $39\frac{13}{15}$.
	Example $8\frac{2}{3} \times 4\frac{3}{5} =$ [8] (2nd) (n/d) [2] [▼] [3] (enter) [×] [4] (2nd) (n/d) [3] [▼] [5] (enter) (2nd) (x10ⁿ) (enter) This key combination only works if the calculator is in MathPrint™ mode.	
Percentages	To calculate with percentages, enter the percent number, then (2nd) (( ).	The correct answer is 360.
	Example $72\% \times 500 =$ [7] [2] (2nd) (( ) [×] [5] [0] [0] (enter)	

Powers & Roots

To calculate with powers and roots, use the x^2 and $\wedge$ buttons for powers and the 2nd x^2 and 2nd $\wedge$ buttons for roots.

Example
$21^2 =$

[2] [1] [x^2] [enter]

The correct answer is 441.

Example
$2^8 =$

[2] [$\wedge$] [8] [enter]

The correct answer is 256.

Example
$\sqrt{729} =$

[2nd] [x^2] [7] [2] [9] [enter]

The correct answer is 27.

Example
$\sqrt[5]{16807} =$

[5] [2nd] [$\wedge$] [1] [6] [8] [0] [7] [enter]

The correct answer is 7.

You can use the 2nd x^2 and 2nd $\wedge$ buttons to also compute squares and square roots.

Scientific Notation

To calculate in scientific notation, use the $x10^n$ button as well as make sure your calculator is in Scientific notation in the mode menu.

Example
$6.81 \times 10^4 + 5.201 \times 10^4 =$

[6] [.] [8] [1] [$x10^n$] [4] [enter] [+]

[5] [.] [2] [0] [1] [$x10^n$] [4] [enter]

The correct answer is 1.2011×10^5.

When you are done using scientific notation, make sure to change back to Normal in the mode menu.

Toggle

In MathPrint™ mode, you can use the toggle button [◄►] to switch back and forth from exact answers (fractions, roots, π, etc.) and decimal approximations.

Example
$\frac{3}{7} =$

[3] [$\frac{n}{d}$] [7] [enter] [◄►]

The correct answer is 0.428571429.

If an exact answer is not required, you can press the toggle button [◄►] immediately to get a decimal approximation from an exact answer without reentering the expression.

GLOSSARY

A

abiotic pertaining to all the nonliving things in an environment

acceleration the rate of change of velocity

acid a chemical with a sour taste that forms a salt when mixed with a base

adaptation any trait that helps an organism survive and reproduce in its environment

allele one of two or more forms of a gene

alveoli tiny air sacs within the lungs where gas exchange occurs

analyze to understand the relationship of parts through examination

ancestry the lineage or bloodline of descendants

anticipate to think of something that will or might happen in the future

apply to put to use, especially for some practical purpose

arteries blood vessels that carry oxygen-rich blood away from the heart

arrange to move or organize into a particular order or position

artificial selection the process by which humans breed other animals and plants for particular traits

assess to make a judgment about

asteroid small, rocky body that orbits the Sun

atmosphere the layer of gases that surrounds Earth

atom the smallest particle of an element that has the properties of that element

autotroph an organism that captures matter and energy from a nonliving source (a producer)

B

base a chemical with a bitter taste that forms a salt when mixed with an acid

biodiversity the variety of life in an area that is determined by the number of species in that area

biogeochemical cycles the recycling systems of an ecosystem

biomass the total mass of living tissue in a trophic level

biome a major ecological system that occupies a large region of land or water and is characterized by the organisms adapted to its particular environments

biotic pertaining to all the living things in an environment

C

calories a measure of the energy stored in food

capillaries microscopic blood vessels that connect arteries and veins

carrying capacity the maximum number of organisms of one species that an environment can support for the long term

cartilage strong but flexible material found in some parts of the body

cells the smallest living unit that carries on the activities of an organism

cell cycle the sequence of events that leads to cell growth and division

cell theory states that cells are the basic units of life, that all organisms are made of cells, and that cells produce new cells

cellular respiration a process in which glucose and other organic molecules are broken down to release energy in the presence of oxygen

characteristics properties or traits that can be used to identify an object or event

chemical bond a force that holds together two atoms in a compound

chemical property the ability or inability of a substance to react with or change into one or more new substances

chemical reaction the process in which one or more substances are changed into new substances

chlorophyll pigment that gives plants their green color and allows plants to capture the energy of sunlight

chromatid one copy of a chromosome that is joined to its exact duplicate sister chromatid

chromosomes structures where genes are located

cladogram diagram that shows the evolutionary relationship of organisms

classify to group into categories based on similar characteristics

climate change a persistent and noticeable change in local or global weather patterns over a long period of time

comet small body of ice and rock that is left over from the formation of the solar system

commensalism a symbiotic relationship in which one organism benefits and the other is not affected

compare to determine how two things are alike or different

compound machines machines made of more than one simple machine

conduction the transfer of thermal energy between particles that collide

constellation recognizable pattern formed by groups of stars in the night sky

construct to make or create something by organizing ideas, words, or objects

contrast to show differences between

convection the transfer of thermal energy by the movement of particles

crossing over the process in which DNA from the father and DNA from the mother switch chromosomes

D

demonstrate to clearly show a process or explain a concept

deposition the process by which material is either laid on the ground or sinks to the bottom of a body of water

design to plan or make something for a specific use or purpose

develop to create or produce something over a period of time

differentiate to see or state the differences between two or more things

discriminate to notice that one thing is different from another thing

disease any condition that disrupts the normal functioning of the body

DNA replication the process in which an extra copy of DNA is made

draw conclusions to interpret or make inferences based on the results of an investigation

E

ecosystem a community of different organisms in an area and all the nonliving surroundings

electromagnetic waves waves created by vibrating electrical charges that can travel through matter or space

element a substance in which all the atoms are the same

endothermic reactions reactions that require the addition of energy to proceed

energy resource a natural material people use to meet their energy needs

energy transformation the change of one type of energy into another type of energy

enzymes molecules, often proteins, that facilitate chemical reactions in organisms

epidemic a disease or illness affecting a large number of people

epigenetics the study of how the chemicals that are not part of the DNA sequence affect the expression of genes

erosion the transport of weathered materials from one place to another by water, ice, wind, or gravity

estimate an approximate calculation

esophagus a muscular tube that moves food from the throat to the stomach

eukaryotic cell a cell with a nucleus and many organelles enclosed in their own membranes

eutrophication when excess nutrients in a body of water causes oxygen depletion

evaluate to determine the quality of

evolution change in living organisms over long periods of time

example an illustration of a rule, method, or topic

exothermic reactions reactions that release energy as the reaction proceeds

experiment a scientific investigation carried out with the goal of solving a scientific question

extinction the death of all members of a species

F

fermentation a process that releases the energy stored in organic molecules in the absence of oxygen

fetus stage of development of an organism eight weeks after fertilization until birth

force a push or pull

fossil the preserved remains of an organism

fossil fuel a fuel formed from the remains of ancient organisms

fossil fuels energy resources that form over millions of years from the remains of once-living organisms

G

galaxy a large group of stars, dust, and gases held together by gravity

gamete sex cell

gas a state of matter made of particles that vibrate and move freely and quickly

gene a segment of DNA that contributes to the characteristics, or traits, of an organism

genetic recombination the redistribution of genes in cells

genetics the field of biology devoted to studying heredity

genotype the genetic makeup of an organism

glands organs that produce and release a substance

graph a diagram (a series of one or more points, lines, line segments, curves, or areas) that represents the variation of a variable in comparison with that of one or more other variables

gravity a force of attraction between two objects because of their mass

greenhouse effect the natural heating of Earth's surface by atmosphere gases

H

habitat destruction the changing of a natural area such that the habitat is no longer able to support the organisms that live there

heat the transfer of thermal energy

heredity the passing of traits from one generation to the next

heterotroph an organism that eats other organisms (a consumer)

homeostasis the regulation of an organism's internal environment to maintain conditions necessary for life

hormones chemical messengers released by glands into the blood that regulate body functions

I

immunity a condition of being able to resist a particular disease

inertia the tendency of an object to resist a change in motion

infer to form an opinion or reach a conclusion based on evidence

integrate bring parts together to make a whole

invasive species an organism that is moved to a new, foreign environment in which that organism causes harm

J

joint point of connection between bones

K

kinetic energy energy that results from motion

L

label to name or describe something in a specified way

law a statement that describes a relationship in nature that has been observed to always occur under certain conditions

law of conservation of energy states that energy cannot be created or destroyed

law of conservation of mass In a chemical reaction, the combined mass of all the reactants is equal to the combined mass of all the products.

law of conservation of momentum states that the total momentum of a system does not change during a collision

M

matter anything that has mass and takes up space

mechanical advantage the amount of mechanical help a machine provides

mechanical energy the sum of an object's kinetic energy and its potential energy

medium the matter through which a wave travels

meiosis a type of cell division that produces gametes

melting point the temperature at which a substance changes from a solid to a liquid

minerals inorganic elements the body needs for metabolic functions

mineral a naturally occurring, inorganic solid that has a specific chemical composition and a definite crystalline structure

mitosis the process that divides the nucleus of a cell

momentum the product of the mass and the velocity of a moving object

monohybrid cross a mating between two parents that differ in only one trait

muscle tissue that can contract

mutation a random change that occurs in the genetic material of a cell

mutualism a symbiotic relationship in which both species benefit

N

natural hazard the natural forces that can result in a serious threat to life

natural resources resources provided by Earth, including organisms, nutrients, rocks, water, and minerals

natural selection a process by which organisms that are best adapted to their environment tend to survive and pass on genetic characteristics to offspring

negative-feedback mechanism a system that responds to a change by shifting values in the opposite direction

neuron cell that transmits or receives signals within the nervous system

niche the role an organism plays in an ecosystem

nonrenewable resource a resource that can be used up

nuclear fission the splitting of a nucleus into two smaller nuclei

nucleus the central organelle of a cell that contains the cell's genetic material

nutrients raw materials needed to sustain healthy life functions

nutrition the process by which an organism takes in and uses food

O

oceans large bodies of water that contain dissolved salts

organelles cell structures that perform a particular function for the cell

organize to arrange or order things so they can be easily understood or easily found

osmosis diffusion of water across a selectively permeable membrane

outline a summary of the main points of a text

ozone atmospheric gas that helps block harmful rays from the Sun

P

parasitism a symbiotic relationship in which one organism, the parasite, feeds off the living body of the other organism, the host

pathogen something that causes disease

percent part of one hundred

periodic table an organized list of all known elements

phenotype observable traits in an organism

phloem tubelike structures that transport organic molecules from the leaves to the rest of the plant

photosynthesis the process by which some organisms capture light energy and change it into chemical energy

physical property a characteristic of matter that can be observed without changing the identity of the matter

placenta a connection between the mother and embryo or fetus

planetesimal solid particle that forms the building blocks of planets

plate tectonics the slow movement of sections of Earth's crust and mantle

pollination the transfer of pollen from a stamen to a pistil

pollution substances that have a harmful effect on an environment

positive-feedback mechanism a system that responds to changes by increasing the change

potential energy energy that is due to its position

power the rate at which work is done

predation when one organism kills and eats another organism

probability the likelihood that a certain event will occur

prokaryotic cell a cell that does not have a nucleus or membrane-bound organelles

Punnett square a chart used to predict the possible genotypes and phenotypes of offspring

R

radiation the transfer of thermal energy as electromagnetic waves

reconcile explain how two ideas are true at the same time

relative dating a process of determining the age of artifacts or events by comparing them to others

renewable resource a natural energy resource that can be replaced

response the reaction to a stimulus

revise to make changes, especially to correct or improve

rock cycle the continuous changing and remaking of rocks over time

S

salinity measure of dissolved salts in a solution

satellite object, such as a moon, that orbits a planet

saturation the state of being combined until there is no further tendency to combine

simple machines devices that make work easier—specifically wedge, wheel and axle, lever, and pulley

solar system consists of the Sun, the planets and other bodies that travel around it

solubility the amount of a substance that will dissolve in a given amount of another substance

solution a mixture in which one substance is completely and uniformly dissolved in another

speciation the evolutionary process by which new biological species arise

species distinct group of organisms that can produce live offspring

speed the distance an object travels per unit of time

spontaneous generation a belief that living things come from nonliving matter

stars hot, glowing balls of gas that generate their own light

state to express in words

states of matter the physical forms in which all matter exists—most commonly solid, liquid, gas, or plasma

statistics the field of study involving the collection and analysis of data

stimulus a condition that causes an organism to react in a certain way

structure an object with a form, composition, or arrangement

subdivide to organize into smaller units

sublimation the change of state from a solid to a gas

summarize to provide a short statement that includes the main ideas of a larger topic

sustainability the ability to maintain resources levels that allow them to be available for future use

symbiosis a close relationship between individuals of two or more species

T

tabulate to arrange in an organized manner for study purposes

temperature the measure of the average kinetic energy in a substance

tendon strong, fibrous connective tissue that joins muscle to bone

theory an explanation of some aspect of the natural world based on knowledge that has been repeatedly confirmed through observation and experimentation

trait a heritable characteristic

transpiration the process by which water vapor exits the leaves of a plant through tiny openings in the leaves

trophic level each step in a food chain or ecological pyramid

U

universe everything that exists throughout space

V

vaccine dead or incomplete portions of pathogens or antigens

valid logical and justifiable

variations different characteristics or traits that, if favorable, can help a species better survive

vascular true land plants that have evolved to survive independent of wet environments

velocity the speed and direction of a moving object

veins blood vessels that carry oxygen-poor blood toward the heart

vitamins complex organic molecules that help the body build new tissues and important molecules

W

water cycle the continuous movement of water from Earth's surface to its atmosphere and back again

wave a repeating disturbance that transfers energy as it travels through matter or space

weather the condition of the atmosphere at a particular place and time

weathering the breaking down of rock into smaller pieces by natural processes

weather systems form when an air mass remains over the same area for days or weeks

weight a measure of the force of gravity on an object

work occurs when a force moves an object

X

xylem tubelike structures that transport water and minerals from the roots to the rest of the plant

INDEX

Climate, 292–293
    and biomes, 65
    definition of, 65
    global warming, 86, 87
    impact of oceans on, 300
    records of, 349
Climate change, 292–293
    definition of, 288
    records of, 349
    and sea level rise, 301
    and use of fossil fuels, 314
Clusters (galaxies), 336
Coal, 313
Cold fronts, 321
Collaboration, 122
Color, as physical property, 256
Comets, 344, 346
Commensalism, 78, 80
Communication, 122, 163
Community(-ies):
    biological, 63
    definition of, 63
    studying, 64
Compare, 228, 229
Competition, as limiting factor, 78
Compound machines, 196, 200
Compounds, 252–253
Compression waves, 236
Concentration:
    and chemical-reaction rate, 269
    definition of, 269, 272
    in describing solutions, 275–276
Condensation, 71, 250
Conduction, 228, 229
Conservation of energy, 212, 216–217
Conservation of mass, 264, 265
Conservation of momentum, 184, 186–187
Constellations, 336, 340
Construct (term), 344, 348
Consumers, 70
Contact forces, 190
Continental-continental convergent boundaries, 308
Continental crust, 304, 307
Contrast, 126, 129
Convection, 228, 230
Convergent boundaries, 307–308
Copper, 313
Coral reefs, 300–301
Core (Earth), 304, 305
    materials in, 305
    parts of, 304–305
Coriolis effect, 298
Corona, 347
Cosmic background radiation, 337
Covalent compounds, dissolving, 273
Creativity, 199
Critical thinking, 43
Cross-cultural skills, 144
Crossing over:
    definition of, 162
    and genetic variation, 162–163

Crust (Earth), 304, 305
    materials in, 305
    parts of, 304
    and plate tectonics, 307
Crystalline structure (minerals), 305
Currents, ocean, 298
Cycles of matter, 72–75
Cytokinesis, 127, 129
Cytoplasm, 104, 107

D

Dams, 316
Darwin, Charles, 156, 157, 168–170, 173
Dating:
    absolute, 349
    relative, 344, 348–349
Daughter cells, 127, 129
Day, 347
Deciduous forest, 66
Decomposers, 70
Demonstrate (term), 312
Density:
    of ocean water, 298
    as physical property of matter, 256
Density currents (oceans), 298
Deposition:
    definition of, 320
    erosion and, 323
Describe data sets statistically (core practice), 80, 146, 291
Desert, 66
Design a scientific investigation (core practice), 111
Determine central ideas (core skill), 18, 265
Determine details (core skill), 235
Determine hypotheses (core skill), 273
Determine the meaning of symbols, terms and phrases as they are used in scientific presentations (core practice), 107
Determine the probability of events (core practice), 153
Develop, 264, 269
Diet, balanced, 45, 50
Differentiate, 104, 106
Digestion, 22
Digestive system, 22–23
Dihybrid cross, 153
Discriminate, 234, 235
Disease, 48
    definition of, 48
    and immune system, 49
    as limiting factor for population, 78
    prevention of, 50–51
Disruptions, ecosystem, 84–87
Dissolving, rate of, 274
Distinguish among reasoned judgments (core skill), 85
Distinguish between cause and effect (core skill), 49, 224
Distinguish between facts and speculation (core practice), 120
Divergent boundaries, 307
DNA (deoxyribonucleic acid), 104, 142–144
    crossing over of, 162–163
    mutated, 164
    replication of, 163